A Special Issue of
Aphasiology

The representation of language in the brain

In honour of John C. Marshall

Edited by

Chris Code

University of Exeter, Exeter, UK

Ψ Psychology Press
Taylor & Francis Group
HOVE AND NEW YORK

First published 2006 by Psychology Press

27 Church Road, Hove, East Sussex BN3 2FA

Simultaneously published in the USA and Canada
by Psychology Press

711 Third Avenue, New York, NY 10017

First issued in paperback 2015

*Psychology Press is an imprint of the Taylor & Francis Group,
an informa business*

British Library Cataloguing in Publication Data
A catalogue record for this book is available from the British Library

ISBN 13: 978-1-138-87769-6 (pbk)
ISBN 13: 978-1-84169-817-5 (hbk)

ISBN 0268-7038

Cover design by Design Deluxe
Typeset in the UK by H Charlesworth & Co Ltd, Wakefield, Yorkshire

APHASIOLOGY*

CONTENTS

(Continued overleaf)

---

* This book is also a special issue of the journal *Aphasiology*, and forms issues 9, 10
& 11 of Volume 20 (2006). The page numbers are taken from the journal and so
begin with p. 819.

Foreword

The form of representation of language in the brain and the influence of John C. Marshall

Chris Code

University of Exeter, UK

Claus W. Wallesch

University of Magdeburg, Germany

In 1977, John Marshall wrote that "the primary goal of neurolinguistics can be simply stated: the discipline seeks to understand the form of representation of language in the human brain" (p. 127). For "neurolinguistics" read any sub-field concerned with the neuropsychology of language and speech. If our understanding of the representation of language and other cognitive functions in the brain has improved since 1977, we contend that it is in no small part due to the activities of John C. Marshall.

Language disorder has not been the only area of neuropsychology to which John has made a major contribution, but his encounters with generative and structural linguistics at the beginning of his career probably contributed to his early interest in aphasia, including subsequent choices of terminology for newly described forms of acquired dyslexia. Language impairments remain the area to which he has contributed most, and is the topic of the contributions to this Special Issue of *Aphasiology*.

JCM is famously known as one of the founding personalities of cognitive neuropsychology, a cornerstone of modern cognitive neuroscience. With him the separate features of the enterprise are encapsulated: a coming together of the information processing metaphor, the notion of a mind organised into modules, and the development and testing of models against the broken cognition of brain-damaged people using psycholinguistically controlled tests. While many early models and investigators in cognitive neuropsychology came out of the psycholinguistics lab, it was the clinic that was to provide the data that drove the enterprise. In John are brought together the separate elements of the enterprise: he was able to combine his work with brain-damaged individuals, his knowledge of linguistics and the

Address correspondence to: Chris Code, School of Psychology, Washington Singer Labs, University of Exeter, Exeter EX4 4QG, UK. E-mail: c.f.s.code@exeter.ac.uk

history of aphasiology, and his work developing single-case methodology to its early development.

John's career shows both his broad interests and how he grew to become what he is. Starting with psycholinguistics and experimental psychology, his first research interest was acquired dyslexia (Holmes, Marshall, & Newcombe, 1971; Marshall & Newcombe, 1966), and he and Freda Newcombe were responsible for the seminal paper describing the acquired impairments in reading that we now know, after Marshall and Newcombe (1973), as deep dyslexia, surface dyslexia, and visual dyslexia, and for introducing a dual-route information processing model of reading aloud. So while it might still be unwise to insist that modern aphasiology began in 1861 with Broca's description of Laborgne, there is some justification for tracing the beginnings of cognitive neuropsychology back to these seminal descriptions of acquired dyslexia. John completed his PhD in 1967 at the University of Reading, a festering hotbed of future cognitive neuropsychologists at that time, including John Morton and Tony Marcel. In the early 1970s, Max Coltheart and Alan Allport too were at Reading. In the late 1970s, JCM moved from the MRC Speech and Communication Research Unit at the University of Edinburgh to the psycholinguistics project at the University of Nijmegen, which was of great importance for the shaping of continental Western European neurolinguistics and neuropsychology. In 1977, a group of people all working on deep dyslexia (including JCM, Max Coltheart, John Morton, Karalyn Patterson, and Eleanor Saffran) coincided at an INS meeting in London out of which grew a plan for a deep dyslexia conference in 1978 that led to the books *Deep Dyslexia* (1980) and *Surface Dyslexia* (1985) edited by Max Coltheart, Karalyn Patterson, and JCM. John visited North American Universities extensively until he settled in Oxford in the mid-1980s. Also in the 1980s, he became a principal proponent of metatheories, or scientific cross-overs (Marshall 1982, 1984) and also a leading cognitive methodologist (Marshall & Newcombe, 1984; Newcombe & Marshall, 1988). At the same time, he started to focus on the tantalising problem of neglect and body representation (Halligan & Marshall, 1988; Marshall & Halligan, 1988), adding a second research focus to language and reading disorders.

But how successful has cognitive neuropsychology been in elucidating "the form of representation of language in the brain"? It may be too early to say, as the field continues to reform and reinvent itself. There have been evolutions back to large group studies and the mapping of cognitive functions to brain structure with developments in imaging and connectionist modelling. However the enterprise has already left a legacy of theoretical and methodological rigour, from which neuropsychology, neurolinguistics, neurology, rehabilitation, and functional imaging have profited. For instance, its intellectual rigour appeals to neurologists concerned with deducing the functional composition of the nervous system from the symptoms of its damage.

The view from the late 1980s was that we knew too little about the architecture of cognitive functions to say useful things about their relationship with brain structure. The 1990s saw the emergence of *cognitive neuroscience* with the rise and rise of functional imaging able to provide images of metabolic activation during cognitive tasks. Cognitive neuropsychology was sceptical to begin with, and many still are, because the actual tasks used in early studies were too general and uncontrolled to provide useful data. It soon became clear that the quality of the result from the sophisticated technical machinery depends on the quality of the question, the specification of tasks, and the experimental design. Formulation of a hypothesis depends on theory, and the methodological rigour and the models derived from cognitive neuropsychology were central for the validity of functional imaging studies designed to investigate the representation of language in the brain. John was among the first to provide guidance and clarity on the search for cognitive methodologies and interpretations of functional imaging (Fink, Halligan, Marshall, Frith, Frackowiak, & Dolan, 1996) and has since been a cognitive and methodological advisor to many investigations using functional imaging.

Occasionally people find themselves at a loss with cognitive theories, especially when more than one theory or model can be applied to a single symptom complex (e.g., paraphasia, dyslexia) in a given patient, producing different interpretations and predictions. So cognitive *neuropsychology* becomes important, because the constraining influence of symptoms in brain damage may help to decide between theories. Single case investigations were championed in early cognitive neuropsychology, but they have fallen out of favour with some in recent years, although theory development is constrained by data from single cases and their theory-driven investigation (Code, Wallesch, Lecours, & Joanette, 1996, 2003; Gurd & Marshall, 2003; Marshall & Gurd, 2004). In addition, cognitive neuropsychology has had a significant impact on treatment studies in aphasia, the earliest in Britain (see Howard & Hatfield, 1987). It brought a new systematic approach to designing treatments for individuals based on controlled hypothesis testing of impairments and capabilities using psycholinguistically controlled tests.

JCM and Jennifer Gurd summarised the goals of the study of pathologies of cognition as threefold (Marshall & Gurd, 2003, p. 7):

> Neuropathological fragmentations of cognition impose strong constraints upon theories of the normal system. The striking dissociations of impaired and preserved performance seen after brain damage indicate which overt behavioural abilities must not be analysed together as manifestations of a single underlying function.
>
> The interpretation of pathological performance by reference to normal theory allows the investigator to move beyond the mere description of overt symptomatology to accounts of the underlying processes that are impaired.
>
> In any complex system, identical overt failures and errors can arise from malfunction of different underlying components. Such ambiguities must be resolved by linking the patterns of impaired and preserved performance to specified (and justified) information-processing components.

Has our understanding of the representation of language in the brain improved in the 40 years or so since John Marshall shone his light on the subject? A full answer to that question is for future historians—we can be sure that knowledge is always provisional and we always face the epistemic cliff edge of our own cognitive limitations. We have certainly seen massive developments over these four decades and John C. Marshall has been in the thick of it. Unlike Kafka's *Joseph K* who was arrested, tried, and executed for a crime of which he knew nothing and about which he was told nothing—*The Trial* (1945) is JCM's favourite novel—John Marshall is guilty as charged. He knew what was going on. In fact, he was a ringleader.

Rumours of John's "retirement" are clearly exaggerated, as work continues to flow from his pen, if not his word processor. Even so, this does seem a good time to organise a *Festschrift* that celebrates his work in the neuropsychology of language thus far. John is justifiably well known as an encouraging supporter of the work of others, and he has long been a friend and associate of *Aphasiology*, having been both an Editorial Board member since 1999 and a regular contributor. This is not the first tribute to John and won't be the last, and we are delighted with the response from colleagues and friends of John's who wanted to contribute to the idea. There are contributions on the history of aphasia, reading, naming, syntax, comprehension, foreign accent syndrome, progressive aphasia, treatment, the evolution of language, calculation, and embodied cognition. The content reflects John's own interests in language and aphasia, and it is therefore no surprise that it also reflects current and central issues in the neuropsychology of language.

REFERENCES

Code, C., Wallesch, C-W., Lecours, A-R., & Joanette, Y. (Eds.). (1996). *Classic cases in neuropsychology.* Hove, UK: Lawrence Erlbaum Associates Ltd.

Code, C., Wallesch, C-W., Lecours, A-R., & Joanette, Y. (Eds.). (2003). *Classic cases in neuropsychology: Volume II.* Hove, UK: Lawrence Erlbaum Associates Ltd.

Coltheart, M., Patterson, K. E., & Marshall, J. C. (Eds.). (1980). *Deep dyslexia.* London: Routledge & Kegan Paul.

Fink, G. R., Halligan, P. W., Marshall, J. C., Frith, C. D., Frackowiak, R. S. J., & Dolan, R. J. (1996). Where in the brain does visual attention select the forest and the trees? *Nature, 382,* 626–628.

Gurd, J. M., & Marshall, J. C. (2003). Dissociations: Double or quits? *Cortex, 29,* 192–195.

Halligan, P. W., & Marshall, J. C. (1988). How long is a piece of string? A study of line bisection in a case of visual neglect. *Cortex, 24,* 321–328.

Holmes, J., Marshall, J. C., & Newcombe, F. (1971). Syntactic class as a determinant of word-retrieval in normal and dyslexic subjects. *Nature, 234,* 418.

Howard, D., & Hatfield, F. M. (1987). *Aphasia therapy.* Hove, UK: Lawrence Erlbaum Associates Ltd.

Kafka, F. (1945). *The trial.* London: Secker & Warburg.

Marshall, J. C. (1977). Disorders in the expression of language. In J. Morton & J. C. Marshall (Eds.), *Psycholinguistics Series 1: Developmental and pathological.* London: Paul Elek Ltd.

Marshall, J. C. (1982). Biological constraints on orthographic representation. *Philosophical Transactions of the Royal Society London B, 298,* 165–172.

Marshall, J. C. (1984). Multiple perspectives on modularity. *Cognition, 17,* 209–242.

Marshall, J. C., & Gurd, J. M. (2003). Neuropsychology: Past, present and future. In P. W. Halligan, U. Kischka, & J. C. Marshall (Eds.), *Handbook of clinical neuropsychology* (pp. 3–12). Oxford, UK: Oxford University Press.

Marshall, J. C., & Gurd, J. M. (2004). On the anatomo-clinical method. *Cortex, 40,* 230–231.

Marshall, J. C., & Halligan, P. W. (1988). Blindsight and insight into visuo-spatial neglect. *Nature, 336,* 766–767.

Marshall, J. C., & Newcombe, F. (1966). Syntactic and semantic errors in paralexia. *Neuropsychologia, 4,* 181–188.

Marshall, J. C., & Newcombe, F. (1973). Patterns of paralexia: A psycholinguistic approach. *Journal of Psycholinguistic Research, 2,* 175–199.

Marshall, J. C., & Newcombe, F. (1984). Putative problems and pure progress in neuropsychological single case studies. *Journal of Clinical Neuropsychology, 6,* 65–70.

Newcombe, F., & Marshall, J. C. (1998). Idealization meets psychometrics: The case for the right groups and the right individuals. *Cognitive Neuropsychology, 5,* 549–564.

Patterson, K. E., Marshall, J. C., & Coltheart, M. (Eds.). (1986). *Surface dyslexia.* Hove, UK: Lawrence Erlbaum Associates Ltd.

Reading disorders in a language with shallow orthography: A multiple single-case study in Italian

Alessio Toraldo

University of Pavia, Italy

Barbara Cattani and Giusi Zonca

Salvatore Maugeri Foundation, Montescano & Pavia, Italy

Paola Saletta

G. Salvini General Hospital, Rho-Passirana, Italy

Claudio Luzzatti

University of Milano-Bicocca, Milano, Italy

Background: This study aimed (i) to verify whether the classical word-naming models developed for English-speaking participants also account for the performance of patients who speak a shallow-orthography language such as Italian, and (ii) to study the effects of word frequency, concreteness, and grammatical class on word naming.
Methods & Procedures: A total of 90 Italian aphasic patients participated in two reading tasks. The first task contained four sets of items: (i) concrete nouns (natural objects and artefacts), (ii) abstract nouns, (iii) function words, (iv) morphologically simple legal nonwords. The second task (trisyllabic words with unpredictable stress position) was designed to test reading ability along the lexical route (the position of the major word stress is the only opaque variable in the Italian reading system). The patients' performances on the two tasks were analysed for strong dissociations, and to test the effect of grammatical class, concreteness, word frequency, and item length. The effect of age of acquisition was tested in a subsequent analysis.
Outcomes & Results: Reading scores were pathological for all patients. The present sample reflected the entire spectrum of reading impairments: phonological (49), surface (4), undifferentiated (32), and letter-by-letter (5) dyslexia, which is in line with data reported for English-speaking aphasic patients. Only one of the phonological dyslexic patients made semantic errors (a reading impairment compatible with the diagnosis of deep dyslexia). The vast majority of Broca's aphasic patients suffered from phonological dyslexia (76%), while fluent aphasic patients were distributed more evenly across dyslexia types; all four surface dyslexic patients belonged to the fluent aphasia group. Overall, grammatical class (concrete nouns vs function words) had a significant effect on 14 patients (15.6%), concreteness (concrete vs abstract nouns) on 15 (16.7%), and word frequency on 5 (5.6%). Grammatical class and concreteness affected the performance of phonological and undifferentiated dyslexic patients, and seemed not

Address correspondence to: Claudio Luzzatti, Department of Psychology, University of Milano-Bicocca, Piazza dell'Ateneo Nuovo 1, 20126 Milano, Italy. E-mail: claudio.luzzatti@unimib.it

This paper is dedicated to John Marshall: a splendid scientist, an extraordinary teacher, an exceptional humanist, and a wonderful friend.The study was partly financed by a Grant from the Italian Ministry of Education (FIRB-01 RBAU01LE9P_006).

to influence the scores of the surface dyslexic patients. Age of acquisition turned out to have a highly significant effect and may account for most of the lexical effects emerging from the first analysis.

Conclusions: The entire spectrum of reading impairments was observed in this group of Italian aphasic patients, thus confirming the validity of contemporary reading models also for shallow-orthography languages. Concreteness and grammatical class effects, present in deep dyslexia, also affected the performance of patients suffering from other types of dyslexia, although both phenomena might derive from a confounding effect of age of acquisition.

Over the last two decades contemporary cognitive psychologists have proposed several models of progressive complexity to describe the processing units underlying normal reading (Coltheart, Patterson, & Marshall, 1980; Patterson, Marshall, & Coltheart, 1985). These models assume the need for at least two processing routes: a lexical route by means of which words are treated as a whole, and a sub-word-level routine (SWL henceforth) based on grapheme-to-phoneme conversion (GPC) rules. The hypothesis of at least two procedures has been suggested for the English language to explain how alphabetised participants can read both words with irregular orthography and legal nonwords (i.e., nonlexical strings of letters, which however respect the phonotactic and graphotactic rules of a given language).

The English language appears to require two reading routes due to its irregular orthography, which frequently renders impossible the enunciation of a (written) word by deduction from the corresponding letter string. Not all alphabetic orthographies are as irregular as English. Italian, for instance, is considered to be a language with shallow orthography, i.e., a language in which the majority of written words can be named through the sub-word-level procedure. However, Italian has also a non-shallow condition, in that it is not possible to predict whether the stress in tri-syllabic or longer words falls on the penultimate or on the antepenultimate position: e.g., the stress in GONDOLA falls on the first syllable ['gondola], and not on the second [gon'dola], whereas in MENTOLO the stress falls on the second syllable [men'tolo], and not on the first ['mentolo].

Studies of patients suffering from acquired dyslexia after brain damage have confirmed the existence of two reading routes. Some patients can still apply GPC rules while having lost (or no longer being able to access) previously acquired orthographic lexical knowledge. In such cases, patients are able to read regular words flawlessly, but make inevitable regularisation errors when asked to name words with non-shallow orthography. This damage is usually called *surface dyslexia* (Patterson et al., 1985). Other patients can name regular and irregular words the orthography of which they are already familiar with, but are unable to read nonwords. This damage is usually called *phonological dyslexia* (Derouesné & Beauvois, 1985). Schwartz, Saffran, and Marin (1980) observed a patient who could read irregular words but was not able to understand them; they interpreted this impairment as the result of a direct connection of the *orthographic input lexicon* to the *phonological output lexicon* (direct lexical route), bypassing the underlying conceptual knowledge. This reading impairment is usually called *direct dyslexia*. There is also a subset of phonological dyslexic patients in whom severe damage to the SWL reading procedure is associated with grammatical class effects (better performance on reading nouns than verbs or function words), concreteness effects (concrete words are read better than abstract words) and semantic errors (e.g., they read *dog* instead of *hound* or *tree* instead of *wood*). This peculiar type of reading disorder, which often characterises the reading performance of agrammatic patients, is known as *deep dyslexia*. One explanation for this phenomenon is that following devastation of the left hemisphere language areas by an extensive perisylvian lesion, right hemisphere linguistic abilities—which are limited to high-frequency concrete nouns—may emerge (Coltheart, 1980b, 2000; Saffran, Boygo, Schwartz, & Marin, 1980; Zaidel, 1990).

There is a further set of patients whose reading impairment is due to early functional damage arising upstream from the bifurcation of the two reading routes described above. This impairment is known as *letter-by-letter* (LBL) *dyslexia* (Coltheart, 1998; Patterson & Kay, 1982). Patients suffering from this type of reading disorder can usually identify and often name single letters; however, this knowledge is ineffective for a functional reading performance both along the lexical and the sub-word-level route. For example, in the case of the word DOG, the patient spells each single letter of the target word ("dee-oh-gee"). Albeit very slow, this procedure may occasionally produce the correct name by means of a backward spelling procedure. This damage corresponds in large extent to the impairment called *pure alexia* in the classical literature (Déjerine, 1892), and is usually caused by a lesion of the left occipital pole (with right hemianopia, i.e., left-hemisphere blindness) and of the splenium of the corpus callosum, thus disconnecting the non-blind right occipital visual areas from the alphabetised left hemisphere (i.e., from the left-hemisphere orthographic lexical knowledge and the GPC routine).

READING AND WRITING IN LANGUAGES WITH SHALLOW ORTHOGRAPHY

While the relevance of two reading routes has been suggested (and demonstrated) by contemporary cognitive psychologists in languages with opaque orthography (such as English), it is possible that they may have a different level of relevance in languages with shallow orthography (such as Italian). The question is whether—and if so, to what extent—shallow languages actually require two processing routes for naming and spelling words (see Ardila, 1991). On the one side there are some general reasons that would suggest the need of two routes. For instance, while the SWL procedure allows the naming of the vast majority of words, it does not provide direct access to meaning, so rapid reading of a text can only be achieved along the lexical route. On the other hand reading with the SWL routine implies a heavier cognitive computational load, i.e., subtraction of cognitive resources from the comprehension of the text to be read. Another variable that may influence the reading and spelling procedures of normal adult participants is how written language has been acquired during the early phases of literacy acquisition. This is predominantly SWL in languages with shallow orthography and lexical in those with opaque orthography. Therefore, in a shallow language in which the early acquisition of reading and writing is SWL, secondary acquisition of the orthographic lexicons can only be achieved through later practice.

THE AIMS OF THE STUDY

The first aim of the present study is to reconsider the issue of a possible difference underlying the reading performance (and its disorders) in aphasic patients whose mother tongue is a shallow-orthography language, such as Italian, with a particular focus on determining the rate of disproportionate damage either to the lexical or to the SWL reading route (surface or phonological dyslexia). A specific reading task was developed to assess the two routes independently in literate adult aphasic patients.

The second aim was to assess the effect of concreteness, grammatical class, word frequency, and word length on a large sample of dyslexic participants. The former three lexical variables are known to influence the reading performance both in normal participants (e.g., Shibahara, Zorzi, Hill, Wydell, & Butterworth, 2003; Strain, Patterson, & Seidenberg, 1995) and in deep dyslexic patients (e.g., Coltheart, 1980a). Some predictions derive from the dual-route reading model and from previous single-case studies. The effects of word frequency, grammatical class, and concreteness are expected to depend on the predominant use of the lexical route and therefore should be minimal in surface dyslexia and stronger/ more frequent in phonological dyslexia. On the other hand, the length effect should be stronger/more frequent in surface dyslexia than in phonological dyslexia, since reading via the SWL routine (the procedure upon which surface dyslexic patients tend to rely) implies an increase in the probability of errors in correspondence with the increase in graphemes to be converted—see Cumming, Patterson, Verfaellie, and Graham, in press; Gold et al., 2005, for a similar effect in patients with semantic dementia.

Subsequent to the start of our data collection phase, several studies have stressed the role of age of acquisition (AA) in determining the reading performance of both normal participants (e.g., Bates, Burani, D'Amico, & Barca, 2001; Juhasz, 2005; Morrison & Ellis, 1995) and aphasic patients (e.g., Barca & Burani, 2002; Barry & Gerhand, 2003), which has led to much debate as to whether it is possible to disentangle AA effects from word frequency effects (see the cumulative-frequency hypothesis by Lewis, Gerhand, & Ellis, 2001; see also Bonin, Barry, Méot, & Chalard, 2004; Zevin & Seidenberg, 2002, 2004). Since initially we did not consider AA when constructing the reading tasks, we ran a first analysis in which the original experimental design was maintained; a second analysis was then made considering AA and its impact on the former lexical variables.

ANALYSIS 1

Participants

A total of 90 right-handed mild to moderate aphasic patients (63 males, 27 females) were recruited from a continuous sample of patients tested at three Northern Italian rehabilitation units from January 1995 to February 2003. Participants were native Italian speakers, with at least 5 years of education and evidence of focal brain damage in the left hemisphere. The age of the patients was 56.8 ± 16.1 (range 14–81) and their education was 8.6 ± 3.7 (range: 5–18) years of schooling. The type and severity of the language disorder was assessed by means of the Italian version of the Aachen Aphasia Test (AAT; Luzzatti, Willmes, & De Bleser, 1996). Of these patients, 65 suffered from ischaemic vascular damage, 13 from cerebral haemorrhage, 7 from traumatic brain injury, 2 from post-anoxic coma, 2 from brain tumours, and 1 from a brain abscess. Table 1 records how the patients were distributed across the aphasia sub-groups.

TABLE 1
Distribution of patients according to aphasia type

Aphasia type	Nonfluent			Fluent						
	B	TM	MT	A	W	TS	C	F/nF	RAS	Total
N	17	1	1	12	28	8	9	8	6	90
%	18.9	1.1	1.1	13.3	31.1	8.9	10.0	8.9	6.7	100

Aphasia type (AAT, Luzzatti et al., 1996): B, Broca's; TM, transcortical motor; MT, mixed transcortical; A, anomic; W, Wernicke's; TS, transcortical sensory; C, conduction; F/nF, unclassifiable along the fluency dimension; RAS, residual aphasic symptoms.

In addition 13 healthy participants, matched for age and years of education to the aphasic sample, participated in the study (age: 56.6 ± 13.2, range 33–77; education: 9.9 ± 3.0, range 5–14 years).

Tasks

Task 1: Reading of words and nonwords (W-nW). Participants were asked to read aloud a list of 61 words and 15 legal nonwords (see Table 2). Words were chosen from different lexical categories; the list included 16 function words, 30 concrete nouns (15 referring to natural objects, 15 to artefacts), and 15 abstract nouns. Subsets of items were balanced for word length. Abstract and concrete nouns were balanced for word frequency. Written word frequency was obtained from a corpus of 3,670,600 words normalised to 10 million occurrences (IBM, 1989). As frequently happens, it was not possible to balance noun frequency with that of function words. The stimuli were written in font Helvetica 26 capitals, and were each printed individually on a separate sheet of white A4 paper. The items were presented in identical randomised order to all participants.

Task 2: Trisyllabic words with unpredictable stress position (TWUS). Participants were asked to read aloud 40 trisyllabic words, of which half carry the stress on the penultimate syllable (e.g., MENTOLO, menthol: /men'tolo/; MISTERO, mystery:

TABLE 2
Reading tasks: Item subtypes and general characteristics

Task	Item classification			N	Length (letters) (median; range)	Frequency (median; range)
W-nW	Words	Function words		16	6; 4–10	4048; 432–23535
		Abstract nouns		15	7; 4–11	120; 35–1346
		Concrete nouns	Natural objects	15	7; 4–10	229; 0–1067
			Artefacts	15	8; 4–11	214; 0–906
	Nonwords			15	7; 4–10	
TWUS	Penultimate stress position			20	6; 6–7	8; 0–50
	Antepenultimate stress position			20	6; 5–7	2; 0–38

W-nW: Words and nonwords reading task; TWUS: Reading of tri-syllabic words with unpredictable stress position.

/mis'tero/), and half on the antepenultimate syllable (e.g., PENTOLA, pot: /'pentola/; ALBERO, tree: /'albero/). The items used in the penultimate- and antepenultimate-stress subsets had same CV structure and same ending, and were balanced for word frequency. It is not possible to derive the stress position of the words from their orthography: it has to be retrieved from lexical knowledge. Stimuli with penultimate and antepenultimate stress positions were given in randomised order in the same list. By applying the criteria discussed in the section "Principles of classification" to the results of this task we were able to estimate the integrity of the lexical route.

Scoring

Responses were scored as correct when given within 2 seconds after stimulus presentation. Latencies longer than 2 seconds, repairs, and hesitations were scored as errors.

Principles of classification

Patients were classified as suffering from *phonological* dyslexia when their performance along the SWL route was significantly more impaired than along the lexical route, and as suffering from *surface* dyslexia in the opposite case. Two independent estimates of the integrity of each route were used to effect this classification (the integrity of a route was computed as the probability of giving a correct output).

SWL route. The rate of successful reading of nonwords provides a good basis on which to estimate the probability of obtaining correct output along this route, i.e., of its integrity. This rate was labelled "S" (for SWL).

Lexical route. In opaque-orthography languages such as English the rate of successful naming of *irregular* words is a direct measure of the integrity of the lexical route. In Italian, due to its shallow orthography, irregular words are virtually absent, which poses the problem of how to estimate the integrity of the lexical route. As mentioned earlier in this paper, Italian orthography has its own form of ambiguity that concerns the positioning of the major stress in words of three or more syllables. Information regarding the stress position cannot be accessed through the SWL route, as it is unpredictable and not diacritically marked. As a result, three-syllable

TABLE 3
Contingency table

	Correct	Incorrect
TWUS task (Lexical route, L)	A = number of words named successfully *minus* number of stress errors	40 − A
W-nW task (SWL route, S)	B = number of nonwords named successfully	15 − B

Contingency table (2 × 2) used as input for the Monte Carlo Method (approximating Fisher's Exact Test) for each patient.
Example: consider a patient with the following raw data. *TWUS Task:* 11 words named successfully, 9 stress errors. *W-nW task:* 12 nonwords named successfully. The resulting contingency table will be: [2, 38; 12, 3]; Monte Carlo Method: $p < .0001$ (surface dyslexia).

words processed via the *SWL route* have a 50% chance of being named successfully.[1] Thus, if a patient made 12% stress errors (right phonology, *wrong* stress position), then it is to be expected that s/he would name words correctly (right phonology, *right* stress) at approximately the same rate (12%) via the SWL routine. The percentage of words that were named successfully via the *lexical* route was then computed by subtracting the percentage of stress errors from the overall percentage of words named successfully (see Equation).[2]

L (estimate of the Lexical route integrity) = % successfully named words – % stress errors.

Classification. According to the principles commonly employed in cognitive neuropsychology, L and S (the integrity levels of the two routes) are said to dissociate within a patient when they differ significantly, but without requiring the better performance to be in the normal range (strong dissociation; Shallice, 1988). In our control sample L turned out to be significantly higher than S (L = .992; S = .944; L–S = .049; Wilcoxon test: $z = 2.213$; $p = .027$). The null hypothesis of no dissociation[3] was tested for each patient by application of the Monte Carlo method ($n = 10000$). Table 3 reports the 2×2 contingency table used to input the Monte Carlo method. If a significant p-value emerged from the Monte Carlo procedure the patient was classified as suffering either from *phonological* (L–S significantly $>.049$) or from *surface dyslexia* (L–S significantly $< .049$). Phonological dyslexic patients producing semantic errors were further classified as suffering from *deep dyslexia*. If no significant difference was found between L and S, patients were classified as suffering from *undifferentiated dyslexia*. Patients suffering from *LBL dyslexia* were defined on the basis of the following criteria: very severe reading impairment (overall performance on both the W-nW and the TWUS tasks less than or equal to 10%) in spite of mild or no oral language impairment. For the few items that could be read successfully, LBL patients showed dramatic length effect and occasionally, backward-spelling reading strategy. The final classification tree is shown in Figure 1.

---

[1] This is true independently of the tendency of each patient to guess whether the stress lies on the penultimate or the antepenultimate syllable because the words in the TWUS task were equally divided between words with penultimate (P, $n = 20$) and antepenultimate (AP, $n = 20$) stress positions. Thus, if a surface dyslexic patient guessed a P stress in 20% of the trials and an AP stress in the remainder (80%), s/he would stress *correctly* 80% of the AP words (i.e., 16 words) and 20% of the P words (i.e., 4 words). Overall, 20 words (50%) would be named correctly. Another patient might prefer a P stress (as most Italian readers would), e.g., 90% P and 10% AP. In this case, the correct stress would be given to 90% of the P words ($n = 18$) and to 10% of the AP words ($n = 2$). The overall number would still be 20 (50%). Therefore, the final success rate of the SWL procedure will *always* be 50%, irrespective of the relative rate of P and AP stresses given by the participant, provided that P and AP words are present in equal numbers in the task and that the SWL route cannot access any information regarding stress position.

[2] An anonymous referee has pointed out that the terms used above suggest that any given word is processed by either one route or the other. Following contemporary cognitive models (see for example Coltheart, 1980a; Coltheart, Rastle, Perry, Langdon, & Ziegler, 2001, for its computational counterpart) Equation 1 assumes that words are processed by both routes simultaneously, and that activation arising from both routes is summed in the phonological output buffer (see Coltheart et al., 2001). Hence, if both routes provide partial activation of a phoneme, the combined activation may then reach the critical threshold and allow the production of the phoneme.

[3] It cannot be expected that the L–S difference will be identical (.049) across the entire pathology range; for instance, a patient with L and S values close to zero can be expected to show a smaller difference. Therefore, instead of using a fixed difference of .049 we adopted a value that decreased as the overall performance approached zero.

Effects of word frequency, concreteness, grammatical class, and word length

Psycholinguistic studies of reading in normal adults have repeatedly shown that reading times are highly correlated with word frequency (words that are more frequent in written form are read faster than words that are less frequent; see Andrews, 1989; Coltheart et al., 2001; Forster & Chambers, 1973; Paap & Noel, 1991; Shibahara et al., 2003; Strain et al., 1995; see Barca, Burani, & Arduino, 2002, for a study in Italian). Studies of acquired dyslexia also report three phenomena that often characterise reading impairments, i.e., concreteness, grammatical class, and word frequency effects (e.g., Coltheart, 1980a). According to the classical dual-route model, the emergence of these effects is to be considered as a marker of reading performance along a partially damaged lexical-semantic route. These variables were therefore included in our experimental design and their effect(s) tested in a group study and in a multiple single-case design. The effect of word length was also tested.

Group study

The group study was based on three "by-item" ANCOVAs. Each ANCOVA had the 61 words of the W-nW reading task as entries; Item Type (concrete noun, function

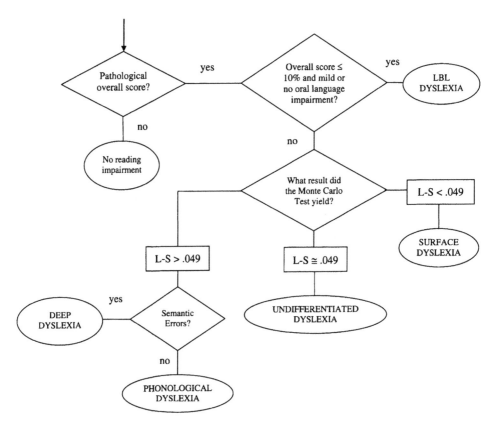

Figure 1. Dyslexia classification flowchart.

word, abstract noun) was used as a factor; Word Length and Word Frequency[4] were used as covariate variables; the percentage of patients who successfully named the item was used as a dependent variable. The three ANCOVAs were carried out on the data from phonological, surface, and undifferentiated dyslexic patients respectively (data from LBL dyslexic patients could not be analysed due to gross violations of the normality assumption).

Multiple single-case study

Word frequency. The effect of word frequency was estimated separately for concrete nouns, abstract nouns, and function words. Three logistic regression analyses (LRA) were performed for each patient, with Word Frequency as predictor and pass–fail scores on the three item types as dependent variables. This analysis was conducted to test the effect of word frequency at the individual level.

Concreteness. Since abstract and concrete nouns were matched for word frequency, it was possible to make a direct comparison of the % success scores for the two item types.

Grammatical class. Since concrete nouns and function words differed massively in word frequency (see Table 2), an adjustment for word frequency had to be introduced in order to make the two terms comparable. The LRA was used to compute the success rate that function words would have had if their word frequency had been identical to that of concrete nouns. This rate was then compared to the *real* success score obtained from concrete nouns by means of Fisher's Exact test. The procedure was carried out for each individual patient.

Word length. An LRA was carried out on each patient's pass–fail scores using word length as a unique predictor (all 61 words of the *W-nW* reading task were employed, since all word types have identical word length distribution).

Results

Comparison between control participants and aphasic patients

As expected, control participants obtained a close-to-ceiling performance on the overall reading score (range: 110–116; median = 115; 5th percentile = 110). The patients' scores were all below or equal to the control participants' 5th percentile, and covered the entire range of performance (range: 2–110; median = 72.5). Therefore, all patients suffered from some degree of dyslexia.

Aphasic patients: Types of dyslexia

Table 4 reports the results of the Monte Carlo statistical test for each individual patient and the final diagnostic classification. Table 5 reports absolute and relative frequencies of each diagnostic category.

---

[4] The logarithmic transformation *log*(frequency+82) was used instead of the original word frequency value in order to meet the linearity assumption required by ANCOVA.

TABLE 4
Results of individual participants (Analysis 1)

Patient	Aphasia type	Dyslexia type	TWUS Words named successfully (/140)	Stress errors (/140)	W-nW Words named successfully (/61)	Nonwords named successfully (/115)	WF	GC	Co	WL	L	S	L–S comparison: Monte Carlo (significant two-tailed p-values)
01	A	Undiff	33	3	47	7				.02	.75	.47	
02	A	Phon	29	2	45	5					.68	.33	.04
03	A	Undiff	13	6	12	5				.01	.18	.33	
04	A	Undiff	26	1	44	5					.63	.33	
05	A	Undiff	31	3	44	6				.01	.70	.40	
06	A	Phon	35	0	54	4					.88	.27	<.01
07	A	LBL	7	0	6	0		.05		.02	.18	.00	.02
08	A	Undiff	40	0	57	13				.01	1.00	.87	
09	A	Phon	23	0	22	0				.04	.58	.00	<.01
10	A	Phon	17	0	18	1				.01**	.43	.07	.01
11	A	Phon	29	0	39	3		.01	.02	.03	.73	.20	<.01
12	A	LBL	2	1	1	0					.03	.00	
13	B	Phon	32	3	45	3				<.01	.73	.20	<.01
14	B	Phon	31	0	45	3		.02	.03		.78	.20	<.01
15	B	Phon	21	0	21	1					.53	.07	<.01
16	B	Phon	25	0	29	1		.02			.63	.07	<.01
17	B	Phon	38	0	55	3					.95	.20	<.01
18	B	Undiff	10	3	3	1					.18	.07	
19	B	Phon	12	2	16	0				<.01	.25	.00	<.01
20	B	Undiff	21	1	40	9					.50	.60	
21	B	Undiff	31	0	41	7					.78	.47	
22	B	Phon	27	0	48	0		<.01			.68	.00	<.01
23	B	LBL	0	0	2	0					.00	.00	
24	B	Phon	15	0	25	0			.04	<.01	.38	.00	<.01
25	B	Phon	36	0	55	3					.90	.20	<.01
26	B	Phon	32	0	52	7					.80	.47	.05

TABLE 4 (Continued.)

Patient	Aphasia type	Dyslexia type	TWUS Words named successfully (140)	Stress errors (140)	W-nW Words named successfully (161)	Nonwords named successfully (115)	WF	GC	Co	WL	L	S	L–S comparison: Monte Carlo (significant two-tailed p-values)
27	B+ag	Phon-Deep	25	0	31	0		<.01	<.01		.63	.00	<.01
28	B+ag	Phon	28	0	44	0					.70	.00	<.01
29	B+ag	Phon	7	1	18	0		<.01	.02		.15	.00	.01
30	C	Phon	31	0	37	5				.01	.78	.33	.01
31	C	Undiff	19	0	24	6				.01	.48	.40	
32	C	Undiff	31	0	46	10				.01	.78	.67	
33	C	Undiff	20	1	44	3	.03		.02	<.01	.48	.20	
34	C	Phon	30	0	19	3		.01*			.75	.20	<.01
35	C	Undiff	13	9	14	0				<.01	.10	.00	
36	C	Phon	30	0	36	6	.04			<.01	.75	.40	.04
37	C	Surface	30	5	52	14				.01	.63	.93	.02
38	C	Phon	38	2	58	9					.90	.60	.04
39	F-nF	Phon	37	1	51	8				.01	.90	.53	.02
40	F-nF	Phon	39	0	56	6	.05			.01	.98	.40	<.01
41	F-nF	Phon	31	0	44	1					.78	.07	<.01
42	F-nF	Phon	39	0	56	6	.02		.02		.98	.40	<.01
43	F-nF	Undiff	32	1	52	8					.78	.53	
44	F-nF	Phon	8	1	18	0				.01	.18	.00	.03
45	F-nF	Phon	33	1	43	1		<.01		<.01	.80	.07	<.01
46	F-nF	LBL	0	0	7	2				.01	.00	.13	
47	MT	Phon	20	0	31	1					.50	.07	<.01
48	RAS	Phon	37	1	58	6					.90	.40	<.01
49	RAS	Phon	29	0	47	0					.73	.00	<.01
50	RAS	Undiff	38	0	53	13					.95	.87	
51	RAS	Phon	40	0	60	7					1.00	.47	<.01
52	RAS	Phon	34	1	51	1				.05	.83	.07	<.01

TABLE 4 (Continued.)

Patient	Aphasia type	TWLS			W–nW								L–S comparison: Monte Carlo (significant two-tailed p-values)
		Dyslexia type	Words named successfully (140)	Stress errors (140)	Words named successfully (161)	Nonwords named successfully (115)	WF	GC	Co	WL	L	S	
53	RAS	Phon	37	1	57	5			.03		.90	.33	<.01
54	TM	Phon	33	1	50	6					.80	.40	.01
55	TS	Phon	17	1	24	0				.01	.40	.00	<.01
56	TS	Phon	26	1	33	0					.63	.00	<.01
57	TS	Phon	17	0	14	0				<.01	.43	.00	<.01
58	TS	Undiff	31	4	45	6		.01			.68	.40	
59	TS	Phon	31	0	46	1					.78	.07	<.01
60	TS	Undiff	37	0	59	11					.93	.73	
61	TS	Phon	34	1	48	2				.01	.83	.13	<.01
62	TS	Surface	11	5	35	8				.01	.15	.53	.01
63	W	Undiff	33	0	48	8				.03	.83	.53	
64	W	Phon	15	0	13	0			.01		.38	.00	<.01
65	W	Phon	33	2	50	3					.78	.20	<.01
66	W	Undiff	14	2	34	3					.30	.20	
67	W	Undiff	34	2	53	10					.80	.67	
68	W	Undiff	21	2	21	4		<.01	.01	<.01	.50	.27	<.01
69	W	Surface	17	10	44	14					.10	.93	
70	W	Undiff	17	5	21	1		.01	.05	<.01	.15	.07	<.01
71	W	Phon	13	0	22	0		<.01		<.01	.33	.00	<.01
72	W	Phon	24	1	27	1					.58	.07	<.01
73	W	Undiff	29	5	49	9					.60	.60	
74	W	Phon	29	4	32	1		.01	.02	.05	.38	.07	.03
75	W	Phon	33	1	56	7				.02	.80	.47	.05
76	W	Undiff	12	6	20	3		<.01		<.01	.15	.20	
77	W	Undiff	15	11	27	4		<.01		<.01	.10	.27	
78	W	Undiff	0	1	8	0				.03	.00	.00	

TABLE 4 (Continued.)

Patient	Aphasia type	Dyslexia type	TWUS				W-nW						L–S comparison: Monte Carlo (significant two-tailed p-values)
			Words named successfully (/40)	Stress errors (/40)	Words named successfully (/61)	Nonwords named successfully (/15)	WF	GC	Co	WL	L	S	
79	W	Phon	28	1	37	3					.68	.20	<.01
80	W	Undiff	16	3	31	1	.04		.01	.04	.33	.07	
81	W	Undiff	31	2	43	9			.02	.01	.73	.60	
82	W	LBL	2	0	4	0					.05	.00	
83	W	Phon	6	0	13	0				.04	.15	.00	.04
84	W	Undiff	36	0	58	11					.90	.73	
85	W	Phon	28	0	33	1					.70	.07	<.01
86	W	Undiff	36	0	55	13					.90	.87	
87	W	Surface	12	15	24	8		.01	.02	<.01	.00	.53	<.01
88	W	Undiff	30	2	51	11					.70	.73	
89	W	Undiff	30	6	46	10			.01	.01	.60	.67	
90	W	Undiff	26	3	45	4				.04	.58	.27	

Aphasia type (AAT, Luzzatti et al., 1996): A, anomic; B, Broca's; B+ag, agrammatic Broca's; C, conduction; F/nF, unclassifiable along the fluency dimension; MT, mixed transcortical; RAS, residual aphasic symptoms; TM, transcortical motor; TS, transcortical sensory; W, Wernicke's.

Dyslexia type: LBL, Letter-by-Letter; Phon, phonological; undiff, undifferentiated.

L and S: levels of integrity of the lexical and SWL routes, respectively (see the Method section for details).

Significant one-tailed p-values are reported for the effects of Word Frequency (WF) in concrete nouns, Grammatical Class (GC), Concreteness (Co), and Word Length (WL).

* Grammatical class effect in paradoxical direction; ** Word length effect in paradoxical direction (two-tailed p-values are reported in the latter two cases).

READING DISORDERS AND SHALLOW ORTHOGRAPHY   835

TABLE 5
Cross-tabulation of the patient sample according to aphasia type and dyslexia type

| Dyslexia type | Aphasia type | | | | | | | | | Total | % |
| | Nonfluent | | | Fluent | | | | | | | |
	B	TM	MT	A	W	TS	C	FlnF	RAS		
Phonological	13*	1	1	5	9	5	4	6	5	49	54.4
Surface					2	1	1			4	4.4
Undifferentiated	3			5	16	2	4	1	1	32	35.6
Letter-by-Letter	1			2	1			1		5	5.6
Total	**17**	**1**	**1**	**12**	**28**	**8**	**9**	**8**	**6**	**90**	
%	18.9	1.1	1.1	13.3	31.1	8.9	10.0	8.9	6.7		

See Table 1 for acronyms. *One patient (P27) produced semantic errors (deep dyslexia).

All the expected dyslexic types were found in the sample. The performance of five patients corresponded to the operational criteria of a LBL reading impairment (5.6%). Most patients suffered from phonological (49, i.e., 54.4%) or undifferentiated (32, i.e., 35.6%) dyslexia. Only four patients (4.4%) could be classified as suffering from surface dyslexia. Finally, only one of the phonological dyslexic patients (P27) produced some semantic errors, thus responding to the operational criteria of *deep dyslexia* (see Luzzatti, Mondini, & Semenza, 2001 for a more extensive description of the case).

Aphasic patients: Relationship between type of aphasia and type of dyslexia

Table 5 illustrates the distribution across dyslexic types according to type of aphasia. Two phenomena emerge from a preliminary examination of the data: almost all nonfluent patients (15 out of 19) suffer from phonological dyslexia, whereas all the surface dyslexic patients (4 out of 4) belong to the fluent aphasia group.

Only two aphasia categories (fluent, nonfluent) and two dyslexia categories (phonological, undifferentiated) contained a sufficient number of participants on which to perform a statistical comparison. This showed a significant relationship ($\chi^2 = 7.48$, $p = .006$) between the two variables: the proportion of phonological vs undifferentiated dyslexia was much higher among the nonfluent (83.3% phonological) than the fluent (46.0% phonological) aphasic patients.

Effects of word frequency, concreteness, grammatical class, and word length

Group analyses: Phonological dyslexic patients. The ANCOVA revealed significant main effects of Word Frequency, $F(1, 50) = 3.85$, one-tailed $p = .028$, Word Length, $F(1, 50) = 38.97$, $p < .001$, and Item Type, $F(2, 50) = 9.55$, $p < .001$. The latter effect derived from a clear advantage of concrete nouns (70.3% patients named them successfully) over both function words (58.6%) and abstract nouns (58.0%). Thus there was both an effect of grammatical class, $F(1, 41) = 5.59$, $p = .023$, and an effect of concreteness, $F(1, 35) = 14.89$, $p < .001$.

Group analyses: Surface dyslexic patients. In the small group of surface dyslexic patients ($n = 4$), there was a highly significant effect of Word Length, $F(1, 50) = 19.39$, $p < .001$, without either an effect of Word Frequency, $F(1, 50) = 0.183$, $p = .67$, or of Item Type, $F(2, 50) = 0.482$, $p = .62$.

Group analyses: Patients with undifferentiated dyslexia. As was found for the phonological dyslexic sample, all three lexical variables turned out to have a significant effect also in patients with undifferentiated dyslexia—Word Length: $F(1, 50) = 70.04$, $p < .001$; Word Frequency: $F(1, 50) = 7.09$, $p = .01$; Item Type: $F(2, 50) = 10.54$, $p < .001$. Concrete nouns were named successfully by 70.7% of the patients, function words by 61.3%, and abstract nouns by 57.2%. Both the concreteness effect, $F(1, 35) = 18.98$, $p < .001$, and the grammatical class effect, $F(1, 41) = 3.76$, one-tailed $p = .03$, were significant.

Group analyses: Comparison between dyslexic subgroups. Figures 2, 3, and 4 show the effects of Word Frequency, Item Type, and Word Length in the four dyslexic subgroups. Surface and LBL dyslexic subsets were too small to allow for direct statistical comparison; marked differences emerged for the lexical effects (word frequency; concreteness, i.e., concrete vs abstract nouns; grammatical class, i.e., concrete nouns vs function words) between surface dyslexic patients, on the one hand, and patients with phonological and undifferentiated dyslexia on the other.

Figure 4 shows the rate of accuracy of the four dyslexic subgroups on short and long words. The effect of word length was maximal in surface dyslexia (43.8%), and more pronounced in undifferentiated (30.6%) than in phonological (23.4%) dyslexia. LBL patients showed an effect of 15.4%. The word length effects in surface and phonological dyslexic patients were significantly different (patients with surface

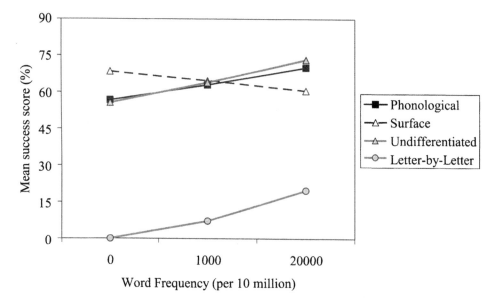

Figure 2. Word frequency effect as a function of dyslexia type (Analysis 1).

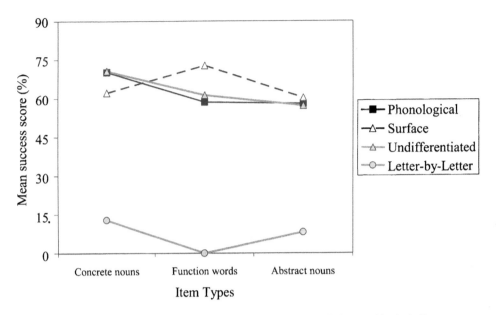

Figure 3. Mean success score as a function of item and dyslexia type (Analysis 1).

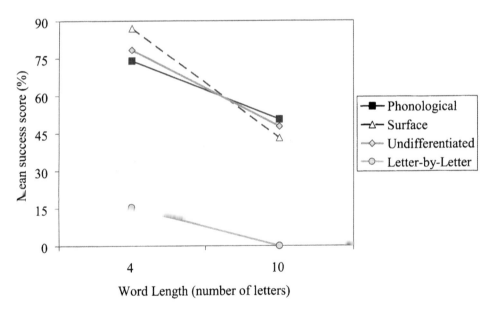

Figure 4. Word length effect as a function of dyslexia type (Analysis 1).

dyslexia < phonological dyslexia), in spite of the limited sample of the former group, $F(1, 50) = 4.77$, $p = .034$.

Single-case analyses: Word frequency. Concrete nouns were used in this analysis because they constituted the largest set of homogeneous items ($n = 30$). An LRA was carried out on the pass–fail scores of each patient on concrete nouns with *Word Frequency* as a unique predictor. Only five patients showed a significant word frequency effect (see Table 4). The apparent discrepancy with the results emerging from the group analysis (see above) can be explained by assuming that word frequency effects were widespread but relatively slight; the individual LRAs could not detect word frequency effects, while the more powerful group analysis picked them up.

Single-case analyses: Grammatical class and concreteness. A total of 15 patients with a significant effect of grammatical class and 15 patients with a significant concreteness effect were identified by Fisher's Exact tests. All the effects were in the expected direction, with the exception of one patient who showed a paradoxical advantage of function words over concrete nouns (P34). Effects co-existed in the deep dyslexic patient (P27), and were rather large ($p < .01$). His naming of concrete nouns was 86% accurate, while he named both function words and abstract nouns with an accuracy of approximately 20%.

Single-case analyses: Relationship between word frequency, grammatical class, and concreteness effects. Table 6 reports the rates of association/dissociation between lexical effects. The number of patients with a significant word frequency effect was too small to analyse the distribution of this variable. A strong association emerged between grammatical class and concreteness effects (Fisher's Exact test: $p < .001$: 57% of the patients with grammatical class effect also had a concreteness effect; this percentage dropped to 7% among patients without grammatical class effect).

Some of the patients showed significant effects of one or the other of the two lexical variables: five patients showed a concreteness effect but no grammatical class effect, and a further six patients showed the latter but not the former. We looked for strong dissociations between the patients' performance on function words and abstract nouns (to test the hypothesis that performance on abstract nouns could dissociate from that on function words) by comparing their success rates (adjusted for word frequency) with a Fisher's Exact test. This was done for each patient showing either a significant concreteness effect ($n = 7$) or a significant grammatical class effect ($n = 6$) or both ($n = 8$). Of the 21 patients, 2 suffered from a disproportionate impairment either of function words or of abstract nouns. Patient P24 named function words significantly better than abstract nouns—9/16 (adjusted for word frequency) vs 3/15; $p = .05$. Patient P71 performed significantly better on abstract nouns than on function words—5/15 vs 0/16 (adjusted for word frequency); $p = .018$.

TABLE 6
Word and nonword naming test

		Word frequency effect			
		Yes		No	
		Concreteness effect		Concreteness effect	
		Yes	No	Yes	No
Grammatical	Yes			8	6
class effect	No	2	3	5	66

Classification of patients according to presence/absence of significant effects of word frequency, grammatical class, concreteness (Analysis 1).

Single-case analyses: Word length. A total of 41 patients showed the expected effect of word length, i.e., they named shorter words more successfully than longer words. One patient (P10) showed a paradoxical advantage for longer words. The word length effect was significant in three out of the four surface dyslexic patients (75%), but only in 37% of the phonological (18/49) and 59% of the undifferentiated (19/32) dyslexic patients; only two out of the five LBL readers showed such an effect. This was to be expected as the measured variable was *accuracy* (within 2 seconds): the performance of the LBL readers was so poor (less than 10%) that not all the effects were able to reach statistical significance.

Discussion

The entire spectrum of dyslexic types predicted by the classical dual-route model was covered by the present sample, with the vast majority being phonological and undifferentiated dyslexic patients, while surface and LBL dyslexic patients were in the minority. Only one patient satisfied the operational criteria for deep dyslexia. Types of dyslexia were distributed unevenly across the various aphasia categories, as most nonfluent aphasic patients suffered from phonological dyslexia and all the surface dyslexic patients suffered from a fluent form of aphasia.

The analysis also studied the effects of word frequency, grammatical class, concreteness, and word length. *Word frequency* significantly affected the performance of the phonological and undifferentiated dyslexic subgroups; however, a similar effect did not emerge in surface dyslexic patients. A significant word frequency effect was seen at individual level in only five patients. This pattern of results may be explained by assuming a *small* but *widespread* effect of word frequency in the entire aphasic/dyslexic population, with the exception of surface dyslexic patients.

The *length of the stimuli* had a dramatic effect on reading performance; this effect is particularly strong in surface dyslexia and relatively less marked in phonological dyslexia and in the undifferentiated reading impairments. Although the reading impairment in LBL dyslexia is very severe, even in such cases word length remains a crucial predictor.

Concreteness and *grammatical class* affected group performance (and individual performances in 21 patients), with concreteness producing a slightly higher effect on the word-naming performance compared to grammatical class. Such effects appeared in both *phonological* and *undifferentiated* dyslexic patients, while they did not emerge in the limited *surface* dyslexic sample (see Figure 3). The absence of concreteness and grammatical class effects in surface dyslexia was predicted by the classical reading models. On the contrary, the performance of the deep dyslexic case (P27) was strongly influenced by both grammatical class and concreteness, as is prototypical of the syndrome.

Age of Acquisition (AA) has been found to be a crucial predictor of the performance of aphasic patients on a number of lexical tasks. For instance, Feyereisen, Van der Borght, and Seron (1988), Hirsh and Ellis (1994), and Hirsh and Funnel (1995) found strong AA effects in *picture naming*. The same effect was recently found by Barry and Gerhand (2003) in the *word naming* performance of a 52-year-old woman (LW) suffering from severe nonfluent language impairment and deep dyslexia. Interestingly, AA turned out to be the main predictor of this patient's performance, with concreteness being as effective as AA and word frequency influencing performance to a lesser extent. LW's pattern of damage was interpreted by the authors in terms of a model of reading in deep dyslexia in which AA affects the ease with which lexical phonology becomes available for spoken word production.

The question therefore arises whether the performance of our deep dyslexic patient (P27) might have been influenced by AA and whether this effect can be generalised to a larger number of patients. Furthermore, as AA correlates negatively with both concreteness and word frequency (Barry & Gerhand, 2003) it might well be that the significant effects of these variables on the performance of our patients were in fact mimicked by AA. This calls for a re-analysis of the data in a design that takes this variable into consideration. Since concrete nouns are usually acquired earlier than function words and these latter earlier than abstract nouns, AA could in fact be the primary explanation of concreteness and grammatical class effects.

ANALYSIS 2: THE ROLE OF AGE OF ACQUISITION

The purpose of the present analysis is to assess the impact of AA on the performance of the only deep dyslexic case identified by analysis of the individual patients' profiles. Since the lexical effects found for this patient in the previous analysis also affected a wider set of dyslexic patients, it was important to test whether this would be the case for the AA effect too.

Materials and methods

Measurement of age of acquisition

A 9-point scale was employed to collect *age of acquisition* ratings for each of the 61 words of the W-nW reading task. A total of 33 normal participants (age: 30.7 ± 8.7; education 17 ± 2.5 years) were asked to estimate the presumable age of acquisition of each word. A rating of 1 corresponded to acquisition within the second year of life, a rate of 2 within the third year of life, and so on (a rating of 9 was attributed to acquisition within the age of 13 or later).

Statistical analyses

The AA scores of the three item types (concrete nouns, abstract nouns, and function words) were compared by means of the Mann-Whitney test.

The effect of AA on the patients' performance *as a group* was assessed. Three "by-item" ANCOVAs were performed; they were identical to those employed in Analysis 1, the only difference being that AA was introduced as an additional covariate. Each ANCOVA also included the remaining lexical variables, i.e., Item Type (concrete nouns, abstract nouns, and function words) and Word Frequency. It was therefore possible to test whether the effects of the variables were in fact genuine or were to be attributed to a more general effect of AA.

At the *single-case* level, a conceptually similar analysis was performed by means of an LRA which considered the following independent variables: AA, Item Type, Word Frequency, and Word Length. The latter variable was included because of its massive effect on performance: its omission would have resulted in a considerable loss of statistical power.

Results

AA by item type

The average AA scores were 3.4 ± 1.3 for concrete nouns, 4.7 ± 1.4 for function words, and 6.5 ± 1.3 for abstract nouns. As predicted, concrete nouns were acquired earlier than both function words (Mann-Whitney: $z = 2.906$, $p = .004$) and abstract nouns ($z = 4.876$, $p < .001$), while function words were acquired earlier than abstract nouns ($z = 3.024$, $p = .002$).

The effect of AA on the patient with deep dyslexia (P27)

The AA effect was not significant (Wald $= 1.041$, one-tailed $p = .154$). After this (non-significant) effect had been partialled out, it was seen that the patient could name concrete nouns with 86% accuracy, abstract nouns with 30% accuracy, and function words with 6% accuracy: concreteness and grammatical class still had a significant influence on the patient's performance (Wald $= 4.673$, one-tailed $p = .016$; Wald $= 5.971$, one-tailed $p = .008$, respectively). After correction for AA, both Word Frequency and Word Length remained non-significant predictors (Wald $= 1.079$, one-tailed $p = .15$; Wald $= .386$, one-tailed $p = .267$, respectively).

ANCOVAs

Phonological dyslexic patients. There was a significant AA effect; words acquired early were named with 69.6% accuracy, while words acquired at a later stage only reached 55.1% accuracy (see Table 7). After AA was included in the design, the lexical effects disappeared or diminished dramatically, losing significance in all cases. The advantage of concrete nouns over both function words and abstract nouns (which was 12% in Analysis 1) decreased to less than 2.5%, and the effect of word frequency dropped from 13.4% to 3.3%.

Surface dyslexic patients. There was no significant AA effect and no substantial change emerged in the lexical effects (Table 7).

Undifferentiated dyslexic patients. The pattern was similar to that observed in phonological dyslexia. A strong AA effect (8.5%) was observed in conjunction with the reduction of the grammatical class (from 9.4% to 3.7%), concreteness (from 13.5% to 7.8%), and word frequency (from 17.7% to 11.9%) effects. All these effects except that of word frequency (see Table 7) lost significance.

Single-case analyses (LRA)

At the individual level, AA significantly affected the performance of 12 patients. The results of these analyses also showed a partial or total disappearance of the concreteness and grammatical class effects. After AA was introduced as a predictor, concreteness had a significant effect in only four patients (including P27), as opposed to 15 in the previous analysis; grammatical class had a significant effect in two patients (including P27), as opposed to 15 in the previous analysis. Thus, patient P27 was the only participant whose performance was still affected significantly by concreteness and grammatical class. Four patients showed a word frequency effect, as opposed to five in the previous design.

TABLE 7
ANCOVA results

	AA				Word Frequency					Item Type				
SD (%)	Low (3.5 yrs)	High (9 yrs)	F(1, 49)	p	0	1000	20000	F(1, 49)	p	Concrete	Function	Abstract	F(2, 49)	p
Phonological 7.7	69.6	55.1	16.67	<.001	58.4	60.0	61.8	.29	.591	61.2	59.5	58.8	.22	.803
Surface 23.0	70.4	59.7	1.00	.322	69.7	62.5	54.4	.60	.442	55.4	73.4	60.9	.84	.437
Undifferentiated 8.4	67.4	58.9	4.73	.035	56.6	62.2	68.6	3.01	.089*	65.5	61.8	57.7	1.96	.152
Letter-by-Letter 11.8	7.5	4.9	—	—	0.0	6.8	18.3	—	—	11.3	0.0	8.3	—	—

Mean success scores (%) as a function of Age of Acquisition, Word Frequency and Item Type (Analysis 2).
Significance test results are not reported for LBL readers as the ANCOVA was invalidated by large normality violations.
SD %, standard deviations of the error term from the specific ANCOVA, in the % scale. Two-tailed p-values are reported.
* The word frequency effect observed in the undifferentiated dyslexic patients is in the expected direction (one-tailed p-value = .0445).

Discussion

AA was introduced in a further analysis to test its effect on the word-naming performance of our deep dyslexic patient and of the entire dyslexic sample; AA did not influence the word-naming performance of the deep dyslexic patient, whereas its effect was crucial in the phonological and undifferentiated dyslexic samples, where the effects of grammatical class, concreteness, and word frequency vanished or diminished. Thus, a certain degree of the lexical effects emerging from Analysis 1 can be explained by the confounding effect of AA. Data are in agreement with results indicating that self-report by adult participants is an important predictor of word retrieval performance in both aphasic patients (e.g., Hirsh & Ellis, 1994) and normal participants (e.g., Bates et al., 2001).

GENERAL DISCUSSION

While studies of patients suffering from reading impairment after brain damage have provided excellent opportunities to test contemporary models of written language, the majority were done with dyslexic patients whose mother-tongue was English or French, two languages with largely opaque orthography. In this paper we address the question of whether contemporary models of word naming are also applicable to languages with shallow orthography. Single cases of phonological, surface, and deep dyslexia have also been reported in Italian (e.g., Caramazza, Miceli, Silveri, & Laudanna, 1985; Job & Sartori, 1984; Miceli, Capasso, & Caramazza, 1994; Miceli, Villa, & Silveri, 1983) and in other shallow languages (Ferreres & Miravalles, 1995; Ruiz, Ansaldo, & Lecours, 1994). However, it is unclear whether these cases constitute a fringe and sporadic phenomenon (as suggested by Ardila, 1991, for the Spanish language), or important evidence that dual-route models of word naming may be generalised to all natural languages, irrespective of their orthography and of the procedures used to teach reading skills during the early phases of literacy acquisition.

Distribution of patients along the dyslexia spectrum

The first aim of the present study was to verify to what extent theoretical inferences derived from dyslexia in English could be extended to aphasic participants speaking a language with highly shallow orthography, such as Italian, and in particular to determine the rate of disproportionate damage of either the lexical or the SWL reading route (surface and phonological dyslexia, respectively).

In analogy with data reported for English-speaking aphasic patients, the reading impairments of the 90 Italian aphasic patients who participated in the present study covered the entire range of reading impairments, but with a majority of phonological dyslexia (54%), followed by relatively high rate of undifferentiated dyslexia (36%), and a much lower incidence of letter-by-letter dyslexia (6%) and surface dyslexia (4%). Of the phonological dyslexic patients only one made semantic errors, showing the features of deep dyslexia.

Interesting inferences might be drawn from a comparison of the distribution of Italian- and English-speaking aphasic patients over the dyslexia spectrum. However, to the best of our knowledge rates of dyslexia subtypes have not yet been systematically described in English speakers or speakers of other opaque-orthography languages. Although it was not possible to make a direct comparison with an English-speaking aphasic sample, two results of the present study are worth mentioning: (i) the surprising disproportion between phonological and surface dyslexic patients, with the former being more than 12 times more frequent than the latter; (ii) the very small number of deep dyslexia cases ($n = 1$) notwithstanding the size of the sample (90). Both results seem to be in agreement with Ardila's (1991) claim that the distribution by dyslexic type differs between samples of aphasic patients speaking languages with shallow and opaque orthographies.

Deep dyslexia

There are two classical accounts that explain the mechanisms underlying deep dyslexia: (i) the emergence of right hemisphere (RH) residual abilities that are usually said to be limited to high-frequency concrete nouns (Coltheart, 1980b, 2000; Zaidel, 1990); (ii) an instability of the conceptual system in the absence of adequate (lexical) phonological control (Buchanan, Hildebrandt, & MacKinnon, 1994; Morton & Patterson, 1980).

Both accounts are compatible with the rarity of semantic paralexia in Italian. In this language, the premorbid over-reliance on the SWL procedure (due to the shallow orthography) offers the dyslexic patient greater opportunities to compensate for the lack of adequate lexical-semantic knowledge and/or (lexical) phonological control, thus reducing the probability of semantic errors in reading.

Damage to the SWL procedure is a crucial element of deep dyslexia; the functional lesion has to be severe enough to prevent correct naming along this route, but some (correct) phonemes might still access the phonological output buffer via the SWL conversion routine (see Coltheart, Curtis, Atkins, & Haller, 1993, p. 596, and Plaut, McClelland, Seidenberg, & Patterson, 1996, p. 102). This phonological information might be sufficiently strong to disambiguate between competing lexical strings arising from semantically related conceptual nodes. For instance, the written word HOUND would activate the appropriate semantic node along the spared lexical route, which in turn would activate the lexical representation [dɔg], i.e., the most commonly used term in English for the four-legged domestic animal which barks; the less frequent phonological word form [haund] would also be activated, although to a lesser extent, and its corresponding phonological string [h][a][u][n][d] would be forwarded to the phonological output buffer. Although the SWL conversion route in its damaged state would not be able to provide complete word naming, it could activate some phonemes, e.g., [h] ... [n], thus making the less frequent phonological string [h][a][u][n][d] predominate over the more frequent [d][ɔ][g]. As a final result, the correct output *hound* would be given instead of the more common, and therefore more intensely activated, semantically related lexical output *dog*.[5] This would explain the very low frequency of deep dyslexia in Italian.

According to this hypothesis, a damaged SWL routine could still provide phonological disambiguation and therefore prevent semantic errors. A patient would

---

[5] Alternatively, functional summation has been said to occur through direct connection between the GPC and the phonological output lexicon (Hillis & Caramazza, 1991), or by backward spreading activation of the phonological output lexicon arising from the phonological output buffer (Dell & Juliano, 1996; Dell, Schwartz, Martin, Saffran, & Gagnon, 1997).

therefore be classified as suffering from phonological dyslexia, although some typical characteristics of deep dyslexia, such as grammatical class, concreteness, and word frequency effects, would still appear. This does in fact appear to be the case (see Analysis 1). Phonological dyslexic patients showed significant grammatical class, concreteness, and word frequency effects as a group (Figures 3 and 4), while surface dyslexic patients did not (although the limited size of the sample, $n = 4$, makes it premature to draw conclusions in this respect). In addition, none of the four surface dyslexic patients revealed significant effects of any of the three lexical variables in the single-case analysis, while these effects were present in many phonological (14 out of 49) and undifferentiated (9 out of 32) dyslexic patients.

Another straightforward prediction of the "SWL phonological control" hypothesis is that in opaque-orthography languages like English, which do not provide such an effective SWL strategy, semantic errors, i.e., deep dyslexia, should be more frequent. In the absence of data on deep dyslexia frequency among English-speaking aphasic patients, this has to be left as an open question deserving further research.

Phonological versus surface dyslexia

The phonological/surface disproportion can be accounted for by assuming a different implementation of the two routes in the brain. If it is assumed that the left hemisphere has both a lexical and a SWL route, while the right hemisphere only has limited lexical knowledge (most likely limited to high-frequency, concrete nouns; see Coltheart, 1980b; Binder, Westbury, McKiernan, Possing, & Medler, 2005), *extensive* unilateral LH lesions would damage both routes and unblock the limited RH lexical knowledge, therefore causing a reading impairment with the characteristics of phonological dyslexia. On the other hand, the emergence of surface dyslexia would require the co-occurrence of two factors: a lesion small enough to leave the SWL route intact and a failure in the activation of the limited RH lexical knowledge. The hypothesis is for the moment only speculative and deserves anatomo-clinical correlative study.

Aphasia and dyslexia

Another issue emerging from the present data is the relationship between aphasia and dyslexia classifications. The majority of Broca's aphasic patients suffered from phonological dyslexia (76%). By contrast, fluent aphasic patients were distributed more evenly across dyslexia types. Surface dyslexia would seem to occur only in fluent aphasia cases with severe input and output lexical damage. It is worthy of note that a similar trend did not emerge for the spelling disorders in Italian aphasic participants, where no relationship could be found between type of aphasia and type of dysgraphia (Luzzatti, Laiacona, Allamano, De Tanti, & Inzaghi, 1998).

Concreteness, grammatical class, word frequency, age of acquisition, and word length

The final aim of this study was to assess the influence of word frequency, AA, concreteness, grammatical class, and stimuli length on the reading performance of a large sample of aphasic patients.

Length effect

The length of the stimuli had a significant effect on the reading performance; this effect is particularly strong in surface dyslexia and much less marked in phonological dyslexia and in the undifferentiated reading impairments. Although the reading disorder in LBL dyslexia is already very severe for short stimuli, word length still also predicts the reading performance in such cases.

Concreteness, grammatical class, and word frequency effects

In Analysis 1, concreteness, grammatical class, and word frequency affected group performance (and individual performances in 24 patients), with effects ranging from 9.3% to 15.5%. Such effects appeared in both *phonological* and *undifferentiated* dyslexic patients, while they did not seem to be present in the small *surface* dyslexic sample (see Figures 2 and 3). These results were maintained both at the group and at the single-case level. The absence of the lexical effects in surface dyslexia is predicted by the classical reading models.

Age of acquisition (AA)

In Analysis 2, AA had only a marginal effect on the performance of the deep dyslexic case, but proved to be the best predictor of the performance of the remaining patients (and particularly for the phonological and undifferentiated dyslexia subgroups). Furthermore, the introduction of AA in the design reduced the size of the other lexical effects, which became non-significant. According to Barry and Gerhand (2003), the effects of AA would arise in the phonological output lexicon. It is highly likely that this unit—or access to it—is damaged in many of the patients of our aphasic sample, which is consistent with the large AA effect found in Analysis 2.

Another question is why AA cancels the other lexical effects (word frequency, grammatical class, concreteness) at group level. One possible explanation is that AA is the only important predictor of word-naming performance in dyslexia. In other words there would be no mental basis (or biological correlate) of the grammatical class distinction and concreteness effect in word naming, but these apparent effects would be an artefact arising from the earlier acquisition of concrete nouns with respect to abstract nouns and function words. However, this explanation is not wholly satisfactory, and it does not account for the large grammatical class and concreteness effects that persisted in our deep dyslexic patient after the effect of AA was removed.

In conclusion, the dyslexia types predicted by the classical dual-route models of reading could also be found in Italian. This suggests that qualitatively similar cognitive architectures for reading are also developed in shallow-orthography languages.

Nevertheless, only 1 out of 90 patients could be classified as suffering from deep dyslexia. This very low rate might be due to over-reliance on the (effective) SWL route in Italian, which, although damaged, might still provide enough phonological control to prevent semantic errors. Several variables predict the patients' word-naming performance: these were (in order of effect size) word length, word frequency, concreteness, and grammatical class. However, the effects of the latter three variables could be partially explained by AA (e.g., Barca & Burani, 2002;

Barry & Gerhand, 2003; Zevin & Seidenberg, 2002, 2004). The nature of this interaction is still unclear and deserves further research.

REFERENCES

Andrews, S. (1989). Frequency and neighbourhood effects on lexical access: Activation or search? *Journal of Experimental Psychology: Learning, Memory and Cognition, 15*, 802–814.

Ardila, A. (1991). Errors resembling semantic paralexias in Spanish-speaking aphasics. *Brain and Language, 41*, 437–445.

Barca, L., & Burani, C. (2002). Word age-of-acquisition and acquired language impairments: A review. *Ricerche di Psicologia, 25*, 73–94.

Barca, L., Burani, C., & Arduino, L. S. (2002). Word naming times and psycholinguistic norms for Italian nouns. *Behavior Research Methods, Instruments & Computers, 34*, 424–434.

Barry, C., & Gerhand, S. (2003). Both concreteness and age-of-acquisition affect reading accuracy but only concreteness affects comprehension in a deep dyslexic patient. *Brain and Language, 84*, 84–104.

Bates, E., Burani, C., D'Amico, S., & Barca, L. (2001). Word reading and picture naming in Italian. *Memory and Cognition, 29*, 986–999.

Binder, J. R., Westbury, C. F., McKiernan, K. A., Possing, E. T., & Medler, D. A. (2005). Distinct brain systems for processing concrete and abstract concepts. *Journal of Cognitive Neuroscience, 17*, 905–917.

Bonin, P., Barry, C., Méot, A., & Chalard, M. (2004). The influence of age of acquisition in word reading and other tasks: A never ending story? *Journal of Memory and Language, 50*, 456–476.

Buchanan, L., Hildebrandt, N., & MacKinnon, G. E. (1994). Phonological processing of nonwords by a deep dyslexic patient: A rowse is implicitly a rose. *Journal of Neurolinguistics, 8*, 163–181.

Caramazza, A., Miceli, G., Silveri, M. C., & Laudanna, A. (1985). Reading mechanisms and the organization of the lexicon: Evidence from acquired lexicon. *Cognitive Neuropsychology, 2*, 81–114.

Coltheart, M. (1980a). Deep dyslexia: A review of the syndrome. In M. Coltheart, K. Patterson, & J. C. Marshall (Eds.), *Deep dyslexia* (pp. 22–47). London: Routledge & Kegan Paul.

Coltheart, M. (1980b). Deep dyslexia: A right hemisphere hypothesis. In M. Coltheart, K. Patterson, & J. C. Marshall (Eds.), *Deep dyslexia* (pp. 326–380). London: Routledge & Kegan Paul.

Coltheart, M. (1998). Seven questions about pure alexia (letter-by-letter reading). *Cognitive Neuropsychology, 15*, 1–6.

Coltheart, M. (2000). Deep dyslexia is right-hemisphere reading. *Brain and Language, 71*, 299–309.

Coltheart, M., Curtis, B., Atkins, P., & Haller, M. (1993). Models of reading aloud: Dual-route and parallel-distributed-processing approaches. *Psychological Review, 100*, 589–608.

Coltheart, M., Patterson, K. E., & Marshall, J. C. (1980). *Deep dyslexia*. London: Routledge & Kegan Paul.

Coltheart, M., Rastle, K., Perry, C., Langdon, R., & Ziegler, J. (2001). DRC: A dual route cascaded model of visual word recognition and reading aloud. *Psychological Review, 108*, 204–256.

Cumming, T. B., Patterson, K., Verfaellie, M., & Graham, K. S. (in press). One bird with two stones: Abnormal word length effects in pure alexia and semantic dementia. *Cognitive Neuropsychology*.

Déjerine, J. J. (1892). Contribution à l'étude anatomo-pathologique et clinique des différentes variétés de cécité verbale. *Comptes Rendus Hebdomadaires des Séances et Mémoires de la Société de Biologie (Paris), 4*, 61–90.

Dell, G. S., & Juliano, C. (1996). Computational models of phonological encoding. In T. Dijkstra & K. de Smedt (Eds.), *Computational psycholinguistics: AI and connectionist models of human language processing* (pp. 328–359). Philadelphia: Taylor & Francis.

Dell, G. S., Schwartz, M. F., Martin, N., Saffran, E. M., & Gagnon, D. A. (1997). Lexical access in aphasic and nonaphasic speakers. *Psychological Review, 104*, 801–838.

Derouesné, J., & Beauvois, M. F. (1985). The "phonemic" stage in the non-lexical reading process: Evidence from a case of phonological alexia. In K. E. Patterson, J. C. Marshall, & M. Coltheart (Eds.), *Surface dyslexia*. Hove, UK: Lawrence Erlbaum Associates Ltd.

Ferreres, A. R., & Miravalles, G. (1995). The production of semantic paralexias in a Spanish-speaking aphasic. *Brain and Language, 49*, 153–172.

Feyereisen, P., Van der Borght, F., & Seron, X. (1988). The operativity effect in naming: A re-analysis. *Neuropsychologia, 26*, 401–415.

Forster, K. I., & Chambers, S. M. (1973). Lexical access and naming time. *Journal of Verbal Learning and Verbal Behavior, 12*, 627–635.

Gold, B. T., Balota, D. A., Cortese, M. J., Sergent-Marshall, S. D., Snyder, A. Z., & Salat, D. H., et al. (2005). Differing neuropsychological and neuroanatomical correlates of abnormal reading in early-stage semantic dementia and dementia of the Alzheimer type. *Neuropsychologia, 43*, 833–846.

Hillis, A. E., & Caramazza, A. (1991). Mechanisms for accessing lexical representations for output: Evidence from a category-specific semantic deficit. *Brain and Language, 40*, 106–144.

Hirsh, K. W., & Ellis, A. W. (1994). Age of acquisition and lexical processing in aphasia: A case study. *Cognitive Neuropsychology, 11*, 435–458.

Hirsh, K. W., & Funnell, E. (1995). Those old, familiar things: Age of acquisition, familiarity and lexical access in progressive aphasia. *Journal of Neurolinguistics, 9*, 23–32.

IBM (1989). *VELI, Vocabolario Elettronico della Lingua Italiana*. Milano: IBM.

Job, R., & Sartori, G. (1984). Morphological decomposition: Evidence from crossed phonological dyslexia. *Quarterly Journal of Experimental Psychology, 36A*, 435–458.

Juhasz, B. J. (2005). Age-of-acquisition effects in word and picture identification. *Psychological Bulletin, 131*, 684–712.

Lewis, M. B., Gerhand, S., & Ellis, H. D. (2001). Re-evaluating age-of-acquisition effects: Are they simply cumulative-frequency effects? *Cognition, 78*, 189–205.

Luzzatti, C., Laiacona, M., Allamano, N., De Tanti, A., & Inzaghi, M. G. (1998). Writing disorders in Italian aphasic patients: A multiple single-case study of dysgraphia in a language with shallow orthography. *Brain, 121*, 1721–1734.

Luzzatti, C., Mondini, S., & Semenza, C. (2001). Lexical representation and processing of morphologically complex words: Evidence from the reading performance of an Italian agrammatic patient. *Brain and Language, 79*, 345–359.

Luzzatti, C., Willmes, K., & De Bleser, R. (1996). *Aachener Aphasie Test (AAT): Versione Italiana*. (2nd ed.). Firenze: Organizzazioni Speciali.

Miceli, G., Capasso, R., & Caramazza, A. (1994). The interaction of lexical and sublexical processing in reading, writing and repetition. *Neuropsychologia, 32*, 317–333.

Miceli, G., Villa, P. L., & Silveri, M. C. (1983). Deficit dei meccanismi di lettura in un caso di dislessia profonda: Componenti centrali e periferiche. *Archivio di Psicologia, Neurologia e Psichiatria, 44*, 185–215.

Morrison, C. M., & Ellis, A. W. (1995). Roles of word frequency and age of acquisition in word naming and lexical decision. *Journal of Experimental Psychology: Learning, Memory and Cognition, 21*, 116–133.

Morton, J., & Patterson, K. (1980). A new attempt at an interpretation, or, an attempt at a new interpretation. In M. Coltheart, K. Patterson, & J. C. Marshall (Eds.), *Deep dyslexia* (pp. 91–118). London: Routledge & Kegan Paul.

Paap, K. R., & Noel, R. W. (1991). Dual route models of print to sound: Still a good horse race. *Psychological Research, 53*, 13–24.

Patterson, K. E., & Kay, J. (1982). Letter by letter reading: Psychological description of a neurological syndrome. *Quarterly Journal of Experimental Psychology, 34A*, 411–441.

Patterson, K. E., Marshall, J. C., & Coltheart, M. (1985). *Surface dyslexia*. Hove, UK: Lawrence Erlbaum Associates Ltd.

Plaut, D. C., McClelland, J. L., Seidenberg, M. S., & Patterson, K. (1996). Understanding normal and impaired word reading: Computational principles in quasi-regular domains. *Psychological Review, 103*, 56–115.

Ruiz, A., Ansaldo, A. I., & Lecours, R. (1994). Two cases of deep dyslexia in unilingual hispanophone aphasics. *Brain and Language, 46*, 245–256.

Saffran, E. M., Bogyo, L. C., Schwartz, M. F., & Marin, O. S. M. (1980). Does deep dyslexia reflect right hemisphere reading? In M. Coltheart, K. E. Patterson, & J. C. Marshall (Eds.), *Deep dyslexia*. London: Routledge & Kegan Paul.

Schwartz, M. F., Saffran, E. M., & Marin, O. S. M. (1980). Fractionating the reading process in dementia: Evidence from word-specific print-to-sound associations. In M. Coltheart, K. E. Patterson, & J. C. Marshall (Eds.), *Deep dyslexia*. London: Routledge & Kegan Paul.

Shallice, T. (1988). *From neuropsychology to mental structure*. Oxford, UK: Oxford University Press.

Shibahara, N., Zorzi, M., Hill, M., Wydell, T., & Butterworth, B. (2003). Semantic effects in word naming: Evidence from English and Japanese kanji. *Quarterly Journal Of Experimental Psychology, 56A*, 263–286.

Strain, E., Patterson, K., & Seidenberg, M. (1995). Semantic effects in single-word naming. *Journal of Experimental Psychology: Learning, Memory, and Cognition, 21,* 1140–1154.

Zaidel, E. (1990). Language functions in the two hemispheres following complete cerebral commissurotomy and hemispherectomy. In F. Boller & J. Grafman (Eds.), *Handbook of neuropsychology, Vol. 4* (pp. 115–150). Amsterdam: Elsevier.

Zevin, J. D., & Seidenberg, M. S. (2002). Age of acquisition effects in word reading and other tasks. *Journal of Memory and Language, 47,* 1–29.

Zevin, J. D., & Seidenberg, M. S. (2004). Age-of-acquisition effects in reading aloud: Tests of cumulative frequency and frequency trajectory. *Memory and Cognition, 32,* 31–38.

Using orthographic neighbours to treat a case of graphemic buffer disorder

Karen Sage

University of Manchester, UK

Andrew W. Ellis

University of York, UK

Background: The characteristics of graphemic buffer disorder have been described by Miceli, Silveri, and Caramazza (1985) and Caramazza and Miceli (1990) and include a length effect in spelling words and nonwords, in both written and oral format. Error patterns typically consist of omissions, substitutions, additions, and movement errors. Recently, lexical effects on spelling accuracy in many buffer cases have been shown (Sage & Ellis, 2004) and, in patient BH in particular, these included an influence of orthographic neighbourhood size (the number of words that can be generated by changing one letter in the target word; Coltheart, Davelaar, Jonassen, & Besner, 1977).

Aims: This paper aims to show that orthographic neighbours used in a therapy programme can bring about improvements in the spelling of targets that have not directly received therapy.

Methods & procedures: This was a single case treatment study of BH, who showed classic features of graphemic buffer disorder in her spelling. Two priming studies contrasting no prime, control primes, and orthographic neighbour primes (both word and nonword) established that positive effects on spelling accuracy and error pattern could be achieved. The use of orthographic neighbours was then extended into a therapy programme. Three word sets contrasted direct therapy to the words themselves (Set1), no therapy at all (Set 2), and therapy to neighbours of the words in a set (Set 3). An errorless learning paradigm was used throughout the therapy programme.

Outcome & results: Improvement was made both to the treated words in Set 1 and to the words in Set 3, even though these words had received no direct therapy. There was no change in accuracy in Set 2, the control set that had received no therapy. The paper also explores changes in error patterns due to therapy, showing that error patterns changed following therapy.

Conclusions: The priming studies showed that changes in accuracy could be achieved when orthographic neighbours were used. Following on from this, a therapy programme based on neighbours was effective in assisting the graphemic buffer. Specifically, the interaction between lexicon and buffer was used therapeutically to improve not only the spelling of words that had received direct treatment but also to a word set that did not directly receive treatment. These changes were brought about using an errorless learning paradigm.

Address correspondence to: Karen Sage, School of Psychological Sciences, University of Manchester, Oxford Road, Manchester M13 9PL, UK. E-mail: karen.sage@manchester.ac.uk

The work was supported by a Health Foundation mid-career award to K. Sage

MODEL OF SPELLING

According to the dual route model of spelling (Barry, 1994; Ellis, 1982), there are two procedures by which spelling is achieved: the semantic/lexical route and the non-lexical route. The non-lexical procedure converts phonemes into graphemes, and is therefore able to spell accurately words that have predictable phoneme-to-grapheme correspondences and to make a good attempt at spelling unfamiliar, unknown, and nonwords by using the conversion method. The semantic/lexical procedure uses word meanings to assist in spelling. This is particularly helpful when the word does not follow the same pattern as other similar sounding words (e.g., SOAP contrasting with HOPE, SLOPE, COPE etc.) or has a completely irregular spelling (e.g., YACHT). Both routes come together at the graphemic output buffer which is a short-term holding mechanism where the graphemes are stored temporarily while the output method is established (e.g., whether a word is to be written, spelt orally, typed etc.).

Graphemic buffer disorder, as described by Miceli, Silveri and Caramazza (1985) and Caramazza and Miceli (1990), is interpreted as a disruption in this short-term holding mechanism. The characteristics of buffer disruption are that more errors occur as target length increases and errors are typically substitutions (e.g., "church" – CHURSH, "lunch" – LANCH), additions (e.g., "anger" – AUNGER, "trunk" – THRUNK), omissions (e.g., "album" – ALUM, "insect" – INECT), movement (e.g., "guard" – GAURD, "third" – THRID), or a combination of these (e.g., "giraffe" – GIRRFFA, "aisle" – IALE). The buffer lies at the intersection with the output methods to be selected and so damage to the buffer should affect all forms of output (whether it be in written, oral, or typed format). In some cases, errors occur more in the middle of words than at the end (e.g., McCloskey, Badecker, Goodman-Schulman, & Aliminosa, 1994; Miceli et al., 1985). In other cases, errors have occurred more frequently towards the end of the word (e.g., Katz, 1991; Schiller, Greenhall, Shelton, & Caramazza, 2001). Because the buffer receives information from both lexical and non-lexical spelling routes, similar accuracy rates have been expected for both nonwords and words. This assumption has recently been challenged by Sage and Ellis (2004), who compared the accuracy for words and nonwords in 17 cases of graphemic buffer disorder and found that in 10 cases, nonword spelling was significantly worse than word spelling, a finding which suggests that the buffer, in these cases, responded more successfully to lexical items. Similarly, early research (Caramazza & Miceli, 1990; Miceli et al., 1985) claimed that lexical qualities such as frequency, age of acquisition, imageability etc. were unlikely to contribute to spelling accuracy. There is, however, increasing evidence that many graphemic buffer cases are affected by such lexical variables (Sage & Ellis, 2004; McCloskey, Marusco, & Rapp, 1999, Pate & Margolin, 1990).

REMEDIATION FOR SPELLING PROBLEMS WITHIN THE GRAPHEMIC BUFFER

There are a number of studies that have described therapy programmes aimed at assisting the graphemic output buffer (Aliminosa, McCloskey, Goodman-Schulman, & Sokol, 1993; de Partz, 1995; Hillis & Caramazza, 1987, 1989; Pound, 1996; Rapp & Kane, 2002; Raymer, Cudworth, & Haley, 2003). In four of these studies (Aliminosa et al., 1993; de Partz, 1995; Rapp & Kane, 2002 and Raymer et al., 2003) locating the spelling problem entirely within the buffer is problematic, and consequently interpreting how therapy achieved improvement remains unclear. In all four cases, spelling output showed that the graphemic buffer was not working effectively. There may have been at least three reasons why the buffer was unable to work effectively: (1) the information arriving in the buffer was itself damaged; (2) the information arriving in the buffer was intact but the buffer was damaged and so could not retain it correctly; (3) a combination of these.

Case details from two of the studies suggest that the primary disruption to spelling was because the target was damaged before it arrived in the buffer (de Partz, 1995; Raymer et al., 2003). AM (de Partz, 1995) was a woman with deep dysphasia who made lexical and semantic errors in word repetition. She was unable to repeat nonwords or write nonwords to dictation. However, spelling tasks that did not use input phonology (such as written picture naming and delayed copying) were also severely disrupted and pointed to a further, specific spelling problem. AM showed a clear length effect and the majority of spelling errors (76% of word errors and 68% of nonword errors) were buffer-like. She made a number of lexical errors, for example, four substitutions of functions words (e.g., "je" [I] spelt as TU [you]), three "lexico-graphemical" errors and spelling accuracy for words was affected by both frequency and imageability. In summary, AM's nonword spelling route was severely impaired, the lexico-semantic route was damaged to a lesser degree, and there may also have been further damage within the graphemic buffer itself.

NM (Raymer et al., 2002) had severe aphasia initially which resolved to minimal verbal language problems. Spelling remained problematic, which the authors suggest arose from damage to both the orthographic output lexicon and the graphemic buffer. Evidence for lexical damage came from the error patterns of phonologically plausible nonwords, no responses, and orthographically similar word errors which made up 32% of all errors. NM was more impaired at delayed copying and spelling of nonwords compared to words and she found high-frequency words easier to spell than low-frequency words and nonwords. Evidence for an additional buffer problem was suggested because of the large number of multiple omission errors made (65% of errors made on spelling to dictation were made because NM could write only the first one or two letters). NM made very few other buffer errors and there was no clear decrease in accuracy as the target increased in length. The balance of evidence would therefore suggest that NM's spelling difficulties arose primarily in the lexicon, with concomitant difficulties in the buffer because of inadequate information placed there.

In view of the lexical damage in each of these cases, therapy might aim to improve the quality of the lexical item before it reaches the buffer and if so, the effects of such therapy might be expected to be item specific. In the first case, AM (de Partz, 1995) was asked to chunk long words into smaller, manageable bites, in the hope that this would become a compensatory strategy that AM could use to assist all long words whether they had been involved in the direct therapy programme or not. However, improvement was seen only when AM worked specifically on targeted words. The second case, NM (Raymer et al., 2003), was trained on six-letter word sets which had been paired with words that shared initial or final orthography (e.g., the trained word "racket" was linked to the untrained words "racoon" and "basket"). NM made most improvement on items that were treated, but also made significant gains on those words with shared orthography, particularly when the shared orthography was at the beginning of the word. In both cases, the improvement was attributed in increasing activation within the orthographic lexicon. Raymer et al. (2002) attributed NM's ability to spell untrained words that shared the same ending as those trained as evidence that improvement at the syllable level within the lexicon had enabled these words to be maintained by the buffer.

Two further studies involved cases where the background information suggested that the primary disruption to their spelling was likely to be as a result of a poorly functioning buffer (Aliminosa et al., 1994; Rapp & Kane, 2002). Following a CVA, JES (Aliminosa et al., 1994) had good language skills in that he could understand spoken and written material, name, repeat accurately, and hold conversations with only mild fluency difficulties. He retained a relatively severe spelling problem, which was characterised by decreasing accuracy as word length increased and errors occurring in the middle of words that were buffer-like. However, his spelling was also influenced by the frequency of the word, lexicality (he was better at words than nonwords), and regularity, making some phonologically plausible errors. RSB (Rapp & Kane, 2002) had moderate language problems following a CVA, particularly with word finding. He also had moderately severe spelling problems, with decreasing accuracy as target length increased and buffer-like errors in his spelling, particularly omissions and substitutions. However, he was more accurate at high-frequency words and made some phonologically plausible errors, suggestive of a mild lexical impairment.

In these two cases, JES's response to a therapy programme of copying was item specific (Aliminosa et al., 1994) while RSB (Rapp & Kane, 2002), with a similar therapy programme of delayed copying, improved his spelling of items that were not in the therapy programme and this improvement was maintained after the end of therapy. Only RSP achieved generalisation across untreated items that were completely unrelated to the treated items. Rapp and Kane (2002) proposed three possible reasons for this: that the buffer's repeated exposure to words improved its capacity to maintain representations; that scanning speed or speed of transfer to the letter-shape level of writing was improved; or that training orthographic representations enabled them to survive buffer damage more effectively.

The current study describes two priming experiments followed by a treatment programme for patient BH, a classic case of graphemic buffer disorder. BH showed a strong length effect in spelling to dictation and oral spelling, and made errors of substitution, omission, addition, and movement, and these errors occurred in the middle rather than beginning or end of words. These features indicated problems maintaining the word to be spelt in the temporary store (the buffer) before output (Caramazza & Miceli, 1990; Miceli et al., 1985). Sage and Ellis (2004) showed that the lexical nature of words also influenced the performance of the buffer, not only in BH's case, but also in the majority of previously reported cases of buffer disruption (e.g., Annoni, Lemay, Pimenta, & Lecours, 1998; Caramazza & Miceli, 1990; Hillis & Caramazza, 1989; Jónsdóttir, Shallice, & Wise, 1996; Katz, 1991; Kay & Hanley, 1994; McCloskey et al., 1994; Miceli et al., 1985; Schiller et al., 2001; Tainturier & Rapp, 2003). BH's spelling accuracy improved when she spelt a word compared to a nonword, an early-acquired word compared to a late-acquired word, a highly imageable word compared to a low-imageable word, and a highly frequent word compared to a less frequent word. Sage and Ellis (2004) suggested that BH's graphemic buffer received top-down support from the lexicon, which enabled her to maintain and output words (or nonwords) that had greater lexical support in the buffer more accurately than words which did not.

Of particular interest for this article was the finding that BH's spelling accuracy improved when she spelled words that had many orthographic neighbours compared to words with no or few neighbours. Orthographic neighbourhood size was defined by Coltheart et al. (1977) as the number of words that could be generated by changing one letter in the target word. For example, the written word "PINT" has 11 orthographic neighbours, which are MINT, PANT, PINE, HINT, PING, PINS, TINT, PUNT, DINT, LINT, and PINK, whereas the word "MONK" has only three which are HONK, MINK, and MOCK. Orthographic neighbours have been shown to influence both normal and brain-damaged performance in a number of linguistic tasks. In rapid decision tasks (e.g., lexical decision), responses may be slower when the target has fewer neighbours (Boyczuk & Baum, 1999; Coltheart et al., 1977; Garlock, Walley, & Metsala, 2001; Grainger, Spinelli, & Ferrand, 2000). In those tasks where an accumulation of evidence to reach a threshold is required (e.g., naming) neighbours are supportive and help in pushing the activation towards accurate and speedier realisation (Arguin, Bub, & Bowers, 1998; Laxon, Masterson, & Moran, 1994). It may be that having many neighbours is beneficial to some decisions/responses and harmful to others (Grainger, Muneaux, Farioli & Ziegler, 2005).

The orthographic neighbourhood effect in BH was evident not only in her spelling of words but also in her spelling of nonwords (Sage, 2004). Sage and Ellis (2004) suggested that words and nonwords that had several neighbours were able to provide extra stabilising support for each letter of the item, so that it was better able to survive within the damaged buffer. Neighbourhood effects have not thus far been explored in remediation studies of spelling. Two initial priming studies were carried out to examine whether neighbours could influence BH's spelling in the short term and, following positive results from these priming studies, a remediation programme was carried out to see whether the short-term priming effects could be maintained over time and whether spelling accuracy for orthographic neighbours that were not treated would be assisted. The therapy study was carried out to test the prediction that boosting activation of neighbours would assist the spelling of not only directly treated targets but also neighbours. This prediction relied on the assumption that there was interactivity between the lexicon and the graphemic buffer. The manipulation of orthographic neighbours became the focus of therapeutic intervention for BH in order to address this theoretical question. Orthographic neighbours were used to bring about change in treated as well as untreated items. This method also allowed generalisation effects to be seen which might not otherwise have been evident. As will be made clear in the general discussion, we are not necessarily advocating the use of orthographic neighbours as a clinical tool.

This paper sets out BH's background neuropsychological profile, describes the priming experiments and the remediation programme which exploit orthographic neighbours, and then draws some conclusions about the nature of rehabilitating disorders of spelling linked to the buffer and the use of neighbours in remediation. The study further serves to illustrate how therapeutic interventions can be used to address theoretical questions about the interaction between lexical and buffer levels in spelling and what effect this may have on generalisation from treated to untreated items in therapy.

CASE HISTORY

BH was a 68-year-old woman at the time of this study who had suffered a CVA in 1996. An MRI scan (see Sage & Ellis, 2004) showed a widespread region of ischaemic damage extending throughout fronto-temporal, parietal, and occipital regions of the left cerebral hemisphere, and a small ischaemic region in the occipital lobe of the right cerebral hemisphere. BH had bilateral moderate sensori-neural hearing loss for which she wore a hearing aid in the right ear at all times. Her vision was corrected with glasses, which she wore through the background testing, priming, and therapy programme. She had mild right-sided hemiparesis but this did not affect her mobility or activities of daily living. BH was well motivated, sociable, and fully involved in her community. She had previously worked as a clothing inspector in a local clothes factory, was an avid reader prior to her CVA, and continued to listen to spoken books post CVA. Her performance on the Raven's Progressive Matrices (Raven, 1985), with a score of 38/60, gave her a grading of III+ (lower average intelligence), while the National Adult Reading Test (Nelson, 1982) provided a pre-morbid IQ estimate of 102.3.

At the time of testing, BH presented with good auditory and written comprehension and excellent spoken output, including normal naming skills and sentence production. She scored 53/60 on the Boston Naming Test (Kaplan, Goodglass, & Weintraub, 1983) and 24/30 on the Graded Naming Test (McKenna & Warrington, 1983), which, under revised norms (Warrington, 1997), was within the 90th percentile. Her reading aloud of single words was good (92%) while nonword reading was impaired (59%). In contrast to her good oral skills, her written output was severely impaired. On further testing she showed the major characteristics of a deficit in the graphemic buffer. A full account of BH's language and spelling skills is available elsewhere (Sage & Ellis, 2004).

BH's graphemic buffer symptoms

One of the defining characteristics of a graphemic buffer deficit is an increasing error rate as word length increases. BH showed a significant effect of length on two tests: the PALPA (Kay, Lesser, & Coltheart, 1992) letter length spelling test and the length × frequency subtest from the Johns Hopkins University Battery (Goodman & Caramazza, 1994). A significant effect of length in oral spelling of the PALPA items was also found. BH's spelling errors were consistent with those seen in other buffer cases (e.g., substitution: "lunch" – LAUNCH; addition: "anger" – AUNGER; omission: "album" – ALUM; movement: "horse" – HOSRE; compound: "reign" – RIANG). She showed similar error numbers and error patterns when she carried out oral spelling of the same test. BH was more likely to make such errors in the middle of the word rather than at the beginning or end of the word (Sage, 2004).

Nonword spelling was significantly more impaired than word spelling. In total, 54/208 (26%) nonwords were spelt correctly compared to 798/1525 (52%) words. BH's accuracy for nonwords was influenced by length and showed the error patterns typical of buffer damage (e.g., substitution: "blisp" – BLIST; addition: "mobe" – MOBER; omission: "shrint" – SHINT; movement: "splank" – SPANLK; compound: "anify" – ANEFIY), and consequently the source of her spelling problem for nonwords was also identified as resulting from buffer damage.

The lexical influences on BH's spelling accuracy are explored fully in Sage and Ellis (2004). The focus of this article is on neighbours and their influence on BH's spelling accuracy. BH was more likely to make an error on a word with few or no neighbours than a word with several. When BH was asked to spell aloud a set of words of contrasting neighbourhood size (Forster & Shen, 1996), she was more accurate on words with many neighbours such as BANNER and SPEAR than words with fewer neighbours such as CANCEL and SPECK. On another set of words, which varied N and spelling–sound regularity while being matched on length, frequency, familiarity, and bigram frequency (Laxon et al., 1994), BH showed no effect of regularity on spelling but a significant effect of neighbourhood size. On a word set that varied length (words of five and eight letters long) while controlling for neighbourhood size (Lavidor & Ellis, 2002), the length effect was considerably reduced. Sage and Ellis (2004) suggested that part of the length effect in BH, and perhaps in other buffer cases, may be a neighbourhood effect that had remained undetected.

The study was carried out 3 years post-onset of BH's CVA and is divided into three parts; two priming experiments (Studies 1 and 2) and the therapy experiment (Study 3). The priming experiments aimed to examine the short-term effects on BH's spelling accuracy following a range of primes (a word neighbour, a nonword neighbour prime, a control word, and no prime at all), whereas the therapy experiment set out to transfer any short-term gains seen in priming into a longer-lasting improvement in spelling, achieved by repeated exposure to the target. All primes and therapy materials were presented in upper case and BH wrote, with her right hand, in upper case throughout.

STUDY 1: PRIMING EXPERIMENT WITH NEIGHBOUR AND CONTROL PRIMES

This experiment aimed to contrast the effect of priming BH's spelling by prior exposure to words that were either neighbours of the target or visually dissimilar words of the same length and frequency as the neighbour primes. BH's spelling accuracy for words and nonwords was directly influenced by lexical support acting on the buffer, such that words with greater lexical support were better able to survive in the damaged buffer and be spelt correctly. In this experiment, the effect of neighbours was examined.

Selection of items

The 30 targets to be primed were all six-letter words that BH had been unable to spell on a previous occasion. There were two sets of words that were used as primes, all of which were also six letters long. In both priming sets, there were three word primes for each target word (a total of 90 primes in each set). The primes in Set 1 were orthographic neighbours of the target words in that they differed from the target by one shared letter (5/6 letters had the same identity and place as the target). For example, for the target word ASSENT, the three neighbour primes were ABSENT, ASCENT, ASSERT. The primes in Set 2 were words matched for frequency to the neighbour primes in Set 1 and were selected to share as few letters as possible with the target. So, for the same target word ASSENT, the frequency primes were POWDER, UNHOOK, TIMBER, which were matched, in pairs, to the orthographic primes using Kucera and Francis (1967) frequencies. There were no significant differences between the Kucera and Francis (1967) frequency means for the three sets, $F(2, 89) = 0.06$, $p = .94$, nor was there a frequency difference when Celex (Baayen, Piepenbrock, & Gulikers, 1995) frequencies were substituted, $F(2, 89) = 1.75$, $p = .18$. The control primes (Set 2) shared as few letters in common with the targets as possible. In the example above, ASSENT shared only one letter (E) with POWDER and TIMBER and no letters with UNHOOK. Overall, 14.4% of the letters in the control primes also occurred in the targets. Of these, only 4% shared the same position as well as letter—e.g., the target HUNTER shared the same letter (R) and its position with the control prime CAVIAR. A full set of items is available in Sage (2004).

Procedure

Three word primes per target were typed, in capital letters, using Arial font size 20, and positioned one at the top, one in the middle, and one towards the bottom of an A4 page. BH was asked to copy each of the word primes on the sheet. This sheet was removed and she was given a fresh sheet of paper on which she was asked to write the target word to dictation, in her own time. This priming procedure was carried out over two sessions, separated by 2 weeks. BH was primed once, on both occasions, for each of the target words. In the first session, half of the targets were primed with neighbour primes and half with the control primes. In the second session, those target words that had received the neighbour primes in session one, received the control primes, and vice versa. Within this constraint, the order of the primes was random.

Results

The results were analysed in two ways: a whole word count of accuracy following the two primes and an analysis of accuracy at a letter level following in the different priming conditions.

Whole words correct. BH spelled 27/30 (90%) target words correctly following the neighbour primes and 17/30 (57%) target words correctly following the control primes. This difference in scores was significant (McNemar exact $p = .002$, two-tailed). There was no discernable difference between the two testing sessions in terms of accuracy (in session one, BH scored 14/15 following the N primes and 8/15 after the control primes, while in session two she scored 13/15 after the N primes and 9/15 on the control primes).

Letter-level analysis. A simple measure of whole words correct or incorrect might underestimate the priming effect because all errors are given an equal weighting (of zero) under that system. A second analysis used in all three studies scored BH's responses according to how many letters from the target were present in the response. Since all targets were six letters long, a single omission error (for example, CORNEA – COREA) gained a score of 5 since five of the six letters were present in the error. Under this system, simple addition and movement errors (for example, DENIAL – DEINAL) all scored 6 points. To reflect that, although all the letters were present there was a difficulty with the spelling provided in these cases and not in the correctly spelled targets, every correctly written response was given two extra points (i.e., scored 8 points). Using this way of analysing BH's spelling, there was a significant difference between BH's responses to N primes (mean = 7.73) and controlled primes (mean = 6.53, t_{29} = 3.84, $p < .001$). BH's errors were all buffer-type in nature and never involved writing any of the primes themselves (i.e., for the target ASSENT, which was primed with the neighbours ABSENT, ASCENT, ASSERT, BH's error was ASENT).

Discussion

This priming experiment demonstrated that BH was more likely to benefit from primes that were neighbours of the target than primes that were the same length and frequency as the neighbour primes but did not share the orthography of the target. Our hypothesis is that the priming of targets was achieved by increasing the activation of the target's neighbours in the orthographic lexicon, providing top-down support to the target when it was in the buffer.

STUDY 2: PRIMING EXPERIMENT WITH NO PRIMES, WORD PRIMES, AND NONWORD PRIMES

In Study 1, more than half of the words primed by frequency alone were spelled correctly and so a second priming experiment was set up with a three-way comparison where one set of targets received no prime, a second set received a word neighbour prime (as in Set 1 of Study 1), and a third set received a nonword neighbour prime. This set was included to look at whether the priming effect was achieved solely by the influence of neighbourhood or whether other lexical properties were also needed to get positive results.

Selection of items

There were 36 targets to be primed. All the targets were six letters long and were words that BH had been unable to spell on a previous occasion. No targets from Study 1 were used in this study. All the targets had only three neighbours. As in Study 1, there were two sets of primes, all of six letters. Again, as in Study 1, there were three primes of each type for each target (a total of 108 primes in each set). The primes in Set 1 were the three orthographic neighbours of the targets. For example, for the target LATENT, there were three neighbours PATENT, LAMENT, and LATEST. The primes in Set 2 were all nonwords that were also orthographic neighbours of the targets. The nonwords were formed by taking the neighbours from Set 1 and making a letter change in the same position as the letter change that was present in the word neighbour compared to the target. For example, for the target word LATENT, the nonword BATENT was made by altering the first letter of the word neighbour PATENT from P to B. The nonword LAWENT was made by altering the M in LAMENT, and the nonword LATERT by altering the S in LATEST. This was to ensure that the position of the letter change in the nonword neighbours was the same as the letter change in the word neighbours when compared to the target. A full set of items is available in Sage (2004).

Procedure

There were three conditions involved in this experiment. The first did not involve a prime, and in this control condition BH was asked to write the target word down directly on a piece of paper. The second and third conditions involved priming, either by word neighbours or by nonword neighbours. Three primes per target were prepared as for Study 1 (that is typed, in capital letters, using Arial size 20, and placed one at the top, one in the middle, and one towards the bottom of an A4 page). BH was asked to copy each of the word or nonword primes on the sheet, in her own time, and then given a fresh sheet of paper and asked to write the target word. The priming was carried out over three sessions over a period of 6 weeks, each session separated by 2 weeks. In session one, BH wrote 18 targets without a prime, 18 targets following three word neighbour primes, and 18 targets following three nonword neighbour primes. This pattern was repeated over sessions two and three until all the targets had been written either with no prime, following three word primes, or following three nonword primes. Within these constraints, the presentation of each 18 was randomised for each session.

Results

As in Study 1, the results were analysed in two ways: a whole word count of accuracy following the two primes and an analysis of accuracy at a letter level following in the different priming conditions.

Whole words correct. BH spelled 21/36 (58%) of the target words correctly without any prime, 29/36 (81%) targets with nonword primes, and 35/36 (97%) with word primes. The differences were compared using McNemar tests. If one-tailed tests are employed on the grounds that priming was predicted following the positive results of Study 1, then there was a significant difference between the word prime condition and the unprimed control condition (McNemar, exact $p = .04$), and between the nonword prime condition and the unprimed control condition (McNemar, exact $p = .03$). The difference between the word and nonword prime conditions was also significant (McNemar, exact $p = .02$). If more conservative two-tailed analyses are employed, only the difference between the word prime and control conditions is significant. There was a tendency for overall performance to improve over the three testing sessions (Time 1, 26/36; Time 2, 28/36; Time 3, 31/36) but this trend was not significant (Jonckheere's Trend Test, $z = 1.29$, two-tailed $p = .20$).

Letter-level analysis. A one-way analysis with priming condition as the factor showed a significant overall difference between priming conditions using the letter-level analysis, $F(2,70) = 11.14$, $p < .001$. The three conditions were compared on a pairwise basis using t-tests. There was a significant difference between the word prime condition (mean = 7.94) and the unprimed control condition (mean = 6.53, $t_{35} = 4.74$, two-tailed $p < .001$), and between the nonword prime condition (mean = 7.39) and the unprimed control condition ($t_{35} = 2.34$, two-tailed $p < .05$). The difference between the word and nonword prime conditions was also significant ($t_{35} = 2.49$, two-tailed $p < .05$). That is, both word and nonword neighbour priming conditions resulted in better spelling than in the control condition but word priming was more effective than nonword priming.

Discussion

This study demonstrated that BH was better able to write correctly if she had been primed using orthographic neighbours than if she received no priming at all. The study also indicated that she showed more priming from word neighbours than nonword neighbours. The nonword primes share the same number of letters with the target words as do the word primes, and so should provide the same amount of practice in executing the correct letter sequences at the level of the graphemic buffer. They should also activate word units in the graphemic output lexicon by virtue of their shared letters. But nonwords will be less effective than words at generating lexical activation. The nonword primes improved spelling of the target words somewhat, but not as much as the word primes. One possible explanation would be that word and nonword primes provided equal levels of support to graphemic buffer processes but that word primes induced a greater amount of additional top-down support from the lexicon. Our preferred interpretation would be that all of the observed priming effects are the result of increased top-down support, with word primes inducing more support than the nonword primes.

STUDY 3: THERAPY PROGRAMME

The therapy programme had two aims: to find out whether the correct spelling of targets could be maintained first for the duration of the programme (3 weeks) and, second, 6 weeks after the end of the intervention (a total of nine weeks), and to establish what effect providing therapy to neighbours of targets would have immediately after therapy and at follow-up. The therapeutic approach differed from previous spelling therapy programmes (e.g., Aliminosa et al., 1993; de Partz, 1995; Rapp & Kane, 2002; Raymer et al., 2003) in that it was designed to reduce errors as much as possible while learning. In previous studies, the patient worked at the correct spelling until this was achieved. Throughout the therapy procedures in this study, BH was prevented (as far as possible) from making errors. This was to avoid erroneous spelling patterns from being reinforced. One of the main ideas behind errorless learning is that in some situations, errant behaviour can be self-reinforcing: the act of producing an error for a certain stimulus can strengthen this incorrect association such that the error will be even more likely the next time the stimulus is attempted. This cycle can be broken if the learner is prevented from making errors, instead allowing only correct stimulus–response associations to be formed and strengthened (Baddeley & Wilson, 1994). Errorless learning has been used most widely in the rehabilitation of amnesic patients (e.g., Parkin, Hunkin, & Squires, 1998; Wilson, Baddeley, Evans, & Shiel, 1994) but some therapy studies in aphasia have used the approach (e.g., Ellis, Lambon Ralph, Morris, & Hunter, 2000; Fillingham, Sage, & Lambon Ralph, 2006; Morris & Franklin, 1995; Sage, Hesketh, & Lambon Ralph, 2005).

Selection of items

BH was asked to spell 72 six-letter words on two separate occasions. From these, 45 targets, which BH had misspelled twice, were selected. The items were divided into three sets of 15, matched for neighbourhood size and Celex combined frequency (Baayen et al., 1995). There were no significant differences between the three groups on neighbourhood size, $F(2, 44) = 0.008$, $p = .99$, or frequency, Celex frequency $F(2, 44) = 0.739$, $p = .48$.

The words in Set 1 received therapy and so were labelled the "direct set". The words in Set 2 did not receive therapy and so were labelled the "control set". The words in Set 3 did not receive therapy but one neighbour of each word did receive therapy and so this set was labelled the "N set".

In order to decide which neighbours from Set 3 (the indirect set) should receive therapy, all the neighbours of the targets in Set 3 were found. Seven of the targets in Set 3 (DECEIT, AERIAL, IODINE, VAPOUR, GENIUS, SHRIEK, SIMPER) had one neighbour only and so this was the neighbour used in the therapy set. There were two targets (PURSER, VERITY) that had two neighbours each, two targets (BOTHER, INSECT) with three neighbours each, two targets (RACKET, HOWLER) with four neighbours, one target (STRIDE) with five neighbours, and one target (TUMBLE) with six neighbours. When selecting a neighbour for those targets that had more than one possible neighbour to choose from, each letter position was represented in terms of letter change. For example, a position 1 letter change was JACKET for the target RACKET, position 2 was BATHER for the target BOTHER, position three was VALOUR for the target VAPOUR, position four was SIMMER for the target SIMPER, position five was STRIFE for the target STRIDE, and position six was PURSES for the target PURSER. A full set of items used in the therapy procedure is available in Sage (2004).

Procedure

Therapy sessions took place over a period of 2 weeks, in two 1-hour sessions with the therapist (KS). Three tasks were used to promote BH's learning of Set 1 (the direct set) and Set 3 (the N set). Each task aimed to reduce errors made by BH by always having the correct prime word present at all times.

Task 1: Pairwise comparisons. The target word was placed at the top of the page, followed by paired versions of the target where one was the correct spelling and one altered using the error patterns seen in BH's own work (e.g., omissions, substitutions, movement errors, additions): for example, SAVAGE: SAVGE. BH selected the word spelt correctly, identified where the other word was misspelt and corrected it.

Task 2: Insert missing letters. The target word was placed at the top of the page and the same target was reproduced several times below with two letters missing in each reproduction. BH had to fill in the missing letters, checking with reference to the correct target at the top of the page, for example, HERESY: H-R-SY.

Task 3: Word search grids. All the targets were hidden in grids of letters. The words were placed in either the vertical, horizontal, or diagonal plane. Beneath the grid, each target was printed so that BH had to search and ring the target once it was found in the grid and remove it from the list below. These low-error techniques were sometimes used to teach neighbour primes rather than the target words themselves (i.e., near errorless learning of *primes*).

Following the two therapy sessions, a third visit 1 week later was carried out to retest BH on all three word sets; that is, the direct therapy set (Set 1), the control set

(Set 2), and the N set (Set 3). The 45 items were presented in random order. BH was asked not to work on her spelling for 6 weeks, after which a further testing session occurred on the 45 items from the three sets.

Performance within therapy programme across the three tasks

On the first therapy task (pairwise comparisons), BH was 100% correct, for all prime words, at both selecting the correct spelling and correcting the mistake in the incorrect version. On the second task (inserting two missing letters) she made three errors overall which she self-corrected. Given that each prime word was practised 40 times, this error rate is very small. However, BH herself reported that this task was more exacting for her than the first one but was not able to specify in what way. In task 1, (pairwise comparison) the correct prime word was always next to the incorrect one and so monitoring of this might have been easier for BH than in the second task (inserting two missing letters) where there was only one correct prime word at the top of the page. Task 3 (word grids) was completed successfully with no errors. These were included in the therapy because BH enjoyed this type of activity and had become very proficient at other word searches she found in quiz books.

Results

Whole target words correct. Table 1 shows the number of whole target words in each set that BH spelled correctly at baseline, immediately post-therapy, and at the 6-week follow-up. Note that only in the direct treatment condition were the words the same as the words practised in the therapy sessions. Every target word was spelled incorrectly at the baseline assessment. Immediately after therapy there was a significant difference between the scores of the three sets of items (overall $\chi^2 = 9.50$, $df = 2$, $p < .01$). The best score was obtained on the set of words given direct treatment, which showed a significant increase from baseline (McNemar, exact $p = .004$, two-tailed). The indirect set, where treatment concentrated on neighbours rather that the target words themselves, also improved significantly relative to the baseline (McNemar, exact $p = .03$, two-tailed). Comparison of the three sets post-therapy found that the direct set was significantly better than the control set ($\chi^2 = 7.11$, $df = 1$, $p < .01$), whereas the difference between the indirect and control sets did not reach significance ($\chi^2 = 2.88$, $df = 1$, $p = .09$) and neither did the difference between the direct and indirect therapy sets ($\chi^2 = 0.52$, $df = 1$, $p = .45$).

At follow-up, the significant difference between the scores of the three sets of items was maintained (overall $\chi^2 = 8.72$, $df = 2$, $p < .01$). BH retained the improvement on both treated sets at the 6-week follow-up, with performance on the indirect treatment

TABLE 1
Results of whole words correct analysis on 45 targets divided by Set, over three time periods

	Baseline	Post-therapy	Follow-up
Set 1 (direct set)	0/15	9/15	10/15
Set 2 (control set)	0/15	1/15	3/15
Set 3 (indirect set)	0/15	6/15	10/15

set not being significantly worse than that of the direct treatment set at this point. Both the direct and indirect sets were significantly better than the control set ($\chi^2 = 4.72$, $df = 1$, $p < .03$).

Letter-level analysis. The results for the letter-level analysis of BH's performance at baseline, post-therapy, and follow-up are shown in Figure 1. A two-way analysis of variance was carried out with word sets as a between factor and time (testing sessions) as a within factor. The main effect of time was significant, $F(2, 84) = 25.75$, $p < .001$, indicating that there was an overall difference in letter accuracy between the three time periods. The main effect of word sets was also significant, $F(2, 42) = 3.52$, $p < .05$, indicating that there was an overall difference in performance between the three word sets. Importantly, the interaction between time and word sets was significant, $F(4, 84) = 4.41$, $p < .01$, indicating that performance on the three word sets changed in different ways over time. T-tests were used to compare performance on each set at baseline and post-therapy and at the post-therapy assessment. Scores on the direct set improved between baseline and post-therapy ($t_{14} = 5.40$, $p < .001$), as did performance on the indirect set ($t_{14} = 3.65$, $p < .01$). At the post-therapy assessment the difference between the direct and control sets was significant ($t_{28} = 3.84$, $p < .001$). The differences between the indirect and control sets and the direct and indirect sets post-therapy were not significant—indirect vs control: ($t_{28} = 1.69$, $p > .05$), direct vs indirect ($t_{28} = 1.55$, $p > .05$). At follow-up, the difference between the direct and control sets remained significant ($t_{28} = 2.56$, $p < .02$) while the difference between the direct and indirect sets was still not significant ($t_{28} = 0.20$, $p > .05$). In contrast to the result immediately post-therapy, the difference between the control set and the indirect set was significant ($t_{28} = 2.90$, $p < .01$).

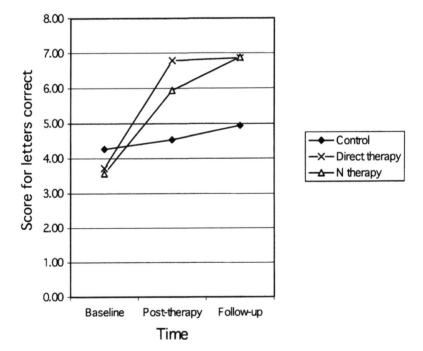

Figure 1. Scores for letters correct in BH's spelling over time and according to the therapy received.

To summarise, both analyses found a significant improvement for the direct treatment set that was sustained at the 6-week follow-up. The untreated control set did not improve. The indirect set did not show significant improvement immediately post-therapy but did so at follow-up.

GENERAL DISCUSSION

BH showed the classic signs of a graphemic buffer disorder (Caramazza & Miceli, 1990; Miceli et al., 1985). Her spelling was strongly affected by length. Her errors (omissions, substitutions, additions, and movements) were typical of problems maintaining graphemes in a short-term holding mechanism. She showed the same pattern whether in writing to dictation, written picture naming, or oral spelling. Her nonword spelling was more severely affected than word spelling but showed a similar length and error pattern. A number of lexical variables, including orthographic neighbourhood size, affected her spelling accuracy (Sage & Ellis, 2004). These effects arose from interaction between the lexical and buffer stages of spelling such that top-down lexical support helped to stabilise the entry in the buffer. Lexical influences have also been shown in other cases of graphemic buffer disorder (e.g., Caramazza & Miceli, 1990; Kay & Hanley, 1994; McCloskey et al., 1999; Pate & Margolin, 1990; Sage & Ellis, 2004).

Two priming experiments were carried out using orthographic neighbours in order to examine the short-term effects on BH's spelling accuracy following a range of primes. The first experiment contrasted orthographic primes with control primes and showed a significant benefit of priming with orthographic neighbours compared to controls. The second experiment contrasted no prime with orthographic neighbour primes that were either words or nonwords and suggested that BH's spelling was assisted most by word neighbours but was also helped by nonword neighbours. The therapy study aimed to see if the short-term effect of increased activation from priming neighbours could be transferred to a longer-term effect within a therapy programme. There were three sets of items in the therapy programme. Set 1 received direct treatment, Set 2 received no attention at all (the control set), and Set 3 did not directly receive treatment but neighbours of the targets were practised. Improvement was measured in two ways; the number of items spelled correctly and the number of letters written correctly. The two analyses yielded similar results. Performance on the direct treatment set improved over the course of therapy. That improvement was sustained at the follow-up. Performance on the untreated control set did not improve significantly.

Figure 2 shows how the increase in activation of a target's neighbours in the orthographic lexicon might allow the target word to receive support within the damaged buffer. The high N word CASK, in the graphemic output lexicon, directly activates the letters C, A, S, and K in their respective positions (i.e., C in first position, A in second position, and so on). This activation is bilateral such that activation in the buffer feeds back to the lexicon. The letter units C, A, S, and K are also linked to word units in the graphemic output lexicon for four-letter words that have C as a first letter, or A as a second letter, or S as a third letter, or K as a final letter. By this means, when the letters in CASK are activated, there will be activation of other word units to the extent that the words represented by those units share letters with CASK. The words that share most letters with CASK are, of course, its orthographic neighbours, which differ by just one letter. When the orthographic

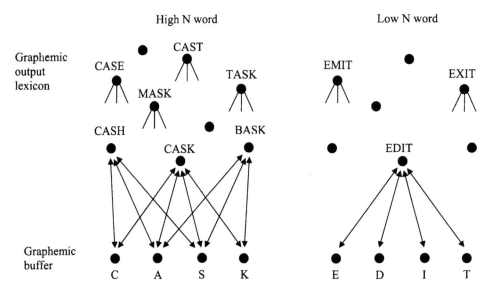

Figure 2. Neighbourhood activation for words between graphemic output lexicon and graphemic buffer.

neighbours are activated through the bottom-up connections from the buffer to the lexicon, they will reciprocate by contributing some top-down support to the letter units at the buffer level. More support will be available for the letters in a word like CASK, which has many neighbours, than for the letters in a word like EDIT, which has few neighbours.

Top-down support from lexical units should assist letter units in the buffer to overcome disturbed functioning of the buffer. Our results imply that the best way to improve the support for a word's letter units is to boost the activation of the word itself through priming or longer-term practice. But letter units can also receive assistance from a neighbour whose activation level has been boosted by priming or practice. In terms of Figure 2, BH's ability to write CASK will be maximally assisted by boosting the word unit for CASK itself, but will also benefit to a lesser degree from boosting the unit for CASE or BASK. As we have shown, those benefits can be long lasting. In practical terms we would predict that the maximum assistance for CASK would be obtained from practising CASK and all its neighbours. That should give the letters of CASK the best chance of overcoming damage to processing within the buffer.

Figure 3 shows how interaction between words in the graphemic lexicon and letter units in the buffer may support nonwords in the buffer, although to a lesser extent than words. The letter units for a nonword like TRAB may be activated by phoneme–grapheme conversion rather than by a lexical unit (because there is no pre-existing lexical unit for a nonword). But the bottom-up connections from the buffer to the lexicon mean that the letter units T, R, A, and B will activate the word units for words that share some of those letters, for example TRAY and CRAB. Boosting those neighbours through priming or practice should help BH to write TRAB more accurately. Again, the effects could be reasonably long lasting (as long as the increased activation of the word neighbours is sustained).

It could be argued that part of the improvement observed was due to better ability of the buffer to retain particular orthographic sequences (not orthographic

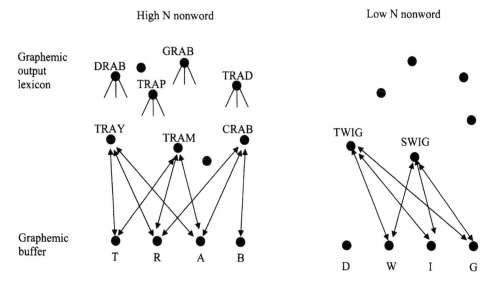

Figure 3. Neighbourhood activation for nonwords in the buffer, receiving some support from the graphemic output lexicon.

sequences in general or we would have observed more improvement in the control set). We note, however, that none of the therapy tasks that induced these improvements involved writing either the directly treated words or the neighbours of the indirectly treated words. One task involved comparing correctly and incorrectly spelled alternatives, one involved writing two letters to complete gaps in words, and one involved finding words in word grids. We believe that these tasks are more likely to have boosted lexical representations than facilitated the maintenance and reproduction of letter sequences at the buffer level.

Previous reports into the remediation of buffer-level spelling problems differ in their predictions (and their findings) about whether to expect an improvement in the spelling of words that have not received direct treatment. RSB (Rapp & Kane, 2002) and NM (Raymer et al., 2003) were able to spell words that had not been included in the treatment programme, whereas AM (de Partz, 1995) and JES (Aliminosa et al., 1994) did not show any generalisation to untreated items. Only the therapy programme carried out by Raymer et al. (2003) made use of orthographic similarity, although the stimuli shared only half their letters either at the beginning or end of the words. NM showed improved ability on words not worked on directly (but which were orthographically linked to the therapy targets), and he was more accurate in particular on words where the initial 2/3 letters had been seen in therapy. The authors suggested that increased activation at syllable level within the lexicon allowed the therapeutic words and linked words to be subject to less decay in the buffer (a significant problem for NM at pre-therapy testing). BH's responses did not show preference for the start of the word; her errors were more likely to be in the middle of words. Nor did BH make errors that were direct neighbours of the targets or show syllabic preference (as NM had done). Whereas the adaptation in NM's performance was attributed to changes in the lexicon itself, this paper suggests that it is the additional increased activation from word neighbours between lexicon and buffer that has assisted BH's improvement in the N set. There has already been some evidence of interaction and feedback between the buffer and the lexicon

(McCloskey et al., 1999; Pate & Margolin, 1990; Sage & Ellis, 2004). In this therapy programme, the use of neighbours enabled BH to make improvements on targets that were not treated but which were linked by neighbourhood to those she had been working on. This result demonstrated that she was able to use top-down lexical support to assist the target's passage through the buffer (Figure 2) over a longer time period.

The use of errorless learning in this study ensured that the feedback between buffer and lexicon was accurate as far as possible. BH made very few errors during the therapy programme and the correct target response was always present. At the two retesting times (immediately after therapy and at 6 weeks follow-up), she did not make errors that were neighbours of the tested items. Errorless learning relies on the correct target being learned and in the direct therapy set this was shown to work well immediately and at follow-up. Figure 2 suggests that directly strengthening the activation between lexicon and buffer will be particularly effective if there is a direct correspondence between the lexicon and buffer (as is the case with the direct set). For the N therapy set, BH was asked to learn a neighbour of the target, not the target itself. The mechanism by which errorless learning was advantageous for this set may be similar to that set out in Figure 3, in that sustained, correct stimulation of the prime's neighbour provided some important additional support when the prime was required to be spelt immediately after therapy and at follow-up. The benefits of this additional support became more evident at follow up when BH's accuracy for the N set was equal to that of the direct therapy set and when no further emphasis had been placed on the neighbour. The clinical speech and language therapist may therefore consider it useful to concentrate on the direct targeting of spellings as the most efficient way to improve in spelling, but may seek to look for generalisation effects via orthographic neighbours.

REFERENCES

Aliminosa, D., McCloskey, M., Goodman-Schulman, R., & Sokol, S. (1993). Remediation of acquired dysgraphia as a technique for testing interpretations of deficits. *Aphasiology, 7*, 55–69.

Annoni, J. M., Lemay, M. A., Pimenta, M. A. D., & Lecours, A. R. (1998). The contribution of attentional mechanisms to an irregularity effect at the graphemic buffer level. *Brain and Language, 63*, 64–78.

Arguin, M., Bub, D., & Bowers, J. (1998). Extent and limits of covert lexical activation in letter-by-letter reading. *Cognitive Neuropsychology, 15*, 53–92.

Baayen, R. H., Piepenbrock, R., & Gulikers, L. (1995). *The CELEX lexical database.* Philadelphia: Linguistics Data Consortium, University of Pennsylvania.

Baddeley, A., & Wilson, B. (1994). When implicit learning fails: Amnesia and the problem of error elimination. *Neuropsychologia, 32*, 53–68.

Barry, C. (1994). Spelling Routes (or Roots or Rutes). In G. D. A. Brown & N. C. Ellis (Eds.), *Handbook of spelling: Theory, process and intervention* (pp. 27–50). Chichester, UK: John Wiley & Sons Ltd.

Boyczuk, J. P., & Baum, S. R. (1999). The influence of neighbourhood density on phonetic categorisation in aphasia. *Brain and Language, 67*, 46–70.

Caramazza, A., & Miceli, G. (1990). The structure of graphemic representations. *Cognition, 37*, 243–297.

Coltheart, M., Davelaar, E., Jonassen, J., & Besner, D. (1977). Access to the internal lexicon. In S. Dornic (Ed.), *Attention and performance, Vol. 6* (pp. 535–556). Hillsdale, NJ: Lawrence Erlbaum Associates Inc.

de Partz, M. P. (1995). Deficit of the graphemic buffer: Effects of a written lexical segmentation strategy. *Neuropsychological Rehabilitation, 5*, 129–147.

Ellis, A. W. (1982). Spelling and writing (and reading and speaking). In A. W. Ellis (Ed.), *Normality and pathology in cognitive functions* (pp. 113–146). London: Academic Press.

Ellis, A. W., Lambon Ralph, M. A., Morris, J., & Hunter, A. (2000). Surface dyslexia: Description, treatment and interpretation. In E. Funnel (Ed.), *Case studies in the neuropsychology of reading* (pp. 85–122). Hove, UK: Psychology Press.

Fillingham, J., Sage, K., & Lambon Ralph, M. A. (2006). The treatment of anomia using errorless learning. *Neuropsychological Rehabilitation, 16*, 129–154.

Forster, K. I., & Shen, D. (1996). No enemies in the neighbourhood: Absence of inhibitory neighbourhood effects in lexical decision and semantic categorisation. *Journal of Experimental Psychology: Learning, Memory and Cognition, 22*, 696–713.

Garlock, V. M., Walley, A. C., & Metsala, J. L. (2001). Age of acquisition, word frequency and neighborhood density effects on spoken word recognition by children and adults. *Journal of Memory and Language, 45*, 468–492.

Goodman, R. A., & Caramazza, A. (1994). *The Johns Hopkins University Dysgraphia Battery*. Baltimore, MD: Johns Hopkins University.

Grainger, J., Muneaux, M., Farioli, F., & Zeigler, J. C. (2005). Effects of phonological and orthographic neighbourhood density interact in visual word recognition. *The Quarterly Journal of Experimental Psychology, 58*(A), 981–998.

Grainger, J., Spinelli, E., & Ferrand, L. (2000). Effects of baseword frequency and orthographic neighborhood size in pseudohomophone naming. *Journal of Memory and Language, 42*, 88–102.

Hillis, A. E., & Caramazza, A. (1987). Model-driven treatment of dysgraphia. In R. H. Brookshire (Ed.), *Clinical aphasiology* (pp. 84–105). Minneapolis, MN: BRK Publishers.

Hillis, A. E., & Caramazza, A. (1989). The graphemic buffer and attentional mechanisms. *Brain and Language, 36*, 208–235.

Jónsdóttir, M. K., Shallice, T., & Wise, R. (1996). Phonological mediation and the graphemic buffer disorder in spelling: Cross-language differences? *Cognition, 59*, 169–197.

Kaplan, E., Goodglass, H., & Weintraub, S. (1983). *Boston Naming Test*. Philadelphia: Lea & Febiger.

Katz, R. B. (1991). Limited retention of information in the graphemic buffer. *Cortex, 27*, 111–119.

Kay, J., & Hanley, R. (1994). Peripheral disorders of spelling: The role of the graphemic buffer. In G. D. A. Brown & N. C. Ellis (Eds.), *Handbook of spelling: Theory, process and intervention* (pp. 295–315). Chichester, UK: John Wiley & Sons Ltd.

Kay, J., Lesser, R., & Coltheart, M. (1992). *Psycholinguistic Assessments of Language Processing in Aphasia*. Hove, UK: Lawrence Erlbaum Associates Ltd.

Kucera, H., & Francis, W. N. (1967). *Computational analysis of present-day American English*. Providence, RI: Brown University Press.

Lavidor, M., & Ellis, A. W. (2002). Word length and orthographic neighbourhood size effects in the left and right hemispheres. *Brain and Language, 80*, 45–62.

Laxon, V., Masterson, J., & Moran, R. (1994). Are children's representations of words distributed? Effects of orthographic neighbourhood size, consistency and regularity of naming. *Language and Cognitive Processes, 9*, 1–27.

McCloskey, M., Badecker, W., Goodman-Schulman, R. A., & Aliminosa, D. (1994). The structure of graphemic representations in spelling: Evidence from a case of acquired dysgraphia. *Cognitive Neuropsychology, 11*, 341–392.

McCloskey, M., Macaruso, P., & Rapp, B. (1999). Grapheme-to lexeme feedback in the spelling system: Evidence from dysgraphia. *Brain and Language, 69*, 395–398.

McKenna, P., & Warrington, E. K. (1983). *Graded Naming Test*. Windsor, UK: NFER-Nelson.

Miceli, G., Silveri, M. C., & Caramazza, A. (1985). Cognitive analysis of a case of pure agraphia. *Brain and Language, 25*, 187–212.

Morris, J., & Franklin, S. (1995). Assessment and remediation of a speech discrimination deficit in a dysphasic patient. In M. Perkins & S. Howard (Eds.), *Case studies in clinical linguistics* (pp. 245–270). London: Whurr.

Nelson, H. E. (1982). *National Adult Reading Test (NART)*. Windsor, UK: NFER-Nelson.

Parkin, A. J., Hunkin, N. M., & Squires, E. J. (1998). Unlearning John Major: The use of errorless learning in the reacquisition of proper names following herpes simplex encephalitis. *Cognitive Neuropsychology, 15*, 361–375.

Pate, D. S., & Margolin, D. I. (1990). Disruption of the spelling system: Evidence for interlevel interaction. *American Academy of Neurology, 40*, 241.

Pound, C. (1996). Writing remediation using preserved oral spelling: A case for separate output buffers. *Aphasiology, 10*, 283–296.

Rapp, B., & Kane, A. (2002). Remediation of deficits affecting different components of the spelling process. *Aphasiology, 16*, 439–454.

Raven, J. C. (1985). *Raven's Progressive Matrices* (23rd ed.). London: H. K. Lewis & Co.

Raymer, A., Cudworth, C., & Haley, M. (2003). Spelling treatment for an individual with dysgraphia: Analysis of generalisation to untrained words. *Aphasiology, 17*, 607–624.

Sage, K. (2004). *The graphemic output buffer: A single case study.* Unpublished PhD thesis, University of York, UK.

Sage, K., & Ellis, A. W. (2004). Lexical effects in a case of graphemic output buffer. *Cognitive Neuropsychology, 21*, 381–400.

Sage, K., Hesketh, A., & Lambon Ralph, M. A. (2005). Using errorless learning to treat letter-by-letter reading: Contrasting word versus letter based therapy. *Neuropsychological Rehabilitation, 15*, 619–642.

Schiller, N. O., Greenhall, J. A., Shelton, J. R., & Caramazza, A. (2001). Serial order effects in spelling errors: Evidence from two dysgraphic patients. *Neurocase, 7*, 1–14.

Tainturier, M.-J., & Rapp, B. (2003). Is a single graphemic buffer used in reading and spelling? *Aphasiology, 17*, 537–562.

Warrington, E. (1997). The Graded Naming Test: A restandardisation. *Neuropsychological Rehabilitation, 7*, 143–146.

Wilson, B. A., Baddeley, A., Evans, J., & Shiel, A. (1994). Errorless learning in the rehabilitation of memory impaired people. *Neuropsychological Rehabilitation, 4*, 307–326.

John Marshall and the developmental dyslexias

Anne Castles

University of Melbourne, and Macquarie University, Sydney, NSW, Australia

Timothy C. Bates and Max Coltheart

Macquarie University, Sydney, NSW, Australia

Background: In 1984, John Marshall made the case that one can use a model of the skilled reading system not only to interpret the acquired dyslexias, but also to interpret the developmental dyslexias, and the particular model of the skilled reading system he favoured for this purpose was the dual-route model. This claim has been a controversial one, with many researchers claiming that static models of adult skilled reading, such as the dual-route model, are inappropriate for understanding the process of reading development and, consequently, the developmental reading disorders.
Aims: In this paper, we examine how Marshall's conjecture has fared over the past 20 years.
Main Contribution: We evaluate Marshall's conjecture by examining evidence for developmental analogues of acquired surface and phonological dyslexia, by reporting new data on cases of "pure" developmental surface and phonological dyslexia, and by assessing the success of dual route versus connectionist accounts of these subtypes. We also report evidence that the dual-route model of skilled reading provides an accurate account of the reading performance of children at all stages of reading development.
Conclusion: We conclude that Marshall's controversial claim has been vindicated by subsequent research.

The cognitive neuropsychology of reading disorders was born as a presentation by John Marshall and Freda Newcombe to the Engelberg meeting of the International Neuropsychology Symposium in 1971, subsequently published as Marshall and Newcombe (1973). This seminal paper was the first attempt at distinguishing between different types of acquired dyslexia (in this case, deep dyslexia, visual dyslexia, and surface dyslexia) and at interpreting all of these acquired dyslexias in relation to a common model of reading: "We wish to emphasize the essential 'normality' of the errors characteristic of acquired dyslexia. That is, we shall interpret dyslexic mistakes in terms of a functional analysis of normal reading processes" (Marshall & Newcombe, 1973, p. 188).

The functional analysis of reading Marshall and Newcombe offered was the dual-route model of reading; their Figure 1 (reproduced here in our Figure 1) was the first

Address correspondence to: Anne Castles, Department of Psychology, University of Melbourne, Parkville VIC 3010, Australia. E-mail: acastles@unimelb.edu.au

This work was funded in part by an NHMRC grant to the authors. We are very grateful to Andy Ellis and Elaine Funnell for insightful comments on earlier drafts of the manuscript.

STIMULUS

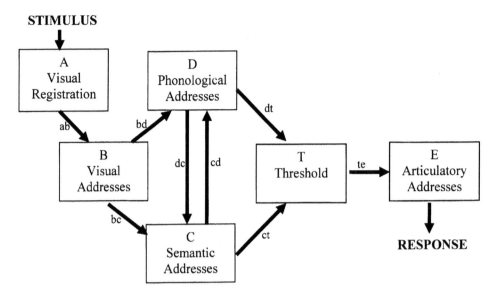

Figure 1. The dual-route model of reading of Marshall and Newcombe (1973).

diagram of the dual-route model to be published.[1] This model portrays two pathways from print to speech. One pathway operates via the use of grapheme–phoneme correspondence rules (Marshall & Newcombe, 1973, p. 191); this has come to be called the nonlexical route for reading aloud. The other pathway operates via access to a semantic system; this has come to be called the lexical route for reading aloud. The nonlexical route successfully reads *nonwords*, which are not real English words but can be pronounced by rule (like GOP or TACHET) and *regular* words, which are real words that conform to typical English grapheme–phoneme conversion rules (like TREE or MARKET). However, it produces regularisation errors to words which disobey the grapheme–phoneme correspondence rules of English, i.e., irregular or exception words such as CHEF, HAVE, or SAID. The lexical route successfully reads all words (and is indifferent to whether these are regular or irregular words), but cannot produce a correct response to nonwords, since these have no representations in the semantic system.

If brain damage has impaired the ability to read aloud via the lexical route, so that sometimes only the nonlexical route can be used to read aloud, then regularisation errors in reading aloud will occur; that is, surface dyslexia. Conversely, the complete inability to read nonwords that is seen in deep dyslexia was interpreted by Marshall and Newcombe as being due to abolition of the nonlexical route by brain damage.

A second salient characteristic of deep dyslexia is the production of semantic errors in reading aloud. How is this symptom related to the complete abolition of the nonword reading system in deep dyslexia? One possible view is that reading via an *intact* semantic system will produce semantic errors (that must at least be true for exact synonyms), which could only be avoided if information about correct pronunciation were available from the nonlexical system. An alternative is that there is a second deficit in deep dyslexia, an impairment of the semantic system itself, and

---

[1] Forster and Chambers (1973) independently put forward the same kind of dual-route account of reading aloud.

that semantic errors arise because of this second deficit. In subsequent work, Beauvois and Derouesné (1979) reported data from patients with severe impairments of the nonlexical route who made no semantic errors in reading aloud. Thus, a new form of acquired dyslexia was defined: *phonological dyslexia* (nonword reading impaired relative to word reading, in the absence of semantic errors in reading aloud), and the view was then adopted by many that the identifying symptom of deep dyslexia was the occurrence of semantic paralexias. This distinction of phonological dyslexia from deep dyslexia implies that reading via the lexical system is not to be exclusively identified with reading via semantics.

If there are different types of acquired dyslexia—different ways in which reading can break down after brain damage—why not different types of developmental dyslexia—different ways in which children can be failing to acquire reading ability? Marshall and his doctoral students Jane Holmes and Christine Temple were exploring this possibility in the 1970s and early 1980s, and they reported cases of developmental surface dyslexia (Holmes, 1973) and developmental phonological dyslexia (Temple & Marshall, 1983).

Given the occurrence of these developmental equivalents of acquired dyslexias, a bold conjecture may be entertained: that one can use a model of the skilled reading system not only to interpret the acquired dyslexias, but also to interpret the developmental dyslexias. Marshall (1984, p. 46) did so conjecture:

> Our own approach to this problem has been somewhat extreme. I shall assume (I hope uncontroversially) that the syndromes of developmental dyslexia must be defined over a functional architecture of visible language processing. But I shall further speculate that the relevant functional architecture is the one that correctly characterizes the normal, fluent, adult reading system. The syndromes of developmental dyslexia will accordingly be interpreted as consequent upon the selective failure of a particular adult component (or components) to develop appropriately, with relatively intact, normal (adult) functioning of the remaining components.

Marshall (1984, p. 47) then proceeded to identify two presuppositions that this approach to the understanding of developmental dyslexia makes:

> This is to adopt a highly modular "preformist" approach to the development of the reading system. The paradigm explicitly denies that developmental failure distorts the architecture of the system as a whole; it also, of course, denies that the *normal* development of reading skill changes in a "stage-wise" manner whereby the character of reading mechanisms at stage *n* is qualitatively distinct from their character at stage *n+1*.

His conclusion from this line of thought was: "To the extent that these presuppositions are true, taxonomies of the acquired dyslexias should map in a one-to-one fashion on to taxonomies of the developmental dyslexias" (Marshall, 1984, p. 47).

So Marshall then considered whether there exist developmental analogues of six documented types of acquired dyslexia, noting particularly the pioneering work of his PhD student Jane Holmes, who had already provided evidence that a developmental form of surface dyslexia can be observed (Holmes, 1973; see also Coltheart, Masterson, Byng, Prior, & Riddoch, 1983). His conclusion (Marshall, 1984, p. 55) from these comparisons of acquired and developmental dyslexias was: "It is somewhat surprising to find that, at least superficially, the study of developmental dyslexia has even now revealed considerable commonality with partitionings derived from the investigation of acquired dyslexia".

Marshall's conjecture that static models of adult skilled reading could play a role in the understanding of learning to read and of developmental dyslexia was received with considerable consternation—not to say outright hostility—by some developmental psychologists:

> "The already existing structural model, useful as it is in describing the skilled reading process, needs to be complemented by a developmental model in order to make sense of the varieties of developmental dyslexia" (Frith, 1985, p. 326).

> "A far greater problem arises when researchers [on children's reading] fail to adopt a developmental perspective when analyzing their data" (Snowling, 1987, p. 83).

> "... dual-route models of adult word reading ... do not provide any adequate account of the development of reading skills in children" (Snowling, Bryant, & Hulme, 1996, p. 449).

> "... we would argue that the idea of trying to formulate a theory of developmental dyslexia in terms of a theory of adult reading is fundamentally misguided (cf. Frith, 1985) ... A static model of adult performance, such as dual-route theory, is inadequate for understanding how children learn to read and why some children learn to read easily while others have difficulties" (Snowling et al., 1996, p. 444).

Marshall offered his conjecture more than 20 years ago. How has it fared since then?

PURE AND IMPURE CASES OF DEVELOPMENTAL DYSLEXIA

Before proceeding with this discussion, some consideration of terminology is required. Suppose a child of 10 achieves a reading accuracy with irregular words that is equivalent to the mean accuracy of a sample of 7-year-old normal readers. This child's ability to use the lexical route for reading is thus well below an age-appropriate level; and that is our definition of developmental surface dyslexia. Suppose a second, comparable child of 10 achieves a reading accuracy with nonwords that is equivalent to the mean accuracy of a sample of 7-year-old normal readers. This child's ability to use the nonlexical route for reading is thus well below an age-appropriate level; and that is our definition of developmental phonological dyslexia.

Now suppose a third child is referred who displays the impairments of both of the two children described above. What are we to say about this child? That he has *both* developmental surface dyslexia *and* developmental phonological dyslexia? We contend that this is a logical position to adopt.

But of course the distinction between, on the one hand, a child whose irregular word reading is well below chronological age while nonword reading is at an age-appropriate level and, on the other hand, a child whose irregular word reading and nonword reading are both below age-appropriate level, is an important one. So we need terminology to express this distinction. The terminology we will use is "pure" versus "impure". By "pure developmental surface dyslexia" we mean that all aspects of reading except use of the lexical route are at age-appropriate levels; and by "pure developmental phonological dyslexia" we mean that all aspects of reading except use of the nonlexical route are at age-appropriate levels. If some cases of developmental surface or phonological dyslexia are pure in this sense, that would imply the important conclusion that it is possible for either of the reading routes to be acquired at a normal rate even when the other route was being acquired abnormally slowly. We will adhere to this terminology throughout the discussion of subtypes of developmental dyslexia below.

For the purposes of achieving comparability with more typically used definitions of dyslexia, we may sometimes also require our definition of "pure" versus "impure" to reflect whether other aspects of functioning, such as IQ, are impaired in these cases, or whether these are also at age-appropriate levels. Therefore, depending on the focus of interest, the term "pure" might also be applied when all aspects of functioning considered relevant to the case—including, say, IQ—were at age-appropriate levels except the reading sub-process in question. In our view, precisely which aspects of functioning are required to be normal depends on the nature of the case and the particular research question being asked.

SUBTYPES OF DEVELOPMENTAL DYSLEXIA

Evidence for developmental forms of surface and phonological dyslexia

Given the dual-route model of reading proposed by Marshall and Newcombe (1973), and the proposals by Marshall (1984) concerning the applicability of static models of adult skilled reading to the analysis of patterns of developmental dyslexia, it follows that children learning to read may have varying degrees of difficulty in acquiring one route or the other. Dissociations of this type in the developmental dyslexic population were precisely what Castles and Coltheart (1993) set out to identify. Some promising evidence was already available in the form of case studies (e.g., Campbell & Butterworth, 1985; Coltheart et al., 1983; Goulandris & Snowling, 1991; Hanley, Hastie, & Kay, 1992; Snowling & Hulme, 1989; Temple & Marshall, 1983), and from group studies based on somewhat different theoretical approaches (Boder, 1973; Mitterer, 1982).

Castles and Coltheart sought to consolidate these findings in a group study of irregular and nonword reading in 53 dyslexic children and 56 age-matched controls. They found that approximately one third of the poor readers were in the normal range for their age on one task but below the 5th percentile on the other. Specifically, eight subjects were identified as exhibiting pure developmental phonological dyslexia: their nonword reading was poor, compared with chronological age-matched controls, but their irregular word reading was within normal range. Another 10 subjects were classified as exhibiting pure developmental surface dyslexia: their irregular word reading was poor but their nonword reading fell within normal range. A further 27 subjects were poor on both tasks, but nevertheless showed a significant discrepancy between their scores on the irregular word and nonword tasks. The remaining subjects were equally poor on both tasks, leading Castles and Coltheart to conclude that, while deficits on the two reading tasks generally co-occur in children with reading difficulties, irregular word reading and nonword reading can be developmentally dissociated—that is, acquisition of the lexical reading route and acquisition of the nonlexical reading route are independent to a degree, just as would be expected from the approach to developmental dyslexia proposed by Marshall (1984). Very similar findings have since been reported in several group studies (Castles, Datta, Gayan, & Olson, 1999; Manis, Seidenberg, Doi, McBride-Chang, & Peterson, 1996; Stanovich, Siegel, & Gottardo, 1997).

"PURE" CASES OF DEVELOPMENTAL SURFACE AND PHONOLOGICAL DYSLEXIA: SOME NEW EVIDENCE

As mentioned above, Castles and Coltheart (1993) did report cases of pure surface dyslexia and cases of pure phonological dyslexia, according to our definition. However, the criteria for normal performance in this study were not particularly stringent: the dyslexic children only had to fall within the 90% confidence band of scores achieved by the age-matched controls. Therefore it could be argued that some of these cases of developmental surface dyslexia were still mildly impaired on nonword reading and that some of these cases of developmental phonological dyslexia were mildly impaired on irregular word reading.

Thus, to further address the question of the existence of pure developmental dyslexia subtypes, we report here some new analyses in which we applied much stricter criteria for normal performance. The question we asked was: are completely pure cases of developmental surface and phonological dyslexia still identifiable under these more stringent conditions?

The analyses were conducted on two large datasets, the first comprising reading scores from a large group of developing readers and the second consisting of scores from a group of adolescents and young adults. The developing reader dataset consisted of the combined data from six separate studies, specifically those of Castles and Coltheart (1993; $N = 56$), Coltheart and Leahy (1996; $N = 420$), Edwards and Hogben (1999; $N = 297$), Alexander and Martin (2000; $N = 812$), Bowey (unpublished data a; $N = 242$), and Bowey (unpublished data b; $N = 309$.[2] Thus, the data were obtained from 2136 developing readers in total. These children ranged in age from 6,5 to 15,9 years, and were selected without reference to their reading ability (that is, none came from an identified dyslexic sample).

The second dataset consisted of reading accuracy scores from a sample of 1024 adolescents and young adults who were participating in a separate study of the genetic bases of reading that we have been conducting (for more detail, see Bates, Castles, Coltheart, Gillespie, Wright, & Martin, 2004). The participants ranged in age from 12 to 21, and were again selected without reference to their reading ability.

The important aspect of these two datasets for the present purposes is that all of the participants from both datasets had been given sets of irregular words and nonwords for reading aloud, and had been scored on their accuracy. In the case of the developing reader dataset, all had been administered the 30 irregular words and 30 nonwords from Coltheart and Leahy (1996). The older readers in the second dataset had been tested on reading aloud 40 irregular words and 40 nonwords from an extension of the Coltheart and Leahy items for older readers that we have recently developed (see Bates et al., 2004).

Thus we were in a position to interrogate both datasets for the existence of pure developmental surface dyslexia and pure developmental phonological dyslexia. Our criteria were very strict. We first converted individual irregular and nonword reading

---

[2] We are very grateful to Judy Bowey, John Hogben, and Frances Martin for kindly providing us with their irregular and nonword reading data for these analyses.

scores to z-scores, using age-specific means. We then looked for participants whose irregular word reading was very impaired (more than 1.64 standard deviations below average for their age) but whose nonword reading was in the normal range or better (no worse than half a standard deviation below the mean for their age). Such cases would constitute examples of pure developmental surface dyslexia. As well, we looked for participants whose nonword reading was very impaired (more than 1.64 standard deviations below average) but whose irregular word reading was normal or better (no worse than half a standard deviation below the mean for their age). These would be cases of pure developmental phonological dyslexia.

We found evidence for completely pure forms of both types of developmental dyslexia in both datasets. The pure surface dyslexic cases identified from the developing reader dataset are presented in Table 1. There were 16 children, ranging in age from 7 to 15, who were extremely impaired in irregular word reading for their age but who performed normally or better at nonword reading.[3] Cases identified from the older reader sample are presented in Table 2. As can be seen, from this sample we identified 13 adolescents and adults (9 male, 4 female) with completely normal nonword reading but severely impaired irregular word reading.

Cases of pure surface dyslexia clearly occur relatively infrequently (why this might be we discuss below). However, the rarity of these cases in our datasets should not be exaggerated, because the two samples of readers we examined were not pre-diagnosed dyslexic readers, but were children, adolescents, and adults selected without reference to their reading ability. Of the 2066 children in the first dataset, 244 (11.7%) could be classified post hoc as having a reading impairment, on the basis that they performed more than 1.64 standard deviations below average on either

TABLE 1
Pure surface dyslexic cases from a large sample of
developing readers (listed in order of severity)

	Age	*z-irreg*	*z-non*
1	11.5	−2.90	1.20
2	9.5	−2.61	0.28
3	13.0	−2.17	0.11
4	9.3	−2.15	−0.29
5	15.8	−2.06	0.76
6	14.9	−2.06	1.05
7	7.2	−2.02	0.66
8	9.3	−2.02	−0.45
9	13.0	−1.97	0.32
10	9.2	−1.90	−0.09
11	7.8	−1.82	−0.29
12	7.6	−1.82	0.02
13	14.0	−1.76	0.76
14	12.7	−1.76	−0.33
15	13.6	−1.65	1.16
16	15.2	−1.65	1.09

---

[3] Unfortunately, as this was a sample collated from many sources, we do not have the male/female breakdown.

TABLE 2
Pure surface dyslexic cases from a large sample of
older readers (listed in order of severity)

	Age	z-irreg	z-non
1	14	−3.24	−0.43
2	21	−2.65	−0.36
3	20	−2.08	0.02
4	20	−2.08	−0.28
5	20	−2.08	−0.28
6	18	−2.06	0.44
7	16	−1.95	0.20
8	21	−1.91	0.11
9	21	−1.91	−0.20
10	17	−1.90	0.35
11	20	−1.85	−0.13
12	13	−1.80	−0.46
13	17	−1.66	−0.17

irregular word reading or nonword reading or both. Of these, 16 children, or 6.6%, showed the pure surface dyslexic pattern described above. Of the 1024 older participants (the second sample), 104 (10.2%) could subsequently be classified as having a reading impairment on the basis that they performed more than 1.64 standard deviations below average on either irregular word reading or nonword reading or both. Of these, 13 participants, or 12.5%, showed the pure surface dyslexic pattern described above. We note that Castles and Coltheart (1993) reported that six of their 53 dyslexic children, or 11.3%, showed a similar pure surface dyslexic pattern. In our view, a proportion of 6.6–12.5% of all dyslexic readers showing a pure surface dyslexic pattern, in both children and adult samples, cannot be described as negligible.

The cases meeting the criteria for pure developmental phonological dyslexia from the developing reader and older reader datasets are presented in Tables 3 and 4 respectively. As can be seen, 22 pure cases of pure developmental phonological dyslexia were identified from the developing reader dataset, which represents approximately 9% of those with a reading impairment within that sample. Ten pure cases (seven male, three female) were identified in the older reader sample, which represents almost exactly the same proportion of those with a general reading problem within that group (9.6%). Again, it is clear that pure cases of developmental phonological dyslexia can be identified and that their incidence in the population of people who are reading poorly is not negligible.

WHY DO DEVELOPMENTAL DEFICITS OF IRREGULAR WORD READING AND NONWORD READING TEND TO CO-OCCUR?

A common query from researchers who argue for non-dual route architectures in reading—either developmentally or in adults—is, given that the two routes are modular to one another, why do the two major forms of dyslexia co-vary so strongly? As Castles and Coltheart (1993) also observed, it is certainly the case that many poor readers are impaired on both irregular word and nonword reading. It is

TABLE 3
Severe phonological dyslexic cases from a large sample of
developing readers (listed in order of severity)

	Age	z-irreg	z-non
1	11.8	0.06	−2.21
2	11.1	−0.17	−2.16
3	7.4	0.72	−2.12
4	11.1	0.48	−2.05
5	11.3	−0.15	−2.05
6	9.1	−0.30	−1.96
7	9.6	−0.15	−1.90
8	10.1	−0.35	−1.90
9	11.4	−0.35	−1.90
10	8.1	−0.12	−1.90
11	8.3	−0.26	−1.90
12	14.2	0.16	−1.86
13	13.8	−0.12	−1.75
14	7.4	0.30	−1.75
15	10.2	−0.40	−1.75
16	9.3	−0.17	−1.74
17	9.1	−0.15	−1.73
18	8.9	0.47	−1.65
19	9.7	−.041	−1.65
20	9.2	−.041	−1.65
21	12.7	0.32	−1.64
22	7.9	0.02	−1.64

also true that one way of accounting for this is to propose that a single reading mechanism is responsible for reading both types of item.

However, there are at least three reasons why a correlation between irregular and nonword reading performance might also be expected on a dual-route account. The first reason relates to the structure of the model itself. Figure 2 represents the dual-route model in its most recent form, as the computational Dual Route Cascaded (DRC) model of Coltheart and colleagues (Coltheart, Curtis, Atkins, & Haller, 1993; Coltheart, Rastle, Perry, Langdon, & Ziegler, 2001). As can be seen, the lexical and nonlexical routes of the DRC are not completely independent, but have three

TABLE 4
Severe phonological dyslexic cases from a large sample of
older readers (listed in order of severity)

	Age	z-irreg	z-non
1	14	0.24	−2.95
2	17	0.06	−2.61
3	16	0.57	−2.37
4	14	−0.50	−2.06
5	21	−0.20	−1.91
6	16	−0.44	−1.82
7	19	−0.16	−1.75
8	17	−0.18	−1.74
9	18	−0.34	−1.68
10	20	−0.08	−1.64

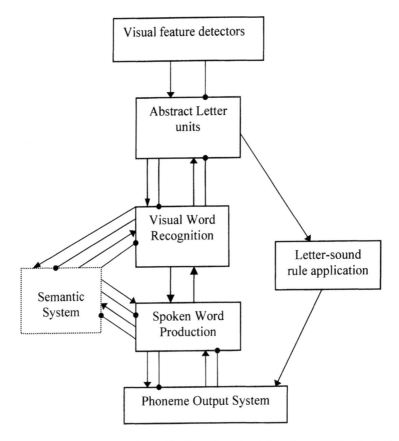

Figure 2. The Dual-route Cascaded Model of reading aloud, based on Coltheart et al. (2001). Implemented modules are in unbroken lines, arrows represent excitatory links and dots inhibitory links.

components in common: *visual feature detectors, abstract letter units*, and the *phoneme output system*. Therefore, a deficit in any one of these components will lead to impairments in both irregular and nonword reading. A specific impairment in either irregular or nonword reading would only ever be expected to occur, even on a dual-route model, on those occasions when there was localised damage to a component of the system that was unique to either the lexical and nonlexical routes.

The second reason why deficits in irregular and nonword reading will often co-occur relates not to the structure of the dual-route model itself but to the distal factors that may have influenced the development of the components of the model in the first place. Even though the processes themselves may be distinct, there are numerous factors—personality, cognitive, social, and educational—that are likely to influence the speed and efficiency of children's acquisition of *both* the lexical and the nonlexical routes, and to an approximately equal degree. For example, a poor teacher who does not engage a child's interest is likely to have a negative impact on that child's ability to learn grapheme–phoneme correspondence rules as well as their ability to build a sight vocabulary. Similarly, a child with attention deficit hyperactivity disorder is likely to fail to pay attention to instruction relevant to the acquisition of components of both the lexical and nonlexical routes. An extended period of illness or emotional upset would again be likely to have a generalised impact on lexical and nonlexical learning.

The third reason why deficits in irregular and nonword reading will often co-occur is that, although the orthographic lexicon and the GPC procedure in the DRC model *operate* independently, this does not mean that they are *learned* independently. Each component might assist the learning of the other. According to the self-teaching hypothesis, being able to recognise unfamiliar printed words auditorily by sounding them out using the GPC procedure assists the development of visual word recognition skills; that is, the use of this procedure helps the orthographic lexicon to develop (Share, 1995). And conversely it is quite plausible to suppose that one of the ways a child learns about the correspondences between graphemes and phonemes is by reflecting upon the relationships between the spellings and the pronunciations of already learned words, as proposed in the Lexicalised Implicit Learning framework of Fletcher-Flinn and Thomson (2004); here the contents of the lexicons help the GPC system to develop. If there is this mutual dependence of the components as children learn to read, then if one of the components is defective it will not be able to assist the acquisition of the other, leading to the co-occurrence of poor irregular word reading and poor nonword reading.

In summary, then, for several reasons the association of irregular word reading and nonword reading in children learning to read, and the co-occurrence of deficits on these tasks in developmental dyslexia, is not inconsistent with the dual-route model of reading.

WHY IS THE OCCURRENCE OF PURE CASES IMPORTANT?

Although deficits in irregular word reading and nonword reading will generally co-occur, we suggest that, for two reasons, the existence of pure cases of developmental surface and phonological dyslexia is of particular importance. The first reason is that, although we think the self-teaching hypothesis (that children make use of the nonlexical reading routes when building up the lexical reading route) and the lexicalised implicit learning hypothesis (that children make use of reflection upon the spelling–sound relationships of words already represented in the lexical route when building up the body of letter–sound rules that constitutes the nonlexical route) are both highly plausible, the existence of pure cases indicates that these aids to learning are not essential. Some children can be acquiring the lexical route at an age-appropriate rate even when their nonlexical route is poor, and some children can be acquiring the nonlexical route at an age-appropriate rate even when their lexical route is poor. It should also be noted that, although we have not considered them here, cases of children who were reading at age-appropriate levels on one task but significantly *above* such levels on the other task, and vice versa, would also support our claim.

The second reason is that the existence of pure cases of developmental surface dyslexia and developmental phonological dyslexia is problematic for connectionist attempts at simulating developmental reading difficulties.

CONNECTIONIST MODELLING OF DEVELOPMENTAL DYSLEXIA

Harm and Seidenberg (1999) present a detailed account of the role of phonology in reading acquisition and of the basis of dyslexia subtypes in the context of a modified version of the connectionist model of Plaut, McClelland, Seidenberg, and Patterson (1996). Summarised briefly, the Harm and Seidenberg model differs from the original Plaut et al. model in that (a) learning in the phonological units is assisted by cleanup units, (b) the phonological units represent phonetic features, not phonemes, and (c) the orthographic units represent letters, not graphemes. They first implement a phonological system that represents phonological knowledge within an attractor network of phonetic features. They then implement a reading model that learned to map orthographic representations onto this phonological knowledge. Having trained the model to achieve satisfactory performance in reading words and nonwords, they go on to examine ways in which the network might be impaired so as to simulate different patterns of developmental dyslexia.

Consistent with the Manis et al. (1996) account, developmental surface dyslexia is conceptualised by Harm and Seidenberg as a general delay, with a range of possible sources. The results of two specific simulations are reported. In one, a general "processing" deficit, or impairment in the capacity of the network to map from orthography to phonology, is simulated by reducing the number of hidden units mediating between the two systems from 100 to 20. In a second simulation, a "learning" deficit is instantiated by reducing the network's learning rate. Harm and Seidenberg also discuss other means by which a general delay might be produced, including (a) simulating a lack of reading experience by reducing the number of training cycles to which the network is exposed, and (b) simulating the possible effects of low-level visual deficits by impairing the orthographic input to the system.

Importantly, all of these causal factors are proposed to produce the same general outcome—a slower mastery of *all* types of reading stimuli, but a particular difficulty in learning to read irregular words. The pattern of findings for the two Harm and Seidenberg simulations of surface dyslexia are consistent with this prediction. Irregular words were the worst affected in both simulations, producing a dissociation between irregular word and nonword reading performance. When a reduction in hidden units was imposed, asymptotic performance on irregular word reading was reduced from 93% to approximately 76%; in the reduced learning rate simulation, asymptotic performance decreased from 93% to about 84%. Note, however, that in both cases nonwords are affected as well, with asymptotic performance dropping from 89% to about 71% in both simulations. So, in these simulations, impaired acquisition of irregular word reading was accompanied by impaired acquisition of nonword reading: that is, pure surface dyslexia was not simulated but instead a generalised reading deficit

In accordance with its proposed basis at the level of phonological units, Harm and Seidenberg simulate developmental phonological dyslexia by damaging the model's phonological system. They did this in two ways. In the first simulation, the network was impaired by imposing a small weight decay on the phonetic feature units during training. This intervention is shown to have a weak effect on the ability of the network to perform phonological tasks such as pattern completion, and is therefore referred to as a *mild* phonological impairment. The second simulation explores a more severe form of damage where, in addition to the weight decay, cleanup units are removed from the network, as are 50% of the connections between the phonetic feature units. This is shown to have a larger effect on the network's ability to perform phonological tasks, and so is referred to as a *moderate* phonological impairment.

In what ways was reading affected by these two forms of network damage? In the case of the mild phonological impairment, irregular word reading was unaffected, but the learning of nonwords was slightly impaired, with asymptotic performance dropping from approximately 79% to 64%. Thus, in this case, the damage to the network resulted in *pure* phonological dyslexia: irregular word reading was not just superior to nonword reading but was normal, while nonword reading was worse than normal. However, it should be noted that, although pure, the phonological dyslexia displayed was very mild. Nonword reading was only 15% worse than normal, and far above zero. In the case of the moderate phonological impairment, nonword reading was indeed more severely impaired than in the mild impairment, with performance dropping from about 79% to 56%. However, in this case, the deficit was also accompanied by a decrease in irregular word reading performance from 93% to 89%.

Thus, in the Harm and Seidenberg simulations, only when the phonological units were degraded very mildly did the model produce a pure pattern of phonological dyslexia, with nonword reading being affected but irregular word reading remaining normal. When the phonological units were degraded more severely, *both* irregular and nonwords were always affected.

To summarise, then, in this connectionist work:

(a)   Pure surface dyslexia was not observed: any lesion of the model that impaired the acquisition of irregular word reading also impaired the acquisition of nonword reading.
(b)   Only when the acquisition of nonword reading was mildly impaired by damaging the network did the acquisition of irregular word reading remain normal; that is, pure phonological dyslexia was not observed in any situation where the impairment of nonword reading acquisition was severe.

As we have described above, however, cases of pure developmental surface dyslexia *are* observed (Tables 1 and 2; see also Castles & Coltheart, 1996, for a detailed description of another such case) and so are cases of pure developmental phonological dyslexia where the nonword reading deficit is severe (see Tables 3 and 4). So these observed extreme developmental dissociations indicate that connectionist modelling has not yet been successful in accounting for developmental disorders of reading. Connectionist modelling of acquired disorders of reading has likewise not yet been successful in explaining features of these acquired dyslexias (Coltheart, 2006).

THE DRC MODEL AND READING ACQUISITION

The DRC model has nothing to say about the processes by which children learn to read, since it is a "static" model of the adult skilled reading system. But that does not mean that the model has nothing to say about reading acquisition. John Marshall's conjecture was that, as children acquire a reading system, they do not proceed through a series of developmental stages, and that there are no qualitative changes in their reading systems over time. All change is quantitative, according to this conjecture: young readers and skilled adult readers have the same architecture for the reading system. Reading acquisition consists simply of making quantitative changes to this architecture—for example, adding words to the sight vocabulary and adding rules to the database of grapheme–phoneme correspondences.

We have tested Marshall's conjecture as follows. Suppose we give a child a set of nonwords, a set of regular words, and a set of irregular words to read aloud. The regular words are matched to the irregular words on all relevant variables, particularly word frequency. Suppose this child correctly reads 70% of the irregular words. According to the DRC model, this indicates that this child's lexical reading route contains 70% of words that have these particular word properties. Because the irregular words are matched with the regular words on all relevant variables, it follows that 70% will also be an estimate of how many of the regular words can be read via the lexical route. So this child should correctly read at least 70% of the regular words.[4]

What of the remaining 30% of regular words? A fully acquired nonlexical reading route would read all of these aloud correctly, of course. But this child might not yet have fully acquired the nonlexical reading route. The child's nonword reading accuracy is a measure of how well the nonlexical reading route has been acquired. Suppose this child's nonword reading accuracy is 40%. Hence we might expect that, of the remaining 30% of regular words, 40% (i.e., 12% of the total set of regular words) will be readable nonlexically. Thus the child should score 70% + 12% = 82% on regular word reading—if the DRC model is an accurate description of this child's reading system.

Thus in general if we know any child's irregular word reading accuracy (IRR) and nonword reading accuracy (NWD), the child's regular word reading accuracy (REG) will, if the DRC model correctly describes this child's reading system, be predictable by the equation:

$$REG = IRR + (1 - IRR)^*NWD$$

To test the validity of this equation, we need data in which children were given regular and irregular words (matched on important variables such as length and word frequency) and nonwords to read aloud. For each child, we can compute Predicted REG from the equation above and plot it against Obtained REG (the actual proportion of regular words the child read aloud correctly). That will tell us how accurately the dual route equation applies to children's reading.

Figure 3 shows the results with the same six datasets that were combined to produce the large developing reader sample described previously, all involving children who were normal readers. The equation fits every dataset excellently: the percentage of variance in regular word reading accuracy the equation explains varies from 73% to 84%.

In order to confirm that both predictor variables are pulling their weight here, we calculated the proportion of variance of REG scores accounted for by IRR and NWD scores in simple regression analyses and compared this to the proportion accounted for in multiple regression analyses using both variables. The results are shown in Table 5. For all six datasets, the proportion of variance of REG scores accounted for by the predictor variables in conjunction was higher than the proportion accounted for by either predictor variable alone.

This provides strong evidence in support of Marshall's conjecture. Even though the children in these samples vary widely in age and level of reading ability, a static model of the architecture of the skilled reading system provides a satisfactory

---

[4] If regular word reading accuracy in this child were significantly less than 70%, that would instantly refute the DRC model. So would the finding of regular word reading accuracy that was significantly below nonword reading accuracy.

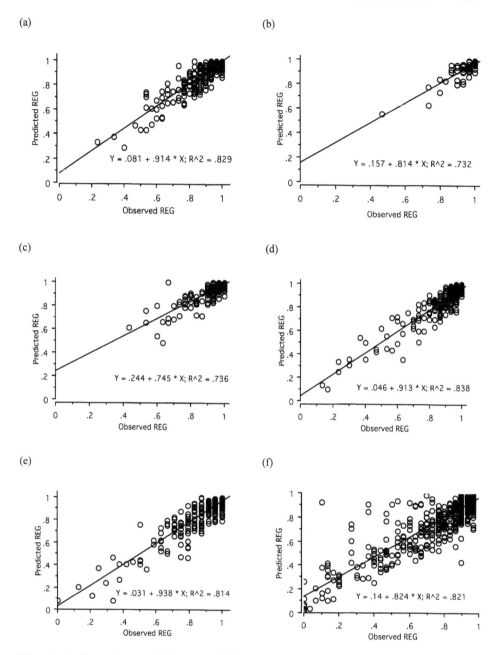

Figure 3. Predictions from the dual-route model for six unselected samples of children: (a) Coltheart and Leahy, 1996: $N = 420$; (b) Castles and Coltheart, 1993: $N = 56$; (c) Edwards and Hogben, 1999: N = 297; (d) Bowey, unpublished (a): $N = 242$; (e) Bowey, unpublished (b): $N = 309$; (f) Alexander & Martin, 2000: $N = 812$.

description of the architectures of these children's reading systems; if this description were not satisfactory, the predictions could not be so accurate.

These children were normal readers. What about children who are abnormal readers? Does the DRC model also offer an adequate description of their reading

TABLE 5
Proportion of variance in REG scores accounted for by IRR and NWD scores separately and jointly, in normal readers

	IRR alone	NWD alone	IRR and NWD jointly
Coltheart & Leahy, 1996	.612	.668	.757
Castles & Coltheart, 1993	.330	.640	.664
Edwards & Hogben, 1999	.461	.618	.660
Bowey, unpublished (a)	.608	.646	.726
Bowey, unpublished (b)	.624	.657	.761
Alexander & Martin, 2000	.780	.455	.791

systems—that is, does the equation for predicting REG from IRR and NWD also hold for such readers?

First, consider developmental dyslexia. Figure 4 shows the results of applying the equation to two samples of developmentally dyslexic children. The equation continues to provide an excellent fit to the data, despite the fact that all the children here have a developmental disorder of reading. So even when reading is developing abnormally, the system that is being used to read aloud appears to possess the same architecture as the adult skilled reading system, since predictions based on that architecture fit the data very well.

Next, consider children who have had strokes. Figure 5 shows the results of applying the equation to a sample of such children.[5] Again, the equation fits the data very well, indicating that childhood stroke, although it can impair reading, does not do so in a way that produces a qualitative change in the reading system.

Again, in order to confirm that both predictor variables are pulling their weight here, we calculated the proportion of variance of REG scores accounted for by IRR and NWD scores in simple regression analyses and compared this to the proportion accounted for in multiple regression analyses using both variables. The results are shown in Table 6. For all three datasets, the proportion of variance of REG scores accounted for by the predictor variables in conjunction was higher than the proportion accounted for by either predictor variable alone.

Lastly, consider age. One might argue that the excellent fits seen in Figure 3 are being driven by the oldest children and that these children are effectively adult readers, so that we don't really have here a demonstration of a static model dealing successfully with a developing system. If that is so, the accuracy with which the equation predicts REG will be lower, the younger the children are.[6] Figure 6 plots difference between predicted and obtained REG scores for the entire sample of 2136 unselected children from Figure 3 (who ranged in age from 6 to 15), as a function of the children's age

It is clear that the accuracy of the equation's predictions is independent of age: the equation is just as good at predicting the performance of 6-year-olds (many of whom can scarcely read at all) as it is at predicting the age of 15-year-olds (many of whom are reading at adult levels). So even when reading is barely developed at all, the system that is being used to read aloud appears to be a system that possesses the same architecture as the adult system—it is just a scaled-down version of the adult system.

---

[5] We thank Nikki Pitchford for providing us with these raw data.
[6] We thank Margot Prior for suggesting this analysis.

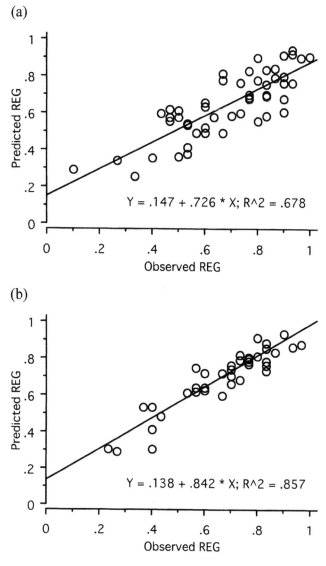

Figure 4. Predictions from the dual-route model for two samples of dyslexic children: (a) Castles and Coltheart, 1993, $N = 53$; (b) Cestnick and Coltheart, 1999, $N = 40$.

These analyses comprehensively vindicate Marshall's conjecture. Regardless of a reader's age, and regardless of whether the person is an intact or impaired reader, a static model of the adult skilled reading system (in these cases, the DRC model) provides an excellent description of their reading performance.

Might this also be achievable by connectionist models of reading? Only actual simulations with such models could provide a definitive answer, but we doubt that comparable accuracy in predicting REG from IRR plus NWD could be achieved. Presumably what would have to be done would be to halt the learning by the model at different points before it had reached asymptotic performance. These different halting points would correspond to children at differing levels of reading development. For each partially trained model, performance on IRR and NWD

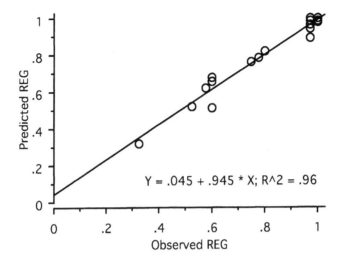

Figure 5. Predictions from the dual-route model for a group of children who had had strokes (Funnell & Pitchford, unpublished data, $N = 17$).

TABLE 6
Proportion of variance in REG scores accounted for by IRR and NWD scores separately and jointly, in impaired readers

	IRR alone	NWD alone	IRR and NWD jointly
Castles & Coltheart, 1993	.552	.659	.835
Cestnick & Coltheart, 1999	.469	.356	.744
Funnell & Pitchford, unpublished	.630	.917	.933

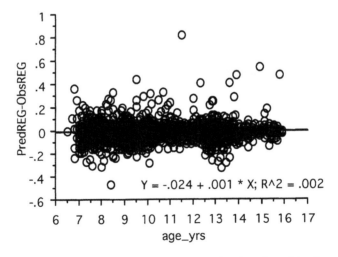

Figure 6. Accuracy of the dual-route model's predictions as a function of age (data from all children in Figure 3; $N = 2136$).

could be calculated and used to predict the model's performance on REG. We have already noted that with the model of Harm and Seidenberg (2004) any lesion of the model that harmed the learning of irregular words also harmed the learning of nonwords, and any lesion of the model that more than mildly affected the learning of nonwords harmed the learning of irregular words. Our opinion is therefore that the acquisition of these three types of item by connectionist models is too interdependent for the models to be able to predict the full range of results seen in large samples of children when reading scores on the three types of items are analysed.

OTHER SUBTYPES OF DYSLEXIA

It would seem abundantly clear now that phonological dyslexia and surface dyslexia occur in both developmental and acquired forms. What about other dyslexia subtypes? Marshall (1984, p. 49) considered four others:

(a) *Attentional dyslexia.* Here, word reading and the naming of individual letters is relatively preserved, but naming letters when they are part of a letter string is impaired. Acquired cases include that of Shallice and Warrington (1987). Marshall (1984, p 51) stated that as far as he knew no cases of a developmental form of this dyslexia subtype had been reported. Subsequently Rayner, Murphy, Henderson, and Pollatsek (1989) have described a developmental case that looks very much like developmental attentional dyslexia.

(b) *Visual dyslexia.* Here, whether the stimulus to be read is a word or a nonword, the response is characteristically a word that has some orthographic resemblance to the stimulus: for example the acquired dyslexic patient MB (Newcombe & Marshall, 1973) produced such errors as *mow* → "now", *rid* → "rib", and *beg* → "big". Again, Marshall (1984, p 51) stated that as far as he knew no cases of a developmental form of this dyslexia subtype had been reported. But cases JM, TW, and AS reported by Snowling, Stackhouse, and Rack (1986, pp. 317–318) seem to be clear examples; their reading errors included *sign* →"sing", *bitter* → "butter", *pint* → "pink", *breath* →"bread", *flood* →"food", and *bitter* → "better". All three were particularly poor at reading nonwords, but that is to be expected in developmental visual dyslexia if the predominant method of reading here is to find in the orthographic lexicon a word that is orthographically close to the input string, and if this matching process is somewhat approximate; this method will always deliver a word as a response even when the input string is a nonword.

(c) *Direct dyslexia.* This is reading aloud without comprehension, including the reading aloud of irregular words despite the fact that they cannot be understood. Acquired cases of this dyslexia subtype include those of Schwartz, Saffran, and Marin (1987) and Blazely, Coltheart, and Casey (2005). This is familiar as a subtype of developmental dyslexia under the name hyperlexia (e.g., Glosser, Grugan, & Friedman, 1997, who observed (p. 234) of their developmental case that "These findings support the assertion that both orthographic and phonological whole-word representations can be acquired, stored, and retrieved in the absence of a functional link to semantic memory").

(d) *Deep dyslexia.* Prominent symptoms of this dyslexia subtype include semantic errors in reading aloud, very poor reading of function words, and the abolition of nonword reading (Coltheart, 1987). Marshall in 1984 knew of no cases of developmental deep dyslexia but such a case has subsequently been reported by Stuart and Howard (1995).

Thus all six of the subtypes of acquired dyslexia considered by Marshall (1984) turned out to occur also as developmental dyslexias. And there are other subtypes unknown in 1984 for which the same is true:

(e) *Neglect dyslexia*: Here reading errors arise only with respect to one end of the word, typically the left. Acquired cases include those of Caramazza and Hillis (1990) and Haywood and Coltheart (2001). A developmental case of left neglect dyslexia (without any general visuospatial neglect) has been reported by Friedmann and Nachman-Katz (2004).

(f) *Letter-position dyslexia*. Reading errors here typically involve wrongly identifying the positions of letters in a word, so that beard might be read as "bread". This occurs in both acquired and developmental forms (Friedmann & Gvion, 2001).

CONCLUSIONS

We have provided evidence in this paper that strongly supports Marshall's proposals that "the syndromes of developmental dyslexia must be defined over *a* functional architecture of visible language processing" and that "the relevant functional architecture is the one that correctly characterizes the normal, fluent, adult reading system" (Marshall, 1984, p. 46). And we have also provided evidence that the particular functional architecture that constitutes this correct characterisation is the kind of dual-route architecture originally proposed by Marshall. Studies of normal readers (see e.g., Coltheart et al., 2001) support the view that the reading system has a highly modular organisation). Studies of acquired dyslexia (see e.g., Coltheart, 2006) support the view that brain damage causes this system to break down in highly modular ways. And the work we have reviewed in this paper supports the view that the way in which the reading system is acquired is also highly modular—that is, that it is profitable, as Marshall (1984, p.47) suggested, "to adopt a highly modular 'preformist' approach to the development of the reading system".

REFERENCES

Alexander, J. R. M., & Martin, F. (2000). Norming tests of basic reading skills. *Australian Journal of Psychology, 52*, 139–148.

Bates, T. C., Castles, A., Coltheart, M., Gillespie, N., Wright, M., & Martin, N. G. (2004). Behaviour genetic analyses of reading and spelling: A component processes approach. *Australian Journal of Psychology, 56*(2), 115–126.

Beauvois, M. F., & Derouesné, J. (1979). Phonological dyslexia: Three dissociations. *Journal of Neurology, Neurosurgery & Psychiatry, 42*, 1115–1124.

Blazely, A., Coltheart, M., & Casey, B. (2005). Semantic dementia with and without surface dyslexia. *Cognitive Neuropsychology, 22*, 695–717.

Boder, E. (1973). Developmental dyslexia: A diagnostic approach based on three typical reading–spelling patterns. *Developmental Medicine and Child Neurology, 15*, 663–687.

Campbell, R., & Butterworth, B. (1985). Phonological dyslexia and dysgraphia in a highly literate subject: A developmental case with associated deficits of phonemic processing and awareness. *Quarterly Journal of Experimental Psychology, 35*A, 435–475.

Caramazza, A., & Hillis, A. E. (1990). Spatial representation of words in the brain implied by the studies of a unilateral neglect patient. *Nature, 346*, 267–269.

Castles, A., & Coltheart, M. (1993). Varieties of developmental dyslexia. *Cognition, 47*, 149–180.

Castles, A., & Coltheart, M. (1996). Cognitive correlates of developmental surface dyslexia: A single case study. *Cognitive Neuropsychology, 13*, 25–50.

Castles, A., Datta, H., Gayan, J., & Olson, R. K. (1999). Varieties of developmental reading disorder: Genetic and environmental influences. *Journal of Experimental Child Psychology, 72*, 73–94.

Cestnick, L., & Coltheart, M. (1999). The relationship between language-processing and visual-processing deficits in developmental dyslexia. *Cognition, 71*, 231–255.

Coltheart, M. (1987). Deep dyslexia: A review of the syndrome. In M. Coltheart, K. Patterson, & J. Marshall (Eds.), *Deep dyslexia* (pp. 22–47). London: Routledge.

Coltheart, M. (2006). Acquired dyslexias and the computational modelling of reading. *Cognitive Neuropsychology, 23*, 96–109.

Coltheart, M., Curtis, B., Atkins, P., & Haller, M. (1993). Models of reading aloud: Dual route and parallel-distributed-processing approaches. *Psychological Review, 100*, 589–608.

Coltheart, M., & Leahy, J. (1996). Assessment of lexical and nonlexical reading abilities in children: Some normative data. *Australian Journal of Psychology, 48*, 136–140.

Coltheart, M., Masterson, J., Byng, S., Prior, M., & Riddoch, J. (1983). Surface dyslexia. *Quarterly Journal of Experimental Psychology, 37*A, 469–495.

Coltheart, M., Rastle, K., Perry, C., Langdon, R., & Ziegler, J. (2001). DRC: A dual route cascaded model of visual word recognition and reading aloud. *Psychological Review, 108*, 204–256.

Edwards, V. T., & Hogben, J. H. (1999). New norms for comparing children's lexical and nonlexical reading: A further look at subtyping dyslexia. *Australian Journal of Psychology, 51*, 37–49.

Fletcher-Flinn, C. M., & Thompson, B. (2004). A mechanism of implicit lexicalized phonological recoding used concurrently with underdeveloped explicit letter–sound skills in both precocious and normal reading development. *Cognition, 90*, 303–335.

Forster, K. I., & Chambers, S. M. (1973). Lexical access and naming time. *Journal of Verbal Learning and Verbal Behavior, 12*, 627–635.

Friedmann, N., & Gvion, A. (2001). Letter position dyslexia. *Cognitive Neuropsychology, 18*, 673–696.

Friedmann, N., & Nachman-Katz, I. (2004). Developmental neglect dyslexia in a Hebrew-reading child. *Cortex, 40*, 301–313.

Frith, U. (1985). Beneath the surface of developmental dyslexia. In K. E. Patterson, J. C. Marshall, & M. Coltheart (Eds.), *Surface dyslexia*. Hove, UK: Lawrence Erlbaum Associates Ltd.

Glosser, G., Grugan, P., & Friedman, R. B. N. (1997). Semantic memory impairment does not impact on phonological and orthographic processing in a case of developmental hyperlexia. *Brain and Language, 56*, 234–247.

Goulandris, N. K., & Snowling, M. (1991). Visual memory deficits: A plausible cause of developmental dyslexia? Evidence from a single case study. *Cognitive Neuropsychology, 8*, 127–154.

Hanley, R., Hastie, K., & Kay, J. (1992). Developmental surface dyslexia and dysgraphia: An orthographic processing impairment. *The Quarterly Journal of Experimental Psychology, 44*, 285–319.

Harm, M. W., & Seidenberg, M. S. (1999). Phonology, reading acquisition, and dyslexia, insights from connectionist models. *Psychological Review, 106*, 491–528.

Heywood, M., & Coltheart, M. (2001). Neglect dyslexia with a stimulus-centred deficit and without visuospatial neglect. *Cognitive Neuropsychology, 18*, 577–615.

Holmes, J. M. (1973). *Dyslexia: A neurolinguistic study of traumatic and developmental disorders of reading.* Unpublished PhD thesis, University of Edinburgh.

Manis, F. R., Seidenberg, M. S., Doi, L. M., McBride-Chang, C., & Peterson, A. (1996). On the bases of two subtypes of developmental dyslexia. *Cognition, 58*, 157–195.

Marshall, J. C. (1984). Toward a rational taxonomy of the developmental dyslexias. In R. N. Malatesha & H. A. Whitaker (Eds.), *Dyslexia: A global issue*. The Hague: Martinus Nijhoff.

Marshall, J. C., & Newcombe, F. (1973). Patterns of paralexia: A psycholinguistic approach. *Journal of Psycholinguistic Reseach, 2*, 175–199.

Mitterer, J. O. (1982). There are at least two kinds of poor readers: Whole word poor readers and recoding poor readers. *Canadian Journal of Psychology, 36*, 445–461.

Plaut, D. C., McClelland, J. L., Seidenberg, M. S., & Patterson, K. (1996). Understanding normal and impaired word reading: Computational principles in quasi-regular domains. *Psychological Review, 103*, 56–115.

Rayner, K., Murphy, L. A., Henderson, J. M., & Pollatsek, A. (1989). Selective attentional dyslexia. *Cognitive Neuropsychology, 6,* 357–378.

Schwartz, M., Saffran, E., & Marlin, O. S. (1987). Fractionating the reading process in dementia: Evidence for word-specific print-sound association. In M. Coltheart, K. Patterson, & J. Marshall (Eds.), *Deep dyslexia* (pp. 259–269). London: Routledge.

Shallice, T., & Warrington, E. (1987). Single and multiple component central dyslexic syndromes. In M. Coltheart, K. Patterson, & J. Marshall (Eds.), *Deep dyslexia* (pp. 119–145). London: Routledge.

Share, D. L. (1995). Phonological recoding and self-teaching: Sine qua non of reading acquisition. *Cognition, 55,* 151–218.

Snowling, M. (1987). *Dyslexia: A cognitive developmental perspective.* Oxford, UK: Blackwell.

Snowling, M. J., & Hulme, C. (1989). A longitudinal case study of developmental phonological dyslexia. *Cognitive Neuropsychology, 6,* 379–401.

Snowling, M. J., Bryant, P., & Hulme, C. (1996). Theoretical and methodological pitfalls in making comparisons between developmental and acquired dyslexia: Some comments on A. Castles and M. Coltheart (1993). *Reading and Writing: An Interdisciplinary Journal, 8,* 443–451.

Snowling, M., Stackhouse, J., & Rack, J. (1986). Phonological dyslexia and dysgraphia: A development analysis. *Cognitive Neuropsychology, 3,* 309–339.

Stanovich, K. E., Siegel, L. S., & Gottardo, A. (1997). Converging evidence for phonological and surface subtypes of reading disability. *Journal of Educational Psychology, 89,* 114–127.

Stuart, M., & Howard, D. (1995). KJ: A developmental deep dyslexic. *Cognitive Neuropsychology, 12,* 793–824.

Temple, C. M., & Marshall, J. C. (1983). A case study of developmental phonological dyslexia. *British Journal of Psychology, 74,* 517–533.

Task-independent and task-specific syntactic deficits in aphasic comprehension

David Caplan

Massachusetts General Hospital, Boston, MA, USA

Gayle DeDe

Boston University, MA, USA

Jennifer Michaud

Massachusetts General Hospital, Boston, MA, USA

We present 42 case studies of aphasic syntactic comprehension performances in sentence–picture matching and object manipulation, examining the data for the existence of deficits referable to particular syntactic structures, or such structures in a single sentence form, in both tasks. No deficits affected performance on all sentence types that contained a particular structure in both tasks. Most deficits affected single sentence forms in only one task, and no isolated deficits occurred. The implications of the pattern of performance for the nature of aphasic deficits are discussed.

For the most part, researchers who have studied disturbances of syntactic processing in comprehension have studied performance on a single task and interpreted deficits in one sentence type as arising from failure of parsing and/or the use of syntactic representations to assign aspects of propositional meaning (e.g., Caplan & Hildebrandt, 1988). Entire theories of the nature of deficits and compensations to deficits have been built on such data (e.g., Caplan & Hildebrandt, 1988; Grodzinsky, 2000), and taken as evidence for aspects of models of normal syntactic structure (e.g., Caplan & Hildebrandt, 1988; Grodzinsky, 2000). However, interpreting sentence-specific deficits on a single task as parsing or interpretive failures would be incorrect if the performances that are taken as evidence for the deficit are restricted to that task and not found on tasks that require the same level of processing. For example, a deficit on passive sentences in sentence–picture matching cannot be taken as evidence for a deficit in parsing passive structures if it co-exists with an intact ability to enact actions in response to passive sentences.

Address correspondence to: David Caplan MD PhD, Neuropsychology Laboratory, Massachusetts General Hospital, 175 Cambridge Street, Suite 340, Fruit Street, Boston, MA 02114, USA. E-mail: dcaplan@partners.org

This research was supported by grants from NIDCD (DC0094 to David Caplan and DC007564 to Gayle DeDe). We wish to thank an anonymous reviewer for pointing out errors in a previous draft and for helpful suggestions regarding statistical analyses.

This has been recognised and discussed for two decades in relationship to a pattern of good performance on grammaticality judgement and poor sentence–picture matching (Linebarger, Schwartz, & Saffran, 1983). While the initial studies of grammaticality judgement did not test patients on the same sentence types on which they had performed abnormally in picture matching, subsequent studies showed this dissociation over the same structures (Linebarger, 1995). This dissociation has led to modifications of the deficit analyses that were based on performances in sentence–picture matching alone. In the face of good performance on grammaticality judgement, abnormal performances on particular sentence types in sentence–picture matching have been attributed to a deficit in using syntactic structures to assign propositional meanings coupled with a retained ability to construct such structures (i.e., a "mapping" rather than a "parsing" deficit).

In the case of good performance on grammaticality judgement and poor sentence–picture matching, this re-analysis of the deficit may be plausible, as a stage of processing that makes use of syntactic representations to assign meaning may exist in sentence–picture matching that is not needed in grammaticality judgement. Even this characterisation of the deficit is suspect, as grammaticality judgement may involve reference to meaning and depends on the nature of the foils (Caplan, 1995), but a dissociation in processing one syntactic structure in two tasks that require comprehension is even harder to explain. To take up the example presented above again, if a patient can understand passive sentences as shown by reliably enacting the meaning of these sentences, and is capable of matching the same meanings derived from active sentences to pictures, why should s/he not be able to match the meaning of passive sentences to a picture?[1]

While less well publicised than the dissociation between good performance on grammaticality judgement and poor performance on sentence–picture matching, dissociations in performance on specific sentence types over tasks that require comprehension have been recorded (Cupples & Inglis, 1993). We have previously found that performance on specific sentence types correlated at about the .6 level in sentence–picture matching and enactment in 17 aphasic patients (Caplan, Waters, & Hildebrandt, 1997)—a level of correlation that, while significant, indicates that many patients differed in their accuracy on a given sentence type in the two tasks. Dissociations of performance over two comprehension tasks have two consequences for theory, one negative and one positive. On the negative side, their existence raises a caution about interpreting sentence-specific deficits in one task as deficits in parsing or interpretation. On the positive side, their existence requires us to develop models of how sentence comprehension and task performance interact and of the stages of those interactions at which sentence-specific deficits might arise.

---

[1] Dissociations of the ability to utilise particular types of propositions over two tasks are more easily explained. For instance, if a patient failed to enact sentences with two propositions but could match such sentences to pictures, and did not show a corresponding dissociation over tasks for sentences with one proposition, this could be due to how limitations in a memory store for propositional knowledge affected enactment. The reason this type of explanation can more readily account for task-specific effects of particular semantic representations is that task performance depends on the meaning of a sentence, not its syntax. Note that either the overall complexity or specific aspects of a task could interact with propositional content, leading to both double dissociations and a more common effect of one task than another on the ability to demonstrate certain propositional representations.

We here present data from 42 aphasic patients showing that such dissociations are the rule, not the exception. We then turn to several possible accounts of their existence.

METHOD

A total of 42 aphasic patients (mean age 60.3 years, range: 24.7–84.5; mean education 14.7 years, range: 9–22; M:F = 26:16) who met entry criteria were tested. Patients were required to be aphasic, right handed, have a single left hemisphere stroke, be able to perform the tests, and be judged to have adequate single word comprehension to avoid failure because of lexical semantic disturbances (patients were screened for disturbances of phoneme discrimination, auditory lexical decision, and spoken word-picture matching). A total of 25 age- and education-matched controls (mean age 68.9 years, range: 52.8–89.9; mean education 14 years, range: 9–21; M:F = 8:17) were also tested.

The ability to construct and understand three syntactic structures—passives, relative clauses, and sentences with reflexive pronouns—was tested by having patients respond to pairs of sentences in which the baseline sentence did not contain the construction/element in question, or could be interpreted on the basis of a heuristic, and the experimental sentence contained the structure/element and required the assignment of a complex syntactic structure to be understood. Each structure was tested with two experimental/baseline contrasts, with 10 examples of each sentence type (Table 1). Participants were tested in object manipulation (OM), picture matching (SPM), and grammaticality judgement (GJ) tasks, the latter two with both whole sentence and self-paced listening presentation conditions, using digitised computer-delivered auditory stimuli. Accuracy and end-of-sentence reaction time (RT) (in SPM and GJ) were measured. We here report on the data from the OM and SPM tasks, which require comprehension (as opposed to GJ,

TABLE 1
Stimulus sentences

Test Sentence	Baseline Sentence
Passive Structures	
The man was scratched by the boy (Full Passive: PF)	The man scratched the boy (Active: A)
The man was scratched (Truncated Passive: PT)	
Object Relatives	
It was the man who the boy scratched (Cleft Object: CO)	It was the boy who scratched the man (Cleft Subject: CS)
The boy who the man scratched pushed the girl (Subject Object:SO)	The boy who scratched the man pushed the girl (Subject Subject: SS)
Reflexives	
The father of the boy scratched himself (Reflexive Genitive: RG)	The father of the boy scratched the girl (Reflexive Genitive Baseline: RGB)
The boy's father scratched himself (Reflexive Possessive: RP)	The boy's father scratched the girl (Reflexive Possessive Baseline: RPB)

which may not), with whole sentence presentation, which is the most natural form of language presentation in a hearing participant.

Interpretive framework

Types of deficits. We examined the accuracy of each patient in each task to identify deficits in particular sentence types and structures. We can identify several types of specific deficits. All consist of poor performance on an experimental sentence and good performance on a baseline sentence chosen to test the ability to comprehend a particular structure (we consider how to measure "good" and "poor" performance below). The differences between the types of deficits depend on where such a pattern is seen. We begin with the most restricted and progress to the most general types of deficits.

A *construction-specific, task-specific deficit* occurs when a patient performs poorly on one experimental sentence and well on the corresponding baseline in one task, and performs well on the second pair of experimental and baseline sentences instantiating the same structure and on the experimental and baseline sentences for both sentence types testing the structure in the second task. For instance, a patient may perform poorly on full passive sentences (i.e., those with a *by*-phrase) and well on actives in SPM, and perform normally on truncated passives in SPM and perform normally on all passives and actives in OM.

A *construction-specific, task-independent deficit* occurs when a patient performs poorly on one experimental sentence type and well on the corresponding baseline in both tasks, and well on the second pair of experimental and baseline sentences instantiating the same structure in both tasks. For instance, a patient may perform poorly on full passive sentences and well on actives in both SPM and OM, and perform well on truncated passives in both tasks.

A *structure-specific, task-specific deficit* occurs when a patient performs poorly on both experimental sentence types instantiating a structure and well on the corresponding baselines in one task, and well on the experimental and baseline sentences in question in the second task. For instance, a patient may perform poorly on both full passive sentences and truncated passives and normally on actives in SPM, and well on passives, truncated passives and actives in OM.

Finally, a *structure-specific, task-independent deficit* occurs when a patient performs poorly on both experimental sentence types instantiating a structure and well on the corresponding baselines in both tasks. For instance, a patient may perform poorly on both full passive sentences and truncated passives and well on actives in both SPM and OM.

Structure-specific deficits, whether task-specific or task-independent, can be defined at various levels of generality (or abstraction). For instance, we have considered a deficit affecting passives. We could consider more general structure-specific deficits, such as the one postulated by the trace deletion hypothesis, which would consist of poor performance on experimental sentences instantiating both passive and object-extracted relative structures, and good performance on baseline active and subject-extracted relative structures. Such a pattern found only in either SPM or OM would be a more general structure-specific task-specific deficit than one affecting only passive or object extracted structures; if found in both OM and SPM, it would be a more general structure-specific task-independent deficit.

The above descriptions are phrased in terms of performance on a particular structure. As the example of a higher-level deficit affecting sentences with traces shows, it is important to consider performance on several structures to identify more general deficits. However, this cuts both ways. Deficits that are seen in one structure or construction are not isolated if the patient has a deficit in another structure. For instance, if a patient has a structure-specific, task-dependent deficit affecting passives (s/he fails on full and truncated passives and not on actives in SPM and does well on all these sentences in OM), that deficit is not *isolated* if the patient also has a second deficit affecting, say, one construction containing a reflexive pronoun. The question that arises about such patterns is whether they are due to separate impairments of two syntactic or interpretive operations, or to a single impairment that affects two constructions. Both analyses are usually possible: deficits of this sort could result from disruptions to multiple specific operations (some possibly interacting with task demands), to a higher-order operation (such as the ability to co-index referentially dependent noun phrases, in Chomsky's theory, again interacting with task demands in some way), to a reduction in resources available for parsing and interpretation, or to other impairments. Before characterising a patient's deficit as "selective" for a structure or construction, we must examine his/her performance on other structures and constructions.

The performance patterns outlined above are ones in which performance on baseline sentences is "good". There are many instances in which this is not the case. A patient may fail to show the pattern of performance needed to establish a specific deficit because s/he does poorly on the baseline sentence in an experimental/baseline pair. Again, this may occur for both baseline sentences relevant to a particular structure in both tasks, for only one in both tasks, for both in only one task, or for only one in one task. These patterns provide data relevant to the nature of aphasic sentence comprehension of syntactically simple sentences and the interaction on such sentences and tasks, but they are hard to interpret because, as with most studies, this study was not designed to allow failure on a baseline sentence to be compared against failures on other baseline sentences for purposes of elucidating deficits. All that can be said about these data is that, if a patient fails on a baseline sentence, his/her deficit cannot be attributed to the selective impairment of the ability to structure or interpret a type of experimental sentence.

Finally, we note that some patterns of performance are ambiguous. Consider a pattern of performance in which patient performs well on both baseline sentences (e.g., CS and SS) in both tasks and poorly on one experimental sentence (e.g., SO) in both tasks and well on the other (e.g., CO) in only one task (e.g., SPM). One way to characterise this is as a task-independent construction-specific deficit for the sentence type on which performance is poor in both tasks; that is, the patient could be said to have a deficit for SO sentences. Alternatively, it could be characterised as a task-dependent structure-specific deficit for the structure on which performance is poor on both sentence types in one task; i.e., the patient could be said to have a deficit for object-extracted sentences in OM. Either of these characterisations would be incomplete, and an additional task-specific construction-specific deficit must be recognised, which would be characterised differently depending on how the deficit is considered (as a deficit for CO in OM if the first characterisation is adopted, and as a deficit for SO in SPM if the second is adopted). Many other mixed patterns are also ambiguous with respect to classification. These are more than terminological ambiguities: what is at issue is the nature of the patient's deficit.

In our presentation, we do not list all the mixed deficits, primarily because, to anticipate, there are so many of them and including them does not change the conclusions of this study. We will consider their implications for aphasic deficits in the discussion.

Determining good and poor performance

Determining whether a deficit exists for a particular sentence type involves comparing performance on an experimental sentence with performance on its baseline. There are two ways in which accuracy could be used classify performance as "good" or "poor".

First, performance could be considered to be "good" in the sense of "normal". We determined the range of normal performance on the basis of the mean percent correct and standard deviation of the control performances corrected for sample size (Crawford & Howell, 1998). By these criteria, patients whose percent correct for any sentence type was within 1.74 SD of the control mean percent correct for that sentence type on a given task were considered to have performed normally on that sentence type in that task, and performance below that level was considered abnormal (Crawford & Howell, 1998; Table 1).

Although this seems to us to be an appropriate sense of the word "normal", its application to the present data presents two problems. First, for some sentence types and tasks, such as cleft subject and cleft object sentences in OM, normal performance was at ceiling with virtually no variance. In these cases, a single error resulted in an abnormal performance on a sentence type, which seems too high a standard to impose. Second, conversely, for some sentence types and tasks, such as sentences with object extracted relative clauses (SO sentences) in OM, normal performance showed so much variance that five correct responses was within normal limits. This is obviously a very lax criterion for "good performance", since it includes levels of correct responses that are at chance. In addition to these considerations, some theories couch their predictions in terms of whether performance is above, or at, or below, chance. Therefore, we also looked for patients whose performance was at or below chance on an experimental sentence type and above chance on the corresponding baseline.

The calculation of chance depends on the number of possible responses. In our version of SPM, the number of choices is always two. In OM, this is not always the case. If any noun phrase (NP) mentioned in a sentence could play any thematic role around any verb, there are 36 possible responses in SO and SS sentences (including reflexive actions), and 6 in the baseline sentences for reflexive structures. However, Caplan and Hildebrandt (1988) showed that patients never make most of these responses, restricting their responses in OM to "linear" responses in which a post-verbal NP is the theme of that verb, and either the preverbal NP or the first NP in the sentence is the agent. Thus, for SS sentences and sentences with reflexives and their baselines, there is only one true alternative to the correct response, and for SO there are two: the first NP could be the agent of both verbs, or the second NP could be the agent of both. We also considered that, in active and CS sentences, a possible error was the inversion of NPs as agent and theme. Accordingly, we set the number of alternatives over which chance should be computed as two for all sentences except SO, where that number was three. Expansion of the binomial then yields the result that eight or more correct responses in any sentence type except SO, and six or more correct responses in SO sentences in OM, constitutes above chance performance.[2] These numbers were adjusted as appropriate for data loss (1.48% of responses: 2.84% in SPM, 0.13% in OM).[3]

Given the overall high level and small variance of normal performance, some above-chance performances will be considered "abnormal" by the 1.74-SD-below-the-mean criterion. This can affect both experimental and baseline sentences. In addition, some chance performances can be normal, as mentioned above. Therefore, the two criteria lead to different patients being classified as having deficits. We did not combine the two criteria; that is, we did not consider a patient to have a deficit on a sentence type if s/he performed either within the normal range or above chance on the baseline sentence and either below the normal range or at or below chance on the experimental sentence. The two sets of criteria are based on different views of what constitutes "good" and "poor" performance that seem to us to be logically independent and therefore not combinable.

Two other aspects of performance need to be considered before ascribing a deficit on a sentence type in a task to a patient on the basis of either of the above criteria.

First, it is possible that although a patient performed "well" on a sentence type on one task and "poorly" on that sentence type on the second task (by either criterion), his/her performance on the two tasks did not differ. One might consider it inappropriate to take two performances that do not differ as representing "good" performance in one case and "poor" performance in another, especially when "good" and "poor" refer to "above chance" and "at or below chance" performance. However, with only 10 examples of each sentence type per task, two performances need to differ by 5 correct responses or more to be statistically different. We therefore determined whether a patient's difference fell within the normal range of performance, where the normal range was based on the mean and standard deviation of the difference in performance of the control participants on each sentence type across the two tasks, adjusted for sample size, as above.[4]

---

[2] Using two-tailed tests, above chance performance requires 9 or 10 correct responses. We used a one-tailed criterion for significance because we do not distinguish here between chance and below chance performance, both of which are taken as indications of "poor" performance. Whether chance and below chance performances should be considered different depends on what models of error generation, cognitive responses to error, and response selection are adopted. For instance, a model that maintains that errors result from universal failure to apply an operation, that responses to these failures lead to ambiguity regarding agents, and that response selection results in random selection from binary choices, predicts chance performance (Grodzinsky, 2000); in this case, it would be important to distinguish chance and below chance performance. A model that maintains that errors arise from intermittent failure to apply an operation, that thematic roles are assigned incorrectly when this occurs, and that response selection is determined by the meaning that has been extracted from the sentence, makes no distinction between chance and below chance performances. As we are not committing to a model of these processes, we did not distinguish between chance and below chance performance.

[3] Three of the sentences in SPM were deemed to have ambiguous accompanying pictures and were excluded from all analyses; the remaining missing data constituted 0.12% of the data (0.11% SPM, 0.13% OM).

[4] Crawford et al. (2003) have developed a test that determines whether a participant's difference in scores on two tasks falls within the normal range of differences. Crawford's test could not be applied in seven sentence types because the control group's performance on a sentence type was too highly correlated across the two tasks. For the four sentence types in which both calculations were done, there were 19 discrepancies (11%) between the two calculations. In all cases, as expected, the discrepancy consisted of the difference in scores being considered outside the normal range by the criteria we adopted and within the normal range by the Crawford and Howell (1998) methods. Our method therefore slightly overestimates the occurrence of differences that are outside the normal range.

Second, the speed with which a patient responds must be taken into account in determining whether a patient has a deficit. RTs were only collected in SPM, because they are often long in OM and we had not thought they would be meaningfully analysed. Patients whose RTs were 1.74 *SD* longer than the mean RT for the controls on a sentence type in SPM were considered to be abnormal on that sentence type. Note that this is a very liberal criterion for calling a performance abnormal because aphasic patients' RTs are often long compared to controls' for reasons unrelated to sentence comprehension. However, its liberalness is compensated for by the fact that it applies to baseline as well as experimental sentences, so a pattern of normal RTs for a baseline sentence and abnormally long RTs for an experimental sentence does suggest a deficit in processing the construction needed in the experimental sentence.

The use of RTs to determine a deficit is not explicitly endorsed by all theorists, in the sense that some theories of aphasic disturbances of syntactic operations do not mention slowed processing as a type of impairment (e.g., the "trace deletion hypothesis" is phrased in terms of the inability to construct certain representations and/or perform certain operations without reference to temporal issues; Grodzinsky, 2000). The identification of additional patients with deficits that are found only in RT thus might not be relevant to such hypotheses. However, it is hard to know whether the authors of such hypotheses truly mean to characterise them as all-or-none losses of representations or operations, or more graded deficits in which extra processing time can compensate for an impairment (very closely related models of deficits in the same patients are phrased in terms of temporal factors; e.g., Swinney, Zurif, Prather, & Love, 1996). Also, there are theories of aphasia which maintain that patients have slowed rise times for syntactic representations and that this affects some syntactic structures more than others (e.g., Haarmann & Kolk, 1991).

RTs can also give hints as to the existence of speed–accuracy trade-offs, in one of two ways. A patient who speeds through an experimental sentence and makes an error might have produced a correct response if s/he had allowed him/herself a normal amount of time to process the stimulus. This pattern, which would constitute the classic speed–accuracy trade-off, did not occur in our data (no patient's performances were 1.74 *SD* below the average mean on any sentence type). On the other hand, it is also possible that good performance on a sentence is related to a patient taking more time than normal on that sentence. If this happens for a baseline sentence that the patient gets consistently correct and RTs are normal on the corresponding experimental sentences that the patient gets wrong, the resulting pattern is hard to interpret. Would the patient have done worse on the baseline sentence if s/he had not taken an unusually long time to process it, and/or normally on the experimental sentence if s/he had? A deficit seen in accuracy in which this pattern of RTs is also seen is an unclear basis on which to say that a patient has a deficit.

RESULTS

Tables 2–7 show the accuracy data. Performances 1.74 *SD* below the normal mean or at or below chance are highlighted. By the criteria according to which abnormal performance is defined as performance falling 1.74 *SD* below the normal mean, there was one case of a task-independent structure-specific deficit—Case 50041 had a deficit for passive structures. By the chance criteria for the determination of a deficit,

TABLE 2
Abnormal performances on passive and baseline structures based on mean normal
performance

subj	SPM		OM		SPM		OM	
	PF	A	PF	A	PT	A	PT	A
50001	abn 77.8	norm 100	abn 80	abn 90	norm 100	norm 100	abn 40	abn 90
50002	abn 88.9	abn 88.9	norm 100	norm 100	abn 88.9	abn 88.9	norm 100	norm 100
50003	norm 100	norm 100	norm 100	norm 100	norm 100	norm 100	abn 90	norm 100
50004	norm 100	norm 100	norm 100	norm 100	abn 88.9	norm 100	norm 100	norm 100
50005	norm 100	norm 100	norm 100	norm 100	norm 100	norm 100	norm 100	norm 100
50006	norm 100	norm 100	norm 100	norm 100	norm 100	norm 100	norm 100	norm 100
50007	abn 33.3	abn 77.8	abn 90	abn 90	abn 55.6	abn 77.8	abn 80	abn 90
50009	norm 100	norm 100	abn 90	norm 100	norm 100	norm 100	norm 100	norm 100
50010	norm 100	norm 100	norm 100	norm 100	norm 100	norm 100	norm 100	norm 100
50011	norm 100	norm 100	norm 100	norm 100	norm 100	norm 100	norm 100	norm 100
50013	abn 88.9	abn 77.8	norm 100	norm 100	abn 77.8	abn 77.8	norm 100	norm 100
50014	norm 100	norm 100	norm 100	norm 100	norm 100	norm 100	norm 100	norm 100
50015	abn 77.8	abn 88.9	norm 100	abn 90	abn 55.6	abn 88.9	norm 100	abn 90
50016	abn 77.8	abn 77.8	abn 20	abn 60	norm 100	abn 77.8	norm 100	abn 60
50017	norm 100	abn 77.8	norm 100	norm 100	abn 88.9	abn 77.8	norm 100	norm 100
50018	abn 44.4	abn 55.6	norm 100	abn 90	abn 77.8	abn 55.6	abn 0	abn 90
50019	abn 22.2	abn 66.7	abn 50	abn 70	abn 44.4	abn 66.7	abn 80	abn 70
50020	norm 100	norm 100	norm 100	norm 100	abn 88.9	norm 100	norm 100	norm 100
50022	norm 100	norm 100	norm 100	norm 100	norm 100	norm 100	abn 90	norm 100
50023	abn 55.6	abn 55.6	abn 60	abn 80	abn 44.4	abn 55.6	abn 90	abn 80
50025	abn 88.9	abn 88.9	norm 100	norm 100	norm 100	abn 88.9	abn 90	norm 100
50026	norm 100	abn 88.9	abn 80	abn 90	norm 100	abn 88.9	abn 70	abn 90
50027	abn 66.7	abn 55.6	abn 80	abn 80	abn 22.2	abn 55.6	abn 90	abn 80

(*Continued*)

TABLE 2
(Continued)

subj	SPM PF	A	OM PF	A	SPM PT	A	OM PT	A
50029	abn 66.7	abn 66.7	norm 100	norm 100	abn 55.6	abn 66.7	abn 50	norm 100
50030	norm 100	norm 100	norm 100	norm 100	norm 100	norm 100	norm 100	norm 100
50034	norm 100	norm 100	norm 100	norm 100	abn 88.9	norm 100	norm 100	norm 100
50036	norm 100	norm 100	norm 100	norm 100	norm 100	norm 100	norm 100	norm 100
50037	norm 100	norm 100	norm 100	norm 100	norm 100	norm 100	norm 100	norm 100
50038	norm 100	norm 100	norm 100	norm 100	norm 100	norm 100	abn 10	norm 100
50041	abn 88.9	norm 100	abn 90	norm 100	abn 88.9	norm 100	abn 40	norm 100
50042	norm 100	norm 100	norm 100	norm 100	norm 100	norm 100	abn 60	norm 100
50043	norm 100	norm 100	norm 100	norm 100	norm 100	norm 100	norm 100	norm 100
50044	abn 66.7	abn 88.9	abn 70	norm 100	abn 77.8	abn 88.9	abn 90	norm 100
50045	abn 55.6	abn 88.9	abn 50	norm 100	abn 88.9	abn 88.9	abn 0	norm 100
50046	norm 100	abn 77.8	abn 90	norm 100	abn 77.8	abn 77.8	abn 10	norm 100
50047	norm 100	norm 100	norm 100	norm 100	norm 100	norm 100	abn 90	norm 100
50048	norm 100	norm 100	norm 100	norm 100	norm 100	norm 100	norm 100	norm 100
50050	abn 44.4	abn 77.8	abn 10	norm 100	abn 55.6	abn 77.8	norm 100	norm 100
50051	abn 44.4	abn 88.9	abn 30	abn 90	abn 22.2	abn 88.9	abn 70	abn 90
50052	norm 100	norm 100	norm 100	norm 100	norm 100	norm 100	abn 90	norm 100
50053	abn 77.8	abn 88.9	abn 80	abn 90	abn 66.7	abn 88.9	abn 70	abn 90
50054	norm 100	abn 88.9	abn 90	norm 100	norm 100	abn 88.9	norm 100	norm 100
PtMean	84.9	89.7	87.1	95.7	84.7	89.7	81.0	95.7
PtSD	22.1	13.8	23.2	8.9	22.2	13.8	29.9	8.9
PtMin	22.2	55.6	10	60	22.2	55.6	0	60
PtMax	100	100	100	100	100	100	100	100
ECMean	99.1	99.6	100	100	100	99.6	99.6	100
EC_SD	3.1	2.2	0	0	0	2.2	2.0	0
ECMin	88.9	88.9	100	100	100	88.9	90	100
ECMax	100	100	100	100	100	100	100	100
cutoff	93.8	95.7	100	100	100	95.7	96.1	100

TABLE 3
Abnormal performances on object extracted and baseline structures based on mean normal performance

subj	SPM		OM		SPM		OM	
	CO	CS	CO	CS	SO	SS	SO	SS
50001	abn 70	abn 90	abn 80	norm 100	abn 60	abn 80	abn 30	abn 50
50002	abn 60	abn 80	abn 80	norm 100	abn 50	norm 90	abn 40	norm 100
50003	abn 70	norm 100	norm 100	abn 90	abn 60	abn 80	abn 40	norm 100
50004	norm 100	abn 90	norm 100	norm 100	abn 70	abn 80	norm 80	norm 100
50005	norm 100	norm 100	norm 100	norm 100	norm 100	norm 100	norm 100	norm 100
50006	norm 90	abn 90	abn 90	norm 100	norm 90	abn 80	norm 100	norm 100
50007	abn 40	abn 80	abn 80	abn 90	abn 50	abn 80	abn 0	abn 60
50009	norm 100	norm 100	norm 100	norm 100	norm 80	norm 100	norm 70	abn 70
50010	norm 90	norm 100	norm 100	norm 100	norm 90	abn 80	norm 50	norm 100
50011	norm 100	norm 100	norm 100	norm 100	norm 90	norm 90	norm 80	norm 90
50013	norm 100	norm 100	norm 100	norm 100	abn 50	norm 100	norm 70	norm 90
50014	norm 100	norm 100	norm 100	norm 100	norm 100	norm 100	norm 100	norm 100
50015	norm 90	abn 90	norm 100	norm 100	norm 80	norm 90	abn 30	norm 100
50016	abn 80	abn 90	abn 80	abn 90	norm 80	abn 80	abn 0	abn 0
50017	norm 100	abn 70	norm 100	norm 100	norm 80	abn 80	norm 50	abn 60
50018	abn 20	abn 60	abn 80	abn 70	abn 50	abn 70	abn 0	abn 22.2
50019	abn 50	abn 80	abn 50	abn 90	abn 40	norm 90	abn 10	abn 10
50020	abn 80	norm 100	abn 90	norm 100	abn 60	abn 60	abn 10	abn 50
50022	norm 90	norm 100	norm 100	norm 100	norm 90	norm 90	norm 60	norm 90
50023	abn 20	abn 60	abn 50	abn 70	abn 70	abn 60	abn 20	abn 80
50025	abn 60	abn 80	abn 20	norm 100	abn 70	abn 70	abn 0	abn 10
50026	abn 70	abn 90	abn 90	norm 100	abn 70	norm 90	abn 20	abn 10
50027	abn 50	abn 90	abn 60	abn 70	abn 60	abn 70	abn 20	abn 0

(Continued)

TABLE 3
(Continued)

subj	SPM		OM		SPM		OM	
	CO	CS	CO	CS	SO	SS	SO	SS
50029	abn 50	abn 80	abn 70	norm 100	abn 40	abn 70	abn 40	abn 10
50030	norm 100	norm 100	abn 90	norm 100	norm 100	norm 100	abn 40	abn 60
50034	norm 90	norm 100	norm 100	norm 100	norm 80	norm 100	norm 60	norm 100
50036	norm 90	abn 90	norm 100	norm 100	abn 70	norm 90	norm 70	norm 90
50037	norm 90	norm 100	norm 100	norm 100	norm 100	norm 100	norm 80	norm 100
50038	norm 90	norm 100	norm 100	norm 100	norm 80	norm 100	abn 10	norm 100
50041	norm 100	abn 90	abn 80	norm 100	abn 60	abn 80	abn 12.5	abn 0
50042	abn 80	abn 90	abn 90	norm 100	norm 90	norm 90	abn 30	abn 70
50043	norm 90	norm 100	abn 90	norm 100	abn 50	norm 100	abn 20	norm 100
50044	abn 50	abn 80	abn 60	norm 100	abn 20	norm 100	abn 20	abn 0
50045	abn 60	abn 90	abn 50	abn 70	abn 40	abn 60	abn 10	abn 10
50046	abn 80	abn 90	norm 100	norm 100	abn 50	abn 60	abn 0	abn 0
50047	norm 100	norm 100	norm 100	norm 100	norm 100	norm 100	abn 20	abn 0
50048	norm 100	norm 100	norm 100	norm 100	norm 80	abn 80	abn 10	norm 100
50050	abn 60	abn 70	abn 30	abn 90	abn 40	abn 30	abn 11.1	abn 0
50051	abn 60	abn 80	abn 60	norm 100	abn 60	norm 90	abn 0	abn 80
50052	norm 100	norm 100	norm 100	norm 100	norm 100	norm 100	norm 90	norm 100
50053	abn 40	norm 100	abn 70	norm 100	abn 20	abn 70	abn 20	norm 100
50054	norm 90	norm 100	norm 100	norm 100	norm 90	norm 90	abn 30	norm 100
PtMean	77.4	90.5	84.3	96.0	69.3	83.8	37.0	62.2
PtSD	23.1	11.3	21.0	9.1	22.1	15.5	31.4	41.1
PtMin	20	60	20	70	20	30	0	0
PtMax	100	100	100	100	100	100	100	100
ECMean	97.6	98.8	100	100	91.2	97.2	79.8	97.6
EC_SD	4.4	3.3	0	0	10.1	4.6	21.2	6.0
ECMin	90	90	100	100	60	90	30	80
ECMax	100	100	100	100	100	100	100	100
cutoff	90.0	93.0	100	100	73.6	89.2	42.9	87.2

TABLE 4
Abnormal performances on sentences with reflexives and baseline structures based on mean normal performance

subj	SPM RG	SPM RGB	OM RG	OM RGB	SPM RP	SPM RPB	OM RP	OM RPB
50001	abn 90	abn 40	abn 0	norm 100	norm 100	norm 100	abn 10	norm 100
50002	abn 90	abn 60	abn 90	abn 90	abn 90	abn 60	norm 100	abn 90
50003	abn 80	norm 90	abn 60	abn 70	abn 90	abn 70	norm 100	norm 100
50004	abn 90	abn 70	norm 100	norm 100	abn 90	norm 100	norm 100	norm 100
50005	norm 100	norm 100	norm 100	norm 100	norm 100	norm 100	norm 100	norm 100
50006	norm 100	norm 90	abn 90	abn 70	norm 100	norm 100	norm 100	abn 80
50007	abn 70	abn 70	abn 50	abn 80	abn 60	abn 50	norm 100	abn 70
50009	norm 100	norm 100	norm 100	norm 100	norm 100	abn 90	norm 100	norm 100
50010	norm 100	norm 100	norm 100	norm 100	norm 100	abn 90	norm 100	norm 100
50011	norm 100	norm 100	norm 100	norm 100	norm 100	norm 100	norm 100	norm 100
50013	abn 80	norm 100	norm 100	norm 100	abn 90	abn 90	abn 90	norm 100
50014	norm 100	norm 100	norm 100	norm 100	abn 90	norm 100	norm 100	norm 100
50015	abn 70	abn 70	abn 70	abn 90	abn 90	abn 90	abn 80	norm 100
50016	abn 70	norm 90	norm 100	abn 10	abn 80	abn 80	norm 100	abn 20
50017	norm 100	abn 60	norm 100	norm 100	norm 100	abn 90	norm 100	abn 90
50018	abn 60	abn 50	abn 50	abn 50	abn 60	abn 70	abn 80	abn 70
50019	abn 60	abn 30	abn 40	abn 40	abn 80	abn 60	abn 80	abn 40
50020	norm 100	abn 80	abn 90	abn 90	norm 100	abn 90	abn 90	norm 100
50022	norm 100	norm 90	norm 100	norm 100	abn 80	norm 100	abn 90	norm 100
50023	abn 40	abn 30	abn 40	abn 50	abn 20	abn 20	abn 10	abn 40
50025	abn 70	abn 60	abn 70	abn 70	abn 50	abn 30	abn 80	abn 80
50026	abn 50	abn 60	abn 30	abn 30	abn 90	norm 100	abn 60	abn 40
50027	abn 70	abn 70	abn 50	abn 20	abn 90	abn 50	abn 70	abn 30

(*Continued*)

TABLE 4
(*Continued*)

subj	SPM		OM		SPM		OM	
	RG	RGB	RG	RGB	RP	RPB	RP	RPB
50029	abn 70	abn 80	abn 0	abn 40	abn 70	abn 90	abn 0	abn 40
50030	norm 100	abn 80	norm 100	norm 100	norm 100	abn 90	abn 90	abn 80
50034	abn 80	norm 90	norm 100	norm 100	abn 88.9	abn 90	abn 90	norm 100
50036	norm 100	norm 100	norm 100	norm 100	norm 100	norm 100	abn 90	norm 100
50037	abn 90	norm 100	norm 100	norm 100	norm 100	norm 100	abn 90	norm 100
50038	norm 100	norm 90	norm 100	abn 90	abn 80	norm 100	abn 80	norm 100
50041	norm 100	norm 100	abn 80	norm 100	abn 90	abn 90	abn 70	abn 90
50042	abn 90	abn 70	norm 100	norm 100	abn 80	abn 90	norm 100	abn 90
50043	abn 70	abn 70	norm 100	abn 90	abn 90	norm 100	abn 90	norm 100
50044	abn 10	abn 20	abn 20	abn 11.1	abn 90	norm 100	norm 100	abn 50
50045	abn 60	abn 60	abn 60	abn 60	abn 90	abn 60	abn 70	abn 60
50046	abn 60	abn 70	abn 80	norm 100	abn 90	abn 70	abn 80	norm 100
50047	norm 100	norm 100	norm 100	norm 100	abn 90	abn 90	norm 100	norm 100
50048	norm 100	norm 90	abn 90	norm 100	norm 100	norm 100	norm 100	norm 100
50050	abn 40	abn 50	abn 40	abn 20	abn 50	abn 60	abn 80	abn 50
50051	abn 90	abn 80	abn 70	abn 10	norm 100	abn 70	abn 90	abn 70
50052	abn 90	norm 100	norm 100	norm 100	norm 100	norm 100	norm 100	norm 100
50053	abn 50	abn 50	norm 100	abn 70	abn 80	abn 70	norm 100	abn 60
50054	norm 100	norm 90	norm 100	abn 80	norm 100	norm 100	norm 100	norm 100
PtMean	80.7	76.2	77.9	76.9	86.6	83.3	84.8	81.9
PtSD	21.7	22.2	29.7	30.5	17.1	20.4	24.4	24.4
PtMin	10	20	0	10	20	20	0	20
PtMax	100	100	100	100	100	100	100	100
ECMean	98.4	96.8	100	100	99.6	98.4	99.2	99.6
EC_SD	3.7	4.8	0	0	2.0	3.7	4.0	2.0
ECMin	90	90	100	100	90	90	80	90
ECMax	100	100	100	100	100	100	100	100
cutoff	91.9	88.5	100	100	96.1	91.9	92.2	96.1

TABLE 5
Performance on passive and baseline structures relative to chance performance

subj	SPM		OM		SPM		OM	
	PF	A	PF	A	PT	A	PT	A
50001	at/below 77.78	above 100	above 80	above 90	above 100	above 100	at/below 40	above 90
50002	above 88.89	above 88.89	above 100	above 100	above 88.89	above 88.89	above 100	above 100
50003	above 100	above 100	above 100	above 100	above 100	above 100	above 90	above 100
50004	above 100	above 100	above 100	above 100	above 88.89	above 100	above 100	above 100
50005	above 100	above 100	above 100	above 100	above 100	above 100	above 100	above 100
50006	above 100	above 100	above 100	above 100	above 100	above 100	above 100	above 100
50007	at/below 33.33	at/below 77.78	above 90	above 90	at/below 55.56	at/below 77.78	above 80	above 90
50009	above 100	above 100	above 90	above 100	above 100	above 100	above 100	above 100
50010	above 100	above 100	above 100	above 100	above 100	above 100	above 100	above 100
50011	above 100	above 100	above 100	above 100	above 100	above 100	above 100	above 100
50013	above 88.89	at/below 77.78	above 100	above 100	at/below 77.78	at/below 77.78	above 100	above 100
50014	above 100	above 100	above 100	above 100	above 100	above 100	above 100	above 100
50015	at/below 77.78	above 88.89	above 100	above 90	at/below 55.56	above 88.89	above 100	above 90
50016	at/below 77.78	at/below 77.78	at/below 20	at/below 60	above 100	at/below 77.78	above 100	at/below 60
50017	above 100	at/below 77.78	above 100	above 100	above 88.89	at/below 77.78	above 100	above 100
50018	at/below 44.44	at/below 55.56	above 100	above 90	at/below 77.78	at/below 55.56	at/below 0	above 90
50019	at/below 22.22	at/below 66.67	at/below 50	at/below 70	at/below 44.44	at/below 66.67	above 80	at/below 70
50020	above 100	above 100	above 100	above 100	above 88.89	above 100	above 100	above 100
50022	above 100	above 100	above 100	above 100	above 100	above 100	above 90	above 100
50023	at/below 55.56	at/below 55.56	at/below 60	above 80	at/below 44.44	at/below 55.56	above 90	above 80
50025	above 88.89	above 88.89	above 100	above 100	above 100	above 88.89	above 90	above 100
50026	above 100	above 88.89	above 80	above 90	above 100	above 88.89	at/below 70	above 90
50027	at/below 66.67	at/below 55.56	above 80	above 80	at/below 22.22	at/below 55.56	above 90	above 80

(*Continued*)

TABLE 5
(Continued)

subj	SPM PF	SPM A	OM PF	OM A	SPM PT	SPM A	OM PT	OM A
50029	at/below 66.67	at/below 66.67	above 100	above 100	at/below 55.56	at/below 66.67	at/below 50	above 100
50030	above 100	above 100	above 100	above 100	above 100	above 100	above 100	above 100
50034	above 100	above 100	above 100	above 100	above 88.89	above 100	above 100	above 100
50036	above 100	above 100	above 100	above 100	above 100	above 100	above 100	above 100
50037	above 100	above 100	above 100	above 100	above 100	above 100	above 100	above 100
50038	above 100	above 100	above 100	above 100	above 100	above 100	at/below 10	above 100
50041	above 88.89	above 100	above 90	above 100	above 88.89	above 100	at/below 40	above 100
50042	above 100	above 100	above 100	above 100	above 100	above 100	at/below 60	above 100
50043	above 100	above 100	above 100	above 100	above 100	above 100	above 100	above 100
50044	at/below 66.67	above 88.89	at/below 70	above 100	at/below 77.78	above 88.89	above 90	above 100
50045	at/below 55.56	above 88.89	at/below 50	above 100	above 88.89	above 88.89	at/below 0	above 100
50046	above 100	at/below 77.78	above 90	above 100	at/below 77.78	at/below 77.78	at/below 10	above 100
50047	above 100	above 100	above 100	above 100	above 100	above 100	above 90	above 100
50048	above 100	above 100	above 100	above 100	above 100	above 100	above 100	above 100
50050	at/below 44.44	at/below 77.78	at/below 10	above 100	at/below 55.56	at/below 77.78	above 100	above 100
50051	at/below 44.44	above 88.89	at/below 30	above 90	at/below 77.78	above 88.89	at/below 70	above 90
50052	above 100	above 100	above 100	above 100	above 100	above 100	above 90	above 100
50053	at/below 77.78	above 88.89	above 80	above 90	at/below 66.67	above 88.89	at/below 70	above 90
50054	above 100	above 88.89	above 90	above 100	above 100	above 88.89	above 100	above 100
PtMean	84.9	89.7	87.1	95.7	84.7	89.7	81.0	95.7
PtSD	22.1	13.8	23.2	8.9	22.2	13.8	29.9	8.9
PtMin	22.2	55.6	10	60	22.2	55.6	0	60
PtMax	100	100	100	100	100	100	100	100
ECMean	99.1	99.6	100	100	100	99.6	99.6	100
EC_SD	3.1	2.2	0	0	0	2.2	2.0	0
ECMin	88.9	88.9	100	100	100	88.9	90	100
ECMax	100	100	100	100	100	100	100	100

TABLE 6
Performance on object extracted relative and baseline structures relative to chance performance

	SPM		OM		SPM		OM	
subj	CO	CS	CO	CS	SO	SS	SO	SS
50001	at/below 70	above 90	above 80	above 100	at/below 60	above 80	at/below 30	at/below 50
50002	at/below 60	above 80	above 80	above 100	at/below 50	above 90	at/below 40	above 100
50003	at/below 70	above 100	above 100	above 90	at/below 60	above 80	at/below 40	above 100
50004	above 100	above 90	above 100	above 100	at/below 70	above 80	above 80	above 100
50005	above 100	above 100	above 100	above 100	above 100	above 100	above 100	above 100
50006	above 90	above 90	above 90	above 100	above 90	above 80	above 100	above 100
50007	at/below 40	above 80	above 80	above 90	at/below 50	above 80	at/below 0	at/below 60
50009	above 100	above 100	above 100	above 100	above 80	above 100	above 70	at/below 70
50010	above 90	above 100	above 100	above 100	above 90	above 80	at/below 50	above 100
50011	above 100	above 100	above 100	above 100	above 90	above 90	above 80	above 90
50013	above 100	above 100	above 100	above 100	at/below 50	above 100	above 70	above 90
50014	above 100	above 100	above 100	above 100	above 100	above 100	above 100	above 100
50015	above 90	above 90	above 100	above 100	above 80	above 90	at/below 30	above 100
50016	above 80	above 90	above 80	above 90	above 80	above 80	at/below 0	at/below 0
50017	above 100	at/below 70	above 100	above 100	above 80	above 80	at/below 50	at/below 60
50018	at/below 20	at/below 60	above 80	at/below 70	at/below 50	at/below 70	at/below 0	at/below 22.22
50019	at/below 50	above 80	at/below 50	above 90	at/below 40	above 90	at/below 10	at/below 10
50020	above 80	above 100	above 90	above 100	at/below 60	at/below 60	at/below 10	at/below 50
50022	above 90	above 100	above 100	above 100	above 90	above 90	above 60	above 90
50023	at/below 20	at/below 60	at/below 50	at/below 70	at/below 70	at/below 60	at/below 20	above 80
50025	at/below 60	above 80	at/below 20	above 100	at/below 70	at/below 70	at/below 0	at/below 10
50026	at/below 70	above 90	above 90	above 100	at/below 70	above 90	at/below 20	at/below 10
50027	at/below 50	above 90	at/below 60	at/below 70	at/below 60	at/below 70	at/below 20	at/below 0

(Continued)

TABLE 6
(Continued)

subj	SPM CO	SPM CS	OM CO	OM CS	SPM SO	SPM SS	OM SO	OM SS
50029	at/below 50	above 80	at/below 70	above 100	at/below 40	at/below 70	at/below 40	at/below 10
50030	above 100	above 100	above 90	above 100	above 100	above 100	at/below 40	at/below 60
50034	above 90	above 100	above 100	above 100	above 80	above 100	above 60	above 100
50036	above 90	above 90	above 100	above 100	at/below 70	above 90	above 70	above 90
50037	above 90	above 100	above 100	above 100	above 100	above 100	above 80	above 100
50038	above 90	above 100	above 100	above 100	above 80	above 100	at/below 10	above 100
50041	above 100	above 90	above 80	above 100	at/below 60	above 80	at/below 12.5	at/below 0
50042	above 80	above 90	above 90	above 100	above 90	above 90	at/below 30	at/below 70
50043	above 90	above 100	above 90	above 100	at/below 50	above 100	at/below 20	above 100
50044	at/below 50	above 80	at/below 60	above 100	at/below 20	above 100	at/below 20	at/below 0
50045	at/below 60	above 90	at/below 50	at/below 70	at/below 40	at/below 60	at/below 10	at/below 10
50046	above 80	above 90	above 100	above 100	at/below 50	at/below 60	at/below 0	at/below 0
50047	above 100	above 100	above 100	above 100	above 100	above 100	at/below 20	at/below 0
50048	above 100	above 100	above 100	above 100	above 80	above 80	at/below 10	above 100
50050	at/below 60	at/below 70	at/below 30	above 90	at/below 40	at/below 30	at/below 11.11	at/below 0
50051	at/below 60	above 80	at/below 60	above 100	at/below 60	above 90	at/below 0	above 80
50052	above 100	above 100	above 100	above 100	above 100	above 100	above 90	above 100
50053	at/below 40	above 100	at/below 70	above 100	at/below 20	at/below 70	at/below 20	above 100
50054	above 90	above 100	above 100	above 100	above 90	above 90	at/below 30	above 100
PtMean	77.4	90.5	84.3	96.0	69.3	83.8	37.0	62.2
PtSD	23.1	11.3	21.0	9.1	22.1	15.5	31.4	41.1
PtMin	20	60	20	70	20	30	0	0
PtMax	100	100	100	100	100	100	100	100
ECMean	97.6	98.8	100	100	91.2	97.2	79.8	97.6
EC_SD	4.4	3.3	0	0	10.1	4.6	21.2	6.0
ECMin	90	90	100	100	60	90	30	80
ECMax	100	100	100	100	100	100	100	100

TABLE 7
Performance on sentences with reflexives and baseline structures relative to chance
performance

subj	SPM		OM		SPM		OM	
	RG	RGB	RG	RGB	RP	RPB	RP	RPB
50001	above 90	at/below 40	at/below 0	above 100	above 100	above 100	at/below 10	above 100
50002	above 90	at/below 60	above 90	above 90	above 90	at/below 60	above 100	above 90
50003	above 80	above 90	at/below 60	at/below 70	above 90	at/below 70	above 100	above 100
50004	above 90	at/below 70	above 100	above 100	above 90	above 100	above 100	above 100
50005	above 100	above 100	above 100	above 100	above 100	above 100	above 100	above 100
50006	above 100	above 90	above 90	at/below 70	above 100	above 100	above 100	above 80
50007	at/below 70	at/below 70	at/below 50	above 80	at/below 60	at/below 50	above 100	at/below 70
50009	above 100	above 100	above 100	above 100	above 100	above 90	above 100	above 100
50010	above 100	above 100	above 100	above 100	above 100	above 90	above 100	above 100
50011	above 100	above 100	above 100	above 100	above 100	above 100	above 100	above 100
50013	above 80	above 100	above 100	above 100	above 90	above 90	above 90	above 100
50014	above 100	above 100	above 100	above 100	above 90	above 100	above 100	above 100
50015	at/below 70	at/below 70	at/below 70	above 90	above 90	above 90	above 80	above 100
50016	at/below 70	above 90	above 100	at/below 10	above 80	above 80	above 100	at/below 20
50017	above 100	at/below 60	above 100	above 100	above 100	above 90	above 100	above 90
50018	at/below 60	at/below 50	at/below 50	at/below 50	at/below 60	at/below 70	above 80	at/below 70
50019	at/below 60	at/below 30	at/below 40	at/below 40	above 80	at/below 60	above 80	at/below 40
50020	above 100	above 80	above 90	above 90	above 100	above 90	above 90	above 100
50022	above 100	above 90	above 100	above 100	above 80	above 100	above 90	above 100
50023	at/below 40	at/below 30	at/below 40	at/below 50	at/below 20	at/below 20	at/below 10	at/below 40
50025	at/below 70	at/below 60	at/below 70	at/below 70	at/below 50	at/below 30	above 80	above 80
50026	at/below 50	at/below 60	at/below 30	at/below 30	above 90	above 100	at/below 60	at/below 40
50027	at/below 70	at/below 70	at/below 50	at/below 20	above 90	at/below 50	at/below 70	at/below 30

(Continued)

TABLE 7
(*Continued*)

subj	SPM		OM		SPM		OM	
	RG	RGB	RG	RGB	RP	RPB	RP	RPB
50029	at/below 70	above 80	at/below 0	at/below 40	at/below 70	above 90	at/below 0	at/below 40
50030	above 100	above 80	above 100	above 100	above 100	above 90	above 90	above 80
50034	above 80	above 90	above 100	above 100	above 88.89	above 90	above 90	above 100
50036	above 100	above 100	above 100	above 100	above 100	above 100	above 90	above 100
50037	above 90	above 100	above 100	above 100	above 100	above 100	above 90	above 100
50038	above 100	above 90	above 100	above 90	above 80	above 100	above 80	above 100
50041	above 100	above 100	above 80	above 100	above 90	above 90	at/below 70	above 90
50042	above 90	at/below 70	above 100	above 100	above 80	above 90	above 100	above 90
50043	at/below 70	at/below 70	above 100	above 90	above 90	above 100	above 90	above 100
50044	at/below 10	at/below 20	at/below 20	at/below 11.11	above 90	above 100	above 100	at/below 50
50045	at/below 60	at/below 60	at/below 60	at/below 60	above 90	at/below 60	at/below 70	at/below 60
50046	at/below 60	at/below 70	above 80	above 100	above 90	at/below 70	above 80	above 100
50047	above 100	above 100	above 100	above 100	above 90	above 90	above 100	above 100
50048	above 100	above 90	above 90	above 100	above 100	above 100	above 100	above 100
50050	at/below 40	at/below 50	at/below 40	at/below 20	at/below 50	at/below 60	above 80	at/below 50
50051	above 90	above 80	at/below 70	at/below 10	above 100	at/below 70	above 90	at/below 70
50052	above 90	above 100	above 100	above 100	above 100	above 100	above 100	above 100
50053	at/below 50	at/below 50	above 100	at/below 70	above 80	at/below 70	above 100	at/below 60
50054	above 100	above 90	above 100	above 80	above 100	above 100	above 100	above 100
PtMean	80.7	76.2	77.9	76.9	86.6	83.3	84.8	81.9
PtSD	21.7	22.2	29.7	30.5	17.1	20.4	24.4	24.4
PtMin	10	20	0	10	20	20	0	20
PtMax	100	100	100	100	100	100	100	100
ECMean	98.4	96.8	100	100	99.6	98.4	99.2	99.6
EC_SD	3.7	4.8	0	0	2.0	3.7	4.0	2.0
ECMin	90	90	100	100	90	90	80	90
ECMax	100	100	100	100	100	100	100	100

TABLE 8

Cases with structure- or construction-specific deficits, showing other abnormal performances

Case 50041: Performance by "normal" criteria

OM		OM		SPM		SPM	
PF	A	PT	A	PF	A	PT	A
abn 90	norm 100	abn 40	norm 100	abn 88.9	norm 100	abn 88.9	norm 100
CO	CS	SO	SS	CO	CS	SO	SS
abn 80	norm 100	abn 12.5	abn 0	norm 100	abn 90	abn 60	abn 80
RG	RGB	RP	RPB	RG	RGB	RP	RPB
abn 80	norm 100	abn 70	abn 90	norm 100	norm 100	abn 90	abn 90

Case 50051: Performance by "chance" criteria

OM		OM		SPM		SPM	
PF	A	PT	A	PF	A	PT	A
at 30	above 90	at 70	above 90	at 44.44	above 88.89	below 22.22	above 88.89
CO	CS	SO	SS	CO	CS	SO	SS
at 60	above 100	below 0	above 80	at 60	above 80	at 60	above 90
RG	RGB	RP	RPB	RG	RGB	RP	RPB
at 70	below 10	above 90	at 70	above 90	above 80	above 100	at 70

Case 50022: Performance by "normal" criteria

OM		OM		SPM		SPM	
PF	A	PT	A	PF	A	PT	A
norm 100	norm 100	abn 90	norm 100	norm 100	norm 100	norm 100	norm 100
CO	CS	SO	SS	CO	CS	SO	SS
norm 100	norm 100	norm 60	norm 90	norm 90	norm 100	norm 90	norm 90
RG	RGB	RP	RPB	RG	RGB	RP	RPB
norm 100	norm 100	abn 90	norm 100	norm 100	norm 90	abn 80	norm 100

Case 50043: Performance by "chance" criteria

OM		OM		SPM		SPM	
PF	A	PT	A	PF	A	PT	A
above 100	above 100	above 100	above 100	above 100	above 100	above 100	above 100
CO	CS	SO	SS	CO	CS	SO	SS
above 90	above 100	below 20	above 100	above 90	above 100	at 50	above 100
RG	RGB	RP	RPB	RG	RGB	RP	RPB
above 100	above 90	above 90	above 100	at 70	at 70	above 90	above 100

there was one case of a task-independent structure-specific deficit—Case 50051 had a deficit for passive structures and for object-extracted relatives. This deficit is one that can be characterised as a deficit affecting the co-indexation of traces.

Both these patients showed other abnormal performances, however (Table 8). Case 50041 had below normal performances on sentences with object extracted structures, CS sentences in SPM, SS sentences in both tasks, and several sentences with reflexives and their baselines. Case 50051 had chance or below chance performance on several sentences with reflexives and their baselines.

There were no task-dependent structure-specific deficits by either the 1.74 SD below the normal mean or chance criteria.

One task-independent construction-specific deficit was seen by the 1.74 *SD* below the normal mean criterion: Case 50022 had a deficit affecting sentences with reflexives and noun phrase subjects with possessive prepositional phrases. By chance criterion, Case 50043 had a deficit for subject-object sentences. Both these patients showed other abnormal performances in unrelated sentence types by the same criteria that were used to establish these deficits (Table 8). Case 50022 performed abnormally low on PT sentences in OM. Case 50043 performed at chance on sentences with reflexive pronouns and genitive noun phrase subjects and their baselines in SPM.

Construction-specific, task-specific deficits, by the 1.74-*SD*-below-normal criterion, occurred in Case 50009 for full passives in object manipulation; Cases 50003, 50022, 50038, 50042, 50047, and 50052 for truncated passives in enactment; Cases 50004, 50020 and 50034 for truncated passives in sentence–picture matching; Case 50013 for SO sentences in sentence–picture matching; Cases 50038 and 50054 for SO in enactment; Case 50052 for sentences with reflexives and genitive subject noun phrases in sentence–picture matching; Case 50048 for sentences with reflexives and genitive subject noun phrases in enactment; Case 50014 for sentences with reflexives and possessive subject noun phrases in sentence–picture matching; and Case 50036 for sentences with reflexives and possessive subject noun phrases in enactment. By the chance criteria, these deficits occurred in Cases 50026, 50038, 50041, and 50042 for truncated passives in enactment; Cases 50004, 50013, and 50036 for SO sentences in sentence–picture matching; Cases 50010, 50015, 50038, 50048, and 50054 for SO in enactment; and Case 50041 for sentences with reflexives and possessive subject noun phrases in enactment. None of the construction-specific, task-specific deficits occurred in isolation. That is, all cases had mixed deficits when all constructions were considered.

A complete listing of all patients with specific deficits is found in Table 9. For each task-specific deficit, we checked to see whether the difference between the "poor" performance on the experimental sentence type on one task and the "good" performance on the experimental sentence type on the other was larger than expected on the basis of the distribution of differences of controls on that sentence type across tasks. In all but two cases, the difference in scores in the patient was more than 1.74 *SD* greater than that in the controls. The two exceptions—Case 50036 and Case 50010—were ones in which the difference in performance on SO sentences was within the normal limit of differences on the two tasks.

Table 10 presents the RT data from the SPM task. Cells in which a patient's RTs are 1.74 *SD* longer than the normal mean are highlighted.[5] By RT criteria, six patients had construction- or structure-specific deficits. Case 50001 was impaired on both passive sentence types; Case 50041 on full passives; Case 50003 on SO sentences; Cases 50038 and 50044 on both sentence types with reflexives, and Case 50042 on sentences with reflexives and subject noun phrases with possessive prepositional phrases.

Turning to speed–accuracy trade-offs, as noted, there were no instances of patients responding 1.74 *SD* faster than the normal mean RT on any sentence type. There were two instances in which a deficit in a construction or a structure in SPM

---

[5] We used all responses as the basis for patients' RTs; several patients would have had a small sample of RTs if RTs to correct responses had been used. The use of the latter basis does not change the overall pattern of results.

TABLE 9
Summary table of all deficits by accuracy criteria

Type of Deficit	Subj	Structure(s)	Task(s)	Criterion
Task-Independent, Structure-Specific Deficits	50041	passives	both	1.74SD
	50051	passives, obj-extr relatives	both	chance
Task-Dep, Struct-Specific	none	NA	NA	NA
Task-Independent, Construction-Specific Deficits	50022	RP	both	1.74SD
	50043	SO	both	chance
Task-Dependent, Construction Specific Deficits	50009	PF	OM	1.74SD
	50003, 50022, 50038, 50042, 50047, 50052	PT	OM	1.74SD
	50004, 50020, 50034	PT	SPM	1.74SD
	50013	SO	SPM	1.74SD
	50038, 50054	SO	OM	1.74SD
	50052*	RG	SPM	1.74SD
	50048	RG	OM	1.74SD
	50014	RP	SPM	1.74SD
	50036	RP	OM	1.74SD
	50026, 50038, 50041, 50042	PT	OM	chance
	50004, 50013, 50036*	SO	SPM	chance
	50010, 50015, 50038, 50048, 50054	SO	OM	chance
	50041	RP	OM	chance
Construction- or Structure-Specific Deficits by RT criteria	50001	passives	SPM	RT
	50041	PF	SPM	RT
	50003	SO	SPM	RT
	50038, 50044	reflexives	SPM	RT
	50042	RP	SPM	RT

* denotes cases where a deficit in a constuction or structure in SPM was rendered less clear by the presence of normal RTs for the experimental sentence and abnormally long RTs for the baseline

determined by the accuracy data (by either criterion) was rendered less clear by the presence of normal RTs for the experimental sentence and abnormally long RTs for the baseline sentence: Case 50052 for sentences with reflexives and genitive subject noun phrases; and Case 50036 for SO sentences.

DISCUSSION

We first register a caveat about these data. We recognise that, with only 10 examples of each sentence type, it is unclear that we have examined each patient carefully enough to be sure that his/her performance is reliably captured in our testing. Also, this small number of examples makes it difficult for a patient to differ on the same sentence type in two tasks. We limited the number of examples of each sentence type in each task because of the total test burden, and 10 sentences is enough to detect chance and above chance performance. Nonetheless, the results here should be considered preliminary and it would be worthwhile to repeat this study with a larger number of examples of each sentence type.

TABLE 10
Patient RTs in SPM: Abnormally long RTs are highlighted

subj	SPM											
	PF	A	PT	A	CO	CS	SO	SS	RG	RGB	RP	RPB
50001	abn 3666	norm 1891	abn 3612	norm 1891	norm 2811	norm 1793	norm 2640	abn 3091	abn 1584	norm 2088	norm 891	abn 2486
50002	norm 756	norm 1331	norm 2429	norm 1331	norm 2551	norm 1629	norm 1798	norm 2588	norm 818	norm 2420	abn 1809	abn 2602
50003	norm 1109	norm 1350	norm 1645	norm 1350	norm 2628	norm 1325	abn 4316	norm 2464	norm 666	norm 1145	norm 424	norm 1267
50004	norm 624	norm 830	norm 1129	norm 830	norm 809	norm 870	norm 1966	norm 533	norm 935	norm 1056	norm 627	norm 954
50005	norm 915	norm 1663	norm 2047	norm 1663	norm 1047	norm 1614	norm 1928	abn 2943	norm 1100	norm 2289	norm 567	abn 2463
50006	abn 2452	abn 2223	norm 2544	abn 2223	norm 2767	abn 2410	abn 4136	abn 5161	abn 2058	abn 3444	abn 1724	abn 2816
50007	abn 4360	abn 6420	abn 7170	abn 6420	abn 4928	abn 4379	abn 4444	abn 7640	abn 2849	abn 6120	abn 3320	abn 3251
50009	norm 1219	norm 1404	norm 2732	norm 1404	norm 1160	norm 1267	norm 3109	abn 3235	norm 758	norm 1184	norm 727	norm 1221
50010	norm 493	norm 853	norm 1312	norm 853	norm 618	norm 749	norm 644	norm 619	norm 366	norm 767	norm 592	norm 1042
50011	norm 1446	norm 1557	norm 1995	norm 1557	norm 2474	norm 1076	norm 1893	norm 2161	norm 894	norm 1256	norm 1317	norm 1948
50013	norm 1929	abn 2146	abn 3698	abn 2146	norm 2715	abn 2268	abn 7642	abn 4747	norm 1396	abn 3693	norm 1085	abn 2479
50014	norm 447	norm 678	norm 1981	norm 678	norm 902	norm 563	norm 735	norm 573	norm 393	norm 724	norm 258	norm 1040
50015	norm 1135	norm 1761	norm 2238	norm 1761	norm 2380	abn 1906	abn 7020	abn 3687	abn 2439	abn 2842	norm 1491	abn 2719
50016	abn 7871	abn 7209	abn 6475	abn 7209	abn 7469	abn 7043	abn 9285	abn 8581	abn 5362	abn 7625	abn 4262	abn 7621
50017	abn 4008	abn 4730	abn 5966	abn 4730	abn 3771	abn 3880	abn 7210	abn 5353	abn 2983	abn 5754	abn 2792	abn 5158
50018	abn 7596	abn 7541	abn 6656	abn 7541	abn 6960	abn 5197	abn 6905	abn 9006	abn 7338	abn 8284	abn 7222	abn 7070
50019	abn 3211	abn 2385	norm 2641	abn 2385	norm 1608	abn 1977	abn 4357	norm 1677	abn 1515	abn 2599	norm 1044	abn 2811
50020	abn 2984	abn 3297	abn 3291	abn 3297	abn 5735	abn 2808	abn 4975	abn 6660	abn 2476	abn 4795	abn 3476	abn 3471
50022	abn 5184	abn 4061	abn 4854	abn 4061	abn 6452	abn 4225	abn 4926	abn 9011	abn 3456	abn 7681	abn 3952	abn 6502
50023	abn 2507	abn 3471	abn 4512	abn 3471	abn 3920	abn 3271	norm 3389	abn 3049	abn 2033	norm 2425	abn 2170	abn 3940
50025	norm 1504	abn 3035	abn 3015	abn 3035	abn 3589	norm 1314	abn 6726	abn 4002	abn 3310	abn 4236	abn 4041	abn 4692
50026	abn 4421	abn 4311	abn 6499	abn 4311	abn 6906	abn 4652	abn 8822	abn 5693	abn 7016	abn 6166	abn 3310	abn 6619
50027	abn 3164	abn 4267	abn 6660	abn 4267	abn 3338	abn 3140	abn 4643	abn 3875	abn 1804	abn 3778	norm 1463	abn 4619

(Continued)

We begin by considering task-independent structure-specific deficits. By the accuracy criteria used in these analyses, examining the results on a structure-by-structure basis, there were two instances of task-independent structure-specific deficits in accuracy. By the 1.74-*SD*-below-normal criterion, Case 50041 showed a task-independent deficit for passive structures. When the chance criterion was applied, Case 50051 had a task-independent deficit affecting passives and one affecting object extracted structures. However, when other sentence types were

TABLE 10
(*Continued*)

subj	PF	A	PT	A	CO	CS	SO	SS	RG	RGB	RP	RPB
50029	abn 4213	abn 5776	abn 5667	abn 5776	abn 5676	abn 5199	abn 10293	abn 7042	abn 4552	abn 8697	abn 4610	abn 7278
50030	norm 1022	norm 1769	norm 2359	norm 1769	norm 2258	norm 1493	norm 2696	abn 3038	norm 381	norm 1731	norm 821	norm 1601
50034	norm 349	norm 765	norm 1375	norm 765	norm 1008	norm 852	norm 994	norm 1176	norm 629	norm 1152	norm 775	norm 1000
50036	norm 1053	abn 2455	norm 1918	abn 2455	norm 1389	norm 1663	norm 3104	abn 4497	abn 1946	abn 3957	norm 1706	norm 1412
50037	norm 773	norm 889	norm 1318	norm 889	norm 994	norm 1377	norm 2487	norm 946	norm 30	norm 1311	norm 310	norm 2164
50038	norm 1195	norm 1528	norm 1794	norm 1528	norm 1061	norm 1098	norm 2171	norm 1732	abn 2726	norm 2137	abn 2047	norm 1454
50041	abn 2877	norm 1844	norm 2416	norm 1844	norm 2236	abn 2082	abn 4157	abn 4695	abn 4169	abn 2592	abn 4512	norm 1638
50042	norm 1097	norm 1748	norm 2452	norm 1748	norm 1919	abn 2003	norm 3439	norm 2634	norm 1400	norm 2118	abn 2266	norm 1780
50043	abn 6059	abn 3448	abn 3812	abn 3448	abn 6863	abn 2503	abn 8560	abn 3734	abn 4387	abn 3715	abn 3693	abn 4666
50044	abn 6054	abn 3654	abn 8052	abn 3654	abn 4147	abn 3357	norm 1752	norm 1814	abn 3730	norm 1311	abn 3313	norm 1785
50045	abn 2228	abn 3146	norm 2797	abn 3146	abn 3293	abn 2562	abn 4263	abn 3596	abn 5624	norm 2238	abn 2405	abn 2317
50046	abn 2527	abn 3094	abn 3523	abn 3094	abn 4028	abn 2573	abn 4212	abn 5170	abn 2930	abn 2968	abn 2479	abn 2799
50047	norm 706	norm 1202	norm 1286	norm 1202	norm 865	norm 798	norm 867	norm 1052	norm 520	norm 979	norm 971	norm 1164
50048	abn 2263	abn 2993	abn 3632	abn 2993	norm 2344	abn 2065	norm 2801	abn 3916	abn 4294	abn 4811	abn 2903	abn 4491
50050	abn 6161	abn 4761	abn 5268	abn 4761	abn 8223	abn 5962	abn 11565	abn 6944	abn 7559	abn 6251	abn 3477	abn 6737
50051	abn 5013	abn 2298	abn 3829	abn 2298	abn 6598	abn 3933	abn 5074	abn 5124	abn 2070	abn 3559	norm 981	abn 2349
50052	norm 1163	norm 1086	norm 1560	norm 1086	norm 1461	norm 1231	norm 1412	norm 1299	norm 1350	abn 2704	norm 1210	norm 1478
50053	abn 2202	abn 3608	abn 4232	abn 3608	abn 3277	abn 3346	norm 3379	abn 4758	norm 1144	abn 2799	norm 1580	abn 2686
50054	abn 3080	abn 3348	abn 5965	abn 3348	abn 3828	abn 3273	abn 4892	abn 5820	norm 1112	abn 2866	abn 2011	abn 2512
PtMean	2691	2805	3532	2805	3310	2541	4324	3937	2479	3340	2158	3098
Pt *SD*	2017	1732	1905	1732	2134	1536	2711	2323	1968	2158	1504	1945
PtMin	349	678	1129	678	618	563	644	533	30	724	258	954
PtMax	7871	7541	8052	7541	8223	7043	11565	9011	7559	8697	7222	7621
ECmean	712	955	1590	955	1245	818	1281	1110	464	1185	624	1125
EC *SD*	725	552	732	552	1110	577	1336	920	586	792	628	626
+1.74*SD*	1973	1915	2864	1915	3177	1822	3606	2711	1484	2563	1716	2215
-1.74*SD*	-550	-6	315	-6	-687	-185	-1044	-492	-556	-194	-469	35

examined, both the cases had other poor performances, judged by the same criteria that apply to determine their deficit.

Task-independent structure-specific deficits could be interpreted as parsing and/or interpretive failures restricted to specific syntactic structures, and could provide evidence regarding the nature of syntactic representations and parsing and/or interpretive operations (Caplan & Hildebrandt, 1988; Grodzinsky, 2000). Unfortunately for the use of data from aphasia for this purpose, clear cases of such deficits are rare, if they exist at all. To our knowledge, all available data regarding such deficits come from studies of patients in single tasks, usually either SPM or OM but not both (Cupples & Inglis, 1993, is an exception, and these authors found dissociated performance over SPM and OM), and in no case was RT considered, so speed–accuracy trade-offs cannot be ruled out. Since task-independent deficits do not occur commonly, we must be cautious about accepting these performances in the literature as being due to parsing/interpretive deficits.

If they exist, task-independent structure-specific deficits could be due to deficits in the operations needed to parse or interpret the structures in question. They could also be due to resource reductions. Double dissociations over performances that can be interpreted as task-independent structure-specific deficits cannot both be due to resource reduction. Caplan and Hildebrandt (1988) discuss the implications for parsing and parsing deficits of a series of such dissociations, in a framework which assumes that performance in one task can be used to support a deficit analysis at the level of the parser/interpreter (an assumption we reject here). The present data show so few cases of task-independent structure-specific deficits that these issues cannot be explored.

There were two instances of task-independent construction-specific deficits. By the 1.74-SD-below-normal criterion, Case 50022 showed a task-independent deficit for sentences with reflexives and possessive noun phrase subjects. By the chance criterion, Case 50043 showed a task-independent deficit for SO sentences. Both these cases came close to having selective deficits for these constructions, with only a few other sentence types on which they performed poorly, and these "discrepant" performances were at high levels.

Task-independent construction-specific deficits can be taken as evidence for a parsing and/or interpretive failure that affects a syntactic structure in one sentential context. The deficits in these cases seem to be related to a combination of operations. Case 50022 seems able to co-index reflexives (as judged by his/her ability to co-index reflexives in sentences with possessive noun phrase subjects), and to structure genitive noun phrases so as to be able to determine which noun in such a phrase is the subject of a sentence (as judged by his ability to determine the subject of the baseline sentences with such structures) but not to combine the two operations. Case 50043 seems able to assign structure and meaning in sentences with object extracted structures (as judged by his/her performance on CO sentences) and to relate the subject of a sentence with a relative clause on the subject to the main verb (as judged by his/her ability to interpret SS sentences) but not to combine these two operations.

In contrast to the rarity of task-independent structure- and construction-specific deficits, there are a large number of task-specific, construction-specific deficits. As noted in the introduction, such deficits pose a problem. If a patient can understand a sentence as shown by, say, reliably matching its meaning to a picture, and is capable of enacting the same meaning derived from a different structure, it is not immediately clear why s/he cannot enact the meaning of that sentence. The form of a sentence itself is not needed to demonstrate the meaning of the sentence; all that is needed is that the sentence be understood. We can imagine two reasons why such patterns might occur.

The first is that syntactic processing and the performance of a task operate in cascade on-line (Tanenhaus, Spivey-Knowlton, Eberhard, & Sedivy, 1995). If listeners are planning actions or matching thematic roles depicted in pictures to sentences as a sentence unfolds, the syntactic structure of a sentence, as well as its meaning, is being activated as the task is being planned and/or performed. Task-specific structure-specific deficits could arise from an inability to integrate the demands of one task with sentence structure building and semantic interpretation.

That is, although goal-directed comprehension appears to be seamlessly integrated with the performance of many operations that constitute sub-goals of the entire task (e.g., encoding propositional meaning into memory, planning action on the basis of propositional meaning, matching propositional meaning onto the products of perception), it is in fact always an instance of a continuous dual-task situation, in which the two tasks are the assignment of sentence meaning and the use of that meaning to accomplish a task. Increases in on-line sentence processing load could affect a patient's ability to do the two together, through resource sharing or bottlenecks, as occur in "psychological refractory periods" effects. On this account, task-specific construction-specific deficits arise in the course of mapping the intermediate products of comprehension onto developing task demands.

Task-specific construction-specific deficits are not limited to either SPM or OM. This indicates that the overall complexity of a set of task demands is not the sole determinant of which task can be associated with sentence- and structure-specific deficits; rather, specific combinations of construction- and task-specific operations must be beyond individual patients' processing capacities (on this account of these deficits).

The second account of task-specific construction-specific deficits is based on the observation that syntactic structure determines not only propositional semantic values such as thematic roles, but discourse-level representations, such as focus, presuppositions, etc. as well. While discourse-level representations are logically irrelevant to the performance of the tasks we used, which only require consideration of thematic roles and co-indexation, they may affect performance, and do so differently in different tasks. For instance, passives and cleft-object sentences place the theme in the discourse focus. If a patient has difficulty formulating an action in which the focused element is the theme, but does not consider focus information when matching thematic roles to pictures, s/he may have trouble with passive and cleft-object sentences only in enactment. On this account, task-specific construction-specific deficits arise in the course of mapping the combination of discourse and propositional meanings onto tasks, and provide evidence that levels of linguistic representations (in this case, aspects of the representation of discourse) affect the performance of tasks that do not logically require their activation.

We have thus far attempted to account for the specific deficits seen in these cases. The explanations we have advanced assume that these deficits occur because of disturbances affecting the ability to assign a particular syntactic structure and/or to interpret that structure, possibly while doing a particular task. These accounts do not capture the fact that all patients had other poor performances, either when compared to normal performance or when compared to chance. They also do not capture the fact that many patients had abnormal performances on baseline sentences. Finally, they do not capture a fact that we have not emphasised to this point—there were instances in which a patient performed poorly on a baseline sentence and well on the related experimental sentence in the same task. These "reversed" patterns did not occur as often as poor performances on experimental sentences and good performances on baseline sentences, but neither were they infrequent, constituting 9.5% of the data by the 1.74-SD-below-normal criterion, 6.7% of the data by the chance criterion, and 13.5% of the data by the RT criterion.[6] The mechanisms we

---

[6] These figures reflect the percent of instances in which the performance on a baseline sentence was "poor" and performance on the corresponding experimental sentence was "good" by these criteria as a function of the total number of baseline–experimental pairs.

have suggested—and, as far as we can see, any mechanism that creates a specific deficit—cannot account for these aspects of performance. It is hard to imagine a deficit that would affect a baseline sentence on a task without affecting the corresponding experimental sentence; accordingly, these performances seem likely to be due to a random error-generating process (i.e., "noise"). Such factors have been invoked to account for aphasic performances in other areas and simulated in various ways (e.g., Dell, Schwartz, Martin, Saffran, & Gagnon, 1997).

In summary, we have found that task-independent deficits affecting particular structures or constructions are rare in aphasia. Task-dependent, construction-specific deficits occurred more frequently. None of these types of specific deficits occurred in total isolation in our data. Theories of the deficits in aphasia need to account for the effects of task on performance on specific sentence types. Models of aphasic performance are likely to need to include parameters related to noise, the demands of each sentence, the overall ability of a patient to handle that demand, as well as operation-specific or task- and operation-specific deficits.

REFERENCES

Caplan, D. (1995). Issues arising in contemporary studies of disorders of syntactic processing in sentence comprehension in agrammatic patients. *Brain and Language, 50*, 325–338.

Caplan, D., & Hildebrandt, N. (1988). *Disorders of syntactic comprehension.* Cambridge, MA: MIT Press (Bradford Books).

Caplan, D., Waters, G., & Hildebrandt, N. (1997). Determinants of sentence comprehension in aphasic patients in sentence–picture matching tasks. *Journal of Speech and Hearing Research, 40*, 542–555.

Crawford, J. R., Garthwaite, P. H., & Gray, C. D. (2003). Wanted: Fully operational definitions of dissociations in single-case studies. *Cortex, 39*, 357–370.

Crawford, J. R., & Howell, D. C. (1998). Comparing an individual's test score against norms derived from small samples. *The Clinical Neuropsychologist, 12*, 482–486.

Cupples, L., & Inglis, A. L. (1993). When task demands induce "asyntactic" sentence comprehension: A study of sentence interpretation in aphasia. *Cognitive Neuropsychology, 10*, 201–234.

Dell, G. S., Schwartz, M. F., Martin, N., Saffran, E. M., & Gagnon, D. A. (1997). Lexical access in aphasic and nonaphasic speakers. *Psychological Review, 104*, 801–838.

Grodzinsky, Y. (2000). The neurology of syntax: Language use without Broca's area, *Behavioral and Brain Sciences, 23*, 47–117.

Haarmann, H. J., & Kolk, H. H. (1991). Syntactic priming in Broca's aphasics: Evidence for slow activation. *Aphasiology, 5*, 247–263.

Linebarger, M. C. (1995). Agrammatism as evidence about grammar. *Brain and Language, 50*, 52–91.

Linebarger, M. C., Schwartz, M. F., & Saffran, E. M. (1983). Sensitivity to grammatical structure in so-called agrammatic aphasics. *Cognition, 13*, 361–392.

Swinney, D., Zurif, E., Prather, P., & Love, T. (1996). Neurological distribution of processing resources underlying language comprehension. *Journal of Cognitive Neuroscience, 8*, 174–184.

Tanenhaus, M. K., Spivey-Knowlton, M. J., Eberhard, K. M., & Sedivy, J. E. (1995). Integration of visual and linguistic information in spoken language comprehension. *Science, 268*, 1632–1634.

Distinguishing semantic and lexical word retrieval deficits in people with aphasia

David Howard

University of Newcastle-upon-Tyne, UK

Claire Gatehouse

Plymouth Teaching Primary Care Trust, UK

Background: Identifying the point of breakdown in people with aphasia with disorders of word retrieval is not straightforward. Evidence has been sought from: (i) the nature of the errors in naming; (ii) the variables affecting naming accuracy; (iii) the effects of correct and misleading cues; (iv) performance in other word comprehension and production tasks. However, previous research has demonstrated that each of these sources of evidence provides information compatible with more than level of breakdown.

Aims: The study investigates whether a combination of information from these sources can provide a coherent account of how word retrieval is breaking down in people with aphasia.

Methods & Procedures: Three people with aphasia (JGr, LM, and KS) took part in four experiments. The first investigated the errors made in picture naming and the factors (target word length, imageability, frequency ...) affecting naming accuracy. The second experiment investigated the effects of correct phonemic cues and miscues on word retrieval. The third examined the participants' performance in tests of spoken and written word and picture comprehension. The fourth experiment investigated whether the participants had the processing abilities necessary to generate their own phonemic cues in spoken naming from orthographic information.

Outcomes & Results: Evidence from these investigations showed different levels of breakdown in the three participants. JGr's naming was characterised by semantic errors, effects of target imageability and familiarity on naming accuracy, improved naming with correct phonemic cues and semantic errors with miscues, and poor performance in word comprehension tasks. This pattern is consistent with a breakdown at a semantic level underlying JGr's difficulty in word retrieval. In contrast, LM shows performance indicating a breakdown in mapping between intact semantic and phonological representations. He makes primarily no response errors in naming and his accuracy is affected only by frequency and familiarity. Correct phonemic cues can improve his naming accuracy to near normal levels, and he makes no semantic errors, although he is slowed by miscues. His word and picture comprehension is intact. KS shows a more complex pattern of impairment. Like JGr, she shows evidence of a semantic

Address correspondence to: David Howard, School of Education, Communication and Language Sciences, University of Newcastle, Newcastle-upon-Tyne NE1 7RU, UK.

E-mail: david.howard@newcastle.ac.uk

This research was supported by grants from the Stroke Association and the Medical Research Council. We would like to thank Wendy Best and Carolyn Bruce for their collaboration in the design of many of the investigations, and Lyndsey Nickels for her helpful suggestions and comments on an earlier draft of the paper. In addition we would like to thank JGr, LM, KS, and their respective families for their invaluable cooperation.

impairment: she makes semantic errors in naming, and her accuracy is affected by target imageability. She makes errors in word comprehension and her word retrieval is adversely affected by miscues. There are two unusual features to her performance: her naming accuracy is not improved by initial phoneme cues (despite effects of miscues and more extensive phonemic cues), and she is better at naming pictures with longer names (a "reverse length effect"). Investigations in experiment four show that KS is using orthographic information on the initial letter of names to generate her own phonemic cues; it is concluded that in addition to her semantic deficit she has an impairment in access to lexical phonological representations.

Conclusions: We conclude that careful investigation of the performance of people with aphasia across a range of tasks can be used to identify underlying levels of breakdown in word retrieval. However, superficial resemblances between people with aphasia can be misleading.

Impairments in word retrieval in people with aphasia have been found to arise from a number of different causes. Semantic specifications can be impaired (e.g., Hillis, Rapp, Romani, & Caramazza, 1990; Howard & Orchard-Lisle, 1984), access to the word in the phonological output lexicon can fail (e.g., Kay & Ellis, 1987), or lexical representations themselves can be lost (Howard, 1995). Three different sources of information have been used in identifying the locus of deficit: analysis of types of naming errors, investigation of the effects of psycholinguistic variables on naming performance, and assessment of semantic comprehension (Butterworth, Howard, & McLoughlin, 1984; Caramazza & Hillis, 1990; Gainotti, Silveri, Villa, & Miceli, 1986; Howard & Orchard-Lisle, 1984). In addition, the investigation of picture naming when the person with aphasia is phonemically cued with either correct or incorrect phonological information has been found to aid our ability to identify the nature of word retrieval deficits in aphasia (Howard & Orchard-Lisle, 1984; Kay & Ellis, 1987; Lambon Ralph, Sage, & Roberts, 2000; Li & Williams, 1991; Myers Pease & Goodglass, 1978; Nickels & Howard, 1994; Stimley & Noll, 1991).

In phonemic cueing participants with aphasia are provided with the first sound of the word for which they are searching to aid word retrieval. These phonemic cues have either comprised the initial consonant of the target word plus the first vowel (Myers Pease & Goodglass, 1978) or just the initial phoneme with a following schwa (Bruce & Howard, 1988; Hillis & Caramazza, 1995; Howard & Orchard-Lisle, 1984; Kay & Ellis, 1987; Li & Canter, 1991; Li & Williams, 1991; Nickels & Howard, 1994; Stimley & Noll, 1991). In addition to assessing cueing effects, Howard and Orchard-Lisle (1984) investigated the effects of phonemically miscueing their patient JCU. In this condition the person with aphasia was given the initial phoneme of a semantic coordinate of the target, such as /tə/ for a picture of a lion, and was induced to produce the response "tiger". JCU was severely non-fluent with a marked semantic comprehension deficit. Whereas she was only able to name 5% of pictures with an unrelated cue, when given a correct phonemic cue her performance improved to 49% correct. In contrast, when miscued JCU's naming performance deteriorated to 1% correct. The miscues, as would be predicted, resulted in a great number of semantic errors (31%) whereas with unrelated cues her predominant error type was "no response". Howard and Orchard-Lisle (1984) concluded that, when naming, JCU's semantic deficit resulted in the available semantic information being insufficient to specify the precise target item to be accessed in the phonological output lexicon (POL). As a result the phonological forms of the target and a range of semantically related items were similarly activated in the POL. No item would be successfully retrieved unless a phonemic cue or miscue added extra activation, allowing one to reach threshold.

A semantic impairment in aphasia may be caused by a degradation of semantic information, resulting in only partial information being available, or because semantic representations have become inaccessible (Lesser, 1989). Since the semantic system is central to all meaningful language processing, patients with such deficits have been found to be impaired in both comprehension and production, and across modalities (Butterworth et al., 1984; Gainotti et al., 1986; Nickels & Howard, 1994). In fact, Butterworth et al. (1984), Gainotti et al. (1986), and Nickels and Howard (1994) all found a significant correlation between patients' performance on semantic comprehension tests and the production of semantic errors, although this was not an item-specific effect. Butterworth et al. (1984) suggested that this impairment arose from a variable ability to retrieve full semantic specification in the damaged system. A reduced semantic specification would then activate a range of semantically related items in the POL with the possibility of one of these competitors reaching threshold before the target item. A severe semantic impairment could even result in semantic activation being so diminished that no response is possible, not even a semantic error. This has been found to be the case in severe semantic dementia (Funnell & Hodges, 1991; Hodges, Patterson, Oxbury, & Funnell, 1992), and for people with global aphasia such as JCU (Howard & Orchard-Lisle, 1984).

Difficulties in word retrieval due to a semantic impairment have been contrasted with impairments in access to the POL. While people with aphasia with this level of breakdown also improve with phonemic cues, in contrast to semantically impaired patients, they are not adversely affected by miscues. This is because the central semantic system remains intact. For example, Kay and Ellis (1987) described a person with fluent aphasia, EST, who was cueable but not miscueable. Investigations of EST's picture naming revealed significant frequency effects, with 37% correct picture naming. In addition, although phonemic cues increased performance by 10%, miscues had no effect. Good performance on comprehension assessments for concrete words excluded any semantic deficit for picturable items. Good repetition of words that could not be produced as picture names compared to repetition of nonwords was taken to show that the phonological lexical representations were intact. Kay and Ellis (1987) therefore concluded that entries in the POL were not lost but merely inaccessible due to a partial disconnection between semantics and the POL. This impairment resulted in reduced activation reaching lexical items; phonemic cues helped EST by providing sufficient additional activation to boost more frequent items to threshold.[1] Many of EST's naming errors were phonological approximations to the target; Kay and Ellis suggest that, in these cases, activation of POL entries was sufficient to elicit only a partial phonological specification of the word.

Difficulties in access to the POL need not necessarily result in phonologically related errors. Caramazza and Hillis (1990) report patient RGB who, like EST, made no semantic errors in spoken word comprehension, was more accurate with higher-frequency targets, and benefited from correct phonemic cues. His naming errors were almost exclusively either semantic errors or circumlocutory descriptions. Caramazza

---

[1] Interpretations of EST's underlying naming impairment have varied. While Kay and Ellis (1987) argue for a partial disconnection of semantics and the lexicon resulting in weak lexical activation, and Kay and Patterson (1985) suggest raised output lexicon thresholds, Smith (1988) and Ellis and Young (1988) prefer an account in terms of insufficient activation at a post-lexical phoneme level. Kay (1992) suggests a dual deficit to the connections between semantics and the lexicon and damage to the lexicon itself.

and Hillis suggest, following Patterson (1979), that when the target phonological representation is inaccessible "the most highly activated, semantically-related lexical-phonological representation is produced in its stead" (p. 112). This mechanism may also apply to EST; Smith (1988) showed that in naming EST produced approximately equal numbers of semantically and phonologically related errors.

It has been argued that in an impairment of access to the POL, the output from the intact semantic system is sufficient but access to the POL does not reliably occur. This failure may be due to abnormally raised activation thresholds (Hillis & Caramazza, 1995) or even fluctuating loss of activation in transmission from the semantic system to the POL (Kay & Ellis, 1987). Whatever the reason for the failure in lexical access, an evaluation of cueing and miscueing effects can be useful in differentiating such an access disorder from a central semantic impairment. This is particularly important since the presence of semantic errors alone is not a reliable indicator of a semantic deficit as Caramazza and Hillis (1990) have shown.

The two people with aphasia (JS and GM) described by Lambon Ralph et al. (2000)—like Katz and Lanzoni's (1997) participant—have good comprehension, and near flawless speech production in repetition and reading, but a severe anomia.[2] This pattern is described by Lambon Ralph et al. (2000) as "classical anomia". The participants' errors in naming are, most frequently, no responses, although semantic errors occur that they immediately reject. All three of these participants are aided by phonemic cues and hindered by miscues. The obvious conclusion is that there is clear evidence that both semantics and phonology are intact and the difficulty is in mapping between the two domains. Miscues are effective because the impairment to the mapping between semantics and phonology results in a set of semantically related items being activated that can then be elicited by a phonemic miscue. The conclusion that these participants' impairments are necessarily post-semantic is, almost certainly, ill founded. Comprehension tasks are easier than production. In naming, the correct target will be produced when the target activation is greater than all the words in the participant's lexicon. Comprehension tasks require only that the target's activation is compared with that of a single competitor or an array of competitors (typically items from the same semantic category). This problem with using comprehension tasks to identify semantic impairments depends, partly, on the nature of the task. Word-to-picture matching may be less sensitive than word–picture verification with semantic foils (Breese & Hillis, 2004), but neither may be able to detect subtle semantic impairments that are sufficient to impact on word retrieval. Alive to this difficulty, Lambon Ralph et al. (2000) suggest that JS and GM's impairments in word retrieval might be due either to an impairment to the mapping between semantics and phonology or an impairment at a semantic level that their word comprehension tasks were not sensitive enough to detect.

Howard (1995) described a patient, EE, who like EST, RGB, JS, and GM showed no impairment in comprehension, and for whom naming was better for higher-frequency targets. Unlike all these people with aphasia, neither correct phonemic cues, nor miscues had any effect on EE's naming, and there was substantial

---

[2] Lambon Ralph, Moriarty, and Sage (2002) have argued that, in aphasia, the degree of anomia is due only to the degree of impairment in semantics and in phonology. This they call the "primary systems hypothesis" (see also Patterson & Lambon Ralph, 1999). We note, in passing, that the patients reported by, for example, Lambon Ralph et al. (2000) among others, who have no impairments at either semantic or phonological levels, are sufficient to falsify this conjecture.

consistency in the availability of names from session to session.[3] This pattern seems to accord better with loss of lexical representations rather than an impairment of access procedures (cf. Shallice, 1988). Although the majority of EE's naming errors were no responses, many errors were semantic circumlocutions, which Howard argues represent offering appropriate semantic information in the absence of the phonological word form. It must therefore be borne in mind that, as with the lexical access deficit, semantic errors may also relate to lexical storage deficits; frank semantic errors and circumlocutions can be indistinguishable when the person with aphasia is very non-fluent or has limited output. Again we must conclude that semantic errors alone cannot be relied on to identify the level of impairment, since they can be the result of a number of different deficits.

Analysis of the effects of psycholinguistic variables on naming performance is another source of evidence that can be used to shed light on levels of language impairment. When a patient's naming is found to be affected by a particular property of a word, this can provide evidence that to helps to identify where in the language-processing system a difficulty might be (cf. Shallice, 1988).

Imageability has been shown to predict some patients' word-finding abilities, with concrete words easier than abstract ones (Goodglass, Hyde, & Blumstein, 1969; Howard, 1985; Nickels, 1995; Nickels & Howard, 1994). Nickels and Howard (1995) were able to show that some people with aphasia were better at naming pictures whose names had higher imageability ratings, even when the effects of other variables are controlled and despite the very limited range of imageability values for picturable items. Nickels (1995) and Nickels and Howard (1994) showed that the imageability of the targets affected the rate of production of semantic, but not phonological naming errors. Because the patients in Nickels' study who made semantic errors in production also had impairments in comprehension, this suggests that the imageability effects in naming are primarily indicative of semantic impairments. However, there is evidence that imageability effects can also be found where the problem in word retrieval is post-semantic. Franklin, Howard, and Patterson (1995) described a patient with a selective difficulty in retrieving low-imageability words, whose comprehension of such words in the written form was normal. This showed that the semantics for such words was intact and the deficit—which was imageability sensitive—was post-semantic.

Frequency has also been considered to be a salient variable in word production, since it has been shown that normal participants' response times in naming and word recognition tasks are inversely related to word frequency (e.g., Oldfield & Wingfield, 1965). Similarly, frequency effects have been found for accuracy of naming by aphasic participants (e.g., Ellis, Miller, & Sin, 1983; Kay & Ellis, 1987; Zingeser &

---

[3] Confusingly, Lambon Ralph (1998) presents the patient, JS, (also reported by Lambon Ralph et al., 2000) as similar to EE. The differences, though, are substantial: (i) JS benefits from correct phonemic cues (Lambon Ralph, 1998, p. 344, where the effect of cueing is very substantial but the statistics incorrect—see also Table 4, Lambon Ralph, 1998, pp. 350–351, where 10/30 items are elicited by a single phoneme cue, and Lambon Ralph et al., 2000, pp. 191–192, where JS shows an effect of single phonemic cues, significant on a one-tailed test), EE does not; (ii) JS's naming is reduced significantly by miscues (Lambon Ralph et al., 2000, p.193), EE's is not; (iii) JS's naming is most strongly affected by target word imageability—a semantic-level variable (Lambon Ralph, 1998, p. 345), EE only shows an independent effect of word familiarity; (iv) JS does not show significant item consistency when confounding variables are accounted for (Lambon Ralph, 1998, footnote 4 pp. 356–357), EE does not. With these differences, it is very unlikely that JS and EE have the same underlying impairment.

Berndt, 1988). However, these naming studies have been criticised for not taking into account the effects of other variables, such as age-of-acquisition (AofA), since there is a high correlation between word frequency and the age at which words are acquired (Carroll & White, 1973). Normal participants' naming latencies have been found to be significantly affected by rated AofA (Morrison, Ellis, & Quinlan, 1992) and AofA has been found to be a good predictor of success in aphasic naming (Feyereisen, Van der Borght, & Seron, 1988; Hirsh & Ellis, 1994; Nickels & Howard, 1995). Morrison et al. (1992) showed that AofA has no effect on latencies for semantic categorisation, and argue that the AofA effect in naming indicates that the variable affects lexical access and not picture recognition or access to the semantic system. They suggested that it might operate by lowering lexical thresholds, by resulting in more complete forms being stored initially or by strengthening the connections between semantic and phonological representations. However, Nickels and Howard (1995) found that AofA predicted the occurrence of semantic errors while familiarity and length predicted phonological errors. These familiarity effects concurred with Gernsbacher (1984) who suggested that it was not frequency that should be considered but familiarity. This she characterised as subjective or experiential familiarity with a word, which she claimed would not only be more contemporary than objective frequency counts but would also encompass experience in all modalities. While Gernsbacher's investigations were into word recognition rather than production, Funnell and Sheridan (1992) were able to find a significant effect of familiarity, independent of frequency, in an aphasic patient who had originally appeared to have a category-specific naming impairment.

Word length, which was found to be the other significant variable affecting normal naming latencies by Morrison et al. (1992), has frequently been identified as affecting some aphasic patients' performance (Ellis et al., 1983; Howard, Patterson, Franklin, Morton, & Orchard-Lisle, 1984; Kohn, 1988, 1989; Nickels, 1995; Nickels & Howard, 2004; Pate, Saffran, & Martin, 1987). Although these latter studies did not all control for independent age-of-acquisition effects, the length effects were always in the direction that short words were easier than longer ones. Because this effect is commonly found with aphasic patients who produce high proportions of phonological errors (Nickels, 1995), it has been assumed the effect reflects deficits in phonological assembly, possibly due to capacity limitations in the post-lexical processing components (Butterworth, 1992). Although length effects have normally been in the direction of worse performance with longer words, Best (1995) described a patient with a "reverse length effect". This patient, CGJ, was better at naming long words than short, although his reading aloud showed the more usual trend in favour of shorter words. Best suggests that this result is most easily explained by a disorder of lexical phonological representation or of access to the lexicon. More recently, Lambon-Ralph and his colleagues have described another patient, IW, with better naming of pictures with long names (Lambon Ralph & Howard, 2000; Lambon Ralph, Howard, Nightingale, & Ellis, 1998); unlike CGJ, whose comprehension was good, IW showed a severe difficulty in both spoken and written word comprehension, and a reverse length effect in both of these tasks.

In conclusion, the analysis of psycholinguistic variables is far from straightforward. Although imageability effects have traditionally been taken to indicate a semantic impairment, these effects can also be found with post-semantic impairments. The reliability of frequency effects has been brought into serious question due to its intercorrelation with so many other variables. While familiarity effects, so far, seem relatively reliable, it is not clear whether they relate to semantic or lexical deficits. Similarly, AofA effects have been taken to indicate either semantic or lexical deficits, depending on the investigation. Even length effects have not consistently been in the predicted direction and reverse length effects may be associated with lexical access deficits. We must therefore conclude that, while the analysis of psycholinguistic variables affecting patient performance offers one source of evidence concerning patients' deficits, these analyses alone cannot be relied on. The review of the literature on error analysis did not prove to be entirely straightforward either. Although semantic errors seemed to generally reflect semantic deficits, they have also been produced by patients with lexical access or storage deficits, while no-response errors abound whatever the level of impairment.

Thus, analysis of naming impairments cannot be based on analysis of errors, or of variables affecting performance, as each of these sources, used alone, provides ambiguous information: convergent evidence from different investigative techniques seems the most useful course of action. More importantly, including cueing and miscueing techniques is essential if we are to identify the locus of deficit in anomic patients reliably. By combining these varying sources of information certain characteristics corresponding to different levels of breakdown do emerge. The two levels of impairment relevant to the three patients to be reported below can now be summarised in Table 1 (note that there are many other possible levels of breakdown in word retrieval with different characteristic patterns of performance; see e.g., Howard, 2000). On the basis of the information summarised in Table 1 we will be able to interpret our findings from the each experiment to be reported below.

Each of the three patients to be reported in this paper was investigated as part of a larger project investigating phonemic cues and their effectiveness when used in therapy. As a result they were all assessed on naming a large set of pictures allowing the analysis of error type and variables affecting correct responses. This investigation and its results will be reported in Experiment 1. From this experiment it will be seen that while patients JGr and KS demonstrate striking similarities to JCU, LM is more

TABLE 1
Characteristics of two levels of impairment in aphasic naming

1.   Semantic impairment
  (a)   Spoken and written naming will be similarly impaired and semantic errors will occur in both modalities of production.
  (b)   Both comprehension and production will be affected by the semantic variables imageability and/or concreteness.
  (c)   Increased correct responses with correct phonemic cues.
  (d)   Production of semantic errors in response to miscues.
  (e)   Similar levels of impairment in semantically mediated tasks such as comprehension of spoken and written words.
2.   Impaired access to the phonological output lexicon
  (a)   Spoken and written naming may be differentially impaired and semantic errors will not be commonly observed.
  (b)   Frequency effects, familiarity effects, and possibly age-of-acquisition effects, but no imageability or concreteness effects in naming.
  (c)   Day-to-day inconsistency over and above frequency effects.
  (d)   Increased correct responses with correct phonemic cues.
  (e)   Semantic errors are not produced in response to miscues.
  (f)   Intact semantic comprehension of both spoken and written words.

like EST. On the basis of these findings, we will make predictions about the patients' responses to cues and miscues, which are investigated in Experiment 2. Further support for the hypotheses will be sought by investigating semantic comprehension in Experiment 3. Finally Experiment 4 is motivated by KS's rather contradictory performance on cueing tasks and serves to clarify this issue. Note that the order in which these data were collected does not necessarily match the order in which they are presented. The structure of this paper is adopted to demonstrate the logical structure of the argument, and does not attempt to present a chronology of our investigations.

THE PARTICIPANTS

JGr was a 56-year-old retired scaffolder who suffered a left cerebrovascular accident (CVA) 2 years prior to the investigation, resulting in a dense hemiplegia and severe non-fluent aphasia. He made some small improvements in language abilities and, while functional comprehension became adequate, spontaneous speech was still severely restricted, relying heavily on responses to yes/no questions. JGr used some single words in an agrammatic manner, but other than a few high-frequency phrases, attempts at phrase production could not usually be completed. JGr scored an Aphasia Quotient (AQ) of 56 and was classified as Broca's aphasic on the Western Aphasia Battery (WAB); (Kertesz, 1982).

LM was a 64-year-old businessman who suffered a left middle cerebral artery infarct 2½ years prior to the current investigation. Initially LM had a dense right hemiplegia, severe dysphagia, and a moderate-severe non-fluent aphasia with good auditory comprehension. Some slow recovery had been made both physically and in speech and language, but his spontaneous speech remained very restricted. Although LM's communication was limited he was aided his by good gesture, pointing, fragmentary phrases, good initial letter information, and questioning by the listener. LM scored an AQ of 64 and was classified as Broca's aphasic on the WAB.

KS was a 64-year-old woman who had worked in good secretarial jobs for much of her life. She had suffered two left CVAs 6 and 2 years prior to study. Although she had no physical disabilities, the second CVA resulted in a mild fluent aphasia, with occasional word-finding difficulties, particularly evident on proper nouns. However, KS's conversational speech was excellent and to the casual observer no difficulties would be evident. Reading and writing were similarly well preserved. KS scored an AQ of 86 and was classified as anomic on the WAB.

All three participants were native British English speakers, were right-handed, and had normal or corrected-to-normal vision and normal hearing.

EXPERIMENT 1: ASSESSMENT OF PICTURE NAMING

This experiment was conducted to investigate picture naming performance, in terms of consistency, variables affecting correct responses, and the types of errors made. In addition we tested word and nonword repetition to give further information on the degree of impairment to output phonological processes.

Stimuli

A set of 194 black and white line drawings beginning with 10 different phonemes/letters was used. A group of 24 middle-aged and elderly control participants, with a mean age of 58 yrs (range 41–76), provided an average name agreement of 96% with a minimum of 87%.

Method

The pictures were subdivided into four sets (A–D) so that naming could be alternated with other tasks, such as phonemic cueing (to be reported in Experiment 2). All participants were assessed on naming the 194 pictures twice (naming 1, naming 2) over four sessions. A 10-second response-time cut-off criterion was used and the final response in this 10-second period was scored. Responses were classified as correct, visual errors, semantic errors, phonologically related errors, unrelated errors, no responses, or other errors. Our classification of semantic errors included shared feature errors (including coordinates, superordinates, and subordinates), associate errors, attempts at circumlocution, semantic followed by phonological errors, and mixed semantic and phonological errors. However, responses that involved identifying another part of the picture (such as ball from the picture of a footballer) were classified as visual errors, included in the other errors category. Responses were classified as being phonologically related if 50% or more of the target's phonemes were contained in the response or if 50% or more of the response's phonemes were contained in the target in roughly the same order. If the responses failed to meet either of these criteria then they were classified as unrelated. "No responses" included the patient saying nothing, responses such as "no" or "don't know" and vague comments such as "I've got one of those" or "I did that yesterday". Any multi-word response containing more semantic information was classified as an attempt at circumlocution, e.g., "It's in the kitchen". "Other" errors included initial letter naming and gestures.

In addition we assessed repetition of a subset of the target words (Set C; $n = 48$), repetition of 30 nonwords varying in length from one to three syllables and repetition of 20 single phonemes.

Analysis

The mean proportion correct and the percentage error distribution from naming 1 and 2 were calculated for each patient and are given in Table 2. A contingency coefficient was calculated to estimate the consistency of correct naming responses over the two presentations. Shallice (1987) suggests that a value of C greater than 0.30 indicates a consistent impairment.

From the corpus of 194 items, matched sets were constructed to assess the effects of a number of psycholinguistic variables on each patient's correct naming responses. Sets were selected so that there was a substantial difference in the variable(s) under consideration, but the sets were matched for all the other variables. The variables available for each item were number of phonemes and number of syllables; word frequency (from Francis & Kucera, 1982); familiarity, concreteness, and imageability (from the MRC Psycholinguistic Database, Coltheart, 1981) and ratings of age-of-acquisition and operativity. Ratings for the latter two variables were collected from 10 normal control participants.

The matched sets were constructed to assess for the effects of the following variables; imageability and concreteness together, familiarity, frequency, familiarity and frequency together, age of acquisition, and number of syllables. Imageability

TABLE 2
Mean proportion of types of responses in naming 194 pictures on two
occasions

	JGR	LM	KS
Correct	0.53	0.63	0.61
Semantic errors	0.10	0.04	0.12
Shared feature errors	0.06	0.01	0.08
Associates	0.02	0.02	0.02
Semantic circumlocutions	0.00	0.01	0.02
Mixed semantic and phonological errors	0.01	0.00	0.01
Semantic-then-phonological errors	0.01	0.00	0.00
Phonological errors	0.02	0.04	0.00
Phonologically related real words	0.01	0.01	0.00
Phonologically related nonwords	0.01	0.02	0.00
Initial phoneme only	0.00	0.01	0.00
Unrelated errors	0.01	0.01	0.01
Unrelated real words	0.005	0.003	0.01
Unrelated nonwords	0.005	0.005	0.00
Other errors	0.05	0.13	0.08
No response	0.29	0.15	0.18
Contingency coefficient	0.30	0.29	0.46

and concreteness were varied together because the variables are highly correlated and we have no theoretical grounds to distinguish their effects. The sets varying frequency or familiarity alone allow us to distinguish independent effects of the variables; the sets varying familiarity and frequency together were to allow comparison with other studies that have not distinguished these effects. The sets used were matched for all the remaining variables with one exception: the sets varying word length necessarily differ in both the number of syllables and the number of phonemes (see Howard & Nickels, 2005, for the difficulties of separating these effects). Each patient's performance on the matched subsets was analysed in terms of proportion correct on naming. The significance of any difference between the sets was calculated using the Wilcoxon-Mann-Whitney Rank Sum Test, and with number of syllables a Jonckheere Trend Test. The proportions correct and the significance levels are given in Table 3.

Results

JGr was on average only 53% correct in naming and had only a moderate degree of item consistency (C = 0.30).[4] He produced a very large proportion of no responses, 29%, and a smaller number of semantic errors, 10%. JGr's naming performance was significantly affected by target imageability/concreteness ($p = .049$), familiarity

---

[4] The consistency shown by these patients could result from item-specific impairments or be due to different probabilities of success to items with different properties. To allow for this, the contingency coefficients were recalculated allowing for the effects of all variables considered here using the method described by Howard (1995). This reduced the values to 0.23 for JGr, 0.24 for LM, and 0.34 for KS, showing that, even when the effects of confounding variables are taken into account, KS shows rather greater consistency than the other two patients.

TABLE 3

Performance in naming subsets matched for psycholinguistic variables

	Patients		
	JGr	*LM*	*KS*
Imageability/Concreteness combined			
High (*n* = 50)	0.66	0.65	0.69
Low (*n* = 50)	0.53	0.61	0.48
Significance	*p* = .049	*ns*	*p* = .005
Familiarity			
High (*n* = 37)	0.63	0.69	0.65
Low (*n* = 37)	0.47	0.57	0.55
Significance	*p* = .026	*ns*	*ns*
Frequency			
High (*n* = 50)	0.52	0.64	0.64
Low (*n* = 50)	0.60	0.58	0.57
Significance	*ns*	*ns*	*ns*
Familiarity & Frequency combined			
High (50)	0.61	0.66	0.63
Low (50)	0.45	0.51	0.55
Significance	*p* = .017	*p* = .024	*ns*
Age of acquisition			
High (n = 40)	0.44	0.54	0.35
How (n = 40)	0.57	0.65	0.66
Significance	*ns*	*ns*	*p* = .002
Number of syllables			
One (*n* = 25)	0.52	0.62	0.46
Two (*n* = 30)	0.42	0.52	0.53
Three (*n* = 25)	0.34	0.58	0.84
Significance	*p* = .050	*ns*	*p* = .001

Performance in naming subsets matched for psycholinguistic variables, in terms of proportions correct and exact levels of significant differences (one-tailed; from Fisher exact test or, for number of syllables, Jonckheere trend test).

(p = .026), and familiarity/frequency together (p = .017). There was, in addition, a marginally significant effect of word length, with longer words named less accurately than shorter words (p = .050).

LM had rather better oral naming than JGr, scoring an average of 63% correct but had a similar degree of item (in)consistency (C = 0.29). LM produced very few semantic errors (4%) and instead produced a lot of "other" responses, usually comprising a gesture and/or initial letter tracing. He was not significantly affected by any of the variables investigated except for familiarity/frequency taken together (p = .024).

KS had a similar degree of naming impairment to LM, scoring 61% correct. However, KS showed a higher degree of item consistency in her naming (C = 0.46). KS, like JGr, produced both no-response and semantically related errors but in more similar proportions (18% and 12% respectively). Again, like JGr, she showed a significant effect of imageability/concreteness (p = .005). KS's significant length effect (p = .001) was the reverse of that found in most other people with aphasia: the longer the word the easier it was for her to produce. KS's naming accuracy was also significantly affected by age of acquisition (p = .002).

The results of testing word and nonword repetition are shown in Table 4. JGr is significantly more accurate in repetition than naming ($p < .001$), but repeats nonwords poorly, indicating that real-word repetition must rely at least in part on lexical mechanisms. LM is more accurate in repetition than naming, but the trend is not significant ($p = .08$). Like JGr he is much less accurate in nonword repetition, again indicating the use of lexical information in word repetition. KM repeats real words flawlessly and is also very good at nonword repetition. All three participants are able to repeat single phonemes.

Discussion of results from Experiment 1

At the end of the introduction, the characteristics of two levels of breakdown in naming were outlined. As a result, from the patients' naming performance alone, it is possible to formulate a working hypothesis as to the level of breakdown in word retrieval for each of them.

JGr had a moderate oral naming impairment and produced a very large proportion of no responses and a smaller number of semantic errors. We argued in the introduction, on the basis of Funnell and Hodges (1991) and Howard and Orchard-Lisle (1984), that both semantic errors and omissions might indicate a semantic impairment. The significant effect of imageability/concreteness supports the hypothesis of a semantic impairment. The effects of familiarity and familiarity/frequency are consistent with a lexical access problem resulting either from the semantic impairment or from an additional problem at the level of the POL. Finally, the possibility of some post-lexical impairment is suggested by the length effect, although JGr made few phonologically-related errors. Our initial hypothesis is that JGr's naming impairment is primarily due to an impairment either to semantics or in the process of output from semantics. Because nonword repetition is impaired, real-word repetition has to rely on a combination of information from impaired lexical and sub-lexical mechanisms resulting in better performance than in naming, but still below normal.

In contrast to JGr, LM produced very few semantic errors, was not significantly affected by imageability/concreteness, and was able at times to gesture or trace the initial letter of a target word. Our initial interpretation was that LM did not have any

TABLE 4
Proportions correct in repetition compared to naming of the same items ($n = 48$)

	JGr		LM		KS	
	Naming	*Repetition*	*Naming*	*Repetition*	*Naming*	*Repetition*
Correct	0.44	0.88	0.50	0.75	0.54	1.00
Semantic errors	0.13	0.00	0.10	0.00	0.15	0.00
Phonological errors	0.02	0.08	0.08	0.10	0.00	0.00
Other errors	0.08	0.02	0.13	0.02	0.04	0.00
No responses	0.33	0.02	0.19	0.13	0.27	0.00
Nonword repetition ($n = 30$)		0.43		0.40		0.93
Phoneme repetition ($n = 20$)		1.00		0.95		0.95

semantic impairment and instead had an impairment at the level of the POL. Since he showed quite low item consistency, a deficit of access rather than an impairment of the lexical representations themselves seems more likely (Shallice, 1987, 1988). He makes few phonologically related errors, and shows no length effect in naming, suggesting that post-lexical phonological assembly is intact. As with JGr, LM has to rely on a combination of impaired lexical and sub-lexical mechanisms in word repetition.

Like JGr, KS made a considerable number of semantic errors and was significantly affected by the semantic variable imageability/concreteness. The effect of age-of-acquisition on performance could be compatible with a semantic deficit, as early-acquired words may be more richly represented at a semantic level. However, this effect is also compatible with a deficit to lexical phonological representations with, as Brown and Watson (1987) suggest, early-acquired words more stably represented. The reverse word length effect might also be interpreted as evidence for an impairment to lexical representations (Best, 1995), and the high level of consistency would be compatible with a storage deficit (Shallice, 1987). The lack of phonological errors and flawless word repetition indicate that post-lexical phonological assembly is intact.

Howard and Orchard-Lisle (1984) argued that correct phonemic cues should aid word retrieval in patients who were addressing the POL with information that activated the target entry (and maybe others) but which was insufficient to make the representation available for output. These cues should, therefore, be effective both with participants with impairment at a semantic level and with those with an impairment of access to the lexicon. Miscues, on the other hand, should only elicit incorrect, semantically related responses from participants with a semantic impairment, since it is only for these participants that semantic coordinates would be partially activated. This first experiment showed that both JGr and KS make substantial numbers of semantic errors and are affected by the imageability/concreteness of the target. We therefore predict that they should both benefit from correct cues and be adversely affected by miscues. LM, on the other hand, shows no evidence of a semantic impairment. There is no evidence of a post-lexical impairment—his naming accuracy is unaffected by word length, and phonologically related errors are rare. As his naming is rather inconsistent, the most plausible interim interpretation is that LM's impairment is in access to the POL where, as with the patients described by Kay and Ellis (1987) and Caramazza and Hillis (1990), correct retrieval is more likely for higher-familiarity/frequency items. We predict, therefore, that LM will benefit from correct cues, but be unaffected by miscues.

EXPERIMENT 2: AN INVESTIGATION OF PHONEMICALLY CUED AND MISCUED NAMING

Stimuli

The stimulus pictures used in this experiment were the same set of 194 black and white line drawings that were used in Experiment 1. However, different subsets of pictures were used for different cueing conditions. Thus, all 194 items (Sets A–D) were used for the initial phoneme (IP) cue condition while only 49 items (Set A) were used for the cue-miscue condition. Rime cues were assessed on a subset of 48 items

(Set B) and consonant-vowel (CV) cues were assessed on 42 items, which comprised Set B but excluding any targets with a CV structure alone. In the IP condition, the cue comprised the initial consonant of the target word followed by schwa. The CV cues comprised both the initial consonant and vowel of the target word while the "rime cues" comprised all of the phonemes of the word excluding the initial phoneme. Miscues comprised the initial phoneme of a semantic coordinate of the target word followed by schwa. Thus for the target word *dog*, the IP cue was /dǝ/, the CV cue was /dɒ/, the rime cue was /ɒg/ and the miscue was /kǝ/ (for cat).

Method

All cueing conditions were administered in parallel with oral naming, over a minimum of four sessions. Thus, on the first assessment session, while sets A and B were presented for naming sets, C and D were presented with initial phoneme cues. On subsequent sessions the sets and conditions were reversed. A second naming baseline of sets A to D was alternated with the other cueing conditions. In the cue-miscue condition, miscues were presented together with correct initial phoneme cues and these cues and miscues were randomly ordered. As a result the cue-miscue investigation took place over two sessions, so that each item was presented twice, on one occasion with the target phoneme and the other with the miscue. In the cue-miscue condition the patients were informed that either the correct sound or the sound of a closely related word might be given to them, and to be careful not to be "caught out" by them. In other cueing conditions the patients were informed to listen for the cue that would provide them with some of the sounds of the target word.

All cues were given to the patient simultaneously with the presentation of the picture. In this way it was possible to use the same 10-second response-time cut-off criterion as used in Experiment 1. In addition we were able to eliminate the risk of confounding the effects of cues with merely giving the patient extra time in which to name (cf. Bruce & Howard, 1988). The same scoring system was used as in Experiment 1 and reaction times for correct responses in all conditions were recorded.

Results

Effects of correct cues. Each patient's correct responses in the uncued naming condition were compared with those in each of the IP cue, CV cue, and rime cue conditions, using McNemar's test. A one-tailed level of significance was used for all statistical analyses as each patient's performance had been predicted after Experiment 1. The proportions correct in each condition for each patient and significant differences as compared with uncued naming of the same items are given in Table 5.

JGr was significantly aided by all three types of cue. IP cues increased correct responses from 53% in uncued naming to 72% ($p < .001$). CV cues increased naming from 52% to 77% ($p = .007$) and rime cues increased naming performance from 63% to 96% ($p < .001$).

LM also benefited significantly from each of the three types of cue. IP cues raised performance from 60% on uncued naming to 71% ($p = .008$). CV cues had a more

TABLE 5
Proportions correct in uncued naming

Task	Uncued (n = 194)	IP (n = 194)	Uncued (n = 42)	CV (n = 42)	Uncued (n = 48)	Rime (n = 48)
JGr	0.53	0.72**	0.52	0.77**	0.63	0.96**
LM	0.60	0.71**	0.62	0.93**	0.63	0.87*
KS	0.61	0.62	0.64	0.86**	0.65	0.87**

Proportions correct in uncued naming compared with initial phoneme cued (IP), CV, and Rime cued naming of same items.
Significance level when compared with uncued naming of same items: * $p < .05$, ** $p < .01$

striking effect, raising correct responses from 62% to 93% ($p = .002$), and rime cues improved naming from 63% to 87% correct ($p = .014$).

In contrast to JGr and LM, KS did not benefit from IP cues: There was no difference between her uncued and IP cued naming performance (61% and 62% respectively). However, CV cues did improve performance from 62% to 93% correct ($p = .008$) and rime cues raised the proportion of correct responses from 65% to 87% ($p = .003$).

Effects of miscues. In the analysis of the cue-miscue condition, each patient's correct responses in the no-cue condition was compared with those in the miscue and the correct cue conditions, using McNemar's test. In addition, McNemar's test was used to compare the number of semantic errors, no-response errors, and "other" errors in uncued naming and miscued naming. The mean response times for correct responses, in seconds, for each of the three conditions were also calculated. Reaction times in each of the cued conditions were compared with RT in the uncued baseline, using related t tests for those items correctly named in both conditions. A one-tailed level of significance was used for each statistical analysis as each patient's performance had been predicted at the end of Experiment 1. The results for all three patients in the cue-miscue condition are presented in Table 6.

Once again, JGr benefited significantly from correct cues ($p = .001$) but he also proved to be significantly miscueable ($p < .001$). Miscueing not only dramatically reduced correct naming from 67% to 18%, but also significantly increased semantic errors to 37%. This proportion was significantly greater than the 10% produced in uncued naming of set A ($p < .005$). In addition, in the miscue condition, 15 of JGr's 18 semantic errors are the targeted miscue coordinate. JGr showed no significant difference in his RTs for correct responses in the miscue condition as compared with uncued naming.

LM was significantly more accurate with correct cues compared with uncued naming (74% and 57% correct respectively; $p = .049$). In contrast, miscues did not significantly affect his naming accuracy ($p = .084$). However, there was clearly a trend towards miscueability, with the proportion of correct responses reduced to 43% when a miscue was given. However, analysis of errors shows no increase in the number of semantic errors in the miscued condition: LM produced just 4% semantic errors in both uncued and miscued naming, and none of his semantic errors was a miscued coordinate. His reaction times in the miscue condition were significantly slower than uncued naming, $t(14) = 5.37$, $p < .0005$: It took LM a mean of 2.94

TABLE 6
Cue–miscue condition

Patient	Response	Naming condition		
		Uncued	Correct cue	Miscue
JGr	Correct	0.49	0.80**	0.18**
	Semantic	0.10	0.08	0.37**
	No response	0.37	0.04**	0.39
	Other errors	0.04	0.08	0.06
	Mean RT (seconds)	2.65	1.88	3.71
LM	Correct	0.57	0.74*	0.43
	Semantic	0.04	0.00	0.04
	No-response	0.16	0.08	0.22
	Other errors	0.23	0.16	0.31
	Mean RT (seconds)	2.94	3.56	6.49*
KS	Correct	0.71	0.76	0.41**
	Semantic	0.08	0.08	0.35**
	No-response	0.12	0.10	0.20
	Other errors	0.09	0.06	0.04
	Mean RT (seconds)	2.16	1.77	2.88

Proportion of correct responses with mean reaction times (RT) and proportion of errors for each patient in cue-miscue condition compared with naming 1 ($n = 49$ in each condition).

Significance level when compared with uncued naming performance on same items: * $p < .05$, ** $p < .005$

seconds to correctly name items when no cue was given but 6.49 seconds when a miscue had been given.

KS's response to IP cues was consistent with her previous performance: she was no better with a correct cue than in uncued naming. However, miscues did have a significant detrimental effect on naming: Correct responses were significantly reduced from 71% to 41% correct when a miscue was given ($p = .001$). In addition, semantic errors significantly increased from 8% with no cue to 35% with a miscue; in the miscue condition, 15 of her 17 semantic errors were the coordinate corresponding to the miscue. In reaction times for correct responses, KS was not significantly slower in the miscue condition than she was with no cue.

Discussion of results from Experiment 2

On the basis of naming performance in Experiment 1, a number of working hypotheses and predictions were made for each of the three patients. These predictions were tested in Experiment 2 by investigating the effects of correct and incorrect phonemic cues as compared to uncued naming. On the basis of his performance in Experiment 1, we argued that JGr had a semantic impairment, and should both benefit from correct phonemic cues and be hindered by miscues. The results of this experiment support those predictions. JGr was significantly better at naming when a correct cue was given, and the greater the amount of phonological information given the greater the benefit. Thus, CV cues were more effective than IP cues, but rime cues were more effective than all other cues. In addition, JGr's naming was found to be significantly poorer when a miscue was given, and he produced significantly more semantic errors in response to miscues, the majority of which were the targeted miscued coordinate. However, JGr was not significantly slower in his correct response reaction times in the miscue condition as compared with those in uncued naming. Therefore, it could not be argued that his reduction in performance with miscues was merely the result of a slowing of his responses making him unable to name before the 10-second cut-off point. All these findings consistently added up to strong support for JGr's hypothesised semantic impairment.

We argued that LM's performance would contrast with JGr's, since LM was thought to have a lexical access deficit. Thus, he would be cueable but not miscueable. Again these predictions were supported. LM was significantly aided by all types of cues, with CV and rime cues rather more effective than IP cues. There was no significant effect of miscues, although there was a trend in this direction. Since there was no increase in semantic errors it seemed unlikely that this was a true miscueing effect. Instead, the large difference between his reaction times in uncued naming and miscued naming suggests that this difference might be explained by a slowing down of LM's production of correct responses when a miscue is given. We therefore concluded that this slowing down reflects an interference effect that resulted from semantic coordinates receiving extra activation from the miscue. Such interference would slow down LM's naming and thus prevent the production of a correct response before that 10-second cut-off. We suggest that this slowing with miscues may be characteristic of patients with intact semantics and an impairment in lexical access. This is because intact semantics would allow the person with aphasia to detect and inhibit any semantic errors. This would prevent them being miscued but may well slow down response times. Similar slowing by the activation of semantic competitors has been observed in normal participants' latencies (Howard, Nickels, Coltheart, & Cole-Virtue, 2006; Wheeldon & Monsell, 1994). This argument is supported by the fact that LM's slowed performance was in marked contrast to that of JGr who, with a semantic deficit, showed no such slowing and did produce semantic errors in the miscue condition.

KS's results are less readily interpreted. We had argued on the basis of Experiment 1 that KS had a semantic impairment, and we predicted that she would, like JGr, benefit from correct phonemic cues and be adversely affected by miscues. However, she did not even show a trend towards being cued by initial phonemes. Nevertheless, partial phonological information about the sought-for word did significantly improve KS's naming: both CV and rime cues resulted in highly significant improvements in naming. One possible interpretation is that KS needed rather more phonological information than the initial phoneme alone provided to facilitate lexical access. Some support for this view came from our finding that JGr and LM's naming also benefited more from CV and rime cues than IP cues. Thus all three participants seemed to benefit from more phonological information. However, this did not explain why a single initial phoneme in the form of a miscue had substantial effects on KS's naming. Miscues both significantly reduced correct responses and significantly increased semantic errors in naming. Although this was in keeping with the working hypothesis regarding KS's semantic impairment, it was difficult to reconcile with the absence of any effect of correct IP cues. An alternative proposal, which we will pursue in Experiment 4, was that the IP cues provided no more information to KS than that which she was already using; we will test the hypothesis that KS does not benefit from IP cues because she is, in effect, already providing her own phonemic cues when she is naming pictures unaided (cf. Howard & Harding, 1998).

Predictions for Experiment 3

In Experiment 3, we tested our patients' ability to access precise semantic information from words and pictures. Our argument that LM had a breakdown in access to the phonological output lexicon from the semantic system was firmly supported by the cueing investigations. We could therefore predict that LM, when investigated in Experiment 3, would demonstrate intact semantic comprehension in either or both the auditory and written modalities, consistent with the view that central semantic representations are intact, at least for picturable items. Our argument that KS and JGr, in contrast to LM, both had a semantic impairment had also been supported by the miscueing investigation. We could, therefore, predict that both JGr and KS would be found to have significant degrees of impairment in semantically mediated tasks such as comprehension of spoken and written words.

EXPERIMENT 3: INVESTIGATION OF SEMANTIC COMPREHENSION

Stimuli and method

Four assessments of semantic comprehension were administered to each patient over the period when the naming assessments in Experiments 1 and 2 were conducted.

Auditory word-to-picture matching and written word-to-picture matching (Kay, Lesser, & Coltheart, 1992). Both these assessments use the same picture stimuli, ordered differently for each modality version. Each of the 40 items takes the form of an array of five black and white line drawings; the target picture (e.g., hat), a close semantic distractor (coat), a distant semantic distractor (sock), a visually related distractor (iron), and an unrelated distractor (ironing board). The patients were tested on the different modality versions on separate occasions. For each version the patients were presented with the five pictures and the written or spoken target word, and simply had to point to the corresponding picture. We consider a normal score to be one within two standard deviations of the normal mean. For the auditory version this is 93% correct or above and for the written version 94% correct or above.

Auditory synonym judgements (Coltheart, 1980). In this test pairs of words were presented to the patients in the auditory modality. Patients had to judge if the two words had the same meaning or not. There were 38 pairs of high-imageability words and 38 low-imageability words, half of which were synonymous and half of which were not. These pairs were randomly ordered and presented one at a time, and the patients simply responded with a yes or a no judgement. A score that is within normal limits is considered to be within two standard deviations of the normal mean. For the high-imageability version this is 97% or above and for the low-imageability items, 94% or above.

Pyramids and Palm Trees: Three picture version (Howard & Patterson, 1992). In this test of non-verbal semantic comprehension each patient was presented with triads of pictures ($n = 52$). The top picture was the target picture to which one of a pair of related pictures below had to be matched. The patient had to simply point to one of the lower pictures, which was more associated with the target picture. For example, the picture of a pyramid had to be matched with either a pine tree or a palm tree. The lower limit of the normal range on this test is 94%. Howard and Patterson argue that normal performance on this test is only possible if complete semantic information is consistently available from pictures.

Picture-name verification. This test used the same set of pictures and semantic coordinates that were used for the miscueing condition in Experiment 2. The patients were presented with each picture on three different occasions. On each occasion they were asked if a spoken word was the appropriate name for the picture. This spoken word could be the correct name (e.g., "lion"), a semantically related word (e.g., "tiger"), or a phonologically related word (e.g., "iron"). The patients simply gave a yes/no response. Correct names, semantic coordinates, and phonologically related items were interspersed and randomly ordered, with each picture presented only once in each session, so the test took three sessions in total. No feedback was given to the patients as to whether they were right or wrong.

Results

The results are shown in Table 7. JGr was outside the range of normal control participants' performance on spoken and written word-to-picture matching, auditory synonym judgements, and the three-picture version of Pyramids and Palm Trees. In picture-name verification he accepted 20% of semantic co-ordinates as correct names for the pictures, which indicated a considerable impairment.

LM, in contrast, was well within the normal range on every assessment, and successfully rejected every semantic coordinate in picture-name verification.

KS was impaired relative to normal controls in spoken word-to-picture matching and her errors were all semantic coordinates. In the three-picture Pyramids and Palm Trees her performance was also below the norm, and in picture-name verification she accepted 20% of semantic coordinates as correct picture names. In synonym judgements, her scores were within the normal range. This task, however, requires less detailed semantics than the other tasks; matching pairs are close synonyms and non-matching pairs are semantically unrelated, so that accurate performance can be achieved with only partial semantic information. KS's data were therefore consistent

TABLE 7
Proportions correct on assessments of semantic comprehension

	JGr	LM	KS
PALPA Word-to-Picture Matching (n = 40)			
Auditory	0.75*	1.00	0.87*
Visual	0.67*	0.97	nt
Picture Name Verification (set A; n = 49)			
Target	1.00	0.98	0.98
Semantic coordinate	0.80	1.00	0.80
Phonologically related	1.00	1.00	0.96
Coltheart Auditory Synonym Judgements (n = 38)			
High imageability	0.84*	1.00	1.00
Low imageability	0.71*	0.95	0.95
Pyramids & Palm Trees (n = 52)			
Three-picture version	0.88*	0.98	0.81*

nt – not tested.
* Scores impaired relative to normal control participants.

with the prediction that she had degraded semantic representations, for some items at least. Therefore representations she retrieved did not reliably distinguish between the correct target and other closely related category members.

Discussion of results of Experiment 3

The results of this experiment supported the characterisations of these patients from the results of Experiments 1 and 2. Both JGr and KS showed evidence of semantic impairment in both word and picture comprehension, as well as in their naming and cueing performance. LM showed no signs of impairment to semantic representations in any of these tasks.

The remaining puzzle was why KS did not benefit from correct initial phoneme cues. The results from all the experiments were consistent with the view that, in naming, KS addressed the output lexicon with partial semantic information, which resulted in activation of a range of semantically related phonological word forms. This resulted in semantic errors in naming when one of the semantically related items reached its output threshold before the target. With an initial phoneme miscue, additional activation to the phonological form of a semantic coordinate from the cue could result in its production as an error. Additional activation from the correct initial phoneme as a cue should also have resulted in an increased rate of correct responses.

In the next experiment we investigate the possibility that KS generates her own phonemic cues internally. Bruce and Howard (1988) argue that patients will be able to generate their own phonemic cues to aid word retrieval if (i) they know the initial letter of words that they cannot produce, (ii) they can generate the sound corresponding to this letter, and (iii) they benefit from therapist-given phonemic cues. With 23 non-fluent aphasic patients, they found no participants who showed all three of these abilities. However, Nickels (1992) trained a patient, TC, who had much better written than spoken naming and who benefited from phonemic cues given by the experimenter to generate his own cues. Initially, TC could not sound any individual letters, but Nickels taught him to do this in a short training programme, and to use this to generate his own cues. This resulted in spoken naming improving to the level of accuracy he achieved in written naming.

To establish whether our three patients had the resources necessary to generate their own cues, in Experiment 4 we investigated their knowledge of initial letters of items presented for naming, their written naming, and knowledge of letter–sound correspondences.

EXPERIMENT 4: GRAPHEME–PHONEME KNOWLEDGE

Stimuli

Two subsets of the 194 black and white line drawings used in Experiments 1 and 2 were used in this experiment. Subset D ($n = 49$) was used to assess written naming, and the 48 items from set C, printed in block capitals, were randomly ordered and used to assess oral reading accuracy. Twenty block capital letters of the alphabet were also used to assess each patient's single grapheme-to-phoneme correspondence knowledge. The patients' ability to indicate initial letters of words was assessed using the 48 pictures of set D; letter knowledge was shown by pointing to an initial letter from a choice of 10 uppercase letters.

Method

All of the tasks in this experiment were conducted over a number of sessions in parallel with other assessments. In the written naming investigation, each of the pictures from set D were presented in turn for the patients to name. They were not allowed to orally name the picture before writing it. In contrast to oral naming, the 10-second time limit was not enforced as JGr and LM both wrote with their non-preferred hands. A modified version of the classification system from Experiments 1 and 2 was used to categorise responses. In the reading aloud task each patient was presented with printed words from set C and asked to read them aloud. In this task the 10-second response-time criterion was enforced. The participants' responses were tape recorded, transcribed, and categorised using the same classification system as in Experiments 1 and 2. In the grapheme-to-phoneme conversion task, a considerable amount of explanation was given. Then each letter was presented to the patient in turn and they were asked to produce the appropriate sound. Their final response was scored, using a right/wrong scoring system. In assessing knowledge of initial letters, patients were asked to indicate the appropriate letter and then name the picture.

Analysis

The proportion correct for each patient in the written naming task was calculated as was the proportion of close spelling errors, the proportion of items where the initial letter was correct, and the proportion of no-responses. All four categories of response for each of the three patients are given in Table 8. In addition, each patient's written naming was compared to their oral naming of the same items both in naming 1 and naming 2 using McNemar's test with a two-tailed significance level. The percentage correct for each patient in reading aloud was calculated and this was also compared with naming of the same items in both naming 1 and 2. Once again McNemar's test and a two-tailed level of significance was used. The proportions

TABLE 8
Written naming, reading aloud, and letter–sound conversion

	JGr	LM	KS
Written naming (set D)			
Correct	0.00	0.02	0.67
Close spelling error	0.00	0.02	0.12
Initial letter written	0.08	0.78	0.06
No response	0.92	0.18	0.15
Spoken naming (set D)	0.50	0.65	0.59
Real word reading aloud (set C)	0.85	0.46	0.96
Letter-to-sound conversion	0.35	0.05	0.95
Indicating initial letters (set D)			
Pictures named correctly	0.29**(24)	1.0***(27)	1.0***(28)
Pictures not named correctly	0.08 (24)	0.81***(21)	0.25* (20)

Proportions correct and errors in written naming ($n = 49$) and proportions correct in reading aloud ($n = 48$) and letter–sound conversion ($n = 20$).
*$p < .05$, **$p < .01$, ***$p < .001$.
Numbers in parentheses indicate the number of items in each cell.

correct in written naming and reading aloud and significant differences from naming 1 or 2 are given in Table 8. Finally, the proportions of sounds correctly derived from their corresponding letters were calculated and are also given in Table 8. The patients' accuracy in indicating initial letters is given separately for items named correctly and incorrectly in Table 8. The exact binomial test was used to assess whether performance was significantly better than chance.

Results

JGr was severely impaired in all aspects of written naming. He was unable to write the name of any single item, and he wrote the initial letter for only four items, with the remaining responses being omissions. He was rather more successful at indicating initial letters from a written choice where, for items he could name correctly, he chose the correct initial letter on 7/24 occasions ($p = .008$). He achieved some success in letter–sound conversion (7/20 correct), and oral reading was significantly better than spoken naming of the same items ($p < .001$ relative to both naming tests).

LM was also severely impaired in written naming with only one correct response, but on 80% of trials he was able to offer at least the initial letter of the word. This good knowledge of initial letters was confirmed by his excellent ability to indicate initial letters of both the words that he could produce and, with a high level of accuracy, even for the pictures that he did not name correctly. However, LM cannot use this initial letter information to generate his own internal phonemic cues, as his knowledge of letter–sound correspondences is very severely impaired. His reading is at an equivalent level to his spoken naming of the same items (46% and 52% respectively). His deficit in accessing lexical phonological representations from semantics affects both reading and naming equivalently, suggesting, together with his letter–sound correspondence impairment, that LM is reading via semantics. His reading errors support this view; there are a number of semantic errors including PYRAMID→"pharaohs", TOMATO→"pineapple, no", and LAMB→"nice meat", and a visual-then-semantic error :BUCKLE→"pail".

KS's written naming was far superior to that of JGr and LM, scoring 67% correct. Since KS had been able to orally name a mean of 58% (naming 1 and 2) of the same items, written naming appeared to be superior, although not significantly. Nevertheless, KS also produced six (12%) close approximations of the target, such as "DINSCORE" for the target "dinosaur" and "CULINDER" for "colander", suggesting that she is better at accessing the appropriate orthographic form of a word than its phonological form. She was perfect in indicating the initial letter of items she could name correctly, and better than chance ($p = .04$) although very inaccurate with those she did not name correctly. She was also very good at letter–sound correspondences, indicating that she had the necessary information to generate her own cues. KS also proved to be near perfect at reading aloud, with 96% correct. This was very much better than her naming of the same items (50% correct).

Discussion of results from Experiment 4

The results of this experiment show that KS has good written naming in comparison to spoken naming, and good knowledge of initial letters. She also has excellent letter–sound conversion abilities. The implication is that she has all the necessary abilities to provide her own phonemic cues in naming. This resolves the puzzle of the ineffectiveness of initial phoneme cues on her naming. She is, we propose, generating her own initial phoneme cues during spoken naming attempts; a cue given by the experimenter simply duplicates the partial phonological information she already has. When the experimenter gives her CV cues or rime cues, KS's naming improves substantially (Experiment 1); this suggests that self-generated cues are probably confined to the initial phoneme of the word.

Two interesting implications follow from these findings with KS. First, her relatively good written naming puts a lower bound on the extent of her semantic impairment. For those items where she can access the correct orthographic lexical specifications for output, she must have reasonably good semantic information. We would suggest that she accesses the correct lexical specification for not only the 67% of items she writes the names of correctly, but also the 12% of items where she produces a close spelling error. Her semantic representations are, therefore, at least sufficient for retrieval of approximately 80% of written picture names.

Second, if KS's uncued naming represents in effect self-cued naming, her (uncued) baseline ability to access phonology on the basis of semantic information alone must be lower than that apparently found. We can roughly estimate this accuracy level on the basis of JGr's performance. His uncued naming accuracy (49%) fell exactly midway between performance with a correct cue (80%) and a miscue (18%). Applying this to KS, we estimate that her uncued baseline naming accuracy might be around 58% (her miscued naming was 41% and her cued naming was 76% correct).

These two interpretations taken together lead us to conclude that KS, in addition to her semantic impairment, also has a difficulty in accessing the phonological output lexicon or impairment to that lexicon. Such a deficit would account for the discrepancy between her written naming ability and her uncued naming ability. Her high level of accuracy with CV cues and rime cues (86% and 87% correct) suggests that lexical representations are largely intact and it is a difficulty in lexical access that is responsible.

GENERAL DISCUSSION

At the end of the introduction two levels of breakdown in aphasic naming were summarised in Table 1. We subsequently conducted a series of experiments in order to discover whether uncued and cued naming investigations could serve to identify the level of breakdown in each of our three patients. In Experiment 1 we investigated the picture-naming performance of JGr, LM, and KS. JGr and KS both produced significant proportions of semantic errors and their naming accuracy was affected by an item's imageability/concreteness, while LM produced few semantic errors and his naming accuracy was unaffected by imageability/concreteness. As a result we argued that JGr and KS had an underlying semantic deficit while LM did not. In the second and third experiments we tested our hypotheses concerning each patient's level of deficit by investigating the effects of phonemic cues and miscues and by assessing semantic comprehension.

Our findings concerning JGr and LM were very straightforward, since all JGr's results pointed towards a semantic deficit and all LM's indicated an impairment of access to the phonological output lexicon. In fact, JGr was found to bear a striking similarity to Howard and Orchard-Lisle's (1984) patient JCU who, like JGr, was cueable, miscueable, and had impaired semantic comprehension. LM on the other hand bore many similarities to Kay and Ellis's (1987) EST as he was cueable but not miscueable and had intact semantic comprehension. While a comparison of EST and JCU has often been used to illustrate the distinction between semantic and post semantic impairments (e.g., Ellis & Young, 1988; Ellis, Franklin, & Crerar, 1994; Ellis, Kay, & Franklin, 1992), there are difficulties in making the comparison. JCU was profoundly aphasic with virtually no ability to access appropriate phonological word forms in her speech production. EST was very much better at naming, and made both semantic and phonological errors in naming; the original descriptions of EST offer no account of these semantic errors. JGR and LM are much more clearly comparable: they have similar levels of naming accuracy, similar degrees of severity of aphasia and the same classification as Broca's aphasics on the WAB. Yet, as we have shown, they have sharply contrasting underlying disorders responsible for their difficulties in word retrieval.

LM seems to be a very clear case of a patient with a difficulty in access to phonological lexical representations for output. All our investigations suggest that semantic representations are intact. Since he produces 93% correct naming responses with CV cues, his phonological representations are largely intact. The correct word is more likely to be retrieved with items that are higher in familiarity and frequency, but naming accuracy is not significantly affected by rated age-of-acquisition. This finding casts severe doubt on Hirsh and Ellis's (1994) suggestion that age-of-acquisition effects will be associated with an impairment in phonological word form retrieval, but accords with Nickels' (1995) demonstration that familiarity effects are associated with post-semantic breakdowns in naming.

We noted in the introduction that patients whose underlying impairment lie, it has been argued, in the process of lexical retrieval make a variety of different patterns of errors. Kay and Ellis's (1987) EST and Caramazza and Hillis's (1990) HW make both semantic and phonological errors in naming. RGB, reported by Caramazza and Hillis (1990), made semantic errors and offered definitions of the item. In contrast, our patient LM characteristically made no responses, produced appropriate gesture, or indicated some partial orthographic knowledge. LM made very few semantic errors and resembles Zingeser and Berndt's (1988) patient HY, who made primarily circumlocution and no response errors, like the patients reported by Lambon Ralph et al. (2000). LM might well have circumlocuted instead of gesturing had he been more fluent. The suggestion here is that true semantic errors do not occur with this level of deficit, but that semantic information may be offered when no appropriate response is available (see Caramazza & Hillis, 1990).[5] This suggests that the production of semantic errors may have been under the patients' strategic control. Such performance would also be in keeping with Howard's (1995) patient EE, who circumlocutes as a result of a lexical storage deficit. Clearly, miscueing is one technique that would help to distinguish the cause of the semantic errors. Note that these different patterns of errors in patients whose primary impairment lies in the mapping from semantics to phonology may be problematic to understand in terms of theories that propose a single stage in this mapping (e.g., Allport, 1985; Caramazza, 1997; Lambon Ralph et al., 2002; Lambon Ralph et al., 2000). They may be much

---

[5] There is some suggestion that the occurrence of semantic errors in Caramazza and Hillis's patients may be under strategic control. While they made substantial proportions of semantic errors in picture naming, there are no clear examples of semantic errors in word retrieval when they are defining written words.

more easily understood in terms of theories that propose an intermediate level of lexical representation—in Levelt's terms, the lemma—(e.g., Butterworth, 1980, 1983; Dell, Schwartz, Martin, Saffran, & Gagnon, 1997; Levelt, 1989; Levelt, Roelofs, & Meyer, 1999; for discussion in relation to disorders of word retrieval see Nickels & Howard, 2000). Impairments in the mapping from semantics to the lemma may result in activation of a range of semantically related lexical items leading to in clear semantic errors. In contrast, deficits in the mapping from lemmas to phonological lexical representations may result in a difficulty in activation of lexical representations and perhaps better retrieval of items that are more distinctive in phonological space—leading to a reverse length effect

JGr's impairment is just that which we predicted should be shown by a patient with a central semantic impairment. His naming is characterised by semantic errors, and naming accuracy is affected by target imageability/concreteness. He can be phonemically cued to produce correct responses, and miscueing elicits semantic errors. Comprehension of spoken and written words is also impaired. The co-occurrence of semantic errors and imageability/concreteness effects is as found by Nickels and Howard (1994). The familiarity effect on JGr's naming was not predicted but fits with the findings of Funnell and Sheridan (1992) that low-familiarity items may be more susceptible to semantic impairment. The effects of both miscues and correct cues on JGr's naming suggest that the impairment results in underspecified semantic representations being used to address output phonology. GLT, a person with aphasia with a central semantic deficit—as demonstrated by, for instance acceptance of semantic foils in word–picture verification—showed, like JGr, improved naming with correct phonemic cues and reduced accuracy with miscues (Hillis & Caramazza, 1995).

While the miscueing effect is consistent with a central semantic impairment that results in a range of phonological word forms being addressed by underspecified semantic representations, we do not wish to claim that all patients with central semantic impairments will necessarily be susceptible to miscueing. It is possible, for instance, that a central semantic impairment could result in underactivation of the correct entry in the phonological lexicon without substantial activation of semantic competitors. Further detailed case studies will be necessary to resolve this issue. It is also possible that, as Caramazza and Hillis (1990) argue for their patient RGB, a post-lexical deficit in the mapping from semantics to the POL can result in activation of a range of semantically related items. In this case, we would also predict both cueing and miscueing effects.

There are two aspects of KS's performance that are unusual. First, she is only the third patient described who is better at retrieving longer words than shorter words—a reverse length effect (the previous cases are described by Best, 1995, and Lambon Ralph & Howard, 2000). Second, all previous reports of patients whose performance is adversely affected by single phoneme miscues also benefit from correct initial phoneme cues (Hillis & Caramazza, 1995; Howard & Orchard-Lisle, 1984; Katz & Lanzoni, 1997; Lambon Ralph et al., 2000). KS is unique in showing substantially reduced performance with miscues, but no benefit from correct initial phoneme cues.

As a result, KS showed a less readily predictable pattern of impairment than JGr or LM. She showed the same characteristics as JGr in naming, comprehension, and cueing, with one striking exception. While she was adversely affected by initial phoneme miscues, correct initial phoneme cues had no effect. In Experiment 4 we showed that she both knew initial letters of words and had good knowledge of grapheme–phoneme correspondences, and we argued that correct initial phoneme cues had no effect because she was generating cues on-line in the process of naming. She was in effect spontaneously adopting the same self-cueing strategy that Nickels (1992) taught to her patient TC, and which Bruce and Howard (1987) used with a series of patients, providing the letter–sound correspondences from a computer aid.

In addition to her semantic deficit, KS clearly has a problem in access to phonological lexical representations; access to orthographic lexical representations is better even than her (self-cued) access to phonology. While the effect of imageability/ concreteness on word retrieval can clearly be attributed to her central semantic impairment, the effects of rated age-of-acquisition and the reverse word length effect are more probably related to the disorder of word retrieval. KS resembles CGJ reported by Best (1995) who also showed a reverse word length effect in word retrieval. One possible account of this is that the word representations for longer words are richer and more distinctive in the phonological domain, and therefore more resistant to degradation. Allport (1985) suggests that lexical phonological specifications may be implemented as an autoassociative phonological network; degradation within such a network will result in better performance for longer, more distinctive words. It is possible that the age-of-acquisition effects may be related to this: Brown and Watson (1987) have suggested that early-acquired words may be more completely represented at a phonological level.[6]

CONCLUSION

Converging information from the investigations of (i) cueing and miscueing, (ii) the properties affecting word retrieval, and (iii) the nature of errors and performance in comprehension tasks can be used to identify the locus of deficit in aphasic patients. The hypotheses made about our three patients on the basis of naming performance were reliably supported by the cueing data. The assessment of semantic comprehension merely served to confirm the reliability of the cueing technique as a basis for the identification of the level of breakdown in naming. This is because, as for example Lambon Ralph et al. (2000) point out, supported by a computational model (Lambon Ralph, McClelland, Patterson, Galton, & Hodges, 2001), there can be semantic impairment that is sufficient to impact on word retrieval, but that cannot be detected by conventional tests of comprehension. It is clear that good performance in tests of comprehension does not necessarily show that patients have semantics good enough to support word retrieval. In addition, we showed that when a patient such as KS does not appear to be cueable it may be necessary to look more

---

[6] This kind of account must be very tentative. First, it is not clear that this is a genuine effect of age-of-acquisition. As Walley and Metsala (1992) point out, when rating age-of-acquisition, participants do so with no direct knowledge of the age at which they acquired the word. They must do so on the basis of their beliefs about what makes words easier to acquire. For instance shorter, more concrete, and more frequent items get lower age-of-acquisition ratings. Some or all of the combination of factors used by normal participants in making age-of-acquisition ratings may be the actual factors influencing KS's word retrieval. Even if one accepts that the ratings do reflect true age-of-acquisition, the effects may occur either because of differences in how early-acquired words are represented (as Brown and Watson suggest), or because (some or all of) the factors that make words easier to acquire (e.g., being shorter, referring to separable objects, being higher in frequency etc., see Markman, 1989, for review) affect KS's word retrieval. One should also note that there is no direct evidence in favour of Brown and Watson's suggestion that early-acquired words differ in their phonological representations from words acquired later in life.

carefully at language-processing abilities and impairments in order to identify a combination of semantic and lexical access deficits. If we had not investigated miscueing in KS, an explanation for the apparent discrepancy with IP cues would not have been pursued and the dual nature of her impairment would not have been identified.

JGr and LM were superficially very similar in their aphasia. Both could be classified as having Broca's aphasia; they had similar levels of impairment in word retrieval. Yet we have clearly established that they have very different underlying levels of impairment in word retrieval. As Caramazza (1986) has pointed out, we should not assume that patients whose superficial appearance is similar necessarily have the same impairments; in-depth assessment employing converging evidence across a variety of tasks is necessary to identify the nature of a participant's impairment. Conclusions are too often drawn on the basis of a superficial and limited assessment.

REFERENCES

Allport, D. A. (1985). Distributed memory, modular subsystems and dysphasia. In S. K. Newman & R. Epstein (Eds.), *Current perspectives in dysphasia* (pp. 32–60). Edinburgh: Churchill Livingstone.

Best, W. (1995). A reverse length effect in dysphasic naming: When elephant is easier than ant. *Cortex, 31*(4), 637–652.

Breese, E. L., & Hillis, A. E. (2004). Auditory comprehension: Is multiple choice really good enough? *Brain and Language, 89*(1), 3–8.

Brown, G. D. A., & Watson, F. L. (1987). First in, first out: Word learning age and spoken word frequency as predictors of word familiarity and word naming latency. *Memory and Cognition, 15*, 208–216.

Bruce, C., & Howard, D. (1987). Computer-generated phonemic cues: An effective aid for naming in aphasia. *British Journal of Disorders of Communication, 22*, 191–201.

Bruce, C., & Howard, D. (1988). Why don't Broca's aphasics cue themselves? An investigation of phonemic cueing and tip-of-the-tongue information. *Neuropsychologia, 26*, 253–264.

Butterworth, B. L. (1980). Some constraints on models of language production. In B. L. Butterworth (Ed.), *Language production, Volume 1: Speech and talk*. London: Academic Press.

Butterworth, B. L. (1983). Lexical representation. In B. L. Butterworth (Ed.), *Language production, Volume 2: Development, writing and other language processes* (pp. 257–294). London: Academic Press.

Butterworth, B. L. (1992). Disorders of phonological encoding. *Cognition, 42*, 261–286.

Butterworth, B. L., Howard, D., & McLoughlin, P. J. (1984). The semantic deficit in aphasia: The relationship between semantic errors in auditory comprehension and picture naming. *Neuropsychologia, 22*, 409–426.

Caramazza, A. (1986). On drawing inferences about the structure of normal cognitive systems from the analysis of patterns of impaired performance – the case for single-patient studies. *Brain and Cognition, 5*(1), 41–66.

Caramazza, A. (1997). How many levels of processing are there in lexical access? *Cognitive Neuropsychology, 14*(1), 177–208.

Caramazza, A., & Hillis, A. E. (1990). Where do semantic errors come from? *Cortex, 26*, 95–122.

Carroll, J., & White, M. N. (1973). Word frequency and age-of-acquisition as determinants of picture-naming latency. *Quarterly Journal of Experimental Psychology, 25*, 85–95.

Coltheart, M. (1980). *Analysing acquired disorders of reading*. Unpublished manuscript: Birkbeck College.

Coltheart, M. (1981). The MRC psycholinguistic database. *Quarterly Journal of Experimental Psychology, 33A*, 497–505.

Dell, G. S., Schwartz, M. F., Martin, N., Saffran, E. M., & Gagnon, D. A. (1997). Lexical access in aphasic and nonaphasic speakers. *Psychological Review, 104*(4), 801–838.

Ellis, A. W., Franklin, S. E., & Crerar, A. (1994). Cognitive neuropsychology and the remediation of disorders of spoken language. In M. J. Riddoch & G. W. Humphreys (Eds.), *Cognitive neuropsychology and cognitive rehabilitation* (pp. 287–315). Hove, UK: Lawrence Erlbaum Associates Ltd.

Ellis, A. W., Kay, J., & Franklin, S. E. (1992). Anomia: Differentiating between semantic and phonological deficits. In D. Margolin (Ed.), *Cognitive neuropsychology in clinical practice* (pp. 207–228). New York: Oxford University Press.

Ellis, A. W., Miller, D. C., & Sin, G. (1983). Wernicke's aphasia and normal language processing: A case study in cognitive neuropsychology. *Cognition, 15*(1–3), 111–144.

Ellis, A. W., & Young, A. W. (1988). *Human cognitive neuropsychology*. Hove, UK: Lawrence Erlbaum Associates Ltd.

Feyereisen, P., Van der Borght, F., & Seron, X. (1988). The operativity effect in naming: A re-analysis. *Neuropsychologia, 26*, 401–415.

Francis, W. N., & Kucera, H. (1982). *Frequency analysis of English usage: Lexicon and grammar*. Boston: Houghton Mifflin.

Franklin, S., Howard, D., & Patterson, K. (1995). Abstract word anomia. *Cognitive Neuropsychology, 12*(5), 549–566.

Funnell, E., & Hodges, J. R. (1991). Progressive loss of access to spoken word forms in a case of Alzheimer's disease. *Proceedings of the Royal Society of London, 243*, 173–179.

Funnell, E., & Sheridan, J. (1992). Categories of knowledge? Unfamiliar aspects of living and non-living things. *Cognitive Neuropsychology, 9*, 135–153.

Gainotti, G., Silveri, M. C., Villa, G., & Miceli, G. (1986). Anomia with and without lexical comprehension disorders. *Brain and Language, 29*, 18–23.

Gernsbacher, M. A. (1984). Resolving 20 years of inconsistent interactions between lexical familiarity and orthography, concreteness, and polysemy. *Journal of Experimental Psychology: General, 113*, 256.

Goodglass, H., Hyde, M. R., & Blumstein, S. E. (1969). Frequency, picturability and availability of nouns in aphasia. *Cortex, 5*, 104–119.

Hillis, A. E., & Caramazza, A. (1995). Converging evidence for the interaction of semantic and sublexical phonological information in accessing lexical representations for spoken output. *Cognitive Neuropsychology, 12*, 187–227.

Hillis, A. E., Rapp, B., Romani, C., & Caramazza, A. (1990). Selective impairment of semantics in lexical processing. *Cognitive Neuropsychology, 7*(3), 191–243.

Hirsh, K. W., & Ellis, A. W. (1994). Age of acquisition and lexical processing in aphasia: A case study. *Cognitive Neuropsychology, 11*(4), 435–458.

Hodges, J. R., Patterson, K. E., Oxbury, S. M., & Funnell, E. (1992). Semantic dementia: Progressive fluent aphasia with temporal lobe atrophy. *Brain, 115*, 1783–1806.

Howard, D. (1985). *The semantic organisation of the lexicon; evidence from aphasia*. Unpublished PhD thesis: University of London.

Howard, D. (1995). Lexical anomia – or the case of the missing lexical entries. *Quarterly Journal of Experimental Psychology, 48A*, 999–1023.

Howard, D. (2000). Cognitive neuropsychology and aphasia therapy: The case of word retrieval. In I. Papathanasiou (Ed.), *Acquired neurogenic communication disorders* (pp. 76–99). London: Whurr.

Howard, D., & Harding, D. (1998). Self-cueing of word retrieval by a woman with aphasia: Why a letter board works. *Aphasiology, 12*(4–5), 399–420.

Howard, D., & Nickels, L. (2005). Separating input and output phonology: Semantic, phonological, and orthographic effects in short-term memory impairment. *Cognitive Neuropsychology, 22*(1), 42–77.

Howard, D., Nickels, L. A., Coltheart, M., & Cole-Virtue, J. (2006). Cumulative semantic inhibition in picture naming: Experimental and computational studies. *Cognition, 100*, 464–482.

Howard, D., & Orchard-Lisle, V. M. (1984). On the origin of semantic errors in naming; evidence from the case of a global aphasic. *Cognitive Neuropsychology, 1*, 163–190.

Howard, D., Patterson, K., Franklin, S., Morton, J., & Orchard-Lisle, V. (1984). Variability and consistency in picture naming by aphasic patients. In F. Rose (Ed.), *Advances in neurology 42; Progress in aphasiology* (pp. 263–276). New York: Raven Press.

Howard, D., & Patterson, K. E. (1992). *The Pyramids and Palm Trees Test*. Bury St Edmunds, UK: Thames Valley Test Company.

Katz, R. B., & Lanzoni, S. M. (1997). Activation of the phonological lexicon for reading and object naming in deep dyslexia. *Brain and Language, 58*(1), 46–60.

Kay, J. (1992). The write stuff: A case of acquired spelling disorder. In R. Campbell (Ed.), *Mental lives: Case studies in cognition*. Oxford, UK: Blackwell.

Kay, J., & Ellis, A. W. (1987). A cognitive neuropsychological case-study of anomia – implications for psychological models of word retrieval. *Brain, 110*, 613–629.

Kay, J., Lesser, R., & Coltheart, M. (1992). *Psycholinguistic Assessments of Language Processing in Aphasia*. Hove, UK: Lawrence Erlbaum Associates Ltd.

Kay, J., & Patterson, K. E. (1985). Routes to meaning in surface dyslexia. In K. E. Patterson, J. C. Marshall, & M. Coltheart (Eds.), *Surface dyslexia: Neuropsychological and cognitive studies of phonological reading* (pp. 79–104). Hove, UK: Lawrence Erlbaum Associates Ltd.

Kertesz, A. (1982). *The Western Aphasia Battery*. New York: Grune & Stratton.

Kohn, S. E. (1988). Phonological production deficits in aphasia. In H. Whitaker (Ed.), *Phonological processes and brain mechanisms*. New York: Springer-Verlag.

Kohn, S. E. (1989). The nature of the phonemic string deficit in conduction aphasia. *Aphasiology, 3*, 209–239.

Lambon Ralph, M. A. (1998). Distributed versus localist representations: Evidence from a study of item consistency in a case of classical anomia. *Brain and Language, 64*(3), 339–360.

Lambon Ralph, M. A., & Howard, D. (2000). Gogi aphasia or semantic dementia? Simulating and assessing poor verbal comprehension in a case of progressive fluent aphasia. *Cognitive Neuropsychology, 17*(5), 437–465.

Lambon Ralph, M. A., Howard, D., Nightingale, G., & Ellis, A. W. (1998). Are living and non-living category-specific deficits causally linked to impaired perceptual or associative knowledge? Evidence from a category-specific double dissociation. *Neurocase, 4*(4–5), 311–338.

Lambon Ralph, M. A., McClelland, J. L., Patterson, K., Galton, C. J., & Hodges, J. R. (2001). No right to speak? The relationship between object naming and semantic impairment: Neuropsychological abstract evidence and a computational model. *Journal of Cognitive Neuroscience, 13*(3), 341–356.

Lambon Ralph, M. A., Moriarty, L., & Sage, K. (2002). Anomia is simply a reflection of semantic and phonological impairments: Evidence from a case-series study. *Aphasiology, 16*(1–2), 56–82.

Lambon Ralph, M. A., Sage, K., & Roberts, J. (2000). Classical anomia: A neuropsychological perspective on speech production. *Neuropsychologia, 38*(2), 186–202.

Lesser, R. (1989). Some issues in the neuropsychological rehabilitation of anomia. In X. Seron & G. Deloche (Eds.), *Cognitive approaches in neuropsychological rehabilitation*. Hillsdale, NJ: Lawrence Erlbaum Associates Inc.

Levelt, W. J. M. (1989). *Speaking: From intention to articulation*. Cambridge, MA: MIT Press.

Levelt, W. J. M., Roelofs, A., & Meyer, A. S. (1999). A theory of lexical access in speech production. *Behavioral and Brain Sciences, 22*, 1–45.

Li, E. C., & Canter, G. J. (1991). Varieties of error produced by aphasic patients after phonemic cueing. *Aphasiology, 5*, 51–61.

Li, E. C., & Williams, S. E. (1991). An investigation of naming errors following semantic and phonemic cueing. *Neuropsychologia, 29*, 1083–1093.

Markman, E. M. (1989). *Categorisation and naming in children: Problems of induction*. Cambridge, MA: MIT Press.

Morrison, C. M., Ellis, A. W., & Quinlan, P. T. (1992). Age of acquisition, not word frequency, affects object naming, not object recognition. *Memory and Cognition, 20*, 705–714.

Myers Pease, D., & Goodglass, H. (1978). The effects of cuing on picture naming in aphasia. *Cortex, 14*, 178–189.

Nickels, L. A. (1992). The autocue? Self-generated phonemic cues in the treatment of a disorder of reading and naming. *Cognitive Neuropsychology, 9*, 155–182.

Nickels, L. A. (1995). Getting it right – Using aphasic naming errors to evaluate theoretical models of spoken word recognition. *Language and Cognitive Processes, 10*(1), 13–45.

Nickels, L. A., & Howard, D. (1994). A frequent occurrence – factors affecting the production of semantic errors in aphasic naming. *Cognitive Neuropsychology, 11*(3), 289–320.

Nickels, L. A., & Howard, D. (1995). Aphasic naming – What matters? *Neuropsychologia, 33*(10), 1281–1303.

Nickels, L. A., & Howard, D. (2000). When the words won't come: Relating impairments and models of spoken word production. In L. R. Wheeldon (Ed.), *Aspects of language production* (pp. 115–142). Hove, UK: Psychology Press.

Nickels, L. A., & Howard, D. (2004). Dissociating effects of number of phonemes, number of syllables and syllabic complexity on word production in aphasia: It's the number of phonemes that counts. *Cognitive Neuropsychology, 21*, 57–78.

Oldfield, R. C., & Wingfield, A. (1965). Response latencies in naming objects. *Quarterly Journal of Experimental Psychology, 17*, 273–281.

Pate, D. S., Saffran, E. M., & Martin, N. (1987). Specifying the nature of the production deficit in conduction aphasia: A case study. *Language and Cognitive Processes, 2*, 43–84.

Patterson, K., & Lambon Ralph, M. A. (1999). Selective disorders of reading? *Current Opinion in Neurobiology, 9*(2), 235–239.

Patterson, K. E. (1979). What is right with "deep" dyslexic patients. *Brain and Language, 8*, 111–129.

Shallice, T. (1987). Impairments of semantic processing: Multiple dissociations. In M. Coltheart, R. Job, & G. Sartori (Eds.), *The cognitive neuropsychology of language* (pp. 111–129). Hove, UK: Lawrence Erlbaum Associates Ltd.

Shallice, T. (1988). *From neuropsychology to mental structure.* Cambridge, UK: Cambridge University Press.

Smith, A. (1988). *A cognitive neuropsychological investigation of the origin of phonological errors in two aphasic individuals.* Unpublished undergraduate dissertation, University of Newcastle, Newcastle-upon-Tyne.

Stimley, M. A., & Noll, J. D. (1991). The effects of semantic and phonemic prestimulation cues on picture naming in aphasia. *Brain and Language, 41*, 496–509.

Walley, A. C., & Metsala, J. L. (1992). Young children's age-of-acquisition estimates for spoken words. *Memory and Cognition, 20*, 171–182.

Wheeldon, L. R., & Monsell, S. (1994). Inhibition of spoken word production by priming a semantic competitor. *Journal of Memory and Language, 33*(3), 332–356.

Zingeser, L. B., & Berndt, R. S. (1988). Grammatical class and context effects in a case of pure anomia – implications for models of language production. *Cognitive Neuropsychology, 5*(4), 474–516.

Foreign Accent Syndrome: In the ear of the beholder?

Cinzia Di Dio
University of Parma, Italy

Joerg Schulz
University of Hertfordshire, Hatfield, UK

Jennifer M. Gurd
University of Oxford, UK

Background: The identification of accent type in patients with acquired accent change following brain damage (Foreign Accent Syndrome; FAS), may vary depending on the judge.

Aims: This experiment tests the accent identification abilities of naïve judges listening to speech samples from FAS patients versus healthy controls.

Method & Procedures: A total of 52 naive judges listened to speech samples from speakers of British English, which were presented over audio CD. They were asked to identify the accent type, but were blind as to the identity of the participants vis-à-vis FAS versus control, and foreign versus native UK. Accuracy, variability, and confidence ratings were assessed as a function of participant and of accent type.

Outcomes & Results: The naïve judges displayed greater accuracy, consistency, and confidence in typing the control versus the FAS accents. There was a positive familiarity effect for the control, but not the FAS accents.

Conclusions: The data provide preliminary support for the view that FAS is not exclusively "in the ear of the beholder".

Foreign Accent Syndrome (FAS) is a term first coined by Whitaker (1982), to refer to cases of acquired accent change following brain damage in adults. In the UK at least, the relevant speech and language therapist sees 1.5 adult cases per decade of practice on average (Coleman & Gurd, in press). It has been assumed that FAS results from damage to higher cortical speech processes, rather than to strictly peripheral motor impairments (i.e., dysarthria), but this has been difficult to substantiate. The literature on FAS has been slow to amass, and it is often difficult to know the extent of motor impairment from published case reports. It is also clear that various motor speech disorders may co-occur with FAS (although not necessarily causally). Nonetheless, FAS can occur in "pure" forms, apparently independent of motor speech deficits (Gurd, Bessel, Bladon, & Bamford, 1988). Each

Address correspondence to: Dr. J. M. Gurd, Neuropsychology Research Unit, University Department of Clinical Neurology, The Radcliffe Infirmary, Woodstock Road, Oxford OX2 6HE, UK.

We are particularly grateful to our colleagues J. Coleman, E. Leinonen, B. Rosner, and J. Ryalls, to the anonymous reviewers, and to the Critchley Charitable Trust for their support of this work.

case is unique with respect to type and severity of accent change and accompanying speech, language, and motor-speech disorders. Generalisations are made difficult by the lack of a diagnostic "acid test" for FAS. This brings listener judgement to the fore. It obviously pivots on expertise, experience, and bias. A trained ear, such as that of a speech scientist, phonetician, or speech and language therapist is typically required.

In everyday life, everyone with whom a FAS patient communicates becomes an unwitting judge. Accent perception is known to vary according to the listeners' regional origin (Edwards, 1999). For example, in the UK, people in the south of the country may in the past have harboured prejudicial attitudes towards those speaking with regional northern accents (e.g., a Castleford accent). To avoid this, some parents might have enrolled their children in elocution lesions. However, there was always the risk of the child's acquiring an altogether anomalous accent, known colloquially as "speaking funny", if the lessons "failed" (Marshall, personal communication). This anecdote is not entirely tongue in cheek; there is an extensive sociolinguistic literature on the significance of social communication (Cavanaugh, 2005) and of the impact of attitude to foreign language perception (Purnell, Idsard, & Baugh, 1999; Ray & Zahn, 1999). Systematic assessment of whether FAS patients *are* actually perceived by naïve listeners as sounding foreign has been limited. As this informs therapeutic treatment of FAS, it motivated the current investigation.

Three different points of view pertaining to FAS are now described. (i) *The generic view* that FAS constitutes a "generic" rather than a "particular" foreign-sounding accent (Kurowski, Blumstein, & Alexander, 1996). If this were the case, then it would *not* be possible to reliably identify the FAS patient's accent type, and hence there would be considerable variation among the identifications from different judges. This would be reflected in terms of low accuracy, low concordance between different expert judges, and low confidence judgements, in comparison to the comparable identification of control participants' accents. Moreover, there would be no distinction between types of accents, and hence no positive effects of familiarity on accuracy or confidence of judgements. (It is somewhat of an open question as to how naïve judges would perform.)

(ii) *The perceptual view*, also referred to fondly as the phoneticians' Rorschach Test, PRT (Rosner, personal communication), is that "... the 'foreign' quality of FAS speech is a perceptual impression of the listener, and not inherent in the patient's vocalizations" (Carbary, Patterson, & Snyder, 2000, p. 78). This places even greater weight on the degree of expertise of the listener. (Again, the performance of naïve judges would be difficult to predict.) This implies that the features of FAS patients' speech do not pertain to any particular foreign accent and therefore listener bias would play a greater part in the accent judgements. Judgements would be at chance for accuracy, with very low confidence ratings, and no effect of familiarity.

(iii) *The linguistic relative view* asserts the importance of "considering" the perception and experience of the listener in the identification and interpretation of FAS: Typically, accents heard are those within the experience of a listener or speech community. Examples from the FAS literature include: "Parisians hear Alsatian; listeners in England hear a change to Welsh, Scots, French; Australians hear a Chinese/Japanese accent; a German accent is heard during the time of German occupation in Norway. Noticeably we do not hear of a British English speaker in England being described as developing an Ibo or Tagalog accent, even though their speech may contain features of these languages. In other words listeners focus on salient elements in speech, and these are interpreted through their experiential and attitudinal filters" (Miller, Lowit, & O'Sullivan, in press). (This view is better adapted to the relevance of the naïve listener's judgements.) Consistent with this view would be significant familiarity effects. (Details of the "consideration" referred to above clearly need to be spelled out in greater detail.) More specific theories will no doubt emerge in future.

The brief study described here focuses on naïve judges' free accent identifications, and compares performance in response to FAS versus healthy controls' speech sample stimuli. Notably, this does not assess the extent to which these results would generalise to other FAS patients. This experiment features eight speech samples, which were played over headphones to 52 naïve judges. Unknown to the listeners, two of the samples were actually from FAS patients who were judged by an expert phonetician (southern English speaker) as sounding Scottish, and French, respectively. The remaining six samples were obtained from control participants who also had Scottish or French accents. All these control participants were non-native speakers of British English, hence their accents were "real". Two experimental hypotheses were that: (1) correct identifications will be lower in response to the FAS, versus control stimuli; and (2) correct identifications will be higher for the more familiar accent.

METHOD

Participants

A total of 52 participants (26 male and 26 female, age 18–54 years) served as naïve judges of speech accent type. Eight different speech samples were played to them over high-quality headphones (this was carried out within the context of a larger study). All volunteer judges spoke (British) English as their first language, and had normal hearing. Of these judges, 68% reported that they had learned French as a second language at school (range: 3–5 years). The FAS samples were both from female patients who had pre-morbidly been monolingual speakers of British English. Further descriptions of the patients may be found in Dankovicova et al. (2001), and in Gurd, Coleman, Costello, and Marshall (2001). Although both had suffered strokes, neither had what could be described as "localising" lesions; there were either multiple lesion sites, sub-arachnoid lesions, or ones that did not show reliably on the MRI or CT scans.

An experienced phonetician (J.C.) described the FAS accents as Scottish and French, respectively. Therefore, three Scottish, and three native French speakers of British English were interviewed to collect the six control speech samples (three each). They were thus matched to the patients by accent and gender. The Scottish controls were all native speakers of Scottish English, who originated from southern Scotland (control 1), Glasgow (control 2), and Edinburgh (control 3). The three French controls were from the south-east of France, but had different regional accents. French control 1 was from Savoia, control 2 was from Lyon, and control 3 was from St. Etienne. They had spent at least 10 years in England. Two of them had learned British English at school in their country of birth, whereas one moved to England with no previous knowledge of English. Because FAS patients' accents are not "naturally" foreign, we did not match the controls with any greater specificity vis-à-vis region of accent. With the exception of gender and English language proficiency, any other factors that could have affected the control speakers' accents, were left free to vary. Factors such as type, extent, and persistence of the original regional accent and its manifestation in spoken English were not further assessed.

Materials and procedures

Speech segments ranging in duration from 1 to 5 seconds were assembled randomly, yielding samples ranging in length from 27 to 30 seconds each. This removed nationality or grammaticality clues, which might betray the speaker's identity. Speech editing and sound modification used Sound Forge 5 which permitted the minimisation of noise, by modifying sound volume, excessively high or low frequencies, background noise, and sound quality, across speech samples. (Removal of excessively high frequencies did not obscure the foreign quality of the speech such as atypical pitch patterns frequently present in FAS speech.) When the adjustment and composition of the nine speech samples was completed, they were transferred to CD.

The stimuli were presented in pseudo-random order within each sequence (with the restriction that consecutive FAS samples, or consecutive control accents of the same type, were not allowed). The audio CD stimuli were presented to participants over high-quality sound headphones (Sennheiser HD 477) connected to a portable CD player (Panasonic SL-S214, S-XBS). The audio speech stimuli were presented in two different sequences (to minimise order effects); half the judges performed the accent identifications under condition 1 (order 1) and half under condition 2 (order 2). The experimenter requested that the judge freely identify each accent immediately following its presentation on the CD. Judges were also requested to indicate their levels of judgement confidence (on a scale ranging from 1 = very confident, to 5 = not confident at all). Each speech sample stimulus was played a maximum of twice (either consecutively, or at the end of the testing session). If *no* accent was detected at all, the experimenter entered a default coding of *English*.

Statistical analyses

A within-participants repeated measures experimental design was employed. The first contrast was between control accent type: French versus Scottish. The second was between FAS and control. The dependent variable was the number of correct accent identifications (or number of "hits"). Depending on the type of data, both nonparametric (Hollander & Wolfe, 1999; Siegel & Castellan, 1988), and parametric statistical procedures were applied. Each FAS stimulus was presented only once during the experiment (unless repeats were specifically requested by the participant). Correct identifications were coded as 1, incorrect as 0. McNemar's test was used to compare the proportion of correct identifications between pairs of different FAS stimuli. Because there were three different stimuli for each control accent (i.e., three Scottish and three French), an average percent correct was calculated per accent type, per participant. We reasoned that a percentage correct, as the dependent variable, would be the most apt statistical representation for a "natural" language accent. (The slight variations in response to the three individual control stimuli per accent type would be balanced out through averaging.) This resulted in a variable with just four different values (0%, 33%, 66%, 100%), therefore the Sign test was used to compare the average percent correct between pairs of control stimuli. The comparisons between FAS versus control stimuli were performed using the Binomial test (the average percent correct for each type of control stimulus was taken as the test value against which the observed proportion correct for the corresponding FAS stimulus was calculated). For the confidence ratings t-tests for dependent samples were used.

RESULTS

Hypothesis 1: FAS < control

The prediction that the percent correct accent identifications for FAS stimuli would be lower than controls' was tested using two planned comparisons (each with a critical p value set at $p = .025$, Bonferroni adjusted, one-sided, to adjust for multiple comparisons.) The mean percent correct identifications were consistently lower for the FAS versus controls' (Table 1, comparison 1a and 1b). To investigate the degree of variation per different control stimuli (per accent type), a follow-up analysis compared each control stimulus with its FAS correspondent (Table 2). Of the three French control stimuli, only one received significantly higher percent correct identifications. Two out of three Scottish control samples evoked significantly higher percent correct identifications compared to their FAS correspondent.

Hypothesis 2: Less familiarity < greater familiarity

It was predicted that the mean percentage correct would be French < Scottish for both the control and the FAS stimuli, based on the assumption that Scottish accents

TABLE 1
Planned comparisons relating to hypotheses 1 and 2

No	Planned comparisons	p values (one-tailed)	Decision
1a	French Control – French FAS (42% – 23%)	$p = .003$ (Binomial Test)	Difference as predicted
1b	Scottish Control – Scottish FAS (59% – 27%)	$p = .0001$ (Binomial Test)	Difference as predicted
2a	Scottish FAS – French FAS (27% – 23%)	$p = .41$ (McNemar Test)	No difference in the % of hits
2b	Scottish Control – French Control (59% – 42%)	$p = .025$ (Sign Test, $Z = -1.97$)	Difference as predicted

TABLE 2
Individual comparisons of percent correct identifications for Scottish and French FAS vs individual controls

	Scottish		French	
FAS speech sample	27%		23%	
1st control	33%	$p = .33$	31%	$p = .26$
2nd control	75%	$p < .001$	39%	$p = .08$
3rd control	69%	$p < .001$	58%	$p < .001$

p-values are one-tailed and relate to the McNemar test; critical p value = .017.

are more familiar than French ones to UK residents. Two sets of planned comparisons were tested (with the critical p value adjusted to $p = .025$, one-sided). The mean percent correct to the control stimuli followed the predicted familiarity pattern, but those to the FAS stimuli, *did not* (Table 1, comparison 2a and 2b).

Variation: Number of different accent types identified in response to control and FAS stimuli

The details of accent type varied considerably across stimuli, and included non-European languages. Figures 1 and 2 show the frequencies of the different accents identified in response to control versus FAS stimuli. Of the three available control stimuli, the first one was used for this comparison; this was done to avoid repetition effects, which might have influenced the judgements of subsequent second and third presentations of the stimuli. Some of the accents identified (i.e., African, Indian, Iranian, Swiss), are not actual languages, but are reported here as the judges' verbatim responses.

With respect to the differences in response to FAS versus control stimuli, the Scottish FAS elicited higher frequencies of different accent types (compared to their controls), a pattern that did not hold for the French FAS contrast. The details are: For the Scottish FAS sample—excluding hits (Scottish), and defaults (standard Southern British English)—three other accents of English were also identified (Irish, Welsh, northern English; sum = 17.3%), as well as four European language accents (Spanish, German, Portuguese, and Polish; sum = 9.6%), and Indian (1.9%): total other = 28.8%. Thus a total of nine different accents (excluding the English default) were assigned. This is a clear increase over the control comparator, for which a total of only four different accents were identified; all of which were accents of English (Scottish, northern English, Irish, and American); hence the total "other" = zero. The French FAS sample was most frequently identified as African (25%). Excluding hits (French), nine other accents were identified; one was an accent of English (Welsh = 3.8%), five were European (Italian, Spanish, Swedish, German, Swiss; sum = 34.6%), and two were non-European (Chinese, Indian; sum = 13.4%); hence total other = 76.9%. However, the number of categories ascribed to French FAS was considerably less than the 15 different control judgements. A noticeable difference was in the small percent of African control identifications (9.62%).

Confidence ratings

Table 3 displays the descriptive statistics for the confidence ratings. A *t*-test for dependent samples revealed a highly significant mean difference in the control confidence ratings between the Scottish and the French stimuli, $t(51) = 7.58, p < .001$, in favour of the Scottish. By contrast, the mean FAS confidence level difference was insignificant: Scottish versus French FAS, $t(51) = 1.48, p = .15$. Table 3 also reveals that each FAS stimulus received lower confidence ratings than its control counterpart. The confidence level for the Scottish FAS versus control accent identifications was significantly higher, $t(51) = 6.16, p > .001$. The mean difference between the French control versus FAS stimuli was also significant, $t(51) = 2.22, p = .03$, but less pronounced.

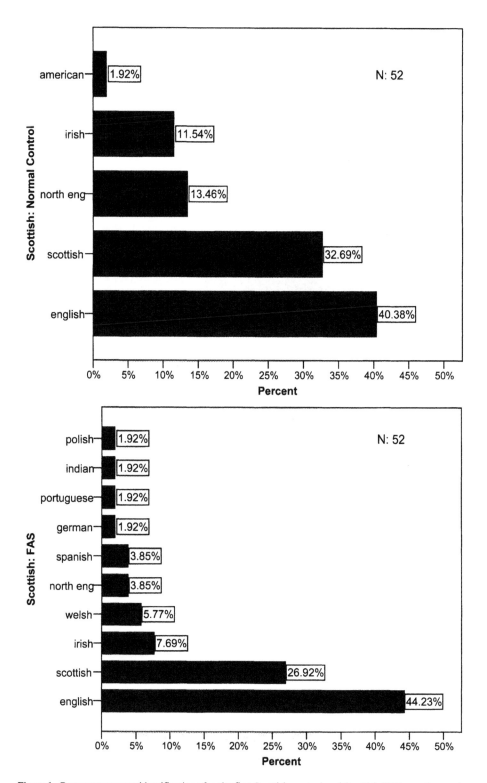

Figure 1. Percentage accent identifications for the first Scottish control and Scottish FAS speech samples.

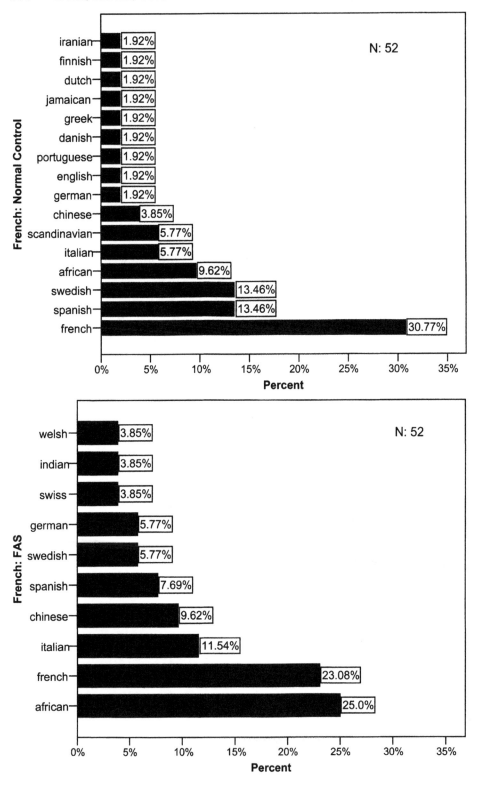

Figure 2. Percentage accent identifications for the first French control and French FAS speech samples.

TABLE 3
Descriptive statistics of the confidence ratings: FAS and control

	N	Minimum	Maximum	Mean	Std. Deviation
Confidence rating Scottish Control	52	2.00	5.00	3.8077	0.77360
Confidence rating French Control	52	1.00	4.67	2.7949	0.90304
Confidence rating Scottish FAS	52	1	5	2.79	1.194
Confidence rating French FAS	52	1	5	2.50	1.000

DISCUSSION

Our first hypothesis predicted a lower hit rate for the FAS versus control stimuli, and this received support. The hit rates for the control Scottish and French stimuli were considerably higher than for their respective FAS stimuli. It is notable that the participants expressed significantly greater confidence in the Scottish versus French control accent identifications. All individual control stimuli were identified with significantly greater confidence than their corresponding FAS stimuli. These results indicate that, although accent identification was quite poor in all instances, there was a difference between FAS versus control accent perception, and thus identification. On average, the controls' stimuli were identified with greater accuracy than the FAS, indicating that the quality of speech accent differed between FAS and controls. Put differently, these results may be interpreted as indicating that the FAS stimuli *were* perceived as sounding foreign, although not to the same extent as the controls'.

With respect to the second hypothesis, there was a significant effect of familiarity on the accuracy judgements for control, but not for FAS stimuli; therefore there was only partial support. (Greater numbers of FAS and control stimuli would be required to probe this finding further.)

Several summary observations can be made about the percent correct identifications. Although none of the accents was terribly well identified, there was a clear pattern of consensual identifications for both the Scottish- and the French-sounding FAS stimuli. The best, the Scottish control, did not even reach 60%. The largest FAS:control difference in percent hits per accent type was for the Scottish, a significant 32% difference (French significant difference = 19%). For the purposes of argument here, view (i) predicts that accent identification of FAS patients' speech samples will be random, compared to that of controls (Hypothesis 1). Since it is not random, our results fail to support this view. But neither is it as good as for controls. Therefore, the explanation needs to be probed further.

It is certainly the case that FAS patients' acquired accents do not contain 100% of the features of the new accent; a significant factor that varies from case to case, which needs to be taken into account (cf. Dankovicova et al., 2001). Nevertheless, partial discrimination between FAS and control accents (both in terms of percent correct and confidence rating) indicates qualitative differences in the perceived speech; FAS patients were not perceived in the same way as unimpaired speakers with an actual foreign accent. This could provide support for the perceptual PRT view (view ii), that naïve listeners *did* recognise FAS patients as sounding foreign, although *not* automatically because of foreign features in the speech. Instead, it is possible that the speech was judged as foreign, simply because it was different. Further experimental manipulations would be required to tease out these distinctions.

Views (ii) and (iii) both predict that accent identification of FAS patients' samples will be a function of familiarity (Hypothesis 2), but for slightly different reasons. More familiar accents will be the more likely identifications for FAS stimuli (Hypothesis 2). ("Familiarity" is assessed as the percent correct on the control stimuli.) Our data do not provide unequivocal support for this prediction. However, view (iii) further predicts the likelihood that accents within the listeners' experience will be ascribed to FAS cases; a prediction for which our data *do* provide some support. (Although, admittedly, the views and their interpretations are not clear-cut.)

We would like to conclude that foreign accent syndrome (FAS), a rare but fascinating acquired disorder of speech accent (Monrad-Krohn, 1947; Ryalls & Reinvang, 1985), is not entirely "in the ear of the beholder"! Although it has been described in several recent case studies (Ardilà, Rosselli, & Ardilà, 1981; Blumstein, Alexander, Ryalls, Katz, & Dworetzky, 1987; Graff-Radford, Cooper, Colsher, & Damasio, 1986; Gurd et al., 1988; Moen, 2000), it remains comparatively underinvestigated (Christoph, de Freitas, dos Santos, Lima, Araujo, & Carota, 2004). Perhaps more importantly, it certainly does *not* constitute a unitary phenomenon. Several diagnostic and explanatory issues remain to be explored on a case-by-case basis. For example, how do patient profiles differ with respect to patterns of motor speech and language impairment, lesion sites, and aetiology? There may be some overlap between aphasia, apraxia of speech, and dysarthria as the clinical diagnostic umbrellas under which to include FAS. Indeed, the degree of language impairment (including aphasic verbal paraphasias), higher-level motor speech programming (apraxic) errors, and bucco-facial movement dysarthrias varies from case to case, and fuels misunderstandings concerning the investigation of FAS (cf. Kent, 2005; Miller, 2002). These issues notwithstanding, the focus here has been on the more background phenomenological issues of listeners' perceptual identifications of FAS accents, since there is considerable interest in whether FAS resembles a specific foreign accent versus a generic one (i.e., it sounds "foreign", but is not readily identified as characteristic of any particular foreign accent of, for example, British English).

In order to increase the robustness of these results, further methodological restrictions could be employed to control for potential sources of variation in accent perception in naïve listeners. These include controlling for the regional accent of controls, as well as their levels of English proficiency. With reference to the regional accent identification of the FAS patients, it would be interesting to test the comparative judgements of experts in contrast to those of naïve listeners. Employing both naïve and trained listeners as judges could be important to highlight the different potential sources of variation in the two groups. To increase the reliability of such results, it is recommended that pre-testing be undertaken to derive categories for forced choice designs.

Other sources of perceptual variation across listeners that were not controlled for, and could potentially have affected the results, are the listeners' socio-cultural background (Giles & Powesland, 1975), and personal experiences (cf. Edwards, 1999); factors that could be manipulated in future studies. In terms of external validity, it is vital to note that during real conversations, listeners' socio-cultural backgrounds and speaker's language may interact to determine the ultimate product of the perceptual experience (Krauss, Freyberg, & Morsella, 2002; Niedzielski, 1999). Accent identification can occur on the basis of a very brief linguistic exposure to phonemic variations or specific acoustic elements (Purnell et al., 1999). Speech rate and pitch variation can also influence one's impression of the traits of a speaker (Ray & Zahn, 1999). Improved understanding of the relationship between speech accent production, perceptual factors, and social judgements (i.e., listeners' attitudes and emotional responses) can inform the development of remedial techniques or strategies to help FAS patients (cf. Bayard, 1995; Boberg, 1999; Doest, Semin, & Sherman, 2002; Ray & Zahn, 1999). This is particularly important, given that an unwelcome accent change may disadvantage one in everyday life (Kalin, 1982; Dixon, Mahoney, & Cocks, 2002).

More than anything, this study contributes a design for the investigation of the bias inherent in perceptual accent identification in healthy versus patient populations. We highlight the role of naïve listeners as judges in such experiments, and link the significance to a patient's day-to-day life experiences of communicating in the real world. It seems clear that naïve judges *are* able to make the distinctions between different accent types. Perhaps unsurprisingly, they are better at this for control versus patient (i.e., FAS) stimuli. (We emphasise that this speaks more to the naïve listeners' judging capacities than to the actual nature of FAS accents or their fit with competing quasi-theoretical views.) Further refinements and increased sample numbers would improve further modifications. Pilot tests of control samples as well as of naïve judges' ranges of responses could be employed to enhance the accuracy levels of control identifications, and to transform the design into a multiple choice one. These preliminary findings are nonetheless thought provoking, in that they probably provide the strongest support for the *linguistic relative* (iii) view of Miller and colleagues, rather than the generic (i) or the perceptual PRT (ii) views. But there is some limited support for all three views, depending on one's perspective. Further evidence is called for.

REFERENCES

Ardilà, A., Rosselli, M., & Ardilà, O. (1988). Foreign accent: An aphasic epiphenomenon? *Aphasiology, 2,* 493–399.

Bayard, D. (1995). *Kiwitalk: Sociolinguistics and New Zealand society.* Palmerston North, New Zealand: Dunmore Press.

Blumstein, S., Alexander, M. P., Ryalls, J. H., Katz, W., & Dworetzky, B. (1987). On the nature of the foreign accent syndrome: A case study. *Brain and Language, 31,* 215–244.

Boberg, C. (1999). The attitudinal component of variation in American English foreign (a) nativization. *Journal of Language and Social Psychology, 18,* 49–61.

Carbary, T. J., Patterson, J. P., & Snyder, P. J. (2000). Foreign accent syndrome following a catastrophic second injury: MRI correlates, linguistic and voice pattern analyses. *Brain and Cognition, 43,* 78–85.

Cavanaugh, J. R. (2005). Accent matter: Material consequences of sounding local in northern Italy. *Language and Communication, 25,* 127–148.

Christoph, D. H., de Freitas, G. R., dos Santos, D. P., Lima, M. A. S. D., Araujo, A. Q. C., & Carota, A. (2004). Different perceived foreign accents in one patient after prerolandic hematoma. *European Neurology, 52,* 198–201.

Coleman, J., & Gurd, J. M. (in press). Introduction to the theme issue on foreign accent syndrome. *Journal of Neurolinguistics.*

Dankovičová, J., Gurd, J. M., Marshall, J. C., MacMahon, M. K. C., Stuart-Smith, J., & Coleman, J. S. et al. (2001). Aspects of non-native pronunciation in a case of altered accent following stroke (foreign accent syndrome). *Clinical Linguistics and Phonetics*, *15*, 195–218.

Dixon, J. A., Mahoney, B., & Cocks, R. (2002). Accents of guilt? Effects of regional accent, race, and crime type on attributions of guilt. *Journal of Language and Social Psychology*, *21*, 162–168.

Doest, L. T., Semin, G. R., & Sherman, S. J. (2002). Linguistic context and social perception. Does stimulus abstraction moderate processing style? *Journal of Language and Social Psychology*, *21*, 195–229.

Edwards, J. (1999). Refining our understanding of language attitudes. *Journal of Language and Social Psychology*, *18*, 101–110.

Giles, H., & Powesland, P. F. (1975). *Speech styles and social evaluation*. London: Academic Press.

Graff-Radford, N. R., Cooper, W. E., Colsher, P. L., & Damasio, A. (1986). An unlearned foreign accent in a patient with aphasia. *Brain and Language*, *28*, 86–94.

Gurd, J. M., Bessel, N. J., Bladon, R. A. W., & Bamford, J. M. (1988). A case of foreign accent syndrome with follow-up clinical, neuropsychological, and phonetic descriptions. *Neuropsychologia*, *26*, 237–251.

Gurd, J. M., Coleman, J. S., Costello, A., & Marshall, J. C. (2001). Organic or functional? A new case of Foreign Accent Syndrome. *Cortex*, *37*, 715–718.

Hollander, M., & Wolfe, D. A. (1999). *Nonparametric statistical methods*. New York: John Wiley.

Kalin, R. (1982). The social significance of speech in medical, legal and occupational settings. In E. B. Ryan & H. Giles (Eds.), *Attitudes towards language variation: Social and applied contexts* (pp. 148–163). London: Arnold.

Kent, R. D. (2005). Speech motor control and its disorders. In H-J. Freund, M. Jeannerod, M. Hallet, & R. Leiguarda (Eds.), *Higher-order motor disorders: From neuroanatomy and neurobiology to clinical neurology* (pp. 249–260). Oxford, UK: Oxford University Press.

Krauss, R. M., Freyberg, R., & Morsella, E. (2002). Inferring speakers' physical attributes from their voices. *Journal of Experimental Social Psychology*, *38*, 618–625.

Kurowski, K. M., Blumstein, S. E., & Alexander, M. (1996). The foreign accent syndrome: A reconsideration. *Brain and Language*, *54*, 1–25.

Miller, N. (2002). The neurological bases of apraxia of speech. Apraxia of speech: From concept to clinic. *Seminars in Speech and Language*, *23*, 223–230.

Miller, N., Lowit, A., & O'Sullivan, H. (in press). What makes acquired foreign accent syndrome foreign? *Journal of Neurolinguistics*.

Moen, I. (2000). Foreign Accent Syndrome: A review of contemporary explanations. *Aphasiology*, *14*, 5–15.

Monrad-Krohn, G. H. (1947). Dysprosody or altered "melody of language". *Brain*, *70*, 405–415.

Niedzielski, N. A. (1999). The effect of social information on the perception of sociolinguistic variables. *Journal of Social Psychology*, *18*, 62–85.

Purnell, T., Idsard, W., & Baugh, J. (1999). Perceptual and phonetic experiments on American English dialect identification. *Journal of Language and Social Psychology*, *18*, 10–30.

Ray, G. B., & Zahn, C. J. (1999). Language attitudes and speech behavior. New Zealand English and Standard American English. *Journal of Language and Social Psychology*, *18*, 310–319.

Ryalls, J., & Reinvang, I. (1985). Some further notes on Monrad-Krohn's case study of Foreign Accent Syndrome. *Folia Phoniatrica*, *37*, 160–162.

Sigel, S., & Castellan, N. J. (1988). *Nonparametric statistics for the behavioral sciences*. New York: McGraw-Hill.

Whitaker, H. (1982). Levels of impairment in disorders of speech. In R. N. Malatesha & L. C. Hartlage (Eds.), *Neuropsychology & cognition* (Vol. 1, pp. 168–207). The Hague: Nijhoff.

The impact of phonological or semantic impairment on delayed auditory repetition: Evidence from stroke aphasia and semantic dementia

Elizabeth Jefferies

University of Manchester, UK

Jenni Crisp

North Tyneside Primary Care Trust and University of Newcastle, UK

Matthew A. Lambon Ralph

University of Manchester, UK

Background/Aims: This study aimed to evaluate the interactive account of repetition by examining the influence of factors that differentially tapped semantic and phonological processing in a case series of patients with semantic or phonological impairment.

Methods & Procedures: We compared two patient groups: predominantly phonologically impaired cases with aphasia following cerebrovascular accident, and patients with semantic dementia. Immediate repetition was contrasted with repetition after a 5-second filled delay, and lexicality, frequency, and imageability were manipulated—therefore both the task and the neuropsychological impairment biased processing in favour of either lexical-semantic or phonological capacities.

Outcomes & Results: Substantial interactivity was observed between phonological/ semantic impairment and variables largely tapping these processes. The phonologically impaired patients showed substantial effects of lexicality and imageability that were larger in delayed than immediate repetition. The semantically impaired patients exhibited the complementary pattern, showing reduced effects of these lexical-semantic variables and a delay effect that was larger for more poorly comprehended, low-frequency items. Semantic errors were related to phonological deficits whereas semantic impairment led to an increase in phonological errors. The phonologically impaired stroke cases also made more perseverative responses.

Conclusions: These findings support the view that repetition is underpinned by interaction between semantics and phonology within a single route and not by distinct lexical and sub-lexical pathways. The results also provide evidence of a continuum between phonological and deep dysphasia.

There are two opposing accounts of the way in which phonological and lexical-semantic representations contribute to auditory repetition. According to dual-route accounts (Hanley & Kay, 1997; Hanley, Kay, & Edwards, 2002; Hillis & Caramazza, 1991; McCarthy & Warrington, 1984, 1987), there are distinct non-lexical and

Address correspondence to: Dr Elizabeth Jefferies, Neuroscience and Aphasia Research Unit, School of Psychological Sciences, University of Manchester, Oxford Road, Manchester, M13 9PL, UK. E-mail: beth.jefferies@manchester.ac.uk

lexical-semantic pathways to repetition. The non-lexical route, which transforms auditory representations directly into an articulatory code without reference to word meaning, is critical for the repetition of nonwords. The lexical-semantic route utilises connections from input phonology to semantics and then to output phonology in order to support word repetition. In contrast, single-route models—for example, the interactive-activation (IA) model of Dell and colleagues (Dell & O'Seaghda, 1992; Dell, Schwartz, Martin, Saffran, & Gagnon, 1997; Foygel & Dell, 2000) and the parallel distributed processing (PDP) framework of Plaut and Kello (1999)— propose that *interactivity* between phonology and semantics underpins the repetition of all items. Within this single route, the repetition of nonwords is supported primarily by phonology, whereas lexical-semantic knowledge provides additional constraints on phonological activation for words.

Patients who have phonological deficits from either stroke or nonfluent progressive aphasia show poor repetition characterised by frequent phonological errors (Croot, Patterson, & Hodges, 1998; Wilshire & Fisher, 2004; Wilshire & McCarthy, 1996). In contrast, individuals who show a profound loss of conceptual knowledge in the context of good phonology, e.g., patients with fluent progressive aphasia/semantic dementia (SD), have relatively intact repetition. This apparent dissociation speaks against the view that semantics plays a necessary role in the repetition of all items (e.g., the proposal of Plaut & Kello, 1999). However, when the phonological system is stressed in delayed repetition or the immediate serial recall (ISR) of several items, SD patients show clearer effects of semantic status on repetition and make errors that resemble those made by phonologically impaired patients (Knott, Patterson, & Hodges, 1997; see below). Interactivity between phonology and semantics may become more critical in repetition tasks that are highly demanding. The present study was motivated by the observation that repetition can look superficially similar in SD patients and phonologically impaired stroke aphasic patients when a delay is interposed between the stimulus and response: nevertheless, these groups should respond differently to variables that tap semantic and phonological processes if their difficulties in delayed repetition are underpinned by diverse impairments.

Several existing lines of evidence support the view that repetition is underpinned by interactivity between semantics and phonology within a single route. Semantically impaired patients, such as those with SD, show superior ISR for words that they still understand relatively well, compared with words that are more semantically degraded according to performance on semantic tests such as naming and word–picture matching (Caza, Belleville, & Gilbert, 2002; Forde & Humphreys, 2002; Jefferies, Jones, Bateman, & Lambon Ralph, 2004a, 2005; Jefferies, Patterson, Jones, Bateman, & Lambon Ralph, 2004b; Knott et al., 1997; Knott, Patterson, & Hodges, 2000; Patterson, Graham, & Hodges, 1994). They make frequent phoneme migration errors when recalling word lists that they no longer fully understand, suggesting that semantic representations may help to constrain the order of phonemes in verbal short-term memory (Patterson et al., 1994). Similarly, normal participants make phoneme migration errors in ISR when lexical-semantic constraints are weak (Jefferies, Frankish, & Lambon Ralph, 2006a; Treiman & Danis, 1988).

Patients with a circumscribed semantic impairment also show poorer ISR for nonwords that are phonologically similar to semantically degraded words, compared with nonwords derived from better-understood words (Caza et al., 2002; Jefferies et al., 2005), suggesting a role for lexical-semantic representations in nonword as well as word repetition. This finding contradicts the strong form of the dual-route hypothesis which proposes that nonword repetition is achieved entirely through the non-lexical route. Lexical variables, such as the number of real-word neighbours, also have a demonstrable impact on nonword repetition in normal participants (Roodenrys & Hinton, 2002).

Converging evidence for interactivity is provided by studies of stroke aphasia. Within this population, phonological and semantic impairment produce dissociable effects on repetition/ISR: poor semantic processing is associated with reduced effects of frequency and imageability, whereas poor phonological processing is associated with increased effects of these variables (N. Martin & Saffran, 1997). In addition, patients can show specific difficulties in the retention of semantic or phonological information (R. Martin & Lesch, 1996; R. Martin, Lesch, & Bartha, 1999; R. Martin, Shelton, & Yaffee, 1994).

A small number of aphasic patients with severe phonological deficits show a pattern termed "deep dysphasia"; that is, they make semantic errors in immediate single word repetition (e.g., camel → "horse"), show a large effect of semantic variables such as imageability in repetition, and are unable to repeat nonwords, suggesting that their repetition relies heavily on word meaning (for example, Howard & Franklin, 1988; Katz & Goodglass, 1990; Majerus, Lekeu, Van der Linden, & Salmon, 2001; N. Martin & Saffran, 1992; Michel & Andreewsky, 1983; Valdois, Carbonnel, David, Rousset, & Pellat, 1995). In accounting for the syndrome of deep dysphasia, the single-route account has the advantage that apparently disparate effects—such as the occurrence of both semantic and phonological errors and effects of lexicality and imageability in repetition—can be explained parsimoniously in terms of a single impairment. N. Martin, Saffran, and colleagues demonstrated that the key symptoms of deep dysphasia could be accounted for in Dell and O'Seaghda's (1992) model by postulating an abnormally fast decay of activation in all units (Martin, Dell, Saffran, & Schwartz, 1994; Martin & Saffran, 1992; Martin, Saffran, & Dell, 1996). In a recent modification of this model, Foygel and Dell (2000) proposed that phonological and semantic processing could be impaired independently; consequently, deep dysphasia might arise from a specific impairment of phonological processing that renders repetition more reliant on lexical-semantic processing (see Wilshire & Fisher, 2004). In contrast, two independent deficits might be postulated to explain deep dysphasia within the dual-route framework. The inability to repeat nonwords is suggestive of an impairment to the non-lexical route, whereas the large imageability effects and semantic errors shown by these patients are interpreted as resulting from additional weakness in the lexical-semantic route (see Hanley, Dell, Kay, & Baron, 2004; Hanley & Kay, 1997; Hanley et al., 2002).

The findings reviewed above are broadly consistent with Dell and colleagues' interactive-activation (IA) model (Dell & O'Seaghda, 1992; Dell et al., 1997), which incorporates three distinct processing levels: phonological, lexical, and semantic. Each level consists of localist nodes, linked by bidirectional connections to the nodes in the adjacent layers. Activation spreads forwards and backwards between the levels during every processing cycle so that in repetition, reverberating input from the lexical and semantic layers helps to sustain rapidly decaying phonological activation. The PDP framework (e.g., Patterson et al., 1994; Plaut & Kello, 1999) makes similar predictions but employs a rather different architecture. This approach posits distinct semantic and phonological representations but not a separate lexical level. The phonological system develops pattern completion properties for familiar items by virtue of the fact that the phonological elements of words are always produced together. A second source of constraint is provided by the semantic system. As semantic activation co-occurs with phonology during word comprehension and production, input from semantic memory helps to bolster the correct phonological pattern and suppresses activation of erroneous phonology. Both of these models predict that semantic impairment will increase phonological errors in repetition.

This study aims to evaluate the interactive account of repetition by examining the way in which factors that differentially tap semantic processing (e.g., lexicality and imageability) and phonological processing (e.g., the presence of a delay prior to repetition) interact with semantic or phonological impairment in SD and stroke aphasia respectively. Patients with phonological impairment should perform poorly when a brief delay is imposed between the stimulus and response because phonological activation is thought to decay rapidly and phonological impairment will therefore be exacerbated by a delay. These patients are also expected to have particular difficulty repeating stimuli such as nonwords, which derive little support from lexical-semantic representations and thus rely more heavily on phonology. Similarly, phonologically impaired patients should show increased effects of semantic variables such as imageability. Highly imageable words have been assumed by a number of authors to have "richer" semantic representations than less imageable words, perhaps because they are associated with a larger number of semantic features (Jones, 1985; Plaut & Shallice, 1991). Consequently, when repetition is forced to rely heavily on lexical-semantic processing due to phonological impairment, items that are well supported by such processing (i.e., highly imageable words) are repeated with a higher degree of accuracy than items that are not well supported (i.e., lower-imageability words). Larger than normal imageability effects emerge as a direct consequence of phonological impairment according to this interactive framework, rather than from additional damage somewhere along the lexical-semantic route (see Martin & Saffran, 1997). The interactive perspective also predicts that semantic effects should be greater following a delay: this biases the system towards greater reliance on semantic processing and will have a more catastrophic impact on the repetition of stimuli that derive little support from lexical-semantic activation, such as nonwords. Finally, the interactive framework anticipates that phonological impairment should increase the likelihood of both phonological and semantic errors in repetition, in line with the performance of deep dysphasic patients (see Martin & Saffran, 1992): phonological errors reflect difficulty in maintaining a veridical phonological representation, and semantic errors reflect an increased reliance on lexical-semantic processing.

In contrast, semantically impaired patients might be expected to show a reduction in the impact of word meaning on repetition. Lexicality effects should be smaller in this patient group, as lexical-semantic support for words over nonwords will be eroded. Previous studies have demonstrated that semantic deficits are also associated with reduced effects of word frequency and imageability in repetition (Martin & Saffran, 1997). However, patients with semantic dementia show degradation of semantic knowledge that is highly sensitive to word frequency. The meaning of lower-frequency words/concepts typically degrades earlier in the condition (Funnell, 1995), so high-frequency words may receive a stronger boost from lexical-semantic representations relative to lower-frequency words. This should increase, rather than decrease, the impact of word frequency on repetition in SD. In addition, word frequency/degree of semantic degradation should interact with delay—in immediate repetition, the good phonology of SD patients might enable them to retain even poorly understood words. However, after a delay, the phonological trace is no longer adequate for accurate repetition, and this should be more apparent for lower-frequency words that are more semantically degraded. It is more difficult to know what to predict for imageability. If highly imageable words have more semantic features (Jones, 1985; Plaut & Shallice, 1991), then they might be expected to be relatively resistant to semantic degradation. If so, SD patients should show enhanced effects of imageability as well as frequency in repetition. On the other hand, given that imageability effects are thought to reflect the normal operation of the semantic system, they might be reduced in size in SD. Finally, semantic impairment is expected to increase the occurrence of phonological errors in repetition due to a lessening of semantic constraints that reinforce the correct phonological pattern. These predictions for phonologically and semantically impaired patients are summarised in Table 1.

In this work we investigated the impact of phonological or semantic impairment on the repetition of a group of 12 CVA and 6 SD patients. SD and CVA patients have previously been studied in order to assess the contribution of phonological and semantic processes in repetition, but they have not been directly compared on the same tasks. We present analyses that (1) compare these two groups directly and (2) collapse across the groups to examine the influence of phonological and semantic skills on repetition. Previous investigations of the role of phonological and semantic processes in repetition (reviewed above) have relied largely on descriptions of single cases (although see N. Martin & Saffran, 1997, for a notable exception). The advantage of the case-series approach adopted here is that it is possible to investigate how factors tapping semantic/phonological processing vary systematically as a function of semantic/phonological impairment. For example, does the size of the imageability effect vary with the degree of phonological impairment (as proposed by Martin & Saffran, 1997) or with lexical-semantic damage (as proposed by Hanley & Kay, 1997; Hanley et al., 2002)? Is there a continuum between phonological and deep dysphasia explicable in terms of the severity of phonological impairment? To what extent does repetition reflect interactivity between semantics and phonology, in line with the predictions in Table 1?

We examined both immediate repetition and delayed repetition following articulatory suppression because theoretical considerations (see above) and empirical

TABLE 1
Predicted impact of semantic and phonological impairment on repetition according to interactive models

	Semantic impairment (semantic dementia)	Phonological impairment
Delay before response	Small effect; biggest for poorly comprehended words	Large effect; biggest for nonwords
Lexicality	Reduced effect	Increased effect
Imageability	Unclear	Increased effect
Frequency	Increased effect reflecting degree of semantic degradation	Increased effect
Phonological errors	Increased in frequency	Increased in frequency
Semantic errors	No semantic errors	Increased in frequency

findings (Jefferies et al., 2006a) suggest that lexical-semantic factors may play a greater role in repetition tasks when phonological maintenance is especially challenging. In delayed repetition, phonological output is not tightly constrained by incoming phonology; consequently long-term knowledge of the sounds and meanings of familiar words should make a larger contribution to phonological output. In line with this suggestion, phonological errors have been observed previously in delayed but not immediate repetition for a few SD patients (Knott et al., 1997, 2000): this study explores the generality of these findings in both SD and CVA. The study therefore presents an opportunity to establish if N. Martin and Saffran's (1997) findings for two-word lists generalise to a new task (delayed repetition) and a new patient population (SD).

METHOD

Participants

A total of 12 phonologically impaired CVA patients (PI-CVA) and 6 semantic dementia (SD) patients took part in the study (see Table 2 for background information). These groups had contrasting deficits: the PI-CVA group had more intact semantic memory but poorer phonological processing, whereas the SD patients had severe semantic impairment but relatively good phonology (see Tables 2 and 3). These groups were compared in order to explore the impact of semantic and phonological impairment on repetition. There was, however, some overlap between the semantic/phonological abilities of the patients in the two groups: some of the CVA patients had semantic as well as phonological difficulties. We therefore also examined associations between repetition and semantic/phonological deficits collapsing across the two groups (following the methods of N. Martin & Saffran, 1997).

Semantic dementia. SD is the temporal variant of frontal-temporal dementia and is associated with progressive bilateral focal atrophy of the anterior infero-temporal neocortex, which results in a specific and progressive impairment of semantic memory (Hodges, Patterson, Oxbury, & Funnell, 1992; Snowden, Goulding, & Neary, 1989). Patients with SD display a highly uniform pattern of impairments: they are anomic in spontaneous speech and picture naming and have impaired comprehension on both verbal and non-verbal tasks. In contrast, their perceptual and spatial skills, new episodic learning, non-verbal reasoning, syntax, and phonology remain largely intact (Hodges et al., 1992; Snowden, Neary, & Mann, 1996). SD patients have fluent speech that is largely free from phonological errors. Likewise, their single word repetition is excellent and they typically have good digit span (Jefferies et al., 2004b). They are able to discriminate between pairs of words that differ by a single phonetic feature (such as hat/cat) and can perform phoneme addition/subtraction (e.g., "shale" → ALE), at least until the late stages of the disease (Jefferies et al., 2005). Even late-stage patients continue to be sensitive to the effects of phonological similarity in ISR (Jefferies, Patterson, Bateman, Jones, & Lambon Ralph, 2006b). These findings support the characterisation of SD as semantic impairment in the context of good phonology. SD patients do show poor repetition of items that they no longer fully understand, especially in demanding tasks such as delayed repetition or ISR (see Jefferies et al., 2004a, for a review),

TABLE 2
Background information and semantic skills for each patient

		PI-CVA												SD						Mean		Controls	
Name	Max	LR	MM	RJ	RS	AB	NS	MR	BN	TJ	PG	TH	DB	SJ	EK	KI	JT	GT	MK	PI-CVA	SD	Mean	Cut-off†
Age		58	58	40	64	83	51	72	52	60	66	48	61	60	60	65	66	71	68	59	65		
Years post-onset		13	10	2	3	1	8	2	4	6	2	3	1	3	5	4	4	5	3	4.6	4.0		
Spoken word–picture match	30	29	29	29	21	30	29	29	25	28	30	30	30	28	23	19	18	11	5	28.3	17.3	‡	‡
Written word–picture match	30	27	28	29	29	29	29	30	24	29	30	29	30	NT	NT	NT	NT	NT	NT	28.6	NT	‡	‡
Picture association	30	20	22	23	26	24	22	22	15	17	27	28	25	21	13	8	16	15	9	22.6	13.7	27.6	24.8
Picture naming	30	12	15	15	15	12	21	22	18	25	25	29	29	13	8	8	4	4	1	19.8	6.3	‡	‡
Graded synonyms																							
Auditory: concrete	25	15	14	14	8	18	18	14	10	17	23	22	14	16	14	NT	NT	14	NT	15.6	14.7	21.0	15.0
Written: concrete	25	9	19	13	18	23	19	11	16	18	22	24	15	NT	NT	NT	NT	NT	NT	17.3	NT	23.9	21.4
Auditory: abstract	25	15	13	14	10	19	18	14	13	19	19	21	16	12	12	NT	NT	9	NT	15.9	11.0	21.0	14.0
Written: abstract	25	16	11	18	11	20	15	15	13	20	24	19	15	NT	NT	NT	NT	NT	NT	16.4	NT	23.3	20.0
Frequency by imageability synonyms	96	46	51	68	54	74	80	60	68	72	85	86	77	78	68	58	NT	48	30	68.4	56.2	94.5	91.0

PI-CVA=phonologically impaired cerebrovascular accident patient. SD=semantic dementia. NT=not tested. †=cut-off for normal performance at 2 SD below the mean. ‡=controls expected to be at ceiling on these easy tests. Picture association test=Shortened Camel and Cactus test used by Bozeat et al., 2000. Graded synonyms test by Warrington et al., 1998. Details of each test are given in the Method section.

TABLE 3

Phonological skills for each patient

| Name | Max | PI-CVA | | | | | | | | | | | | SD | | | | | | Mean | | Controls | |
		LR	MM	RJ	RS	AB	NS	MR	BN	TJ	PG	TH	DB	SJ	EK	KI	JT	GT	MK	PI-CVA	SD	Mean	Cut-off†
ADA nonword min pairs	40	40	31	36	22	30	18	31	36	39	37	39	40	NT	NT	NT	NT	NT	NT	33.3	NT	39.4	37.5
PALPA word min pairs	72	NT	NT	NT	NT	NT	NT	NT	NT	NT	NT	NT	NT	72	71	69	70	64	58	NT	67.3	70.1	63.4
PALPA nonword min pairs	72	NT	NT	NT	NT	NT	NT	NT	NT	NT	NT	NT	NT	70	71	71	70	60	59	NT	66.8	70.9	65.1
Nonword min pairs (proportion)	–	1	.8	.9	.6	.8	.5	.8	.9	1	.9	1	1	1	1	1	1	.8	.8	.83	.93	–	–
Segmentation total	96	67	0	11	0	71	0	16	50	19	0	47	61	92	81	83	90	66	nu	28.5	82.4	91.1	–
Phoneme addition	48	20	0	11	0	31	0	16	32	0	0	16	23	45	37	38	44	32	nu	12.4	39.2	–	–
Phoneme deletion	48	47	0	0	0	40	0	0	18	19	0	31	38	47	44	45	46	34	nu	16.1	43.2	–	–
Rhyme judgement	48	40	31	40	24	46	48	34	42	41	38	41	43	43	42	40	46	nu	nu	39.0	42.8	47.8	47.0
Rhyme production	24	15	13	13	–	10	15	11	9	9	–	9	13	21	20	20	17	nu	nu	11.9	19.5	22.0	17.3

PI-CVA=phonologically impaired cerebrovascular accident patient. SD=semantic dementia. NT=not tested. nu=not understood. †=cut-off for normal performance at 2 SD below the mean. Min pairs=minimal pairs. ADA=Action for dysphasic adults (Franklin et al., 1992). PALPA=Psycholinguistic Assessments of Language Processing in Aphasia (Kay et al., 1992). Details of each test are given in the Method section.

indicating that semantic memory makes a crucial contribution to phonological stability/maintenance. It should also be noted that as the disease progresses, patients show increasing difficulty on tasks such as phoneme segmentation and nonword repetition/recall. Although this pattern is consistent with the notion that additional phonological problems develop in late-stage SD, these tasks are not *purely* phonological and are demonstrably sensitive to semantic degradation. For example, nonwords that are phonologically similar to relatively well-understood words are recalled more accurately than nonwords that are derived from more semantically degraded words (Jefferies et al., 2005). Therefore, late-stage SD patients' difficulties on "phonological" tasks, which are observable in some of the patients examined here, may result from their severe semantic deficits.

Phonologically impaired cerebrovascular accident (PI-CVA) group. The PI-CVA group were recruited for a study on phonological and deep dyslexia (Crisp & Lambon Ralph, 2006) and were therefore selected according to their reading performance, rather than their phonological skills. However, neuropsychological tests revealed that all the PI-CVA patients had moderate to severe phonological impairment (see Table 3). A subset of this group also showed deficits on tests of semantic memory although these problems were milder than those shown by the SD cases (see Table 2). This group can therefore be characterised as phonologically impaired but relatively semantically intact. Both fluent and non-fluent speakers were included. None of the patients had marked apraxia of speech (although subtle difficulties of this nature were possibly present in case RS). Further details of these patients are provided by Crisp and Lambon Ralph (2006).

Phonological and semantic abilities in the two groups

We examined the performance of the two patient groups on a battery of semantic and phonological tests to allow consideration of the impact of semantic/phonological impairment on repetition. Four semantic tests were used. (1) Auditory word–picture matching: this test required patients to select the picture named aloud by the experimenter. There were 30 targets, each presented with 9 semantically related foils. The PI-CVA patients were also asked to perform a written version of this task. Their performance was largely comparable across the two versions, although one patient (RS), with auditory input problems/word deafness, was more accurate for written than spoken word–picture matching.[1] (2) The Camel and Cactus test of semantic association (Bozeat, Lambon Ralph, Patterson, Garrard, & Hodges, 2000). This was similar to the Pyramids and Palm Trees test (Howard & Patterson, 1992) and used the same 30 items as the word–picture matching test described above. Patients were asked to decide which of four pictures was most closely related in meaning to a target picture (e.g., camel: tree, sunflower, cactus, rose). The four choices were drawn from the same semantic category. (3) Patients were asked to name the same 30 targets from black and white line drawings. (4) Imageability by frequency synonym judgement test. Participants were asked to choose which of three written words was most similar in meaning to a written target (e.g., keep: become, save, put). There were 96 trials that orthogonally varied

---

[1] Despite this difference, the PI-CVA patients showed better performance than the SD patients on the auditory version of the task.

imageability (low, medium, high) and frequency (low and high). All four words within a trial were matched for these two factors such that the trials as a whole varied consistently on these two variables. The words were read aloud to the SD patients during the test because of their marked surface dyslexia. As the words were not also read aloud to the PI-CVA patients, the test is unlikely to be a pure measure of the comprehension of this reading-impaired group. However, the PI-CVA patients also completed the graded synonyms test (Warrington, McKenna, & Orpwood, 1998) using auditory and written presentation and the majority of patients showed little difference between the two modalities.

There were also four phonological tests. (1) Phoneme manipulation (Patterson & Marcel, 1992). There were two versions of this task. In the phoneme subtraction version, the patients were asked to delete the first sound of an item and say what remained (e.g., vale → ale). In the phoneme addition version, patients were asked to add a phoneme to the rhyme of an item (e.g., ale → vale). All of the items were monosyllabic and the same 48 items were used in the two versions of the task. The lexicality of the stimulus and the target response was manipulated. There were four conditions: word → word; word → nonword; nonword → word; nonword → nonword. (2) Rhyme judgement (Patterson & Marcel, 1992): This task required patients to judge whether or not two spoken words rhymed (e.g., white–kite). There were 48 trials. Half of the 24 non-rhyming trials were composed of two phonologically similar words (e.g., tick–tin). (3) Rhyme production (Patterson & Marcel, 1992): Patients were asked to produce a word that rhymed with 24 spoken words. (4) Minimal pairs: Patients made same/different judgements for pairs of auditorily presented nonwords that differed by a single phonetic feature (e.g., miv–niv). The available data for the two patient groups on this task are from two comparable tests: the PI-CVA patients were tested on the nonword minimal pairs test from the ADA battery (Franklin, Turner, & Ellis, 1992), whereas the SD patients were tested on the minimal pairs test from the PALPA (Kay, Lesser, & Coltheart, 1992). While it is obviously less than ideal that the patients were tested on different sets of items, these data still provide a guide to the auditory discrimination abilities of the two groups.

Several of the PI-CVA patients were unable to perform the phoneme manipulation and rhyme production tasks. For these patients, testing was discontinued and a score of zero was assumed. There are also missing data on the phoneme manipulation and rhyme tests for two of the later-stage SD patients. These cases were unable to comprehend the task instructions (for example, they did not understand the notion of "rhyme"). These values are treated as missing below.[2]

Across these tests, the SD patients were semantically impaired yet relatively phonologically intact, whereas the PI-CVA patients were phonologically impaired but more semantically intact (see Tables 2 and 3). The SD patients showed greater impairment than the PI-CVA group across a range of semantic tests: spoken word–picture matching, $t(16) = 4.26$, $p = .001$; semantic association, $t(16) = 4.26$, $p = .001$; and picture naming, $t(16) = 4.77$, $p = .0002$. However, they did not differ significantly on the synonym judgement test, $t(15) = 1.55$, ns, possibly because the PI-CVA

---

[2] Nevertheless, the patient groups were significantly different on these tasks even when the zeros obtained by the PI-CVA patients were treated as missing values.

patients' poor reading (their phonological/deep dyslexia) contributed to their difficulties on this task. The PI-CVA patients performed more poorly than the SD patients on two measures of phonological skill: phoneme manipulation, $t(15) = 4.05$, $p = .001$, and rhyme production, $t(14) = 3.63$, $p = .003$. However, the two groups did not differ significantly on two other measures: rhyme judgement $t(14) = 1.09$, ns, and minimal pair discrimination $t(16) = 1.25$, ns.

Collapsing across groups, there were strong correlations between the four semantic tasks (word–picture matching and semantic association: $r = .72$, $p = .001$; word–picture matching and naming: $r = .77$, $p = .0002$; naming and semantic association: $r = .71$, $p = .001$; word–picture matching and synonym judgement: $r = .73$, $p = .001$; naming and synonym judgement: $r = .74$, $p = .001$; semantic association and synonym judgement: $r = .58$, $p = .02$). There were also marked correlations between the phonological tasks. Phoneme manipulation correlated with all three of the other phonological tasks (rhyme judgement: $r = .53$, $p = .04$; rhyme production: $r = .78$, $p = .0004$; minimal pairs: $r = .59$, $p = .01$). Rhyme production also correlated with rhyme judgement ($r = .71$, $p = .002$).

Word–picture matching, semantic association, and naming did not positively correlate with any of the phonological measures. Similarly, phoneme segmentation, rhyme production, and minimal pair discrimination did not positively correlate with any of the semantic measures.[3] However, there was a positive correlation between synonym judgement and rhyme judgement ($r = .58$, $p = .02$), possibly because both tasks tapped working memory and required decision making.

An overall estimate of each participant's semantic and phonological performance was obtained using factor analysis (as in Lambon Ralph, Moriarty, & Sage, 2002). For semantics, we used the three semantic tasks for which data were available for every patient (word–picture matching, naming, semantic association). The single-factor solution accounted for 82% of the variance. For phonology, we used the two phonological tasks for which there were least missing data (phoneme manipulation and minimal pair discrimination).[4] Again, a single-factor solution was derived that accounted for 79% of the variance. We did not obtain a composite measure of phonology for one SD patient, MK, due to missing data. The factor scores from these analyses were used as a measure of each patient's semantic/phonological impairment in subsequent analysis.

Repetition tasks

In each of three tasks, immediate and delayed repetition was assessed in a single trial. The experimenter presented the items auditorily. Participants attempted to repeat

[3] There were some *negative* correlations between phonological and semantic measures, presumably reflecting the fact that the semantically impaired SD patients had relatively good phonology whereas the phonologically impaired CVA patients had relatively good semantics.

[4] Several of the stroke aphasic patients were unable to complete the segmentation task, presumably due to their severe phonological difficulties, and were assigned a score of zero which was included in the factor analysis. We also computed a phonological factor score using minimal pair discrimination and rhyme judgement; for these tasks, all of the stroke patients were off floor. The two factor scores were very highly correlated ($r = .85$; $p < .0001$). Both significantly correlated with the size of the imageability effect in delayed repetition although the alternative phonological factor score did not correlate with the effect of delay in repetition.

each one both immediately and again after a 5-second delay. The delay was filled with phonological production (see below). No feedback was given about the accuracy of responses.

(1) The first task involved 96 words and crossed two levels of word frequency with three levels of imageability (the targets from the imageability by frequency synonym judgment test; referred to as Word Set 1 below). As the high-imageability words in Set 1 were significantly shorter than the low-imageability words, a matched subset of 72 items was selected. In this subset, syllable and phoneme length were held constant across the different levels of frequency and imageability. The characteristics of these words are shown in the Appendix. For the PI-CVA patients, the delay between the immediate and second repetition was filled with rehearsal of their own name.[5] The SD group was asked to count aloud from 1 during the delay.

(2) Both groups of participants were asked to count aloud from 1 during the 5-second delay for Word Set 2, making it possible to see if the results from the first word set would hold for a new set of items when the two patient groups performed identical tasks. There was some variation in the rate of participants' counting, with the SD patients typically counting faster than the PI-CVA group. This word set also crossed frequency with imageability and contained two levels of each variable. The 56 items considered here comprised a matched subset of those tested (62 for the SD patients and 120 for the PI-CVA patients). The high- and low-frequency/imageability words were equivalent in terms of phoneme and syllable length (see Appendix).

(3) The third task involved nonword repetition. The 48 nonwords were derived from the low-frequency words in Word Set 1 and were matched to them for syllable length and number of phonological neighbours. Other methodological details were as described for Word Set 1.

RESULTS

Accuracy: Difference between patient groups

As the results were very similar for the complete word sets and the matched subsets in which length was held constant across the levels of frequency/imageability, only the matched subsets are considered below. Immediate self-corrections were counted as correct in these analyses.

Words: Set 1. Immediate and delayed repetition data were obtained for 11 PI-CVA patients and 6 SD patients. One PI-CVA patient was unable to complete the delayed repetition task and was excluded from the analysis. The results for each group are shown in Figure 1 and individual patient data are provided in Table 4. The influence of delay, frequency, and imageability on repetition in the two patient groups was compared by subjects (F_1) and by items (F_2) using analysis of variance (ANOVA). Delay had a greater impact on the repetition of the PI-CVA patients, in line with their more severe phonological impairments, $F_1(1, 15) = 7.6$, $p = .02$; $F_2(1,$

---

[5] Pilot work had identified this as the most reliable method of getting this group with sometimes severe expressive aphasia to fill the delay with overt articulatory suppression.

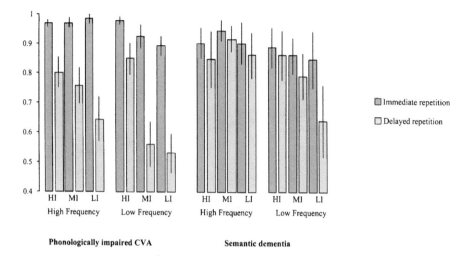

Note: Each set of bars shows immediate and delayed repetition for one level of frequency (high/low) in one group of patients at three levels of imageability (HI = high imageability; MI = medium imageability; LI = low imageability). Error bars show standard error of mean.

Figure 1. The influence of frequency and imageability on immediate and delayed repetition.

66) = 70.8, $p < .0001$. Immediate repetition was superior to delayed repetition for both the PI-CVA patients, $F_1(1, 10) = 29.2$, $p = .001$; $F_2(1, 66) = 231.2$, $p < .0001$, and the SD patients, $F_1(1, 5) = 7.6$, $p = .04$; $F_2(1, 66) = 28.0$, $p < .0001$.

High-frequency words were repeated more accurately than low-frequency words by both the SD patients, $F_1(1, 5) = 12.03$, $p = .02$; $F_2(1, 66) = 7.3$, $p = .01$, and the PI-CVA patients, $F_1(1, 10) = 20.1$, $p = .001$; $F_2(1, 66) = 10.0$, $p = .002$. Frequency had an equivalent effect on the two groups, $F_1(1, 15) < 1$; $F_2(1, 66) < 1$. For the SD patients, the effect of the delay was modulated by frequency, $F_1(1, 5) = 11.0$, $p = .02$; $F_2(1, 66) = 4.9$, $p = .03$: delay had relatively little impact on the high-frequency, more semantically intact items, Bonferroni $t_1(5) = 1.3$, ns; $t_2(35) = 3.0$, $p = .01$, but a more substantial effect on the poorly comprehended/low-frequency items, Bonferroni $t_1(5) = 4.3$, $p = .01$; $t_2(35) = 3.9$, $p = .0008$. In contrast, delay did not interact with frequency for the PI-CVA group, $F_1(1, 10) = 3.8$, $p = .08$; $F_2(1, 66) = 1.7$, ns. The three-way interaction between patient group, frequency and delay did not reach significance, $F_1(1, 15) < 1$; $F_2(1, 66) < 1$.

High-imageability words were repeated more accurately than low-imageability words by the PI-CVA patients, $F_1(2, 20) = 13.7$, $p = .0002$; $F_2(2, 66) = 15.2$, $p < .0001$. In contrast, the SD patients did not show a significant main effect of imageability, $F_1(2, 10) = 1.8$, ns; $F_2(2, 66) = 2.0$, ns. Imageability affected the repetition of the PI-CVA patients more strongly than the SD patients, $F_1(2, 30) = 2.5$, $p = .1$; $F_2(2, 66) = 3.6$, $p = .03$. In both groups, the delay had a greater influence on words that were lower in imageability, PI-CVA: $F_1(2, 20) = 11.4$, $p = .0005$; $F_2(2, 66) = 12.2$, $p < .0001$; SD: $F_1(2, 10) = 7.5$, $p = .01$; $F_2(2, 66) = 3.9$, $p = .03$. This interaction between delay and imageability was larger for the PI-CVA patients, $F_1(2, 30) = 2.8$, $p = .08$; $F_2(2, 66) = 3.5$, $p = .04$.

There was an interaction between frequency and imageability, $F_1(2, 30) = 7.1$, $p = .003$; $F_2(2, 66) = 4.5$, $p = .02$, which did not vary significantly with patient group, $F_1(2, 30) < 1$; $F_2(2, 66) < 1$. The size of the frequency by imageability interaction was

TABLE 4
Accuracy for individual patients on Word Set 1 as a function of delay, frequency, and imageability

		PI-CVA												SD					
		RS	NS	MM	LR	TJ	AB	BN	DB	MR	TH	PG	RJ	SJ	EK	JT	KI	GT	MK
Immediate	HF HI	.33	1	1	1	1	.92	1	1	.92	1	.92	.92	1	1	1	.92	.75	.75
	HF MI	0	1	1	1	.92	1	.92	1	1	1	1	.83	1	1	1	1	.83	.83
	HF LI	0	1	.92	1	1	1	1	1	1	1	1	.83	.92	1	1	1	.58	.83
	LF HI	.08	1	1	1	1	1	1	1	1	1	.92	.92	1	.92	.92	1	.83	.58
	LF MI	0	1	.75	1	1	.92	.92	1	.92	.83	.92	.58	.92	1	.92	.92	.58	.83
	LF LI	0	.92	1	1	1	.92	.83	.83	.83	1	1	.75	1	.92	1	.92	.75	.42
	High frequency	.11	1	1	1	.97	.97	.97	1	.97	1	.97	.86	.97	.97	.97	.97	.72	.81
	Low frequency	.03	.97	.89	1	1	.97	.92	.94	.92	.94	.94	.75	.96	.97	1	.94	.72	.61
	High imageability	.21	1	.96	1	1	.96	.92	1	.96	1	.92	.92	1	.96	.96	.96	.79	.67
	Medium imageability	0	1	1	1	.96	1	.92	.92	.96	.92	.96	.92	.96	1	.96	.96	.71	.83
	Low imageability	0	.96	.88	1	1	.96	.92	.92	.92	1	1	.71	1	.96	.96	.96	.67	.63
	All	.07	.99	.94	1	.99	.97	.94	.97	.94	.97	.96	.79	.99	.99	.99	.96	.72	.71
Delayed	HF HI	NT	1	.75	.92	.42	.67	.83	.92	.83	1	.83	.67	1	1	1	.92	.75	.42
	HF MI	NT	.83	.83	.75	.50	.58	.67	1	.83	.83	.92	.42	1	1	.92	1	.83	.75
	HF LI	NT	.50	.42	.92	.58	.42	.67	1	.92	1	.58	.25	.92	1	1	1	.58	.67
	LF HI	NT	.92	.75	.92	.42	.92	.92	1	.92	.92	.92	.67	.92	1	1	1	.75	.50
	LF MI	NT	.75	.25	.75	.25	.42	.33	.75	.83	.92	.58	.33	.92	.92	.75	.96	.50	.67
	LF LI	NT	.50	.25	.58	.50	.33	.50	.75	.58	1	.58	.25	.92	.83	.75	.67	.58	.08
	High frequency	NT	.78	.67	.86	.50	.56	.72	.97	.86	.94	.78	.44	.97	1	.97	.97	.72	.61
	Low frequency	NT	.72	.42	.75	.39	.56	.58	.83	.78	.97	.69	.42	.92	.92	.83	.89	.61	.42
	High imageability	NT	.96	.75	.92	.42	.79	.88	.96	.88	1	.88	.67	.96	1	1	.96	.75	.46
	Medium imageability	NT	.79	.54	.75	.38	.50	.50	.88	.83	.96	.75	.38	.96	.96	.83	1	.67	.71
	Low imageability	NT	.50	.33	.75	.54	.38	.58	.88	.75	.92	.58	.25	.92	.92	.88	.83	.58	.38
	All	NT	.75	.54	.81	.44	.56	.65	.90	.82	.96	.74	.43	.94	.96	.90	.93	.67	.51

Figures show proportion of items correct. PI-CVA = phonologically impaired cerebrovascular accident patient. SD = semantic dementia. HF = high frequency, LF = low frequency, HI = high imageability, MI = medium imageability, LI = low imageability. NT = not tested.

affected by the delay, $F_1(2, 30) = 3.8$, $p = .03$; $F_2(2, 66) = 4.1$, $p = .02$. The frequency by imageability interaction reached significance for delayed repetition, $F_1(2, 32) = 8.7$, $p = .001$; $F_2(2, 66) = 5.8$, $p = .005$, but not immediate repetition, $F_1(2, 32) = 2.7$, $p = .09$; $F_2(2, 66) = 1.4$, ns.

Words: Set 2. The six SD patients and seven of the PI-CVA patients provided data on an additional set of words. A comparison of the two groups replicated many of the findings for Word Set 1 (see Table 5, which shows the mean performance for each group, and Table 6, which shows the outcome of analyses by subjects and items). Both groups showed poorer repetition after a delay; however, the delay had a greater

TABLE 5
Accuracy for each patient group on Word Set 2

	SD (N = 6)		Phonologically impaired CVA (N = 5)	
	Immediate	*Delayed*	*Immediate*	*Delayed*
High frequency, high imageability	.99 (0.41)	.99 (0.41)	.99 (0.38)	.94 (1.07)
High frequency, low imageability	.89 (1.76)	.86 (1.67)	.94 (1.07)	.72 (2.97)
Low frequency, high imageability	.92 (2.04)	.83 (1.97)	.99 (0.38)	.84 (1.80)
Low frequency, low imageability	.80 (3.31)	.70 (3.54)	.91 (1.50)	.70 (4.10)
High frequency	.94	.92	.96	.83
Low frequency	.86	.77	.95	.77
High imageability	.95	.91	.99	.89
Low imageability	.84	.78	.92	.71
All	.90	.85	.96	.80

Figures show mean proportion of items correct for each group (standard deviation in parentheses).

TABLE 6
Analysis of differences in repetition accuracy between the two patient groups for Word Set 2

	Semantic dementia (N = 6)	Phonologically impaired CVA (N = 7)	Cross-group comparison (N = 13)
Delay	$F_1 = 27.0$, $p = .01$ $F_2 = 7.4$, $p = .01$	$F_1 = 11.5$, $p = .01$ $F_2 = 52.6$, $p = .0001$	$F_1 = 4.0$, $p = .07$ $F_2 = 19.3$, $p = .0001$
Frequency	$F_1 = 6.1$, $p = .06$ $F_2 = 13.6$, $p = .001$	$F_1 = 4.7$, $p = .07$ $F_2 = 2.4$, ns	$F_1 = 2.8$, ns $F_2 = 4.7$, $p = .03$
Frequency by delay	$F_1 = 30.0$, $p = .01$ $F_2 = 2.3$, ns	$F_1 = 1.1$, ns $F_2 = 1.1$, ns	$F_1 < 1$ $F_2 < 1$
Imageability	$F_1 = 6.3$, $p = .05$ $F_2 = 12.2$, $p = .001$	$F_1 = 7.6$, $p = .03$ $F_2 = 21.2$, $p = .0001$	$F_1 < 1$ $F_2 < 1$
Imageability by delay	$F_1 = 1.0$, ns $F_2 < 1$	$F_1 = 5.7$, $p = .05$ $F_2 = 5.1$, $p = .03$	$F_1 = 2.4$, $p = .15$ $F_2 = 4.4$, $p = .04$
Frequency by imageability	$F_1 < 1$ $F_2 < 1$	$F_1 < 1$ $F_2 < 1$	$F_1 < 1$ $F_2 < 1$

F_1 denotes analysis by subjects (degrees of freedom = (1, 5) for semantic dementia group; (1, 6) for phonologically impaired CVA group; (1, 11) for cross-group comparison). F_2 denotes analysis by items (degrees of freedom = (1, 52) for all comparisons). ns = not significant (all $p > .1$).

impact on the PI-CVA patients. Both groups also showed effects of frequency and imageability (although the frequency effect was only marginally significant for the PI-CVA group). In the by-participants analysis, the SD group showed an interaction between frequency and delay. The delay impaired the SD patients' repetition of low-frequency words that were presumably semantically degraded, Bonferroni $t_1(5) = 5.8$, $p = .004$, but did not affect the repetition of high-frequency words, Bonferroni $t_1(5) = 2.2$, ns. There was no interaction between frequency and delay for the PI-CVA patients. For the PI-CVA but not the SD patients, there was an interaction between imageability and delay. The delay had a larger effect on the PI-CVA patients' repetition of low-imageability words, Bonferroni $t_1(6) = 3.2$, $p = .04$; $t_2(27) = 6.0$, $p = .0001$, although there was also a significant effect of delay for high-imageability words, Bonferroni $t_1(6) = 3.1$, $p = .04$; $t_2(27) = 4.0$, $p = .001$.

Words vs nonwords. A total of 11 PI-CVA patients and 6 SD patients performed immediate and delayed repetition of 48 nonwords matched to the low-frequency words from Set 1. The group results are shown in Figure 2 and individual patient data are shown in Table 7. In the complete set of items collapsing across syllable length, lexicality had a highly significant effect on the repetition of the PI-CVA group, $F_1(1, 10) = 136.2$, $p < .0001$; $F_2(1, 94) = 99.9$, $p < .0001$, and a somewhat smaller influence for the SD patients, $F_1(1, 5) = 2.6$, ns; $F_2(1, 94) = 18.2$, $p < .0001$. The interaction between lexicality and patient group reached significance, $F_1(1, 15) = 3.5$, $p = .08$; $F_2(1, 94) = 16.2$, $p = .0001$. There was an interaction between lexicality and delay for the PI-CVA patients, $F_1(1, 10) = 16.9$, $p = .002$; $F_2(1, 94) = 30.9$, $p < .0001$, which reflected the fact that the delay impaired the repetition of nonwords, Bonferroni $t_1(10) = 9.2$, $p < .0001$; $t_2(47) = 19.5$, $p < .0001$, more substantially than the repetition of words, Bonferroni $t_1(10) = 5.6$, $p = .0004$; $t_2(47) = 9.9$, $p < .0001$. In contrast, the lexicality effect did not vary with the delay for the SD patients, $F_1(1, 5) < 1$; $F_2(1, 94) < 1$. The three-way interaction between

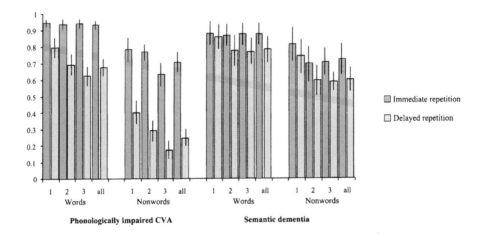

Note: Each set of bars shows immediate and delayed repetition for words/nonwords at three syllable lengths and combining across length. Error bars show standard error of mean.

Figure 2. Lexicality and item length effects for the two patient groups.

TABLE 7
Accuracy for individual patients as a function of delay, lexicality, and item length

	Syllables	PI-CVA													Semantic dementia				
		RS	NS	MM	LR	TJ	AB	BN	DB	MR	TH	PG	RJ	SJ	EK	JT	KI	GT	MK
Immediate word	1	0	1	1	1	1	1	.86	1	.86	1	.86	.86	1	1	1	.86	.57	.86
	2	.05	1	.80	1	1	1	.95	1	.95	.90	.95	.75	.95	.95	.95	1	.75	.60
	3	0	.94	1	1	1	.89	.94	.89	.94	1	1	.72	.94	1	1	.94	.72	.61
	all	.02	.98	.90	1	.98	.96	.94	.94	.94	.96	.94	.73	.96	.98	.98	.96	.71	.65
Delayed word	1	NT	1	.43	.86	.71	.86	.57	1	.86	1	.86	.57	1	1	1	.86	.57	.71
	2	NT	.85	.45	.80	.30	.70	.55	.90	.80	.95	.75	.55	.90	.90	.90	.95	.60	.40
	3	NT	.56	.50	.72	.50	.39	.67	.72	.78	1	.67	.33	.94	.89	.78	.89	.67	.44
	all	NT	.75	.48	.77	.44	.60	.58	.81	.79	.98	.73	.46	.94	.90	.88	.90	.63	.46
Immediate nonword	1	.14	1	.57	.86	.86	.86	.86	1	.86	1	.29	.43	.43	.86	1	1	.57	1
	2	0	.95	.55	.90	.80	.50	.90	.90	.75	.90	.60	.65	.30	.80	.85	.95	.45	.80
	3	0	.94	.39	.94	.78	.39	.78	.67	.50	.78	.44	.33	.39	.72	.89	.89	.56	.78
	all	.02	.92	.48	.92	.75	.50	.85	.83	.67	.88	.48	.46	.35	.77	.90	.94	.52	.83
Delayed nonword	1	NT	.57	0	.29	.29	.57	.29	.43	.57	.86	.29	.29	.43	.86	1	.86	.43	.86
	2	NT	.55	.10	.45	0	.15	.20	.40	.30	.65	.30	.10	.30	.70	.65	.85	.35	.70
	3	NT	.33	.11	.33	0	.11	0	.28	.06	.50	.22	0	.39	.78	.61	.56	.50	.67
	all	NT	.44	.08	.35	.04	.19	.13	.33	.23	.60	.25	.08	.35	.75	.69	.71	.40	.69

Figures show proportion of items correct. PI-CVA = phonologically impaired cerebrovascular accident patient. NT = not tested.

patient group, lexicality, and delay reached significance, reflecting this difference between the two groups, $F_1(1, 15) = 5.4$, $p = .03$; $F_2(1, 94) = 13.5$, $p = .0004$.

Items contained one syllable ($N = 7$), two syllables ($N = 20$), three syllables ($N = 18$), or four syllables ($N = 3$). We considered the effect of syllable length on the repetition of nonwords, excluding the small number of items with four syllables from the analysis. The number of syllables had a significant effect on repetition accuracy for both the PI-CVA patients, $F_1(2, 20) = 10.1$, $p = .001$; $F_2(2, 42) = 3.9$, $p = .03$, and the SD patients, $F_1(2, 10) = 7.1$, $p = .01$; $F_2(2, 42) < 1$. There was no interaction between syllable length and patient group, $F_1(2, 30) = 1.9$, ns; $F_2(2, 42) = 1.5$, ns.

Accuracy: Correlations with composite semantic and phonological scores

For each patient, the size of the lexicality, frequency, and imageability effects in delayed repetition were estimated by determining the difference between words/nonwords, high/low-frequency words and high/low-imageability words (medium-imageability words were discarded). Similarly, we computed the difference between immediate/delayed repetition to examine the effect of the delay for words and nonwords. Correlations were calculated between the effect size for each patient and the composite measures of semantic and phonological impairment. This analysis included 11 PI-CVA patients and 6 SD patients who were tested on Word Set 1 (although we were unable to obtain a composite phonological score for one SD case, patient MK). The significance values reported below are one-tailed. Positive correlations indicate an association between *good* semantics/phonology and a large effect of the variable in question, whereas negative correlations indicate that semantic/phonological *impairment* was coupled with a large effect of the variable.

There was a significant negative correlation between the semantic and phonological composite measures, presumably indicating that the semantically impaired SD patients were generally good at the phonological tasks, whereas the phonologically impaired CVA patients had relatively good semantics ($r = -.43$, $p = .05$). Good performance on semantic tasks was associated with a large influence of lexicality in delayed repetition ($r = .81$, $p < .0001$). This correlation was significant for the SD group alone, despite the small sample size, indicating that the milder SD patients showed larger lexicality effects ($N = 6$, $r = .92$, $p = .009$). Semantic deficits were linked to large frequency effects both for all of the cases combined ($r = -.40$, $p = .05$) and the SD group separately ($r = -.84$, $p = .03$). Finally, combining the two groups, there was a correlation between semantic abilities and delay effects in nonword repetition ($r = .43$, $p = .04$), reflecting the SD patients' insensitivity to delay.

Preserved phonological skills were linked to a reduced effect of delay on both word repetition ($r = -.50$, $p = .02$) and nonword repetition ($r = -.36$, $p = .08$). Patients with poor phonological skills also showed a more substantial effect of imageability ($r = -.63$, $p = .004$).

Errors

Errors that were immediately and spontaneously self-corrected were excluded from this analysis. Incorrect responses were classified in the following way: Semantic errors were semantically or associatively related to the target word (e.g., KITTEN →

"mouse"). Derivational errors included both inflectional errors (PRIVATE → "privately") and completions (WINDOW → "window cleaner"). There were two categories of phonological error. Close phonological errors shared at least 50% of the target phonemes (e.g., SUFFIX → "sussex"). Distant phonological errors shared at least one phoneme with the target, excluding the neutral schwa sound (ARBITOR → "abudy"). Formal (i.e., real word) errors were coded separately from nonword paraphasias, making it possible to consider influences on phonological errors (combining words and nonwords) and lexicality of responses (combining phonological and unrelated responses). A small number of errors were both phonologically and semantically related to the target words (WICKET → "cricket"). These are combined with the other semantic errors in the analysis below. Perseverations occurred when a previous response was repeated (e.g., Trial 1: QUAKE → "quake"; Trial 2: CRUSH → "quake"). A second category of incomplete or altered perseverations comprised responses that contained a significant degree of perseveration (e.g., Trial 1: STRENGTH → "strength"; Trial 2: CONSTANT → "struh"). Omissions were failures to respond, or responses such as "forgot it". Unrelated errors did not fall into any of these categories. The lexicality of close/distant phonological errors and unrelated responses was recorded.

Word Set 1. This analysis is based on the matched subset of words ($N = 72$) discussed above. There were too few errors in immediate repetition to conduct a formal analysis. Only one PI-CVA patient (PS) made a substantial number of errors in this task—these were primarily omissions. Two SD patients (GT and MK) also had accuracy below 80%—most of their errors were close phonological approximations. The other patients in both groups made small numbers of close phonological errors.

Figure 3 shows average errors of each type as a proportion of total errors in delayed repetition for each patient group. Phonological errors (combining across the close and distant categories) were more numerous for the SD than the PI-CVA

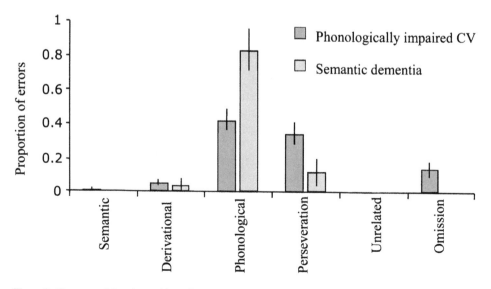

Figure 3. Errors on delayed repetition of Word Set 1. Errors are expressed as a proportion of total errors. Error bars show standard error of the mean.

patients, $t(15) = 3.33$, $p = .005$. The PI-CVA patients made more semantic/derivational errors than the SD patients, $t(10.5) = 2.82$, $p = .02$; collapsing these two categories. Thus semantic impairment was associated with relatively large numbers of phonological errors, whereas phonological impairment produced semantic/derivational errors (although it should be emphasised that semantic errors were a small proportion of the total number of errors and were only made by 3 out of 11 participants—in contrast, derivational errors were made by 8 of the CVA cases). Perseverations (combining the complete and partial perseveration categories) were also more frequent for the PI-CVA group, $t(15) = 2.07$, $p = .06$, as were omissions, $t(15) = 2.55$, $p = .02$. The majority of perseverations were complete repetitions of a previous response (83%). Although the number of errors of some types was small, these effects were all significant in nonparametric tests (Mann Whitney $U < 12.5$, $p < .04$). The pattern of results was also unchanged when errors were expressed as a proportion of items presented (as opposed to a proportion of total errors).

The PI-CVA patients made more real word responses in delayed word repetition than the SD patients: 40% vs 18% of phonological and unrelated errors; $\chi^2(1) = 8.50$, $p = .004$. This difference may have reflected the PI-CVA patients' increased reliance on semantics in the repetition task.

Correlations between the number of errors in each category (expressed as a proportion of total errors) and the composite measures of semantic and phonological impairment were calculated, combining the two patient groups. There was a negative correlation between the phonological factor and semantic/derivational errors ($r = -.49$, two-tailed $p = .06$), indicating that these errors were associated with phonological impairment. These errors were also associated with poor nonword repetition, both immediately ($r = -.61$, two-tailed $p = .01$) and after a delay ($r = -.67$, two-tailed $p = .004$). There was no association between semantic/derivational errors and the semantic factor ($r = .32$, two-tailed $p = .21$). There was a strong negative correlation between the semantic factor and phonological errors ($r = -.76$, two-tailed $p = .0004$), indicating that phonological errors were associated with semantic impairment. Conversely, there was a positive correlation between the phonological factor and phonological errors ($r = .51$, two-tailed $p = .04$), indicating that the patients with good phonology (i.e., the SD patients) typically made more phonological errors. Phonological impairment was associated with a higher incidence of omission errors ($r = -.85$, two-tailed $p < .0001$). In addition, semantically impaired patients made fewer perseverative errors ($r = .61$, two-tailed $p = .009$), presumably reflecting the fact that these errors were uncommon amongst the SD patients.

Word Set 2. An analysis of delayed repetition errors for Word Set 2 replicated many of these findings (see Table 8). The SD group made more phonological errors than the PI-CVA patients, $t(11) = 4.90$, $p = .0005$. The PI-CVA patients made more perseverations, $t(11) = 2.48$, $p = .03$, and showed a trend towards making more omissions, $t(6) = 2.10$, $p = .08$. The difference in phonological errors reached significance in a nonparametric test (Mann-Whitney $U = 1.0$; $p = .004$). The difference in perseverations approached significance (Mann-Whitney $U = 8.0$; $p = .06$). However, there was no significant difference between the groups in the number of semantic/derivational errors due to the small number of errors of this type, $t(11) < 1$; Mann-Whitney $U = 16.0$, $p = .4$.

TABLE 8
Errors on delayed repetition of Word Set 2

	PI-CVA (N = 7)		Semantic dementia (N = 6)	
	M	SD	M	SD
Semantic & derivational	.16	.37	.04	.10
Phonological	.31	.18	.86	.22
Perseverations	.41	.28	.10	.15
Unrelated	.02	.05	0	0
Omission	.10	.12	0	0

Errors are expressed as a proportion of total errors. Figures show mean and standard deviation for each group. PI-CVA = phonologically impaired cerebrovascular accident patient.

Nonwords. Table 9 shows the errors made by the two patient groups in immediate and delayed nonword repetition. One PI-CVA patient, RS, was not tested on the delayed repetition task and was excluded from this analysis. In immediate repetition, the errors made by both groups were almost exclusively phonological in nature (although patient RS made a larger number of errors in immediate repetition, 60% of which were omissions). In delayed repetition, the majority of errors were again phonological. This category represented a larger proportion of the total number of errors for SD patients compared with PI-CVA patients, $t(15) = 2.74$, $p = .02$; Mann-Whitney $U = 3.0$, $p = .002$. The PI-CVA group made more omissions, $t(15) = 2.95$, $p = .01$; Mann-Whitney $U = 0.0$, $p = .001$, and perseverations, $t(15) = 1.96$, $p = .07$;

TABLE 9
Errors on immediate and delayed repetition of nonwords

			PI-CVA (N = 11)		Semantic dementia (N = 6)	
			M	SD	M	SD
Nonwords	Immediate	Semantic & derivational	0	0	0	0
		Phonological	.97	.08	1	0
		Perseveration	0	0	0	0
		Unrelated	0	0	0	0
		Omission	.03	.08	0	0
	Delayed	Semantic & derivational	0	0	0	0
		Phonological	.72	.23	.99	.03
		Perseveration	.19	.21	.01	.03
		Unrelated	.01	.03	0	0
		Omission	.08	.06	0	0
Words (matched subset)	Delayed	Semantic & derivational	.10	.11	.06	.14
		Phonological	.52	.25	.89	.27
		Perseveration	.22	.21	.06	.14
		Unrelated	.01	.03	0	0
		Omission	.15	.14	0	0

Errors are expressed as a proportion of total errors. Figures show mean and standard deviation for each group. PI-CVA = phonologically impaired cerebrovascular accident patient.

Mann-Whitney $U = 12.5$, $p = .04$. The majority of perseverations were partial (84%; e.g., pomor → "porg"; gintry → "forg").

Effect of lexicality. Patients' errors on nonwords and the matched subset of words were compared (see Table 9). The SD patients' errors on both delayed word and nonword repetition were almost exclusively phonologically related to the target (97% and 99% of errors respectively, combining across the patients). The fact that this group did not show any differences in the errors they made to words and nonwords might have reflected their severe semantic impairments, with the repetition of unknown words resembling that of nonwords. In contrast, the PI-CVA group made more semantic errors in word than nonword repetition, $t(10) = 3.00$, $p = .01$; Wilcoxon Signed Ranks Test $Z = 2.52$, $p = .01$, and more phonological errors in nonword than word repetition, $t(10) = 2.58$, $p = .03$; Wilcoxon Signed Ranks Test $Z = 2.05$, $p = .04$. They also showed a trend towards making more omission errors in nonword repetition, $t(10) = 1.98$, $p = .08$; Wilcoxon Signed Ranks Test $Z = 1.87$, $p = .06$.

Perseverative errors. It is somewhat surprising that the more phonologically impaired group, who showed poorer repetition following a delay, also made more perseverative responses in delayed repetition. We examined the perseverations of the PI-CVA patients during delayed repetition of the complete group of 96 items included in Word Set 1 in more detail. This analysis included perseverations that were spontaneously self-corrected. The number of perseverations per patient ranged from 2.1% to 44.8% of trials ($M = 11.8\%$; $SD = 13.0$). On most of these trials, the perseveration occurred despite accurate immediate repetition (e.g., Trial 1: RIVER → "river"... "river"; Trial 2: HUMOUR → "humour"... "river"). A preceding target word was produced in its entirety in 70% of these perseverations; the remaining trials were either complete perseverations of an error (e.g., rogue → "curtains"; winter → "curtains") or were partial perseverations (e.g., window → window; helmet → "win"). Considering only complete perseverations of targets, 71% involved the repetition of high-frequency words, as opposed to 29% on which low-frequency words were reproduced. These values significantly differed from the expected ratio of 1:1 (Binomial $p = .001$), suggesting that high-frequency words were more likely to be perseverated. However, highly imageable words were not more likely to be reproduced on subsequent trials (34% high imageability; 18% medium imageability; 32% low imageability). As well as considering the frequency/imageability of perseverated items, we can also consider whether perseverations were more likely to occur for low-frequency or less imageable words. Perseverations, expressed as a percentage of incorrect trials, occurred at a rate of 47% for high-frequency words and 33% for low-frequency words. The values for high-, medium-, and low-imageability words were 53%, 41%, and 33% respectively. Therefore, perseverations did not occur at an elevated rate relative to overall accuracy for either low-frequency or low-imageability trials.

The majority of perseverations reflected the repetition of the immediately preceding response (74%; e.g., river → river; humour → river). On 11% of trials, the penultimate response was repeated (e.g., river → river; humour → humour; master → river) and a further 6% of perseverations reproduced the response three trials back; 4% of perseverations were repetitions of items between four and ten trials back; and 5% of perseverations were over a lag of more than 10 trials. The majority of items were only produced in a single perseverative error (78%). However, there were instances in which the same word was produced repeatedly: 19% of words were perseverated from two to four times and 4% of words were involved in more than four perseverative errors. The performance of one patient in particular (TJ) was characterised by strings of continuous perseveration.

The proportion of each PI-CVA patient's errors that were perseverative did not correlate with the composite measures of semantics ($r = .15$, $N = 11$, $p = .6$) or phonology ($r = .01$, $N = 11$, $p = .99$). Therefore, although perseverations characterised the performance of the PI-CVA group who were relatively phonologically impaired/semantically intact, the frequency of these errors did not appear to relate to these capacities. We will consider why the PI-CVA patients made more numerous perseverations in the General Discussion.

GENERAL DISCUSSION

This work investigated the impact of phonological and semantic impairment on immediate and delayed repetition in CVA and semantic dementia (SD). Lexicality, frequency, and imageability were varied in order to manipulate the extent to which lexical-semantic knowledge could act to constrain and maintain phonological activation. If semantic memory and phonology underpin repetition in an interactive way as envisaged by single route theories (Dell et al., 1997; Foygel & Dell, 2000; Patterson et al., 1994; Plaut & Kello, 1999), the degree of semantic and phonological impairment should interact with experimental factors purported to tap semantic and phonological processing. Our findings supported this hypothesis.

The phonologically impaired CVA patients showed relatively good immediate repetition but much poorer performance after a delay. This finding is consistent with the view that delay-dependent phonological decay or interference exacerbates the effects of phonological impairment. The PI-CVA patients also showed substantial effects of lexicality and imageability that were larger in delayed than immediate repetition; this result suggests that lexical-semantic knowledge plays a greater role in repetition when the contribution of phonology is minimised due to brain damage or the nature of the task. The semantically impaired SD patients, on the other hand, showed smaller effects of lexicality and imageability in repetition, reflecting the reduced impact of lexical-semantic processing in this condition. For these patients, the delay had a more substantial effect on the repetition of poorly understood, low-frequency words relative to high-frequency words that were better understood, suggesting that phonology plays a critical role in the repetition of items not adequately supported by lexical-semantic representations. A complementary finding was that phonological and not semantic impairment led to an increase in the number of semantic/derivational errors in repetition. It seems likely that these errors reflected the predominance of semantic processing in the PI-CVA group. Conversely, semantic impairment increased the incidence of phonological errors, in line with the hypothesis that semantic representations help to constrain phonological activation (Patterson et al., 1994).

The "semantic-phonological" computational model of Foygel and Dell (2000) is able to capture many of these findings (see http://langprod.cogsci.uiuc.edu/cgi-bin/webfit.cgi). This model incorporates three layers of phonological, lexical, and semantic nodes linked by bidirectional connections. Activation across all of these nodes decays at a predetermined rate. Variation between aphasic patients is accommodated by altering two parameters, the strength of semantic and phonological connections. Specific damage to the phonological-lexical weights produces rapidly decreasing repetition performance. As the level of phonological impairment is increased, repetition shows an increasing influence of semantic memory: the errors change from phonologically related nonwords to include a larger number of real words that are sometimes semantically related to the target. Therefore, the model successfully accommodates the correlation that we observed between phonological impairment and semantic errors in repetition. If the number of steps between the initial activation and the output is increased to simulate delayed repetition (as in Martin et al., 1996), semantic errors emerge with milder phonological problems: this is also consistent with our data. When the semantic-lexical weights are specifically impaired in a model with intact phonology (perhaps reflecting the pattern in semantic dementia[6]), there is very little impact on immediate repetition (accuracy remains at 96% even when the semantic weights are set to zero). However, delayed repetition is more substantially impaired by this selective impairment of semantic memory, in line with our findings. A combination of semantic and phonological damage in this model produces a more striking impairment of repetition, demonstrating the interactive nature of semantic and phonological processing. An extension of the model might also be able to account for the interactions that we observed between task variables (e.g., lexicality, frequency, imageability, and delay) and the degree of semantic and phonological damage. Nevertheless, some of our findings do not fit comfortably within this framework: the model is only concerned with single trials and therefore cannot explain perseverations. It also appears that the model cannot fit the pattern of errors shown by SD patients in naming and delayed repetition. In picture naming, as acknowledged by Foygel and Dell, the model greatly underestimates the rate of semantic errors and predicts the presence of phonologically related words and unrelated responses, which rarely occur for SD patients. Additionally, in delayed repetition, the model overestimates the proportion of errors that are real words for SD patients.

The pattern of performance displayed by the PI-CVA group, i.e., large effects of lexicality and imageability in repetition, together with a predominance of phonological errors, has been termed "phonological dysphasia" (Hanley & Kay, 1997; Hanley et al., 2002), in order to distinguish it from the "deep dysphasic" syndrome characterised by semantic errors in repetition. It is interesting to note that in this study the PI-CVA patients began to make semantic as well as phonological errors when repetition was delayed, suggesting that these two disorders may lie on a continuum of impairment (as has been suggested in the reading domain for phonological and deep dyslexia: Crisp & Lambon Ralph, 2006; Friedman, 1996). Cases with more severe phonological problems might generate semantic errors in repetition, whereas more mildly impaired patients might only produce phonological errors. The deep dysphasic patient studied by N. Martin and colleagues (1996) resolved into a phonological dysphasia during recovery, in line with this view. The presence of a delay in the repetition task apparently aggravated the patients'

---

[6] The semantic impairment in SD is multimodal: the meanings of words are degraded (corresponding to damage of lexical-semantic weights) but other modalities of input are equally affected suggesting damage to the semantic representations themselves. This type of damage is not incorporated in these computational implementations of the interactive activation model.

phonological problems, increasing their reliance on lexical-semantic activation. The emergence of semantic errors, therefore, might have reflected the normal operation of the lexical-semantic system unconstrained by phonological activation that would otherwise have inhibited semantic neighbours of the target. In our study, semantic/ derivational errors correlated with phonological and not semantic abilities, supporting this viewpoint. Hanley and Kay (1997) have also suggested that phonological as opposed to semantic errors occur in repetition when there is partial preservation of the non-lexical (phonological) route.

The source of the imageability effect in deep/phonological dysphasia remains a point of contention. Hanley and Kay (1997) proposed that two separate impairments to both the non-lexical and lexical-semantic routes underlie this disorder. By this view, substantial imageability effects reflect the impairment of the lexical-semantic route. In the current study, however, the size of the imageability effect was correlated with phonological and not semantic impairment. Martin and Saffran (1997) obtained a similar finding and showed how it could be elegantly accommodated by an interactive, single-route model in which lexical-semantic processing plays a greater role in repetition in the face of phonological impairment. Our findings build on this study by demonstrating that lexical-semantic factors such as lexicality, frequency, and imageability not only interact with the degree of semantic and phonological impairment in a neuropsychological population, but also interact with the presence of a delay in the repetition task and influence the types of errors that are made.

One issue that warrants further discussion is the circumstances in which semantic/ phonological impairment increases or decreases the effect of semantic/phonological variables in repetition. In the Introduction we noted that, in SD, exaggerated imageability effects might occur if highly imageable words are more resistant to semantic degradation by virtue of their richer representations; however, imageability effects might be reduced if the normal advantage for processing highly imageable words is eroded by the semantic impairment. According to the interactive framework, there should be *reduced* effects of semantic variables (and *enhanced* effects of phonological variables) in the face of semantic impairment, as processing shifts away from the semantic units, which are sensitive to these variables, and draws more heavily on phonology. For phonological impairment, the reverse should be true. In the present study, there are several examples of this type of interactivity. The SD patients showed a smaller imageability effect than the PI-CVA group overall, and the impact of the delay was larger for low-frequency and low-imageability items. However, the SD patients also showed a substantial frequency effect and the PI-CVA patients were more severely affected by the delay than the SD group. In some situations, therefore, semantic/phonological impairment can result in exaggerated effects of variables that purportedly tap these processes. We have argued that the increased delay effect for the PI-CVA group occurred because immediate repetition is not a highly phonologically demanding task, whereas delayed repetition exacerbates the effects of phonological impairment. Similarly, SD patients almost universally show large effects of frequency and it is thought that this is because low-frequency words and concepts degrade at an earlier stage of the condition (Funnell, 1995). It is interesting to note that Martin and Saffran (1997) found a positive and often non-significant relationship between semantic ability and frequency in a group of CVA patients, whereas we observed a significant negative correlation: the semantically impaired SD patients showed larger not smaller effects of frequency. This difference might have reflected the nature of the comprehension impairment in the two groups: although high-frequency items might be more robust in the face of semantic degradation in SD, frequency effects may be weakened in comprehension-impaired CVA patients who do not have degradation of the semantic representations themselves, but instead show difficulty accessing semantics effectively (Warrington & Cipolotti, 1996).

Other differences in the repetition performance of the SD and PI-CVA patients might have stemmed from the distinct aetiologies involved. The PI-CVA patients made significantly more perseverative errors than the SD patients, despite their difficulties in delayed repetition. Indeed, all of the PI-CVA cases made at least some perseverative errors, although the rates of perseveration were highly variable. In contrast, this error type almost never occurred in the SD group. One possible explanation of this group difference is that perseverations arose from the PI-CVA patients' relatively intact and durable semantic memory combined with poor processing of phonological input, which prevented new items from overriding the lingering activation of older items. Two findings speak against this view, however: (1) the proportion of errors that were perseverative did not correlate with either semantic or phonological abilities; (2) substantial perseveration was observed in both word and nonword repetition. An alternative possibility is that perseverations arise in CVA but not SD because of differences in the nature of the underlying brain damage. Several researchers have argued that perseverations are the product of a neuromodulatory failure resulting from low levels of acetylcholine, which purportedly makes cells more sensitive to feed-forward input (Gotts, della Rocchetta, & Cipolotti, 2002; Sandson & Albert, 1987). In perseverative CVA patients, there may be a cholinergic deficit that prevents new inputs from overriding current processing. Subcortical involvement is comparatively common in stroke, potentially producing deficits of this nature: in contrast, subcortical regions are relatively well preserved in SD (Galton et al., 2001; Mummery, Patterson, Price, Ashburner, Frackowiak, & Hodges, 2000).

Although we acknowledge that the nature of the underlying brain damage is likely to have important behavioural consequences, we observed evidence of substantial interactivity between semantics and phonology in the repetition performance of both stroke and semantic dementia patients. The PI-CVA patients showed sizeable effects of lexicality and imageability that were larger in delayed than immediate repetition, whereas the semantically impaired SD patients showed a reduced influence of these lexical-semantic variables and a delay effect that was larger for more poorly comprehended low-frequency items. In addition, patients with severe phonological deficits in the context of nonfluent progressive aphasia can resemble the phonologically impaired CVA cases reported here. Tree, Perfect, Hirsh, and Copstick (2001) described one such progressive aphasic patient who showed strong influences of lexicality/imageability and made semantic errors in repetition. Therefore, converging evidence for the interactive account of repetition is provided by patients with both fluent (SD) and non-fluent progressive aphasia, as well as CVA cases.

REFERENCES

Baayen, R. H., Piepenbrock, R., & van Rijn, H. (1993). *The CELEX Lexical Database.* [CD-ROM]. Philadelphia, PA: Linguistic Data Consortium, University of Pennsylvania.

Bozeat, S., Lambon Ralph, M. A., Patterson, K., Garrard, P., & Hodges, J. R. (2000). Non-verbal semantic impairment in semantic dementia. *Neuropsychologia, 38*, 1207–1215.

Caza, N., Belleville, S., & Gilbert, B. (2002). How loss of meaning with preservation of phonological word form affects immediate serial recall performance: A linguistic account. *Neurocase, 8*, 255–273.

Crisp, J., & Lambon Ralph, M. A. (2006). Unlocking the nature of the phonological–deep dyslexia continuum: The keys to reading aloud are in phonology and semantics. *Journal of Cognitive Neuroscience, 18*, 348–362.

Croot, K., Patterson, K., & Hodges, J. R. (1998). Single word production in non-fluent progressive aphasia. *Brain and Language, 61*, 226–273.

Dell, G. S., & O'Seaghda, P. G. (1992). Stages of lexical access in language production. *Cognition, 42*, 287–314.

Dell, G. S., Schwartz, M. F., Martin, N., Saffran, E. M., & Gagnon, D. A. (1997). Lexical access in aphasic and nonaphasic speakers. *Psychological Review, 104*, 801–838.

Forde, E. M. E., & Humphreys, G. W. (2002). The role of semantic knowledge in short-term memory. *Neurocase, 8*, 13–27.

Foygel, D., & Dell, G. S. (2000). Models of impaired lexical access in speech production. *Journal of Memory and Language, 43*, 182–216.

Franklin, S., Turner, J., & Ellis, A. W. (1992). *The ADA comprehension battery: Action for dysphasic adults*. York, UK: York Human Neuropsychology Laboratory.

Friedman, R. B. (1996). Recovery from deep alexia to phonological alexia: Points on a continuum. *Brain and Language, 52*, 114–128.

Funnell, E. (1995). Objects and properties: A study of the breakdown of semantic memory. *Memory, 3*, 497–518.

Galton, C. J., Patterson, K., Graham, K., Lambon Ralph M., A., Williams, G., & Antoun, N. et al. (2001). Differing patterns of temporal atrophy in Alzheimer's disease and semantic dementia. *Neurology, 57*, 216–225.

Gotts, S. J., della Rocchetta, A. I., & Cipolotti, L. (2002). Mechanisms underlying perseveration in aphasia: Evidence from a single case study. *Neuropsychologia, 40*, 1930–1947.

Hanley, J. R., Dell, G. S., Kay, J., & Baron, R. (2004). Evidence for the involvement of a nonlexical route in the repetition of familiar words: A comparison of single and dual route models of auditory repetition. *Cognitive Neuropsychology, 21*, 147–158.

Hanley, J. R., & Kay, J. (1997). An effect of imageability on the production of phonological errors in auditory repetition. *Cognitive Neuropsychology, 14*, 1065–1084.

Hanley, J. R., Kay, J., & Edwards, M. (2002). Imageability effects, phonological errors, and the relationship between auditory repetition and picture naming: Implications for models of auditory repetition. *Cognitive Neuropsychology, 19*, 193–206.

Hillis, A., & Caramazza, A. (1991). Mechanisms for accessing lexical representations for output: Evidence from a category specific semantic deficit. *Brain and Language, 40*, 106–144.

Hodges, J. R., Patterson, K., Oxbury, S., & Funnell, E. (1992). Semantic dementia: Progressive fluent aphasia with temporal lobe atrophy. *Brain, 115*, 1783–1806.

Howard, D., & Franklin, S. (1988). *Missing the meaning*. Cambridge, MA: MIT Press.

Howard, D., & Patterson, K. (1992). *Pyramids and Palm Trees: A test of semantic access from pictures and words*. Bury St. Edmunds, UK: Thames Valley Test Company.

Jefferies, E., Frankish, C., & Lambon Ralph, M. A. (2006a). Lexical and semantic binding in verbal short-term memory. *Journal of Memory and Language, 54*, 81–96.

Jefferies, E., Jones, R., Bateman, D., & Lambon Ralph, M. A. (2004a). When does word meaning affect immediate serial recall in semantic dementia? *Cognitive, Affective and Behavioral Neuroscience, 4*, 20–42.

Jefferies, E., Jones, R. W., Bateman, D., & Lambon Ralph, M. A. (2005). A semantic contribution to nonword recall? Evidence for intact phonological processes in semantic dementia. *Cognitive Neuropsychology, 22*, 183–212.

Jefferies, E., Patterson, K., Bateman, D., Jones, R., & Lambon Ralph, M. A. (2006b). The natural history of "pure" late-stage semantic dementia. *Neurocase, 12*, 1–14.

Jefferies, E., Patterson, K., Jones, R. W., Bateman, D., & Lambon Ralph, M. A. (2004). A category-specific advantage for numbers in verbal short-term memory: Evidence from semantic dementia. *Neuropsychologia, 42*, 639–660.

Jones, G. V. (1985). Deep dyslexia, imageability and ease of prediction. *Brain and Language, 24*, 1–19.

Katz, R. B., & Goodglass, H. (1990). Deep dysphasia: Analysis of a rare form of repetition disorder. *Brain and Language, 39,* 153–185.

Kay, J., Lesser, R., & Coltheart, M. (1992). *Psycholinguistic Assessments of Language Processing in Aphasia.* Hove, UK: Lawrence Erlbaum Associates Ltd.

Knott, R., Patterson, K., & Hodges, J. R. (1997). Lexical and semantic binding effects in short-term memory: Evidence from semantic dementia. *Cognitive Neuropsychology, 14,* 1165–1216.

Knott, R., Patterson, K., & Hodges, J. R. (2000). The role of speech production in auditory-verbal short-term memory: Evidence from progressive fluent aphasia. *Neuropsychologia, 38,* 125–142.

Kucera, H., & Francis, W. N. (1967). *Computational analysis of present-day American English.* Providence, RI: Brown University Press.

Lambon Ralph, M. A., Moriarty, L., & Sage, K. (2002). Anomia is simply a reflection of semantic and phonological impairments: Evidence from a case-series study. *Aphasiology, 16,* 56–82.

Majerus, S., Lekeu, F., Van der Linden, M., & Salmon, E. (2001). Deep dysphasia: Further evidence on the relationship between phonological short-term memory and language processing impairments. *Cognitive Neuropsychology, 18,* 385–410.

Martin, N., Dell, G. S., Saffran, E. M., & Schwartz, M. F. (1994). Origins of paraphasias in deep dysphasia: Testing the consequences of a decay impairment to an interactive spreading activation model of lexical retrieval. *Brain and Language, 47,* 609–660.

Martin, N., & Saffran, E. M. (1992). A computational account of deep dysphasia: Evidence from a single case study. *Brain and Language, 43,* 240–274.

Martin, N., & Saffran, E. M. (1997). Language and auditory-verbal short-term memory impairments: Evidence for common underlying processes. *Cognitive Neuropsychology, 14,* 641–682.

Martin, N., Saffran, E., & Dell, G. (1996). Recovery in deep dysphasia: Evidence for a relation between auditory-verbal STM capacity and lexical errors in repetition. *Brain and Language, 52,* 83–113.

Martin, R. C., & Lesch, M. (1996). Associations and dissociations between language impairment and list recall: Implications for models of STM. In S. E. Gathercole (Ed.), *Models of short-term memory* (pp. 149–178). Hove, UK: Psychology Press.

Martin, R. C., Lesch, M. F., & Bartha, M. C. (1999). Independence of input and output phonology in word processing and short-term memory. *Journal of Memory and Language, 41,* 3–29.

Martin, R. C., Shelton, J., & Yaffee, L. S. (1994). Language processing and working memory: Neuropsychological evidence for separate phonological and semantic capacities. *Journal of Memory and Language, 33,* 83–111.

McCarthy, R., & Warrington, E. K. (1984). A two-route model of speech production: Evidence from aphasia. *Brain, 107,* 463–485.

McCarthy, R. A., & Warrington, E. K. (1987). The double dissociation of short-term memory for lists and sentences: Evidence from aphasia. *Brain, 110,* 1545–1563.

Michel, F., & Andreewsky, A. (1983). Deep dysphasia: An analogue of deep dyslexia in the auditory modality. *Brain and Language, 18,* 212–223.

Mummery, C. J., Patterson, K., Price, C. J., Ashburner, J., Frackowiak, R. S. J., & Hodges, J. R. (2000). A voxel-based morphometry study of semantic dementia: Relationship between temporal lobe atrophy and semantic memory. *Annals of Neurology, 47,* 36–45.

Patterson, K., Graham, N., & Hodges, J. R. (1994). The impact of semantic memory loss on phonological representations. *Journal of Cognitive Neuroscience, 6,* 57–69.

Patterson, K., & Marcel, A. J. (1992). Phonological ALEXIA or PHONOLOGICAL alexia? In J. Alegria, D. Holender, J. Junca de Morais, & M. Radeau (Eds.), *Analytic approaches to human cognition* (pp. 259–274). Amsterdam: Elsevier.

Plaut, D. C., & Kello, C. T. (1999). The emergence of phonology from the interplay of speech comprehension and production: A distributed connectionist approach. In B. MacWhinney (Ed.), *The emergence of language.* Mahwah, NJ: Lawrence Erlbaum Associates Inc.

Plaut, D. C., & Shallice, T. (1991). Deep dyslexia: A case study in connectionist neuropsychology. *Cognitive Neuropsychology, 10,* 377–500.

Roodenrys, S., & Hinton, M. (2002). Sublexical or lexical effects on serial recall of nonwords? *Journal of Experimental Psychology: Learning, Memory and Cognition, 28,* 29–33.

Sandson, J., & Albert, M. L. (1987). Perseveration in behavioral neurology. *Neurology, 37,* 1736–1741.

Snowden, J. S., Goulding, P. J., & Neary, D. (1989). Semantic dementia: A form of circumscribed cerebral atrophy. *Behavioural Neurology, 2,* 167–182.

Snowden, J. S., Neary, D., & Mann, D. M. A. (Eds.). (1996). *Frontotemporal lobar degeneration: Frontotemporal dementia, progressive aphasia, semantic dementia.* London: Churchill Livingstone.

Tree, J. J., Perfect, T. J., Hirsh, K. W., & Copstick, S. (2001). Deep dysphasic performance in non-fluent progressive aphasia: A case study. *Neurocase, 7*, 473–487.

Treiman, R., & Danis, C. (1988). Short-term memory errors for spoken syllables are affected by the linguistic structure of the syllables. *Journal of Experimental Psychology: Learning, Memory and Cognition, 14*, 145–152.

Valdois, S., Carbonnel, S., David, D., Rousset, S., & Pellat, J. (1995). Confrontation of PDP models and dual-route models through the analysis of a case of deep dysphasia. *Cognitive Neuropsychology, 12*, 681–724.

Warrington, E. K., & Cipolotti, L. (1996). Word comprehension: The distinction between refractory and storage impairments. *Brain, 119*, 611–625.

Warrington, E. K., McKenna, P., & Orpwood, L. (1998). Single word comprehension: A concrete and abstract word synonym test. *Neuropsychological Rehabilitation, 8*, 143–154.

Wilshire, C. E., & Fisher, C. A. (2004). "Phonological" dysphasia: A cross-modal phonological impairment affecting repetition, comprehension, and production. *Cognitive Neuropsychology, 21*, 187–210.

Wilshire, C. E., & McCarthy, R. A. (1996). Experimental investigations of an impairment in phonological encoding. *Cognitive Neuropsychology, 13*, 1059–1098.

APPENDIX

Characteristics of stimuli

	Imageability		Frequency		Syllable length		Phoneme length	
Word Set 1 – matched subset (N = 72)								
High frequency (N = 36)	449.9 (141.0)	ns	201.7 (209.7)	p < .001	2.1 (0.6)	ns	5.6 (1.4)	ns
Low frequency (N = 36)	450.7 (146.4)		6.5 (7.2)		2.2 (0.6)		5.6 (1.4)	
High imageability (N = 24)	622.8 (15.0)	p < .001	131.6 (240.1)	ns	2.2 (0.5)	ns	5.6 (1.4)	ns
Medium imageability (N = 24)	449.2 (26.9)		86.0 (122.3)		2.2 (0.8)		5.8 (1.4)	
Low imageability (N = 24)	278.9 (16.0)		93.3 (149.5)		2.2 (0.6)		5.5 (1.5)	
Word Set 2 (N = 56)								
High frequency (N = 28)	468.0 (127.6)	ns	260.0 (223.3)	p < .001	1.93 (0.54)	ns	4.36 (1.16)	ns
Low frequency (N = 28)	473.0 (141.5)		11.3 (6.8)		1.93 (0.72)		4.46 (1.23)	
High imageability (N = 28)	598.5 (28.2)	p < .001	126.5 (203.3)	ns	1.89 (0.63)	ns	4.21 (1.23)	ns
Low imageability (N = 28)	342.3 (36.1)		149.7 (203.4)		1.96 (0.64)		4.61 (1.13)	

Figures show mean for each group (standard deviations in parentheses). ns = not significant (all $p > .1$). Frequency values for Set 1 show Lemma frequency from Celex (Baayen, Piepenbrock, & van Rijn, 1993). Frequency values for Set 2 are from Kucera and Francis (1967). For Set 2, we were unable to obtain imageability scores for two words and frequency counts for one item.

Morpho-syntactic and morpho-phonological deficits in the production of regularly and irregularly inflected verbs

Judit Druks

University College London, UK

Background: The background to the study is the debate in relation to the English regular/irregular past tense forms.

Aims: The purpose of the investigation was the evaluation of the dual mechanism (DMT: Pinker, 1999; Marslen-Wilson & Tyler, 1997, 1998; Ullman, Corkin, Coppola, Hickok, Growdon, Koroshetz, et al., 1997) and connectionist single mechanism models (SMT: Bird, Lambon Ralph, Seidenberg, McClelland, & Patterson, 2003; Joanisse & Seidenberg, 1999; Patterson, Lambon Ralph, Hodges, & McClelland, 2001) through exploring the reading and oral production of regular and irregular past tense forms and other verbal and nominal inflections by a Broca's type aphasic and phonological dyslexic patient.

Methods & Procedures: Eight experimental tasks are reported. Three involved the reading of stems and inflected verbs and nouns in differently organised lists, two involved the oral production of past tense verbs and plural nouns, and three explored the ability to distinguish between written verbs inflected with various affixes.

Outcomes & Results: In reading randomly organised list of nouns, verb stems, and regular and irregular past tense forms the patient displayed dissociation between regular and irregular past tense forms as predicted by DMT. When the same items were presented in a list with present and past tense forms paired, and in the oral transformation task, the dissociation disappeared, and performance in regular and irregular past tense forms became comparable. There was a difference in the patient's reading of plural nouns and progressive verbs, which was good, and of past tense forms and third person forms, which was impaired. The recognition/comprehension tasks revealed that the patient was aware of the presence of an affix, but he could not reliably distinguish between different affixes.

Conclusions: Performance on regular/irregular past tense forms and the variable levels of performance in producing different regular inflections are in conflict with both DMT and SMT on a number of grounds. The task-related differences between randomly organised lists and paired present and past tense forms are accounted for by distinguishing between morpho-phonological and morpho-syntactic effects. It is argued that deficits confined to the production of regular past tense forms are morpho-phonological in nature, while deficits in both regular and irregular past tense forms originate in morpho-syntax. Since SMT and DMT are theories of morpho-phonological processes, they cannot account for the complex performance pattern presented by the patient in the present study and by other similar patients. The differences attested in the availability of differently affixed words and deficits in irregular past tense forms are only accountable at the level of morpho-syntax.

Aphasic patients with predominantly anterior damage are known to have problems with the production of grammatical morphemes. Recently, however, it has been

---

Address correspondence to: Judit Druks, Department of Human Communication Sciences, University College London, Chandler House, 2 Wakefield Street, London WC1 1PF, UK. E-mail: j.druks@ucl.ac.uk

shown that the deficit in relation to grammatical morphemes is selective. Some researchers claim that the selectivity is between nominal and verbal inflections (e.g., Tsapkini, Jarema, & Kehayia, 2002; Shapiro, Shelton, & Caramazza, 2000; Shapiro & Caramazza, 2003), others between tense and agreement marking verbal inflections (e.g., Friedman & Grodzinsky, 1997), and others between regular and irregular inflections (Pinker, 1999; Ullman, 2001; Ullman et al., 1997). The present paper relates to some of these questions by exploring the reading, oral production, and grammaticality judgement of nominal and verbal inflections in a Broca's type patient with phonological dyslexia. While English is not an appropriate language to test dissociations between tense and agreement since it has only a single agreement marker, it is particularly suited to exploring any putative differences between regular and irregular inflections. This works especially well for the past tense form because English has a single productive regular past tense affix that is applicable to the majority of verbs alongside a set of few hundred irregular verbs. A comparison of the availability and use of English regular and irregular past tense forms, potentially, may decide between different theoretical positions to language representation and processing.

According to the single mechanism theory (SMT), both regular and irregular past tense verbs are learnt and processed by creating associations between the phonology of the verb stem and its past tense form, without the involvement of a morphological interface and/or resort to internalised rules such as *add -ed* when past tense is required (e.g., Joanisse & Seidenberg, 1999; Rumelhart & McClelland 1986). According to the dual mechanism theory (DMT), regular and irregular past tense verbs are represented and processed differently. While regular past tense forms are constructed by applying the past tense rule, irregular past tense forms are learnt by rote and are stored in associative lexical memory (e.g., Pinker, 1991; 1999).[1]

The initial evidence for both theoretical positions is derived from experiments with normal participants, language acquisition, and computer simulations (e.g., Bybee, 1985, 1995, 1999; Bybee & Moder, 1983; Daugherty & Seidenberg, 1992; MacWhinney & Leinbach, 1991; Plunkett & Marchman, 1991, 1993; Prasada & Pinker, 1993; Rumelhart & McClelland 1986; Ullman & Gopnik, 1999). It has been pointed out, however, that most of the findings could be accounted for by both single and double mechanism theories (Joanisse & Seidenberg, 1999). For this reason, research efforts have been directed to the potential of data derived from neurologically impaired patients to distinguish between the competing theories. Accordingly, therefore, increasing numbers of studies have been carried out with aphasic patients (e.g., Bird et al., 2003; de Diego Balaguer, Costa, Sebastian-Galles, Juncadella, & Caramazza, 2004; Faroqi-Shah & Thompson, 2004; Izvorsky & Ullman, 1999; Marslen-Wilson & Tyler, 1997, 1998; Penke, Janssen, & Frause, 1999; Thompson, Fix, & Gitelman 1999; Ullman et al., 1997), Parkinson's and Huntington's disease patients (Ullman et al., 1997), patients with dementia (Patterson et al., 2001), and SLI children (e.g., van der Lely & Ullman, 2001).

Patterson et al. (2001), working within the single mechanism framework, found that a group of semantic dementia patients were able to produce regular past tense forms, but were impaired in producing irregular past tense forms. Despite the

---

[1] A third approach according to which both regular and irregular past tense forms are learnt and produced by the involvement of (phonological) rule application (Chomsky & Halle, 1968; Halle & Mohanan, 1985) is not prominent in up-to-date debates.

evidence of dissociation that appears to support the DMT, Patterson et al. argued that the data are better accounted for by the constraint satisfaction parallel distributed processor (PDP) of Joanisse and Seidenberg (1999). This is a variant of PDP models (e.g., Rumelhart & McClelland, 1986) that consists of two interacting layers, semantic and phonological. In Joanisse and Seidenberg's model, when the semantic layer is lesioned, predominantly irregular past tense verbs are affected, and when the phonological layer is lesioned, regular past tense verbs suffer more. In a companion paper, Bird et al. (2003) argue that Broca's aphasic patients' selective deficit in producing regular past tense forms is due to their phonological impairments. Thus, in Joanisse and Seidenberg's model, the double dissociation between regular and irregular past tense forms is accounted for by (non-specific) selective deficits in one of two interacting components of the language system— phonology and semantics—that underlie *all* aspects of language production and comprehension.

Other reports of relatively more impaired regular past tense forms in Broca's aphasia have supported the dual mechanism view (Marslen-Wilson & Tyler, 1997; Ullman et al., 1997). According to Ullman (e.g., Ullman, 1999; Ullman et al., 1997), patients with lesions involving the frontal/basal ganglia circuit—underlying motor and other cognitive *skills*, including the use of grammatical rules—are impaired in the production of regular past tense forms. Patients with lesions in the temporal lobe circuits, which underlie *lexical knowledge*, are impaired in producing irregular past tense forms. Marslen-Wilson and Tyler (1998), on the other hand, define the difference between regular and irregular past tense forms in terms of their morphological structure. Regular past tense forms have internal morphological structure, and in order to comprehend or construct the regular past tense form, a segmenting or combinatorial operation is required. Irregular past tense forms, on the other hand, are unstructured and are processed as whole forms.

Both the SMT and DMT, for different reasons, maintain that Broca's aphasic patients have disproportional deficits in producing regular past tense forms. According to SMT (Bird et al., 2003), the reason for deficits in regular verb production in Broca's aphasia is the phonological deficits that these patients typically have. Bird et al. showed that regular past tense forms are often phonologically more challenging due to the consonant cluster created when the past tense morpheme is added to many stems, and the dissociation disappears when the regular and irregular past tense forms are matched in terms of phonological complexity. According to DMT (Ullman, 1999; Ullman et al., 1997), the reason for Broca's aphasic patients' problems with regular inflections is that, due to a lesion in the motor circuit, they have lost the ability to apply and follow rules. Since irregular forms are stored in memory like all uninflected words, they remain (relatively) unaffected in Broca's aphasia.

However, the evidence in studies involving aphasic patients is not uniformly supportive of these theories. Only a few reported cases of Broca's aphasia show disproportional deficits for regular past tense forms, and the majority of patients are also impaired at irregular past tense production (e.g., Faroqi-Shah & Thompson, 2004; Izvorsky & Ullman, 1999). It is, therefore, uncertain that Broca's aphasic patients are a suitable population to distinguish between SMT and DMT, or that these theories (or one of them) are capable of accounting for the full set of observed problems in relation to past tense production in Broca's aphasia. Therefore, in order to assess the extent to which SMT and/or DMT can account for the evidence, the present study explores the deficits that a Broca's aphasic patient has in relation to inflectional morphology (see also de Diego Balaguer et al., 2004, who posed a similar question using cross-linguistic evidence).

In the study the patient's production of regularly and irregularly inflected past tensed verbs is compared. In addition to oral production, oral reading and written word recognition and comprehension were also included. One of the reasons for including reading tasks is that it allowed testing of the production of inflected words in intermixed lists in which the patient is unaware of the nature of the task, instead of the repeated production of past tense forms in response to the present tense form in the often used transformation paradigm (e.g., Ullman et al., 1997), which is likely to lead to task-induced errors. Testing in the written modality was made possible by the specific profile of the patient described in this study. The patient displayed a reliable reading pattern of phonological dyslexia and was only able to read lexically (Druks & Froud, 2002).

The principal question addressed in the present study is to what extent and under what conditions a morpho-phonological (Marslen-Wilson & Tyler, 1997; Ullman et al., 1997) and/or phonological (Bird et al., 2003) distinction between regular and irregular inflections may account for the performance of this patient, and others like him in producing and comprehending inflected words. It is possible, and it will be so argued here, that the bulk of the problems these patients have in relation to inflected words, and, in particular, tensed verbs, are rooted within morpho-syntax (see also de Diego Balaguer et al., 2004, for a similar argument on the basis of Spanish and Catalan data). In this case neither SMT or DMT can provide an explanation for the deficits in Broca's aphasia, and Broca's aphasia cannot contribute to the debate between SMT and DMT. Studies that try to do so (e.g., Bird et al., 2003; Ullman et al., 1997) are misleading, at least to some extent.

Both SMT and DMT explicate their respective theories and provide empirical evidence predominantly in relation to the English regular and irregular past tense forms (but see de Diego Balaguer et al., 2004; Penke et al., 1999) despite the fact that the notions of regularity (e.g., Ullman et al., 1997), phonological complexity (e.g., Bird et al., 2003), and morphological structure (e.g., Marslen-Wilson & Tyler, 1997) are relevant not only to past tense forms but also to other (English) verbal and nominal affixations. In the present study, therefore, the production of differently affixed words was also explored. Performance on these forms, like performance in languages with different morphological systems, may provide additional tests of SMT and DMT.

CASE STUDY

MC is a right-handed 76-year-old male who suffered a left hemisphere embolic CVA in 1990. Prior to his stroke MC was a successful music impresario.[2] An assessment on the Boston Diagnostic Aphasia Examination (Goodglass & Kaplan, 1983) showed a diagnostic profile similar to that of Broca's aphasia, although his articulatory agility is greater than would be expected of a Broca's patient, and his

---

[2] MC participated in the study with interest and enthusiasm and was fully aware that our work together was for research purposes. MC sadly died some time after the data for this paper were collected. This paper was written in his memory, with gratitude for his commitment to my and Karen Froud's research.

speech, though structurally ungrammatical, is not devoid of inflected and derived words or free-standing grammatical morphemes (see MC's diagnostic profile on the BDAE in Druks & Froud, 2002).

MC is a phonological dyslexic patient whose ability to convert graphemes into phonemes is seriously impaired. His reading performance has been described in detail in Druks and Froud (2002). He could only read 6% of a large number of pseudowords. In addition to his nonword reading deficit MC is also seriously impaired in reading free-standing and bound (inflectional and derivational) grammatical morphemes. In contrast, MC reads most stems well, including highly abstract and low-frequency nouns and verbs, and his speech, though often ungrammatical, includes many correctly used grammatical morphemes. Thus while single written grammatical morphemes are inaccessible to him, he can use them relatively well in (connected) speech. This includes the correct use of the past tense, both regular and irregular, at times (see Appendix 1 for examples of MC's past tense use in connected speech, and Appendix 2 for a summary of his language profile in Druks & Froud, 2002).

In Druks and Froud (2002) we concentrated on MC's reading of function words, but we also explored, to a limited extent, his ability to process derivational and inflectional morphology attached to nouns and verbs. As these aspects of his performance are directly relevant for the present investigation, our findings will be summarised here. In reading a long list of derived and inflected words intermixed with stems, MC made approximately 50% errors on both types of words. All his errors (apart from few stem errors) were of affixation, and were well-formed words in the language. While he made no errors in reading plural nouns, and frequently read the progressive form of the verb correctly, his reading of all other inflected forms was poor. No difference between the availability of derived and inflected words was found, and there was no difference between the number of omissions and substitutions. Inflected verbs were also shown to be impaired in sorting and sentence completion tasks with a choice of verb forms. This was in contrast with MC's ability to understand the meaning of many free-standing grammatical morphemes (locative prepositions, quantifiers, and determiners) and derived words (agentive derived nominals and gender marked nominals) that he could not read (see Appendix 2 for a summary of MC's language profile in Druks & Froud, 2002).

EXPERIMENTAL STUDIES

All eight experimental tasks focused on MC's ability to read, to recognise, and to produce inflected words. The first three tasks consisted of reading stems and inflected verbs and nouns in differently organised lists. In the following two tasks, the oral production of the past tense forms of present tense verbs and the plural form of singular nouns was tested. Finally, in the last three tasks, MC's ability to distinguish between (written) verbs inflected with various affixes was explored.

Materials

For the purposes of the present study 102 verbs, 51 with regular and 51 with irregular past tense, were selected. The past tense forms of the verbs were matched for frequency using Celex (Baayen, Piepenbrock & van Rijn, 1993). Frequencies ranged from very low (0, e.g., *wrung, wilted, trod, slew*) to very high (over 1000, e.g., *told, found, began, remembered*), but no verbs with "super" frequencies (such as *went* and auxiliaries such as *was, got, had*) were included, as these could not be matched with regular past tense forms. Verbs that do not change their form in the past tense (e.g., *hit, put*) were also excluded (the matched list is in Appendix 3). Since the same verbs were used in the different tasks, to minimise retest effects, session were separated by several weeks, although it is known from previous work with MC that he is not affected by practice. The verbs were presented in the different tasks in a different random order and were intermixed with other words as the tasks required.

Task 1: The reading of single verbs—uninflected and regular and irregular past tense forms

Materials and procedure. The objective of the first task was to explore MC's reading of single regular and irregular past tense forms. The 102 past tense verbs were intermixed with the stem form of the same verbs and with 100 concrete nouns selected randomly from other lists. The whole list consisted of 304 words and was presented to MC to read as a list during two sessions, so that the stem and past tense forms of the same verb were seen during different sessions.

Results and summary. MC made no errors in reading the noun filler items, and read 92/102 present tense (stem) forms correctly (he produced three past tense forms, two progressive forms, two nominalisations, two omissions, and one visual error). He read correctly 4/51 regular past tense verbs (*discussed, tried, died,* and *cried*) and 26/51 irregular past tense verbs. A chi square test showed that the difference was highly significant, $\chi^2(1) = 22.86; p < .001$. The majority (32) of the errors among the regular verbs were the omission of the past tense *-ed*. In seven instances MC produced the progressive form, in three instances he nominalised the verb, and he made three semantic and two visual errors. The four past tensed verbs that MC managed to read correctly were among the more frequent items in the list, but since they were very few and MC did not read very many other equally frequent or more frequent words, not much significance need to be attached to this.

Eleven errors among the irregular past tense verbs were the production of the present tense stem form; two, the production of the progressive form; three, the production of the past participle; and one the nominalisation of the verb. Thus 17/25 (68%) of the errors were morphologically related to the target words. See Table 3 below for the breakdown of errors. No frequency effect was apparent: MC was equally likely to produce high (9/17), medium (10/17), and low frequency (7/17) irregular past tense forms. The comparison using chi square was not significant, $\chi^2(2) = 1.481$.

There was a quantitative difference between MC's ability to read regular and irregular past tense verbs. While in the case of regular past tense verbs he invariably omitted the marker of the past tense, he managed to read the irregular past tense form of half of the verbs well. MC's reading of this list, therefore, is compatible with the dual mechanism model: his poor reading of regular past tense forms may reflect an inability to access or to implement the rule required for regular past tense formation. The results, however, may also be compatible with the Joanisse and

Seidenberg model, if the poor performance on the regular past tense morphology can be linked to phonological deficits, and with that of Marslen-Wilson and Tyler's theory of combinatory deficits.

In relation to MCs phonological knowledge, in Druks and Froud (2002) we reported that his speech has normal prosody and he rarely makes phonological errors. He is capable of carrying out phonological tasks such as rhyme detection, and can repeat about 80% of the nonwords in Glushko's (1979) list, showing that he does not have major phonological deficits. However, MC is incapable of carrying out tasks involving phonological segmentation and assembly (see Appendix 2 for a summary of MC's language profile in Druks & Froud, 2002). This could, according to Marslen-Wilson and Tyler, be the reason for his serious problem in reading inflected words, although phonological segmentation and assembly are meta-phonological tasks that could be difficult for MC for this reason. Furthermore, MC's connected speech production, which consists of many inflected words including regular past tense forms, and his performance in subsequent tasks (3 and 4) in this study where he improves considerably at producing regular past tense forms does not indicate the involvement of *general* phonological deficits that would inhibit his regular past tense production.

The significant difference between MC's ability to read regular and irregular past tense forms seem to support the DMT. However, MC is also very impaired in reading irregular past tense forms, making errors on half of them. This is a very large number of errors for MC, whose reading of morphologically simple content words including verbs (while not perfect) is very good (see Appendix 2), since both SMT and DMT assume that irregular past tense verbs are stored in the lexicon similarly to stems (e.g., in Pinker & Ullman, 2002, p. 456, it is argued that "irregular forms are just words, acquired and stored like other words"). Moreover, his errors with both regular and irregular past tense targets demonstrate a strong awareness of the morphological make-up of the past tensed forms. Similar types of errors in regular and irregular verbs argue against DMT, and errors that reflect MC's awareness of the morphological structure of words argue against all explanations that deny the involvement of morphological knowledge in the formation of the past tense.

Task 2: The reading of stems and inflected and derived words

In order to expand the data base that is used to evaluate DMT and SMT, the second reading list consisted of 50 simple singular and plural nouns, 50 regular and 50 irregular verbs in both present and past tense forms, the progressive, and the third person singular forms (the same regular and irregular verbs as in the previous task were used, but due to experimenter error, one regular and one irregular verb were omitted), and 100 derived words (abstract nouns, adjectives, and adverbials). The whole list consisted of 600 words presented in a quasi-random order during four sessions, so that the same stem appeared only once during a single session.

Although DMT makes explicit predictions only in relation to (English) regular and irregular past tense production, it implicitly predicts deficits in producing all regular inflections (i.e., plural -s, regular past, progressive, and third person singular -s) and preserved performance for stored forms (i.e., singular nouns, verb stems, irregular past tense forms, and derived words). In particular, DMT predicts no differences in producing the plural -s, third person -s, progressive, and regular past tense, all being regular. According to Joanisse and Seidenberg's version of the SMT, regular past tense forms are predicted to be difficult for agrammatic patients because many of them are phonologically complex. However, the progressive -*ing* form, being a syllabic affix, is expected to be well preserved, and no difference in performance is expected between plural nouns and third person singular verbs. Marslen-Wilson and Tyler predict deficits in all inflected forms (i.e., plurals, progressive, regular past, and third person present) due to their being morphologically complex. All three theories predict good performance on the stem forms, both verbs and nouns, and also on derived words. Derived words are predicted to be well preserved because they are believed to be stored as full forms (e.g., Ullman et al., 1997), usually do not create consonant clusters (Bird et al., 2003), and are known to be better preserved in Broca's aphasia than inflected words (Grodzinsky, 1990; Miceli & Caramazza, 1988).

Results and summary. The results are summarised in Table 1, and a breakdown of the errors is shown later in Table 3. Comparisons between the different word types were carried out using chi square analyses. Derived words were read as well as present tense (stem form) verbs, $\chi^2(1) = 0.76$; *ns*, and irregular past tense verbs, $\chi^2(1) = 2.27$; *ns*, but were significantly better preserved than regular and irregular past tense forms pooled together, $\chi^2(1) = 12.56$; $p < .001$. The reading of plural nouns was relatively well preserved, similar to the reading of progressive verbs, $\chi^2(1) = 0.05$; *ns*, and derived words, $\chi^2(1) = 1.58$; *ns*, and were significantly better preserved than third person present tense verbs, despite the phonological equivalence of the affix, $\chi^2(1) = 29.74$; $p < .001$. MC made significantly more errors in reading regular than irregular past tense forms, $\chi^2(1) = 6.42$; $p < .02$, and past than present tense forms, $\chi^2(1) = 19.24$; $p < .001$. Among the inflected verbs a hierarchy of difficulty was observed. The progressive -*ing* was better preserved than any other verb form: better than the third person singular, $\chi^2(1) = 27.75$; $p < .001$, regular past tense forms, $\chi^2(1) = 21.37$; $p < .001$, and irregular past tense forms, $\chi^2(1) = 4.94$; $p < .05$. Verbs inflected for the third person singular were more impaired than irregular past tense forms, $\chi^2(1) = 10,52$; $p < .001$, and were as impaired as regular past tense forms, $\chi^2(1) = 0.58$; *ns*.

TABLE 1
Number (%) and type of errors made on different word types in Task 2

Type of word	Number of errors (%)	Main error types
Concrete nouns singular	0/50 (0)	n.a.
Concrete nouns plural	15/50 (30)	sing.form (5)
Present tense verbs	35/100 (35)	-*ing* form (20) deriv (1) past tense (3)
Verbs – progressive	16/50 (32)	stem (6) past tense (5)
Verbs – third person present	42/50 (84)	-*ing* (23) stem (9) past tense (2)
Verbs – regular past tense	39/50 (78)	-*ing* (24) stem (9)
Verb – irreg. past tense	27/50 (54)	present tense (10)
Derived words	41/100 (41)	stem (15) subst (17) add -*ing* (8)

In conclusion, the predictions in relation to stems, derived forms, and regular and irregular past tense forms were supported. MC made no errors on uninflected nouns and his errors in reading verb stems involved the additions of a permissible affix, mainly -*ing*, and he made no stem errors. Regular past tense forms were more impaired than irregular past tense forms. However, MC's performance in reading the progressive and the third person singular forms of verbs and the plural of nouns poses serious questions concerning all three theories under scrutiny here, and will be discussed in the General Discussion.

Task 3: The reading of 102 present and past tense verbs—half regular and half irregular as a paired list

In Tasks 1 and 2, MC read lists in which present and past tense verbs were randomly intermixed with a large number of other word types. MC, therefore, was presumably unaware of the focus of the task on testing the reading of past tense verbs. In the following task, however, he was told in advance that the first word in the pairs of words he was presented with was always a present tense verb, and the second its past tense form.

Results and summary. Under these conditions MC read 82/102 present tense and 61/102 past tense forms—30 regular and 31 irregular—correctly. The results were analysed using chi square statistics. While the difference between present and past tense verbs was significant, $\chi^2(1) = 10.31$; $p < .01$, the difference between regulars and irregulars clearly was not. His errors continued to be predominantly morphological in nature, involving the substitution and deletion of affixes (a breakdown of errors is given in Table 3). Since the dramatic improvement in reading regularly inflected past tense forms was surprising, to test the reliability of the results MC was asked to read the same list again with the same instructions 6 weeks later. Similar results were obtained.

It seems that here MC was able to activate his (relatively) preserved knowledge of the past tense form of regular verbs (see Appendix 1) and apply this knowledge to the reading task. As a consequence, the difference between regular and irregular forms disappeared. He continued to make errors on approximately half of the items and the type of errors on regulars and irregulars remained similar. It will be argued that this pattern of performance reflects his general *morpho-syntactic* problems in relation to tense that are particularly acute in single word tasks where there is no context to facilitate the production of the correct verb form or affix (Druks & Froud, 2002).

Summary of the reading tasks

MC's reading of past tense verbs is affected by the context in which the list is presented. When past tense verbs are intermixed with other words, he invariably omits the regular past tense marker and his reading of irregular past tense verbs is significantly better. However, when he reads the present and past tense forms as pairs of words, and is told what the words signify, the difference between regular and irregular past tense disappears. Performance on irregular past tense forms, on the other hand, remains constant in all three reading tasks. This shows that the improvement in performance on the regulars is not due to this task being easier than the earlier ones. The majority of MC's errors are morphological in response to both present and past tense verbs, regular and irregular forms, and derived words. Errors in which an affix is *added* to a target stem are particularly revealing. These errors are unlikely to be caused by either phonological deficits (Bird et al., 2003) or deficits in phonological assembly (Marslen-Wilson & Tyler, 1997).

Task 4: Single word production—present to past tense verbs

The following two tasks involve spoken single word production, similar to tasks reported in previous studies with patients and normal children and adults (e.g., Izvorsky & Ullman, 1999; Ullman et al., 1997). MC was presented with the spoken form of 51 regular and 51 irregular verbs, the same as in previous lists, randomly intermixed, and was asked to produce their past tense form. When MC did not respond or produced an erroneous response, he was prompted with "*yesterday?*".

Results and summary. The results are given in Table 2 and the breakdown of errors is in Table 3. In the oral transformation task, MC does not show an advantage for irregular past tense forms, in fact he produces more correct regulars than irregulars, although the difference in the chi square analysis is not significant, $\chi^2(1) = 2.55$; *ns*. There were three no-responses, but the majority of the errors were other legal morphological forms of the verb, and regularisations (16), half of which were self-corrected when queried. In order to allow a comparison between the availability of verb and noun inflections, a similar task was carried out involving nouns.

Task 5: Single word production—singular to plural nouns

A list of 50 morphologically simple nouns were selected (a few derived words slipped in, however), 10 very frequent (up to 300 per million), 10 frequent (from 200–150 per million), 10 of medium frequency (from 150–100 per million), 10 of low frequency (from 100–50 per million) and 10 of very low frequency (below 50 per million) words. They were presented one after the other and MC was asked to produce their plural.

Results and summary. The results are summarised in Table 2. In order to use the plural, MC occasionally needed a prompt such as *many, two* or *three*—at other times, he was able to provide the prompt for himself. He was unable to produce the plural of two nouns (*answer* and *government*) and on two occasions he first produced the progressive form of a related verb (*driver → driving; conductor → conducting*), but was able to correct himself.

TABLE 2

Number of errors (%) made in oral production of regular and irregular past tense and plural forms in Tasks 4 and 5

	Regular past tense verbs n = 51	Irregular past tense verbs n = 51	Plural nouns n = 50
Number of errors (%)	19 (37)	25 (49)	2 (3.9)

Summary of the production tasks

MC's spoken production of past tense verbs is similar to his reading of the same items in Task 3. No difference was found between the numbers of correctly produced regular and irregular past tense forms, and the errors were predominantly morphologically related to the targets. In this task, however, there were many regularisation errors. Since MC does not make regularisation errors in spontaneous speech, it is most likely that these were task-induced errors. In chi square analyses, significant differences were found between MC's ability to inflect verbs and nouns: regular past tense forms vs. plural nouns, $\chi^2(1) = 16.95$, $p < .001$; irregular past tense forms vs. plural nouns, $\chi^2(1) = 26.13$; $p < .0001$. It is noteworthy that often, though not always, MC pronounced both the past tense -*ed* and the plural -*s* with somewhat unnatural emphasis.

An overview of the errors in the reading and production tasks

Table 3 shows all errors made in the production tasks. Derived words were better preserved than inflected words, showing that these are either differently represented or that there is a different relationship between a stem and a derivational affix and between a stem and an inflectional affix (e.g., Marslen-Wilson & Tyler, 1998).

Since the errors on derived words were different from the errors on inflected words, they could not be included in Table 3, therefore their breakdown is summarised here. In 15 items, MC omitted a derivational affix (e.g., *density* → *dense*; *purely* → *pure*). There were seven substitution errors (e.g., *reality* → *realism*; *kindly* → *kindness*), and in five words a derivational affix was added. No illegal inflections were ever produced but all verbal inflections (-*ed*, -*s*, -*ing*, the participle form, and derivational affixation) were substituted for present tense, past tense, third person, present singular, and progressive forms, showing intricate relationships among these affixes.

TABLE 3
Number and type of errors in the production tasks (Tasks 1, 2, 3, & 4)

Tasks	1	1	2	2	2	2	2	3	3	3	4	4	
Targets (n):	Rg (51)	irg (51)	prs (50)	rg (50)	irg (50)	-ing (50)	3rd (50)	prs (51)	rg (51)	irg (51)	rg (51)	irg (51)	Total
Type of errors	—	—	—	—	—	—	—	—	—	—	—	—	—
Omission infl.	32	11	—	9	10	6	9	—	1	1	1	1	81
Produce past*	—	—	4	—	—	5	2	9	—	—	—	—	20
Produce -ing	7	2	20	24	3		23	3	10		6	6	104
Produce participle**	—	3		—	—	—	—	2	—	5	—	—	10
Third person	—	—	2	3	2	3	—	—	6	2	7	4	29
Mixed errors	—	—	—	—	—	—	—	—	7	—	—	7
Regularisation	—	—	3	—	3	—	—	—	—	—	—	10	16
Produce deriv. affix	3	—	—	—	—	—	—	—	—	—	—	—	3
Other	6	9	8	3	9	4	8	6	4	4	5	4	70
Total	48	25	37	39	27	18	42	20	21	19	19	25	340

*includes regular and irregular past tense forms.
** all irregulars.

Among the verbs, MC's reading of the progressive -*ing* form is the best and it is on a par with verb stem production. MC also made comparatively large numbers of errors by adding -*ing* to the present tense/stem form of the verb. Clearly, this form of the verb is available to him, as to many other Broca's aphasic patients (e.g., Goodglass & Geschwind, 1976; Saffran, Schwartz & Marin, 1980; Druks & Carroll, 2005). Four possible reasons have been suggested for the preservation of the –*ing* form. One is that it is a well-practised and frequent form of the verb; the second is that it is a syllabic affix; the third is that the -*ing* form is ambiguous, being either the progressive or the gerund, and patients use the nominalised gerund form, not the progressive verb form. The fourth explanation is in terms of morpho-syntax. According to this account, the progressive form of the verb is well preserved in Broca's aphasia because it is not inflected for tense, only for aspect, tense being marked on the auxiliary (i.e., *John is reading* vs *John was reading*). This account is supported by the well-documented finding that, in contrast to the -*ing* form, the production of tensed verbs is difficult not only for MC but for other Broca's aphasic patients (e.g., Druks & Carroll, 2005; Friedman & Grodzinsky, 1997; Tsapkini et al., 2002; Wenzlaff & Clahsen, 2004). Further support comes from the status of the past particle that, similarly to the progressive, is also marked only for aspect, not tense. Although the availability of the past participle was not explored systematically in this study, it was explored that the participle form of (irregular) verbs was on 10 occasions produced as a substitution error (see Table 3). Unfortunately, it is impossible to identify the same error type for regular verbs because the participle of regulars is indistinguishable from their past tense form. Finally, a fifth possibility is that the preservation of the -*ing* form is determined by multiple factors.

While plural nouns were relatively well preserved, third person present tense verbs similarly affixed with -*s* was the most impaired category. Since the plural -*s* is a regular, rule-following, productive inflection, there is no reason, according to DMT, why it should be better preserved than other regular inflections such as the regular past tense or the third person -*s*. Thus, the prediction of DMT, that all regular inflections are equally impaired, was not supported in this study.

The phonological account of SMT also breaks down when the plural -*s* and the third person -*s* are compared. SMT (Bird et al., 2003; Joanisse & Seidenberg, 1999) is unable to explain the better preservation of plurals compared to third person -*s* since they are expected to result in similar phonological difficulties. A potential counterargument is that the semantics of plurality compensated for the phonological weakness, while the third person marker, being a semantically redundant agreement marker, does not provide such support. However, there is no other evidence in the data for the facilitatory effects of semantics. In particular, the semantics of tense did not facilitate the production of regular past tense forms.

The recognition of written past tense forms

In the following three tasks the questions asked are whether MC is able to perceive the graphemic representation of the past tense marker and whether he can understand the meaning of the written past tense marker.

Task 6: A sorting task in which the present and the past tense forms of the verb were presented together and MC had to make a binary decision

MC was presented with the same 102 verbs as in the previous tasks: 51 regulars and 51 irregulars. The present and past tense forms of the same stem were printed next to each other. In 25 of the regular and 26 of the irregular verbs the present tense form was printed first, and in the rest of the items the past tense form was printed first. MC was asked to identify the form in each pair of words that represented the past tense. The task was completed during a single session.

Results and summary. MC made no errors in selecting the regular past tense forms, thereby demonstrating awareness of the written past tense marker or, at least, the presence of an affix. In contrast, he made 10 errors on verbs with irregular past tense: *drink, catch, hang, grow, pay, send, shake, slay, swear,* and *throw.* Thus in 20% of the irregular verb pairs he was uncertain which designated the past tense. Since this task was easy in so far that it could be completed by eliminating the least likely form, in the next task the decision was made harder as it had to be carried out on the basis of a single form.

Task 7: Sorting present and past tense verb forms

MC was presented with the same 102 uninflected verb forms, and their 51 regular and 51 irregular past tense forms, as in the previous task. The words were printed individually on small cards. He was asked to sort the verbs into two piles—present and past tense. The sorting task was carried out during two sessions separated by two weeks, and the same stems did not appear twice during a single session. When MC had made his decision, the word was covered to minimise the influence of one selection on the next one.

Results and summary. MC made no errors in placing regular past tense verbs in the pile of the past tense, made 8/102 (8%) errors in placing present tense verbs in the pile of the past tense ones, and 23/51 (45%) errors in placing irregular past tense verbs in the present tense pile.

The results again demonstrate that MC is aware of the presence of the regular past tense marker, or at least the presence of an affix. The increased task difficulty is reflected in the increased number of errors MC made in sorting the irregular past tense forms. He is clearly unsure which form is the past and which is the present. His eight errors on the stem forms could be due to mistakenly believing that they are irregular past tense forms.

Task 8: A sentence completion task

In this task the correct verb form has to be selected out of a choice of four—the present, the past tense, the progressive form, and the third person singular present tense form. The sentence frame provided a meaningful context for the missing past tense form. The task consisted of 72 items each of which consisted of two sentences, one in the present tense and the second required the past tense form of the same verb (e.g., *Every day I sleep eight hours. Yesterday I ...... only five*). There were 36 sentences requiring regular and 36 sentences requiring irregular verbs. The verbs used were a subset of the 102 verbs featuring in previous tasks, and were selected according to their suitability to form around them meaningful and naturally sounding sentences. The regular and irregular verbs so selected were matched for frequency. The sentences were presented in written form but were also read out for MC. In the written form, the verbs in both sentences were replaced by a series of dots (in order to prevent the comparison of the orthographic forms of the verbs), but in the oral presentation, the present tense verbs were provided. MC was asked to circle the form that correctly completes the second sentence out of four—the target past tense, the stem, third person singular form, and the progressive—printed below each item in a quasi random order.

Results and discussion. In this condition, MC performed poorly. He made only 28/76 (37%) correct choices, 15 on the regular and 13 on the irregular verbs, suggesting random selection. No difference between regulars and irregulars was evident, $\chi^2(1) = 0.25$; *ns*. Most of MC's erroneous choices were other inflected forms. On eight items (five irregular and three regular) he selected the present tense form of the verb instead of the target past tense. As he often confuses the present and past tense forms of written irregular verbs, this makes only three genuine stem selections in the whole set.

Summary of the recognition tasks

In the word-sorting tasks, MC is reliable in detecting regular past tense forms. The situation is different in relation to irregular past tense forms, however. In the first, simplest task, MC made 10 errors of confusion between present and past tense forms. In Task 7, a considerable proportion of irregular past tense forms remained unrecognised (45%). Furthermore, in both tasks, some present tense forms were wrongly classified as past tense. These errors are, most likely, due to the fact that MC is unable to sound out the present and past tense forms of irregular verbs, in the same way that he cannot sound out the past tense forms of regular verbs. Unfortunately, MC was not tested on the auditory version of the verb-sorting task, which could establish that his problem in distinguishing between present and past tense forms is indeed confined to written input.

MC's success in recognising regular past tense forms in Tasks 6 and 7 shows the fact that MC is aware of the presence of a (written) inflectional marker but when a choice of inflections *(-ed, -s, -ing)* is provided in the response array, he cannot distinguish among them due to his inability to convert graphemes into phonemes. Crucially, this deficit is equally evident in reading inflected words and in sounding out the present and past tense forms of irregular verbs.

GENERAL DISCUSSION

The study explored MC's ability to read, comprehend, and orally produce the past tense forms of regular and irregular verbs and the plural form of nouns, and to read verbs inflected with other affixes. The objective was to examine current theories of English past tense production—SMT and DMT. It was expected that the performance of MC, who has Broca's aphasia and is a typical phonological dyslexic patient, would be instrumental in evaluating the two theoretical positions. The following questions will be addressed in the discussion: Are MC's most frequent errors indeed morphological in nature? How do SMT and DMT fare in the light of MCs performance? How can we explain the discrepancy in his ability to produce regular past tense forms in tasks 1 and 2, on the one hand, and in other production tasks, on the other?

Morphological errors?

MC's errors in reading tensed verbs were predominantly morphological. Morphological errors, however, can arguably be seen as indistinguishable from visual and semantic errors (e.g., Badecker & Caramazza, 1989; Funnell, 1987) since they are both visually and semantically similar to the target, and patients who tend to make morphological errors, often also make visual and/or semantic errors (i.e., phonological and deep dyslexic patients). Since MC also makes some visual and semantic errors, in Druks and Froud (2002), the diagnostic of Funnell (1987) was used to determine the true nature of his errors. In this diagnostic test, MC read the pseudo-affixed words significantly better than the morphologically complex words, showing that he makes more errors on morphologically complex words than on monomorphemic words with identical endings. The results were interpreted as supporting the hypothesis that MC's errors on morphologically complex words are morphological, rather than semantic or visual.

Further evidence comes from a comparison between the percentages of morphological and visual/semantic errors MC makes. In Druks and Froud (2002), we reported that MC read 83% of 1093 content words (mostly stems and a few derived words) without error, and only 8% of his errors were semantic. The proportion of visual errors in this large list is not reported, but in smaller lists his visual error rate is around 10%. For example, in the most demanding list consisting of 43 morphologically simple content words, he made five visual (*abstruse* → *abstract; extent* → *extenuate*) and one visual-semantic error (*synod* → *synagogue*). In another list of 100 words, MC made four visual (e.g., *facility* → *faculty; jeopardy* → *leopard*) and one visual-semantic error (*birch* → *beech*). In reading 60 abstract nouns and 60 abstract verbs, he made 6.5% visual errors on the nouns and 8.3% on the verbs. In contrast, the proportion of his errors on regular and irregular past tensed verbs in Druks and Froud (2002; see Appendix 2) and in the present study is between 40 and 50% (see Tasks 1–3). In light of the quantitative differences between visual/ semantic and morphological errors, the conclusion that they derive from different underlying deficits seems strongly suggestive. MC's errors in reading past tense verbs, both regular and irregular, and other inflected words, therefore, may plausibly be considered as morphological in nature.

DMT and SMT in light of MC's performance

The disproportionate problems MC displayed in producing regular past tense forms in Tasks 1 and 2 show that MC's performance is relevant for the examination of theories about regular and irregular past tense production. The fact that some of the evidence is derived from oral reading and not from the more usual oral transformation may seem problematic, however. The evidence is thought to be admissible because MC is a pure case of phonological dyslexia, who is incapable of grapheme/phoneme conversion, but whose content word reading is remarkably good. Thus, he is expected to read well the majority of lexically represented word forms: both regulars and irregulars, according to SMT, and irregulars, according to DMT. His oral reading therefore has the potential of deciding between the claims of SMT and DMT (see also Ullman et al., 1997, where patients who were unable to carry out the oral transformation task, were tested in the written modality. However, their data are less reliable than the data here, because the patients' ability to use the sublexical route was not explored).

MC's performance in Tasks 1 and 2 shows that the pattern often described in the literature (e.g., Marslen-Wilson & Tyler, 1998; Ullman et al., 1997) is replicable: that it is indeed difficult for Broca's-type patients to combine stem with affix and/or to follow the *add -ed* past tense rule. MC, however, is also impaired in producing irregular past tense forms. This could be explained by DMT, by arguing that MC must have additional deficits in associative memory. This is unlikely, however. The errors MC makes on irregular past tense verbs (around 50%) far outnumber the errors he usually makes on morphologically simple content words, including low-frequency and low-imageability words (see Appendix 2). Even more damaging for DMT is the fact that MC's errors on regular and irregular verbs are very similar and predominantly morphological in nature. This pattern of performance is in conflict with DMT, which assumes that irregular verbs are processed and produced in associative memory without the involvement of morphology, and so there is no (adequately convincing) explanation for the predominantly morphological nature of MC's errors (unless these are masked visual or semantic errors, a position against which I argued earlier). Thus, while his very poor reading of regular past tense forms in Tasks 1 and 2 appear to support DMT, the pattern of errors in reading irregulars does not.

MC's good reading and oral production of plural nouns poses an even more serious problem for DMT. There are numerous reports of other Broca's aphasic patients whose production of plural nouns is similarly better preserved than tensed verbs (e.g., De Bleser & Bayer, 1988 [in German]; Druks & Carroll, 2005; Nanousi, 2004 [in Greek]; Shapiro & Caramazza, 2003; Tsapkini et al., 2002). The plural -*s* is a regular inflection with wide applicability, not different from -*ed*, and therefore DMT would predict its impaired production. A hypothetical counterclaim, that there are intrinsic differences between the plural and the past tense and, therefore, evidence from the plural cannot be used in arguing against DMT cannot work, because the case of the German plural -*s* is widely used in support of DMT (e.g., Marcus, Brinkmann, Clahsen, Wiese, & Pinker, 1995).

The -*ing* form of the verb, like the plural -*s* is a well-preserved form not only for MC but for other Broca's aphasic patients, (e.g., Goodglass & Geschwind, 1976; Schwartz, Marin, & Saffran, 1980; Druks & Carroll, 2005), while the third person -*s* is known to be impaired (e.g., Druks & Carroll, 2005). These inflectional affixes are similar at the level of morpho-phonological concatenation (the plural and the third person -*s* are maximally similar, although the -*ing* form, being syllabic, may be easier to attach to the stem), and therefore DMT would predict similar, impaired performance on all of them. However, the data from Task 2, and evidence from other Broca's aphasics, show that the plural -*s* and the -*ing* form are well preserved, while the third person -*s* is very impaired. The finding that some regular inflections are not as impaired as the regular past tense demonstrates that DMT is only able to account for a very limited part of aphasic performance in relation to inflectional morphology. The generalisation that regularity/productivity of an affix determines its availability is not supported by the performance of MC and of many other Broca's aphasic patients.

MC's performance on regular and irregular past tense forms does not support single mechanism models either. For Joanisse and Seidenberg's model to be able to account for MC's performance, it would be necessary to demonstrate that MC has both phonological *and* lexical deficits. Although MC's phonological abilities were not studied as carefully as the patients in Bird et al. (2003), I argued earlier that he has no major phonological deficits. Nevertheless, MC's deficits in phonological combinatory operations may indeed explain his problem in producing regular past tense forms, although, again, the explanation is in conflict with his good performance on the plural and the progressive. Moreover, the dissociation between the plural form and the third person -*s* is difficult to explain in terms of phonological complexity, since there is little phonological difference between them.

MC's deficits in producing irregular past tense forms are also difficult to explain in the terms of SMT. Patterson et al. (2001) claim that problems with irregulars are linked to lexical/semantic deficits. While the complete absence of semantic deficits is difficult to demonstrate conclusively, there is not a shred of positive evidence that MC has semantic deficits, and a great deal of evidence that he has no lexical deficits. The latter is demonstrated by his excellent reading of all content words, including low-frequency, abstract, and irregular words, in the absence of sublexical reading (see Appendix 2). MC is therefore very different from the semantic dementia patients described by Patterson et al.

The morphological nature of MC's errors argues against models of past tense production that are based on simple associations between present and past tense forms. Connectionist models to date cannot account for the range of errors that MC and similar patients make when attempting to produce past tense target forms. The models are limited in their scope (with the exception of MacWhinney & Leinbach, 1991, whose model is capable of making a variety of errors involving other forms of the verb), because they artificially isolate present and past tense forms from other morphological markers associated with verbs. The limited range of errors that such models are capable of producing may correspond to errors that normal adults and children, in experimental conditions, may make in past tense formation (i.e., the omission of the past tense marker, regularisations, and irregularisations), possibly, because the intact morphological system is likely to produce only some types of errors and not others. Aphasic patients such as MC, however, make a variety of errors (e.g., producing the -*ing* form or the third person present tense form, the participle form, or even a derived form), most of them are recognisably morphological in nature. These errors demonstrate, first of all, the relatedness of the verbal affixes within the morphological system, and second that some knowledge of this system is accessible to MC and patients like him, eliciting morphological rather than random (and/or visual or semantic) errors.

According to Marslen-Wilson and Tyler (1998) who accept a variant of DMT, the difficulty involved in producing the regular past tense form is the combinatorial operations involving morphologically complex words. The difference between regular and irregular verbs is due to their different morpho-phonological make-up. While irregular past tense forms are stored as full forms, regular past tense forms need to be generated when produced, and parsed when heard. This creates the combinatorial difficulty for processing the regular past tense. There is evidence for this in MC's data in Tasks 3, 4, and 5, in so far that MC, at times, made a noticeable articulatory effort when producing the past tense (and the plural) marker. The articulatory effort was clearly task induced, however. It did not occur in connected speech or in the mixed reading lists (in Tasks 1 and 2), therefore the reason for it is not entirely clear. Moreover, the difficulty in past tense production clearly cannot only be due to phonological concatenation, since MC's production of the plural marker and of the progressive is considerably better than his processing of the past tense form. Indeed, Marslen-Wilson and Tyler (1997) show that the "combinatorial operations" distinguish between the morphological and/or syntactic functions of the affix. This was demonstrated in their study by normal performance on derived words and impaired performance on past tensed verbs by Broca's aphasic patients. This suggests that similar morpho-syntactic differences may account for the observed differences between different verbal and nominal affixes too in the present study.

To conclude this section, MC's performance over a wider range of inflected words than is usually probed in English studies is shown to be in conflict with both single and dual mechanisms theories. SMT (Bird et al., 2003; Patterson et al., 2001) and DMT (e.g., Ullman et al., 1997) can only account for superficial morpho-phonological differences between regular and irregular past tense forms. They are unable to account for the selectivity in the availability of other inflectional affixes.

Morpho-phonological vs morpho-syntactic deficits

MC's performance in Tasks 1 and 2 and in Tasks 3 and 4 is very different. A possible interpretation of the discrepancy is that MC performs differently in reading and in oral production. However, it is more likely that MC performs better when the task is constrained; when he knows that the words represent present and past tense verbs as in Task 3, a structured reading task, and Task 4, a structured oral production task. When the task is reading a list of unrelated words, however, MC, who is unable to convert graphemes onto phonemes, is unable to sound out the affix on the past tensed verbs.

It is suggested here that MC's performance in Task 1 (and 2) and Task 3 (and 4) reflects two different forms of impairment associated with morphologically complex forms. One is what Badecker (1997) calls a morpho-phonological output deficit that affects regular verbs in English due to their componential make-up, similar to that ascribed to SJD (Badecker & Caramazza, 1991). The second form, impairment of tense at the deeper morpho-syntactic level, involves the making of morphological errors not only in conjunction with regular but also with irregular tensed forms, and in comprehension/recognition tasks with regular and irregular tensed verbs. This form of the deficit is similar to that of FM, described by Badecker and Caramazza (1987) and Badecker (1997), who argued that errors in producing irregular past tense forms (e.g., *fought* → *fighting*) cannot be attributed to a disruption of combinatory operations because irregular past tense forms are not compositional at the output level. Irregular past tense forms, however, are similar to regulars at a deeper morpho-syntactic level (Badecker, 1997 p. 368). In the case of MC too, the variable performance on different nominal and verbal affixation cannot be accounted for by morpho-phonological effects. Only morpho-syntactic differences between nominal (plural *-s*) and verbal/agreement inflections (third person *-s*) and between tense (*-ed*) and aspect (-*ing*) marking inflections may explain why some inflections are better preserved than others.

MC's performance is interesting because it provides evidence of both morpho-phonological and morpho-syntactic deficits. His reading in Task 1 reveals a disproportionate deficit in regular past tense forms, showing therefore that the regular and irregular systems differ. DMT thus appears supportable at the morpho-phonological level. At this level regulars and irregulars are processed differently and (some) Broca's aphasic patients display a dissociation between the two forms. This dissociation may also be accounted for by the Joanisse and Seidenberg model (see Bird et al., 2003), if a correlation between general phonological deficits and deficits in regular past tense production can be demonstrated (see Tyler, Randall & Marslen-Wilson, 2002 for a similar argument).

However, the puzzle remains why we do not observe morpho-phonological effects in the production of the plural and the progressive marker. A possible explanation is that there are complex interactions between the levels of morpho-phonology and morpho-syntax. Accordingly, only those inflections (i.e., tense and agreement marking inflections) that are impaired at the level of morpho-syntax will show *additional* deficits at the level of morpho-phonology, as MC showed in Tasks 1 and 2. In contrast, inflections that are intact at the level of morpho-syntax will remain relatively well preserved at the level of morpho-phonology too.

CONCLUSIONS

The investigations involving MC allowed the distinction between two different patterns to be made in a single patient's performance: one tapping morpho-phonological output deficits, and a second tapping morpho-syntactic deficits, similar to the distinctions made by Badecker (1997). This complex performance pattern cannot fully be accounted for by either SMT or DMT—both being theories of morpho-phonological processes. The Joanisse and Seidenberg model has no mechanism to implement morphological knowledge, and as for DMT, morpho-syntactic processes remain external to the domain of the theory. Indeed, their core data of normal participants carrying out the past tense transformation task (e.g., Bybee & Moder, 1983; Prasada & Pinker, 1993), or young children acquiring past tense forms, are likely to tap morpho-phonological processing only. However, Broca's aphasic patients, in addition to morpho-phonological deficits, have morpho-syntactic problems too. This is the reason why it is doubtful that the performance of Broca's aphasic patients will shed light on the debate between SMT and DMT. Ullman et al. (1997; Ullman, Pancheva, Love, Yee, Swinney, & Hickock, 2005) and Bird et al. (2003), overlook the more fundamental morpho-syntactic deficits this patient group has in producing, in addition to regular past tense, irregular past tense forms and the verbal agreement marker, along with (often) well-preserved verbal and nominal inflections. A major problem for both theories is that the effects of regularity/productivity (and phonological complexity) in this study were only observable in past tense production, but not in the production of the plural and the progressive. This too, I have argued, is due to the morpho-syntactic differences between the different affixes.

REFERENCES

Baayen, H., Piepenbrock, R., & van Rijn, H. (1993). *The CELEX Lexical Databas* [CD-ROM]. Linguistic Data Consortium, University of Pennsylvania, PA.

Badecker, W. (1997). Levels of morphological deficit: Indications from inflectional regularity. *Brain and Language, 60,* 360–380.

Badecker, W., & Caramazza, A. (1987). The analysis of morphological errors in the case of acquired dyslexia. *Brain and Language, 32,* 278–305.

Badecker, W., & Caramazza, A. (1991). Morphological decomposition in the lexical output system. *Cognitive Neuropsychology, 8,* 335–367.

Bird, H., Lambon Ralph, M. A., Seidenberg, M. S., McClelland, J. I., & Patterson, K. (2003). Deficits in phonology and past tense morphology. *Journal of Memory and Language, 48,* 502–526.

Bybee, J. (1995). Regular morphology and the lexicon. *Language and Cognitive Processes, 10,* 425–455.

Bybee, J. L. (1985). *Morphology: A study of the relation between meaning and form.* Philadelphia: John Benjamins.

Bybee, J. L. (1999). Use impacts morphological representation. *Behavioral and Brain Sciences, 22,* 1016–1017.

Bybee, J. L., & Moder, C. L. (1983). Rules and schemes in the development and use of the English past tense. *Language, 59,* 251–270.

Chomsky, N., & Halle, M. (1968). *The sound pattern of English.* Cambridge, MA: MIT Press.

Daugherty, K., & Seidenberg, M. S. (1992). The past tense revisited. *Proceedings of the 14th Annual Meeting of the Cognitive Science Society.* Hillsdale, NJ: Lawrence Erlbaum Associates Inc.

De Bleser, R., & Bayer, J. (1988). Inflectional morphology in agrammatism. In M. Hammond & M. Noonan (Eds.), *Theoretical morphology: Approaches in modern linguistics.* San Diego, CA: Academic Press.

De Diego Balaguer, R., Costa, A., Sebastian-Galles, N., Juncadella, M., & Caramazza, A. (2004). Regular and irregular morphology and its relationship with agrammatism: Evidence from two Spanish–Catalan bilinguals. *Brain and Language, 91,* 212–222.

Druks, J., & Carroll, E. (2005). The crucial role of tense for verb production. *Brain and Language, 94,* 1–18.

Druks, J., & Froud, K. (2002). The syntax of single words: Evidence from a patient with a selective function word deficit. *Cognitive Neuropsychology, 19,* 207–244.

Druks, J., & Masterson, J. (2000). *Object and Action Naming Battery.* Hove, UK: Psychology Press.

Faroqi-Shah, Y., & Thompson, C. K. (2004). Regular and irregular inflections in agrammatism: Dissociations and associations? *Brain and Language, 89,* 484–498.

Friedman, N., & Grodzinsky, Y. (1997). Tense and agreement in agrammatic production: Pruning the syntactic tree. *Brain and Language, 56,* 397–425.

Funnell, E. (1987). Morphological errors in acquired dyslexia: A case of mistaken identity. *Quarterly Journal of Experimental Psychology, 39A,* 497–538.

Glushko, R. J. (1979). The organisation and activation of orthographic knowledge in reading aloud. *Journal of Experimental Psychology: Human Perception and Performance, 5,* 674–691.

Goodglass, H., & Geschwind, N. (1976). Language disorders (aphasia). In C. Carterette & M. P. Friedman (Eds.), *Handbook of perception, Volume 7.* New York: Academic Press.

Goodglass, H., & Kaplan, E. (1983). *The assessment of aphasia and related disorders.* Philadelphia: Lea & Febiger.

Grodzinsky, J. (1990). *Theoretical perspectives on language deficits.* Cambridge, MA: MIT Press.

Halle, M., & Mohanan, K. P. (1985). Segmental phonology of modern English. *Linguistic Inquiry, 16,* 57–116.

Izvorski, R., & Ullman, M. T. (1999). Verb inflection and the hierarchy of functional categories in agrammatic anterior aphasia. *Brain and Language, 68,* 289–291.

Joanisse, M. F., & Seidenberg, M. S. (1999). Impairments in verb morphology after brain injury: A connectionist model. *Proceedings of the National Academy of Sciences, 96,* 7592–7597.

MacWhinney, B., & Leinbach, J. (1991). Implementations are not conceptualisations: Revising the verb learning model. *Cognition, 40,* 121–157.

Marcus, G., Brinkman, U., Clahsen, H., Wiese, R., & Pinker, S. (1995). German inflection: The exception that proves the rule. *Cognitive Psychology, 29,* 189–256.

Marslen-Wilson, W., & Tyler, L. K. (1997). Dissociating types of mental computation. *Nature, 387,* 592–594.

Marslen-Wilson, W., & Tyler, L. K. (1998). Rules, representations, and the English past tense. *Trends in Cognitive Sciences, 2*, 428–435.

Miceli, G., & Caramazza, A. (1988). Dissociation of inflectional and derivational morphology. *Brain and Language, 35*, 24–65.

Nanousi, V. (2004). *Morphological deficits in Greek speaking aphasic patients*. Unpublished doctoral dissertation, University of Essex, UK.

Patterson, K., Lambon Ralph M., A., Hodges, J. R., & McClelland, J. L. (2001). Deficits in irregular past-tense verb morphology associated with degraded semantic knowledge. *Neuropsychologia, 39*, 709–724.

Penke, M., Janssen, U., & Krause, M. (1999). The representation of inflectional morphology: Evidence from Broca's aphasia. *Brain and Language, 68*, 225–232.

Pinker, S. (1991). Rules of language. *Science, 253*, 530–535.

Pinker, S. (1999). *Words and rules: The ingredients of language*. London: Weidenfeld & Nicolson.

Pinker, S., & Ullman, M. T. (2002). The past and future of the past tense. *Trends in Cognitive Sciences, 6*, 456–463.

Plunkett, K., & Marchman, V. (1991). U-shaped learning and frequency effects in a multilayered perceptron: Implications for child language acquisition. *Cognition, 38*, 43–102.

Plunkett, K., & Marchman, V. (1993). From rote learning to system building: Acquiring verb morphology in children and connectionist nets. *Cognition, 48*, 21–69.

Prasada, S., & Pinker, S. (1993). Generalisation of regular and irregular morphological patterns. *Language and Cognitive Processes, 8*, 1–56.

Rumelhart, D. E., & McClelland, J. L. (1986). On learning the past tenses of English verbs. In J. L. McClelland & D. E. Rumelhart (Eds.), *Parallel distributed processing*. (Vol. 2). Cambridge, MA: MIT Press.

Saffran, E., Schwartz, M. E., & Marin, O. (1980). The word-order problem in agrammatism. II. Production. *Brain and Language, 10*, 263–280.

Schwartz, M. E., Marin, O., & Saffran, E. (1980). The word-order problem in agrammatism. I. Comprehension. *Brain and Language, 10*, 249–262.

Shallice, T., & Saffran, E. M. (1986). Lexical processing in the absence of explicit word identification: Evidence from a letter-by-letter reader. *Cognitive Neuropsychology, 3*, 429–458.

Shapiro, K., & Caramazza, A. (2003). Grammatical processing of nouns and verbs in left frontal cortex? *Neuropsychologia, 41*, 1189–1198.

Shapiro, K., Shelton, J., & Caramazza, A. (2000). Grammatical class in lexical production and morphological processing: Evidence from a case of fluent aphasia. *Cognitive Neuropsychology. 17*, 665–682.

Thompson, C. K., Fix, S., & Gitelman, D. R. (1999). Selective impairment of morphosyntactic production in a neurological patient: Evidence for impaired feature processing. *Brain and Language, 68*, 285–288.

Tsapkini, K., Jarema, G., & Kehayia, E. (2002). Regularity revisited: Evidence from lexical access of verbs and nouns in Greek. *Brain and Language, 81*, 103–119.

Tyler, L. K., Randall, B., & Marslen-Wilson, W. D. (2002). Phonology and neuropsychology of the English past tense. *Neuropsychologia, 40*, 1154–1166.

Ullman, M. T. (1999). Naming tools and using rules: Evidence that a frontal/basal-ganglia system underlies both motor skill knowledge and grammatical rule use. *Brain and Language, 68*, 317–318.

Ullman, M. T. (2001). The declarative/procedural model of lexicon and grammar. *Journal of Psycholinguistic Research, 30*, 37–69.

Ullman, M. T., Corkin, S., Coppola, M., Hickok, G., Growdon, J. H., & Koroshetz, W. J. et al. (1997). A neural dissociation within language: Evidence that the mental dictionary is part of declarative memory, and that grammatical rules are processed by the procedural system. *Journal of Cognitive Neuroscience, 9*, 266–276.

Ullman, M. T., & Gopnik, M. (1999). Inflectional morphology in a family with inherited specific language impairment. *Applied Psycholinguistics, 20*, 51–117.

Ullman, M. T., Pancheva, R., Love, T., Yee, E., Swinney, D., & Hickok, G. (2005). Neural correlates of lexicon and grammar: Evidence from the production, reading, and judgement of inflection in aphasia. *Brain and Language, 93*, 185–238.

van der Lely, H., & Ullman, M. T. (2001). Past tense morphology in special language impaired and normally developing children. *Language and Cognitive Processes, 16*, 177–217.

Wenzlaff, M., & Clahsen, H. (2004). Tense and agreement in German agrammatism. *Brain and Language, 89*, 57–68.

APPENDIX 1

Examples of past tense forms taken from recordings of MC's spontaneous speech and story telling

- He was talking to the moor and planted inside a bit of a jealousy.
- And eventually she killed herself, he, she killed herself.
- And the moor also died.
- That was in St. Peterburg and it was lovely opera.
- The story is of Joan of Arc. She fought and fought but it is of no avail.
- He did so.
- But she differed.
- Because she was in battle and the French mourned her.
- She went to the spot.
- She was lying down and they appeared the witches which were very fierce and the angel came down and rescued her.
- She fought and she died.
- She was in love with Carlo but the angels that other plans and she took the sword and the armour and Joan of Arc was the hero.
- She sort of liberated France.
- Joan of Arc was in battle and she died but in the arms of Carlo.
- All the court assembled and she died in the arms of the French.
- Once upon a time there was a prince and princess.
- The baby is arrived.
- All the gentry were present.
- Each one took to point to the baby.
- [The prince] hacked and hacked and hacked and there was the castle.
- He broke in.
- The prince kissed her.
- But they are escaped.
- They are woken by a strange noise, and investigated, and is a little house.
- We were looking at the door and things like that and they went in.
- Just before the cow was sold .... the man appeared.
- And so he said okay and counted them out and so the cow and the man disappeared.
- The little boy went home.
- And the mother exclaimed.
- And so we threw them out of the window.
- And went to bed.
- So they, this boy started to climb.
- And .. he went into the clouds and over, and a house appeared.
- And a castle appeared.
- So .... he looked and entered and the giant appeared.
- He hides and the giant was eating and a harp appeared. Which .. played for it.
- The money ... and escaped and down the beanstalk it fell.
- The mother has gobbled it up first.
- And she was in bed.
- And the wolf was devoured her.

- Popped Riding Hood and the grandmother, safe. They are good idea. That's all.
- I waited and then a bus came.
- We went to Cologne because that is a lovely city.
- It was very funny because the driver took me out and into the building.
- I've been everywhere else but I've never been to Geneva.

APPENDIX 2

A summary of MC's language performance as reported in Druks and Froud (2002). Numbers (%) correct.

I. Semantics and naming

Pyramids and Palm Trees	52/52 (100)
Boston Naming Test	48/60 (80)
Object and Action Naming (an early version of	Objects: 129/140 (92)
Druks & Masterson, 2000)	Actions: 108/140 (77)

II. Orthographic processing

Visual letter identification PALPA 18, 19, 20	100%
Letter discrimination in words and nonwords PALPA 21	100%
Lexical decision with pseudowords PALPA 25	52/60 (87%)
Lexical decision with illegally affixed words PALPA 26	Nonwords 15/30 (chance) Words 26/30 (87%)
Orthographic segmentation – 100 items (Druks & Froud, 2002)	100%

III. Phonological processing

Rhyme judgement PALPA 15	59/60 (98%)
Same/different discrimination PALPA 1	67/72 (93%)
Nonword repetition PALPA 8	20/30 (66%)
Glushko's (1979) list of nonwords	60/74 (81%)
Auditory lexical decision PALPA 5	Words 80/80 (100%)
	Nonwords 77/80 (96%)
Phonological segmentation and assembly (Druks & Froud, 2002)	0%

IV. Graphemes to phonemes conversion

Letter naming	5/52 (9%)
Letter – sounding out PALPA 22	6/52 (11%)
Matching written letters with their sound PALPA 23	11/26 (42%)
Homophone decision with written words PALPA 28	35/60 (58%, chance)
Rhyme judgement with written words PALPA 15	32/60 (53%, chance)

IV. Reading

Nonwords PALPA 36	2/24 (8.3%)
Nonwords Glushko's (1979) list	4/43 (9.3%)
Nonwords – Shallice & Saffran (1986)	6/126 (4.8%)
Concrete nouns	127/132 (96%)
Concrete verbs	140/145 (97%)
Abstract nouns	47/60 (78%) mainly derivational errors
Abstract verbs	42/60 (70%) mainly derivational errors
Derived words of different grammatical class	35/75 (47%)
Inflected words	30/75 (40%)
Content words and	31/43 (72%)
function words (matched for imageability)	7/43 (16%)
Concrete words and	47/50 (94%)
abstract words (matched for frequency)	41/50 (82% including derivational errors)

APPENDIX 3

List of frequency matched regular and irregular verbs used throughout the study

wilted	0	wrung	0
barked	0	dwelt	0
juggled	0	slew	0
coughed	0	trod	0
travelled	9	shrank	15
knitted	12	strove	11
yawned	14	bled	14
bounced	22	froze	23
posted	24	arose	26
prayed	31	swore	31
crawled	31	swam	32
floated	35	wept	33
begged	37	leapt	38
roared	43	hid	43
borrowed	44	spent	48
kicked	59	fled	59
solved	66	tore	67
folded	84	sang	83
knocked	95	forgot	96
washed	104	woke	104
approached	105	fought	128
controlled	120	fed	138
climbed	121	slept	118

APPENDIX 3 continued.

crossed	153	chose	145
destroyed	154	drank	154
enjoyed	167	rang	156
cried	173	ate	180
discussed	183	hung	197
entered	191	threw	210
mentioned	208	taught	216
dropped	267	won	235
loved	280	bought	296
explained	287	wore	265
talked	307	shook	304
pulled	311	grew	311
played	387	caught	386
died	434	paid	420
followed	462	ran	490
opened	469	led	476
worked	484	met	505
stopped	501	spoke	502
walked	545	wrote	539
decided	552	sent	524
started	673	lost	727
tried	723	held	753
turned	1146	heard	954
remember	1138	began	1585
wanted	1138	gave	1244
called	1399	told	1706
asked	1610	found	1650
looked	1788	knew	1988

Progressive non-fluent aphasia is not a progressive form of non-fluent (post-stroke) aphasia

Karalyn Patterson and Naida L. Graham

MRC Cognition & Brain Sciences Unit, Cambridge, UK

Matthew A. Lambon Ralph

University of Manchester, UK

John R. Hodges

MRC Cognition & Brain Sciences Unit, Cambridge, UK

Background: The speech of patients with progressive non-fluent aphasia (PNFA) has been described as similar to that in non-fluent aphasia (NFA) consequent on stroke. There are, however, few direct empirical comparisons of these two patient populations in the literature.

Aims: To test the hypotheses that PNFA cases differ from NFA (a) in the extent to which their speech production deficit varies as a function of speaking task, and (b) in the nature of their phonological deficit.

Methods & Procedures: Groups of PNFA and NFA patients ($N = 10$ each), matched on scores in a picture-naming test, were assessed on tasks of narrative picture description, reading aloud of text and single words, and phonological abilities such as rhyme judgement and rhyme production.

Outcomes & Results: (a) The NFA cases showed equivalent speech rates in self-generated speech and reading text aloud, and equivalent error rates when reading text or isolated single words. In contrast, the PNFA cases spoke more rapidly when reading aloud than when producing narrative speech, and achieved higher accuracy when reading single words aloud than when reading words in text. (b) Variation in success rate for reading different types of words (e.g., content words, function words, and nonsense words), error types in reading, and performance on phonological tasks all indicated a different and better quality of phonological processing in PNFA than NFA.

Address correspondence to: Karalyn Patterson, MRC Cognition and Brain Sciences Unit, 15 Chaucer Road, Cambridge, CB2 2EF, UK. E-mail: karalyn.patterson@mrc-cbu.cam.ac.uk

This contribution, like the others in this Special Issue, is dedicated to John C. Marshall: he and his work have been a considerable inspiration to all of the authors of this paper.

This research was supported in part by a (USA) NIMH Interdisciplinary Behavioural Science Centre Grant (No. MH64445: KP, NLG and MALR) and by a (UK) MRC Programme Grant (No. G9724461: JRH).

We are grateful to Natalie Braber and Katherine Ellis for assistance with data collection for the NFA cases, to Peter Watson for statistical assistance, and to Peter Nestor for helpful discussions regarding the PNFA patients.

Conclusions: Despite some surface similarities, there are telling differences between the speech impairments in PNFA and NFA. The deficit in PNFA particularly compromises self-generated connected speech.

Descriptions of *non-fluent aphasia* resulting from left-hemisphere cerebrovascular accident (CVA) have been in the literature since the time of Broca (1861). Some 120 years later, a similar form of language disorder resulting from neurodegenerative disease was brought to widespread attention by Mesulam (1982, 2001). Although some authors continue to use Mesulam's terminology of "primary progressive aphasia" without specifying speech character, others have now adopted the label *progressive non-fluent aphasia* to refer to the pattern of slowly progressive aphasia in which speech output is notably dysfluent (Gorno-Tempini et al., 2004; Grossman & Ash, 2005; Hodges & Patterson, 1996; Snowden, Neary, & Mann, 1996; Thompson, Ballard, Tait, Weintraub, & Mesulam, 1997). Thus, there are two syndrome labels, non-fluent aphasia (NFA) and progressive non-fluent aphasia (PNFA), differing only in the presence/absence of the adjective *progressive*. These labels give the impression that—apart from the fact that one of these disorders emerges abruptly after a CVA whereas the other develops gradually as a consequence of a neurodegenerative condition—they are two versions of a single aphasic profile.

Furthermore, it is not only the labels that foster this view: although almost all discussions of PNFA comment on the heterogeneity of the language disorder, the pattern most commonly described is effortful, dysfluent speech coupled with phonological and syntactic impairments, which is the typical picture of NFA (Brown, 1972; Caplan, 1987; Saffran, Schwartz, & Marin, 1980). For example, Gorno-Tempini et al. (2004, p. 335) characterised PNFA as comprising "... laboured speech, agrammatism in production and/or comprehension, variable degrees of anomia, and phonemic paraphasias, in the presence of relatively preserved word comprehension". Unlike several large-scale comparisons of PNFA with language disruption in Alzheimer's disease (Grossman et al., 1996; Kertesz, Davidson, McCabe, Takagi, & Munoz, 2003; Mendez, Clark, Shapira, & Cummings, 2003), the literature offers few direct and empirical (as opposed to descriptive) comparisons between PNFA and NFA from stroke. In one major exception (Thompson et al., 1997), the authors used a variety of linguistic measures in the realms of both word and sentence processing, and concluded that three of the four cases of PNFA that they tracked longitudinally had a pattern resembling the NFA cases in their study.

Our own observations have led to the hypotheses that there are at least three potentially salient differences between the language disorders in these two conditions. One of these pertains to the claim that the expressive language of patients with PNFA is typically agrammatic. Contrary to this view, Graham, Patterson, and Hodges (2004) have recently reported that the narrative speech (as measured by picture description) of a group of 14 PNFA cases, relative to that of age-matched controls, was reduced in quantity but had normal ratios of verbs to nouns and of function words to content words. The remaining two hypothesised differences are explored in the current study comparing PNFA with NFA. First, a set of tasks was designed to address the hypothesis that the speech production deficit in PNFA, whilst not exactly milder than that in NFA, is significantly more modifiable by the nature of the language task. More specifically, we predicted that the deficit in PNFA, by contrast to NFA, would primarily disrupt performance in tasks requiring self-generated connected language. Second, we predicted marked differences in the nature of the phonological deficit in PNFA versus NFA.

METHOD

Statistical analyses

The majority of statistical tests reported in this paper, apart from a few correlations, are non-parametric two-tailed Mann-Whitney U tests (for between-group contrasts) and Wilcoxon tests (for within-group comparisons) because of inhomogeneity of variance in the clinical populations.

Participants

Two groups of patients were the source of the data reported here. The first comprised 10 right-handed individuals who had suffered a single left-hemisphere CVA, referred by several consultant neurologists and speech therapists in both Cambridge and Manchester, UK. They were selected for this study on the basis of slow effortful speech containing phonological and/or phonetic errors. Five of these cases had participated in a set of experiments on past-tense verb inflection in non-fluent aphasia (Bird, Lambon Ralph, Seidenberg, McClelland, & Patterson, 2003).

The second experimental group comprised 10 PNFA patients (9 right-handed, 1 left-handed) selected from a slightly larger sample ($N = 14$, reported in Graham et al., 2004) with the goal of matching to the 10 NFA cases just described. They were all recruited from either the Memory Disorders Clinic or the Early Dementia Clinic at Addenbrooke's Hospital, Cambridge, UK, where they presented with a predominant complaint of speech difficulty. In varying degrees, all had slowed, effortful output with phonological errors in spontaneous speech or on formal testing. Every patient in this sub-group has deteriorated on follow-up, supporting the progressive diagnosis. MRI in all cases ruled out stroke, and was often rather unremarkable apart from a degree of abnormal widening of the left Sylvian fissure. Of the 10 reported here, 5 were included in a study of resting cerebral metabolism (FDG-PET), which demonstrated that the most significant region of hypometabolism was the left anterior insula/frontal operculum (Nestor, Graham, Fryer, Williams, Patterson, & Hodges, 2003). In general, the patients in this group fulfilled the standard Mesulam criterion of at least a 2-year history of language disruption in the context of preserved activities of daily living. None of the cases had a clear dementia, although neuropsychological testing revealed a range of function.

It was not obvious *a priori* how the groups should be matched, but picture naming—which is not a taxing speech task but does require both semantic and phonological processing as well as communication from the former to the latter—seemed one appropriate variable. Accordingly, the 10 PNFA cases were selected in order to achieve the closest possible pair-wise matching of cases from the two patient groups in terms of their scores on a picture-naming test from the Hodges and Patterson semantic battery (Bozeat, Lambon Ralph, Patterson, Garrard, & Hodges, 2000), which consists of 64 line drawings of common objects from the Snodgrass and Vanderwort corpus (1980). The suitability of this variable as a basis for matching is supported by the fact that the two groups turned out to be similar on a number of other language measures, which fortunately included speech rate on a narrative task (see below).

Many of the tests included here are either tasks for which normal accuracy would clearly be at ceiling (e.g., single-word reading or naming of common objects) or tests for which we had previously collected control data from normal participants in the age range of the two patient groups; therefore, no dedicated control group was tested for this study. Control scores from these other groups of normal participants will be reported where appropriate.

Table 1 provides demographic and background data for the two groups of patients who are ordered according to their pair-wise matching on picture naming (i.e., the first case listed under NFA was matched with the first case listed under PNFA, and so on). Not surprisingly for a contrast of CVA with progressive disease,

TABLE 1
Basic information on the patient participants

Case	Age	Sex	Years post	Naming	WPM	PPT	TROG	Digits F	Digits B	WCST
NFA										
DC	39	F	2	64	64	52	71	6	1	6
JL	48	F	7	54	64	51	79	5	3	6
PG	68	M	3	53	63	51	71	4	0	5
JS	47	F	6	51	62	42	58	4	2	6
DM	62	M	5	50	61	50	64	3	2	5
GN	74	M	4	48	60	45	62	4	2	1
AB	62	F	7	42	62	47	55	3	2	3
MB	85	F	5	35	60	47	55	3	0	4
IB	55	F	13	33	62	49	63	2	0	NT
GD	66	M	3	27	63	48	69	8	2	2
Mean	60.6			45.3	62.1	48.2	64.7	4.2	1.4	4.2
SD	13.8			11.3	1.4	3.1	7.8	1.8	1.1	1.9
PNFA										
MC	61	F	2+1	62	63	49	66	6	3	1
SA	78	M	3+1	59	63	51	74	5	3	5
DC	73	M	4+3	56	62	47	51	5	2	0
JM	67	M	3+2	53	63	52	75	4	3	6
HK	73	F	7+1	52	63	50	61	4	3	1
MR	67	M	2+1	46	63	45	42	2	2	1
WK	69	M	5+4	44	63	49	64	3	2	0
DJM	71	M	6+2	41	63	45	60	3	—	2
CH	81	M	4+2	41	56	40	69	6	4	1
BR	62	M	5+2	27	60	NT	44	3	2	1
Mean	70.2			48.1	61.9	47.6	60.6	4.1	2.7	1.8
SD	6.4			10.4	2.3	3.7	11.6	1.4	0.7	2

"Years post" = number of years between CVA and testing for the NFA cases; for the PNFA patients, the two numbers represent the time since presentation to a neurological clinic + years of self-/carer report of symptoms prior to presentation. Naming = scores out of 64 on the picture-naming test from the Cambridge Semantic Battery (controls are essentially at ceiling on this naming test); WPM = scores on a 10-alternative forced-choice word-to-picture matching test on the same 64 items as in naming (controls are at ceiling on this WPM test); PPT = scores on the picture version of the Pyramids and Palm Trees 52-item test of associative knowledge (normal controls make a maximum of 3 errors on this test); TROG = scores out of 80 on the Test for the Reception of Grammar (controls are near ceiling on this sentence–picture matching test); Digits F and B = each patient's digit span forwards and backwards; WCST = the number of categories achieved out of 6 on the Wisconsin Card Sorting test (normal controls typically achieve all six categories).

the NFA group had a wider age range than the PNFA patients, and on average the progressive cases were older, with a trend towards significance ($Z = 1.7, p = .09$). As one would expect given that the patient pairs were selected according to this measure, the groups did not differ on naming ($Z = 0.45, p = .65$). A simple test of comprehension for the same 64 items as those used in naming—word–picture matching in which the patients were asked to point to one of 10 semantically related pictures in response to a single spoken word—also did not distinguish between the two groups ($Z = 0.36, p = .72$), and no patient other than PNFA-case CH had a notable impairment on this test. A second, entirely non-verbal assessment of concept knowledge, the PPT (Pyramids and Palm Trees test: Howard & Patterson, 1992) revealed a similar picture: no, or only mild, abnormality (with the exceptions of NFA-case JS and PNFA-case CH), and no significant group difference ($Z = 0.33$, $p = .74$).

On a standard test of syntactic comprehension, the TROG (Test for the Reception of Grammar: Bishop, 1989), both patient groups had substantially abnormal scores (controls = 78.8, $SD = 1.85$); the PNFA cases as a group were numerically but not significantly worse than the NFA patients ($Z = 0.61, p = .55$). The two groups did not differ on forwards digit span ($Z = 0.08, p = .94$) but there was a reliable advantage in backwards digit span for PNFA relative to NFA ($Z = 2.53, p = .01$). Finally, in the non-language domain, although some of the NFA cases achieved fewer than six categories on the Wisconsin Card Sorting Test (Nelson, 1976), almost all of the NFPA patients were impaired at this standard test of frontal function, resulting in a significant group difference ($Z = 2.38, p = .01$).

Experimental tasks and procedures

Cookie Theft. This sub-test of the Boston Diagnostic Aphasia Examination (Goodglass, Kaplan, & Barresi, 2001) was administered in the standard manner, with the participants being asked to "say everything that you can about what is going on in the picture". Descriptions were transcribed on-line but also audiotaped for subsequent checking and scoring. Descriptions were timed, beginning when the participants started to speak and terminating when they indicated that they were finished.

Exceptional Passage. This task, designed by our research group, is a 130-word paragraph consisting of a short story about a birthday dinner. Participants were given a printed version of the paragraph and asked to read it aloud; their reading accuracy was coded by the experimenter on-line, and the whole event was timed and audiotaped for later checking. Distributed throughout the paragraph are 18 words with exceptional spelling–sound correspondences (e.g. *pint, steak, suede, gloves, gauge*) and, on another occasion, these individual 18 words were presented on cards to be read aloud.

Reading lists.

(1) Content vs function words. There are two solutions, neither very adequate, to the problem of comparing performance on word sets like content and function words that have minimally overlapping frequency distributions in natural language. The first is to insist on genuine frequency matching, which can only be

done by choosing longer and less common function words such as *neither* and *except*. The second is to choose the highest-frequency content words available in a ranked frequency list like Kucera and Francis (1967), e.g., *say, old, life, place*, and not to fret too much about the fact that the function words are still, on average, higher in frequency. The latter was the solution adopted by Patterson (1982), and the words from that study were employed here. There are 120 items, 60 content and 60 function words matched pairwise for length; the words were printed on cards and presented in random order for oral reading.

(2) Effects of imageability. This list, consisting of 240 words, was created by Howard and Franklin (1988) to enable assessment of the impact of several different variables on reading. For current purposes, the relevant factor is that the words can be divided into subsets with high- vs low-imageability ratings (means of 5.85 vs 3.39 on a 7-point scale; examples of high = *choir, glove, steam*; low = *soul, trust, cite*) with the two subsets matched for frequency (Kucera & Francis, 1967). Again, words were printed on cards and presented in random order for oral reading.

(3) Finally, the patients were asked to read a set of 40 nonwords (from Patterson et al., 1994). They are all single-syllable strings, four or five letters in length, with common spelling patterns (e.g., *kead, larp, fove*). Any legitimate pronuncia-tion—i.e., one that applies to a real word with the same spelling pattern—is accepted as a correct response; thus either /kid/(as in *bead*) or/kɛd/(as in *head*) would be scored as correct for *kead*.

Phonological judgements/manipulations. The patients were asked to perform two tests (from Patterson & Marcel, 1992) of phonological manipulation at the phoneme level. In the segmentation task, the participant is offered a single-syllable spoken word or nonword and asked to strip off the initial sound and say what remains. For example, the stimulus "task" should yield the response "ask", and "nisk" should yield "isk". In a second task, blending, the experimenter presents a spoken stimulus phoneme (plus schwa) that constitutes the onset of a single-syllable word or nonword and then the vowel + coda of the target response, and the participant is asked to blend these together into a single utterance. Using the same two items as examples, "t" followed by "ask" should yield the response "task", and the correct response to "n" + "isk" is "nisk". There were 48 trials for each of segmentation and blending; the two tasks were completed in separate sessions, and each was preceded by a substantial set of practice items because these are rather unnatural tasks. There were also two tests based on rhyme (derived from materials used by Patterson, Vargha-Khadem, & Polkey, 1989). For the rhyme judgement task, the patient hears a sequence of 48 pairs of single-syllable spoken words, half of which rhyme (e.g., "speak–bleak") and half of which do not (e.g., "speak–break") and is asked to respond yes to rhyming pairs and no to the rest. In a rhyme production task, the patient is offered a single-syllable spoken word ($N = 24$) and asked to produce a rhyming word.

RESULTS

Sensitivity of language performance to task

We begin with some between- and within-group comparisons that are germane to the first hypothesis, namely that the deficits in PNFA are more susceptible than those in

TABLE 2
Connected speech and success on word reading

	NFA	PNFA	Controls
Cookie Theft: words/min	25.2 (11.0)	27.8 (18.7)	137.4 (35.4)
Paragraph reading: words/min	22.5 (17.7)	50.1 (37.0)	171.4 (35.0)
Paragraph reading: total time (sec)	342.0 (175.1)	182.5 (111.2)	47.0 (9.8)
Exception words correct: in context	13.0 (3.4)	12.4 (5.7)	18.0 (0.0)
Exception words correct: single	13.1 (6.3)	16.1 (1.7)	17.7 (0.5)

Five measures concerning rate of connected speech (in either picture description or paragraph reading) and success on word reading in or out of context. Values in the table are means, with standard deviations in brackets. The calculation of words/min for paragraph reading is based on the number of words that each patient produced, not the number presented.

NFA to modification by the nature of the language task. Table 2 displays the following five measures: (i) speech rate (words per minute) in producing a description of the Cookie Theft picture; (ii) speech rate (ditto) in reading aloud the "exceptional passage" described above (note that the measure here is obtained for each patient by dividing the number of words that he or she produced by the total time taken to produce them; where patients omitted words, the numerator is less than 130); (iii) total time to read aloud this passage; (iv) accuracy in reading aloud the 18 words with atypical spelling–sound correspondences embedded in the exceptional passage when patients were asked to read the whole paragraph; (v) accuracy in reading aloud the same 18 words when these were presented as single words.

As one might expect from patients all classified as non-fluent, average speech rate on the Cookie Theft description (see Table 2) was markedly slow in both groups relative to normal speakers, and it did not differ between the patient groups ($Z = 0.38$, $p = .71$). Now consider what happened when the patients were still required to produce connected speech but did not have to generate its form or content because they were reading aloud a paragraph. The speech rate of the NFA cases in text reading was very similar to its value for self-generated speech, but the average speech rate for PNFA nearly doubled. The group difference (PNFA > NFA) in words per minute for reading the paragraph reaches only a trend towards significance ($Z = 1.72$, $p = .09$); but total time taken was significantly less for PNFA than NFA ($Z = 2.29$, $p = .02$). Having the message externally specified thus facilitated speech rate in PNFA but not in NFA. Given that normal speakers read the paragraph aloud in about 40–50 seconds, the PNFA patients were certainly not completing this task in a normal amount of time; but their speech rate was task sensitive in a way that the NFA patients' speed was not.

The next relevant result concerns success in reading aloud the 18 words with atypical spelling–sound correspondences, with a shift from comparing performance in the same conditions across the two patient groups to comparing performance within groups across two conditions. The paragraph dubbed "the exceptional passage" was actually designed to determine whether patients who are impaired at reading aloud words with atypical spelling–sound correspondences when tested in standard single-word reading paradigms would produce more correct responses to such words in context than in isolation. For any type of patient or normal reader, we envisaged only two possible outcomes from this contrast for exception-word reading:

either *context = single* or *context > single*. As Table 2 shows, performance of the NFA patients matched the former of these two patterns, *context = single* ($Z = 1.27$, $p = .21$). We had not considered that performance might ever reveal a pattern of *single > context*; but that is what the PNFA cases showed ($Z = 2.53$, $p = .01$). It is important to emphasise that, although this effect can only be demonstrated for the 18 exception words because they are the only items assessed both singly and in context, the same discrepancy would almost certainly apply to other words in the paragraph. That is, the implication to be drawn is not about words with an atypical spelling–sound relationship. Our conclusion from this contrast is that the requirement to produce (in this case, to read aloud) connected speech rather than single words is a sufficient struggle for patients with PNFA that it actually harms their word production.

The third pertinent contrast in this section concerns the patients' performance in another aspect of reading the whole paragraph: errors to function words. The paragraph contains 59 tokens and 20 types of function words, all extremely common words like *the, and, she, with, in* etc. These words are notoriously difficult for NFA patients to read (as well as to produce in spontaneous speech): this point was strikingly established by Gardner and Zurif's (1975) demonstration that such patients often succeed in reading the nouns *inn* and *bee* but fail on the function words *in* and *be*, despite the orthographic resemblance and phonological equivalence of the two pairs, and the far higher word frequency of the function words than the nouns. Accordingly, it is no surprise that the NFA patients in this study made a number of errors on the function words when reading this paragraph (see Table 3). Slightly more than half of these (60%) were omissions and the remainder were substitutions, mostly by another function word (e.g., *a →"the"*, *was → "is"*, *with → "in"*, etc). The PNFA cases also made function word errors in reading the paragraph, although their mean error rate was almost precisely half that of the NFA group. Of the total of 111 function word errors by the PNFA group in the paragraph, 74% were omissions, and the remaining 26% were substitutions, again typically with a different function word. The striking contrast between patient groups comes not from these figures in the top row of Table 3 but rather from the comparison of row 1 with row 2. The exact set of function words embedded in the exceptional paragraph was not given to the patients to read singly. As indicated in the Method section, however, on another occasion the patients were asked to read a set of 60 function words as single items, including most of those from the exceptional passage. As Table 3 reveals, the likelihood of function word misreadings in the NFA group was similar, indeed slightly higher, when such words were presented in isolation; but in the PNFA group, function word errors more than halved from context to single. A three-factor χ^2 from a loglinear model demonstrated that the interaction between group and task was highly significant, $\chi^2(1) = 39.44$, $p < .001$. This constitutes another indication of

TABLE 3
Error rates (%) for reading of function words in or out of context

	NFA	PNFA
Error rate for function words ($N = 59$) in paragraph reading	19%	36%
Error rate for function words ($N = 60$) in list of single words	44%	08%

the enhanced difficulty of producing connected speech relative to single words for PNFA but not NFA.

Nature of the phonological deficit

The results remaining to be presented from this study all concern, from a rather broad perspective, the phonological abilities of the NFA and PNFA cases. First are accuracy measures for reading single words or nonwords aloud, displayed in Figure 1. No control data are included because normal readers are at ceiling on these tests. NFA patients almost invariably have an acquired reading disorder in the phonological-/deep-dyslexic spectrum (Balasubramanian, 1996; Caramazza, Berndt, & Hart, 1981; Crisp & Lambon Ralph, 2006; Friedman, 1996). The hallmark of this kind of reading impairment might be summarised in the following fashion: success in reading aloud is positively correlated with the degree of richness of semantic content in the target words to be read (Shallice & Warrington, 1975). Thus, meaningless nonwords of even the simplest structure pose extreme difficulties; function words, whose role is more syntactic than semantic, are easier than nonwords but not much; low-imageability content words are somewhat easier than function words; and highly imageable or concrete content words yield the best performance. This rank ordering was not developed on the basis of any findings from the current study but rather from an extensive published literature on phonological and deep dyslexia (Coltheart, 1996; Coltheart, Patterson, & Marshall, 1980). Nevertheless, as can be seen in Figure 1, the reading performance of the NFA cases in this study precisely matches the predicted rank ordering. Recall that the 60 high-frequency content words were selected to be as high as possible in frequency, as approximate mates for the 60 even-higher-frequency function words. This criterion selects words that are rather general and thus somewhat abstract (e.g., *part*, *fact*, *think*).

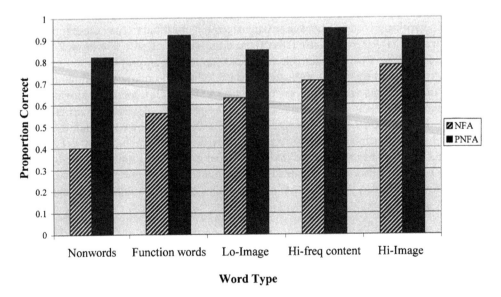

Figure 1. Mean proportion correct for the NFA patients (slanted bars) and PNFA patients (solid black bars) on five different word-reading lists.

If the critical variable that determines reading success in NFA is indeed semantic richness, why do we nest these results under the heading of phonological impairment? The reason is that phonological and deep dyslexia are frequently interpreted as arising from a general phonological disorder (Crisp & Lambon Ralph, 2006; Farah, Stowe, & Levinson, 1996; Patterson, Suzuki, & Wydell, 1996). In the "triangle model" (Plaut, McClelland, Seidenberg, & Patterson, 1996; Seidenberg & McClelland, 1989), reading aloud is primarily achieved by direct activation from orthographic to phonological processing units, but semantic information about the word also contributes to activation of the spoken response. The consequence of this shared responsibility is that, when the phonological system is impaired, achieving sufficient phonological activation for response production requires a larger contribution from word meaning. Nonword reading, to which there can be essentially no contribution from word meaning, might be seen as a kind of gold (or dross!) standard for gauging impaired phonological processing.

From this perspective, a comparison of the NFA and PNFA scores on the five reading lists in Figure 1 suggests a very different quality of phonological processing in the two groups. The PNFA cases achieved significantly higher scores on four of the five stimulus sets (Z values from 2.05 to 2.98, p values from .04 to .003), the one exception being a non-significant advantage for PNFA in reading the words at which the NFA cases do best: high-imageability words. The more important point, however, is the degree to which reading varies within group across the five tests: substantially for NFA and minimally for PNFA. Note also that when difference scores between the two matched pairs of lists in Figure 1 are calculated, which is the equivalent of measuring an interaction, there was a significant group difference for high- minus low-imageability words (difference score for NFA = 15%, for PNFA = 6%, $Z = 2.00$, $p = .04$) and a nearly reliable difference for content minus function words (difference score for NFA = 15%, for PNFA = 3%, $Z = 1.87$, $p = .06$).

We now return, briefly, to performance on the exceptional passage task. As already established in Table 2, the NFA patients made an equivalent number of errors on the 18 target exception words in the two conditions, whereas for the PNFA group, the total number of errors on these target words increased from single-word to text-reading conditions. What types of errors did patients in the two groups make? Table 4 provides an error analysis for each individual patient and for each group as a whole. For single-word reading in NFA, where the majority of errors were produced by patients GN, AB, and MB, the most common error type by far was phonological (or phonetic or articulatory: volumes have been written on how to distinguish the exact level of the speech production process responsible for errors resembling their target words in sound; we acknowledge the importance of these distinctions but our study was not addressed to this question). Many of these errors seem best described as phonological simplifications of the target (e.g., *pint* →/pait/; STEAK →/seik/). Apart from this main error type (or family of types) in this short test of single-word reading, the NFA patients made a few omissions, a few morphological or semantic errors (examples of the latter two types are *poured* → "pour" and *favourite* → "wonderful") and one regularisation error, where the target was pronounced as if it had a typical spelling–sound relation (*mauve* pronounced with the vowel as in "caught" rather than its correct vowel as in "rove"). The NFA patients' errors when reading the same words embedded in text followed a similar pattern except that a few patients (particularly AB) omitted some of the target words in text reading.

For these 18 items as single words, the PNFA patients did not make many errors but, in contrast to NFA, these were as likely to be regularisation errors (e.g., *pint* → /pɪnt/ rhyming with mint; *put* → /pˆt/ rhyming with cut) as phonological misreadings. Regularisation errors indicate *good* processing of the word's orthography and phonology (and the canonical relationship between them), because the word has been pronounced according to the phonological segments typically associated with that spelling pattern. Regularisations reflect not impaired phonology but failure to take account of word-specific lexical/semantic information in computing the word's correct pronunciation. The fact that regularisations, of which there was only one for the whole NFA group, were the most common error type for the PNFA group is another strand of evidence suggesting considerably different and better phonological processing in the PNFA than the NFA cases. In text reading, most errors for the PNFA patients (especially HK and DJM) were omissions, although there were still some regularisations.

Finally we come to the explicit phonological manipulation tasks of phonemic segmentation and blending, and rhyme judgement and production. The first two are somewhat unnatural tasks even for a normal speaker, and patients with phonological deficits are often completely unable to score on these tests, even when given many examples and extended practice. Indeed, perhaps the most important thing to note about the present results is this: for segmentation, 5 of the 10 NFA patients were completely unable even to attempt the task, and for blending the same 5 plus another patient (thus $N = 6$) could not even make a start. The means given in Table 5 for NFA performance on these two tasks are therefore based on a very small number of cases (five and four respectively), and also no doubt represent the least impaired patients who were able to grasp what manipulation was needed and sometimes to perform it correctly. In the PNFA group, two patients could not attempt segmentation and one could not grasp the blending task. For what they are worth, then, the scores on these tasks are given in Table 5. Not surprisingly, with so few observations from the NFA group in particular, neither the numerical PNFA > NFA advantage for segmentation nor the numerical NFA > PNFA advantage for blending was statistically reliable (both Z values < 1). By contrast, no patient tested in either group failed to score on the two rhyming tasks; and here the advantage for PNFA > NFA approached significance for rhyme judgement ($Z = 1.8$, $p = .07$) and achieved it for rhyme production ($Z = 2.21$, $p = .03$), again suggesting generally and genuinely better phonological processing in PNFA.

We argued above that the NFA patients' exaggerated sensitivity to semantic characteristics of words in reading (characteristics such as imageability or content vs function words) is a consequence of their phonological difficulties rather than reflecting a semantic impairment. This claim leads to the prediction that reading success for NFA cases should correlate much more highly with a phonological than a semantic performance measure. Now that results for the phonological measures have been presented, we can indicate that this prediction is correct. Choosing performance on two of the reading lists in Figure 1—the function words and the high-frequency content words—and correlating the NFA patients' scores on these with rhyme production as a phonological measure yields Pearson correlations of 0.92 ($p < .001$) for function words and 0.86 ($p < .003$) for content words. On the other hand, the relationship between reading performance on the same two lists with Pyramids and Palm Trees scores as a semantic measure is characterised by non-significant Pearson correlations: 0.32 ($p = .40$) for function words and 0.25 ($p = .53$) for content words.

TABLE 4
Errors

Case	Single words					Words in context				
	Total errors	Phonological	Regularisation	Omission	Sem/Morphol	Total errors	Phonological	Regularisation	Omission	Sem/Morphol
NFA										
DC	2	1	1	0	0	2	1	1	0	0
JL	2	2	0	0	0	2	2	0	0	0
PG	1	0	0	0	1	3	3	0	2	0
JS	2	2	0	0	0	4	2	0	2	0
DM	0	0	0	0	0	1	1	0	0	0
GN	12	12	0	0	0	8	3	0	4	1
AB	7	3	0	2	2	11	1	0	9	1
MB	18	18	0	0	0	NT				
IB	NT					7	2	0	4	1
GD	0	0	0	0	0	5	3	0	2	0
Sum	44	38	1	2	3	43	18	1	21	3
Proportion		0.86	0.02	0.04	0.06		0.42	0.02	0.49	0.07
PNFA										
MC	0	0	0	0	0	1	0	1	0	0
SA	0	0	0	0	0	2	0	0	2	0
DC	0	0	0	0	0	1	0	1	0	0
JM	3	0	3	0	0	5	1	4	0	0
HK	2	1	1	0	0	13	3	0	10	0
MR	1	0	1	0	0	0	0	0	0	0
WK	4	1	3	0	0	9	4	4	1	0
DJM	4	4	0	0	0	17	2	0	15	0
CH	1	0	1	0	0	4	3	1	0	0
BR	4	2	2	0	0	5	0	4	1	0
Sum	19	8	11	0	0	57	13	15	29	0
Proportion		0.42	0.58	0	0		0.23	0.26	0.51	0

A classification of the errors in reading the set of 18 words with atypical spelling–sound correspondences presented either as single words or in the context of a short story. The table provides numbers of the different errors types for each of the 20 patients plus proportions of error types for each of the two patient groups.

DISCUSSION

The purpose of this study was to question the largely unchallenged assumption that progressive non-fluent aphasia (PNFA) arising from neurodegenerative disease is a gradually emerging facsimile of the non-fluent aphasia (NFA) often consequent on left middle cerebral artery stroke. The assumption is not a surprising one. Speech fluency is one of the main dimensions of variation in the language disorders in both abrupt-onset and slowly developing aphasia. Realistically speaking, fluency is more of a continuous than a bimodal distribution in both aetiologies, but at the two ends of the distribution, fluent and nonfluent aphasia are strikingly different. Because this is true whether the disturbance arises abruptly or gradually, it is perhaps natural to think that the similarity in spectrum equates to similarity in pattern. Furthermore, as Dame Iris Murdoch sagely commented in her novel *The Black Prince*, "we tame the world by generalising". There are enough similarities between NFA and PNFA that, with more than a century of information on NFA to hand, it is tempting to tame the newer world of PNFA by generalising to it what we already know about NFA. Our conclusion from this study and its sister article (Graham et al., 2004), however, is that a deeper understanding of PNFA requires attention to its differences from, as well as its similarities to, NFA.

We should note that we are aware of two considerations that might plague a prediction of theoretically relevant differences between the two patient groups. The first and more general is the inevitable heterogeneity to be found between patients, even within any single group. The second and more specific is the fact that cognitive disorders from cerebral disease or accident are not static conditions. This is of course especially true for disorders associated with neurodegenerative disease, with its inevitable decline, but it also applies to some extent to deficits following stroke, which may improve or change their character as a result of treatment, spontaneous recovery, or reorganisation of function. It is therefore possible that performance patterns in the *same* two patients, one from each group, could be quite discrepant at one point in time but more closely resemble each other at another time of testing. These are not completely surmountable problems, but we have at least been concerned about them and have circumvented them as best we could (a) by selecting NFA patients who were at least 2 years post-insult and hence probably past the period of most striking change, (b) by selecting PNFA patients who were neither too mild nor too severe, and (c) by matching the two groups on a pair-wise basis for picture-naming scores.

As mentioned in the Introduction, the study by Graham et al. (2004) demonstrated that the narrative speech production of a group of 14 PNFA cases

TABLE 5
Proportions correct

	NFA	PNFA
Phoneme segmentation (48)	0.50 (0.24)	0.68 (0.21)
Phoneme blending (48)	0.61 (0.33)	0.48 (0.28)
Rhyme judgement (48)	0.70 (0.20)	0.86 (0.16)
Rhyme production (24)	0.43 (0.32)	0.78 (0.25)

Proportions correct (means, with *SD* in brackets) for the two patient groups on four tests of phonological ability.

was reduced in quantity, speed, and information content relative to the control participants, but was not abnormal in ratios of either content-to-function words or nouns-to-verbs. Saffran et al. (1980) provided clear examples of the severely agrammatic speech that can be observed in NFA patients, for example: "Ah … Monday … ah Dad and Paul … hospital. Two … ah doctors … and ah … thirty minutes … And, er, Thursday … ten o'clock … doctors … and ah … teeth, yeah, fine" (p. 227). Such patients even tend to be agrammatic in sentence repetition, for example: "Experimenter: 'Repeat after me, "No, I do not like fish"'" → Patient: 'No … fish'" (p. 226). Graham et al. (2004) concluded that, perhaps with the exception of late-stage PNFA when patients are often approaching muteness, this frank agrammatism is not typical of PNFA.

The current study extends the differences between NFA and PNFA to two other features. First, the speech-production deficits of the group of $N = 10$ NFA cases studied here were relatively unmodulated by the nature of the task, whereas those in the PNFA group were markedly more circumstance dependent. Both groups had slow and laboured speech in a self-generated narrative speech task, but when the self-generation requirement was withdrawn by asking the patients to read a paragraph aloud, speech rate remained the same in NFA but almost doubled in PNFA. Although the error rate was lower for PNFA than NFA, both groups made errors of omission and substitution on function words in the paragraph-reading task, but when the connected-speech component of function-word reading was withdrawn by asking the patients to read function words as single items, error rate remained the same (or even increased) in NFA but more than halved in PNFA. The two groups made equivalent numbers of errors in reading aloud a set of words with atypical spelling–sound correspondences embedded in the paragraph-reading task, but when the connected-speech requirement of this task was withdrawn by asking the patients to read the exception words as single items, error rate remained the same in NFA but dropped significantly in PNFA. It is important to emphasise that the speech output of PNFA patients is still slower and more error prone than normal even under the least demanding conditions. Nevertheless, our results suggest that, by contrast with NFA, the aphasia in PNFA is more especially a disorder of self-generated connected speech.

The second feature to which our results speak is the degree and nature of the phonological deficit. Impaired phonological ability, like impaired grammatical ability, is typically included in descriptions of PNFA as well as NFA; and at a gross level, this characterisation seems appropriate. For example, like the NFA cases in our study, the PNFA cases made some frank phonological/phonetic errors in all of the speech-production tasks. At a more detailed level of description, however, the PNFA cases revealed phonological-processing capacities far better than those of the NFA patients, in tasks like rhyme production and nonword reading. Of particular note are the following two facts about performance when the only demand was to read aloud single words. First, the PNFA cases made a number of regularisation errors to exception words; this error type, which demonstrates reasonably accurate phonological processing of the stimulus word, virtually never occurs in NFA. Second, the patients were asked to read a set of word lists varying in the amount of lexical/semantic support available (with nonwords at the low end of this dimension and high-imageability content words at the other) and hence varying inversely in the need to rely solely on phonological processing of the orthographic input. This factor substantially and monotonically predicted reading success for NFA patients but had a minimal and non-monotonic impact on success in PNFA.

At the risk of boring our readers, we would like to emphasise once again that, when we say "phonological processing" or "phonological difficulties", we are referring to a fairly broad range of component skills relating to language sound, including the maintenance and manipulation of phonological representations that might be best captured by the concept of auditory-verbal working memory, and also speech production processes that might be better described as phonetic encoding and/or articulation rather than phonology per se. Of course it will be vital for a growing understanding of the kinds of tasks employed here to specify exactly how they "load" on the various components under this broad rubric. And it will be vital for a growing understanding of the deficits in these patient groups to specify exactly which components might actually be responsible for a claim of "better phonological processing" in PNFA vs NFA. These are goals for future research.

We are working towards, but are some way from achieving, a satisfactory functional account of PNFA, in particular an explanation for the fact that the production of connected speech is such a (relatively selective) challenge for these patients. One clue might come from performance on the Wisconsin Card Sorting Task (Nelson, 1976). Among the ten NFA cases included here, one was not available to be tested on the WCST, five had normal scores (five to six categories), four were impaired and, of these latter four, only one patient (GN) failed to get beyond the first category. By contrast, in the PNFA group of ten, only two cases had normal scores of five or six categories; six scored only one or two; and two patients never even managed to sort consistently on a single criterion and thus had scores of zero. The PNFA patients' poor performance on this task, which is designed to measure frontal executive ability, may suggest a significant contribution of poor executive function to the patients' difficulty in connected speech production. In the meantime, as we and other researchers hunt for further clues, our interim conclusion is that the interpretation of the language disorder in PNFA will need to be at least somewhat distinct from accounts of NFA: the two disorders have some resemblances but a number of notable differences.

REFERENCES

Balasubramanian, V. (1996). Deep dyslexia and dysgraphia in a Broca's aphasic. *Brain and Language, 55,* 115–118.

Bird, H., Lambon Ralph, M. A., Seidenberg, M. S., McClelland, J. L., & Patterson, K. (2003). Deficits in phonology and past-tense morphology: What's the connection? *Journal of Memory and Language, 48,* 502–526.

Bishop, D. V. M. (1989). *Test for the Reception of Grammar* (2nd ed.). London: Medical Research Council.

Bozeat, S., Lambon Ralph, M. A., Patterson, K., Garrard, P., & Hodges, J. R. (2000). Non-verbal semantic impairment in semantic dementia. *Neuropsychologia, 38,* 1207–1215.

Broca, P. (1861). Remarques sur la siège de la faculté du langage articulé, suivies d'une observation d'aphemie (perte de la parole). *Bulletin de la Société d'Anatomie (Paris), 36,* 330–357.

Brown, J. W. (1972). *Aphasia, apraxia and agnosia.* Springfield, IL: Charles C. Thomas.

Caplan, D. (1987). *Cambridge studies in speech science and communication.* Cambridge, UK: Cambridge University Press.

Caramazza, A., Berndt, R., & Hart, J. (1981). 'Agrammatic' reading. In F. Pirozzolo & M. Wittrock (Eds.), *Neuropsychological and cognitive processes in reading.* New York: Academic Press.

Coltheart, M. (Ed.). (1996). Phonological dyslexia [Special issue]. *Cognitive Neuropsychology, 13*(6).

Coltheart, M., Patterson, K., & Marshall, J. (1980). *Deep dyslexia*. London: Routledge & Kegan Paul.

Crisp, J., & Lambon Ralph, M. A. (2006). Unlocking the nature of the phonological–deep dyslexia continuum: The keys to reading aloud are in phonology and semantics. *Journal of Cognitive Neuroscience, 18*, 348–362.

Farah, M. J., Stowe, R. M., & Levinson, K. L. (1996). Phonological dyslexia: Loss of a reading-specific component of the cognitive architecture? *Cognitive Neuropsychology, 13*, 849–868.

Friedman, R. (1996). Recovery from deep alexia to phonological alexia: Points on a continuum. *Brain and Language, 52*, 114–128.

Gardner, H., & Zurif, E. (1975). BEE but not BE: Oral reading of single words in aphasia and alexia. *Neuropsychologia, 13*, 181–190.

Goodglass, H., Kaplan, E., & Barresi, B. (2001). *Boston Diagnostic Aphasia Examination*. Baltimore, MD: Lippincott Williams & Wilkins.

Gorno Tempini, M., Dronkers, N., Rankin, K., Ogar, J., Phengrasamy, L., & Rosen, H. et al. (2004). Cognition and anatomy in three variants of primary progressive aphasia. *Annals of Neurology, 55*, 335–346.

Graham, N., Patterson, K., & Hodges, J. (2004). When more yields less: Speaking and writing deficits in nonfluent progressive aphasia. *Neurocase, 10*, 141–155.

Grossman, M., & Ash, S. (2005). Primary progressive aphasia: A review. *Neurocase, 10*, 3–18.

Grossman, M., Mickanin, J., Onishi, K., Hughes, E., D'Esposito, M., & Ding, X-S. et al. (1996). Progressive nonfluent aphasia: Language, cognitive, and PET measures contrasted with probable Alzheimer's disease. *Journal of Cognitive Neuroscience, 8*, 135–154.

Hodges, J. R., & Patterson, K. (1996). Non-fluent progressive aphasia and semantic dementia: A comparative neuropsychological study. *Journal of the International Neuropsychological Society, 2*, 511–524.

Howard, D., & Franklin, S. (1988). *Missing the meaning?*. Cambridge, MA: MIT Press.

Howard, D., & Patterson, K. (1992). *Pyramids and Palm Trees: A test of semantic access from pictures and words*. Bury St Edmunds, UK: Thames Valley Test Company.

Kertesz, A., Davidson, W., McCabe, P., Takagi, K., & Munoz, D. (2003). Primary progressive aphasia: Diagnosis, varieties, evolution. *Journal of the International Neurological Society, 9*, 710–719.

Kucera, H., & Francis, W. (1967). *Computational analysis of present-day American English*. Providence, RI: Brown University Press.

Mendez, M. F., Clark, D. G., Shapira, J. S., & Cummings, J. L. (2003). Speech and language in progressive nonfluent aphasia compared with early Alzheimer's disease. *Neurology, 61*, 1108–1113.

Mesulam, M. (1982). Slowly progressive aphasia without generalized dementia. *Annals of Neurology, 11*, 592–598.

Mesulam, M. M. (2001). Primary progressive aphasia. *Annals of Neurology, 49*(4), 425–432.

Nelson, H. E. (1976). A modified card sorting test sensitive to frontal lobe defects. *Cortex, 12*, 313–324.

Nestor, P. J., Graham, N. L., Fryer, T. D., Williams, G. B., Patterson, K., & Hodges, J. (2003). Progressive non-fluent aphasia is associated with hypometabolism centred on the left anterior insula. *Brain, 126*, 2406–2418.

Patterson, K. (1982). The relation between reading and phonological coding: Further neuropsychological observations. In A. W. Ellis (Ed.), *Normality and pathology in cognitive functions*. London: Academic Press.

Patterson, K., Graham, N., & Hodges, J. (1994). Reading in dementia of the Alzheimer type: A preserved ability? *Neuropsychology, 8*(3), 395–407.

Patterson, K., & Marcel, A. (1992). Phonological ALEXIA or PHONOLOGICAL alexia? In J. Alegria, D. Holender, J. Junca de Morais, & M. Radeau (Eds.), *Analytic approaches to human cognition*. Amsterdam: North Holland.

Patterson, K., Suzuki, T., & Wydell, T. N. (1996). Interpreting a case of Japanese phonological alexia: The key is in phonology. *Cognitive Neuropsychology, 13*, 803–822.

Patterson, K., Vargha-Khadem, F., & Polkey, C. E. (1989). Reading with one hemisphere. *Brain, 112*, 39–63.

Plaut, D. C., McClelland, J. D., Seidenberg, M. S., & Patterson, K. (1996). Understanding normal and impaired word reading: Computational principles in quasi-regular domains. *Psychological Review, 103*, 56–115.

Saffran, E., Schwartz, M., & Marin, O. (1980). Evidence from aphasia: Isolating the components of a production model. In B. Butterworth (Ed.), *Language production* (Vol. 1). London: Academic Press.

Seidenberg, M. S., & McClelland, J. L. (1989). A distributed, developmental model of word recognition and naming. *Psychological Review, 96*, 523–568.

Shallice, T., & Warrington, E. (1975). Word recognition in a phonemic dyslexic patient. *Quarterly Journal of Experimental Psychology, 27*, 187–199.

Snodgrass, J., & Vanderwart, M. (1980). A standardized set of 260 pictures: Norms for name agreement, image agreement, familiarity, and visual complexity. *Journal of Experimental Psychology: Human Learning and Memory, 6*, 174–215.

Snowden, J. S., Neary, D., & Mann, D. (1996). *Frontotemporal lobar degeneration: frontotemporal dementia, progressive aphasia, semantic dementia.* New York: Churchill Livingstone.

Thompson, C. K., Ballard, K. J., Tait, M. E., Weintraub, S., & Mesulam, M. (1997). Patterns of language decline in non-fluent primary progressive aphasia. *Aphasiology, 11*(4), 297–321.

Syntactic impairments can emerge later: Progressive agrammatic agraphia and syntactic comprehension impairment

Chris Code

University of Exeter, UK, and University of Sydney, Australia

Nicole Müller

University of Louisiana at Lafayette, LA, USA

Jeremy T. Tree

University of Exeter, UK

Martin J. Ball

University of Louisiana at Lafayette, LA, USA, and University of Wales Institute, Cardiff, UK

Background & Aims: Recent studies suggest that agrammatism is not a major feature of progressive nonfluent aphasia, at least not in the earlier years post-onset. We investigated the emergence of syntactic impairments over a 3-year period in CS, a 63-year-old man 8 years post-onset of progressive speech difficulties. CS has a range of progressive cognitive impairments, including progressive nonfluent aphasia, and limb and other apraxias (with a progressive non-aphasic and mostly non-dysarthric speech deterioration), but relatively intact intelligence, perception, orientation, long-term memory, semantics, and phonology. Writing impairments did not emerge until some 8 years after naming and speech impairments were first noticed, and after CS became mute.

Methods & Procedures: We undertook detailed longitudinal examination of word and sentence writing and syntactic comprehension across a range of tasks and examined the impact of short-term memory. We were concerned to examine the data for evidence of agrammatic features, particularly in noun and verb use, and use of formulaic and simplified syntactic structures as the condition progressed.

Outcomes & Results: Analysis showed a progressive emergence of deficits on tests of written syntax, syntactic comprehension, and auditory-verbal short-term memory. There was a progressive reduction in verb and noun use, but this was related to the kind of stimulus used. Features of agrammatism were evident in writing with a progressive dependence on formulaic and simplified syntax.

Address correspondence to: Chris Code, School of Psychology, Centre for Cognitive Neuroscience, Washington Singer Labs, University of Exeter, Exeter EX4 4QG, UK. E-mail: c.f.s.code@exeter.ac.uk

CS has worked with us over a number of years. We are grateful to him for always being willing to participate in our investigations of his problems, so that he and we can learn more about them and are able to provide information to help him and his family manage his condition. Thanks to Martin Edwards and Jo Mason for help with some of the testing, and to Karalyn Patterson and Andy Ellis for generous feedback while reviewing the paper.

Conclusions: It may be that agrammatism in PNFA is a feature that develops late in the progression, showing up only in writing because it is masked in speech by motor speech impairment. Increasing reliance on formulaic and simplified structures with progression suggests compensatory adaptation of CS's system. Impairments appeared to emerge in parallel with deterioration of syntactic comprehension and phonological short-term memory.

Extensive study in recent years has revealed that language and speech can be impaired in a variety of ways by progressive neurological damage in the absence of significant impairments to other cognitive processes (Ball, Code, Tree, Dawe, & Kay, 2004; Croot, Paterson, & Hodges, 1998; Garrard & Hodges, 1999; Harasty, Halliday, Kril, & Code, 1999; Jefferies, Crisp, & Lambon Ralph, 2006 this issue; Mesulam, 1982; Patterson, Graham, Lambon Ralph, & Hodges, 2006 this issue; Snowden, Goulding, & Neary, 1989; Tree, Kay, & Perfect, 2005; Tree, Perfect, Hirsh, & Copstick, 2001). This primary progressive form of aphasia was first described in modern times by Mesulam (1982). Different kinds of progressive speech and language impairment have been identified and two broad forms have been described in recent years (e.g., Kertesz, Hudson, Mackenzie, & Munoz, 1994; Patterson et al., 2006 this issue; Snowden et al., 1989). Semantic dementia (SD) (Garrard & Hodges, 1999; Snowden et al., 1989) arises from progressive damage either restricted to the mainly anterior/inferior temporal lobe or temporal lobe plus some frontal parieto-temporal damage, and is characterised by fluent speech with significant impairment of semantic processing. Progressive nonfluent aphasia (PNFA) arises mainly from progressive left frontal damage extending into subcortical areas, which can include varying severities of motor speech impairment, naming and syntactic processing deficits, and disturbances of comprehension. Currently therapy for those with progressive aphasia can do little more than help to prepare individuals and their families for an inevitable decline in speech and language skills. The differential emergence with time of impairments in people with progressive conditions allows the possibility of examining relationships between different components of the language, and greater, cognitive processing system.

In this mainly exploratory study we describe detailed analysis of the progressively deteriorating written syntax of CS, who has an 8-year history of progressive impairment to various components of his cognitive system including features of progressive nonfluent aphasia (PNFA) with progressive apraxias, some form of apraxia of speech, a recently emerging agrammatic agraphia, and an impairment of syntactic comprehension. At the start of the testing period described below, CS had relatively intact semantics, syntax, phonology intelligence, perception, orientation, and memory.

A significant number of cases and case series of PNFA have been described recently, and progressive writing disorders are often noted, but few studies have attempted any detailed analysis of written grammar. Graham, Patterson, and Hodges (2004) carried out a study of connected written output where they compared the written and spoken production of a group of participants with PNFA and age-matched controls, and examined a range of syntactic variables. Most of the participants with PNFA "exhibited some characteristics of apraxia of speech" (p. 142), and six of Graham et al.'s participants had some form of dysarthria. Eight of them who participated in a PET scanning study (Nestor, Graham, Fryer, Williams, Patterson, & Hodges, 2003) showed damage in the left anterior insula.

Graham et al. observed a pattern of poorer spoken and written output associated with either longer vs shorter single words or connected language sentences vs single words. Most participants produced no evidence of spoken agrammatism, with no reduction of verb production and mainly normal proportions of content and function words, nouns, and verbs. However, there was some evidence of agrammatism in the written narratives of some of their participants. Onset of progressive neurological impairment in this cross-sectional study ranged from 1 to 6 years in participants (Mean = 3.28 years).

To our knowledge there are few longitudinal data available on progressive impairments in written syntax. Such data are required given that, by definition, the theoretically interesting feature of such conditions is their progression over time. Agrammatism following stroke is known to change over time, with some recovery from acute to chronic stages with a milder form at more chronic stages more likely reflecting systemic adaptation and compensation (e.g., Guasti & Luzzatti, 2002). A trivial prediction is that progressive agrammatism becomes worse with time, but a more interesting question is to what extent, and at what times, it displays features of compensation. Recent studies (Graham et al., 2004; Patterson et al., 2006 this issue) suggest that speech and writing are differently impaired in PNFA and aphasia following stroke. They showed that PNFA participants are slower and produce more errors in speaking and writing on longer, connected, self-generated tasks like picture descriptions than on shorter single word tasks. This was in contrast to matched participants with non-fluent post-stroke aphasia.

In January 2002, 8 years after onset of his speech difficulties, CS's writing began to deteriorate in graphic and syntactic quality, and the investigations we report here took place between January 2002 and November 2004. Our main motivation for this study was therefore a detailed exploratory longitudinal examination of emerging progressive impairment in written syntax and syntactic comprehension, and we focused our attention on several research questions. We were concerned to examine writing (a) for evidence of progressive deterioration, (b) for the features of agrammatism in written sentences generated from picture descriptions and from noun and verb stimuli, (c) for increasing dependency on formulaic and simplified syntactic structures as indication for an increase in compensatory strategies, and (d) for dissociations in self-generated vs externally stimulated tasks. There was also evidence for an increasing impairment in CS's syntactic comprehension emerging with the deterioration in writing, and we examined longitudinal performance on a range of tests of syntactic comprehension and working memory.

Some preliminary data on CS's progressively deteriorating speech are described in Ball et al. (2004), and investigation of his progressive limb apraxia is ongoing and will be reported in a future publication.

METHOD

CS (DOB: 23/08/40) is a right-handed man with a "First Class" degree in Chemistry from University College, London. He was Head of Chemistry at a well-known British Public (i.e., private) School before retirement because of increasing speech problems, which he first noticed in November 1994 when he was 54 years old. Structural MR scanning in March 2001 (at age 61 years) revealed some mild atrophy, considered near normal for his age. However, recent scanning (October,

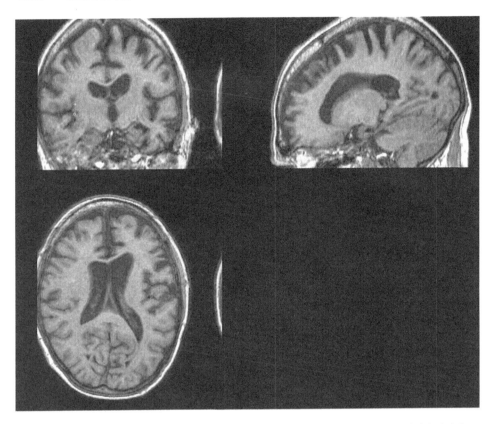

Figure 1. Structural MRI scan: sagittal, coronal and transaxial slices. Left is right and right is left.

2003, age 63 years) shows significant generalised, bilateral atrophy (Figure 1), more prominent in the left frontotemporal area.

A clear neurological diagnosis has never been forthcoming for CS, although Pick's disease was considered a possible cause early on, and some symptoms of progressive suprabulbar palsy and corticobasal syndrome were also present in the early stages. Provisional diagnoses are not unusual in clinical neurology, significant overlap between syndromes is common, and progressive conditions often do not enjoy a clear medical diagnosis. For instance, PNFA can progress to corticobasal syndrome (Gorno-Tempini, Murray, Rankin, Weiner & Miller, 2004). Autopsy is the only way to be sure of the disease process. However, as detailed above and below, CS satisfies well current neurological and neuropsychological diagnostic criteria for PNFA (Mesulam, 2003; Nestor et al., 2003; Snowden, Neary, & Mann, 1996).

By December 2004 a wide range of longitudinal testing had been completed of intelligence, perception, memory, orientation, language, speech and action/gesture. In this study we focus on CS's writing, and do not discuss in any detail his performance in other domains except where directly germane (but see Table 1 for a summary of cognitive testing). Speech difficulties were the first symptoms of his progressive condition to emerge. Phonetic analyses of the speech deterioration are reported in Ball et al. (2004). Extensive examinations of motor speech excluded any frank or marked motor-sensory impairments or dysarthria, although there were some ataxic and spastic features. Analysis revealed many features of apraxia of

TABLE 1
CS's performance on a range of tests of general neuropsychological function and semantic processing over four years

	(Max)	2001	2002	2003	2004
General functioning					
Raven's B&W Matrices	(12)	10	11	7	8
Mini-Mental	(30)	–	28	28	24
WRMT – Faces	(50)	41	41	43	41
WRMT – Words	(50)	36	33	38	35
Executive functioning					
WCST (Norm: 5.4)	(6)	6	6	6	–
Rey – Figure	(36)	36	–	36	–
- Aged-Matched Controls Mean = 34.0;					
- PNFA Mean = 29.93 (Graham et al., 2004)					
Visual perception					
Benton Faces	(21)	20	21	21	–
BORB, Object Decision	(128)	–	116	–	–
BORB, Item Match,	(32)	32	32	–	–
BORB, Foreshortened	(25)	25	25	–	–
BORB, Minimal Features	(25)	25	25	–	–
Semantic processing					
PALPA 49, Auditory	(60)	59	58	58	57
PALPA 50, Visual	(60)	58	59	57	59
PALPA 47, Spoken W/Pix	(40)	40	40	40	40
PALPA 48, Written W/Pix	(40)	40	40	40	40
PALPA 51, Word Assoc.	(30)	–	29	27	26
PPT, Pictures	(52)	49	51	50	52
PPT, Words	(52)	51	–	52	52
Barry Synonyms	(80)	–	80	79	78
Orthographic processing					
Lexical decision					
PALPA 24, Visual LD					
Legality	(60)	60	60	60	60
PALPA 25, Visual LD					
Imageability Vs Frequency	(120)	120	117	116	115
PALPA 26, Visual LD					
Morphoplogical Endings	(60)	–	53	59	54
PALPA 27, Visual LD					
Regularity	(60)	60	60	58	52
Reading					
NART	(50)	30	–	–	–
Full scale IQ: 111					
PALPA Tests 29–35					
Oral Word Reading			No errors		
PALPA 36, Nonwords	(24)	15	–	–	–
Three letters 6/6					
Four letters 3/6					
Five letters 4/6					
Six letters 2/6					

(*Continued*)

TABLE 1
(Continued)

	(Max)	2001	2002	2003	2004
Writing to dictation					
PALPA 39, letter length	(24)	24	24	24	–
PALPA 40, Imageability Vs					
Frequency	(40)	40	39	–	–
PALPA 44, Regularity	(40)	40	40	–	–
PALPA 45, Nonwords	(24)	22	19	–	–

Aud = Auditory, BORB = Birmingham Object Recognition Battery, LD = Lexical Decision, Cats = Categories, Homoph = Homophone, Judge/Jud = Judgement, NART = National Adult Reading Test; PPT = Pyramids & Palmtrees, Reg = Regularity, Rec Mem = Warrington Recognition Memory, Writ = Written.

speech (sometimes referred to as *aphemia* or *anarthria*) caused by speech planning and/or programming impairments. Errors of articulation were inconsistent, and difficulty with initiation of speech was a major feature, with hesitation between words, and less within words. Speech was particularly impaired on longer and connected tasks, like reading a long passage or describing a picture. This pattern is similar to that described by Patterson et al. (2006 this issue) for PNFA. CS's speech gradually became more and more laboured and delayed, and he was mute by the winter of 2002.

Over the 4-year testing period described in this paper, CS had mostly intact phonological and semantic systems, but with some nonword processing problems and anomia. Long- and short-term memory, general intellectual processing, orientation, and visual perception were mostly unimpaired, although there was some deterioration in the Mini Mental State and Raven's matrices by 2004. CS has significant ideomotor, buccofacial, and oculomotor apraxia, tested in detail and the subject of ongoing investigation. These apraxias also progressed slowly, although by December 2004 there was no sign of ideational apraxia, suggesting that action semantics too was mostly unimpaired. In January 2002 there was no sign of agrammatism in speech or in writing and he performed normally on tests of syntactic comprehension. There was some indication of executive impairment on testing, and on some tests of naming, but some of these results may be confounded by speech initiation and control problems.

RESULTS

Results of analyses are reported in three sections: syntactic analysis of sentence generation from noun and verb stimuli and picture description; performance on tests of syntactic comprehension; performance on tests of short-term memory.

Investigations of written syntax

We analysed CS's written syntax, and conducted error analyses on a range of sentence-writing tasks cataloguing changes over this period of sentence, clause, and phrase structure. We examined writing a sentence including a stimulus noun, writing a sentence including a stimulus verb, and writing a connected description of a scene

TABLE 2
Number of main structures in sentences generated to a noun stimulus

Sentences to nouns	August 2002	June 2003
Function words	55	26
Verbal predicates	24	18
Pronouns	15	0
% Pronouns	11.6	0
"I" Initial	13	0
Total words	137	103
Mean words per sentence	5.7	4.3
Total arguments	47	34
Arguments per verbal predicate	1.96	1.89
Total inappropriate arguments	5 (10.6%)	9 (26.5%)
Determiner omissions	6	12
Preposition errors	8	4

(the Cookie Theft Picture from the *Boston Diagnostic Aphasia Exam* and the Picnic Picture from the *Western Aphasia Battery*). Tables 2 to 6 detail the results.

Writing sentences including a stimulus noun. CS completed an adaptation of PALPA 39 (Kay, Lesser, & Coltheart, 1992) twice, 11 months apart, in which he was asked to write a sentence given each of the 24 high-imageability, high-frequency, object stimulus nouns. We analysed sentences in terms of their structure across all test periods, including an analysis of predicate argument structure (PAS: Berndt, Haendiges, Mitchum, & Sandson, 1997; Webster, Franklin, & Howard, 2004; Webster, Morris, & Franklin, 2005). Failure to retrieve a PAS—i.e., retrieving the semantically related argument structure (predominantly noun phrases) from a predicate (a verb)—is said to reflect semantic-level impairments (Berndt et al., 1997). Results are shown in Table 2.

There was a significant reduction in the total number of words produced ($\chi^2 = 4.816$; $df = 1$; $p < .025$; all tests are one-tailed) and a marked but not significant

TABLE 3
Writing sentences including a stimulus verb

Sentences to verbs	October 2003	February 2004	October 2004
Function words	42	35	37
Nouns	19	18	19
Pronouns	23	16	11
% Pronouns	23.6	20	13.8
"I" as subject	17	15	10
Words	89	85	87
Mean words per sentence	3.5	3.5	3.5
Total arguments	30	29	23
Arguments per verbal predicate	1.2	1.2	1.3
Stimulus verb not used as main verb	1	2	8
Sentences without main verb	1	1	3
Determiner omissions	7	3	2
Preposition errors	5	4	2
Inflection errors	7	2	5

TABLE 4
Connected written sentence generation over time (November 2002–February 2004)

November 2002 Cookie Theft	December 2003 Cookie Theft	February 2004 Picnic Picture
1. Washing	1. Biscuit of a boy	1. Sailing boat
2. Sinks overflowing	2. Boy of stool	2. Kite
3. Boy is falling down stool	3. Girl of an happy	3. Dog
4. Mother is drying plate	4. Flood of an sink	4. Sand
5. Girl is a receiving the cookie	5. Mother of (s?)lothing	5. Wine
6. Boy is cookie sister	6. Mother of an dry plate	6. Man the book
7. Garden is in the window	7. Garden is a pretty place	7. Car
8. Path is in the window	8. Curtains of place	8. Bungalow
9. Cupboards in the	9. Cupboards of an usual	9. Tree
		10. Flag
		11. Pier
		12. Boy and kite
		13. wood
		14. forest
		15. radio
		16. basket

reduction in the total number of arguments ($\chi^2 = 2.086$; $df = 1$; ns) between August 2002 and June 2003. Verbs reduced over the test period from 24 to 18 (χ^2 0.8; $df = 1$; ns) and the number of arguments produced per verbal predicate remained stable (1.96 in 2002; 1.89 in 2003). At both dates CS produced a number of inappropriate arguments, which rose from five (2002) to nine (2003) ($\chi^2 = 3.468$; $df = 1$; $p < .05$). We comment below on the syntactically and lexically formulaic character of many of CS's productions.

There was little variation in the verbs used at both testing times. However, in 2002 there was a balance between the use of the copula "is" and "have" as a main verb, (nine versus eight instances, respectively), with seven other verbs altogether. As noted, there were also six sentences that did not contain a form functioning syntactically as a verb.

TABLE 5
Written picture descriptions over time (November 2002 – February 2004)

	November 2002	December 2003	February 2004
Time (mins)	7.9	8.32	5.22
WPM	4.37	4.2	4.02
Total word	35	35	21
Total nouns	15	15	18
Sentences	9	1	1 (possible)
Mean sentences	3.8	3.8	0
Determiners	4	6	1
Inflections: Totals	12	1	0
Main verbs	7/8	1	1 (possible)
Pronouns	0	0	0
Arguments	14	0	1 (possible)
Mean arguments	1.5		
Verbless constructions	0	8	2

TABLE 6

CS's performance over time on the three written picture descriptions compared to age-matched controls (N = 11) and a PNFA (N = 14) group's written descriptions of the Cookie Theft picture (from Graham et al., 2004).

Totals	Controls	PNFA	CS
WPM	18.8	5.1	4.37/4.2/4.02
Words	73.5	34.3	35/35/21
Nouns	16.1	8.5	15/15/18
Verbs	10.7	4.7	7 (or 8)/1/1 (possible)
Function words	38.9	16.2	14/15/2
Content words	33.4	15.9	20/21/19
Info units	31.8	13.0	9/9/0

WPM = words per minute; Info. Units = information units.

There were 15 pronouns of which 14 were "I" in 2002, reducing to zero in 2003. Function words decreased significantly ($\chi^2 = 10.38$; $df = 1$; $p < .005$; one-tailed test) and there was a marked increase in Determiner plus Noun structures between tests ($\chi^2 = 3.24$; $df = 1$; $p < .05$). However, two error types predominated: the omission of determiners (e.g., 2003; "Cricket bat is good" [test items are underlined]) and of prepositions (e.g., 2003; "The bus is the bridge"). The former shows a clear increase from 2002 to 2003, while the latter decreases. This increase in omissions of determiners contrasts with the finding above that dependence on the formulaic use of Det + N for phrase structure increases over the testing period.

At both test times CS relied on very few syntactic structures in the production of clauses and phrases. In 2002 the predominant structure is S(ubject)V(erb)O(object) or SVA(adverbial) ($N = 14$) with "I" as S and "have" as full verb (e.g., "I have a girlfriend, 'bird'!"). CS only used one action verb in the SVO structure. The second most common structure was S(ubject) c(opula)C(omplement) or S(ubject) c(opula)A(dverbial) ($N = 10$), with subject incorporating the stimulus (e.g., "Bed is glorious, comfortable").

In 2003 the dominant structure was ScC or ScA ($N = 16$), where "c" stands for the copula "is", and there was a marked increase in structures where the Subject incorporates the stimulus ($N = 13$) (e.g., "Ship is Mersey"; CS was brought up near the River Mersey). Both in 2002 and 2003 there was a predominance of *static* predicates, a reliance on so-called "light" or semantically comparatively non-specific verbs, and no (or few) *dynamic* verbs. While in 2002 there was a balance in the use of the copula "is" and "have" as a main verb, in 2003 the copula clearly dominated, suggesting that CS had difficulties in processing change of state or action predicates, and tense/aspect morphology, with the exception of the more formulaic (i.e., irregular verb form) "is".

There was a marked decrease over 11 months in the variety and complexity of noun phrases used, and by 2003 CS relied mainly on simpler Noun or Determiner + Noun phrases, which had doubled by then. The three-element phrases he did produce all occurred in incomplete sentences, perhaps indicating that the increased complexity at the phrase level was incompatible with the effort needed to also produce a complete sentence. There are two nominalisations of verbs in 2003; on both occasions a potential verb is coupled with a determiner (e.g., "The sleep", "The riding") making the verbs function as true nouns.

A markedly increasing feature is a formulaic reliance on very few syntactic structures. Using formulas appeared to provide CS's system with an effective strategy to minimise effort while complying with the test instructions. Insistence on favourite syntactic structures was carried to the extent where CS at times formulated semantically awkward sentences (e.g., 2003: "The riding is the horse"), and sentences that did not accommodate the stimulus word, which was then added as a free-floating noun (e.g., 2002: "I have a girlfriend, 'bird'!" ["bird" is British-English slang for a girl]; "I have a pipe – smoke!").

Writing sentences including a stimulus verb. We administered the *Verb Generation Test* (Webster, 1999; Webster et al., 2004; Webster et al., 2005) on three occasions over the 12-month period October 2003 to October 2004, where CS was asked to write a sentence that included each of 26 verbs. We analysed sentences in terms of structures and error patterns across all test periods. Results are presented in Table 3.

For many variables there was little change over time. Number of words, nouns, function words, and pronouns were relatively stable, although the latter did reduce at the third testing but not significantly ($\chi^2 = 0.925$; df-1; ns). Recall that in generating a sentence from a noun 4 months earlier, CS did not produce any pronouns. This highlights the crucial role of the nature of the task and the stimuli. CS had not lost pronouns completely, and what looked like a problem in producing pronouns to noun stimuli probably surfaced because pronouns are less likely to occur with a strategy of placing the stimulus noun in subject position and using a light verb. Sentence length in terms of number of words remained stable, but there was a clear reduction over the three testing periods in structures of three elements or more. Presenting a stimulus verb appeared to provide information that allowed CS to write a more structurally complete sentence than providing him with a noun, but over time the ability to treat the stimulus verb as a verb decreased markedly (see below).

The number and type of inflection errors (predominantly omissions) does not show a clear pattern over time. CS used many bare verb stems at all testing times and inflections were omitted, including present participle -ing, third person singular -s, past tense, and past participle ending, but there was no clear pattern over time. In fact, there were fewer clear verb inflection errors at October 2004 than at October 2003, because at October 2004 fewer verbs were attempted, as verbs.

The dominant sentence types at all three dates were S(ubject)V(erb)O(object) and SVA(dverbial), with "I" as S. "I" (the most frequent word used) gradually decreased as subject, although it was the dominant subject throughout. This was just short of significance ($\chi^2 = 1.88$; $df = 1$; ns), with "I" accounting for nearly 14% of words produced by October 2004 (October 2002: "I carry on suitcase"; February 2003: "I am not earn"; October 2004: "I disagree in the TV").

The total number of arguments produced did not decrease significantly over time, nor did the number of arguments per verbal predicate. However, in October 2004 only 18 of the 25 stimulus verbs were treated as verbs, and produced 23 arguments. The great majority of all structures had semantically appropriate arguments, but some that used the stimulus as adjective or noun were semantically and structurally problematic ("I made in fetch"; note also the light verb "made"; "Hide are about").

As noted above, there was an increase in nominalisations of verbs compared to nominalisations of verbs on noun stimulation in May 2003. However, by that time CS produced only one full verb. A progression seems to be demonstrated in the three examples of sentences generated from the stimulus "die" (October 2003: "The mother <u>die</u> March last year"; February 2004: "Mother is Australia <u>die</u> 2000"; October 2004: "Mum is Australia 30 years <u>dead</u>"). In October 2003 "die" was uninflected. At February 2004 the verb stem was used, but inappropriately, together with the copula "is". By October 2004 CS used the semantically equivalent adjective "dead".

Connected sentence generation in picture description. CS's written picture descriptions on three separate testing occasions are reproduced in full in Table 4 and our analyses summarised in Table 5. For the first two tests, the Cookie Theft picture was used. CS had described this picture in speech and writing many times and because of this we varied pictures for description in our testing. For the third occasion the Picnic Picture from the *Western Aphasia Battery* was used.

Picture description began in November 2002 with separate, and mainly complete, sentences, but by February 2004 it consisted of a string of mainly nouns with one possible verb, one determiner ("man the book"; the man is reading a book in the picture) and one example of "and" ("boy and kite"). Total number of words and overall time reduced significantly ($\chi^2 = 3.5$; $df = 1$; $p < .05$). Words per minute remained stable, however. While verbs disappeared over the period, nouns were stable, reflecting the increasing dependence on nouns, as verbs disappeared. Function words remained stable at the first two testing times, but dropped to just two at final testing.

There was a great deal of structural recycling in the first description. It is not unusual to see apostrophes omitted and this interpretation corresponds with the repetitive structures CS used. Item 2 "Sinks overflowing" sets up the structure for the whole description (the choice of structure is largely appropriate, but note incomplete structures in 6 and 9). In November 2002 CS recycled the "is" structure as a universal functional connector, reminiscent of the frequent use in the sentence generation tasks (note that the function of the form "is" changes: whereas in items 2–6 "is" is an auxiliary, it is the main verb in items 7–9). In December 2003, CS replaced the use of "is" with an "of/a(n)" as his universal functional connector, irrespective of the relationship between elements. However, there were perseverations of not only "of a(n)" but also "of an happy", followed by "of an sink" and "of an dry plate". By February 2004 he had lost most of his ability to signal connective relationships between words, even access to a formulaic universal connector, and there was no clear indication of predicate argument structure.

As in November 2002, CS produced nine information units/sentence attempts in December 2003. The NP patterns were similar, with regular omissions of determiners outside the "of a(n)" structure. There were no change-of-state verbs (see below), the only main verb that was syntactically treated as a verb was the copula. Also note there was only one three-element noun phrase (DAdjN), and only two attempts at verbs; but note here also (items 5 and 6) the presence of "of". At this time there was only one copula with an obvious use of "of"/"of a(n)" as a universal connector, irrespective of the relationship between the elements.

By February 2004 CS produced no verbs (with one possible exception, "sailing"), and only two function words but 18 nouns. Even the copula "is" was no longer available to him. He indicated three possible links between two elements. In November 2002 he produced predicates, and largely appropriate and complete argument structures, although there were gaps. In December 2003 there were two possible predicates. At this time he did not specify events any longer, but rather grouped together participants in events without specifying their role. By February 2004, CS was almost totally dependent on nouns. In addition, he hardly grouped event participants together any longer—in other words, he had lost most of his ability to signal connective relationships between words, even access to a formulaic universal connector. In effect, his picture description at this stage consisted of labels. The almost complete absence of predicates and the required argument structures could be interpreted to indicate impaired semantics (Berndt et al., 1997), but we will argue below that there is good evidence of a significantly intact semantic system from extensive testing of semantic processing (see Table 1), which does not support an interpretation of reduced PAS as semantic impairment, and that CS's failure to construct PAS is likely due to other more basic impairments. In his sentence generation, even where the predicates are off target, the information elements that he grouped together make sense together; i.e., there is a clear semantic relationship between "knife" and "lunch", "ship" and "Mersey", etc.

Table 6 shows a comparison of CS's performance on picture description to written performance on the Cookie Theft picture with data from age-matched controls and PNFA participants (from Graham et al., 2004). Compared to controls CS is clearly very impaired on most variables. He produced a similar number of nouns to controls, but this was at the expense of other structures. More interestingly, he is comparable to an age-matched group of PNFA participants on the total number of words he produced, total function words at the earlier testing dates, and words per minute, but well below the PNFA mean on verb production at later testing dates. He produced at all dates more nouns and content words than the PNFA group. The comparison confirms that CS becomes progressively more agrammatic with time on this self-generation language task compared to the PNFA group.

Comparisons between written sentence generation tasks. We would predict that providing CS with a noun or a verb with which to generate a sentence would show dissociations, particularly perhaps between the production of new nouns or verbs, depending on the task. Recall that testing sentence generation to verb stimuli followed 4 months after writing sentences to noun stimuli, and there are unfortunate gaps in testing. A comparison of Tables 2 (noun stimulus condition) and 3 (verb stimulus condition) is interesting, as it shows that determiners increased on noun stimulation over time and reduced in the verb condition. Ruigendijk and Bastiaanse (2002) found that determiners increased in sentences produced from verb stimuli in agrammatic speakers. Pronoun production reduced on verb stimulation, and was completely absent on noun stimulation; nouns in the verb sentences remained stable; but verbs in the noun condition almost disappeared. Given that the noun tests were administered some months before the verb test, this would suggest that verbs were particularly vulnerable. The reduction in function words on noun stimulation ($\chi^2 = 10.38$; $df = 1$; $p < .005$) appeared to continue on the later testing with verb stimulation, but was lower in the verb condition, although stable over the 12 months. The number of arguments per verbal predicate was marginally higher on noun stimuli over the test period. However, nouns to verb sentences remained stable over 10 months, as did verbs to noun sentences over 12 months. Table 7 shows little difference in totals of nouns or verbs across tasks over the 26-month period. Producing verbs to noun stimuli reduces a little, but not significantly ($\chi^2 = 0.57$; $df = 1$; *ns*) and nouns to verb stimuli totals are stable over the 12-month period.

TABLE 7
Nouns generated from verbs and verbs generated from nouns over time

	Aug 02	June 03	Oct 03	Feb 03	Oct 04
Verbs in noun tests	24	18	–	–	.
Nouns in verb tests	–	–	18	20	18

Mean sentence length declined a little in the noun condition, and was lower overall in the verb condition, although stable over the 12 months of testing.

Also, the difficulty with handling verbs that became quite prominent in June 2003 in the noun condition did not really emerge until the second test date in the verb condition. In both test conditions a striking feature was a perseverative use of similar structures *within* tests, although the structures were different *between* tests.

The virtual absence of verbs and increase in nouns in the picture descriptions confirms that CS had a particular and increasing problem generating his own verbs compared to nouns where there is no verb stimulus. However, it is not only the number of verbs that is notable, but also the lack of diversity in the self-generation of verbs. CS relied almost exclusively on light verbs: there is no "action".

Overall totals of nouns were similar in the picture description and verb stimulus tests, and the same is the case for verbs between the noun stimulus tasks and picture descriptions. It is worth noting that these numbers appeared stable in different tasks across a 26-month period, but these quantitative data mask the deterioration in the quality of verb production, as noted above. Written verb production simplified and narrowed in range and scope with time. Pronouns, so favoured on noun and verb stimulation, were completely absent from the self-generated picture descriptions, where CS did not have the opportunity to use well-rehearsed personal information grounded in his own experience and where the use of pronouns would only be appropriate in elaborations on previously introduced information. The self-generation of argument structure, which deteriorated gradually on the noun/verb stimulus tasks, all but disappeared on picture description. Generation of function words too was reduced, and the total number was significantly lower in the picture descriptions than on the word stimulus tasks. We examined the effects of time and task on function word production by comparing function word totals in picture description (November 2002), to noun stimuli (November 2002), and to verb stimuli (the mean of the three testing periods October 2003 to October 2004) over an 11-month period. This showed that function word production to verb stimuli held up significantly better ($\chi^2 = 9.06$; $df = 2$; $p < .01$) than function word production to nouns or in picture descriptions, where they nearly disappeared. This is a known feature of agrammatism from stroke (Menn, O'Connor, Obler, & Holland, 1995), where function words most likely to be retained are those that do not require syntactic integration into a clause, such as those occurring in clause-initial position (e.g., "I"). CS's performance on picture description appears to confirm that the self-generation of more taxing language became so impaired that he was only able to produce a laboured list of concrete nouns.

Syntactic comprehension

Impairments on tests of syntactic comprehension are well established in people with agrammatic speech and in progressive aphasia. We were therefore concerned to

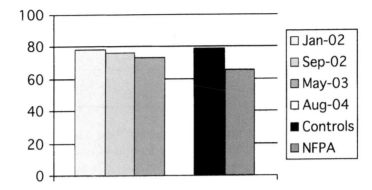

Figure 2. CS's TROG scores over time (maximum 80) compared to means for age-matched control and PNFA participants (from Graham et al., 2004).

monitor changes in syntactic comprehension and to examine associations between syntactic production and comprehension. Figure 2 shows performance on the *Test of Reception of Grammar* (TROG; Bishop, 1989) from January 2002 to August 2004, and shows a gradual deterioration in general syntactic comprehension from a near normal 78/80 to 60/80 (age-matched controls = 78.8; *SD* = 1.85; Graham et al., 2004; Patterson et al., 2006 this issue). At May 2003 and August 2004 CS's score was 2 *SD* below the control mean.

The gradual reduction in scores on the TROG appears to parallel, to some extent, the emergence of agrammatism in writing. Syntactic disturbance in writing was first noticed in August 2002 (see Table 2), but TROG performance was normal at that time. While there was gradual deterioration over time, it was not really until August 2004 that the TROG score resembled the mean performance of a group of participants with PNFA. The gradual deterioration on the TROG prompted us to investigate syntactic comprehension further, with a battery of tests covering a range of processes thought to underlie syntactic comprehension. We examined comprehension of reversible sentences (*Reversible Sentences Test*: Byng & Black, 1999), event processing (*The Event Perception Test*: Dean & Black, 2005; Marshall, Pring, & Chiat, 1993, 1999) and locative relations (*Auditory and Written Comprehension of Locatives* – PALPA 58/59: Kay et al., 1992). Results are detailed in Table 8 and Figure 3.

Performance on these tests showed perhaps some slight, but not increasing, difficulties with event processing and a deficit in processing locatives, which was stable and without marked deterioration over time. A feature of performance on all tests that stands out is a deficit in processing reversible sentences, and by 2003 all errors were on reversible sentences. This might be taken as evidence to support a working memory component to CS's syntactic comprehension impairments.

Figure 4 shows an analysis of CS's proportion of errors that were reversible errors on three tests conducted in 2003 and 2004. While CS scored 29/40 at both testing times on the Reversible Sentence Comprehension Test, there was an increase of lexical distractor errors, but only from 2 to 4, which accounts for the reduced proportion of reversible errors. While CS improved between tests on PALPA 58 (locative prepositions) (from 14/24 to 19/24), all errors were on reversible sentences. The figure illustrates that there was no real change in CS's ability to deal with reversible sentences between tests.

TABLE 8
Performance on tests of syntactic comprehension (correct responses)

Correct scores	2002	2003	2004
Test of Reception of Grammar (TROG) Contl. Mean = 78.8 PNFA = 65.38	Jan – 78/80 (97.5%) 2 reversible errors Sept – 76/80 (95%)	73/80 (91.2%) 2 reversible errors	60/80 (75%)
Reversible Sentences Test		Nov – 29/40 9 Errors on reversible non-action verbs	Nov – 29/40 7 Errors on reversible non-action verbs; 4 lexical
Event Perception Test (Cntrl Med 57)		Nov – 56/60 (93.3%)	Nov – 57/60
Auditory Comp. of Locatives, PALPA 58.		Dec – 14/24 all 10 errors reversible (Cntrl 22)	Nov – 19/24 all 5 errors reversible
Written Comp. of Locatives, PALPA 59.			Feb – 20/24 all 3 errors reversible
Aud. Sentence-Picture Matching – PALPA 55		Dec – 50/60 (83.3%) 5/20 reversible errors	

The *Auditory Sentence Picture Matching* task (PALPA 55), conducted in December 2003, required CS to point to the appropriate picture depicting active and passive sentences varying in reversibility and directionality. He made 10 errors in 60 sentences, but with equal active/passive, reversible/non-reversible errors. To test the idea that phonological short-term memory (phonSTM) was an important variable underlying CS's syntactic comprehension, we examined STM on a range of tasks.

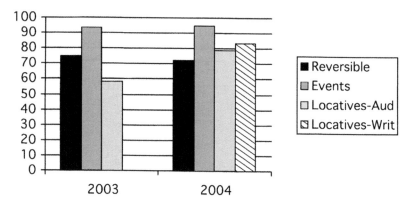

Figure 3. Performance on tests of syntactic comprehension over time (scores converted to percentage correct).

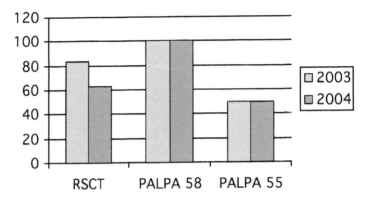

Figure 4. Proportion of errors that were reversible errors on three tests of syntactic comprehension (RSCT = Reversible Sentence Comprehension Test).

Phonological STM (phonSTM) testing

Results on tests of phonological short-term memory (phonSTM) are shown in Table 9. There was evidence of mild, gradual deterioration on digit span over time, and this could suggest a phonSTM impairment, but given that responding to this task requires good articulation, more likely it was the need for overt verbal responses that caused CS's decline. By 2003 the task had to be abandoned. On other tasks known to tap phonSTM that did not involve overt production (i.e., rhyme judgement; Howard & Nickels, 2005), early in his condition CS consistently performed well, suggesting little impairment. Note also that his good performance on rhyme judgement indicates that he could still access and manipulate phonology, despite his severe production impairments, suggesting an unimpaired phonological input buffer (Howard & Nickels, 2005).

We attempted to examine aspects of phonSTM using non-oral response methods. In February 2004 we tested pointing span for noun-verb sequences (PALPA 60) increasing in length from SV (two words) to SVO/SVO (six words). CS began to fail at SV/SV sequences entailing holding four words in memory and then pointing to the correct sequence of pictures. So holding the sequence "shed, boil, mouse, pin, cut" in memory and then pointing to the appropriate picture was particularly difficult for

TABLE 9
Performance (correct responses) on tests of auditory-verbal short-term memory

Tests	2001	2002	2003	2004
PALPA 2 – Aud Dis Minimal Pairs	72/72	70/72	72/72	72/72
PALPA 5 – Auditory Lexical Decision	157/160	74/80	76/80	77/80
PALPA 13 – Digit Span (Contls. Mean = 6.8)	F7, B3	F5, B3	F5, B3	–
PNFA (Mean = 4.15, Graham et al., 2004)				
PALPA 15 – Rhyme Judgement – Auditory	–	57/60	–	56/60
PALPA 15 – Rhyme Judgement - Visual	58/60	58/60	57/60	54/60
PALPA 60 – Pointing Span N/V Sequences	–	–	–	5/12
WMS-III – Spatial Span	F5, B4	–	F4, B4	–

Aud Dis = auditory discrimination; F = forward; B = back; Lex Dec = lexical decision; N/V = noun/verb; PNFA = progressive nonfluent aphasia; Vis = visual; WMS = *Wechsler Memory Scales*.

TABLE 10
Letter pointing span increasing from 1 to 6 letters (response array of 12 uppercase letters),
CS and controls.

Number of letters	1	2	3	4	5	6
CS correct	10/10	10/10	7/10	4/10	2/10	0/10
Controls: Mean correct	10	10	10	10	9.2	8

him. This impairment for longer sequences suggests a relatively mild word span difficulty, which provides some support for the idea that a relatively mild deficit in phonSTM may have contributed to his performance on tests of syntactic comprehension.

In February 2004 we devised a non-oral response task where CS was asked to point to a recited series of 1 to 6 uppercase letters from an arrayed choice of 12 letters. Performance was compared to five age- and education-matched controls. Results in Table 10 appear to confirm an increasing problem for CS as the series became longer. He scored 10/10 on single letters, confirming that he has no difficulties recognising the letters. However, the action initiation delay characteristic of his limb apraxia prevents us excluding the possibility that his failures were simply caused by delay in motor initiation. As noted above, CS has an oculomotor apraxia, with a marked voluntary–involuntary dissociation, and lateral and vertical eye movements to command were almost impossible for him. While his involuntary movements appear to be unimpaired, the condition may nonetheless affect visual scanning of the 12-letter response array, contributing to response delay.

DISCUSSION

Analysis shows a progressive emergence of deficits on tests of written syntax, syntactic comprehension, and phonological STM. When CS was able to speak there was no evidence of agrammatism, but it was first noticed in his writing in August 2002, emerging as he became mute. A syntactic comprehension impairment began to emerge in the summer of 2003. Spelling was entirely intact throughout testing of writing.

The syntactic analysis of sentence writing shows some classic agrammatic features: loss of function words and articles, omission of morphological inflections and nominalisation of verb forms (Caplan, 1987). There is a dependence on "light" verbs (Berndt et al., 1997), like "be" and "have", when generating sentences, and a progressive loss of full verbs to a stage where few, if any, were available. There was a gradual loss of complex verb forms and complex noun phrases, coupled with a strategic use of (relatively) intact structures used formulaically at earlier stages. By the final examination there was little evidence of predicate argument structure (PAS) remaining in CS's connected writing.

A particular deficit in verb production is a common feature of agrammatism and most other forms of aphasia (Bastiaanse & Jonkers, 1998; Luzzatti, Aggujaro, & Crepaldi, in press; Miceli, Silveri, Villa & Caramazza, 1984). Luzzatti et al. have shown that there is a clear dissociation between nouns and verbs across aphasia types, and CS showed the same pattern. This is in contrast to the recent finding

(Graham et al., 2004; Patterson et al., 2006 this issue) that most PNFA speakers and writers do not show a particular problem with verbs over nouns, at least in the early years—Graham et al.'s group were of relatively recent onset (Mean = 3.28 years) compared to CS (8 years). CS produced a reduced number of content words compared to controls on picture description, but this was better than the participants with PNFA. But it is likely that the apparent maintenance of content over function words is due to the fact that CS produced only two function words at final testing, all other words being nouns. Function word production for CS decreased dramatically over time from 14 to 2 at final testing—comparable, at first testing at least, to Graham et al.'s group with PNFA (mean = 16.2), although with progression CS showed an almost total deficit in function word production. In addition, again in contrast to Graham et al.'s group, verbal inflection was largely restricted to the use of the present progressive ending "-ing", and to the form "is"; the latter produced formulaically, rather than productively.

The gradual deterioration in CS's ability to use verbs and function words as connectors for sentence attempts led to a parallel reduction in predicate argument structure (PAS) (Berndt et al., 1997; Webster et al, 2004; Webster et al., 2005). Failure to retrieve a PAS, which entails retrieving the semantically related argument structure from a predicate, is said to reflect semantic-level impairments (Berndt et al., 1997). At the earliest verb-testing date argument structures of the stimulus verbs were largely appropriate, even though some arguments were omitted, and the stimulus verbs were treated as verbs. In February 2004 a tendency to transform stimulus verbs into nouns began, while those that were treated as verbs had appropriate arguments, with some omissions. In October 2004 only 17 stimulus verbs (of 25) were treated as main verbs. A pattern emerged of a difficulty in treating stimulus verbs *as verbs*, and the strategy of replacing the target PAS with simpler copula or verbless structures that incorporated the target verbs as nouns. Good performance on tests of semantic processing does not support a central semantic deficit explanation for CS's PAS deficit, although there were some examples of inappropriate verb semantics (October 2004: "Toss made up"; "I made in fetch"; "Hide are about"). These examples would seem to indicate that a problem with verbal semantics was developing, and the reliance on copulas might support such an interpretation. However, the greater part of CS's constructions consisted of semantically compatible elements, sometimes without a verb (e.g., "The house at build"), or an off-target predicate (e.g., "The bus is the bridge"). This may suggest that CS had access to lexical semantics (in the sense that "house" is semantically compatible with "build") at some level, but was having increasing difficulties in combinatory semantics and syntax, and with encoding processes as processes; i.e., verbs as verbs.

The omission of argument structure and the reliance on simple argument structure can be the manifestation of different underlying impairments in acquired aphasia from stroke. Webster et al. (2004) showed that omission of arguments in their four participants with impairments in PAS could result from failure to retrieve a word, failure to recognise that the argument is necessary, or not being able to assign a thematic role to an argument. Two of their participants (GW and KD) had problems with thematic role assignment that were associated with an increased proportion of reverse role errors in comprehension. CS also has significant problems with reversible sentences in comprehension.

In summary, this individual pattern of syntactic impairment suggests that with progression, agrammatism can develop in writing when speech is no longer possible, particularly on tasks requiring self-generation.

Impairments in syntactic comprehension have been described in participants with progressive apraxia of speech (or anarthria). Four of Broussolle et al.'s (1996) eight cases of progressive apraxia of speech were reported to have syntactic comprehension difficulties. Caplan, DeDe, and Michaud (2006 this issue) and DeDe and Caplan (2006) conducted an analysis of published studies of syntactic comprehension in aphasic participants and conclude that the evidence suggests that a general resource deficit more parsimoniously explains results, rather than a specific deficit in comprehension of syntax. CS's performance on a range of tests of syntactic comprehension was mainly characterised by a difficulty with reversible sentences across most tasks, but good performance on event processing, which is dependent on being able to process the verb in the sentence. The predominance of static predicates in CS's sentence writing, together with significant difficulties in processing dynamic verbs, tense/aspect morphology, and prepositional structures expressing locative relations, led us to test comprehension of locative relations. Performance was variable and reversible sentences again caused most problems, suggesting that CS's problem are mostly explained as a specific problem with reversible sentences rather than a general syntactic comprehension impairment. Impairment to phonological STM has been commonly suggested to be the underlying deficit for problems with reversible sentences in a number of reports (Caramazza, Basili, Koller & Berndt, 1981; Romani, 1994; Saffran & Marin, 1975; Vallar & Baddeley, 1984), although a review by Caplan and Waters (1990) found little or no good evidence to support the view (see Romani, 1994, for discussion), suggesting that in order to demonstrate a contribution of phonological STM impairment, then additional impairments, apart from problems with reversible sentences, must be demonstrated together with evidence that syntactic impairment is linked to the STM impairment. CS appears to only partially satisfy Caplan and Waters' criteria for a phonological STM impairment: he has additional problems in processing syntax and evidence of a, relatively mild, STM impairment across tasks. Processing reversible sentences may depend on phonological STM, and we suggest that a phonological STM impairment contributed to CS's difficulties with reversible sentences.

Performance over time on these tests did not vary greatly, where a progressive deterioration mirroring that in written syntax might have been expected. This would argue against the notion that CS was experiencing a general progressive deterioration in syntactic processing. His mild STM impairment across tasks may explain more parsimoniously his problems on tests of syntactic comprehension, although the reliability of the results of all forms of testing attempted may have been significantly reduced by the presence of apraxic impairments in speech and action. The process of subvocal rehearsal does not appear to depend on the capacity for overt articulation. Baddeley and Wilson (1985) showed that participants with severe dysarthria are still able to use subvocal rehearsal. Participants with apraxia of speech, however, appear unable to use rehearsal because of problems in assembling programs for speech-motor control (Caplan & Waters, 1995), implying that rehearsal is maintained by the ability to establish speech-motor programs rather than by overt articulation (Baddeley, 2003). Thus it would seem appropriate to claim that CS's apraxia of speech had an impact on his phonological rehearsal mechanism and this could account for his reduced span (although this claim must be made tentatively, given our lack of systematic testing of this issue). We can also note that his scores on the *Token Test* remained within the normal range throughout the testing period, which is surprising given that most of the commands of this test have information content above six items (Lesser, 1976), demonstrating that CS did not have a generalised syntactic comprehension deficit—rather it seemed specific to reversible sentences and similar syntactic structures, a sub-set of items that are vulnerable to impairment in the event of phonological STM disruption (Baddeley, Vallar, & Wilson, 1987). It would appear, therefore, that CS's apraxia of speech might have been contributing to performance on tests of syntactic comprehension, causing a mild phonological STM impairment mainly affecting subvocal rehearsal.

Can progressive degeneration reveal relationships between cognitive functions?

Variability in the pattern of emerging deficits would appear to be a hindrance to attempts to reveal general relationships between functions following progressive neural degeneration. The emergence of CS's symptoms may be purely coincidental, and explainable better in terms of the gradually progressing and increasingly extensive neural damage than as a reflection of putative relationships between cognitive functions or systems. But longitudinal investigations of progressive cognitive deterioration have the potential to test the idea that this process can reveal something about the relationships between cognitive functions—this is the promised outcome of investigations of progressive conditions. Specifically, it may be that the greater temporal distance between the emergences of symptoms in progressive disease can be a useful heuristic for testing putative associations between functions (Croot et al., 1998). Impairment to separate functions for CS emerged on testing at different times.

The TROG score was not observed to be impaired for 6 months after agrammatic writing was first observed, although the gradually decreasing TROG score apparent in September 2002 would indicate that syntactic comprehension had started to deteriorate before this. If, as we suggest, a general buffering impairment made a significant contribution to CS's writing and syntactic comprehension impairments, then it would imply an increasingly rapid trace decay affecting functions dependent on working memory. However, perfect performance on rhyme judgement, requiring good phonological working memory, suggests that CS's working memory impairment was not an across-the-board impairment: it does not appear to affect all domains and, specifically, visual and phonological working memory appeared to be relatively less impaired.

CS's writing problems did not emerge until after he had become mute and severely limb apraxic: the progressive impairment to his output modalities (speech, writing, gesture) means that he is becoming effectively "locked-in", despite a relatively intact semantics and intelligence. The later emergence of writing deficits may provide further data on the nature of the degenerating language system. Graham et al. (2004) note that agrammatism in speech is not typical of PNFA, with the possible exception of late-stage PNFA when patients are virtually mute. There was no sign of agrammatism in CS's speech when he was able to speak, although his phrase length was reduced and he was clearly nonfluent. However, and in contrast, Luzzi and Piccirelli (2003) describe a case whose progressive apraxia of speech did not result in mutism for some 7 years after the emergence, first, of a pure agraphia. Luzzi and

Piccirelli suggest that a STM deficit is the cause of both impairments in their case. The reverse pattern of temporal emergence of speech and graphic impairments in Luzzi and Piccirelli's case, compared to CS, would appear again to underline the pitfalls of interpreting the relative timing of the emergence of deficits in individual cases as a basis for inferring associations between functions or processes. The observation that "nonfluency" in PNFA is not necessarily associated with agrammatic speech in the earlier years post-onset (Graham et al., 2004), but emerges as the individual becomes mute, may be of particular significance for the relationship between the planning and programming of articulation and syntactic processing.

The agrammatism of CS appeared to share many features of agrammatism following stroke (Menn et al., 1995). As with agrammatism following stroke, our analysis suggests that progressive agrammatic writing shows a gradual emergence of compensatory strategies, as evidenced by the increasing dependence on formulaic strategies, whether conscious or unconscious. Therefore progressive agrammatism, in CS at least, does not show a reverse picture to that of agrammatism in recovering stroke, but a similar picture. Agrammatism may therefore show increasing adaptation in both progressive and "recovering" agrammatism.

Some see agrammatism as a central syntactic disorder (for review see Caplan, 1987; DeBleser, Bayer & Luzzatti, 1996; Grodzinsky, 2000; Perlman Lorch, 1989), but agrammatism is unlikely to be a unitary syntactic disorder, and a range of alternative underlying impairments have been posited including: impaired working memory; verb and other lexical access deficits; theta-role assignment impairments; systemic adaptation to impaired mechanisms; economy of effort, among others (see Perlman Lorch, 1989, and Caplan, 1987, for reviews of the contenders). But it is also clear that agrammatism itself can evolve with time, changing the pattern of syntactic deficit with recovery from severe to milder forms (e.g., Guasti & Luzzatti, 2002) with features more likely reflecting systemic adaptation and compensation emerging at more chronic stages. A "motor" element to agrammatism has been directly claimed or implied by a number of theories (e.g., Goodglass, 1976; Isserlin, 1922; Lenneberg, 1975) supporting theories claiming a gestural basis to syntax (e.g., Armstrong, Stokoe, & Wilcox, 1994). It may therefore be profitable for future research to examine more closely the evolving relationships between agrammatism and apraxias following stroke and in progressive conditions.

There have been many studies of progressive aphasia and apraxia, many of them describing individuals with "primary" and relatively selective impairments and substantially retained abilities in other areas. CS had a variety of cognitive impairments ranging through the speech, language, and action systems, but he had dramatically retained cognitive abilities too, despite widespread atrophy, mainly to frontal and subcortical areas and predominantly in the left. He had good verbal and action semantics, and while there was significant ideomotor apraxia affecting limb and orofacial actions, he did not have ideational apraxia, suggesting that his action semantics too was unimpaired. He had a substantially intact phonology, and his orientation and general intelligence, perception, and long-term memory were relatively intact.

CS had some frontal executive difficulties, including a partly disinhibited compulsion to respond to tasks prematurely, but at the same time a significant problem in initiating actions and delay between limb, speech, and graphic actions.

He now has a masked expression, which only occasionally allows him to produce an automatic facial expression, with no apparent significant motor or sensory loss.

Investigation of the parallel, or otherwise, emergence of symptoms in other participants with progressive conditions would throw light on the possible relationships between cognitive functions, and further data may provide information on which to base approaches to management. For CS, despite a 10-year history of progressing difficulties leading to a locked-in state, substantially retained cognitive abilities provide important information for his therapists, his family, and himself.

REFERENCES

Armstrong, D. F., Stokoe, W. C., & Wilcox, S. E. (1994). Signs of the origin of syntax. *Current Anthropology, 35*, 349–368.

Baddeley, A. (2003). Working memory and language: An overview. *Journal of Communication Disorders, 36*, 189–208.

Baddeley, A., Vallar, G., & Wilson, B. (1987). Sentence comprehension and phonological memory: Some neuropsychological evidence. In M. Coltheart (Ed.), *Attention and performance XII: The psychology of reading* (pp. 509–529). Hove, UK: Lawrence Erlbaum Associates Ltd.

Baddeley, A. D., & Wilson, B. A. (1985). Phonological coding and short-term memory in patients without speech. *Journal of Memory and Language, 24*, 490–502.

Ball, M. J., Code, C., Tree, J., Dawe, K., & Kay, J. (2004). Phonetic and phonological analysis of progressive speech degeneration: A case study. *Clinical Linguistics & Phonetics, 18*, 447–462.

Bastiaanse, R., & Jonkers, R. (1998). Verb retrieval in action naming and spontaneous speech in agrammatic and anomic aphasia. *Aphasiology, 12*, 951–969.

Berndt, R. S., Haendiges, A. D., Mitchum, C. C., & Sandson, J. (1997). Verb retrieval in aphasia: 2. Relationships to sentence processing. *Brain and Language, 56*, 107–137.

Bishop, D. (1989). *Test for Reception of Grammar.* Windsor, UK: Medical Research Council.

Broussolle, E., Bakchine, S., Tommasi, M., Laurent, B., Bazin, B., & Cinotti, L. et al. (1996). Slowly progressive anarthria with late anterior opercular syndrome: A variant form of frontal cortical atrophy syndromes. *Journal of the Neurological Sciences, 144*, 44–58.

Byng, S., & Black, M. (1999). *Reversible Sentence Comprehension Test.* Bicester, UK: Winslow Press.

Caplan, D. (1987). *Neurolinguistics and linguistic aphasiology.* Cambridge, UK: Cambridge University Press.

Caplan, D., DeDe, G., & Michaud, J. (2006). Task-independent and task-specific syntactic deficits in aphasic comprehension. *Aphasiology, 20*, 895–922.

Caplan, D., & Waters, G. S. (1990). Short-term memory and language comprehension: A critical review of the neuropsychological literature. In G. Vallar & T. Shallice (Eds.), *Neuropsychological impairments of short-term memory* (pp. 337–389). Cambridge, UK: Cambridge University Press.

Caplan, D., & Waters, G. S. (1995). On the nature of the phonological output planning process involved in verbal rehearsal: Evidence from aphasia. *Brain and Language, 48*, 191–220.

Caramazza, A., Basili, G., Koller, J. J., & Berndt, R. S. (1981). An investigation of repetition and language processing in a case of conduction aphasia. *Brain & Language, 14*, 235–271.

Croot, K., Patterson, K., & Hodges, J. R. (1998). Single word production in nonfluent progressive aphasia. *Brain & Language, 61*, 226–273.

Dean, M. P., & Black, M. (2005). Exploring event processing and description in people with aphasia. *Aphasiology, 19*, 521–544.

DeBleser, R., Bayer, J., & Luzzatti, C. (1996). Linguistic theory and morphosyntactic impairments in German and Italian aphasics. *Journal of Neurolinguistics, 9*, 175–185.

DeDe, G., & Caplan, D. (2006). Factor analysis of aphasic syntactic comprehension disorders. *Aphasiology, 20*, 123–135.

Garrard, P., & Hodges, J. R. (1999). Semantic dementia: Implications for the neural basis of language and meaning. *Aphasiology, 13*, 609–623.

Goodglass, H. (1976). *Agrammatism.* In H. Whitaker & H. A. Whitaker (Eds.), *Studies in neurolinguistics, Vol. I.* New York: Academic Press.

Goodglass, H., Kaplan, E., & Barresi, B. (2001). *Boston Diagnostic Aphasia Examination*. Baltimore, MD: Lippincott Williams & Wilkins.

Gorno-Tempini, M. L., Murray, R. C., Rankin, K. P., Weiner, M. W., & Miller, B. L. (2004). Clinical, cognitive and anatomical evolution from nonfluent progressive aphasia to corticobasal syndrome: A case report. *Neurocase, 10*, 426–436.

Graham, N., Patterson, K., & Hodges, J. (2004). When more yields less: Speaking and writing deficits in nonfluent progressive aphasia. *Neurocase, 10*, 141–155.

Grodzinsky, Y. (2000). The neurology of syntax: Language use without Broca's area. *Behavioral and Brain Sciences, 23*, 1–21.

Guasti, M. T., & Luzzatti, C. (2002). Syntactic breakdown and recovery of clausal structure in agrammatism. *Brain & Cognition, 48*, 385–391.

Harasty, J., Halliday, G. M., Kril, J., & Code, C. (1999). Specific temporoparietal gyral atrophy reflects the pattern of language dissolution in Alzheimer's disease. *Brain, 122*, 675–686.

Howard, D., & Nickels, L. (2005). Separating input and output phonology: Semantic, phonological and orthographic effects in short-term memory impairments. *Cognitive Neuropsychology, 22*, 42–77.

Howard, D., & Patterson, K. (1992). *Pyramids and palm trees: A test of semantic access from pictures and words*. Bury St Edmunds, UK: Thames Valley Test Company.

Isserlin, M. (1922). Ueber Agrammatismus. *Zeitschrift für die gesamte Neurologie und Psychiatrie, 75*, 332–410.

Jefferies, E., Crisp, J., & Lambon Ralph, M. A. (2006). The impact of phonological or semantic impairment on delayed auditory repetition: Evidence from stroke aphasia and semantic dementia. *Aphasiology, 20*, 965–994.

Kay, J., Lesser, R., & Coltheart, M. (1992). *Psycholinguistic Assessments of Language Processing in Aphasia*. Hove, UK: Psychology Press.

Kertesz, A., Hudson, L., Mackenzie, I. R. A., & Munoz, D. G. (1994). The pathology and nosology of primary progressive aphasia. *Neurology, 44*, 2065–2072.

Lenneberg, E. (1975). In search of a dynamic theory of aphasia. In E. Lenneberg & E. Lenneberg (Eds.), *Foundations of language development: A multidisciplinary approach, Vol 2*. New York: Academic Press.

Lesser, R. (1976). Verbal and non-verbal memory components of the Token Test. *Cortex, 14*, 79–85.

Lucchelli, F., & Papagno, C. (2005). Is slowly progressive anarthria a "pure" motor-speech disorder? Evidence from writing performance. *Neurocase, 11*, 234–241.

Luzzatti, C., Aggujaro, S., & Crepaldi, D. (in press). Verb-noun double dissociations in aphasia: Theoretical and neuroanatomical foundations. *Cortex*.

Luzzi, S., & Piccirelli, M. (2003). Slowly progressive pure dysgraphia with late apraxia of speech: A further variant of the frontal cerebral degeneration. *Brain and Language, 87*, 355–360.

Marshall, J., Pring, T., & Chiat, S. (1993). Sentence processing therapy: Working at the level of the event. *Aphasiology, 7*, 177–199.

Marshall, J., Pring, T., & Chiat, S. (1999). *Event Perception Test*. Bicester, UK: Winslow Press.

Menn, L., O'Connor, M., Obler, L. K., & Holland, A. (1995). *Non-fluent aphasia in a multilingual world*. Amsterdam: John Benjamin's Publishing Co.

Mesulam, M. M. (1982). Slowly progressive aphasia without generalized dementia. *Annals of Neurology, 11*, 592–598.

Mesulam, M. M. (2003). Primary progressive aphasia – a language-based dementia. *New England Journal of Medicine, 349*, 1535–1542.

Miceli, G., Silveri, M. C., Villa, G., & Caramazza, A. (1984). On the basis of agrammatics' difficulty in producing main verbs. *Cortex, 20*, 217–220.

Nestor, P. J., Graham, N. L., Fryer, T. D., Williams, G. B., Patterson, K., & Hodges, J. R. (2003). Progressive non-fluent aphasia is associated with hypometabolism centred on the left anterior insula. *Brain, 126*, 2406–2418.

Patterson, K., Graham, N. L., Lambon Ralph, M. A., & Hodges, J. R. (2006). Progressive non-fluent aphasia is not a progressive form of non-fluent (post-stroke) aphasia. *Aphasiology, 20*, 1020–1036.

Perlman Lorch, M. (1989). Agrammatism and paragrammatism. In C. Code (Ed.), *The characteristics of aphasia*. Hove, UK: Psychology Press.

Romani, C. (1994). The role of phonological short-term memory in syntactic parsing: A case study. *Language & Cognitive Processes, 9*, 29–67.

Ruigendijk, E., & Bastiaanse, R. (2002). Two characteristics of agrammatic speech: Omission of verbs and determiners, is there a relation? *Aphasiology, 16*, 383–395.

Saffran, E. M., & Marin, O. S. M. (1975). Immediate memory for word lists and sentences in a patient with a deficient auditory short-term memory. *Brain & Language, 2,* 420–433.

Snowden, J. S., Goulding, P. J., & Neary, D. (1989). Semantic dementia: A form of circumscribed atrophy. *Behavioral Neurology, 2,* 167–182.

Snowden, J. S., Neary, D., & Mann, D. M. A. (1996). *Fronto-temporal lobar degeneration.* London: Churchill Livingstone.

Tree, J. J., Kay, J., & Perfect, T. J. (2005). "Deep" language disorders in non-fluent progressive aphasia: An evaluation of the "summation" account of semantic errors across language production tasks. *Cognitive Neuropsychology, 22*(6), 643–659.

Tree, J. J., Perfect, T. J., Hirsh, K. W., & Copstick, S. (2001). Deep dysphasic performance in non-fluent progressive aphasia: A case study. *Neurocase: Case Studies in Neuropsychology, Neuropsychiatry, and Behavioural Neurology, 7*(6), 473–488.

Vallar, G., & Baddeley, A. (1984). Fractionation of working memory: Neuropsychological evidence for a phonological short-term memory store. *Journal of Verbal Learning and Verbal Behavior, 23,* 151–161.

Webster, J. (1999). *Sentence Generation Task (shortened version) [from: A semantic and syntactic analysis of aphasic speech].* Unpublished PhD Thesis, University of Newcastle Upon Tyne, UK.

Webster, J., Franklin, S., & Howard, D. (2004). Investigating the sub-processes involved in the production of thematic structure: An analysis of four people with aphasia. *Aphasiology, 18,* 47–68.

Webster, J., Morris, J., & Franklin, S. (2005). Effects of therapy targeted at verb retrieval and the realisation of the predicate argument structure: A case study. *Aphasiology, 19,* 748–764.

Phrenology and methodology, or "playing tennis with the net down"

Marjorie Perlman Lorch

Birkbeck College, University of London, UK

Background: In 1835, the British Association for the Advancement of Science exhumed the skull of Jonathan Swift, author of *Gulliver's Travels*, to submit it to phrenological scrutiny and ascertain the cause of his final illness. The behaviour Swift exhibited during the final 3 years of his life—including memory impairment, personality alterations, language disorder, and facial paralysis—was the cause of much speculation among his contemporaries.

Aims: This paper will review the debate between Phrenologists and Alienists, which was focused on the significance of the physical evidence presented by Swift's skull, and its implications for explaining behavioural patterns during his lifetime. His skull was the subject of research and rebuttal over a 12-year period, played out in the major medical publications of the day.

Main Contribution: The focus of the arguments hinged on two issues that resonate today in research on cortical localisation of function: the correlation between anatomy and physiology, and the implications of pathology for both.

Conclusion: Examination of the 19th-century debate over the evidence represented by Jonathan Swift's skull for brain/behaviour correlations illuminates methodological and theoretical assumptions.

Whoever would not remain in complete ignorance of the resources which cause him to act ..., should know, that it is indispensable, that the study of the organization of the brain should march side by side with that of its function.

(Gall, cited in Young, 1968, pp. 266–267.)

There is something about Phrenology that will not go away.

(Kosslyn, cited in Marshall & Gurd, 1996, p. 297)

In his great work on the functions of the brain (1835), Franz Joseph Gall (1758–1828) included a large portion devoted to methodological issues, taking great pains to establish the scientific basis for his research. Gall enumerated nine empirical approaches in establishing facts, including correlation, counter-proof, and measurements of living heads, skulls, and brain casts of notable individuals. The correspondence between the skull and underlying organs was stated by Gall to be consistent for those brains that were "sound"—that is, healthy and middle-aged.

Address correspondence to: Marjorie Perlman Lorch, School of Languages, Linguistics and Culture, Birkbeck College, University of London, 43 Gordon Square, London, WC1H OPD UK. E-mail: m.lorch@bbk.ac.uk

Gall argued away counter-examples by stating that "[a particular] talent might have been lost due to excesses or disease" (Young, 1970, p. 43).

The eminent historian Robert Young has suggested that scrutiny of the Phrenologists' writings can aid attempts to clarify the historical sources of "... the confusion in current attempts to relate the concepts used in the explanation of normal and abnormal behaviour to the physiology of the organism" (Young, 1970, p. xxii). This paper investigates a methodological debate that took place in the first half of the 19th century over the use of phrenological evidence for normal and pathological psychological inference of brain physiology. There was a great deal of discussion in the medical journals from 1835 to 1847 over the use of phrenological measurements in pathological cases. The focus of the dispute was clinico-pathological correlations represented by the skull and brain cast of Jonathan Swift (1667–1745), the author of *Gulliver's Travels* and Dean of St. Patrick's Cathedral in Dublin. While the Phrenologists rejected this skull as evidence for personal propensities owing to the effects of age and mental illness, the rising tide of British "Alienists" (i.e., clinicians interested in mental illness) used such cases (among others) as counter-evidence for the phrenological predictions of individual personality traits. This paper will examine the arguments put forward by the various contributors to this debate and consider how they illuminate implicit methodological assumptions about obtaining evidence regarding brain and behaviour relations.

BACKGROUND

In 1835, works were undertaken to address flood damage to the foundations of St. Patrick's Cathedral Dublin. In making these repairs it was necessary to expose several coffins, among which were those of Jonathan Swift and "Stella"—Esther Johnson, his lifetime correspondent. Coincidentally, the British Association for the Advancement of Science (BAAS) meeting was held in Dublin that summer, with a meeting of the Dublin Phrenological Society held the week after. Upon hearing of the repairs at the cathedral, the BAAS committee requested that they be permitted to exhume the skull of Swift for examination, with a view to elucidating the illness from which he had chronically suffered and that had caused his death.

Jonathan Swift was a leading figure in 18th-century Ireland—famous and infamous for his political satire. He also wrote extensively on mind/brain relations as well as language reform and machine translation. He suffered ill health throughout his life—now believed to have been Ménière's disease (Wilson, 1940). Contemporaries and subsequent biographers all note that there was a change in his language and behaviour towards the end of his life. At the age of 73, Swift made a will that testified him to be "of sound mind although weak in body". Two years later, Swift was found by the courts to be "not capable of taking care of his person or fortune", and management of his large estate was given over to relations (Malcolm, 1989). In 1742, Swift suffered what appears to be a severe eye infection, which his biographers have taken as a turning point in his behaviour. Samuel Johnson (1890, from http://lee.jaffebros.com/gulliver/biography/johnslife.com) described this dramatically:

> ... an inflammation in his left eye, which swelled it to the size of an egg, with boils in other parts; he was kept long waking with the pain, and was not easily restrained by five

attendants from tearing out his eye. The tumour at last subsided; and a short interval of reason ensuing, in which he knew his physician and his family, gave hopes of his recovery; but in a few days he sunk into lethargick [sic] stupidity, motionless, heedless, and speechless. But it is said, that, after a year of total silence, when his housekeeper, on the 30th of November, told him that the usual bonfires and illuminations were preparing to celebrate his birth-day, he answered, 'It is all folly; they had better let it alone'. It is remembered that he afterwards spoke now and then, or gave some intimation of a meaning; but at last sunk into perfect silence, which continued till about the end of October, 1744, when, in his seventy-eighth year, he expired without a struggle.

It should be pointed out that Dr Johnson, who had never met Swift, was writing three decades after his death. The only documentary evidence of his language and behavioural changes recorded from eyewitnesses were letters written by the same family relations who had taken over his estate. There are only three short passages that are relevant (Williams, 1965, pp. 214, 215):

He would attempt to speak his mind, but could not recollect words to express his meaning.

...[he] endeavoured, with a good deal of pain, to find the words to speak to me; at last, not being able after many efforts, he gave a heavy sigh, and, I think, was afterwards silent.

Sometimes he will not utter a syllable, at other times he will speak incoherent words; but he never yet as far as I could hear, talked nonsense, or said a foolish thing.

There is no other documentary evidence on which to base any kind of (retrospective) diagnosis, nor should we wish to make one. The point is that there was repeated concern about a change in Swift's behaviour towards the end of his life and its cause, which has been revived by a dozen authors over the past 250 years. (See Lorch, 2005, for a detailed discussion of the representation of his cognitive and linguistic disorders.)

At the time of Swift's death, a death mask was cast and an autopsy was performed "to ascertain the cause of his insanity" (Wilde 1847, p. 3). This autopsy, as was the practice of the day, consisted only of cutting open the skull, which was found to be "loaded with water". Swift was buried in St. Patrick's Cathedral, Dublin where he had been Dean for most of his life (1713–1745).

THE 19TH-CENTURY PHRENOLOGISTS' INVESTIGATION

The investigation instituted by the British Association for the Advancement of Science (BAAS) of Swift's skull was led by Dr John Houston (1802–1845), a pathologist and phrenologist noted for his use of the microscope to investigate cancer. The phrenological examination of the skull and taking of brain casts was carried out in Sir Henry Marsh's House (past president of the Royal College of Physicians, Dublin) adjacent to the cathedral (now the Marsh library). Extensive drawings were also made.

Among those present was Mr George Combe (1788–1858) representing the Edinburgh Phrenological Society at the BAAS. Combe had helped to found the

Phrenological Society in Edinburgh in 1820. Under his impetus, The *Phrenological Journal and Miscellany* began publishing in 1823. By 1832 there were 29 Phrenological Societies in Britain (Cooter, 1984). Since the early days of Gall, and subsequently Spurzheim, Britain had become a stronghold of phrenology, aided to a large extent by George Combe and his brother Dr Andrew Combe.

The Dublin Phrenological Society meeting was held the day after the exhumation occurred. Dr Houston stated that the examination had been agreed on the grounds of "advancement of scientific knowledge". In his report Houston insisted that: "It was no idle curiosity, neither can we boast of its being zeal for the cause of science, which led to the disinterment; it was purely a matter of accident" (Houston, 1834/6, p. 604) (cf. Hagner, 2003). While there was no mention of this investigation in the BAAS report that appeared in *The Lancet* that year, the *Phrenological Journal* carried extensive descriptions and discussion of the case (Anon., 1835/6).

Houston examined the skull and dictated his findings to Combe, which were published (Anon., 1834/6a, p. 466) as "Account of the skull of Dean Swift, recently disinterred at Dublin":

> It is my opinion, that the bones cannot be regarded as free from indications of previous chronic disease. ... the condition of the cerebral surface of the whole of the frontal region is evidently of a character indicating the presence, during life-time, of diseased action in the subjacent membranes of the brain. The skull in this region is thickened, flattened, and unusually smooth and hard in some places, whilst it is thinned and roughened in others. The marks of the vessels on the bone exhibit, moreover, a very unusual appearance; they look more like the imprints of vessels which had been generated *de novo*, in connexion with some diseased action, than as the original arborescent trunks. The impressions of the middle arteries of the dura mater are unnaturally large and deep, and the branches of those vessels which pass in the direction forwards are thick and short, and terminate abruptly by dividing into an unusual number of minute twigs; whilst those of the same trunks which take their course backwards are long and regular, and of graduated size from the beginning to the end of their course ... The skull shewed [sic] clearly increased vascularity of the dura inater in the basilar and anterior regions. The anterior fossae were small both in the longitudinal and in the transverse directions. The middle fossae were of ordinary size; the posterior fossae very large, wide, and deep. The internal parts corresponding to the frontal protuberances were unequal in concavity: at neither was there any depression corresponding to the great prominences on the outer surface. The two hemispheres were regular and symmetrical.

Houston makes a methodologically significant point in his conclusion (Anon., 1834/6a, p. 469):

> ... shape of skull no longer represents accurately that of the Brain. Skulls of aged cannot be used as evidence of talents or dispositions at the time of vigorous maturity due to decreasing volume with age. Cases of disease are also excluded due to morbid action. Increased and at other times diminished mental energy. The relation between organic size and functional power can no longer be depended upon ... Due to Jonathan Swift's very advanced age, known to have died from 'water in the brain', the effect of longstanding disease, the phrenologist would not hold himself warranted to infer, from mere inspection of the skull, what had been the talents and dispositions of its possessor in the prime of life. All he could do would be to point out the relative proportions of the

organs *as they existed*, and compare them, for purposes of illustration rather than proof, with their accompanying manifestations.

A discussion is reported to have taken place at this meeting on the evidence that this skull represented, and the significance it held for phrenological interpretation. One unidentified contributor (Anon., 1834/6b, 559) suggested:

> It would appear from the depression on the anterior part of the head that the man must have been apparently an idiot. The bones must have undergone considerable change during the 10 or 12 last years of his life, while in a state of lunacy.

Another member of the meeting, Dr Richard Tonson Evanson (Professor of Physic, Royal College of Surgeons of Ireland; Anon., 1834/6b, p. 560), remarked that:

> ... the bones of the anterior part of the head were considerably thickened, and the internal surface did not exhibit those impressions of convolutions which are to be found in healthy subjects ... It was not fair to condemn the science if this head were not found to give an idea of the Dean's character; for Phrenology paid regard only to developments occurring in the brain of a person in full heath and vigour.

A conversation then ensued with reference to a cast of a bust of Swift executed during his lifetime. However, this evidence was rejected as "the artists of those days were not accustomed to pay that attention to the developments of the head which is now given ..." (Anon., 1834/6b, p. 560) After the bones were re-interred (except for the larynx), Houston sent the cast of Swift's skull to Combe to be kept in the Edinburgh Phrenological Society Library.

Reports and discussions regarding Swift's skull were published in *The Times*, the *London Medical Gazette, Phrenological Journal*, and *The Lancet*. An editorial appeared in *The Lancet* (Anon., 1836c) regarding the report of the findings on Swift's skull at the London Phrenological Society by Mr Hawkins and an anti-phrenological pamphlet written by a Dr Roderick Macleod of St. George's Hospital London based on the examination of Swift. Curiously, in a letter to the *London Medical Gazette*, Macleod (1836) denies having written anything,

The editors of the *London Medical Gazette* continued to pursue the matter over many issues: "How could any set of men be so demented as to publish facts [regarding Swift's skull measurements] so damning to their doctrine?" (Anon., 1835, p. 116). However, they do go on to make an important statistical point: "When five or six and thirty guesses are made, it would be wonderful [amazing] indeed if some of them did not happen to be right" (Anon., 1835, p. 117). As for the changes in behaviour attributed to Swift, and their relevance to what was found in his skull and brain cast, they concluded: "If you contend, that perhaps these changes occurred ... during the last three or four melancholy years of the Dean's life, we leave you in the hands of the pathologists; they will settle the matter" (Anon., 1835, p. 117).

After printing two earlier reports of meetings of the London Phrenological Society where Swift's skull was discussed, the *London Medical Gazette* (Anon., 1836b) published a review of the book *An Introduction to Phrenology* by Robert Macnish. A remark was included (Anon., 1836b, p. 297) which refers to the obviously still ongoing debate over Swift's skull a year later:

Phrenologists positively declare, that no correct inference can be deduced in cases of old age and diseased brain; yet we had lately the skull of Dean Swift brought forward as an evidence against the Science, in the face of the notorious fact, that the Dean died at the age of seventy-eight, had been subject to loss of memory, and frantic fits of passion, eleven years before his death, and that the last five years his life was passed in idiocy.

The discussion reported in *The Lancet* (Anon., 1836c) emphasised the contentious nature of differing views of Swift's personality and accomplishments. Like the present day cult of celebrity, the 19th-century British also prejudicially concerned themselves with the private lives of public figures. Swift was of interest not only because of his great literary achievements, his political reforms, and social significance but also because of his radical speeches, eccentric behaviour and mysterious unrequited (?) affair with Mrs Johnson (aka, "Stella"). However, *The Lancet* (Anon., 1836c, p. 505) concluded a colourful discussion with the following endorsement for phrenology:

> We [the editor] have suffered the subject to occupy so large a space in our Journal, chiefly because the skull of Swift has furnished, through misrepresentations and want of information, the most important occasion that has offered for many years to the enemies of the doctrines of Gall; and because, while the science of phrenology is one of great interest to medical men, too many of them have not time to examine the facts on which it is based, for themselves. ... we cordially concur with Andral ... that the science of which Gall is the founder must henceforward be included among the grave and serious studies of physiology.

Ten years later, an anonymous review of two books appeared in the *British Quarterly Review* (1846) on *Contributions to the Mathematics of Phrenology* by James Straton and *The Brain and its Physiology; a Critical Disquisition on the Methods of Determining the Relations Between the structure and Function of the Encephalon* by Daniel Noble. The article in fact included little in the way of review, but rather presented original research on the validity of phrenological measurements. Ten skulls of "notables and murderers" lodged at the Edinburgh Phrenological Museum were selected, including four recently hanged for murder, and compared with the skulls of Robert Burns, La Fontaine, Robert the Bruce, Heloise, Jonathan Swift, and Stella. The article concluded: "... [the skull of] Swift had less *Wit* in relation to the size of his brain and his other organs than all the other nine [skulls measured] and yet that phrenology can be true?" (Anon., 1846, p. 408). It goes on to detail Swift's phrenological measurements (p. 413):

> Swift, who (c.f. the Poacher) had the largest organ [of Acquisitiveness], and the least of Benevolence of the whole ten, was not a thief; but altogether frugal ... The measurements of the organ of Wit require no comment; Swift has the smallest: Indeed, on carrying an eye over the tables, we think that the worst head of the series is that of Swift ... With reference to the energy which the predominating faculties of these ten individuals were manifested, ... the smaller heads were, generally speaking, the most energetic. Swift and Haggart [a criminal], who are rather below the mean and should therefore have been the least energetic and active, displayed the greatest energy and intrepidy [sic] of character; the one was the most absolute monarch of the populace of Dublin that ever governed; and the other displayed the most unwearied energy and perseverance in crime.

George Combe felt it necessary to address some of the points raised in this review, which he published in *The Lancet* (1846/7) and identified the anonymous author of the review as Dr David Skae (1814–1873), Medical Superintendent of the Royal Edinburgh Asylum. Combe pointed out that "Dr. Skae knows as well as most men that the 'facts and observations of anatomy and physiology' differ widely from those of 'chemistry and mechanics'. Physiology is an *estimative*, and chemistry and mechanics are *exact*, sciences" (Combe, 1846/7, p. 611). Combe challenged the method that Skae employed to generate his measurements as invalid, pointing out that the comparisons must be made within and not between individuals (p. 662):

> ...[the talent for a given thing] in any individual, depends, not on the size of any organ in his head in proposition to that of the same organ in another head, but on the sized of the respective organs in comparison with each other in his own head.

Combe went on to reject in detail the basis on which Skae made his measurements. He pointed out that they only consider breadth not length of individual organs; that they were based on arbitrary landmarks that introduced artefacts when comparing individuals; and that Skae falsely normalised his measurements using a non-standard reference (Swift), which failed to maintain the relative of proportions of each organ within each individual. All of the methodological procedures detailed in Skae's investigation, Combe insisted, violated phrenological "good practice" and could therefore only lead to invalid data.

He also made the point (Combe, 1846/7, p. 663) that the selection of subjects was in violation of good methodological practice on scientific grounds:

> Phrenologists had stated that individuals free from disease, and not above the middle period of life, are the proper subjects for observation, with a view to test the truth of the science. Disease diminishes, exalts, or perverts, the normal action of the brain, as well as of other organs; and old age infallibly diminishes it, besides generally, if not always, being attended with a lessening of the cerebral substance itself, and with such cranial changes as render the form and size of the head an extremely uncertain index of the form and size of the brain.

Specific objections are made (Combe, 1846/7, p. 9) to the use of Jonathan Swift's skull for the purposes of investigating phrenological measurements of individual propensities:

> Dr Skae acted preposterously in selecting, for the purposes of testing phrenology, not the skull of a sane individual, not beyond the middle period of life, but that of a morbidly irritable and eccentric man, who, as his biographers inform us, died at the age of seventy-eight, in a state of idiocy so complete and long-continued as, with other evidence, to render it next to certain, that a great change had taken place in both the brain and its coverings. Had the phrenologists perpetrated any similar folly, under the plea of "scientific" investigation, the would have been scouted as fit to become the inmates of a lunatic asylum; but Dr. Skae's solemn farce is quietly admitted, under the garb of science, into the pages of a philosophical and enlightened Review! The phrenologists have all along rejected the skull of Swift as affording evidence of the forms and dimensions of his head at forty years of age, and in sound health ... [and] given ample reasons for not seeking proofs of the truth of phrenology from cases of disease.

Combe went on to consider the validity of inclusion of several of the other skulls, pointing out that they were not free from disease either. One was the case of Pollard who committed murder and suicide. Combe argued that he was suffering from cerebral disease rather than criminal propensities. This again raised the issue of whether abnormal behaviour is the result of organic or functional disorder. The Phrenologist, in contrast to the Alienists, upheld the view that behavioural impairment had a physical source.

Skae published a letter of reply to Combe in a subsequent issue of *The Lancet* (1847a). In it he admitted that the first publication contained the wrong table, with "calculated" rather than "actual" measurements. In this paper he presented the correct version (see Figure 1). Skae argued (1847a, p. 126) that the use of "well-known geometrical rules" allowed him to convert all the measures of individual crania to a uniform capacity based on one of the ten, i.e., Swift's:

> True, the measurements of all the crania are brought to those of a crania having the *capacity* or size of Swift's; but if we had brought them all to those of the capacity of the head of a walrus, it would not have vitiated in the least the comparisons instituted. The simple object was, to bring them all to the *same* size, and then to institute a comparison. ... The skull of Swift was taken as being nearly the mean size; but if the whole had been converted into the measurements of a skull, of what Mr. Straton calls *standard* capacity, they would still have occupied the same relative position in the tables.

Skae (1847a, p. 126) is therefore satisfied that these subjects' skulls could be used to infer normal phenomena:

> I deny that Swift died in a state of idiocy or insanity ... But even admitting the assertion that Swift did labour under mental disease, am I to be called upon by Mr. Combe 'to prove the adequacy of diseased heads to furnish conclusive evidence of normal phenomenon' in the question at issue? If the *form* of the cranium of an *adult* is altered by imbecility or by any other form of insanity, it is for Mr. Combe to adduce evidence of the fact. The presumption is against him. I deny that there is a vestige of evidence in support of the *hypothesis*; for such it is.

It is notable that it is Skae, the director of an Insane Asylum, who rejected the phrenological idea of pathophysiology—that is, that idiocy or insanity would change a person's brain and correspondingly the skull measurements over time. It must be remembered that issue of materialism and the sources of insanity were viewed in a different light then, but these issues may parallel current discussions regarding reductionism and psychiatric disease.

The phrenologist had always insisted that "It was not fair to condemn the science if this head were not found to give an idea of the Dean's character; for Phrenology paid regard only to developments occurring in the brain of a person in full health and vigour." (Report of the Dublin Phrenological Society Meeting: Anon., 1834/6b, p. 559).

At the beginning of the 19th century Gall and his followers employed a primarily correlative approach, which led them to the theory of localisation of function. Young (1970) pointed out that statistical methods were not available to Gall to verify the significance of his observed correlations. Yet this is what Skae offered in 1846 to argue against phrenological correlations. Skae compared the phrenologists

CRANIA CHOSEN	BURNS Actual	BURNS Calculated	SWIFT Actual	SWIFT Calculated	M'KANE Actual	M'KANE Calculated	LA FONTAINE Actual	LA FONTAINE Calculated	POLLARD Actual	POLLARD Calculated	BRUCE Actual	BRUCE Calculated	HAGGART Actual	HAGGART Calculated	SPELL Actual	SPELL Calculated	HELOISE Actual	HELOISE Calculated	LOCKEY Actual	LOCKEY Calculated
Capacity in cubic inches	147.7	129.15	129.15	129.15	111.05	129.15	149.6	129.15	122.9	129.15	136.5	129.15	128.6	129.15	119.3	129.15	142.7	129.15	142.05	129.15
Occipital spine to Individuality	8.	7.64	7.6	7.60	7.35	7.60	7.8	7.52	7.7	7.83	7.8	7.66	7.45	7.46	6.9	7.09	7.76	7.496	7.8	7.557
,, Comparison	7.8	7.45	7.4	7.4	7.23	7.5	7.7	7.34	7.4	7.52	7.4	7.26	7.43	7.44	7.	7.19	7.79	7.53	7.9	7.557
Meatus ,, Meatus	4.9	4.68	4.5	4.50	4.5	4.73	5.2	4.95	4.5	4.58	5.4	5.3	4.2	4.206	4.5	4.62	5.	4.836	4.8	4.71
Caution ,, Caution	5.8	5.54	5.6	5.6	5.5	5.78	6.	5.72	5.4	5.49	5.7	5.59	5.4	5.47	5.3	5.44	5.2	5.03	5.8	5.62
Meatus { ,, Occipital Spine } (Amativeness)	4.1	3.92	4.2	4.2	3.84	4.04	3.95	3.76	4.3	4.37	4.57	4.48	3.77	3.78	3.65	3.75	3.98	3.85	4.2	4.08
,, Philoprogenitiveness	4.8	4.599	4.7	4.7	4.4	4.63	4.65	4.426	5.1	5.18	4.9	4.81	4.52	4.53	4.44	4.56	4.9	4.74	4.95	4.807
,, Concentrativeness	5.3	5.06	5.	5.	4.8	5.05	5.04	4.8	5.4	5.49	5.4	5.3	5.1	5.11	4.64	4.76	5.27	5.09	4.77	4.62
Combativeness ,, Combativeness	5.0	4.78	5.6	5.6	5.1	5.36	4.2	4.003	4.5	4.58	4.8	4.71	4.	4.01	4.5	4.62	4.04	4.69	3.94	3.89
Destructiveness ,, Destructiveness	5.4	5.16	5.8	5.8	5.7	5.99	6.1	5.81	5.65	5.74	6.2	6.1	5.36	5.37	5.62	5.77	5.85	5.658	6.1	5.91
Secretiveness ,, Secretiveness	5.7	5.45	5.6	5.6	6.78	6.08	6.3	6.09	5.77	5.86	6.05	5.94	5.6	5.61	6.5	6.65	5.68	5.49	6.3	6.1
Acquisitiveness ,, Acquisitiveness	5.5	5.25	5.5	5.5	5.23	5.5	5.6	5.34	5.26	5.34	5.26	5.15	4.95	4.96	5.02	5.16	5.27	5.09	6.	5.81
Meatus to opposite Adhesiveness	5.36	5.12	5.6	5.6	5.4	5.68	5.3	5.04	5.75	5.85	6.	5.89	5.7	5.71	5.3	5.44	5.8	5.61	5.61	5.43
Meatus to Self-Esteem	5.4	5.16	5.1	5.1	5.1	5.36	5.43	5.17	5.45	5.54	5.6	5.49	5.5	5.51	5.	5.13	5.5	5.33	5.1	4.94
,, Firmness	5.5	5.25	5.3	5.3	5.2	5.48	5.8	5.53	5.4	5.49	5.65	5.55	5.5	5.51	5.13	5.26	5.68	5.49	5.3	5.13
,, Veneration	5.5	5.26	5.1	5.1	5.05	5.31	5.74	5.47	5.2	5.29	5.4	5.3	5.3	5.31	4.9	5.03	5.5	5.38	5.2	5.04
,, Benevolence	5.7	5.46	4.8	4.8	5.1	5.36	5.7	5.43	5.15	5.23	5.15	5.035	5.3	5.31	4.9	5.03	5.35	5.17	5.4	5.35
,, Comparison	5.3	5.06	4.8	4.8	4.93	5.18	5.45	5.19	5.1	5.18	5.1	5.007	4.93	4.94	4.87	5.0	5.1	4.896	5.2	5.04
,, Eventuality	5.0	4.78	4.6	4.6	4.82	5.07	5.3	5.04	4.85	4.93	4.9	4.81	4.8	4.81	4.53	4.65	4.8	4.64	5.1	4.94
,, Causality	4.8	4.59	4.3	4.3	4.3	4.52	4.95	4.72	4.5	4.58	4.7	4.61	4.5	4.51	4.2	4.31	4.85	4.69	4.7	4.55
,, Individuality	4.9	4.68	4.5	4.5	4.7	4.94	5.15	4.91	4.7	4.78	4.83	4.74	4.6	4.61	4.35	4.47	4.66	4.49	4.9	4.75
,, Wit	4.0	3.82	3.4	3.4	4.	4.21	4.	3.81	3.6	3.66	3.85	3.77	4.83	4.84	3.5	3.59	4.1	3.93	4.1	3.97
Wit ,, Wit	3.72	3.55	3.55	3.55	3.8	4.0	4.1	3.907	3.7	3.76	3.7	3.63	3.8	3.81	3.4	3.49	4.44	4.25	4.4	4.26
,, Ideality	5.0	4.78	4.7	4.7	4.8	5.05	4.73	4.51	4.8	4.88	4.65	4.56	4.3	4.31	4.7	4.83	4.76	4.6	5.5	5.33
,, Number	4.1	3.92	4.3	4.3	4.46	4.69	4.57	4.35	3.6	3.66	3.9	3.83	3.83	3.84	3.8	3.9	3.92	3.79	4.4	4.26
,, Tune	4.4	4.21	3.9	3.8	4.5	4.73	4.62	4.4	3.84	3.9	4.1	4.02	3.9	3.91	3.9	4.	4.07	3.93	4.78	4.63

Figure 1. Skae's revised table.

to "the monkey who got his tail chopped off trying to persuade his companions that *he knew the fashions*" (Skae, 1847a, p. 124).

At the same time as this debate was appearing in *The Lancet*, Dr William Wilde (1815–1876, father of Oscar), the Dublin surgeon and eye specialist, took up an investigation into "The Closing Years of Dean Swift's Life" prompted by a letter inquiring about the significance of Swift's reported eye infection. He wrote a long article in the *Dublin Journal of Medical and Chemical Sciences* (1947), which was reprinted as a book and came out in a second edition in 1849. Wilde (1849) determined that Swift had suffered from periodic attacks of cerebral congestion which increased in frequency and severity over time. Wilde (1847, part 2, p. 22) offered the opinion that:

> Most of the so-called pathological appearances here detailed [in Houston's 1835 report] are, however, it is well known, common and natural occurrences in old crania, and no wise indicative of disease. The foramina alluded to are no evidence whatever of a fungous state of the dura mater; but the deep sulci for the meningeal arteries are certainly abnormal, and shew [sic] a long-continued excess of vascular action, such as would attend cerebral congestion.

In making this final point Wilde seems to be implying that vascular disease, which he used to account for the documented language and behavioural defects, was evident on the skull. What he appears to rule out is mental disease as a functional rather than organic process of madness. Wilde specifically argued against the effects of mental disease on the cranium. He cited (1847, part 2, pp. 22–23) Esquirol's study of skulls of the insane and imbecile, which showed that there were no changes over the period of mental illness:

> All these discrepancies [between his known character and the phrenological reading of Swift's skull] are endeavoured to be accounted for by the fact, that the skull then presented was not that of Swift the wit, the caustic writer, and the patriot, – but that of Swift, the madman and the fool; and to explain this it has been asserted, that the skull had collapsed during the period of his mental disease; although, in the previous instances to which we have alluded, at the Richmond Asylum [of the measurement of lunatic inmates] the periscope was made without taking into account this item in the physical as well as moral change of the lunatics ... We at once deny the fact of Swift's skull having altered during life, or of insanity ever producing the effects therein stated; and we may confidently defy its conductors to the proof. Esquirol, one of the highest authorities on the subject, found, from a long series of careful observations, that the skull previously normal does not alter its form or capacity from long-continued insanity or imbecility.

Wilde contacted an eyewitness to the original phrenological examination a decade earlier (Hamilton, personal communication reported in Wilde, 1847, pt 2, pp. 7–8):

> Mr. Hamilton has kindly furnished us [Wilde] with the following communication, accompanied by drawings of the skull, which he made at the time. 'In September, 1835, I had the skulls of Swift and Stella in my possession. ... On looking at Swift's skull, the first thing that struck me was the extreme lowness of the forehead, those parts which the phrenologists have marked out as the *organs of wit, causality, and comparison, being scarcely developed at all*; but the head rose gradually, and was high from benevolence backwards. The portion of the occipital bone assigned to the animal propensities,

philoprogenitiveness and amativeness, &c., appeared excessive ... On the inside of the upper segment of the skull the groove for the middle meningeal artery was remarkably deep, as were also the depressions for the glandulae Pacchionae. The frontal bone was very thick, but the osseous structure did not appear to me to be diseased. It was, however, when looking into the interior, and examining the base, that the wonderful capacity of the skull became apparent. From the flatness of the orbital plates, and the great width of the forehead, the room for the anterior lobes of the cerebrum was very great, the depressions, also, for the middle lobes, were very deep. Although, viewed *externally*, the cerebellum would have been pronounced large, yet, in consequence of the tentorium having been exceedingly low, the cerebellum must have been very small, and the posterior lobes of the cerebrum, consequently, very large. In the temporal regions the skull was thin and semi-transparent; the frontal sinuses were small, though their external appearances would have led to a different conclusion.

Hamilton (reported in Wilde, 1847, pt 2, pp. 7–8) went on to describe his own comparative study, which differed in approach to that discussed earlier by Skae:

Although the skull, phrenologically considered, might be thought deficient, yet its capacity was, in reality, very great, capable of containing such a brain as we might expect in so remarkable a genius. I took an ordinary skull, and making a section of it on the same level with that of Swift's, I compared their outlines (drawn on paper) together, and found that the latter exceeded it in a very remarkable manner, particularly in its transverse diameter.

The final word was had by the Phrenologists. In an anonymous review of Wilde's paper in the *Phrenological Journal* (Anon., 1847), there was agreement over his representation of the physical findings. Where there was a difference of opinion was in the interpretation. While Wilde asserted that all the evidence indicated Swift was not insane, the *Phrenological Journal* insisted it showed that he was, but that this behaviour had a physical source plain to be seen on his skull.

This episode in the research field of phrenology demonstrates their interest in using skull and brain cast information, not for inferring individual manifestations of personality traits, but rather as indirect evidence of pathology. The distinction between mental disease and organic neurological disorder was also considered to be relevant to the interpretation of phrenological findings.

DISCUSSION

In a series of papers, John Marshall and colleagues (Marshall, 1982, 1984, 1995, 2001; Marshall & Fink, 2003; Marshall & Gurd, 1996) have explored the significance of our phrenological heritage for present day cognitive neuropsychology. Indeed, 20 years ago Marshall suggested that neuropsychology is simply "the currently fashionable name for phrenology" (Marshall, 1984, p. 210). The issue dealt with in the present paper is how implied methodological assumptions of principle can be revealed by discussion of exceptions to the rule. Jonathan Swift's skull and brain cast were thought by the Phrenologists to represent forensic evidence, which would reveal the source of his behavioural changes at the end of his life. As such, it was thought to reflect the effects of disease on Swift's brain. In contrast, the Alienist anti-phrenologists viewed it as counter-evidence, which disproved the Gall/Spurzheim/

Combe theory of localisation of mental faculties because the measured organs did not correspond to the personal propensities for which Swift was famous.

As Marshall (1982) pointed out, how counter-examples are dealt with is crucial for maintaining the integrity of any theory. He suggested that Phrenologists weakened the value of their results by only looking for confirmatory cases and invoking ancillary hypotheses for contrary cases. Marshall pleaded, "One hopes that we [neuropsychologists] are not going to repeat this fashion of playing tennis with the net down" (Marshall, 1982, p. 111).

One of the basic empirical premises for phrenology, as practised in the first half of the 19th century in Britain, was that one could study the contours of the skull and infer things about the brain. This was an attempt to derive an objective measure for modular functions in specific locations and correlate them with observed behavioural performance.

Like phrenology, present day neuroimaging techniques use indirect factors to infer function in the living brain. Volume, density, blood flow, metabolism of oxygen or glucose, etc. are taken as (secondary) measures of neuronal activity by correlation: "The current search for local areas of high activation in studies that deploy positron emission tomography (PET) or functional magnetic resonance imaging (fMRI) is coming suspiciously close to the search for bigger, better, and *more* bumps that characterized the demise of the original phrenological movement" (Marshall & Gurd, 1996, p. 297).

In 2001, a book by William Uttal appeared, entitled *The new phrenology: The limits of localising cognitive processing in the brain*. This attracted dozens of book reviews in a variety of journals both paper and virtual. In John Marshall's review (2001, p. 152), he aptly points out that "what needs to be debated here is the extent to which they reflect our failure to design good experiments rather than the brain's failure to instantiate distributed localisation of function". Indeed, this is the same basis for debate as that played out in the pages of *The Lancet* over one and a half centuries ago. The modern debate can be viewed on a webcast: On 23 April 2003 Uttal debated with Michael Posner at Northwestern University, Chicago on the question "Is cognitive neuroscience the new phrenology?" (http://nuamps.at. northwestern.edu/cogsci).

Consideration of the issues faced 150 years ago over clinico-pathological correlation and localisation of function is revisited periodically as technology, methodology, and theory evolve (e.g., Franz, 1912). Phrenology, like the neurofunctional imaging techniques used today, attempted to make connections between the living brain and behaviour by inference from secondary measurements. Refinements in technology must be joined with scrutiny of theoretical and methodological assumptions to ensure good science.

REFERENCES

Anon (1834/6a). Account of the skull of Dean Swift, recently disinterred at Dublin. *Phrenological Journal and Miscellany, 9*, 466–470.

Anon (1834/6b). Dublin Phrenological Society Meeting, August 17, 1835. *Phrenological Journal and Miscellany, 9*, 558–560.

Anon (1835). Phrenology in a quandary. *London Medical Gazette, October 24*, 115–119.

Anon (1836a). Proceedings of the Panton Square Philosophers. Report on the second meeting of the London Phrenological Society. *London Medical Gazette, January 2*, 530–533.

Anon (1836b). Review of An Introduction to Phrenology in the form of question and answer by Robert Macnish. *London Medical Gazette, May 21*, 296–297.

Anon (1836c). London Phrenological Society. Skull of Dean Swift. *Lancet, December 26*, 502–506.

Anon (1846). Book Review of Straton and Noble. *British Quarterly Review, November*, 397–419. [In the subsequent exchange in the Lancet David Skae claims authorship.]

Anon (1846). Review of Contributions to the Mathematics of Phrenology by James Straton and The Brain and its Physiology; a Critical Disquisition on the Methods of Determining the Relations Between the structure and Function of the Encephalon by Daniel Noble. *British Quarterly Review, November*, 397–419.

Anon (1847). Review: On Dean Swift's Death and Post-Mortem Examination: in which the question of his insanity is considered. *Phrenological Journal and Magazine of Moral Science, 20*, 441–443.

Combe, G. (1846/7). On criticisms upon phrenology: a review reviewed. *Lancet, December 19*, 661–663: *January 2*, 8–11.

Combe, G. (1847). Phrenology Mr. Combe's rejoinder to Dr. Skae. *Lancet, August 21*, 194–196.

Cooter, R. (1984). *The cultural meaning of popular science: Phrenology and the organization of consent in nineteenth-century Britain*. Cambridge, UK: Cambridge University Press.

Franz, S. I. (1912). New phrenology. *Science, N.S. 35*, 321–228.

Gall, F. J. (1835) *On the functions of the brain and each of its parts* (6 vols). [Trans. W. Lewis.]. Boston: Marsh, Capen & Lyon.

Hagner, M. (2003). Skulls, brains, and memorial culture: On cerebral biographies of scientists in the nineteenth century. *Science in Context, 16*, 195–218.

Houston, J. (1834/6). On the authenticity of the skulls of Dean Swift and Stella. *Phrenological Journal and Miscellany, 9*, 603–608.

Johnson, S. (1890). Jonathan Swift. In, *Lives of the Poets* (Vol. III, pp. 2–45). London: George Bell & Sons, [Original, 1781.].

Lorch, M. (2005). Jonathan Swift's language: Mind and brain in life and after death. In H. Whitaker, C. U. M. Smith, & S. Finger (Eds.), *Brain, mind and medicine: 18th century perspectives on the neurosciences*. Berlin: Springer-Verlag.

Macleod, R. (1836). Letter to the Editor. *London Medical Gazette, January 2*, 543–544.

Malcolm, E. (1989). *Swift's hospital: A history of St. Patrick's Hospital Dublin (1748–1989)*. Dublin: Gill & MacMillan.

Marshall, J. C. (1982). On the biology of language acquisition. In D. Caplan (Ed.), *Biological studies of mental process*. Cambridge, MA: MIT Press.

Marshall, J. C. (1984). Multiple perspectives on modularity. *Cognition, 17*, 209–242.

Marshall, J. C. (1995). Franz Joseph Gall: Genius or charlatan? *Journal of Neurolinguistics, 8*, 289–293.

Marshall, J. C. (2001). Bumps on the brain: Review of The New Phrenology by W. Uttal. *Nature, 414*, 151–152.

Marshall, J. C., & Fink, G. R. (2003). Cerebral localisation, then and now. *NeuroImage, 20*(Suppl. 1), S2–S7.

Marshall, J. C., & Gurd, J. M. (1996). Johann Gaspar Spurzheim: Quack or Thomist? *Journal of Neurolinguistics, 9*, 297–299.

Skae, D. (1847a). Phrenology, Dr. Skae in reply to George Combe, Esq. *Lancet, July 31*, 123–126.

Skae, D. (1847b). *Phrenological Journal and Magazine of Moral Science, July*.

Uttal, W. (2001). *The new phrenology: The limits of localising cognitive processing in the brain*. Cambridge, MA: MIT Press.

Wilde, W. (1847). Some Particulars respecting Swift and Stella, with Engravings of their Craina; together with some Notice of St. Patrick's Hospital. *Dublin Journal of Medical and Chemical Sciences, 3*, part 1, 384–434: *4*, part 2, 1–33.

Wilde, W. (1849) *The Closing Years of Dean Swift's Life* (2nd enlarged and revised edition). Dublin: Hodges & Smith.

Williams, H. (1965). *Correspondence of Jonathan Swift*. Oxford, UK: Oxford University Press.

Wilson, T. G. (1940). Swift's deafness; and his last illness. *Annals of Medical History, 3rd Series, 3*, 291–305.

Young, R. (1970). *Mind, brain and adaptation*. Oxford, UK: Clarendon Press.

The psycholinguistic approach to aphasia of Chajim Steinthal

Paul Eling

NICI, Radboud University of Nijmegen, The Netherlands

Background: Aphasiology developed in the 19th century as a primary area of research for the localisatio n of function in the brain. It was based on a rather primitive notion of language as a psychological function: input and output of words, in particular nouns. Aphasiology turned into neurolinguistics in the second half of the 20th century, when researchers realised that a linguistically based theory should form the basis of the analysis of language performance deficits.

Aims: The current paper argues that in a very early stage of aphasiology the claim was already formulated that a psycholinguistically oriented approach was necessary. This claim was made by Chajim Steinthal (1823–1893), but it was completely neglected.

Main Contribution: In this paper, I will present Steinthal's psycholinguistic views on aphasia, described in his textbook on psycholinguistics in 1871.

Conclusions: Steinthal formulated a psycholinguistically based theory of language disorders, in which a distinction was made between disorders at the word level and at the sentence level. Moreover, the nature of the deficit was a reduction of the capacity to activate representations and not a loss of word forms. Steinthal thus may be considered a founder not only of psycholinguistics, but also of neurolinguistics.

Nineteenth-century aphasiology was dominated by the works of physicians, who concentrated on the consequences of brain lesions as a means to verify or falsify Franz Joseph Gall's principle of localisation of function in the cerebral cortex. They analysed these effects virtually always in terms of problems in word recognition or word production, even when they admitted that language was a more complicated system, with other levels of representations. The German linguist Chajim Steinthal[1] produced one of the first psycholinguistic models in his handbook. As an addendum, he applied his model to aphasic phenomena. In this paper I will describe Steinthal's psycholinguistic approach to aphasia.

CHAJIM STEINTHAL (1823–1893): HIS CURRICULUM VITAE

Chajim Steinthal was born on 16 May 1823 in Gröbzig, approximately 100 km southwest of Berlin, to Jewish parents. His father, David Steinthal, was a textile

---

[1] Wiedebach and Winkelmann (2002) indicate that first name Heymann, mostly used in the literature, is not the one used by Chajim Steinthal. For his official publications he used "H.", not Heymann. I will follow Wiedebach and Winkelmann.

Address correspondence to: Paul Eling, Biological Psychology, NICI, Radboud University Nijmegen, P.O. Box 9104, 6500HE, The Netherlands. E-mail: p.eling@nici.ru.nl

Chajim Steinthal (1823–1893)

merchant and his mother was Henrietta Heinemann. When Chajim Steinthal was 9 years old his father died, and the family suffered financial problems. In 1836 he went to high school at Bernburg, where he was a good student and passed his examinations to enter university in 1842.

Steinthal then went to the University of Berlin to study theology, philosophy, and general linguistics. In his first semester he soon became acquainted with Humboldt's book *Über die Verschiedenheit des menschlichen Sprachbaus und ihren Einfluß auf die geistige Entwicklung des Menschengeschlechts* (On the diversity of the structure of human languages and its effect on the mental development of the human species). The reading of this book determined Steinthal's scientific work. On 1 November 1847 he became—in absentia—doctor in philosophy and magister in the liberal arts in Tübingen. His thesis had a long title: "De pronomine relativo commentatio philosophico-philologica cum excursu de nominativa particular" (On the relative pronoun, a philosophical-philological commentary with an excursion on the nominative particle). This thesis contains a programme for his scientific explorations, where he formulates the notion that the task for general linguistics is to demonstrate how language is expressed in many different ways and what language has accomplished over the course of history. He remained in Berlin, studying the works of Humboldt, Herbart, general linguistics, and a large number of languages.

On 24 November 1849 Steinthal received his "habilitation"[2] in Berlin with a thesis on Humboldt and Hegel. In 1852 he received the Volney prize for his article on "Die Mande-Negersprachen, psychologisch und phonteisch betrachtet" (The language of the Mande-Negroes[3] from a psychological and phonetic viewpoint), which enabled him to go to Paris where he continued his studies. Without any prospects of a job he returned to Berlin, where he applied for an extraordinary professorship in general linguistics and "Völkerpsychologie", but his request was rejected. He was then forced to earn his living as a "Privat Dozent",[4] but few students were interested in his lessons and even fewer could follow his complex reasoning. He soon became very sceptical about wasting his energy in hopeless attempts to teach his views on general linguistics to these students.

In December 1862 Steinthal received his extraordinary professorship but, because of an anti-Semitic movement led by the Berlin Court Chaplain Stöcker, he never got a full professorship. In 1863 he married Jeanette Lazarus, the sister of his friend Moritz. They had two children, a son and a daughter, who both died at a young age. In 1873 they had a second daughter, Irene, who outlived her father. In 1872 he became a teacher at the newly founded High School for the Science of Judaism in Berlin. In 1893 he fell ill, necessitating daily care from his wife, his sister-in-law, and his daughter. Finally, in 1899 he died at the age of 76 and was buried at the Jewish Cemetery Berlin Weißensee.

An extremely informative and concise description of Steinthal as a person and a colleague, and also of his views on different aspects of language science, can be found in a book written by Waltraud Bumann (1965). However, Bumann does not discuss Steinthal's "revolutionary" ideas concerning language disorders.

INSPIRATION

Many teachers whose lectures Steinthal followed at the University of Berlin have been traced. Among them were philosophers and linguists with good reputations, but Steinthal did not rely on their teachings. He seems to have taught himself. Apparently he was independent, or even isolated, going his own way. Essentially he can be regarded as a commentator on Wilhelm Humboldt. Other important sources of inspiration were Herbart and Heyse.

Wilhelm Humboldt (1767–1835)

Steinthal not only studied Humboldt extensively, but he was also a great admirer and claimed to have saved him from becoming obscure, since other linguists neglected the work of Humboldt. Steinthal had a clear view of the importance of Humboldt's work, but was also critical of Humboldt's weaknesses.

---

[2] "Habilitation" is the highest academic exam, after which someone receives the "venia legendi", the right to teach or to become a professor.

[3] The name Mandingo refers to a group of peoples in West Africa. The name is probably a corruption of the term "Mande-nka" or "Mande-nga". Steinthal argues that the name for the language should be "Mande".

[4] "Privat Dozent" is a private lecturer at the university without a chair; he teaches but has no formal position at the university.

Three statements of Humboldt's were particularly important for Steinthal. First of all, language is not a product ("energon"), but an ongoing process ("energeia"). If one wants to examine language, one should not study products such as written texts. Second, language is a function with which thoughts are formulated. Through language, images can be "fixed" in consciousness, and words enable an individual to become conscious of the outer world but also of him/herself. Finally, language is always a function of the way a particular society perceives the world and communicates about it. There are no a priori language structures.

Steinthal's own scientific merits lie in the extension and incorporation of Humboldt's linguistic concepts into a psycholinguistic theory capable of explaining the phylogenetic and ontogenetic development of linguistic structures and language use, and in the attempt to deal with language disorders within the same framework. At that time, when the study of language was dominated by the study of comparative and historical linguistics, Steinthal pointed out that instead of looking for the roots and the "Ursprache" (primitive language) from which all language apparently has evolved, we should take a closer look at the differences between languages. The underlying constancies are not grammatical categories, but the nature of the workings of the mind.

Johann Friedrich Herbart (1776–1841)

Steinthal relied heavily on Herbart's psychology. The synthesis of Herbart's apperception notion to the linguistic theory of Humboldt forms Steinthal's major contribution. Herbart's psychology was very influential in Germany until Wundt founded a new empirical psychology. So it seems relevant to take a closer look at it here.

Herbart was a bright student and showed remarkable aptitude for mathematics, physical science, and music. He started his studies in philosophy in Jena but interrupted these to become a tutor for the sons of the governor of Interlaken. This triggered his interest in pedagogy, for which he became known later on. He finished his studies in Gottingen and in 1809 he was called to the chair of Kant in Konigsberg, and stayed there for 24 years. In 1816 he published his *Lehrbuch zur Psychologie* and in 1825 his *Psychologie als Wissenschaft*. In 1833 he returned to Gottingen and worked as professor of philosophy until his death in 1841.

Following Kant, Idealists assumed that it was not interesting or even possible to study the mind of an individual. One should study the nature of the Absolute Mind. Herbart was opposed to this idealistic approach to the mind. He seems to relate more directly to Leibniz. He attempted to establish a scientific, empirical psychology, just as the subtitle of his second book promises: *Psychologie als Wissenschaft, neu gegrundet auf Erfahrung, Metaphysik, und Mathematik* (Psychology as science, newly founded on experience, metaphysics and mathematics).

Just as Newton tried to describe the interactions of objects in space in mathematical terms, so Herbart developed a mathematics of the mind. He conceived of the mind as a collection of elementary ideas ("Vorstellungen") of varying intensity ("Kraft"; strength) or clearness. This intensity may be regarded as a tendency of an idea towards self-preservation. Herbart thought of this tendency as the fundamental principle of mental mechanics, much as gravity is the fundamental principle of physical mechanics. Ideas have intensities and interact with other ideas. Intensities and strength of relations with other ideas can be formulated in mathematical terms. An approach like this turns psychology into a scientific discipline.

Ideas that are opposed to each other struggle with one another for access. Some of these ideas are strong enough to cross the threshold of consciousness. Others reside in unconsciousness. "Every movement of the ideas is confined between two fixed points: their state of complete inhibition, their state of complete liberty"; and there is "a natural and constant effort of all the ideas to revert to their state of complete liberty (absence of inhibition)" (Boring, 1957, p. 255). If there were no opposition between ideas, all ideas would form a single mental act. It appears that we are generally conscious of only a restricted number of ideas.

The composition of consciousness at any moment is the result of the mechanical interplay of many ideas. Of all the unconscious ideas, only those that fit in with the conscious ideas find little resistance and can rise above the threshold. This process of "selecting" ideas from unconsciousness is called apperception. Although for Leibniz it only meant that an idea became conscious, Herbart also assumes that the process of apperception results in the assimilation of that idea in the totality of conscious ideas, or in Herbart's terms, the apperceiving mass.

Steinthal borrowed from Herbart his views on ideas and apperception rather than a clear description of psychological processes related to language. But given that Steinthal assumes that language is the expression of the working of mind, these views play a central role in his own theory on language.

Carl Wilhelm Ludwig Heyse (1797–1855)

The final teacher I want to mention here is Carl Heyse. In 1848 Steinthal met Heyse, a language philosopher, who introduced Steinthal to the work of Hegel. Through Heyse, Steinthal became acquainted with Moritz Lazarus, the founder of the "Völkerpsychologie" and developed a lifelong friendship with him. The two, Heyse and Steinthal, must have had many scientific discussions. Perhaps these discussions started as lessons from the senior philosopher to the junior, but in general the two regarded each other as colleagues and honoured their differences of opinion. Steinthal had a great admiration for Heyse, more than for Hegel. That this admiration was mutual is expressed by Heyse's last wish that Steinthal would publish his (Heyse's) *System der Sprachwissenschaft* (System of Language Science), on which he had worked for so many years. Steinthal edited the text and the book was published in 1856.

STEINTHAL'S PSYCHOLINGUISTICS

Others have examined Steinthal's views on language (Bumann, 1965; Christy, 1987, 1998; see also various chapters in Wiedebach & Winkelmann, 2002). First of all— this was how he thought of himself—he can be regarded as a commentator on, or rather conservator of, Humboldt's views on language. Second, he contributed significantly to these ideas by claiming that language and language change should be conceptualised from a psychological point of view. And thus he is regarded by Wundt (1901), as well as by one of the founders of current psycholinguistics, Levelt (1992), as the founder of psycholinguistics. Levelt, however, does not mention Steinthal's work on aphasia. But I would like to propose that, to the best of my knowledge, Steinthal may be considered the first neurolinguist. One may argue that neurolinguistics aims to reveal the linguistic regularities that govern patterns of language loss after brain lesions, rather than the localisation of so-called language organs.

Let us first look at Steinthal's views on language. The lowest level of language, he argues, is formed by an emotion-based representation of experiences or impressions ("Wahrnehmung"). At this level the utterance of sounds is a reflex action. By "sound" Steinthal means the sound representation of a word, which in infant speech may not be a regular word. The sound represents the " totality", i.e., a person or animal or object in action, in motion, or following a movement. One can never observe just a person or an object, nor is it possible to see only a movement or a situation. The two are always observed together. At this level the conceptualisation of an object always contains an activity or a situation, so that at the onset the mind has comprehensive images of events (processes, actions, "Vorgänge"). For instance, the expression "waf" of a child may refer to a barking dog. The onomatopoeic sound reflex is a sound sign because, and as long as, it represents entire perceptions and impressions.

Only when it signifies a single moment of an impression—an object or a feature—does it become a word At the same time, this means that the close relationship between meaning and feelings is lost. The role of feelings now becomes increasingly weaker. Impressions can be evoked directly through the sound. How does a human mind get from a "word-less" stage to the level at which speech is produced in sentences? The development of real language requires social interaction. The major impetus underlying the development of speech is the desire to know what the other party does, where they are, or to communicate to a third party what the other is doing. An extremely important condition is the development of the notion of a person, an individual, or a subject. Perceiving people in action, with varying features, is a basis for this. However, more important is the perception of changes in the child-self: This results in self-consciousness. Self-consciousness is stimulated particularly by play activity, by the manipulation of objects, where form changes occur without changing the material.

A child begins with understanding and imitating onomatopoeic expressions from adults: e.g., bow-wow. This bow-wow is neither a noun nor a verb nor an adjective; it is not object, action, or feature but it stands for everything the dog is and does. The entire meaning cluster, the interwoven mass of related impressions, is represented, replaced in the child's consciousness. Soon the child finds out that there are more bow-wows, and that his bow-wow can be in different positions or conditions, where bow-wow becomes a centre to which perceived differences and distinctions are attached. In this way, bow-wow becomes subject and the changing features the predicate. This leads to the notion that there first is an object, which is related to the second object in a particular way. In psychological terms: first the child has an impression AN, and later an impression AO (e.g., mother sitting inside the house and mother walking outside the house), and these two have to be connected to each other. The fused common part of the connected impressions will stimulate the development of the subject, and the inhibiting specific aspects will be transformed into the predicate, according to the following formula:

$$AN + AO = (A2 - O + N)R$$

where A is the subject, N and O the predicate, and R is the copula, indicating the rule according to which A can be both O and N. R is the hyphen between the impressions AN and AO.

Later in development, the specific elements are not inhibited by the general impression and a struggle begins between the different impressions that are related to each other ("Verflechtung"; interwoven cluster of elements). The hyphen between related impressions becomes the copula, and the impression-cluster turns itself into a subject and a predicate. Language makes it possible to fixate the analysed elements by replacing them with symbols, namely words. Speaking about how the form or structure of an utterance is produced, Steinthal claims the following: There is only so much structure and exactly that structure which is necessary to represent a meaning. A language has a structure in the sense that it represents meanings in forms. There is no general scheme of categories underlying the development of all languages. What Steinthal is trying to say here is that there are no grammatical structures independent of content. Grammatical complexity derives from the differentiation of images.

LANGUAGE DISORDERS

Having explained the language system in general, Steinthal turns to several pathological phenomena in order to provide a more detailed illustration of the language system (Steinthal, 1871, pp. 599–649). In his view *stammering* is the incapacity to produce certain individual sounds, which is due to an anatomical fault either in the speech organs or in the brain. It is an articulation failure. *Stuttering*, however, is a momentarily occurring disorder of speech, elicited by particular states of mind (moods). It is conditioned by cramps in the muscles that should function during speech. It is a defect in breathing and sounding. The speech organs or the brain are not affected. *Anarthria* is, according to Steinthal, a permanent incapacity to utter words that the patient has in consciousness since he/she can write them. In this disease the speech organs are intact—however, either the motor centre for speech is affected or the pathway between this motor and the psychic centre for speech is inhibited, so that the commands of the latter are not executed.

Steinthal defines all this within a single page without giving any further considerations. Apparently, to him, this is all very clear and simple. The concepts for motor and psychic centres for speech are obviously concepts that do not require any further clarifications, just like the idea that there is a pathway between these two centres, and that this connective pathway can be disrupted, leaving the centres intact and nevertheless resulting in a language disorder. All this was written in 1871, three years before the publication of Wernicke's book! This suggests that the notion of language centres connected to each other (and disconnected by lesions) was already more widely accepted.

Finally, Steinthal describes several phenomena that fall under the notion of *aphasia*. Aphasia is commonly understood, so Steinthal writes, as the acquired inhibition or abolishment of the inner word formation ("Wort-Bildung") caused by a deficit in the functioning of the psychic centre for speech without the articulation mechanism being affected. Consequently, either no sound form of a word ("Wortlaut") or a wrong sound form is found for the images available. When a word is uttered, it is done without any effort or overtly visible difficulty. In these cases the disorder concerns the inner word itself.

Steinthal says that different gradations of aphasia can easily be observed. First of all, there can be a complete absence of words ("Wortmangel"). In these cases intelligence may often be affected and anarthria can also be observed. But, even so, some words are usually still available and these are then used on every occasion. These words are, for example, a date, a name, or a frequently used curse. We would refer to these as "recurring utterances".

Steinthal regards the cases with pure aphasia of more interest where particular word groups are affected. In these cases the words that represent certain images simply do not come forward, although they are at the patient's disposition. The categories that are usually lost are nouns, in particular names, while verbs and other word classes remain available. Speech is fluent and the patient may even be talkative ("red-selig")! The patient may start a sentence properly, but then stop as soon as a main word is accessed. It is also possible that wrong names are used, such as stick for hat. In these cases the patient knows that an error has occurred and expresses regret or frustration. We would refer to this as anomia or amnestic aphasia. An even higher grade of aphasia is present when the patient no longer understands words. A general lack of understanding of symbols is described as asemia; a disorder described by Finkelnburg in 1870 in Berlin.

APHASIA EXPLAINED

Let us now consider Steinthal's explanation of aphasic phenomena. He starts by describing the conclusions of "the neurologists"; the views of Broca spread across France and Germany in a few years, and in the discussions of the Berlin Anthropological Society, to which I shall return later, the neurologists speak with great admiration of Broca's work. These neurologists, so Steinthal argues, had reached the conclusion that, apart from the general centre for intelligence, the function of speech is governed by two independent centres: first, a centre steering the materialistic mechanism of articulation, that is, the motor or sound centre, and second a centre for the psychic side of language. Steinthal subscribed wholeheartedly to this trinity but believed that additional evidence was necessary. There is no doubt about the function or the localisation of the motor centre. It lies beneath the corpora quadrigemina and stretches from the pons to the olivaries. It contains the origin of all nerves that go to the muscles of the tongue, the palate, the larynx, and the face (hypoglossus, vagus, and facialis). Damage to this centre will result in anarthria. With respect to the second centre, there is not only much discussion but also the entire conceptualisation is, from Steinthal's point of view, defective. Damage to this centre was thought to result in aphasia. In an effort to find the exact site, the doctors neglected to observe, in detail, the psychological phenomena of the disorder.

Words and sentences: Aphasia and akataphasia

We now get to the point where Steinthal explains different aphasic phenomena. He starts from the assumption that our mental possessions consist of several larger and smaller clusters of knowledge ("Erkenntnis-Gruppen") and judgements, which are each independent to a large extent, even when they are related to each other. According to the purely psychological theory, it is easy to understand that symbolic clusters are, in comparison to object clusters ("Sach-Gruppen"), more vulnerable and restore more slowly after damage—the reason being that all associations based on unnatural or artificial hyphens (and symbols belong to these) have less power and are more easily deranged than those based on objective relations. This also explains why proper names disappear from memory first, since they are related to a person or a place with an individual association. Steinthal also believed that from his exposition of the development of the sentence form it follows that verbs and adjectives are retained better than nouns. It is obvious that the word is much more important for the formulation of motion (or activity) images and qualitative images than it is for the images of objects, which are much closer to the impressions. One can have the image of an object without having the word for it, but a feature or an activity is mostly thought of in words, since they are abstract.

Steinthal now distinguishes the following pathological conditions. First, aphasia may occur primarily in the form in which the reproduction of the word form is impossible. The problem lies in the activation of the word form (the string of sounds). The patient may produce the wrong words, but is aware of erring.

In a second form the patient does not notice mistakes, but believes he/she has used the right word; in this case judgement is affected. Judgement implies comparison, and this is, as with relations in general, not possible without sufficient "reproduction power".[5] Patients may echo words, perseverate, and use words that are associated to words heard. Usually, in this form of aphasia the patient will understand what has been said. Sometimes, however, the reproduction capacity for sound forms is so weakened that the patient cannot comprehend.

Third, at first this lack of judgement and freedom extends over words as mere sound forms. However, the sound forms are associated to an image, causing a more serious language capacity disorder in which the patient is incapable of reproducing not only the sound form but also the image itself. In this case the speech process itself whereby the function of transforming a concept into an image occurs, i.e., the sentence formation, is inhibited. These two levels (mentioned in the first and third points) should be distinguished. This distinction between the two forms seems to be so important to Steinthal that he suggests naming the first *aphasia* and the second *akataphasia*.

This distinction can also be formulated in another way. Language as a psychic mechanism consists on the one hand of an immense number of images An (subjects) and Nn (predicates); on the other hand there are methods (laws, rules) and means (particles, forms) to connect these images in order to form sentences. Accordingly, apart from expressing the meaning, the correct construction of sentences is a purpose of language, indeed its second purpose. Of course, as a means, it is subordinate to the content, nevertheless is something that has to be achieved in itself. Whenever it happens that the mechanism of consciousness does not produce the An (e.g., mother) and Nn (e.g., walking) necessary for representing the content, *aphasia* occurs. However, it is also possible that the power is lacking to apperceive, or connect, the images according to the grammatical laws: this we call *akataphasia*.

Fourth, there may be a disturbance of intelligence, with or without aphasia. These patients may for instance use general formula, without a specific content (empty speech).

Fifth, there is sometimes a lack of control where the patient cannot voluntarily stop. This may occur in slightly affected patients or during recovery. Other impressions take over the formulation process.

---

[5] We would probably use terms like "activation" or "resources".

Sixth, often, but not always, both symbolic speech production and understanding are disturbed. However, understanding may remain while the production is disturbed. Apparently Steinthal does not believe that it can be the other way round: intact speech production with disturbed understanding is impossible!

BERLIN ANTHROPOLOGICAL SOCIETY

Interesting information about Steinthal's views on aphasia can be found in the minutes of a meeting of the members of the Berlin Anthropological Society, which occurred in 1874, three years after the publication of his book (see also Jacyna, 1999). This meeting was a continuation of two earlier meetings during which Hitzig had argued that the individual psychic faculties are focally localised in the cortex, followed by a presentation by Westphal, who claimed that the symptoms of the language disorders he had presented demonstrated that the faculty of speech cannot be definitely localised in the cortex.

The discussants were Virchow, Westphal, Hitzig, Simon, Steinthal, and Lazarus, but the main speaker was Steinthal. The point he wanted to make was that neurologists, when analysing aphasic phenomena, should do this with a more sophisticated notion in the back of their minds on how the language system operates. He felt that they should respect the distinctions that psychologists had made; namely, the sound, the images, and the process of analysing images and thus forming sentences.

Steinthal seemed to disagree with both Hitzig and Westphal, but he mostly revealed his opinion by asking difficult questions. For example, he asked Hitzig whether he believed that the three different aspects that are to be distinguished in language behaviour are localised on the same spot. He asked this question despite the fact that Hitzig had already expressed his belief in the single spot localisation of language. In contrast to Westphal, Steinthal felt that a classification of symptoms would be possible, if one began from a psychological description of the speech process. In this context he explicitly warns against the erroneous procedure of classifying patients instead of symptoms, a mistake also noticed by Ria de Bleser (1987) in her historical review of the concepts of agrammatism and paragrammatism.

It seems that in the meeting there were two distinct camps: the neurologists and the psychologists. In fact, Steinthal, supported by Lazarus, formed the latter party. Virchow referred to them belittlingly as "the gentlemen of the language side". Steinthal was accused of thinking too lightly about the complex phenomena, and Westphal simply stated that the "gentlemen psychologists" should make the effort to study the phenomena of aphasic speech in the patients themselves, and they were invited to do so in his clinic. Steinthal snappily replied that he had already extensively described (in the "Abriss" in 1871) the phenomena and how they could be interpreted. Apparently Westphal knew this work but believed it to be based on only reading about aphasia rather than observing aphasic speech.

DISCUSSION

Taking a closer look at Steinthal's classification of language disorders and his explanation of the underlying nature of the functional deficit, some remarks can be made. First of all, he starts from a psychological theory of normal language functioning, the main text of the 1871 book preceding the "addendum" on language disorders. Starting from a (more or less) elaborated theory of normal language processing is not a common procedure in 19th- or even 20th-century aphasiology. Nineteenth-century aphasiologists focused on the issue of localisation, and mostly took for granted the idea that language can be regarded as word production and word perception. Broca, for instance, indicated that he realised there was more to language than speaking a word, but what he wrote about that can hardly be called a language-processing model (Eling, 1994). Wernicke (1874) discussed the necessity or rather the superfluity of a "concept" as an independent representation, but to him language was very much a sensory-motor process, relating incoming images to motor images for words. He did use the notion of a concept centre, but he argued that this centre cannot be localised in a circumscribed spot on the cortex—rather, it involved the entire cortex (Eggert, 1977).

Unlike most aphasiologists Steinthal did not bother to write much about localisation, at least not in terms of cortical centres. Yet he used the notion of cortical centres. It is sometimes assumed that Wernicke introduced this manner of localising psychological functions in centres, connected to each other by pathways. But of course this was done by others before Wernicke, for instance by Bastian in 1869 (Marshall, 1994) and by Adolf Baginsky in 1871 (Eling, 2005). As argued above, the fact that Steinthal used the concept of centres without bothering to elaborate on it suggests that the notion was quite familiar. And indeed Wernicke (1874) himself argued that his view of language centres was not new at all, but he claimed to have found clinical and anatomical evidence for the localisation of the various centres and the pathways connecting them. Although Steinthal subscribed to a trinity of centres, it is doubtful whether the psychic centre for language can be compared to any of the centres in Wernicke's model from 1874, or to the conceptual centre in Lichtheim's (1885) adaptation of that model. For instance, according to Steinthal the language centre is responsible for transforming images into sentences and vice versa. Sentences are not discussed in the work of Wernicke or Lichtheim.

Steinthal did make a distinction between brainstem lesions affecting motor processes and other lesions causing language disorders. However, in his view lesions affecting the language process do not result in a *loss* of specific linguistic representations or images, but they cause a reduction of "reproductive power" or capacity to activate clusters of associated elements, a processing problem. This is a different paradigm from the one the aphasiologists were using. Yet Steinthal's approach was based on a view of the working of the mind that was widely accepted. Herbart's books on psychology were generally used as introductory texts and indeed formed the framework in which Wundt developed his general psychology. This suggests that a rejection or neglect of Steinthal's neurolinguistic approach cannot easily be ascribed to unfamiliarity with the psychological processes described by Steinthal. In the discussion in the Berlin Anthropological Society the medical doctors do not reject the psycholinguistic model as such, but accuse the psychologists of having no idea what aphasia looks like.

Another important feature that distinguishes Steinthal's theory from that of most contemporary aphasiologists was the absence of input and output representations. Reduction of reproductive power may lead to difficulties in activating word images but this will cause problems in both language comprehension and production. Akataphasia is a problem in connecting elements, nouns and verbs, into a complex image (comprehension), or analysing a complex image into its constituting elements. Both modalities suffer from a reduction in activation. To Steinthal, language processing was essentially a process, in which (abstract) symbols replaced (concrete) images. In contrast, most aphasiologists, even in the 20th century, made a distinction between disorders of language production and language perception. Only very severe aphasic patients, now diagnosed as suffering from global aphasia, were considered to have problems in both modalities. But patients suffering from Broca's aphasia were generally considered to have intact comprehension. The notion that Broca patients not only have problems producing grammatically correct sentences, but also cannot understand sentences correctly, as suggested by Zurif, Caramazza, and Meyerson (1972), would have been obvious to Steinthal. This difference in conceptualisation of language as a sensori-motor function versus a process involving abstract symbols may well be the result of the fact that aphasiologists attempted to emphasise that language disorders should be explained in terms of physiological and anatomical terms, while Steinthal stressed the psychological processes.

CONCLUSION

Steinthal did a fine job by stressing the need for a good psychological theory as a basis for analysing the physiology of the brain. Perhaps one cannot sympathise with his views on the relation between psychology and linguistics, and his beliefs about the origin of linguistic regularities. Nevertheless, one must credit him for his attempt to construct a consistent language system, useful for understanding language phenomena in completely different areas of language science. At least he attacked brain damage and aphasia from the "right" side: the psychological side.

It seems to me that many of Steinthal's contemporaries, philologists as well as physicians, had problems understanding the value of his insights. Some of the lessons that these scientists, as well as many after them, neglected are the following:

- One should study aphasia using a theory of (normal) language processing.
- One should study psycholinguistic phenomena, symptoms, rather than patients or syndromes.
- Language belongs to the domain of psychology.
- It all starts with feelings that need to be expressed.

My favourite lesson from Steinthal is one that I think is worth remembering in these modern times of brain imaging, carrying the risk of "neophrenology" (Uttal, 2001): "Psychology is a work most necessary to be done before one can start a physiology of the brain and it allows also for a rational psychiatry" (Steinthal, 1871, p. 473, par. 631).

REFERENCES

Boring, E. G. (1957). *A history of experimental psychology* (2nd ed.). Englewood Cliffs NJ: Prentice Hall.

Bumann, W. (1965). *Die Sprachtheorie Heymann Steinthals*. Meisenheim an Glan: Anton Hain.

Christy, T. C. (1987). Steinthal and the development of linguistic science: The convergence of psychology and linguistics. In H. Aarsleff, L. G. Kelly, & H. J. Niederehe (Eds.), *Papers in the history of linguistics*. Amsterdam: Benjamins.

Christy, T. C. (1989). Reflex sounds and the experiential manifold: Steinthal on the origin of language. In J. Gessinger & W. von Rahden (Eds.), *Theorien vom Ursprung der Sprache*. Berlin: Walter de Gruyter.

De Bleser, R. (1987). From agrammatism to paragrammatism: German aphasiological traditions and grammatical disturbances. *Cognitive Neuropsychology*, *4*, 187–256.

Eggert, G. (1977). *Wernicke's works on aphasia. A sourcebook and review*. The Hague: Mouton.

Eling, P. (1994). Broca. In P. Eling (Ed.), *Reader in the history of aphasia*. Amsterdam: Benjamins.

Eling, P. (2005). Baginsky on aphasia. *Journal of Neurolinguistics, 18,* 301–315.

Finkelburg, F. (1870). Niederrheinische Gesellschaft in Bonn: Medizinische Section. *Berliner klinische Wochenschrift, 7,* 449–450, 460–461.

Jacyna, S. (1999). The 1874 aphasia debate in the Berliner Gesellschaft fuer Anthropologie. *Brain and Language, 69,* 5–15.

Levelt, W. (1992). Psycholinguistics. In W. Bright (Ed.), *International encyclopedia of linguistics Vol. 3.* New York: Oxford University Press.

Lichtheim, L. (1885). On aphasia. *Brain, 7,* 433–484.

Marshall, J. (1994). Bastian. In P. Eling (Ed.), *Reader in the history of aphasia*. Amsterdam: Benjamins.

Steinthal, H. (1871). *Abriss der Sprachwissenschaften*. Berlin: Harrwitz und Gossmann.

Uttal, W. (2001). *Brain imaging and the new phrenology*. Cambridge, MA: MIT Press.

Wernicke, C. (1874). *Der aphasische Symptomenkomplex. Eine psychologische Studie auf anatomischer Basis*. Breslau: Cohn & Weigert.

Wiedebach, H., & Winkelmann, A. (2002). Einleitung. In H. Wiedebach & A. Winkelmann (Eds.), *Chajim Steinthal: Sprachwissenschaftler and Philosoph im 19. Jahrhundert*. Leiden: Brill.

Wundt, W. (1901). *Sprachgeschichte und Sprachpsychologie*. Leipzig: Engelmann.

Zurif, E., Caramazza, A., & Meyerson, R. (1972). Grammatical judgements of agrammatic aphasics. *Neuropsychologia, 10,* 405–417.

Was Sigmund Freud the first neogrammarian neurolinguist?

Hugh W. Buckingham

Louisiana State University, Baton Rouge, LA, USA

Background: Over 30 years ago in a paper, John C. Marshall suggested that Sigmund Freud was the first neogrammarian neurolinguist. This claim has only rarely been assessed in any depth as to its plausibility. Nevertheless, the issues, ideas, and personalities that Marshall in his study considered were significant in 19th-century neuropsychology, were being debated at the time he wrote his paper, and are still among the major questions being asked today in the "mind/brain" approach to modern neuroscience.

Aims: The primary objective of the present contribution to John's Festschrift is to revisit his evaluation of Freud as the first neogrammarian neurolinguist. The basic point Marshall was considering was that Freud not only seriously read, understood, and incorporated the current works of anatomy and classical aphasiology, but also brought to bear on his theories works from the newly formed fields of evolutionary psychology and historical linguistics. The present paper will show how Freud wove these areas together within a framework of "mind and brain", opting to work at the abstract levels of language description that were more in line with the ways in which psychologists and linguists approached the study of human language.

Main Contribution: The paper demonstrates the value of Marshall's claim as a focal point for an historical analysis of the contributions from psychology and linguistics to the early scientific study of language and the brain, and traces the often unappreciated role of 19th-century Indo-European linguistics, especially in the case where those, such as Berthold Delbruck, dared to delve into the data of aphasia—largely the anomias.

Conclusions: The compatible descriptive levels of psychology and linguistics served to guide the early formulations of a more mentalistic and less physicalistic nature of the aphasias, an account that reflects the 19th-century coalescence of the fields of historical, psycho- and neuro-linguistics. Whether Berthold Delbruck, the neogrammarian, deserves to be given equal billing as the first neogrammarian neurolinguist is considered, and the conclusion is that, indeed, he does.

In this paper I would like to assess John Marshall's (1974, p. 359) claim that, "Historically, then, Freud falls into place as the first neo-grammarian neurolinguist." In earlier work (Buckingham, 1980, 1982a), I discussed Marshall's proposition and traced how he arrived at his conclusion about Freud, the interdisciplinarian. For the most part, Marshall seems to have been right on target. Freud did not partake in the physicalist exuberance of August Comte's positivism of the period, a concept of science as deterministic and crucially grounded in physical reality. Positivism reflected a major contemporary movement in European science and thought, and played into the classical positions on language localisation in the

Address correspondence to: Hugh W. Buckingham PhD, Department of Communication Sciences & Disorders, Louisiana State University, Baton Rouge, LA 70803, USA. E-mail: hbuck@lsu.edu

brain throughout the 19th century from the phrenologists (see Lorch, 2006 this issue) through the major works of the "diagram makers". Freud nevertheless naturally sought support from the less positivist positions on the nature of language and the brain extant in this period. In addition to a certain few later 19th-century non-localisationists practising medicine and seeing patients—neurologists such as Jean-Martin Charcot, John Hughlings-Jackson, and Adolph Kussmaul, but there were a growing number of psychological theorists such as Herbert Spencer and Heymann (Chajim) Steinthal—there was a growing number of linguists out of the tradition of philological studies, largely devoted to the study of the historical formation of words, mainly etymologies.

In the late 18th and early 19th centuries there was an upsurge of studies of human language families and the evolutionary/linguistic history of these families—the overwhelming focus being the Indo-European family, its subdivisions, and the history of each. A natural outcome of this study was the development of techniques of working backwards to arrive at the best approximation of earlier forms of each language grouping—the so-called ancestral or "proto-language". In turn, the regression from the group of "mother languages" back to even earlier forms uncovered through "reconstruction" a "proto-Indo-European" language, perched at the top of the family tree (the "stammbaum" of August Schleicher) of the Indo-European language family (Robins, 1967).

These evolutionary and historical reconstruction analyses took increasing complexity in shape and form, and the linguistic techniques and procedures used in the inquiry unfolded into a paradigm of linguistic analysis, the linguists involved eventually becoming collectively referred to as the "neogrammarians", or the new grammarians. The study of "grammar" had been practised for centuries, but the "new" grammarians brought with them an ever-increasing sophistication of language analysis, and a set of epistemological and metaphysical assumptions that for the most part aligned them with non-positivist thinking regarding the psychological and functional levels of mentality. Essentially, a psycholinguistic descriptive level was slowly developing in the study of linguistic phenomena, some of which was directed at the aphasias but not directly mappable to any physical disruption.

Freud turned to these studies in his book on aphasia (1891) and thus there is reason to believe that he was indeed the first *neogrammarian* neurolinguist. Marshall is thus vindicated, and in this present paper I want to extend the discussion of the issues and refer to some recent work that sheds more light on the issues. One important recent study (Greenberg, 1997) will be treated in this paper, although the author of that study claims (p. 42, footnote 21) that Marshall stated the case for calling Freud the first neogrammarian neurolinguist more strongly than she would. I will also integrate the recent work of Stephen Jacyna (2000) in my exploration of Freud's theory and method.

WHAT WAS A NEOGRAMMARIAN?

In the spirit of positivism, inviolable "laws" in science began to appear, and it was not long until the term "law" was applied to the many observed sound changes in language families, laws that were then claimed to be regular and to have no exceptions. A combination of the search for a "law-like" dynamism, and then sub-laws that would explain exceptions, became the signpost of the work of a growing group of language researchers who came to be known as the "young grammarians" (in the sense of "young Turks"); these "Junggrammaticker" were the "neogrammarians". Their linguistic analytical techniques and influence solidified in the mid 1870s, and some of the principal scholars included Berthold Delbruck and many others such as Brugmann, Leskien, Osthoff, and Hermann Paul (Campbell, 2001, p. 92). Campbell (2001, p. 92) points out that "sound laws" in actuality meant "sound changes" patterned and characterised as laws. At the time, the term "law" linked linguistics (inherently mentalistic) with the "harder" sciences and their more rigorous "law like statements" (p. 92); in this sense, the neogrammarians fell into line with the reigning positivism of the day. Those linguists who studied dialect variation at any one time in a language community began to doubt the veracity of law-like consistency. The variation observed among dialects of the same language seemed to cast doubt on strict lawfulness in language systems, but eventually it was realised that many of the puzzling exceptions to the "laws" nevertheless had lawful or patterned conditions themselves. Many have noted the prodromes of structural linguistics in the work of the "Junggrammatiker", the "young Turks" of grammar (my English translation).

Historical linguistics and the methods of reconstruction of proto-forms achieved a great vigour towards the close of the 19th century. A psychological historicism enveloped the methods and assumptions of the neogrammarians. In a real sense, these early linguistics were crafting a science for the study of human language, and thus were reflecting the positivism of the day. Theories of evolution held sway, and in line with Herbert Spencer's psychology, the neogrammarians took both and suggested that there was a proper evolution of the mind—language being of the mind. Sound change as sound substitution naturally led to the comparison of sound alterations in distinct domains: dialect variation, historical change, and variations noted in child language-learning patterns. Substitution was the primary mechanism thought to be involved in diachronic sound change and in synchronic dialect variation. Children's language errors during ontogeny were also described as substitutions of segments or of full words—the principal elements investigated by language scientists of the day. The notions of "deeply" rooted historical forms in diachrony and the "underlying" structures in synchrony began to look like two sides of the same coin. "Underlying" also mirrored the notion of recondite elements resting just beneath activation thresholds, or abstract forms and representations that had to undergo a set of "derivations" in order to arrive at the surface level of utterance from the "deep structure". The historicism and psychologism became cornerstone assumptions in the work of the neogrammarians.

Interestingly, these two assumptions influenced a smaller group of physicians, such as John Hughlings-Jackson, Karl Finkelnburg, Adolph Kussmaul and, of course, Sigmund Freud. In addition, many of these language investigators used the "organ" metaphor and began referring to language as an "organ". Unlike the metaphor of "faculty", the organ metaphor, developed earlier by Johann Gottfried von Herder, had a physical ring to it but was nonetheless simply a metaphor. The deeply mentalistic assumptions of the linguists of the time, their psychology of the mind and its historical bent, were extremely attractive to Freud and turned out to offer him an alternative model of language with which to investigate aphasia, but also, more importantly, with which to do battle with the classical aphasiologists of the last quarter of the 19th century, such as Karl Wernicke and Ludwig Lichtheim.

WHO DID FREUD READ?

Hughlings Jackson

Every account of Freud's book on aphasia mentions his profound debt to John Hughlings Jackson, who had from his earliest publications worked within the framework laid down by Herbert Spencer (1855), an admixture of evolution and psychology that focused on the mind in terms of the mental idiom that its analysis required. Hughlings Jackson was a physician and no neogrammarian, although his theoretical perspective on language and aphasia fell in line with theirs. Throughout his writings, Jackson stressed the need to keep clearly separate the physical and its descriptive argot from the cant of psychology, cast as it was at some remove from the physical level. Although Freud tended to eschew the strict wording of Jackson's notion of mind–brain concomitance and psycho-physical parallelism (see Buckingham, 1986; Engelhardt, 1975; Greenberg, 1997, p. 45; Jacyna, 2000, p. 126; Marx, 1967), the two physicians were in complete accord in their strict separation of mind and brain, psychology and physiology, both hastening to point out that as language is essentially a psychological (and therefore mental) object, it is more properly understood as a non-physical object. Wallesch (2004, p. 394) quotes Freud on the mind–matter correlation (or interaction), where the latter wrote:

> The chain of physiological events in the nervous system is probably [note Freud's hedge—HWB] not causally related to psychological processes. The physiological events do not stop when psychological events start. Instead, the physiological chain continues, although from a certain point in time onward, its links correspond with psychological phenomena. Therefore, the psychological is a parallel process of the physiological.

Jackson's and Freud's reasoning was that since language was a psychological object, and therefore "of the mind", its natural history would follow the dictates of Spencer who had just called for a sort of Darwinian evolution of mind as opposed to the body. In addition, both incorporated Charcot's notion that the disturbed behaviour of non-organic and organic hysterias revealed few qualitative differences, both requiring descriptions in functional terminology (Greenberg, 1997, p. 18, fn 15; pp. 94–100; pp. 153–154). Jackson and Freud also appeared to make a "lapsus linguae" analogue of the non-organic hysterias. That is, Freud cited Jackson when he noted that the paraphasias of patients with aphasia are essentially like the slips-of-the-tongue in non-pathologically compromised human speakers. More on slips later. In sum, Freud was thoroughly familiar with the work of Hughlings Jackson, and accolades were numerous throughout his book on aphasia.

Jean-Marie Charcot

As with Hughlings Jackson, most writers on Freud's aphasia study mention his several months' visit to Charcot's clinic at the Salpetrière in Paris from September 1885 to February of the following year (e.g., Greenberg, 1997, pp. 94–95; Marshall, 1974, pp. 354–345; Wallesch, 2004, p. 390). There is some disagreement in the literature as to precisely how long Freud stayed in Paris (Buckingham, 1999, p. 80; Eling, 1994, p. 171). In any event, Freud was largely interested in Charcot's patients who had no known nervous system damage, but whose behaviour mirrored much of the behavioural aberrances of patients with discernable brain damage. For the non-pathologically involved, Charcot considered that there was a "functional" lesion, and that the proper way to describe the patients' actual disturbed behavioural patterns rested with a scientific terminology that was psychological in nature and at some remove from a physical level. In fact, it was fully proper as well, therefore, to describe the hysterias caused by nervous system damage at the same mentalistic level used for the hysterias from a "functional lesion". This stance more or less fell in line with Hughlings Jackson, and his very important slip analogy to the hysterias caused by a "functional" lesion. Hughlings Jackson had introduced the non-pathological linguistic error of the lapsus linguae, or the slip-of-the-tongue (Buckingham, 1999, p. 81). Like the non-pathological hysterical behaviours, the slip in normals was due to a derailment in focus, attention, increased emotionality, and in other minimally altered states of mind. The paraphasia, then, came to be appreciated as the analogue to the patho-physiologically caused hysterias. In similar fashion, the paraphasias were increasingly analysed and explained with like functional vocabularies. The full segmental appreciation of the paraphasias below the level of the word was obviously not appreciated until a bit later than the appearance of Freud's book. Freud more or less came to agree with the linguistic analyses of Delbruck, but Delbruck's accounts reflected earlier theories of language production by investigators such as Jacques Lordat (Bay, 1969; Lecours, Nespoulous, & Pioger, 1987; Nespoulous, Code, Virbel, & Lecours, 1998), where the sequential ordering of lexical segments was felt to be routinely automatised over time to such a degree that words were felt to be produced by an overlearned motoric chaining of the segmental makeup of words—a process that rendered the segmental level cognitively chunked with unparsable segments. The term "segment" is best here, since de Courtnay's ultimate fashioning of the unit called the phoneme had not yet made its appearance (Robins, 1967). Words, however, were segmentable, and so the paraphasias were initially cast at that level. In any event, it was Charcot's notion of the "functional lesion" that most impressed Freud.

Chajim Steinthal

Any study of the neogrammarian influence on Freud must appreciate the crucial role of Steinthal (1823–1899) and his cross-discipline contributions to 19th-century psycholinguistic and neurolinguistic thought (see Eling, 1994). A student of Wilhelm von Homboldt, Steinthal was well read in the classics, in the language sciences of the day, and in the historical transition from philosophy to "natural philosophy" and from there to the 19th-century "birth" of the discipline of psychology, although historically it is often difficult to find "births". Greenberg (1997, p. 42) stresses that it was Steinthal's inquiries into aphasia and his psychological approach to its study that influenced Freud. His psychologism, and the mentalistic functionalism it assumed, ensured that his analyses would fall in line with the linguistic studies of the day. According to Greenberg (1997, p. 42), "His interest in aphasia from the linguistic perspective makes Steinthal a lynchpin in the connections that tie Freud's study to language theory" and that in terms of the neogrammarian connection, Steinthal's work, "... passes via Hermann Paul to Berthold Delbruck, who is the only linguist-philologist Freud cites." Steinthal was critical of the localisationist emphasis on aphasia description and classification, noting often that the medical publications lacked any sophisticated awareness of the underlying complexities of human language, preferring rather to locate more closely the regions whose damage gave rise to one or another of the classical syndromes of aphasia. The overwhelming strength of resolve of the localisationists in the 19th century, and in fact of the 20th-century neo-localisationist model of Norman Geschwind (Devinsky & Schacter, 1997; Schacter & Devinsky, 1997), served to play down the competing functional/psychological takes on aphasia and brain correlations that went beyond a mere continuation of the century's old association psychology (Buckingham, 2002). That is, the subtitle of the localisationist Karl Wernicke was "A psychological study of an anatomic base". The psychology, however, was the psychology of the classical models, and that in turn was simply an extension of the same psychological theories that actually led to behaviourism and more comfortably agreed with the positivism of the late 19th century. It was natural to incorporate associationistic accounts of paraphasic errors, because the early descriptions of the error–target relationships highlighted the ancient parameters of associative bonding by similarity, and even more importantly by contiguity (or collocation), or by function (Buckingham, 2002). Greenberg (1997, p. 42) points to the overarching dominance of associationism, concluding that Steinthal and Freud were essentially associationists as far as their linguistics went. She draws from Katherine Arens (1984) who wrote that the redefinition of philology by Steinthal and others was "... on semantics as based on psychological rules of associationism" (p. 42). If Steinthal's psychology was, indeed, scaffolded across association psychology, it should nevertheless be made clear that his superimposition of the model onto the lateral surface of the left hemisphere was not the cornerstone of his claims. The classical localisers of language function made these superimpositions (Jacyna, 2000, p. 107) of their associational "diagrams" with a vengeance. Teasing apart the tenets of association psychology from other non-associationist psychologies has been part and parcel of the history of the psycho- and neuro-linguistic investigations of the cognition of human language structure and function.

Nevertheless, Freud owes much to Chajim Steinthal, who plays a crucial role in the history of psycholinguistics, and who influenced another major player in the formation of Freud's thought: Adolf Kussmaul, a physician with a non-physical appreciation of the cognitive and linguistic epiphenomena of brain damage (Buckingham, 1982a; Greenberg, 1997; Jarema, 1993; Marx, 1967).

Adolf Kussmaul

Adolf Kussmaul (1822–1902), not considered a neogrammarian, was thoroughly integrated by Freud in his book on aphasia. Greenberg (1997) delves deeply into Kussmaul's position on language, aphasia, and the brain. Although Kussmaul's psychology of language was largely associationistic, he superimposed none of his models on the brain; he was a non-localiser physician in the sense of Hughlings Jackson and Charcot, and thus would not reject the notion of a "functional lesion". Although a physician, Kussmaul delved into the Spencerian evolution of the mind and adopted the evolutionary historicism of Steinthal and the neogrammarians. According to Greenberg (1997), he synthesised the associationistic, the evolutionary, and the linguist's view of language "disinvolution" from aphasia or from ageing from breakdown in language association structure. It was Kussmaul who, according to Greenberg (1997, p. 41), "... was a key figure in early aphasia studies and perhaps the only researcher who truly bridged the medicine/linguistics gap." I would hasten to point out, however, that no physician—even Kussmaul—despite being well versed in the complexities of language, ever dared to write an article on proto-Balto-Slavic reconstruction or on the syntax of the Sanskrit dative. However, at least Delbruck (1886) and Baudouin de Courtenay (1886/1972), wrote papers on aphasia (Buckingham, 1982a). Greenberg (1997, p. 43) points out that Kussmaul's historicism extends even to historical linguistic themes, and to a footnote in one of Kussmaul's publications on the etymology of the Indo-European root MAR, tracing it through time and variations in form from Latin, Greek, Irish, Bohemian, Lithuanian, Sanskrit, and some others, up to modern German.

Crucially, Kussmaul felt language was the product of "unconscious", implicit knowledge, and in fact, he stressed that all conscious/volitional activity is prepared "... in the unconscious" (Greenberg, 1997, p. 44). In fact, Kussmaul's notions come very close to using the unconscious as a planning stage for language production— and, of course, Freud linked to this notion and added to it a wider range of preconscious segments and ideas that may be aroused by the semantic, the phonological, or a combination of both of the target items being readied for some current message-driven utterance. At certain times and under certain conditions, these un-targeted but nonetheless associated elements that are subliminally aroused impose themselves on the ultimate utterance. This picture was crafted by Hughlings Jackson, Charcot, and Kussmaul, and was incorporated directly into Freud's model. It was not long until the analogies between non-organic language hysterias and non-organic slips-of-the-tongue were extended to the analysis of paraphasia. Freud considered that all stemmed from damage to the "language apparatus". Kussmaul operated under each of these assumptions, and consequently appears so often cited in Freud's book. But there can be no doubt that it was the neogrammarian, Berthold Delbruck, whose linguistics most impressed Freud.

Berthold Delbruck

As mentioned above, Steinthal had levelled heavy criticism on the "misguided" (Marshall, 1974, p. 358) classical aphasia theories of the physicians. Their localisation hypotheses were guilty of the "category mistake", whereby an overly strong and direct mind–brain mapping was assumed. Steinthal argued that their clinical descriptions were incomplete and inaccurately recorded, and that "Our physicians have as yet no clear concept of what the function of language is" (Marshall, 1974, p. 358). The physician Kussmaul and the neogrammarian Berthold Delbruck (see Greenberg, 1997, p. 52; Sebeok, 1966) were in agreement with Steinthal, and thus their positions were in accord with those of Freud, who considered Steinthal's critique reasonable. Marshall (1974) and Greenberg (1997) have devoted extensive discussions to the work and influence of the neogrammarian Delbruck on Freud's aphasia book. I will discuss Greenberg's (1997, pp. 51–73) detailed assessment of Delbruck's influence on Freud in the present paper, largely because the linguists are typically skipped over in the early history of aphasia, although they accepted and worked within a mentalistic psychology and a historicism that focused on earlier forms in diachrony, as well as underlying forms in synchronic description. For the first time, de Bleser (in press) presents, evaluates, and discusses Delbruck's relatively short paper, originally delivered as a public lecture at the University of Jena and published in 1886. This short publication was the sole reference that Freud made to the work of Delbruck, and thus the eight-page paper has achieved an importance little known by most historians of aphasia. To my knowledge, there is no published English translation of this cross-discipline lecture, and so de Bleser's paper is ground breaking.

Greenberg begins her extended consideration of Delbruck by pinpointing Freud's consideration of paraphasia as the locus in his book where he cites the neogrammarian's paper; Delbruck himself did not use the term "paraphasia". Further, Delbruck was the sole "linguist/philologist" (p. 51) that Freud utilised. Delbruck, whose professor was Steinthal, worked on Indic and Indo-Germanic linguistics at Jena. He collaborated on a comparative grammar on Germanic syntax with Karl Brugmann, and worked with Sanskrit and other ancient Indic languages. The public lecture at Jena, subsequently published, was entitled "Amnestic aphasia". There, Delbruck observed and recorded various lexical substitutions that bore relationships of similarity or more often contiguity in terms of local collocation or contextual function. Although, as just mentioned, Delbruck did not use the term "paraphasia", the derailments he considered were analogous to those Freud had observed. Aphasiologists had adopted the prefix "para-", indicating that substitution was the primary error mechanism in sensory aphasia. Delbruck noted that full word substitutions tended to agree in part of speech, that the agrammatism ("sketchy utterances") he observed showed maintenance of nouns, verbs, and other contentives, and that they were nevertheless sequentially ordered according to Germanic word-order typology. The lexical errors observed by Delbruck indicated that the architecture of the lexicon comprised word bondings in terms of etymological relations, conceptual groupings (categories) and part of speech, and that most all target–error substitutions shared one of these relations.

Furthermore, Delbruck felt that words belonging to single-item categories were lost sooner, for the simple reason that they had no strength of bonding; they were in a field of one. Delbruck felt that this is the reason why proper names are lost first, since proper names are single and isolated—free of associative bonds with any other proper name form. The semantic connections within fields were based on Aristotelian dimensions of similarity (paradigmatic) and contiguity (syntagmatic). Similarity bonds were basically co-hyponymic, while contiguity bonds included contextual effects, functional relationships, metonomy, and localistic collocation. Again, these parameters followed closely along the lines of association psychology, which dates back to Aristotle (Buckingham, 2002).

Relating more to pragmatics than to the semantics of associationism, Delbruck attempted to differentiate what he called "external" words (or strings of them) and "internal" words (or strings of them). For Delbruck, the external words were somehow less deeply embedded in the minds of speakers and referred to objects and events in the world to which we can *point*; these are nouns. They are less complex in their cognitive linguistic make-up, and tend to be lost sooner than "internal" words, which according to Delbruck refer to purely internal events (mind states), facts, and *moods*. Verbs have much more complex functional structuring, and thus verbs tend to resist disruption in aphasia better than nouns. Delbruck noted a dissociation of noun retrieval from verb retrieval, claiming that most often, and earlier, noun retrieval difficulties appear first, and are often the most severe. Working around noun retrieval blocks, the patient with aphasia will supply the function "it's for telling time" or the contiguous function "time" or "that's time" when unable to name a picture (or the actual object) of a watch. Delbruck's example uses scissors, where the noun cannot be accessed but where the patient can nevertheless talk of its function. Mood is importantly resistant to aphasia, patients often producing modalising phraseology such as "I don't feel I know it", or "Well, I would say that ...", or "Well, that might be what you would call a ...", or "I know what it is but I can't say it." Recall that Hughlings Jackson distinguished between what he called "automatic" language and "propositional" language. For "automatic" language, his examples were often the modalised phrases as shown above. The parallels between Delbruck and Hughlings-Jackson are not tight, but they concur that the proposition represents the willful and intentional verbal report of a piece of knowledge—a speech act referred to as a "representative". They report facts, events, etc., and according to Hughlings Jackson require a higher degree of volitional direction than the typical "automatisms" he mentions. The dissociation between propositionalising and modalising in language production has been raised again in the recent work of Nespoulous et al. (1998), Van Lanker Sidtis (2004), Jacyna (2000, p. 139), and Greenberg (1997, p. 59), and it appears that Delbruck was at least partially sensitive to these distinctions in his patient.

Delbruck's description of substitutions of sound and word was adopted by Freud. Delbruck, of course, had seen numerous analogues of these errors in his work with historical change, and also from his observations of synchronic variation within a language—i.e., dialect variation. Diachronic linguistics (and its obviously assumed historicism and evolutionism) quickly led to the study of variations at one time in history—i.e., synchronic variation, which is, of course, dialectology. One of the earliest realisations of historical linguists was that dialect variations provided intriguing analogues to the processes of historical change. Now Delbruck was observing analogues to these processes of change and alteration in sound and word errors in aphasia, having also noted similarities in the alterations of sounds and words in child language acquisition. Below I will show that slips-of-the-tongue were soon brought to bear in the study of aphasia, revealing as they did further interesting analogues with diachrony, synchrony, and ontogeny.

Freud considered that "letters of the alphabet are the fundamental building blocks of language" (Greenberg, 1997, p. 121). He used the word "umordnung" as a process of rearrangement of the ordered letters of words—a "scrambling of letters (p. 121)." Unfortunately, Freud did not have the phoneme concept at his disposal. That linguistic unit of abstraction at the segmental level did not enter the scene until Baudouin de Courtenay, a short time later (Robins, 1967), reasoned that what linguists were taking as "sounds" were in reality *units* of minimally different sounds (themselves abstractions as well; see Hammarberg, 1976) that were dubbed "phonemes", the minimally differing sound elements within the units subsequently called "allophones". The prefix "allo" indicates "one of a group of minimally distinct elements, together which constitute a structural unit", the structural unit here being the phoneme. Each sound considered individually is referred to as the "phone". (The morpheme is structured in the same taxonomic hierarchy: morph, allomorph, and morpheme.) Accordingly, the word "literal" came to be used—stemming as it did from the pre-phoneme concept of the letter as the basic segmental level. One still sees "literal paraphasia" in modern studies of aphasia—well after it should be clear that the phoneme is what is truly involved. However, the history of alphabetic writing indeed shows that the alphabetic systems are mappable to the phonemes of the specific language to differing degrees. So it is not without interest that earlier aphasiologists used "literal" for phonemic in their descriptions of segmental level errors—or what they perceived to be at the level of the segment.

Delbruck, on the other hand, avoided the analysis of sound error qua sound error because, like Jacques Lordat in the early 19th century (Bay, 1969; Nespoulous, et al., 1998), Delbruck felt that word forms were learned as whole units, the sound segments being concatenated localistically, in strict linear order, where a neuromuscular automaticity would develop over time with frequent usage resulting in an automatised segmental chaining, not unlike the context-free, elementary motor response units of Wayne Wickelgren (1969). In a sense the segments were felt to be locked into the word as a whole, and as the word went, so did the sounds. Delbruck postulated that what might seem like a sound substitution was tightly conditioned by a lexical effect. Of course his examples of this would have to show an error form that was nevertheless a word in the dictionary of the patient's language. Delbruck's example of Vatter → Vutter might be analysed at the segmental level of [a]→[U], but Delbruck, no doubt in wording that attracted Freud's attention immediately, claims that the error may very well have taken place at the level of lexical—not segmental—selection. Greenberg (1997, p. 54) quotes Delbruck: "Someone may say, for example, 'Vutter' instead of 'Vatter' because at the same time he has in mind 'Mutter.' Externally, of course, a confusion of sounds is apparent; in truth, however, there exists a mingling of ideas in the mind." This quotation more than most reveals the strong affinity between Delbruck and Freud concerning what are called in modern terminology "competing plans". The close connection between sound structure and semantic relations is often such that errors share both phonetic and semantic relations with their targets. This is often referred to as a "lexical bias" in current work, and connectionist modelling has given us further reason to consider lexical biases in paraphasias, and, incidentally, in slips-of-the-tongue, which we will discuss later. No doubt there will be more work by historians of aphasia on Berthold Delbruck's short but significant paper on "Amnestic aphasia".

Moses Allen Starr

As far as M. Allen Starr's role in Freud's book on aphasia, it is important to specify what Freud was discussing when he first cites Starr's work. Freud was discussing Jackson's parallels between paraphasia and slips-of-the-tongue. On the analogy I proposed that slips had with non-organic hysterias, and on the corollary assumption that there is no sharp boundary between health and disease, Freud was claiming that slips-of-the-tongue and paraphasias were "purely functional symptoms" and were both an indication of "reduced efficiency of the apparatus of speech associations" (Buckingham, 1999, p. 79). The reasoning of Hughlings Jackson and of Freud was the same. If slips are the non-organic counterpart of paraphasias, then it makes little sense to look for some specific region in the human brain that, if damaged, will give rise to paraphasia. A weaker version of this would be that at best there would be no *one* region for the "localisation" of paraphasia. It is at this point where Freud cites the recent study of Starr (1889), where Starr had combed the extant literature of cases with autopsy of sensory aphasia; clinically, there was no indication of Broca's aphasia. Starr collected well over 50 cases of clinically evaluated patients exhibiting no functional signs of a Broca's aphasia and all with at least partial symptomatology of sensory aphasia. He was very cautious in paring down the large set to the 50 he ultimately analysed. First, he discarded all subjects where the lesion had, indeed, infiltrated Broca's area or had extensively damaged the insula. Second, he threw out all cases where death had followed too soon post-onset, because there would have been no way to ensure that within a few more weeks, etc., the patient's symptoms would not have undergone considerable moderation. Starr also excluded patients with large tumours, arguing that increased cranial pressure may have produced indirect symptomatology from regions at some remove from the actual tumour location. He ended up with only 50 cases, but he felt these to be clearer examples of sensory aphasia with pathological indications more tightly linking to sensory aphasia with posterior left lesions.

The gyri involved were first and second temporal, inferior parietal, angular, and supramarginal. He also noted that some sensory aphasias had additional occipital lesions. Each patient had a typical array of sensory aphasic signs. Only 2 of the 50 seemed to have aphemic-like "impairments in the power to talk" (Starr, 1889, p. 87). Following this caveat, Starr (p. 87) writes, "In all others it consisted of the use of wrong words, or unintelligent phrases, a series of words whose connection was deficient." Starr here, as did certain other physicians and non-linguists, left more or less undifferentiated the myriad of "wrong word" errors. Closer observations, however, had noted "literal paraphasias" (segmental errors) and full word errors bearing different types of associative bonding—specifically "similarity" or "contiguity", as mentioned above. Starr (p. 87) continued writing: "Paraphasia is therefore the usual accompaniment of sensory aphasia. In these cases the lesion was wide in extent, involving the temporal, parietal and occipital convolutions."

What clearly most interested Freud was the following citation by Starr (p. 87):

It was impossible to ascertain any constant pathological difference between the cases of sensory aphasia without and with paraphasia. Nor did the power to repeat words one after another seem to depend upon the relative situation of the lesion, as might be supposed from Wernicke's assertion that this defect appears with paraphasia when the temporo-frontal tract is involved. For paraphasia with inability to repeat words was found in a few cases where the lesion lay too far back to affect this tract. Paraphasia therefore may be caused by lesions in very various locations.

Space does not permit full-fledged coverage of Starr's most impressive study of the newly "discovered" (RIP: Gesner and Bastian) sensory aphasias by Wernicke 15 years earlier. The issue of the non-localisability (or the underdetermined localisability within a large perisylvian language area) of paraphasias was what attracted Freud in his book and ultimately what Freud utilised in reasoning about his "1st order aphasia", or what he called "verbal aphasia". Freud's diagram will be treated later in this paper. Interestingly, Starr's 1889 work appeared one year after the preliminary version of Freud's book, which appeared in 1888; Freud continued reading. Starr starred in the 1891 version.

Greenberg (1997, p. 37, fn #13) discusses some interesting personal ventures and writing of Starr, reported by Ernest Jones. It was possible that Starr, who had worked in Meynert's laboratory from October 1881 to March 1882, had worked for a while with Freud. At that time Freud was still in Brucke's institute, where Meynert was. Jones claims to have seen a letter from Freud sometime in 1912 in the *New York Times* reporting on a previous letter in the *Times* attacking him, written by Starr, who claimed to have worked with Freud, although Freud denies ever knowing him. We are left wondering what Freud may or may not have done that apparently had upset Starr.

Other than Greenberg (1997), several others have mentioned M. Allen Starr, but in my opinion, not enough. Finger (1994), Jacyna (2000), and Buckingham (1999) have commented on Starr and Freud's incorporation of his findings.

SLIPS OF THE TONGUE AND PARAPHASIA

The organic and non-organic hysterias of Charcot

Jean-Martin Charcot was fully aware of the complex nature of both hysterias and epilepsy. Each could arise from damage to various regions of the brain, making their behaviour symptomatologies puzzlingly unlocalisable in any strict sense. Of course this functional localisation quandary was in complete accord with what Hughlings Jackson had written about and what was of crucial importance to Freud.

As I pointed out earlier, what eventually accrued was the enigmatic appreciation of two sets of very similar behavioural features, with only one set being unambiguously linked to a certain region of brain damage, or brain damage at all. The upshot of this observation was that the functional level of behavioural description achieved scientific merit, and was in complete accordance with the Spencerian mental functionality of the day.

Slips-of-the-tongue

A basic tenet with the study of slips-of-the-tongue is that they are cast at phonemic, morphological, syntactic, lexical selection, and semantic/conceptual levels of language production, lesions in the physical sense being eschewed; the "functional lesion" comes to mind readily. The oft-mentioned reasons for slips are usually explained in terms of altered focus, emotional instability, momentary attentional derailments, and various and sundry fleeting alterations of "normal" states of mind. These, in turn, may ultimately have physiologic causes in some aspect of the reticular activating system, but on-line studies of slip productions have not been forthcoming. The difficulties for this type of study are legion, since slips are, unless solicited in non-spontaneous speaking laboratory settings (e.g., Motley & Baars, 1976), discourse phenomena.

It has been pointed out that early studies of aphasic language, and language theory in general, often focused exclusively on the word. This was true for Freud, although he recognised a phonetic similarity as well as a conditioning factor for his lexical-level errors—a point he attributed to Delbruck as shown above. Echoing the driving force for Greenberg's (1997) book on Freud's book, although apparently unaware of her publication, Jacyna (2000, p. 174, fn #10) writes, "Freud's work on aphasia has drawn attention chiefly because of its supposed foreshadowing of certain aspects of his later psychoanalytic writing, such as verbal slips." But, again, what is crucial to keep in mind is that Delbruck and Freud pointed to the interaction of whole words and their segmental content. Note, also, that none of this goes through for slips that result in non-words on Freud's account, since a frank non-word would not be in the lexicon of the speaker.

Although these phenomena are referred to as slips *of the tongue* in English, they are referred to in Spanish as "linguistic slip" (*desliz lingüístico*), or in Argentina as "failed act" (*acto fallido*), that occur at non-motoric levels and involve linguistic units at some remove from anything physical. Accordingly, from the beginning their explications or accounts have fallen in line with functional levels of description—a level comfortably accepted by psychologists such as Steinthal, by physicians such as Kussmaul, and by the typical neogrammarian—in our case, Delbruck.

This tradition received a major boost in significance with the seminal publication on slips by Rudolf Meringer and Carl Mayer (1895), four years after Freud's book (see Cutler & Fay, 1978). Meringer was a language scholar; he did the bulk of the writing. Mayer, a neurologist, contributed very little in terms of writing the monograph, but Meringer was curious as to just how alike the paraphasias of the clinic were to the slips-of-the-tongue corpus he had amassed. At this point, Mayer's contribution was (1) to provide Meringer with the clinical literature of the day on paraphasia, (2) to share his own patient data with Meringer, and finally (3) to arrange for Meringer to interview patients himself at Mayer's clinic. This appears to be one of the first major neurolinguistic interdisciplinary efforts between a linguist and a cooperative physician, curious and interested enough in the epiphenomenological language behaviour of his patients to allow the linguist to work directly with them. The physician, Mayer, was also to scrutinise the slip corpus of Meringer, compare it with his corpus of paraphasias, and read Meringer's account closely in order to "... give it his seal of approval by attesting that it did not conflict with the known neurological facts" (Cutler & Fay, 1978, p. xxiv).

Recall that a major effort was devoted by the neogrammarians to establishing deep functional parallels between processes of historical change, dialect variation, and child language acquisition errors and alterations. Aphasiologists such as Hughlings Jackson, Kussmaul, and Freud were intent on showing the parallels between paraphasias and slips-of-the-tongue. Linguists such as Meringer were becoming quite interested not only in the parallels between slips and historical change, but also between slips and paraphasia. He also pointed to the similarities between adult slips and errors in childhood language acquisition. Later, Arnold Pick (1931/1973) would consider the telegraphic syntax of non-native foreign language speakers' errors and the telegraphic speech of Broca's aphasia, while even later Derek Bickerton (1990) would point to the parallels between telegraphic speech and the syntax of pidgin languages. The series of observations of these parallels among language changes, alternations, variations, and errors is referred to by some as "the continuity thesis" (e.g., Buckingham, 1999; Dell, Schwartz, Martin, Saffran & Gagnon, 1997), and it is safe to say that these efforts began with the early considerations of slips-of-the-tongue and the paraphasias in what were most often sensory, posterior, or fluent patients with aphasia, and this is precisely the overriding claim in Meringer and Mayer's (1895) publication.

FREUD'S SO-CALLED "CONTINUITY THESIS"

Slips of the tongue and paraphasias

As implied in all that has been said before, Hughlings Jackson was the first that I can find to craft the continuity claim between paraphasias and slips. After providing some samples of paraphasias, he wrote (1879, p. 194), "Such blunders occur, I think, in persons whose speech is only very slightly defective: I mean in those who, for the most part, speak well." He continues on to provide some slips he had observed. Freud (1891, p. 13) also wrote that "... the paraphasia observed in aphasic patients does not differ from the incorrect use and the distortion of words which the healthy person can observe in himself in states of fatigue or divided attention or under the influence of disturbing affects ..." As mentioned above, Freud used Delbruck's typology of linguistic changes and dialect variations for his understanding of the processes of slips and paraphasia.

These parallels in turn seem to support Spencer's evolutionary view of the mind, whereby there is a deep historicity in human language function and that the historical changes of all languages, the Indo-European family serving as a specific group in the early treatments of the neogrammarians, reflect this view. Herder and Grimm had speculated on language evolution, but seem to have lost ground to the historical studies of extant languages with documents from early forms in conjunction with methods that were developed to "uncover" early proto-forms, which had no direct attestations at all.

So-called "deep" forms or "underlying" forms were part and parcel of linguistic methodology, and this too was in line with the growing mentalist functionalism of the day. The notion that synchronic productions in the phonology of languages derive from or "flow" from, at least to some extent, the deep or remote historical forms of those languages was obviously apparent in generative phonological models and reached its zenith in Chomsky and Halle's (1968) analysis of the sound patterns of English. There is an ongoing battle over how much and to what extent synchronic descriptions are scaffolded off diachrony. Nevertheless, there are clear Spencerian notions in all of this.

Health and disease

Deeply embedded in the continuity between slips and paraphasias, or in fact between parapraxias in normality (action slips; Roy, 1982) and parapraxias in brain damage (the ideational apraxias of Liepmann, 1905/1980), is implied a certain continuity between the healthy human and the diseased human. In a recent discussion of "William James and the case of the epileptic patient" (Menand, 1998), the point is made that there is a continuum of severity of more or less automatised motor movement from the "spasms" of coitus and the involuntary jerking of muscles when being tickled or when asleep. For Charles Brown-Sequard and his student, William James, it was thought that, "... degree by degree we are led to look on epilepsy as an incr[eased] degree of the normal reflex excitability of certain parts of the nervous centers" (Menand, 1998, p. 91). Menand continues to the general position held by James on health and disease (p. 91): "This concept, much amplified, grew to occupy a central place in James's own psychology. His thought was that there is no sharp line to be drawn between 'healthy' and 'unhealthy' minds, that all have something of both." The difference rests with degree, not quality—and this is the claim that relates slips-of-the-tongue in healthy speakers and paraphasia in diseased speakers. And the extension to other domains of language variation in healthy speakers (children, language change, dialect variation, and foreign language errors) is to be expected, as all of these variations are also on continua with disease. Recall, for example, the telegraphic syntax of aphasic speakers with what is usually a motor aphasia, and the telegraphic speech as a level in language acquisition, or foreign language errors. Arnold Pick (1931/1973) comments at length on foreign language telegraphic structure and its parallels to the syntax of motor aphasic patients (see Buckingham, 1999, for more discussion of Pick and the continuity thesis).

FREUD'S DIAGRAM

Is it fair to superimpose Freud's diagram on the left perisylvian region?

Freud's diagram (!) has been analysed by many recent investigators (Buckingham, 1999; Greenberg, 1997; Hommes, 1994; Jacyna, 2000).

The dominant hemisphere peri-sylvian region (originally referred to as the "circonvolution d'enceinte", Foville, 1844, and used by Broca in an attempt to account for negative cases of aphemia, where autopsy demonstrated lesions in more posterior portions, sparing the inferior third frontal gyrus, but nonetheless along the rim of the Sylvian fissure, Schiller, 1979) is supplied by the middle cerebral artery, and its overall extension houses several important language functions. Hommes (1994, p. 178) takes Freud's original diagram (Figure 1), stylises it and superimposes it on the left peri-sylvian region (Figure 2). Jacyna (2000, p. 179) importantly notes that with Freud's original diagram of the speech association field, "No brain profile was depicted." Likewise, Greenberg (1997, p. 180) writes that Freud drafted a diagram, "... which disregards the anatomic situation."

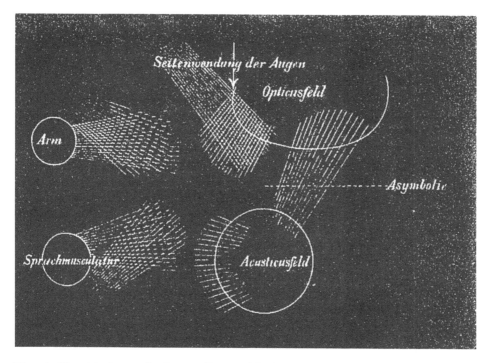

Figure 1. The original anatomic scheme or diagram of the "language association field" from Freud (1891) *Zur Auffassung der Aphasien.* Also reprinted in Greenberg, 1997 (p. 180), and in Jacyna, 2000 (p. 179). Note the total lack of cortical reality. The connecting pencil sketches indicate associations with the "inner" language apparatus as well as associations between the motor and sensory systems themselves. One uses one's imagination to assume that the "inner" language system may reside somewhere in the black space internal (or central) to the outer motor/sensory systems. Greenberg and Jacyna stress that Freud did not want to accept the metaphysical baggage of grafting this scheme on to the peri-sylvian region of the left lateral surface of the cortex. The rhetorical force of his diagram was to contradict the "diagram makers". It was an "anti-diagram" (Jacyna, 2000, p. 179).

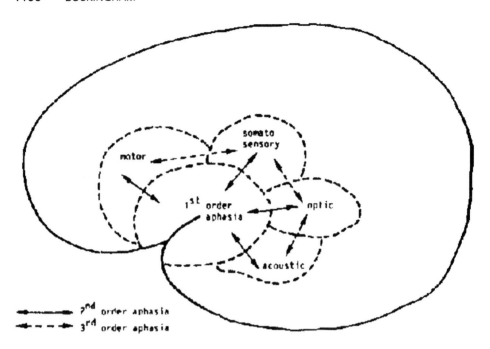

Figure 2. Freud's less anti "anti-diagram" (Jacyna, 2000, p. 179), but scaffolded on the left peri-sylvian region by Hommes (1994, p. 178) and showing the interior zone, a language module of continuous linguistic function (seat of Freud's "language apparatus"). Damage anywhere in this region produces paraphasia and other purely language/associative errors. Also shown are the connections of outer motor-sensory regions with the inner zones, disconnections of which gave rise to "asymbolic aphasias", or "second order aphasias". The second set of connecting arrows is at an even greater remove from language. They represent recognition breakdowns within the somatosensory projection zones, where significant embodied memories are organised. Freud called these disconnections "agnosias", or "third order aphasias". There are no interactions with the language apparatus, and so these "aphasias" were certainly not aphasias at all; they are agnosias. [From Hommes, 1994, p. 178. Reprinted with permission in Buckingham, 1999, p. 80.]

That original diagram was NOT superimposed on the lateral surface of the left hemisphere, and so Jacyna's point is that accordingly it was even less related to the brain. This, of course, is not unlike many of the original diagrams of the localisers, such as Bastian's. His early diagram was like Freud's; no brain profile was depicted. These non-scaffolded diagrams were obviously not committed to localisations to nearly the point that those superimposed on left lateral cortical surfaces were (see Buckingham, 1982b for a discussion of this point as regards Bastian's diagrams). Greenberg (1997), in similar fashion to Jacyna's notion of the "anti-diagram", focuses on Freud's rhetorical use of the diagram, whereby he actually uses one ironically to question the whole enterprise of diagram making in the classical sense. Greenberg and Jacyna are arguing that there was a method to Freud's madness in crafting a diagram, while intentionally avoiding the metaphysical baggage of superimposing it on the cortex.

Otto Hommes (1994) interprets Freud's functional descriptions correctly and relates them logically to the neuroanatomical geography and its finer geo-logical function, *but* takes poetic licence and creatively stylises and grafts that diagram onto a left peri-sylvian region of a human brain—without Freud's permission!

Hommes's diagram shows the distinct depictions of Freud's "first order aphasia", his "second order aphasia", and his "third order aphasia". The second and third order aphasias were somewhat less of "... a complexity beyond comprehension" (quoted in Jacyna, 2000, p. 178), than was verbal aphasia. The second and third types were less puzzling because they were essentially grounded in the less recondite sensory and motor functions of the cortex (motor, somatosensory, optic, and acoustic). Second order aphasias disturbed the connections of the inner zone with one or another of these surrounding motor or sensory functions. Freud termed these second order disruptions "asymbolic aphasia". Third order aphasias (even further removed from an aphasia, according to Freud) disturbed the connections between the above motor and sensory functions. The disturbances here did not encroach on Freud's inner zone, and therefore were clearly at a remove from aphasia—and, in turn, from language. Freud referred to these third order aphasias as "agnostic aphasia", thus introducing for the first time the term "agnosia".

It was Freud's first order aphasia that was the real focus of his claims regarding *true* aphasia, and where he carefully incorporated Starr's conclusions on paraphasia. Recall what Starr (1889, p. 87) had written. There he claimed that he had observed extensive underdetermination as to which areas in the sylvian zones for language would or would not produce adults with paraphasia when damaged. Any lesioned area within this zone may or may not produce adults with paraphasia. Paraphasia, therefore, could be caused ("correlated"? HWB) by lesions in various locations. Both Jacyna (2000, pp. 174–181) and Greenberg (1997, pp. 178–182) cogently describe the uncomfortable mental–physical tension when Freud locates a zone for paraphasic breakdown, but where that function at the same time is *not* localisable in that same zone. For Freud, the classical speech and language centres (e.g., Broca's centre, Wernicke's centre, visual, somatosensory, and writing) were the "far corners of the speech field" (Jacyna, 2000, p. 178). Freud's "speech apparatus" was located in the interior zone, and when lesions occurred in *this* functional continuum, paraphasia was the result. Moreover, it was that same apparatus that was fleetingly interfered with in slips-of-the tongue, and slips, of course, could not be explained by Broca's or Wernicke's area dysfunction. The same held for paraphasia—thus the mystery. Historians of aphasia can judge whether Hommes's superimposition of Freud's diagram is a help or a hindrance. This mind–brain tension lives on today, and in the present discussion is apparent in evaluating the consequences when a purely geometric diagram is subsequently grafted onto the cerebral cortex.

CONCLUSIONS

In this paper I have described a wide swath of influential ideas and authors that influenced Freud's views of aphasia and in many cases portended them. I have attempted to demonstrate, as several other writers have before me, that Freud was a thinker more than a physician, that he embraced (1) a mentalistic psychology that incorporated the non-localisations tenets of those neurologists who dared to counter the established doctrine of the day, (2) the functional psychology of the Spencerian natural philosophers, soon to call themselves psychologists, and (3) the early linguists, etymologists, and philologists, the younger of which came to be known as the "junggrammatiker", or less derisively, the "neogrammarians". Each of these groups of scholar-writers was forging a science of the mental, motivated by the growing sentiment that, in contradistinction to Darwin, there should be an evolutionary theory of the mind.

The admixture of academic, theoretical, and research backgrounds gave rise to an interdisciplinary spirit that engendered a host of compound designations for its adherents. They could be called "cognitive neurobiologists", "neurolinguists", "cognitive aphasiologists", "neuropsychologists", "cognitive neuropsychologists", and one could be trained in "diseases of the mind and nervous system". The prodromes of Freudian psychiatry abounded, and many have stated that the seeds of his psychoanalysis are to be found here. Moreover, certain few linguists of the day, whose principal academic and investigative responsibilities were historical Indo-European linguistics, were occasionally to engage in considering aphasia: de Courtenay, Meringer, and Delbruck. The neogrammarian, Delbruck, delivered a short but insightful lecture on word substitution errors in 1886 and later published it. He claimed the patient was a sensory aphasic, and used the term "amnesic" for it. As Starr (1889, p. 83) pointed out, "ataxic" aphasia eventually came to be called "motor" aphasia, while "amnesic" aphasia came to be called "sensory" aphasia. Freud, while working on the second version of his aphasia book, came upon Delbruck's paper. In that paper, Delbruck made the insightful comment that subconscious competing external plans, semantically and phonologically related to the planned internal message, may substitute for it in paraphasia. The very same claim had been suggested for certain lexical slips-of-the-tongue, as well. Freud ran with it.

John Marshall (1974, p. 359), describing this exciting exchange of ideas, claimed that Freud should go down in history as the first neogrammarian neurolinguist. Some have taken umbrage at this. De Bleser (in press), for example, claims that title for Delbruck himself. Greenberg (1997, p. 42, fn 21) only slightly shares Marshall's exuberance; I don't care. "Firsts" or "births" are difficult to fix unambiguously, as I mentioned earlier in the paper. Science is social and therefore very much a shared enterprise. No one works in vacuums. Finger (2000, pp. 304–305) claims "we stand on the shoulders of giants". Jacyna (2000, p. 16) claims that an important feature of scientific history is its "... insistence on the cumulative, progressive nature of the growth of knowledge. Each giant stands on the shoulders of his predecessor in order to build an ever more imposing edifice." As John Robert Ross said at the outset of his doctoral dissertation in linguistics at MIT in 1967, "... it's giants all the way down". He said "turtles" of course, and they were holding up the earth. This is my take on "firsts" in the history of science, and so, I remain demure.

A further social class issue in our field, whatever it may be called, is that "you pays your money and takes your title". Freud could be a "neurolinguist" and Delbruck a "linguistic aphasiologist", although Freud in truth studied little if any linguistics, and it is not likely that Delbruck read anatomy texts, leaving his Indic comparative grammars aside. What I would say in closing is that the spirit of the present paper should play a part in the history of linguistics, and that more input from linguists should be sought out in studies of 19th-century aphasiology.

REFERENCES

Arens, K. (1984). *Functionalism and fin de siècle: Fritz Mauthner's Critique of Language* (Stanford German Studies, Vol. 23). New York: Peter Lang.

Bay, E. (1969). The Lordat case and its import on the theory of aphasia. *Cortex*, 5(3), 302–308.

Bickerton, D. (1990). *Language and species*. Chicago: University of Chicago Press.

Buckingham, H. W. (1980). *Critical issues in the study of aphasia 100 years after the death of Broca*. Special symposium, 18th annual meeting of the Academy of Aphasia, South Yarmouth, MA, October 5.

Buckingham, H. W. (1982a). Critical issues in the linguistic study of aphasia. In N. J. Lass (Ed.), *Speech and language: Advances in basic research and practice* (pp. 313–337). New York: Academic Press.

Buckingham, H. W. (1982b). Neuropsychological models of language. In N. J. Lass, L. McReynolds, J. Northern, & D. Yoder (Eds.), *Speech, language and hearing: Normal Processes* (pp. 323–347). Philadelphia: Saunders.

Buckingham, H. W. (1986). Language, the mind, and psychophysical parallelism. In I. Gopnik & M. Gopnik (Eds.), *From models to modules: Studies in cognitive science from the McGill workshops* (pp. 209–228). New York: Ablex.

Buckingham, H. W. (1999). Freud's continuity thesis. *Brain and Language, 69*, 76–92.

Buckingham, H. W. (2002). The roots and amalgams of connectionism. In R. G. Daniloff (Ed.), *Connectionist approaches to clinical problems in speech and language* (pp. 265–311). Mahwah, NJ: Lawrence Erlbaum Associates Inc..

Campbell, L. (2001). The history of linguistics. In M. Aronoff & J. Rees-Miller (Eds.), *The handbook of linguistics* (pp. 81–104). Malden, MA: Blackwell Publishing.

Chomsky, N., & Halle, M. (1968). *The sound pattern of English*. New York: Harper.

Cutler, A., & Fay, D. (1978). Introduction. *Versprechen und verlesen: Eine psychologisch-linguistische studie* (reprinted). Amsterdam: John Benjamins.

de Bleser, R. (in press). A linguist's views on progressive anomia: Evidence for Delbruck (1886) in modern neurolinguistic research. *Cortex*.

de Courtenay, J. B. (1885–1886/1972). On pathology and embryology of language. In E. Stankiewicz (Ed. and Trans.), *A Baudouin de Courtenay anthology*. Bloomington, IN: Indiana University Press.

Delbruck, B. (1886). Amnesic aphasia. *Jenaische Zeitschrift fur Naturwissenschaft, 20*, 91–98 [Unpublished translation from the German by Ria de Bleser, 2005.].

Dell, G., Schwartz, M., Martin, N., Saffran, E., & Gagnon, D. (1997). Lexical access in aphasic and non-aphasic speakers. *Psychological Review, 104*, 801–838.

Devinsky, O., & Schachter (Eds.) (1997). *Norman Geschwind: Selected publications on language, behavior and epilepsy*. Boston: Butterworth.

Eling, P. (Ed.) (1994). *Reader in the history of aphasia: From Gall to Geschwind*. Amsterdam: John Benjamins.

Eling, P. (2006). The psycholinguistic approach to aphasia of Chajim Steinthal. *Aphasiology, 20*, 1074–1086.

Engelhardt, H. T. Jr. (1975). John Hughlings Jackson and the mind–body relation. *Bulletin of the History of Medicine, 49*, 137–151.

Finger, S. (1994). *The origins of neuroscience*. New York: Oxford University Press.

Finger, S. (2000). *Minds behind the brain: A history of the pioneers and their discoveries*. New York: Oxford University Press.

Freud, S. (1891/1953). *On aphasia: A critical study* (Translation and introduction by E. Stengel). London: Imago.

Greenberg, V. (1997). *Freud and his aphasia book: Language and the sources of psychoanalysis*. Ithaca, NY: Cornell University Press.

Hammarberg, R. (1976). The metaphysics of coarticulation. *Journal of Phonetics, 4*, 353–363.

Hommes, O. R. (1994). Introduction to Sigmund Freud. In P. Eling (Ed.), *Reader in the history of aphasia: From Gall to Geschwind* (pp. 169–179). Amsterdam: John Benjamins.

Hughlings Jackson, J. (1879–1880). On affections of speech from disease of the brain (III). *Brain, 2*, 323–356.

Jacyna, L. S. (2000). *Lost words: Narratives of language and the brain, 1825–1926*. Princeton, NJ: Princeton University Press.

Jarema, G. (1993). *In sensu non in situ:* The prodromic cognitivism of Kussmaul. *Brain and Language, 45*, 495–510.

Liepmann, H. (1905/1980). The left hemisphere and handedness. *Muenchener Medizinische Wochenschrift, 49*, 2322–2326, 2375–2378. [Trans. from the German by D. Kimura. *Translations of Liepmann's essay on apraxia*. Research Bulletin #506. London, Ontario: Department of Psychology, University of Western Ontario.]

Lorch, M. P. (2006). Phrenology and methodology, or "playing tennis with the net down". *Aphasiology, 20*, 1061–1073.

Marshall, J. C. (1974). Freud's psychology of language. In R. Wollheim (Ed.), *Freud: A collection of critical essays* (pp. 349–365). New York: Anchor.

Marx, O. M. (1967). Freud and aphasia: An historical analysis. *American Journal of Psychiatry, 124*, 815–825.

Menand, L. (1998). William James and the case of the epileptic patient. *New York Review of Books, December 17* 81–93.

Meringer, M., & Mayer, Co. (1895/1978). *Versprechen und verlesen: Eine psychologisch-linguistische studie* (reprinted with introduction by A. Cutler & D. Fay). Amsterdam: John Benjamins.

Motley, M. T., & Baars, D. J. (1976). Semantic bias effects on the outcomes of verbal slips. *Cognition, 4*, 177–187.

Lecours, A. R., Nespoulous, J. L., & Pioger, D. (1987). Jacques Lordat or the birth of cognitive neuropsychology. In E. Keller & M. Gopnik (Eds.), *Motor and sensory processes of language* (pp. 1–16). Hillsdale, NJ: Lawrence Erlbaum Associates Inc.

Nespoulous, J. L., Code, C., Virbel, J., & Lecours, A. R. (1998). Hypotheses on the dissociation between 'referential' and 'modalizing' verbal behavior in aphasia. *Applied Psycholinguistics, 19*, 311–331.

Pick, A. (1931/1973). *Aphasia* (translation and introduction by Jason. W. Brown. Biography by F. Stieglmayr). Springfield, IL: Charles C. Thomas.

Robins, R. H. (1967). *A short history of linguistics*. Bloomington, IN: Indiana University Press.

Roy, E. (1982). Action and performance. In A. W. Ellis (Ed.), *Normality and pathology in cognitive functions* (pp. 265–298). London: Academic Press.

Schacter, S. C., & Devinsky, O. (Eds.) (1997). *Behavioral neurology and the legacy of Norman Geschwind*. New York: Lippincott-Raven.

Schiller, F. (1979). *Paul Broca: Founder of French anthropology, explorer of the brain*. Berkeley, CA: University of California Press.

Sebeok, T. (Ed.) (1966). *Portraits of linguists: A bibliographical sourcebook for the history of western linguistics* (2 Vols.). Bloomington, IN: Indiana University Press.

Spencer, H. (1855). *The principles of psychology*. London: Longmans.

Starr, M. A. (1889). The pathology of sensory aphasia, with an analysis of fifty cases in which Broca's centre was not diseased. *Brain, 12*, 82–101.

Van Lancker Sidtis, D. (2004). When novel sentences spoken or heard for the first time in the history of the universe are not enough: Toward a dual-process model of language. *International Journal of Language and Communication Disorders, 39*, 1–44.

Wallesch, C-W. (2004). Freud as an aphasiologist. *Aphasiology, 18*, 389–399.

Wickelgren, W. (1969). Context-sensitive coding, associative memory, and serial order in (speech) behavior. *Psychological Review, 76*, 1–15.

On knowing about nothing: The processing of zero in single- and multi-digit multiplication

Carlo Semenza

Università degli Studi di Trieste, Italy

Alessia Granà

Università degli Studi di Trieste, and Istituto di Medicina Fisica e Riabilitazione, Udine, Italy

Luisa Girelli

Università degli studi di Milano-Bicocca, Milano, Italy

Background: Zero has a special role in calculation: indeed it is not obvious which representation may be invoked in multiplication or division by zero. In particular, zero as an operand, unlike any other operand, makes any quantity disappear.
Aims: The study is intended to shed light on the mechanisms mediating the manipulation of zero.
Methods & Procedures: Three neuropsychological patients, AF, FV, and FS, are described, whose specific pattern of preserved/impaired performance with single- and multi-digit multiplication shows selective problems with the use of zero ($N \times 0$ and $0 \times N$).
Outcome & Results: AF's performance in single- and multi-digit multiplication showed a clear dissociation between spared fact-based problems and impaired 0 rule-based problems. FV was totally unable, in multi-digit multiplication, to apply adequately the 0 rule that he could master in simple calculation. Finally, FS showed, within the rule-based problems, a clear-cut dissociation between a preserved performance on $N \times 0$ problems and an impaired performance on $0 \times N$ problems, a difficulty that almost disappeared in multi-digit multiplications.
Conclusions: Overall the reported dissociations indicate that a full grasp of the concept of zero may not be used in routine calculation, and that processing of zero rather appears to rely on a collection of independent, shallow representations.

How does our mind manipulate the concept of nothingness in the numerical domain? Indeed, as will be reported in some detail in the discussion, zero as a number appeared very late in the history of mathematics (Butterworth, 1999; Kline, 1972). The delay in its appreciation by infants (Wynn, 1998) and preschoolers (a full

Address correspondence to: Carlo Semenza, Dipartimento di Psicologia, Università degli Studi di Trieste, Via S., Anastasio 12, 34134 Trieste, Italy. E-mail: semenza@univ.trieste.it

We wish to thank Professor Paolo Di Benedetto of the Istituto di Medicina Fisica e Riabilitazione "Gervasutta", Azienda per i Servizi Sanitari, n. 4 "Medio Friuli", Italy for his support throughout this study. The present research has been supported by the European Union (Marie Curie Action Contract "NUMBRA" 504927) and by a MIUR grant 2003 to Carlo Semenza.

appreciation of the use of zero is not expected before the second grade; Wellman & Miller, 1986), and the difficulties associated with its use, may be grounded in its unique mathematical function. In fact, although adding a null quantity or subtracting it from a given quantity can easily be represented (e.g., by visual imaging), it is less obvious which representation may be invoked in multiplication or division by zero. In particular, zero as an operand, unlike any other operand, makes any quantity disappear. The three neuropsychological cases reported here, which show contrasting performances in solving 0-problems in simple and complex multiplication, seem to suggest that a full grasp of the concept of zero may not be used in routine calculation, which rather appears to rely on a collection of independent, shallow representations.

CASE REPORTS

Case 1

AF was a 71-year-old retired skilled manual worker, with 8 years of education, who sustained a vascular injury in the left anterior parietal lobe, extending deeply to the internal capsule (documented by CT scan). His spontaneous speech was non-fluent, characterised by phonemic and phonetic errors and frequent word-finding difficulties. The Aachener Aphasie Test (Italian version, Luzzatti, Willmes, & DeBleser, 1991) classified him as having Broca's aphasia. His short-term memory was just within normal limits for his age (digit span = 4).

Case 2

FV was a 55-year-old right-handed geometer, with 13 years of education, who had a lesion of vascular origin, documented by CT scan, in the posterior parieto-temporal area of the left hemisphere. His spontaneous speech was fluent, although rich in neologisms and paraphasias. The Aachener Aphasie Test classified him as having Wernicke's aphasia. His short-term memory was poor (digit span = 3).

Case 3

FS was a 35-year-old right-handed craftsman, with 8 years of education, who suffered from a traumatic brain injury. A CT scan showed a temporo-parietal contusion in the left hemisphere and a small area of hypodensity in the fronto-parietal region of the right hemisphere. FS's spontaneous speech was fluent with no sign of aphasia. His digit span was normal (5), while in long-term memory tasks both learning and retrieval difficulties emerged. Executive functions tests indicated signs of frontal dysfunction. On the Raven CPM, FS was well within the normal range.

For all the three patients pre-morbid elementary arithmetical abilities were reported to be intact and rather efficient. It remains unclear, and matter of speculation, whether and how their different degrees of competence and experience might have influenced their pathological performance.

METHOD

All the three patients were examined with a preliminary assessment of numerical skills that indicated efficient production and comprehension of up to three-digit

Arabic numerals in AF and FV and well-preserved number processing in FS. As reported in Table 1, all patients showed specific difficulties in calculation. These latter were the object of our investigation. The performance of AB and FV was investigated over a short time span, while for FS a longer and more intensive study was carried out.

The patients were presented with single-digit operations. Overall, 196 single-digit operations (50 additions, 50 subtractions, and 96 multiplications) were presented to AF and FV, while 655 single-digit operations (100 additions, 55 subtractions, and 100 multiplications over five different sessions) were presented to FS. Stimuli included both fact-based and rule-based problems. The former are assumed to be directly retrieved from long-term memory where they are stored in the form of individual representations, e.g., $5 + 2$; 7×5, while the latter are assumed to be stored in the form of general rules, e.g., $N \times 1 = N$; $0 \times N = 0$, for any number N (the stored facts/rules dichotomy is exhaustively treated in McCloskey, Aliminosa, & Sokol, 1991, and in Miceli & Capasso, 1999). Problems consisted of all combinations of operands between 0 and 9, and were visually presented blocked for each operation. Aphasic patients (AF and FV) were required to answer in writing, while FS answered orally.

Once the arithmetical fact battery was completed, patients were visually presented with multi-digit problems. A total of 66 multi-digit problems (14 additions, 16 subtractions, and 36 multiplications) were presented to AF and FV, and 110 multi-digit problems (50 additions, 60 subtractions, and 50 multiplications) to FS. At the end of the same session in which FS was tested with the last block of 100 single-digit multiplications, he was also presented with a further 51 multi-digit multiplications. All stimuli included problems with and without carrying and borrowing, and with or without operands containing "0" as a factor. In multiplication problems the relative position of zero was balanced in both the multiplicand (e.g., $N0N \times NNN$; $NN0 \times NNN$) and the multiplicator (e.g., $NNN \times N0N$; $NNN \times NN0$). Patients were asked to work out the solution of each problem with no time pressure and were encouraged to comment on the operational steps used. The experimenter noted errors and strategies.

RESULTS

All patients showed a specific difficulty with multiplications, while they behaved differently with additions and subtractions.

TABLE 1
Performance in calculation

Subtest	AF's score	FV's score	FS's score
Arithmetical signs	4/4	4/4	12/12
Reading of operation	8/8	8/8	8/8
Writing down an operation	6/6	6/6	6/6
Definition of operation	3/4	4/4	4/4
Arithmetical facts (1/4 add, 1/4 sub, 2/4 mult)	18/20	14/20	63/66
Approximate calculation	3/8	3/8	8/8
Mental calculation	7/28	7/28	16/28
Written calculation (1/3 add, 1/3 sub, 1/3 mult)	6/12	2/12	4/12

AF was correct with addition and subtraction in both single- and multi-digit calculation (respectively, 98% and 87.7% correct for additions and 94% and 87.5 % correct for subtractions). On the other hand, FV's performance in fact retrieval was equally impaired in addition (76% correct), subtraction (72% correct), and multiplication (76% correct), while in written multi-digit calculation his difficulties emerged mainly in subtraction and multiplication, where he performed at floor. FS scored flawlessly in single-digit addition (100% correct) and subtraction (100% correct), while in single-digit multiplication he showed a clear-cut dissociation between spared fact-based problems (98.5% correct) and impaired rule-based problems (50% correct). In his written multi-digit calculation, additions were almost perfect (94% correct), while subtractions (22% correct) and multiplications (5% correct) were characterised by systematic procedural errors. The following analysis of the patients' performance is focused on multiplication only (see Table 2).

Patient AF

AF's performance in single-digit multiplication showed a clear dissociation between spared fact-based problems (95.8% correct) and impaired rule-based problems (0% correct) where the errors were of the type $0 \times N = N$ (e.g., $3 \times 0 = 3$, $0 \times 5 = 5$). The difficulty with the 0-rule also emerged in multi-digit problems. AF correctly applied the algorithm to solve multi-digit multiplication but showed a systematic error with 0-facts when the 0 was in the multiplicand (32% correct). However, when the 0 was in the multiplicator he bypassed the repeated application of the 0-rule, writing directly as many 0s as the number of digits in the multiplicand (thus reaching the level of 94.2% correct).

Patient FV

Interestingly, FV showed a different, somewhat opposite, pattern of performance. In fact, in simple multiplication, his performance was impaired on fact-based problems (75% correct), but well preserved on rule-based problems (100% correct, including those featuring zero). The solution of multi-digit multiplication was instead affected by difficulties with both procedural and arithmetic facts: besides the application of

TABLE 2
Percentages of correct rule-based and fact-based problems

	One-digit calculation			Multi-digit calculation	
	$N \times 0$	$0 \times N$	$N \times M$	0 in multiplicand	0 in multiplicator
	Correct/n % correct	Correct/n % correct	Correct/n % correct	Correct/n % correct	Correct/n % correct
AF	0/8 0.0	0/8 0.0	77/80 96.3	16/50 32.0	31/33 94.2
FV	8/8 100	8/8 100	62/80 77.5	0/14 0.0	0/9 0.0
FS	0/45 0.0	45/45 100	404/410 98.5	55/64 86	39/44 89
				5/172* 3	90/90* 100

AF's, FV's, and FS's percentages of correct rule-based and fact-based problems in single-digit and multi-digit multiplications.

*Further multiplication problems administered to FS at the end of the investigation.

systematic procedural errors consisting in multiplying each number only by the number in the same column, FV was totally unable to apply adequately the $0 \times N = 0$ rule (0% correct) that he could master in simple calculation.

Patient FS

Finally, FS's performance in single-digit multiplications, across the five experimental sessions, showed a clear-cut dissociation between spared fact-based problems (98.5% correct) and impaired rule-based problems (only 50% correct). Moreover, within the rule-based problems, FS showed a further clear-cut dissociation between a preserved performance on $N \times 0$ problems and an impaired performance on $0 \times N$ problems. Errors consistently took the form $0 \times N = N$ (e.g., $0 \times 4 = 4$) whereas $N \times 0$ problems were always correctly solved (e.g., $4 \times 0 = 0$). Interestingly, the difficulty with the 0-rule almost disappeared in multi-digit multiplications. Although FS solved all multiplications by applying an incorrect algorithm (5% correct), in which he systematically wrote down the complete intermediate products before summing them, he was quite good at manipulating 0-facts both with 0 in the multiplicand (86% correct) and in the multiplicator (89%). Moreover, his pattern of performance on multi-digit multiplications changed over the 2 months of the experimental investigation. In fact in the last session, while he was wrong on $N \times 0$ problems (solving them as $= N$), he was also presented with a further 51 multi-digit multiplications including 0 as a factor. In his written multi-digit calculation FS showed systematic errors with 0-facts when 0 was in the multiplicand (3% correct), whereas he managed correctly the 0-rule when 0 was in the multiplicator (100% correct).

DISCUSSION

We reported three case studies who showed different patterns of performance in solving 0-problems in single- and multi-digit multiplications. A behaviour like that found in AF has occasionally been reported in the literature (Sokol, McCloskey, Cohen, & Aliminosa, 1991). However, his performance demonstrates more systematically, with respect to previous sporadic reports, the working of "special case procedures". McCloskey (1992) defined special case procedures as an alternate "path" in the general multi-digit multiplication algorithm that allows the participant to avoid difficulties linked to the use of the $\times 0$ rule. For example, as reported above, when 0 was in the multiplicator AF bypassed the repeated application of the 0-rule by writing directly as many zeros as the number of digits in the multiplicand. This strategy is made possible by the nature of the algorithm and AF seems to systematically profit.

FV, on the other hand, shows that success in solving $\times 0$ problems in isolation does not necessarily imply the transfer of this ability to solve $\times 0$ problems in the context of an operation. Thus, whatever representation FV used to successfully solve $N \times 0/0 \times N$ as a single problem, and whatever appreciation he might have had of the operation of multiplying a given quantity for a null one, this knowledge was not applied in multi-digit calculation.

Interestingly, FS provided further evidence of a dissociation in rule-based problems (McCloskey et al., 1991). Mathematically equal but formally different problems involving zero may occupy separate representations, even in single- digit problems, depending on whether 0 is the multiplicand ($0 \times N$) or the multiplicator ($N \times 0$). FS was disturbed only in $N \times 0$. Interestingly, while FS's error pattern on $N \times 0$ single-digit multiplications was consistent across the different sessions, on his ability to manipulate 0-facts in written multi-digit multiplication, while initially almost entirely correct, he later made $N \times 0 = N$ as with single-digit problems.

These findings support the contention that the calculation system may breakdown in a highly modular way. Not only may knowledge of facts, rules, and procedures all dissociate from one another and from conceptual knowledge (Dehaene & Cohen, 1997; Delazer & Benke, 1997; Girelli & Delazer, 1996; Hittmair-Delazer, Sailer, & Benke, 1995; Hittmair-Delazer, Semenza, & Denes, 1994), but even the same type of knowledge, i.e., the 0-rule in multiplication, may be correctly retrieved or not dependent on the arithmetic context.

Overall, the reported dissociations, along with previous reports in this direction (McCloskey et al., 1991; Pesenti, Depoorter, & Seron, 2000; Sokol et al., 1991), indicate that processing of zero in arithmetic is likely to be mediated by shallow, context-bound rules and procedures, whose binding with conceptual knowledge is rather marginal. Indeed, although automatic and routinised procedures may efficiently support calculation in fully-functioning individuals, they may become isolated and neglected pieces of knowledge in the context of disturbed cognitive systems.

The disconnection between conceptual and procedural knowledge has indeed been identified as a major obstacle to the mastery of arithmetic in scholars of different ages (Resnick, 1982). Yet there are reasons to believe that the critical link between everyday arithmetic algorithms and underlying principles does not characterise the performance of well-educated and expert adults either (Girelli, Delazer, & Butterworth, 2006).

Independence from conceptual knowledge is reflected in the historical and ontological development of zero. The idea of a collection with no members or, in mathematical terms, of an empty set, is neither new nor difficult to grasp, yet it took an exceptionally long time for our ancestors to develop an efficient procedure to represent zero within a numerical system. Indeed, zero was not part of the ancient formal number systems. For example, it took the Babylonian notation system, which originated around 1800 BC and was possibly the most advanced one among the earliest, about 1500 years to include a symbol for zero. Even then it simply had the function of place holder in the absence of any value in a given place. Mathematicians in classical Greece and Rome, including Archimedes, ignored zero altogether. Only much later (in approximately the early seventh century AD, by mathematicians operating in the Indus valley) did this symbol develop a meaning in its own right. The notion took about another 150 years to be adopted by Arabs, whose traders passed it to the Europeans only in the twelfth century. Independent from this mainstream history, the Maya are believed to have preceded everybody by developing a system representing zero 200–600 years before the Hindus. This historical delay, even more surprising when confronted with the extraordinary mastery of other mathematical principles, reflected well the intrinsic difficulty of manipulating a null quantity in arithmetic. The same story holds within individual development. Young children, once they have learned to deal with positive integers and have learned both the word "zero" and the corresponding Arabic symbol, take a considerable time to appreciate that zero is a numerical value corresponding to nothingness (Wellman & Miller, 1986). It appears that this notion then remains somehow segregated in the brain, as demonstrated in the present investigation.

REFERENCES

Butterworth, B. (1999). *The mathematical brain.* London: MacMillan.

Dehaene, S., & Cohen, L. (1997). Cerebral pathways for calculation: Double dissociation between rote verbal and quantitative knowledge of arithmetic. *Cortex, 33,* 219–250.

Delazer, M., & Benke, T. (1997). Arithmetical facts without meaning. *Cortex, 33,* 697–710.

Girelli, L., & Delazer, M. (1996). Subtractions bugs in an acalculic patient. *Cortex, 32,* 547–556.

Girelli, L., Delazer, M., & Butterworth, B. (2006). *Is 160 × 36 equal to 150 × 46? Misconceptions in simple arithmetic.* Manuscript submitted for publication.

Hittmair-Delazer, M., Sailer, U., & Benke, T. (1995). Impaired arithmetic facts but intact conceptual knowledge: A single-case study of dyscalculia. *Cortex, 31,* 139–147.

Hittmair-Delazer, M., Semenza, C., & Denes, G. (1994). Concepts and facts in calculation. *Brain, 117,* 715–728.

Kline, M. (1972). *Mathematical thought from ancient to modern times* (Vol. 1). Oxford, UK: Oxford University Press.

Luzzati, C., Willmes, K., & De Bleser, R. (1991). *Aachener Aphasia Test; Versione Italiana.* Gottingen: Hogrefe.

McCloskey, M. (1992). Cognitive mechanisms in numerical processing: Evidence from acquired acalculia. *Cognition, 44,* 107–157.

McCloskey, M., Aliminosa, D., & Sokol, S. M. (1991). Facts, rules, and procedures in normal calculation: Evidence from multiple single-patient studies of impaired arithmetic fact retrieval. *Brain Cognition, 17,* 154–203.

Miceli, G., & Capasso, R. (1999). Calculation and number processing. In G. Denes & L. Pizzamiglio (Eds.), *Handbook of clinical and experimental neuropsychology.* Hove, UK: Psychology Press.

Pesenti, M., Depoorter, N., & Seron, X. (2000). Noncommutativity of the $N + 0$ arithmetical rule: A case study of dissociated impairment. *Cortex, 36,* 445–454.

Resnick, L. B. (1982). Syntax and semantics in learning to subtract. In T. P. Carpenter, J. M. Moser, & T. A. Romberg (Eds.), *Addition and subtraction: A cognitive perspective* (pp. 136–155). Hillsdale, NJ: Lawrence Erlbaum Associates Inc.

Sokol, S. M., McCloskey, M., Cohen, N. J., & Aliminosa, D. (1991). Cognitive representations and processes in arithmetic: Inferences from the performance of brain-damaged subjects. *Journal of Experimental Psychology: Learning, Memory, and Cognition, 17,* 355–376.

Wellman, H. M., & Miller, K. F. (1986). Thinking about nothing: Development of concepts of zero. *British Journal of Developmental Psychology, 4,* 31–42.

Wynn, K. (1998). Psychological foundations of numbers: Numerical competence in human infants. *Trends in Cognitive Sciences, 2,* 296–303.

Gestural knowledge evoked by objects as part of conceptual representations

Daniel N. Bub and Michael E. J. Masson

University of Victoria, BC, Canada

Background: Theories of embodied knowledge argue that the representation and recruitment of motor processes may be important for deriving the meaning of many linguistic and perceptual elements.
Aims: We examined the conditions under which gestural knowledge associated with manipulable objects is evoked.
Methods & Procedures: A priming paradigm was used in which an object was presented in advance of a photograph of a hand gesture that participants were to mimic. On related trials, the target gesture was the same as the gesture typically used to interact with the object prime. On unrelated trials, the target gesture was not related to the object. In another set of experiments, a Stroop-like paradigm was used in which participants learned to produce manual responses to colour cues. After training, coloured photographs of manipulable objects were presented. The colour-cued gesture was either one typically used with the object or was unrelated to it.
Outcomes & Results: In the priming experiments, response latencies were shorter in the related condition, but only when participants also made an identification response to the object prime. In the Stroop experiments, interference effects indicated that gestures to colour were affected by gestural knowledge associated with the object.
Conclusions: These results indicate that conceptual representations of manipulable objects include specific forms of gestural knowledge that are automatically evoked when observers attend to an object.

Sentences often describe actions dealing with manipulable objects. For example, consider the sentence *Before the interview, Mary hastily applied some lipstick*. One view of sentence comprehension might take the meaning of this sentence to simply require an abstract understanding of the generic function that lipstick entails. Thus, the essential meaning of the sentence might rest on the knowledge that Mary is changing the colour of her lips by means of a cosmetic. But, clearly, the implications of a sentence may depend on more precise knowledge of how the action described is carried out. Suppose we are informed that Mary manipulated the lipstick by holding the cylinder in a clenched fist. Given our conventional understanding of how lipstick is used, it is immediately apparent that there is something anomalous about Mary or

Address correspondence to: Daniel Bub, Department of Psychology, University of Victoria, P.O. Box 3050 STN CSC, Victoria BC V8W 3P5, Canada. E-mail: dbub@uvic.ca

The authors made equal contributions to the work reported here. This research was supported by discovery grants from the Natural Sciences and Engineering Research Council of Canada to Michael Masson and to Daniel Bub, and by a grant from the Perceptual Expertise Network, which is funded by the James S. McDonnell Foundation. We are grateful to Marnie Jedynak for conducting the experiments.

at least about her present situation. We can also be sure that the result of her cosmetic effort is likely to be less than ideal.

The meaning of sentences involving actions on objects may therefore include either explicit or tacit information about how objects are actually manipulated. Indeed, recent accounts of language comprehension suggest that understanding manipulable objects or words referring to such objects requires a mental simulation of action. The knowledge of how a tube of lipstick is manipulated and used constitutes an essential part of the meaning of the concept "lipstick". Theories of embodied knowledge argue for an even more central role of action; the representation and recruitment of motor processes may be important for deriving the meaning of many linguistic elements, and the embodiment of meaning through action extends into abstract domains, including the comprehension and use of metaphor (Barsalou, Simmons, Barbey, & Wilson, 2003; Gallese & Lakoff, 2005; Glenberg & Kaschak, 2002).

There may be important functional relationships between motor representations and language, but how do we distinguish between different possibilities? At present we lack an adequate experimental approach that would reveal the dynamic evocation of actions when objects, words, and sentences are processed for meaning. Consider a number of important questions for which no answers are available at present: Are motor representations evoked by objects even when there is no accompanying intention to carry out an action on the object by the observer? If yes, then what is the nature of these representations? What role do they play in various language tasks? Do words evoke motor representations and under what circumstances? Do these motor representations differ from those evoked by objects? Objects inherently afford multiple actions; for example, we manually interact with a common object like a pocket calculator in several different ways when using it. Which of these actions, if any, are represented as part of the meaning of the object or word?

Functional imaging studies remain an ambiguous source of evidence, although widely cited as support for the claim that manipulable objects, or words and sentences referring to such objects, automatically recruit motor processing. Some experiments (e.g., Chao & Martin, 2000; Creem-Regehr & Lee, 2005) have indicated that passive viewing of tools is sufficient to evoke a range of specific cortical responses associated with motor processes. However, other findings suggest that visual objects do not invariably evoke motoric activation, but that such activation is task dependent. For example, Gerlach, Law, and Paulson (2002) showed premotor cortex involvement in a categorisation task (natural vs manmade), but not in object decisions (real vs non-real). Devlin et al. (2002) reported a meta-analysis of seven studies that used positron emission tomography to examine specific activation patterns for man-made objects, especially tools, in relation to other object classes (e.g., fruits and vegetables). They found evidence for activation in left posterior temporal regions that was specific to tools, but only when participants engaged in naming or semantic classification tasks, not during passive viewing. Clearly, the relationship between participants' task orientation to objects and the kind of premotor representations evoked remains an issue.

In this article we describe the progress we have made in developing experimental methods to reveal the evocation of specific hand actions in response to pictured objects or written words. For example, part of knowing what actions to carry out with a pocket calculator includes the depressing (poking) of keys. A crucial goal in evaluating the claim that lexical meaning includes access to action representations is to have ways of measuring the dynamic evocation of specific hand postures in a variety of tasks involving objects, words, and sentences.

Before describing our research, we summarise previous work in other laboratories that has gone some way towards establishing that certain aspects of hand movement are automatically recruited by objects or their names. We point out the limits of inferences allowed by this work. We then outline the logic of our own experimental approach, and we discuss what we have learned so far on the evocation of specific hand actions in relation to the meaning of manipulable objects and words that refer to them.

A number of previous studies have examined whether words or manipulable objects evoke the representation of hand actions. The basic design of these experiments requires participants to produce a manual response that is potentially influenced by knowledge of how one interacts with an object that is in view. Tucker and Ellis (1998), for example, had participants press a response button with the right or the left hand to classify the orientation of manipulable objects as upright or inverted. Each object was seen in profile and had a handle on its left or right side (e.g., a teapot). When the response hand was aligned with the handle of the object, participants were faster, implying the automatic evocation of a grasp response that affected the generation of the task-defined button press. Evidence that words can affect the generation of actions was provided by Glover, Rosenbaum, Graham, and Dixon (2004), who showed that at early stages of grasping a target block, the aperture between thumb and forefinger was affected by the presence of a word referring to a small or large manipulable object (e.g., apple or grape).

Although these studies demonstrate the evocation of some components of manual action (e.g., left versus right hand and finger aperture), neither addresses the central question of whether objects or words evoke specific hand postures (e.g., a poke gesture to a calculator) and under what circumstances. More recent studies by Tucker and Ellis (2001, 2004) have shown that semantic judgements about graspable objects were faster when the response action to signal the decision (a power or a precision grip) was compatible with the hand action usually associated with the target object. These results go some way towards establishing that specific hand postures are evoked by objects under certain task conditions. We note, however, that a wide range of hand actions in addition to prehensile grasps is typically needed to interact with objects, especially when using manmade objects for their intended purpose. Moreover, we wish to develop a more flexible task than one that requires manual responses driven by decisions that depend on explicit identification of an object. Thus, we present experiments that require manual responses to arbitrary cues and we examine how these responses are altered in the presence of manipulable objects. In addition, we measure a variety of possible hand gestures potentially evoked by objects including, but not limited to, prehensile grips.

EXPERIMENTS 1–3: PRIMING FUNCTIONAL GESTURES

Our approach to measuring the evocation of motor affordances is based on the development of a task that requires participants to initiate a pantomime gesture in response to a cue that defines some specific hand posture. These cues are relatively transparent; they are actual photographs of a hand in a posture that participants are asked to mimic (e.g., a hand with forefinger extended as a poke gesture). We measure the time to initiate each cued action by detecting when the response hand lifts away from a depressed response button. On each trial, we present an object either in advance of or simultaneously with a hand cue. The set of objects and associated hand actions are shown in Figure 1. Our method is analogous to a standard priming paradigm in the psycholinguistic literature, but instead of word recognition as the target task, we use the generation of a pantomime cued by the depiction of hand posture. The relationship between the object displayed as a prime and the hand cue is as follows. On *related* trials, the action denoted by the hand cue matched the action typically associated with the function of the object shown as the prime, as illustrated in Figure 1. On *unrelated* trials, the hand cue was paired with one of the other objects in the set, resulting in an unrelated object–hand pairing. If merely viewing an object without making a response to it elicits pertinent gestural knowledge, then participants should be able to generate actions to the cue more readily on related trials. Alternatively, it may not be the case that passive viewing is sufficient to elicit actions to objects. At least some evidence from the neuroimaging literature implies that semantic processing objects is required to generate motorically based cortical activity (Devlin et al., 2002). We therefore compared priming effects in two situations: participants passively viewed the object and responded to the hand cue or they were instructed to name the object after first responding to the hand cue.

In each of the experiments in this series, participants were shown greyscale photographs of objects and hands. The full set of items is shown in Figure 1. On each trial an object, serving as a prime, and a hand cue were presented. The participant's

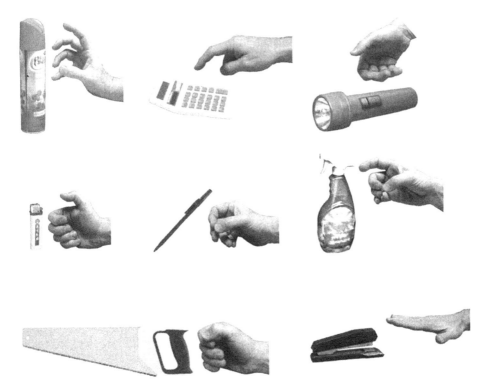

Figure 1. The set of eight objects and corresponding hand gestures used in Experiments 1–3. Each gesture depicts the typical manual action applied when using an object for its intended purpose.

task was to mimic the posture formed by the hand cue. The critical trials began with the participant's dominant hand resting on a response key. To make a response, the participant lifted his or her hand from the key and used the dominant hand to mimic the posture shown in the cue. Latency to initiate this pantomime response was recorded automatically when the response was released. To ensure smooth responding, participants began a test session with a series of practice trials in which they repeatedly mimicked each of the hand gestures represented by the set of hand cues but in the absence of any prime stimulus.

In Experiment 1, participants passively viewed the object prime and no task requirement was associated with that stimulus. The prime was in view for 105 ms or 750 ms, then was replaced by the hand cue. The object prime on each trial was either related or unrelated to the hand posture that was to be made on that trial. For example, the calculator was a related prime for the poke gesture, whereas any of the other objects (e.g., hand saw) were unrelated primes. We tested 24 healthy undergraduate students. The manipulation of prime duration (105 vs 750 ms) did not interact with the prime relatedness factor in any of the experiments in this series, so we present the data collapsed across prime duration. Figure 2 shows the mean response latency in Experiment 1 as a function of prime relatedness. It is clear from the figure that no priming effect was obtained in this experiment. Mere passive viewing of the prime objects apparently failed to elicit gestural knowledge of the type that could influence production of a manual response.

In Experiment 2 we sought to have participants engage with the object primes by requiring them to report the name of the prime after they had mimicked the cued gesture on each trial. By having participants identify the prime object, we expected that they would need to recruit conceptual knowledge associated with the object. If this knowledge includes representations for gestural interactions with the object, then we should find shorter response latencies when the object and target gesture are related than when they are unrelated. The procedure in Experiment 2 was the same as in Experiment 1, except that after pantomiming the target gesture, participants also named the prime object. The mean response latency, shown in Figure 2, revealed

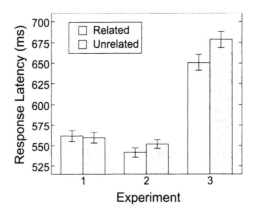

Figure 2. Mean response latency in Experiments 1–3 as a function of prime type. A related object prime represented an object to which the target gesture would typically be applied; unrelated object–prime/gesture–target pairs were created by reassigning objects and gestures. Error bars represent 95% within-participant confidence intervals (Loftus & Masson, 1994; Masson & Loftus, 2003).

a clear priming effect of about 11 ms ($n = 20$, $p < .01$). This result supports our expectation that identifying an object would potentially recruit gestural knowledge.

We attempted to produce a more robust priming effect in Experiment 3. Here, we modified the displays so that the prime object and the hand cue were presented simultaneously, side by side. As in Experiment 2, the task was to first pantomime the cued gesture, then to report the name of the object. By presenting the object and hand cue simultaneously, while requiring the participant to make a selective response to each stimulus, we expected to enhance the interaction between object identification processes and gestural knowledge. The mean response latency for pantomiming the indicated gestures is shown in Figure 2. Overall latencies in this experiment are longer because participants had to encode the object identity while viewing the hand cue and before initiating the manual response—the display was erased as soon as the participant's hand was lifted from the response key. The priming effect was magnified to 28 ms ($n = 21$, $p < .001$) in this experiment, relative to Experiment 2.

The evidence indicates, then, that merely looking at an object like a calculator is not enough to evoke a precise enough representation of hand action to prime the execution of a pantomime corresponding to the gesture normally made when using the object. Rather, objects generate representations of actions when classified and labelled. Our results cast some doubt on over-interpretations of functional imaging experiments that show evocation of motor-related activity when participants passively view objects. Either such activity occurs because objects are displayed long enough to encourage elaborative processing (e.g., speculation on how an object is used) or the motor representations observed in these experiments do not include the detailed parameters of action that led to priming in our task.

When participants are asked to name manipulated objects, however, specific hand actions are potentiated. Representations of hand actions are therefore evoked by the meaning of objects. A sentence like "Calculators are used for adding numbers" should not be taken as a literal index of the contents of semantic memory. Rather, such statements also reflect the fact that the knowledge of adding with a calculator includes elements of motor actions carried out on the physical device (Allport, 1985). Classifying and naming an object like a calculator involves access to this knowledge, yielding evocation of the corresponding representation of hand actions.

EXPERIMENTS 4–7: DISTINGUISHING GESTURES OF FORM AND FUNCTION

Objects normally elicit many kinds of manual actions. When using a calculator, for example, we often begin by picking it up and moving it to a convenient location for operating. A thumbtack requires that one pick it up with a pinch gesture before pressing it into a surface with an extended thumb. The prior history of an object is associated with multiple gestures. We can assume that frequently used actions are all represented as part of object knowledge. This assumption implies that hand actions for manipulable objects include actions corresponding to both the function of an object and its form. In some cases, form- and function-based actions are identical or nearly so. For example, we pick up and use a glass in virtually the same way. Other objects, though, have distinct actions for using and for picking up or moving them. A stapler is typically used to attach pages of paper by depressing its top component using a flat palm, but it is picked up using an inverted open grasp. We refer to form-based actions as *volumetric*, to reflect their sensitivity to details of weight distribution and shape. Actions based on conventional use of the object we refer to as *functional* gestures. This distinction is similar to one made by Johnson and Grafton (2003), who classify object-based actions as "acting on" and "acting with". The former, they assume, occurs when objects are grasped without a specific purpose, whereas the latter relies on knowledge of tool use. However, we do not consider volumetric gestures to be devoid of intentions or goals. Rather, they are executed for purposes such as picking up or moving, and in the case of familiar objects are influenced by memory for prior experience in much the same way as functional gestures.

In considering the possibility that the representations of both functional and volumetric gestures are part of the meaning of an object, we note that both types of gesture are ineluctably part of our prior motor experience with the object. If the knowledge of an object includes this prior history, then there is no reason to assume that functional gestural knowledge alone is maintained at the expense of volumetric knowledge. Indeed, functional gestures depend in crucial ways on knowledge of an object's shape and size encapsulated in volumetric constraints. The keys on a calculator are spatially arrayed within the confines of a particular volume, which determines their separation and therefore the positioning of the finger movements during calculation. We present a series of experiments, therefore, establishing that action representations evoked by objects include volumetric as well as functional gestures, and that both are part of the meaning of an object. After describing this evidence, we discuss the implications of our findings for the interpretation of motor-based activity elicited by objects in functional imaging studies and we consider the possible role that representations of volumetric and functional actions may play in the processing of words and sentences.

This series of experiments used a paradigm introduced by Bub, Masson, and Bukach (2003). The method was designed to provide evidence of the automatic nature of the recruitment of gestural knowledge when viewing an object, and is based on a variant of the Stroop colour-word interference task (Stroop, 1935). In the Stroop task, participants are instructed name the colour in which a stimulus is printed. If the stimulus is an incongruent colour word (e.g., *red* printed in green), participants take much longer to name the colour than if the stimulus is a neutral form such as a row of Xs or a congruent colour name (e.g., *red* printed in red). The long response latencies found in the incongruent condition are generally thought to indicate that participants automatically process word identity even though doing so can only interfere with their ability to efficiently perform the colour-naming task.

In our variant of the Stroop task, participants were first trained to associate each of four gestures with a unique colour. We used four functional gestures and four volumetric gestures in these experiments, testing different groups of participants with each set of four gestures. Figure 3 shows two examples of each type of gesture and an object for which each gesture would be appropriate. After learning the set of colour–gesture associations, participants were then given a series of trials on which they were to respond as quickly as possible to a colour stimulus by making the associated gesture. On these trials, colour was carried by an object (e.g., a green calculator). Colour–object pairs were arranged so that on congruent trials the target gesture was relevant to or congruent with the object (e.g., a green calculator shown to a participant who had learned to respond to green with a poke gesture). On incongruent trials, however, the object's colour was associated with one of the other gestures in the set, which always was an inappropriate gesture for that object (e.g., a

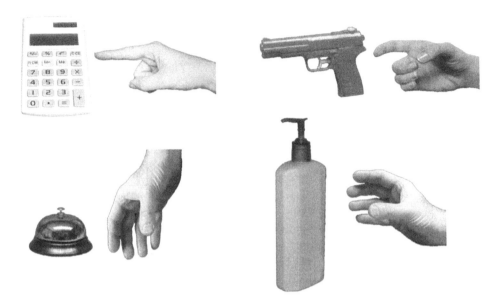

Figure 3. Example objects and gestures used in Experiments 4–7. The top row presents two functional gestures and an associated object for each. These gestures are the ones typically made when using the object for its intended purpose. The bottom row shows two volumetric gestures and an associated object for each. Volumetric gestures are the ones typically made when picking up an object, rather than using it.

red calculator shown to a participant who had learned to respond to red with a trigger gesture).

In this situation, participants are not required to make any response to the objects, but they must examine them to determine the colour in which they appear. However, participants should not attempt to recruit gestural knowledge about the object if they wish to avoid conflict on incongruent trials. But if participants are unable to control the evocation of gestural knowledge when viewing objects (because it occurs automatically), then we can expect that on incongruent trials participants will be slowed in making their responses, relative to congruent trials. For now, we leave aside the question of how the type of object viewing required in this task is different from the passive viewing assumed to operate in Experiment 1, but we will return to this issue in the General Discussion. In addition, one might ask whether participants were induced to recruit gestural knowledge about objects in these experiments because we included congruent trials, where gestural knowledge associated with the object would benefit production of the required response. This issue was addressed across Experiments 4–6 by varying the proportion of congruent trials included in the experiment.

In Experiment 4, we used congruent object–gesture pairs on 50% of the trials and incongruent pairs on the other 50%. In Experiment 5, we reduced the proportion of congruent trials to 25%. Finally, in Experiment 6, we dispensed with congruent trials and introduced a set of "neutral" objects that were large, non-manipulable entities (e.g., boat, airplane, sofa). In this latter case, there could be no motivation for participants to recruit gestural knowledge associated with objects because doing so could serve only to impede generation of the colour-cued gesture. Mean response latency for each of these experiments is shown in Figure 4. It can be seen that in nearly all cases, there was a clear disadvantage for responding in the incongruent

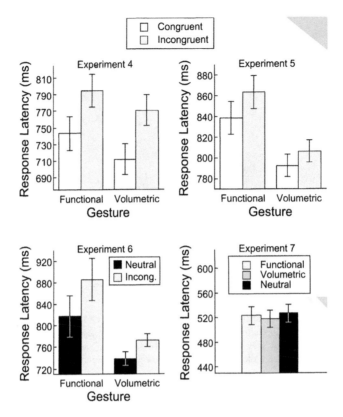

Figure 4. Mean response latency in Experiments 4–7. The data for Experiments 4–6 show gesture latency as a function of object–gesture relationship and type of gesture (functional or volumetric). The data for Experiment 7 show colour naming latency in the control experiment as a function of the type of object used to carry colour. Error bars represent 95% within-participant confidence intervals.

condition. The only exception is for volumetric gestures in Experiment 5, which produced a trend for longer durations in the incongruent condition. The incongruency effect in Experiment 6 is especially important because it shows that gestural knowledge seems to be evoked even when participants had no reason to strategically call upon their gestural knowledge of the objects they were shown, and indeed had reason to try to suppress such knowledge. This result speaks strongly in favour of the automatic nature of the evocation of gestural knowledge.[1]

One might argue that the reason for the incongruency effect seen in Experiment 6 is that participants could more easily discriminate colours when they were carried by the neutral objects than when the gesture-relevant objects were presented. After all, we could not counterbalance assignment of objects to congruency condition in Experiment 6, as we had done in the other two experiments. To dispense with this possibility, we had a group of participants perform a speeded colour-naming task in

---

[1] A reviewer pointed out that the trigger hand gesture physically resembles its associated object (the water pistol) and wondered whether this similarity might have played a major role in the congruency effects. This concern pertains only to the data from the functional gesture condition because the trigger gesture and the water pistol were only used there. We reanalysed the data for the functional condition in each experiment, excluding trials involving this object. A congruency effect emerged in each case even when this item was removed.

Experiment 7. Participants were shown the eight objects we used for functional gestures, the eight objects used for volumetric gestures, and the eight neutral objects. Each object appeared multiple times in each of the four colours used in Experiments 4–6 and the task was to name the colour as quickly as possible. Mean colour-naming latency is shown in Figure 4. It is clear that the three object sets did not differ with respect to colour-naming latency, indicating that colours were equally discriminable regardless of which set of objects carried them.

GENERAL DISCUSSION

The act of identifying manipulable objects evokes gestural representations associated with an object's function, and also with the object's form. These representations are part of object knowledge, but there are important constraints on the kind of the task context that elicits them. It is not the case that passive viewing alone is sufficient; pantomiming actions in response to a photograph of a hand denoting a particular posture was not affected by the accompanying image of an object unless participants were also instructed to name the object after carrying out the pantomime. Yet, surprisingly, an alternative experimental procedure yielded strong evidence that objects automatically evoke gestural representations. If participants pantomimed an action using colour as a cue, and the colour was a surface feature of an object, then both functional and volumetric gestures were elicited and interfered with production of the pantomime when there was a mismatch between it and the gestures conventionally associated with the object.

The paradox between these two outcomes—objects fail to elicit motor affordances in one context but readily do so in another—can easily be resolved if we consider that participants' use of colour as a cue required them to manually respond to an attribute of the depicted object (its colour) without also responding to its form. This is a very unusual filtering task: We are generally never in a situation demanding one kind of action to a surface property of an object, like colour, that is different from actions we normally execute when picking up or using it. Under these circumstances, the intention to act on the colour would not be easily segregated from the more habitual intention to carry out an action on the object, and motor representations afforded by the object are automatically evoked. When the cue to pantomime is a hand shape instead of an arbitrary colour, the response is to a depicted shape (a hand in a particular posture) that is completely distinct from the accompanying object. In this situation, no effect of the object is seen on pantomiming the hand cue, unless the participant also identifies and labels the object. We conclude that visual processing of manipulable objects does not invariably yield precise motor affordances. Gestural knowledge about form and function is evoked if participants attend to the meaning of an object (e.g., when asked to name it), but without intentions to act on the object, passive viewing alone does not automatically elicit gestural representations.

Nevertheless, the evidence we have obtained suggests that objects can readily generate motor representations in semantic tasks, and these representations concern both the function of an object and its volumetric properties. The fact that part of the manipulation knowledge associated with an object like a calculator includes parameters of hand actions executed when lifting the object seems surprising. We generally consider that familiarity with the meaning of an object entails knowing how to manually interact with it according to its conventional function, but this knowledge inevitably requires also knowing how to shape the hand when moving or lifting the object. Indeed, there is good reason on neuropsychological grounds to assume that familiar objects evoke stored knowledge of volumetric manual action as part of their meaning. Jeannerod, Decety, and Michel (1994) reported a case of optic ataxia in which hand configurations for grasping novel objects like a cylindrical tube were severely impaired, but manual interactions with familiar objects like a tube of lipstick were relatively preserved. Knowledge of a familiar object must include a representation of the volumetric gestures associated with shape-based properties, and this knowledge can modulate action even when cortical damage disrupts manual grasping of novel objects.

The fact that both functional and volumetric representations are triggered by objects is of considerable interest in regard to the interpretation of patterns of activation observed in neuroimaging experiments. Cortical areas known to mediate motor function are invoked when participants carry out tasks with tools and other manipulable objects, including tasks that do not require explicit consideration of manual actions (Devlin et al., 2002). It is generally assumed that this activation concerns manipulation knowledge dealing with the function of the object (e.g., Chao & Martin, 2000). Our evidence that hand actions pertaining to object shape, independent of function, are a crucial part of manipulation knowledge raises an important question. Specifically, are regions of activation associated with tools indeed indicative of functional knowledge, or do they represent both function and form? The finding that fruits and vegetables can yield activation of motor cortex (Gerlach et al., 2002) suggests that the representation of shape-based grasping is an important potential component of the observed patterns of activation.

How central are functional and volumetric gestural representations to the meaning of object concepts? Our experimental approach can be adapted to an examination of language tasks in order to determine the conditions generating manual representations evoked by words and sentences referring to manipulable objects. For example, written words instead of depicted objects can be used to carry colours that participants have learned to associate with particular gestures. Colour–word pairings can be arranged so that the gesture cued by the colour matches or mismatches the gestural knowledge associated with the manipulable object denoted by the word. For matching word–colour pairs, the relationship between the colour and the word can be volumetric or functional. Surprisingly, words show exactly the same evocation of functional and volumetric gestural knowledge as picture of objects (Bub, Masson, & Cree, 2006). This evidence strongly implies that gestural knowledge is part of the meaning of words and confirms a recent result reported by Myung, Blumstein, and Sedivy (in press). These authors found that making word–nonword decisions was facilitated on positive trials when the target word was preceded by another word that shared the same kind of manual action (e.g., typewriter, piano). In addition, Zwaan and Taylor (2006) showed that during comprehension of sentences referring to actions involving hand rotation, participants invoked motor representations that interacted with their perceptual judgements of a rotating image.

If gestural knowledge is recruited in processing the meaning of words, then the dynamic role of sentence context on motor representations raises some interesting questions. We have already clear evidence that the word concept "calculator" includes functional as well as volumetric gestural representations. Consider, however, a sentence like "John gave the calculator to Mary". The meaning of this sentence implies an action in which a calculator is being handed from one person to another. What kind of motor representations would be evoked?

Clues to the dynamics of motor representations evoked by sentences can be obtained by considering neurophysiological and computational accounts of contextual influences on action selection in primates (Fagg & Arbib, 1998; Sakata, Taira, Kusunoki, Murata, & Tanaka, 1997). In these accounts, the anterior-inferior parietal lobe (AIP) receives input from ventral pathways and generates multiple grasps afforded by an object. Grasp selection requires input to AIP from the inferior premotor cortex, based on contextual information that includes task demands and intentions. Irrelevant affordances are then suppressed, leaving only the affordance corresponding to the selected grasp.

In the human, we propose a similar dynamic resolution of affordances driven by factors such as sentence context. If understanding a sentence requires a mental simulation of action, then for a sentence like *John gave the calculator to Mary*, multiple affordances evoked by a calculator's shape and function would become available in AIP. The parameters for the relevant hand posture (open grasp) implied by the sentence would emerge over time and parameters for irrelevant gestures, such as poke, would dissipate. A sentence referring to function (*John added the numbers*) should generate the reverse pattern.

We return to the question of the causal role that gestural knowledge plays in language comprehension. The strongest claim is that understanding the meaning of words and sentences often or even invariably requires embodied action. The consistent effects of volumetric and functional gestural representations that we have described would then arise inevitably as a result of the operations required for language understanding. In a recent communication to us, John Marshall indicated that he was sceptical of this idea. We, who wish simply to follow the dictates of empirical evidence, suggest the following rejoinder. If a sentence that makes no appeal to visual or manual interactions with an object (e.g., *Jane remembered the calculator*) still evokes gestural knowledge, then we need to consider carefully the linguistic processes that generate motor representations and the possibility that these representations are an integral part of conceptual knowledge.

REFERENCES

Allport, D. A. (1985). Distributed memory, modular systems and dysphasia. In S. K. Newman & R. Epstein (Eds.), *Current perspectives in dysphasia*. Edinburgh, UK: Churchill Livingstone.

Barsalou, L. W., Simmons, W. K., Barbey, A. K., & Wilson, C. D. (2003). Grounding conceptual knowledge in modality-specific systems. *Trends in Cognitive Sciences, 7*, 84–91.

Bub, D. N., Masson, M. E. J., & Bukach, C. M. (2003). Gesturing and naming: The use of functional knowledge in object identification. *Psychological Science, 14*, 467–472.

Bub, D. N., Masson, M. E. J., & Cree, G. S. (2006). *Evocation of functional and volumetric gestural knowledge by objects and words*. Manuscript submitted for publication.

Chao, L. L., & Martin, A. (2000). Representation of manipulable man-made objects in the dorsal stream. *NeuroImage, 12*, 478–484.

Creem-Regehr, S. H., & Lee, J. N. (2005). Neural representations of graspable objects: Are tools special? *Cognitive Brain Research, 22*, 457–469.

Devlin, J. T., Moore, C. J., Mummery, C. J., Gorno-Tempini, M. L., Phillips, J. A., & Noppeney, U. et al. (2002). Anatomic constraints on cognitive theories of category specificity. *NeuroImage, 15*, 675–685.

Fagg, A. H., & Arbib, M. A. (1998). Modeling parietal–premotor interactions in primate control of grasping. *Neural Networks, 11*, 1277–1303.

Gallese, V., & Lakoff, G. (2005). The brain's concepts: The role of the sensory-motor system in conceptual knowledge. *Cognitive Neuropsychology, 22*, 455–479.

Gerlach, C., Law, I., & Paulson, O. B. (2002). When action turns into words: Activation of motor-based knowledge during categorization of manipulable objects. *Journal of Cognitive Neuroscience, 14*, 1230–1239.

Glenberg, A. M., & Kaschak, M. P. (2002). Grounding language in action. *Psychonomic Bulletin & Review, 9*, 558–565.

Glover, S., Rosenbaum, D. A., Graham, J., & Dixon, P. (2004). Grasping the meaning of words. *Experimental Brain Research, 154*, 103–108.

Jeannerod, M., Decety, J., & Michel, F. (1994). Impairment of grasping movements following a bilateral posterior parietal lesion. *Neuropsychologia, 32*, 369–380.

Johnson, S. H., & Grafton, S. T. (2003). From "acting on" to "acting with": The functional anatomy of object-oriented action schemata. In C. Prablanc, D. Pelisson, & Y. Rossetti (Eds.), *Neural control of space coding and action production. Progress in brain research, Vol. 142* (pp. 127–139). Amsterdam: Elsevier.

Loftus, G. R., & Masson, M. E. J. (1994). Using confidence intervals in within-subject designs. *Psychonomic Bulletin & Review, 1*, 476–490.

Masson, M. E. J., & Loftus, G. R. (2003). Using confidence intervals for graphically-based data interpretation. *Canadian Journal of Experimental Psychology, 57*, 203–220.

Myung, J-Y., Blumstein, S. E., & Sedivy, J. C. (in press). Playing on the typewriter, typing on the piano: Manipulation knowledge of objects. *Cognition*.

Sakata, H., Taira, M., Kusunoki, M., Murata, A., & Tanaka, Y. (1997). The TINS Lecture – The parietal association cortex in depth perception and visual control of hand action. *Trends in Neurosciences, 20*(8), 350–357.

Stroop, J. R. (1935). Studies of interference in serial verbal reactions. *Journal of Experimental Psychology, 18*, 643–662.

Tucker, M., & Ellis, R. (1998). On the relations between seen objects and components of potential actions. *Journal of Experimental Psychology: Human Perception and Performance, 24*, 830–846.

Tucker, M., & Ellis, R. (2001). The potentiation of grasp types during visual object categorization. *Visual Cognition, 8*, 769–800.

Tucker, M., & Ellis, R. (2004). Action priming by briefly presented objects. *Acta Psychologica, 116*, 185–203.

Zwaan, R. A., & Taylor, L. J. (2006). Seeing, acting, understanding: Motor resonance in language comprehension. *Journal of Experimental Psychology: General, 135*, 1–11.

Aphasia, apraxia and the evolution of the language-ready brain

Michael A. Arbib

University of Southern California, Los Angeles, CA, USA

Background: The Mirror System Hypothesis offers the mirror system for grasping (i.e., neural mechanisms active for both execution and observation of grasping) as a neural "missing link" between the brains of our non-human ancestors of 20 million years ago and the modern human language-ready brain, stressing the importance of manual gesture in the evolution of mechanisms supporting language.
Aims: To assess the view that neural mechanisms for both praxis and language share an evolutionary relationship to the ancestral mirror system for grasping.
Main Contribution: The praxis system receives a new analysis based on the attempt to link human praxis to computational models of execution and observation of grasping in the macaque as well as the analysis of parallels between language and praxis.
Conclusions: The conceptual analysis presented here may prove insightful for clinicians seeking to relate and differentiate aphasia and apraxia.

Since humans can learn language and monkeys and chimpanzees cannot, we seek brain regions that are *homologous* across these species (i.e., there is evidence for a shared ancestry) so that we may infer from analysis of both their similarities and differences what might have been the brain architecture of our common ancestor, and what may have changed along our varied evolutionary paths. The present discussion is rooted in the homology between human Broca's area, traditionally thought of as a speech area, and premotor area F5 of the macaque brain (Rizzolatti & Arbib, 1998). But first some definitions:

Address correspondence to: Michael A. Arbib, Computer Science Department, Neuroscience Program, and USC Brain Project, University of Southern California, Los Angeles, CA 90089-2520, USA. E-mail: arbib@pollux.usc.edu; web page: http://www-hbp.usc.edu/).

This work was supported in part by NIH under grant 1 P20 RR020700-01 to the USC/UT Center for the Interdisciplinary Study of Neuroplasticity and Stroke Rehabilitation (ISNSR).

In addition to thanking John Marshall, David Caplan, and Giacomo Rizzolatti for their early stimulus to my research on computational neurolinguistics and then the mirror system hypothesis, I want particularly to thank Anna Barrett, Anne Foundas, and Kenneth Heilman for the critique of the hypothesis that laid down the gauntlet that the present article picks up, and Chris Code, Laurel Buxbaum, Scott Frey, Rafaella Rumiati, and Angela Sirigu for guiding me through a number of relevant intricacies of the literature on apraxia and aphasia.

1. A mirror *neuron* for an action x is a neuron that is active in the brain of an animal both when that animal executes an action of type x and when it observes another animal execute an action of type x.
2. However, this does not imply that such a neuron of itself encodes action x; for example, the neuron might encode a feature of action x (whether of the movement performed during action x, or the goal to which x is directed, or both) and thus be part of a population code for x or some other process associated with x.
3. A mirror *system* for a class X of actions is a region of the brain that, compared with other situations, becomes more active both when actions from class X are observed and when actions from class X are executed.

Neurophysiological studies have shown mirror neurons for a wide range of actions in the macaque monkey, and brain-imaging experiments have demonstrated a mirror system for grasping in the human, but we have no single neuron studies proving the reasonable hypothesis that the human mirror *system* for grasping contains mirror neurons for specific grasps.

More specifically, area F5 (the fifth region in a numbering for areas of the macaque frontal lobe) in ventral premotor cortex contains, among other neurons, a set of neurons that fire when the monkey executes a specific manual action (e.g., one neuron might fire when the monkey performs a precision pinch, another might fire when the monkey executes a power grasp). A subset of these neurons, the so-called *mirror neurons*, also discharge when the monkey observes meaningful hand movements made by the experimenter which are similar to those whose execution is associated with the firing of the neuron (Rizzolatti, Fadiga, Gallese, & Fogassi, 1996). By contrast, the *canonical neurons* are those belonging to the complementary, anatomically segregated subset of grasp-related F5 neurons that fire when the monkey performs a specific action but not when it observes a similar action. We further stress that mirror neurons for grasping have also been found in parietal areas of the macaque brain. Moreover, brain-imaging studies demonstrate that there are mirror systems for grasping (i.e., regions active for both observation and execution of grasping) in Broca's area and parietal cortex. (For more information on the anatomy and neurophysiology, see Rizzolatti, Luppino, & Matelli, 1998; and Rizzolatti, Fogassi & Gallese, 2001). These findings are the basis for:

- The Mirror System Hypothesis (MSH): The *parity requirement for language in humans*—that what counts for the "communicator" [e.g., speaker] must count approximately the same for the "communicatee" [e.g. hearer]—is met because Broca's area evolved atop the mirror system for grasping with its capacity to generate and recognise a set of actions. Here, hand and face gestures may be used as well as, or instead of, vocal gestures for communication (Arbib & Rizzolatti, 1997; Rizzolatti & Arbib, 1998).

When we explore the relation between praxis and communication, we will ask whether the same mirror neurons—accepting the hypothesis of (3)—are involved in both functions. Whether the answer is yes or no, it will be worth stressing that we must go "beyond the mirror"—it is not mirror neurons alone that serve the various functions that interest us, but rather the larger systems (whose delimitation is a challenging task for present and future research) of which they form part.

Although this article is not based on the work of John Marshall, its roots can in part be traced back to his influence and generosity. One morning in 1976, shortly after my family and I arrived in Edinburgh for a year's sabbatical, there came a ring at the doorbell and there on the doorstep stood John Marshall, arriving unheralded to welcome us to Edinburgh. The friendship and conversations of the following year contributed to a rekindled interest in neurolinguistics that laid the basis for the paper by Arbib and Caplan (1979) and the two subsequent workshops at the University of Massachusetts at Amherst that eventually led to the book edited by Arbib, Caplan, and Marshall (1982); related efforts yielded the book by Arbib, Conklin, and Hill (1987). After that, my work on language entered a dormant stage but my work on brain mechanisms for the visual control of action proceeded apace, yielding among other things a partnership with Marc Jeannerod, Giacomo Rizzolatti, and Hideo Sakata (see Jeannerod, Arbib, Rizzolatti, & Sakata, 1995, for one result) that spanned the discovery of macaque mirror neurons in Parma and the linkage to Broca's area that provided the foundation for MSH.

Arbib (2005a) gives a comprehensive review of the current state of MSH, stressing that the formulation offered above is just a starting point for more detailed analysis. That review is accompanied by numerous commentaries and the author's response. Of particular concern here is the commentary by Barrett, Foundas, and Heilman (2005) who discuss functional and structural evidence supporting differential localisation of the neuronal modules controlling limb praxis, speech and language, and emotional communication. They argue that such data rule against MSH. This paper will advance the debate, seeking to refute elements of their critique while conceding that definitive arguments in favour of MSH are still not available.

EVOLUTIONARY PARCELLATION OF THE BRAIN

As background for what follows, it will be useful to recall some key ideas from comparative neurobiology on the evolutionary parcellation of the brain. Butler and Hodos (1996) show that the course of brain evolution among vertebrates has been determined in great part by (a) formation of multiple new nuclei through elaboration or duplication; (b) regionally specific increases in cell proliferation in different parts of the brain; and (c) gain of some new connections and loss of some established connections.

Increases in the overall size of mammalian neocortex are paralleled by increases in the number of its functional subdivisions and the complexity of the internal organisation of the subdivisions, although the differences between primates and other mammals, and between humans and other primates, appear to involve specific changes in circuitry beyond those related to the general sequelae of increase in brain size (Striedter, 2004, Chapter 9).

Kaas (1993) and Krubitzer (1998) offer a detailed perspective on the evolution of cerebral cortex. The neocortex in mammals is divided into many functional subunits, each with a distinct variation on cortical cellular architecture and a unique pattern of connections. New cortical fields might be created by novel combinations of inputs, yielding new functions through varied processing of the patterns of activity in the inputs. Modules could then form within a field that are specialised for a given novel process (with these modules dispersed across the brain region to sample diverse parts of the input manifold). These modules might be of various column-like, band-like, or dot-like shapes, or even form layers or sublayers. Examples include the ocular dominance bands that subdivide primary visual cortex of some monkeys, cytochrome oxidase blob and interblob regions of primary cortex of primates, and the irregular bands of cortex related to slowly adapting and rapidly adapting cutaneous receptors in SI of monkeys. The somatosensory cortex of rodents contains barrel-like structures, one for each of the vibrissae of the face. As Kaas and Krubitzer observe, redistribution of functionally similar modules could then yield new brain regions with new representations of the sensory periphery, and these in turn could yield reorganisation of association and motor cortices. This parcellation into classes of modules, the progressive fusion of modules of like class, and the eventual separation of fused modules into two or more areas, would allow proper function at all stages, and indeed intermediate stages might persist where they prove truly functional. Moreover, new modules may serve to modulate and enrich existing capabilities of the ancestral brain so that (in general) much of the old capability is retained but with an enriched repertoire (Arbib, Érdi, & Szentágothai, 1998). Thus reduplication of circuitry may form the basis for differential evolution of the copies to serve a variety of functions. Hence data on differential localisation of limb praxis, speech and language, and emotional communication may not so much provide arguments against MSH as offer insight into what form these patterns of reduplication and subsequent differentiation might have taken.

MODELLING THE CONTROL AND RECOGNITION OF HAND MOVEMENTS

We briefly recount here our models of the systems in which the canonical and mirror neurons of macaque F5 are embedded, since they highlight certain features of the human brain that will be essential to our analysis of the way in which systems for praxis provide the core for the human brain mechanisms that support language. (I apologise to readers who have seen the next two figures more than once before, but they are needed to anchor certain points below.)

The parietal area AIP (the Anterior region of the Intra-Parietal sulcus) and area F5 together anchor the canonical cortical circuit in macaque which transforms visual information on intrinsic properties of an object into hand movements for grasping it. AIP processes visual information to implement perceptual schemas for extracting grasp parameters (affordances; Gibson, 1979) relevant to the control of hand movements (Taira, Mine, Georgopoulos, Murata, & Sakata, 1990) and is reciprocally connected with the canonical neurons of F5. Discharge in most grasp-related F5 neurons correlates with an action rather than with the individual movements that form it, so that one may relate F5 neurons to various *motor schemas* corresponding to the action associated with their discharge. By contrast, primary motor cortex (F1, aka M1) formulates the neural instructions for lower motor areas and motor neurons.

The basic control system for grasping is modelled by the FARS model (named for Fagg, Arbib, Rizzolatti, and Sakata; Fagg & Arbib 1998) which embeds F5 canonical neurons in a larger system (the model has been implemented, and various examples of grasping simulated). The distinction, for FARS, is between seeing how to grasp an (unclassified) object versus recognising a specific object. The dorsal stream (i.e., that which passes through AIP) does not know "what" the object is, it can only see the object as a set of possible affordances, whereas the ventral stream (from primary visual cortex to inferotemporal cortex, IT) is able to recognise what the object is. This information is passed to prefrontal cortex (PFC), which can then, on the basis of the current goals of the organism and the recognition of the nature of

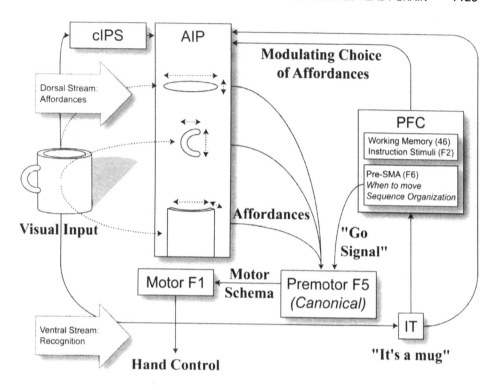

Figure 1. "FARS modificato". The original FARS diagram (Fagg & Arbib, 1998) is here modified to show PFC acting on AIP rather than F5. The idea is that AIP does not "know" the identity of the object, but can only extract affordances (opportunities for grasping for the object consider as an unidentified solid); prefrontal cortex uses the IT identification of the object, in concert with task analysis and working memory, to help AIP select the appropriate action from its "menu".

the object, bias the affordance appropriate to the task at hand. The original FARS model suggested that the bias was applied by PFC to F5; subsequent neuroanatomical data (as analysed by Rizzolatti & Luppino, 2003) suggest that PFC and IT may modulate action selection at the level of parietal cortex rather than premotor cortex. Figure 1 gives a partial view of "FARS Modificato", the FARS model updated to show this modified pathway. AIP may represent several affordances initially, but only one of these is selected to influence F5. This affordance then activates the F5 neurons to command the appropriate grip once it receives a "go signal" from another region, F6 (pre-SMA), of prefrontal cortex. F5 also accepts signals from areas 46 (dorsolateral prefrontal cortex), and F2 (dorsal premotor cortex)—all in prefrontal cortex (PFC)—to respond to working memory, and instruction stimuli, respectively, in choosing among the available affordances. Note that this same pathway could be implicated in tool use, bringing in semantic knowledge as well as perceptual attributes to guide the dorsal system (Johnson-Frey, 2003; Johnson-Frey, Funnell, Gerry, & Gazzaniga, 2005).

It is worth briefly relating this model to data on patients DF (Goodale, Milner, Jakobson, & Carey, 1991) and AT (Jeannerod, Decety, Michel, 1994) which showed a dissociation between the praxic use of size information (parietal) and the "declaration" of that information either verbally or through pantomime (inferotemporal). We may talk about "how/parameterisation of action" versus "what/

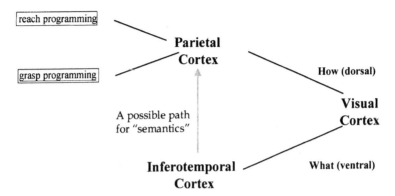

Figure 2. The dorsal "how/parameterisation of action" and ventral "what/knowledge of action" pathways.

knowledge of action" (Figure 2). DF had a lesion allowing signals to flow from V1 towards posterior parietal cortex but not from V1 to inferotemporal cortex (IT), and could preshape accurately when reaching to grasp an object even though she was unable to declare, either verbally or through pantomime, the visual parameters that guided the preshape. By contrast, AT had a bilateral posterior parietal lesion, and could use her hand to pantomime the size of a cylinder, but could not preshape appropriately when asked to grasp it.

Thus what at first sight appear to be the same parameters have two quite different representations—one for determining "How" to set the parameters for an action, the other expressing "What" an object and its describable properties (including appropriate actions involving it) might be. However, although AT could not preshape for a generic object like a cylinder, for which there is no associated size range, she was able to preshape for an object like a lipstick whose "semantics" included a fairly narrow size range. We thus suggest that the IT "size-signal" has a diffuse effect on grasp programming—enough to bias a choice between two alternatives, or provide a default value when the parietal cortex cannot offer a value itself, but not enough to perturb a single sharply defined value established in parietal cortex by other means. Note the corresponding path from IT to AIP—both directly and via PFC—in FARS Modification.

This is consistent with a path from IT to AIP (the choice in Figure 1) or some other part of the grasping system which ensures that when size information is available within the semantics of an object identified by the ventral system, then that information (which may have only limited precision) will be made available to the ventral system. Zhong and Rockland (2003) show that much of the inferior parietal lobule (IPL) has direct connections to anterior-ventral TE (TEav) around the anterior middle temporal sulcus (amts); they also note evidence (Distler, Boussaoud, Desimone, & Ungerleider, 1993; Webster, Bachevalier, & Ungerleider, 1994) for direct connections between TE and the parietal lobe. They view this as consistent with evidence from macaque fMRI (Sereno, Trinath, Augath, & Logothetis, 2002) that the region around the amts may be part of a network involved in three-dimensional shape, which is distributed across both "what" and "where" processing streams. I would speculate that such a reciprocal path might enable the activation of a set of affordances to constrain elicitation of a semantic representation for an action via the ventral path.

If this is accepted, we would then hypothesise that DF's lesion is such that this pathway has been damaged too much to allow such use of her affordances.

With this, we turn to the macaque mirror system for grasping, which we posit to be homologous to a system in the human brain shared with the common ancestor of human and monkey. Macaque mirror neurons do not discharge in response to simple presentation of objects even when held by hand by the experimenter, and require a specific action—whether observed or self-executed—to be triggered. Indeed, macaque mirror neurons for transitive actions do not fire when the monkey sees the hand movement unless it can also see the object or, more subtly, if the object is not visible but is appropriately "located" in working memory because it has recently been placed on a surface and has then been obscured behind a screen behind which the experimenter is seen to be reaching (Umiltà et al., 2001). Moreover, all mirror neurons show visual generalisation. They fire when the instrument of the observed action (usually a hand) is large or small, far from or close to the monkey. They may also fire even when the action instrument has shapes as different as those of a human or monkey hand. A few neurons respond even when the object is grasped by the mouth.

Developing a new capability requires not only the mastery of the relevant motor control but also the attunement of sensory signals for the feedback control of the novel actions. Just as reaching towards an object under visual guidance requires feedback on the position of the hand relative to the object, so too does grasping of a complex object require careful attention to motion of, e.g., fingertips relative to the affordances of the object. Such considerations ground my opinion that the primary evolutionary impetus for the mirror system was *not* for recognising the action of others, but was rather to facilitate feedback control of dexterous movement. I will not attempt to prove this point here, but will instead show how *parameters relevant to such feedback* could be crucial in enabling the monkey to associate the visual appearance of what it is doing with the task at hand, with self-recognition so structured as to also support recognition of the action when performed by others.

The MNS model of Oztop and Arbib (2002) provides some insight into the anatomy while focusing on the learning capacities of mirror neurons. Here, the task is to determine whether the shape of the hand and its trajectory are "on track" to grasp an observed affordance of an object using a known action. The model (Figure 3) is organised around the idea that the AIP $\rightarrow$ F5$_{canonical}$ pathway emphasised in the FARS model (Figure 1) is complemented by 7b ($\approx$PF/PFG) $\rightarrow$ F5$_{mirror}$. As shown in Figure 3, the MNS model can be divided into three parts.

Middle diagonal: Object features are processed by AIP to extract grasp affordances, these are sent on to the canonical neurons of F5 that choose a particular grasp. *Top diagonal*: Recognising the location of the object provides parameters to the motor programming area F4 which computes the reach. The information about the reach and the grasp is taken by the motor cortex M1 to control the hand and the arm. *Essential elements for the mirror system*: The third part of the figure provides components that can learn and apply key criteria for activating a mirror neuron, recognising that (a) the preshape that the monkey is seeing corresponds to the grasp that the mirror neuron encodes; (b) the preshape that the observed hand is executing is appropriate to the object that the monkey can see (or remember); and (c) that the hand is moving on a trajectory that will bring it to grasp the object. Making crucial use of input from the superior temporal sulcus (STSa; Carey, Perrett, & Oram, 1997; Perrett, Mistlin, Harries, & Chitty, 1990), two schemas at bottom left recognise the shape of the hand of the actor being observed

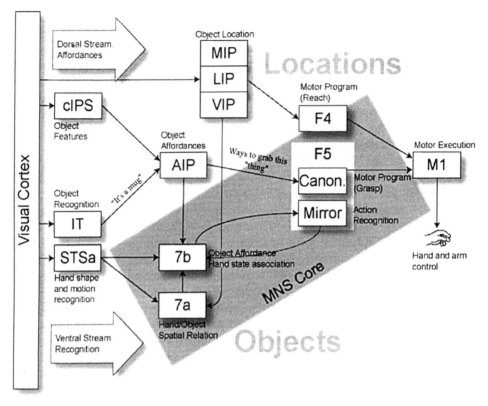

Figure 3. The MNS (Mirror Neuron System) model (Oztop & Arbib, 2002). Note that this basic mirror system for grasping crucially links the visual process of the superior temporal sulcus (STS) to the parietal regions (7b ≈ PF/PFG) and premotor regions (F5), which have been shown to contain mirror neurons for manual actions.

by the monkey whose brain we are interested in, and how that hand is moving. Just to the right of these is the schema for hand–object spatial relation analysis. It takes information about object features, the motion of the hand, and the location of the object to infer the relation between hand and object. Just above this is the schema for associating object affordances and hand state. Together with F5 canonical neurons, this last schema (in 7b≈PF/PFG) provides the input to the F5 mirror neurons.

In the MNS model, the *hand state* was defined as a vector whose components represented the movement of the wrist relative to the location of the object and of the hand shape relative to the affordances of the object. Oztop and Arbib (2002) showed that an artificial neural network corresponding to PF and $F5_{mirror}$ could be trained to recognise the grasp type from the *hand state trajectory*, with correct classification often being achieved well before the hand reached the object. The modelling assumed that the neural equivalent of a grasp being in the monkey's repertoire is that there is a pattern of activity in the F5 canonical neurons that commands that grasp. During training, the output of the F5 canonical neurons, acting as a code for the grasp being executed by the monkey at that time, was used as the training signal for the F5 mirror neurons to enable them to learn which hand–object trajectories corresponded to the canonically encoded grasps. As a result of this training, the appropriate mirror neurons come to fire in response to viewing the appropriate trajectories even when the trajectory is not accompanied by F5 canonical firing. Crucially, this training prepares the F5 mirror neurons to respond to hand–object relational trajectories even when the hand is of the "other" rather than the "self" because the hand state is based on the view of movement of a hand relative to the object, and thus only *indirectly* on the retinal input of seeing hand and object, which can differ greatly between observation of self and other.

Bonaiuto, Rosta, and Arbib (in press) have developed MNS2, a new version of the MNS model using a recurrent architecture that is biologically more plausible than that of the original model. Moreover, MNS2 extends the capacity of the model to address data on audio-visual mirror neurons, i.e., mirror neurons that respond to the sight and sound of actions with characteristic sounds such as paper tearing and nut cracking (Kohler, Keysers, Umiltà, Fogassi, Gallese, & Rizzolatti, 2002), and on response of mirror neurons when the target object was recently visible but is currently hidden (Umiltà et al., 2001). Modelling audio-visual mirror neurons rests on a Hebbian association between auditory neurons and mirror neurons, whereas recognition of hidden grasps employs circuits for working memory (encoding data on the currently obscured hand and object) and dynamic remapping (to update the estimate of the location of the hand relative to the object).

In either case, the key point is that the actual or "virtual" visual input to the F5 mirror neurons encodes the trajectory of the relation of parts of the hand to the object rather than the visual appearance of the hand in the visual field; this training prepares the F5 mirror neurons to respond to hand–object relational trajectories even when the hand is of the "other" rather than the "self". What makes the modelling worthwhile is that the trained network responded not only to hand state trajectories from the training set, but also exhibited interesting responses to novel hand–object relationships. Learning models such MNS and MNS2, and the data they address, make clear that *mirror neurons are not restricted to recognition of an innate set of actions but can be recruited to recognise and encode an expanding repertoire of novel actions.*

Ferrari, Gallese, Rizzolatti, and Fogassi (2003) found what they call "tool-responding mirror neurons" in the lateral sector of monkey ventral premotor area F5. After much training of the monkey, these neurons discharge when the monkey *observes* actions performed by an experimenter with a tool (a stick or a pair of pliers). This response is stronger than that obtained when the monkey observes a similar action made with a biological effector (the hand or the mouth). These neurons also respond when the monkey executes actions with both the hand and the mouth. The visual and the motor responses of each neuron are congruent in that they share the same general goal; that is, taking possession of an object and modifying its state. Ferrari et al. propose that tool-responding mirror neurons enable the observing monkey to extend action-understanding capacity to actions that do not strictly correspond to their motor representations. They hypothesise that after a relatively long visual exposure to tool actions a visual association between the hand and the tool is created, so that the tool becomes recognised as a kind of prolongation of the hand. The idea is that these cells recognise actions with the same goal, even if that goal is achieved by different means.

Escola, Intskirveli, Umiltà, Rochat, Rizzolatti, and Gallese (2004) went further, training a macaque monkey to perform hand grasping actions by means of two especially designed pincers-like tools. One was like normal (spring-loaded) pincers, requiring finger extension to open the pincers and finger flexion to close it. The other tool, the "reverse pincers", required finger flexion to open the pincers, and finger extension to close it. They found that many of the recorded hand grasping neurons in area F5 responded during hand grasping and also during grasping with the two kinds of tool, in spite of the completely different finger movements required to achieve the same goal. These results again suggest that F5 neurons recognise actions with the same goal, even if that goal is achieved by different means.

The above modelling and data yield two challenges to the terminology:

(a) Is a neuron in F5 to be called a mirror neuron if it has not yet learned to fire in relation to execution and observation of a related set of grasps?

(b) Is a neuron in F5 to be called a mirror neuron if it fires for the recognition of an action the animal cannot perform?

For (a), I would say that there are *potential* mirror neurons, a pool that can be recruited by suitable training. For (b), I would say that these are certainly mirror neurons if training has simply broadened their congruence, as in the case where a mirror neuron for the precision pinch comes to respond even when the precision pinch observed is applied using a pair of pliers. However, there is a deeper issue here that seems not to have been addressed in the literature. In both cases we have a set of neurons so situated that it is possible for them to become active in both the observation and execution of actions. It seems a reasonable scientific goal to understand the actual and potential capabilities of such neurons. If, even after adaptation, some of these neurons are not active for both execution and observation of similar movements, then one has a terminological choice as to whether or not to still call them mirror neurons. As a placeholder let us say that, through adaptation, a potential mirror neuron may become a mirror neuron or a *quasi-mirror neuron*. I would argue that quasi-mirror neurons are crucial to the evolution of language, supporting the ability to perceive actions outside one's own repertoire but anchoring them in vaguely related movements that (in the human, not the macaque) can support pantomime. For example, when I flap my arms to suggest a bird's flying, this may involve mirror neurons effective for execution only of arm flapping but for observation of both arm flapping and bird flight. This may then be a crucial stage intermediate to the abstraction of purely symbolic gestures whose mirroring is separated from actions more iconically related to the symbolised action and object.

IMITATION AND COMPOUND ACTIONS

In much of the human brain-imaging literature, it seems to be implied that having mirror neurons is a sufficient base for imitation. This is a myth. The reality is that in macaques we do not see imitation to any significant degree.

From object-based imitation to pantomime

Voelkl and Huber (2000) talk of "true imitation" in marmoset monkeys. In their study, marmosets observed a demonstrator removing the lids from a series of plastic canisters to obtain a mealworm. When subsequently allowed access to the canisters, marmosets that had observed a demonstrator using his hands to remove the lids used only their hands. In contrast, marmosets that had observed a demonstrator using his mouth also used their mouth to remove the lids. In this case, "imitation" is based on the choice of effector to achieve a certain goal, not, I would claim, on the reproduction of a specific, observed movement of that effector. We might call this "effector priming" rather than "true imitation". As far as the neurophysiology of mirror neurons is concerned, all that has been demonstrated is that if a specific action is within a macaque's repertoire, then observation of that action when executed by another will activate the appropriate mirror neurons, not that the monkey will or can imitate the action. Imitation goes from observation of an action to execution of that action. For this purpose one must augment the macaque system captured by the FARS and MNS models as follows:

(i)   For imitation of an action in the repertoire, one needs to add a link from mirror neurons that recognise an action to neurons that will control the execution of that action.

(ii) Imitation may involve using observation to acquire an action not already in the repertoire.

Arbib and Rizzolatti (1997) offered the equation *Action = Movement + Goal*. Monkeys need both movement and goal to recognise the action (recall our discussion of Umiltà et al., 2001). In either case, the trajectory and hand shape must match the affordance of the object. Humans can infer the goal from seeing the movement—a capability that has two quite different consequences: (a) Imitation may be based on attending to the structure of subgoals or the movements that link them, or both; and (b) the human brain can support pantomime, whereas the brains of other primates cannot. (See Arbib & Rizzolatti, 1997, for the linkage of this to inverse and direct models in motor control. For more recent accounts see Miall, 2003; Oztop, Kawato, & Arbib, 2006.)

When explaining MSH below, I will thus claim that hominid evolution extended the capacity of the mirror system first to support imitation, and then to support pantomime, and finally to support protolanguage. Pantomime goes beyond imitation of praxis and establishes mechanisms that can then support the production and recognition of arbitrary gestures that have no relation to external physical goals, but are rather codified in terms of a series of hand shapes and their locations. Note, though, that this evolutionary process is probably not confined to the circuitry homologous to that containing mirror neurons in the macaque, but also involves major extensions of the larger circuitry of which they are part.

Augmented competitive queuing

Turning from single actions to sequences, Fagg and Arbib (1998) hypothesise that the part of the supplementary motor area called pre-SMA (Rizzolatti et al., 1998) has neurons whose connections encode an "abstract sequence" Q1, Q2, Q3, ..., with sequence learning then involving learning that activation of each Qi triggers appropriate F5 neurons for that action of the sequence. Other studies suggest that administration of the sequence (inhibiting extraneous actions, while priming imminent actions) is carried out by the basal ganglia on the basis of its interactions with the pre-SMA (Bischoff-Grethe, Crowley, & Arbib, 2003; see Dominey, Arbib, & Joseph, 1995, for an earlier model of the possible role of the basal ganglia in sequence learning).

Fogassi, Ferrari, Gesierich, Rozzi, Chersi, and Rizzolatti (2005) studied the activity of neurons (both motor and mirror) in the inferior parietal lobule (IPL) when monkeys performed grasping as part of different overall actions, such as grasping a piece of food prior to eating it versus grasping it prior to placing it in a container. They found that the activity of motor IPL neurons coding a specific act was very different depending on the overall action of which it was part. Many of these IPL neurons had the mirror property of discharging during the observation of acts done by others, and most "mirror neurons" responded differentially when the same observed act was embedded in different overall actions. The cue that determines the overall action (whether the monkey's own action or the observed action of the experimenter) is the presence or absence of the container—if the container is present the food is to be placed in it; if not, the food is to be placed in the mouth. The authors suggest that these IPL mirror neurons mediate "intention understanding" since they encode not the current act so much as its role within the overall action of which it is part.

Chersi, Fogassi, Rozzi, Rizzolatti, and Ferrari (2005) outline a model of these findings based on neuronal chains. Suppose that a sequence A→B→C is required to achieve goal G while another sequence A→D→E is required to achieve goal H. The work of Fogassi et al. (2005) suggests that different neurons—let us call them A\G and A\H (leaving aside population coding for now)—are required to code action A in the first and second cases, respectively. Then the Chersi et al. (2005) model postulates neuronal connections A\G→B\G→C\G activating neurons that control the actions required to achieve goal G, while another sequence A\H →D\H →E\H encodes actions leading to H. These chains that Chersi et al. (2005) posit in IPL for action recognition are very similar to those posited by Fagg and Arbib (1998) in pre-SMA: it is the chain of activity rather than the actions themselves that are encoded. However, the very different localisation of the two models poses real challenges for further experiments in both macaque neurophysiology and human brain imaging.

In work currently under way, we have developed a new methodology, which we call augmented competitive queuing (ACQ; Bonaiuto & Arbib, 2006) that explains how it is that apparently fixed chains of behaviour may actually be modified under different circumstances—we behave differently, for example, depending on whether or not wine is in our wine glass. Our approach starts from, but goes beyond, the observation that a sequence may also result from "competitive queuing" (Arbib & Didday, 1975; Houghton & Hartley 1995; Rhodes, Bullock, Verwey, Averbeck, & Page, 2004): At any time neurons representing different actions are activated with different priority signals; a winner take all (WTA) process then selects the action associated with the largest priority signal and initiates its execution. The "winner" is then inhibited and the competition begins anew to choose the next action. Clearly, by setting the initial activation appropriately, one may be able to guarantee the execution of a specific sequence. However, augmented competitive queuing has the advantage that the sequence of actions need not be fixed, but can be determined "on-line" to adjust to changing circumstances.

To motivate ACQ, we consider the case of "Alstermark's Cat": Alstermark, Lundberg, Norrsell, and Sybirska (1981) experimentally lesioned the spinal cord of the cat in order to determine the role of propriospinal neurons in forelimb movements. A piece of food was placed in a horizontal glass tube facing the cat. To eat the food, the cat had to reach its forelimb into the tube, grasp the food with its paw, and bring the food to its mouth. Lesions in spinal segment C5 of the cortico- and rubrospinal tracts interfered with the cat's ability to grasp the food, but not to reach for it. In contrast, both reaching and grasping were defective after a corresponding transection of the cortico- and rubrospinal tracts in C2. It was concluded that the C3 – C4 propriospinal neurons can mediate the command for reaching, but not for grasping which instead can be mediated via interneurones in the forelimb segments C6–Th1. The cat would reach inside the tube, and repeatedly attempt to grasp the food and fail. Alstermark (personal communication to Arbib) reported that these repeated failed grasp attempts would eventually succeed in displacing the food from the tube, and the cat would then grasp the food from the ground with its jaws and eat it. *After only two or three trials*, the cat began to rake the food out of the tube, a more efficient process than random displacement by failed grasps. Rather than learning an entirely new skill, or refining and tuning an already-learned skill, it seems that decision variables have been rapidly modified to adaptively change the deployment of motor schema.

ACQ can explain this because, for one thing, the activation level of motor program elements is dynamically computed in each "time step" rather than being completely specified before sequence execution as in classical CQ. We dissociate the *executability* (based on available *affordances*) of a motor program element from its learned *desirability*. The desirability of each motor element is learned via temporal difference (TD) learning (Sutton & Barto, 1998), which basically provides over time a measure of how likely a given action is to lead to a state in which the organism will receive positive reinforcement. The greater the likelihood, the more desirable the action. These values are multiplicatively combined when calculating an element's activation level for the competitive choice (WTA) process. We thus define the (context-dependent) *priority* of an action A at any particular time t by the formula

$$priority(A, t) = executability(A, t) * desirability(A, t)$$

Our next innovation was to have learning work not only with efferent copy of motor commands—what action was *intended*—but also the perceptions of which actions were *apparently* executed. The intuition is that if we succeed unexpectedly at a task, we may recognise that an apparently random motion can in fact be classified as an action that helped lead to success. We ascribe this "recognition of apparent action" to a mirror system in the cat—making the intriguing point that a mirror system can classify an action on the basis of observing what one is doing oneself as well as observing what the other is doing. Although mirror systems for action recognition have only been found in the macaque and in humans, we think it reasonable to posit mirror systems in other species (making the case for further experiments). In summary, we suggest that success should reinforce not only the action that was actually executed but also any action the mirror system recognises during the course of that execution.

ACQ's method of motor program representation implicitly encodes sequences of motor elements in terms of goals and subgoals. For example, the goal of opening a bottle requires a motor program with two distinct movement patterns: turning the cap and pulling the cap off. The act of turning the cap is a single motor element repeated until the next motor element (pulling the cap off) is executable. In this way, the state of having the cap turned until it can be pulled off can be seen as a subgoal of opening the bottle. This scenario is easily represented within ACQ. If a reward is given for opening the bottle, TD learning would eventually leave the cap-pulling motor schema with a higher desirability value than the cap-turning motor schema. Until the cap-pulling schema is executable, the cap-turning motor schema would repeatedly be selected, unscrewing the cap. Once executable, the cap-pulling schema's higher desirability value will dominate the ACQ network, it will be selected for execution, and the bottle will be opened. The dissociation of motor schema executability from desirability allows motor programs to be represented as dynamic, goal-oriented sequences of motor elements.

Complex imitation

A striking example of complex behaviour in a nonhuman primate is given by the flow diagram offered by Byrne (2003) to summarise the interwoven sequences of coordinated actions by both hands used by a right-handed mountain gorilla when preparing a bundle of nettle leaves to eat. The process starts with acquiring a nettle plant and ends when a folded handful of leaves is put into the mouth. Byrne asserts that non-human great apes acquire such skills by what he calls "imitation by behaviour parsing". The gorilla does not acquire this skill by paying explicit attention to the subgoals that define the tests in Byrne's diagram. Rather, the statistical regularities in the organisation of another agent's behaviour—correlations in circumstances of use, effects on the environment, etc.—can guide the observer's behaviour without his understanding the intentions of the other, or the pattern of cause-and-effect. Thus, Byrne asserts (2003, p. 529) that "imitation of complex, novel behaviour may not require mentalising, but conversely behaviour parsing may be a necessary preliminary to attributing intention and cause … in contrast to the frequent assumption that imitation [must depend] on prior understanding of others' intentions."

What I would stress is that "behaviour parsing" as defined by Byrne is a statistical process very different from the explicit recognition of a nested hierarchy of subgoals and actions posited in what I call *complex imitation*, defined as the combination of (a) the ability to recognise when another's performance combines actions approximatable by variants of actions already in the observer's repertoire with (b) the ability to use that analysis as the basis for imitating (more or less skilfully) the observed compound action. Complex imitation as defined here seems very close to what Wohlschläger, Gattis, and Bekkering (2003) call *goal-directed imitation*. They assume that imitation is guided by cognitively specified goals. According to this view, the imitator does not imitate the observed movement as a whole, but rather decomposes it into its separate aspects. These aspects are hierarchically ordered, and the highest aspect becomes the imitator's main goal. Other aspects become subgoals. On this view, the main goal activates the motor program that is most strongly associated with the achievement of that goal. When executed, this motor program sometimes matches, and sometimes not, the model's movement. However, the main goal extracted from the model movement is almost always imitated correctly.

I have said that complex imitation seems very close to goal-directed imitation, yet the former focuses on a sequence of actions, whereas the latter focuses on a hierarchy of goals. However, I return to the equation *Action = Motion + Goal*. Depending on the focus of attention, we may focus on the goal (e.g., bringing the cup to the lip) or the motion (as in ensuring that a V for victory sign does not appear to be an obscene gesture). If we know how to achieve the subgoals, then they alone may suffice to yield the new behaviour. Otherwise, we may need to pay attention to the exact motion to master the action (oh, you insert it *then* twist it to lock it in place ...). While many skills can be imitated by compounding known actions, others will complement the action/subgoal decomposition by learning new affordances and effectivities and the relation between them. I would emphasise, then, that there is no "magic" in complex imitation that automatically yields the right decomposition of a movement. Rather, it may be the success or failure of a "high-level approximation" of the observed action that leads to attention to crucial subgoals—or crucial "twists" that refine what had been thought originally to be the movement—which were not observed at first, and thus leads, perhaps somewhat circuitously, to successful imitation. But the point remains that this process is in general much faster than the time-consuming extraction of statistical regularities in Byrne's "imitation by (implicit) behaviour parsing"—we might refer to complex (goal-directed) imitation as imitation by *explicit* behaviour parsing.

THE MIRROR SYSTEM HYPOTHESIS EXPANDED

Arbib (2002, 2005a) modified and developed the original MSH argument to hypothesise seven stages, S1 through S7, in the evolution of language, with imitation grounding two of the (possibly overlapping) stages:

- S1: A control system for grasping.
- S2: A mirror system for grasping shared with the common ancestor of human and monkey.
- S3: A simple imitation system for grasping shared with the common ancestor of human and chimpanzee.
- S4: A complex imitation system for grasping.
- S5: Protosign, a manual-based communication system.
- S6: Protolanguage as the combination of protosign and protospeech.
- S7: Language, as going beyond protolanguage.

My view is that this final stage involved little if any biological evolution, but instead resulted from cultural evolution (historical change) in *Homo sapiens*. This view remains highly controversial and lies outside the scope of this paper.

Using the distinctions offered above, I have argued (Arbib, 2002, 2005a) that (i) the common ancestor of monkeys and apes had no greater imitative ability than present-day monkeys; and (ii) the ability for simple imitation shared by chimps and humans was also possessed by their common ancestor; but (iii) only humans possess a talent for *complex imitation*. This supports the two hypotheses:

- Stage S3 Hypothesis: Brain mechanisms supporting a simple imitation system—imitation of short novel sequences of object-directed actions through repeated exposure (which combines tuning of new actions with implicit behaviour parsing)—for grasping developed in the 15 million year evolution from the common ancestor of monkeys and apes to the common ancestor of apes and humans
- Stage S4 Hypothesis: Brain mechanisms supporting a complex imitation system—acquiring (longer) novel sequences of more abstract actions (linked via subgoals) in a single trial—developed in the 5 million year evolution from the common ancestor of apes and humans along the hominid line that led, in particular, to *Homo sapiens*.

To bridge from complex imitation (Stage S4) to protolanguage, I argue that the evolution of *Homo sapiens* yielded a brain that could support not only complex imitation (S4) but also (S5a) the ability to engage in pantomime and (S5b) the ability to make conventional gestures to disambiguate pantomime. This yielded a brain that could support "protosign", a manual-based communication system that broke through the fixed repertoire of primate vocalisations to yield an open repertoire of communicative gestures.

Building on the scaffolding of protosign, and prior to the emergence of *Homo sapiens*, the brain came (S6) to support "proto-speech" through the "invasion" of the vocal apparatus by collaterals from the "protosign" system, and the brain and body mechanisms as well as social institutions supporting protosign and protospeech thereafter evolved in an expanding spiral. Attempting to delineate these social mechanisms is outside my present scope, but the idea is that protosign was only useful to the extent that protohumans had a social structure that made communication adaptive. Just as the altruistic drive to warn others to escape the predation of leopards presumably provided the selective pressure for the *biological* evolution of the vervet alarm call, so the drive to hunt together or share food could provide the context for the *social* evolution of a variety of novel gestures or calls. But once the group had these new mechanisms for social coordination, so new interactions could arise that would provide the "cultural niche" for the emergence of a richer protolanguage. But it was the special *biological* evolution of humans that made this social evolution possible.

Here it is worth stressing the distinction between pantomime and protosign—and the signs of modern signed languages (Arbib, 2005a, Section 5.2). Even those signs of today's "fully linguistic" sign languages (e.g., American Sign Language, ASL) that resemble pantomimes are conventionalised and are thus distinct from pantomimes. Indeed there is a dissociation between the neural systems involved in sign language and those involved in pantomime. Corina, Poizner, Bellugi, Feinberg, Dowd, and O'Grady Hatch (1992) document the dissociation of pantomime from signing in a lesioned ASL signer. Jane Marshall, Atkinson, Smulovich, Thacker, and Woll (2004) offer related data on a BSL signer for whom gesture production was superior to sign production even when the forms of the signs and gestures were similar. Conversely, patient IW is unable to perform instrumental actions without vision, but continues to perform speech-synchronised, co-expressive gestures that are virtually indistinguishable from normal (Cole, Gallagher, & McNeill, 2002). We thus see pantomime as a step towards protosign, not as being itself protosign.

As briefly noted in our discussion of MNS2, Kohler et al. (2002) studied mirror neurons for actions that are accompanied by characteristic sounds, and found that a subset of these are activated by the sound of the action (e.g., breaking a peanut in half) as well as sight of the action. However, the sounds studied by Kohler et al. (2002) cannot be created in the absence of the object and there is no evidence that monkeys can use their vocal apparatus to mimic the sounds they have heard. Complementing studies on hand neurons in macaque F5, Ferrari et al. (2003) studied mouth motor neurons in F5 and showed that about one-third of them also discharge when the monkey observes another individual performing mouth actions. The majority of these "mouth mirror neurons" become active during the execution and observation of mouth actions related to ingestive functions such as grasping, sucking, or breaking food. Another population of mouth mirror neurons also discharges during the execution of ingestive actions, but the most effective visual stimuli in triggering them are communicative mouth gestures (e.g., lip smacking). Here, I would suggest that the "Mirror" neuron is more strongly related to a particular aspect of the ingestive action involving the lips than to the overall action itself, and that this lip movement is more apparent in lip smacking than in the original ingestive action. Thus the neuron becomes associated with a whole range of performances that contain the salient component. This fits with the hypothesis that neurons learn to associate patterns of neural firing rather than being committed to learning specifically pigeonholed categories of data. Thus a potential mirror neuron is in no way committed to becoming a mirror neuron in the strict sense, even though it may be more likely to do so than otherwise. The observed communicative actions (with the effective executed action for different "mirror neurons" in parentheses) include lip smacking (sucking and lip smacking); lips protrusion (grasping with lips, lips protrusion, lip smacking, grasping and chewing); tongue protrusion (reaching with tongue); teeth-chatter (grasping); and lips/tongue protrusion (grasping with lips and reaching with tongue; grasping). We thus see that the communicative gestures (effective observed actions) are a long way from the sort of vocalisations that occur in speech in which movement of articulators is coupled to voicing.

Once an organism has an iconic gesture, it can both modulate that gesture and/or symbolise it (non-iconically) by "simply" associating a vocalisation with it. Once the association had been learned, the "scaffolding" gesture (like the pantomime that supported its conventionalisation, or the caricature that supports the initial understanding of some Chinese ideograms) could be dropped to leave a symbol that need have no remaining iconic relation to its referent (i.e., is "arbitrary" in the linguistic sense), even if the indirect associative relationship can be recalled on some occasions. One open question is the extent to which protosign must be in place before this scaffolding can effectively support the development of protospeech. Since there is no direct mapping of sign (with its use of concurrency and signing space) to phoneme sequences, Arbib (2005a) separated S6, the evolution of protospeech, from S5, the evolution of protosign, to stress the point that the role of F5 in grounding the evolution of a protolanguage system would work just as well had we and all our ancestors had been deaf. However, primates do have a rich auditory system that contributes to species survival in many ways, of which communication is just one (Ghazanfar, 2003). The hypothesis here, then, is not that the protolanguage system had to create the appropriate auditory and vocal-motor system "from scratch" but rather that it could build on the existing mechanisms to derive protospeech. In any case, the issue of whether or not protospeech needed protosign for its scaffolding remains controversial (see Arbib, 2005b; Fogassi & Ferrari, 2004; and MacNeilage & Davis, 2005, for the pros and cons).

Several studies provide behavioural evidence supporting the hypothesis that the system involved in observation and preparation of grasp movements has strong links with cortical areas involved in speech production. Gentilucci (2003) had subjects pronounce either the syllable "ba" or "ga" while observing motor acts of hand grasp directed to objects of two sizes, and found that both lip aperture and voice peak amplitude were greater when the observed hand grasp was directed to the large object. Conversely, Glover and Dixon (2002) presented participants with objects on which were printed either the word "LARGE" or "SMALL" (see "SMALL". An effect of the words on the grip aperture was found, though this effect declined continuously as the hand approached the target. See Gerlach, Law, & Paulson, 2002, and Glover,

Rosenbaum, Graham, & Dixon, 2004, for related results). Gentilucci, Santunione, Roy, and Stefanini (2004a) asked each participant to bring a fruit of varying size (a cherry or an apple) to the mouth and pronounce a syllable instead of biting the fruit. They found an effect of the fruit size not only on the kinematics pattern of the mouth aperture but even on the vocalisation of the participants. The second formant, whose frequency is tightly linked to the shape of the vocal tract, was actually higher when bringing the large fruit rather than the small one to the mouth. Gentilucci, Stefanini, Roy, and Santunione (2004b) asked participants to observe two types of manual action, a bringing to the mouth action and a prehension movement. In each case, the action was performed with a small or a large fruit and the participants had to pronounce the syllable at the end of the movement. The vocal parameters affected by the fruit size changed according to the type of movement observed. While the second formant varied during the bringing to the mouth task, the first formant varied during the prehension task. Such results suggest that the emergence of voice modulation and thus of an articulatory movement repertoire could have been associated with, or even prompted by, the pre-existing manual action repertoire.

Between them, stages S5 and S6 yield a brain endowed with "protolanguage", but not necessarily language; i.e., the possessors of protolanguage may be able to learn an open-ended set of symbols and use them for communication, yet not have the use of a syntax and compositional semantics that allows more than two or three of these symbols to be readily combined to convey new meanings which can almost as readily be understood.

Arbib and Bota (2006) sought to diagram some aspects of the Mirror System Hypothesis by giving a figure offering a high-level view of the cumulative emergence of three fronto-parietal systems. Although the surrounding text offered some useful qualifications, the diagram made it too easy to simply focus the analysis of praxis, action understanding, and language production on the following parallel parieto-frontal interactions:

(i)   object → AIP →$F5_{canonical}$ praxis
(ii) action → PF → $F5_{mirror}$ action understanding
(iii) scene → Wernicke's → Broca's   language production.

To see the problem with this, recall the lesion studies dissociating the roles of human dorsal and ventral streams whose effect was shown in Figure 2. The view that (iii) above is a simple lifting of (i) and (ii) runs into an apparent paradox since the AT and DF data suggest the following scheme:

(iv) Parietal "affordances" → preshape
(v) IT "perception of object" → pantomime or verbally describe size.

In other words, one cannot pantomime or verbalise an affordance; but rather one needs a "recognition of the object" (IT) with which attributes can be associated before one can express them. Note that these data put manual communication (symbols and sign) and pantomime on one side of the divide, and object-based action on the other. Here we face the fact that if one links words too closely to the dorsal stream of the mirror system, one may face a paradox from the AT-DF data, which show a "dissociation between the praxic use of size information (parietal), and the 'declaration' of that information either verbally or through pantomime (temporal)". DF is a visual form agnosic patient who does not have access to conscious declarative information about form (temporally mediated) but can use form information to guide grasping (superior fronto-parietal). AT can pantomime grasp but cannot preshape based on current form information (superior fronto-parietal). What is worth recalling (cf. our discussion of Figure 2) is that AT can preshape appropriately to grasp familiar objects (inferior parietal) Thus there are three different functions partially dissociating here—grasp, pantomime, and object knowledge. Buxbaum (personal communication) argues that F5 does not play the crucial role in gesture representations. Patients with impairments in gesture production and recognition most frequently have left inferior parietal lesions. Conversely, patients with lesions to the putative homologue of F5 (BA 44 or 45) do not often have evidence of loss of gesture knowledge. The role of the IPL in the MNS model (area PF/PFG) of the *macaque* mirror system is circumscribed to the "visual analysis of the trajectory of the hand relative to object affordances". Patients with IT lesions do not suffer deficits in positioning hands with respect to objects for skilled use (or for unskilled use, for that matter) (cf. patient DF). On the other hand, patients with left IPL lesions (apraxics) have striking deficits in hand posture for skilled use (e.g., Buxbaum, Sirigu, Schwartz, & Klatzky, 2003). In line with our discussion in the section "From Object-Based Imitation to Pantomime", I hypothesise that the central importance of the left IPL in human object-specific gesture production and recognition may reflect the difference between a macaque-like IPL, which requires the presence of the object (movement and goal) to recognise an action, and a human-like system that can readily classify hand movements even in the absence of objects, thus supporting the recognition of even meaningless intransitive gestures.

Saussure distinguishes the Signifier from the Signified (or words from concepts), but then highlights the "Sign" as combining these with the linkage between them. My action-oriented view (Arbib, 1989) is that the basic concepts are realised as the perceptual and motor schemas of an organism acting in its world, and that that there is no direct labelling of one word for one concept. Rather, the linkage is many-to-one, competitive, and contextual, so that appropriate words to express a schema may

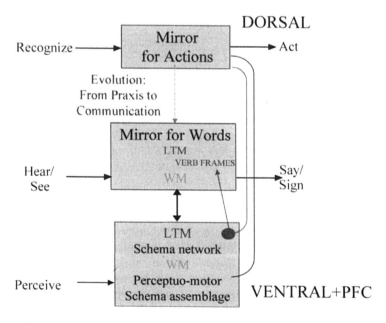

Figure 4. Words link to schemas, not directly to the dorsal path for actions.

vary from occasion to occasion, both because of the assemblage in which the schema instance is currently embedded, and because of the state of the current discourse. Let us diagram this in a way that makes contact with all that has gone before. The lower two boxes of Figure 4 correspond to the words and concepts of Figure 1, but we now make explicit that, following the Mirror System Hypothesis, we postulate that a mirror system for phonological expression ("words") evolved atop the mirror system for grasping to serve communication integrating hand, face, and voice. We also postulate that the concepts—for diverse actions, objects, attributes, and abstractions—are now seen to be represented by a network of concepts stored in LTM, with our current "conceptual content" formed as an assemblage of schema instances in Working Memory (WM). Analogously, the Mirror for Words contains a network of word forms in LTM and keeps track of the current utterance in its own working memory (cf. Baddeley's phonological buffer).

The perhaps surprising aspect of the conceptual model shown here is that the arrow linking the "Mirror for Actions" to the "Mirror for Words" expresses an evolutionary relationship, not a flow of data. Rather than a direct linkage of the dorsal representation of an action to the dorsal representation of the phonological form, we have two relationships between the dorsal pathway for the Mirror for Actions and the schema networks and assemblages of the ventral pathway and prefrontal cortex (PFC). The rightmost path shown in Figure 4 corresponds to the paths in the FARS model whereby IT and PFC can affect the pattern of dorsal control of action. The path just to the left of this shows that the dorsal representation of actions can only be linked to verbs via schemas.

Hickok and Poeppel (2004) observe that early cortical stages of speech perception involve auditory fields in the superior temporal gyrus bilaterally (although asymmetrically), but offer evidence that this cortical processing system then diverges into two streams: (1) A *dorsal stream* mapping sound onto articulatory-based representations, which projects dorso-posteriorly. It involves a region in the posterior Sylvian fissure at the parietal–temporal boundary (area Spt), and ultimately projects to frontal regions. This network provides a mechanism for the development and maintenance of "parity" between auditory and motor representations of speech. (2) A *ventral stream* mapping sound onto meaning, which projects ventro-laterally towards inferior posterior temporal cortex (posterior middle temporal gyrus) that serves as an interface between sound-based representations of speech in the superior temporal gyrus (again bilaterally) and widely distributed conceptual representations.

We may further note the availability of compatible data on the macaque auditory system. Romanski, Tian, Fritz, Mishkin, Goldman-Rakic, and Rauschecker (1999), among others, offer evidence for a dorsal and a ventral stream that process auditory spatial and auditory pattern/object information, respectively. Both streams eventually project to the frontal cortex, which integrates both auditory spatial and object information with visual and other modalities. In human and nonhuman primates, auditory objects, including speech sounds, are identified in anterior superior temporal cortex, which projects directly to inferior frontal regions. This same anatomical substrate may support both the decoding of vocalisations in nonhuman primates and the decoding of human speech. This would seem to correspond to further processing of the result of low-level auditory analysis by the direct route and via the phonological lexicon, respectively.

But now we suggest that we extend the linkage from words to "constructions". Consider that idiomatic expressions like *kick the bucket* or *take the bull by the horns* are an integral part of the speaker's knowledge of his/her language, but their meaning cannot be inferred from the meaning of the individual words and highly general rules of grammar. This suggests that the meaning of each idiom must be stored in each speaker's mind. Fillmore, Kay, and O'Connor (1988) took a radical step: Instead of adding idioms to a generative model that separates the lexicon from syntax considered as a highly general and abstract set of rules for combining words, they argued that the tools they used in analysing idioms could form the basis for *construction grammar* as a new model of grammatical organisation—blurring the division between grammar and lexicon. Itti and Arbib (2006) link this back to the study of vision. They note that the computer scene-recognition system VISIONS (Draper, Collins, Brolio, Hanson, & Riseman, 1989) employs a wide variety of basic "subscene schemas" such as those relating *sky and roof* (one way to recognise a roof is as a form of a certain geometry and size immediately below a region that has been recognised as sky) and *roof, house, and wall* (if you see a roof, check whether the region below it can be recognised as a wall to confirm that together they constitute views of parts of a house). This suggests that an approach to visual scene interpretation with a large but finite inventory of subscene schemas (*from the visual end*) may provide the linkage with constructions (*from the language end*) rich enough to encompass an exemplary set of sentences. A similar argument may link sentences describing courses of actions to "motor constructions" (cf. the coordinated control programs [CCPs] of Arbib, 1981), which may be related to sentence constructions (cf. Kemmerer, 2006). We thus argue that development yields acquisition of subscene schemas (visual and motor and more) that are enriched by their linkage to constructions in the sense of the construction grammar approach to linguistics. "Praxic constructions" viewed as converters from cognitive form to temporal behaviour thus become augmented by constructions for communicative action and perception. The central role of action (praxis) and verb (language) in these two forms leads us to extend the mirror system for words in Figure 4 to encompass constructions as well.

THE MIRROR SYSTEM HYPOTHESIS CRITICISED AND DEFENDED

Barrett et al. (2005) discuss functional and structural evidence supporting localisation of neuronal control of limb praxis, speech and language, and emotional communication, and assert that this evidence supports completely independent limb praxis and speech/language systems. However, I reject the jump from a measure of separation in syndromes to the outright rejection of an evolutionary relationship between the underlying mechanisms. For example apraxic patients are often but not always aphasic. Papagno, della Sala, and Basso (1993) studied 699 patients with cortical or subcortical CT documented vascular lesions in the left hemisphere: 10 patients were found to be apraxic but not aphasic and 149 aphasic but not apraxic. This suggests that praxis and language make use of two different, partly overlapping networks. Note that MSH does not claim that language and praxis are coextensive, rather that the former evolved from the latter. It is thus open to debate whether the machinery supporting language overlaps the machinery for praxis or rather exploits an evolved variant (Roy & Arbib, 2005) (as is suggested in Figure 4). Since one can name actions, and since observing an action may lead one to think of its name, we know there is a linkage between the praxis and naming systems. The issue is whether their coupling implies the evolutionary linkage posited by MSH.

Dissociation is compatible with shared homology

Kimura (1993) argued that the left hemisphere is specialised not for language but for complex motor programming functions that are, in particular, essential for language production. However, one might ask if (i) hominid evolution yielded circuitry used for all forms of complex motor control, so that whether or not specific neurons are involved in control of language behaviour is purely a result of experience-based learning, or (ii) evolution at some stage duplicated the circuitry used for complex motor control, with one copy then becoming specialised for the type of motor sequencing mechanisms needed for language (e.g., those involving the coordinated control of speech apparatus, hands, and facial expression) while the other copy remained available for other forms of coordinated behaviour.

Although disorders of skilled purposive limb movements (limb apraxia) may co-occur with disordered speech (speech apraxia) and language disorders (aphasia), we have already seen (citing Papagno et al., 1993; see also Heilman & Rothi, 2003; Kertesz, Ferro, & Shewan, 1984; Liepmann, 1920) that these three conditions can be anatomically and functionally dissociable. The data surveyed by Code (1998) support the notion that there is at least some segregation of circuitry. He notes that Broca's (1861) first patient Leborgne had a severe inability to articulate in the absence of muscular paralysis or incoordination, what is now called *apraxia of speech*—as distinct from *oral apraxia*, an inability to move the tongue and lips to command or in imitation, although spontaneous action is unimpaired and the patient is able to eat, drink, and smile normally. Code (personal communication) adds that Broca observed that Leborgne also had some ability to gesture spontaneously. Oral sensory perceptual deficits occur frequently among apraxic speakers (Deutsch, 1984). DeRenzi, Pieczuro, and Vignolo (1966) found that the majority of patients with apraxia of speech had oral apraxia and a high coexistence of oral and limb apraxia, while Marquardt and Sussman (1984) found that all 15 of their patients with Broca's aphasia had oral apraxia (12 had apraxia of speech and 5 had limb apraxia). But double dissociations occur in individual cases. Thus, as noted by Code, either separate networks of neurons are engaged in the generation of speech and nonspeech movement of the same muscles, or the same general network underlies speech and nonspeech movements, but (perhaps as a result of some type of self-organisation, such as that described below) these have separate control mechanisms which can be differentially damaged.

Patients demonstrate many dissociations: Some apraxic patients can recognise gestures but not produce them; others can gesture to command but not imitate or recognise gesture, or show input-modality-specific deficits (see Mahon & Caramazza, 2005, for a review), e.g., inability to pantomime or imitate to visual input; and Ochipa, Rothi, and Heilman (1994) report a patient with intact gesture recognition in the context of moderately impaired gesture to command and severely impaired imitation. Barrett et al. assert that Arbib (2005a) treats four forelimb gesture classes interchangeably: volitional meaningless movements or movements unrelated to tool use (e.g., reaching or grasping movements), movements standing for objects (emblems, e.g., flapping hands for "bird"), tool use pantomimes (limb praxis), and movements carrying linguistic meaning (signs). However, MSH offers an evolutionary progression in motor control, stressing that changes in neural circuitry occurred at each stage. I see these functions as evolutionary cousins, but this does not require that the same circuitry subserves each function. Indeed, we have earlier noted the dissociation between the neural systems involved in sign language and those involved in pantomime (Cole et al., 2002; Corina et al., 1992; Jane Marshall et al., 2004), while our discussion of left IPL and gesture makes clear the crucial role of circuitry "beyond the mirror" in yielding a "language-ready" brain.

The fact that apraxia often occurs with aphasia might just be due to the anatomical proximity of systems for praxis and language. Of course this begs the question of why praxis and language might be anatomically proximate, but that is not tantamount to evidence that one system evolved atop the other. Indeed, aphasic patients very frequently have no difficulty with grasping. Unfortunately, the current form of MSH is not specific enough to make predictions about what functions ought to be impaired together/spared together. In my analysis (Arbib, 2005a), I distinguished stage S5a, the ability to engage in pantomime, from Stage S5b, the ability to make conventional gestures to disambiguate pantomime, with these two stages combining to support protosign. I argued that S5a required a biological change. I would now (contra Arbib, 2005a) insist that S5b must have required further biological innovations beyond those of S5a. As a step in further theory building, we will need to develop more explicit models of how (p. 1142 above) "the brain [might come] (S6) to support 'proto-speech' through the 'invasion' of the vocal apparatus by collaterals from the 'proto-sign' system, and [how] the ... mechanisms ... supporting protosign and protospeech thereafter evolved in an expanding spiral" in a form testable by analysis of data on both the macaque and human brain.

Barrett et al. (2005) cite the report by Tonkonogy and Goodglass (1981) that a patient with a lesion restricted to the pars triangularis had linguistic deficits, whereas a patient with a lesion to the pars opercularis had disordered articulation and fluency, but preserved higher-order language functions. Similarly, an fMRI study by Paulesu et al. (1997) found that phonemic and semantic fluency tasks activated the pars triangularis, whereas only phonemic fluency tasks activated the pars opercularis. Barrett et al. (2005) thus argue that the pars triangularis of human Broca's area comprises higher-order heteromodal association cortex suited to complex cross-modal associations typical of higher-order linguistic functions (e.g., syntax, lexical-semantics), whereas the pars opercularis comprises motor association cortex suited to articulatory and motor speech functions. Hence, rather than being a pars triangularis homologue (Brodmann's area 45), area F5 in the monkey may represent the human pars opercularis (Brodmann's area 44), more directly linked to voice and articulation. Certainly, smooth assembly at the level of phonemes/ articulators requires a different level of processing, and different inputs and outputs, than does assemblage of words into sentences. But one need not deny that each set of circuits may have exploited evolutionary variants of core circuitry for hierarchical motor control. Indeed, the skill for complex imitation may have modified each— again in related but specialised ways. Arbib and Bota (2006) and Roy and Arbib (2005) provide further analysis.

Lateralisation, briefly

Although detailed analysis of lateralisation is beyond the scope of this article, it is worth recalling that the left hemisphere in most humans is dominant for language, so that Broca's area (or, at least, area 44) refers to the F5 homologue in only one hemisphere. However, the F5 mirror system in monkeys is bilateral and thus has homologues in the right as well as the left hemisphere of humans and, indeed, the "mirror" responses in human neuroimaging tend to be bilateral and distributed in both frontal and parietal cortex.

Just as the neural representations for language are lateralised, so too are those underlying skilled praxis—even for tasks involving skilled use of the ipsilateral hand. In left-handed subjects, brain regions supporting limb praxis may be localised in the right hemisphere, and those supporting speech and language in the left hemisphere (Heilman, Coyle, Gonyea, & Geschwind, 1973; Valenstein & Heilman, 1979), although left hemisphere dominance for skilled praxis may occur even in left-handers (see Frey, Funnell, Gerry, & Gazzaniga, 2005, for further discussion). Indeed, Meador et al. (1999) demonstrated that the link between language and praxis is different from the link between hand preference and language. Their participants were patients with intractable seizures undergoing the intracarotid amobarbital procedure (IAP) as part of their preoperative evaluation for epilepsy surgery, and the study included patients with atypical cerebral language dominance, i.e., those with bilateral or right hemispheric language function. Hand preference was determined by the Benton Handedness Questionnaire. During left IAP, patients with typical language dominance made more ideomotor apraxic errors than did patients with atypical language dominance. During right IAP, patients with atypical language dominance made more ideomotor apraxic errors than did patients with typical language dominance. Overall, patients with atypical language dominance made fewer ideomotor apraxic errors than did patients with typical language dominance. These relationships were present irrespective of hand preference. Meador et al. conclude that language dominance is more closely associated with the laterality of temporal and spatial movement representations (i.e., ideomotor praxis dominance) than is hand preference. Patients with atypical language dominance exhibit more bilateral cerebral distribution of both language and praxis function. Note that there is one possible confound here. Praxis was assessed by the participant's performance when pantomiming the use of four pictured tools—but we have stressed that skill at pantomime of praxis may itself be dissociable from skilled praxis. For example, the deficits shown by patients with left IPL lesions (apraxic patients) in pantomiming, imitating, and responding to questions about object-related gestures are frequently improved to some degree when the patients are permitted to contact and use objects and tools directly (Buxbaum et al., 2003; and recall our discussion of apraxic patients preceding Figure 4).

Continuing with the mysteries of lateralisation, note that in most humans the left hemisphere may be dominant in the stringing together of words associated with propositional speech, but the right hemisphere often controls the accompanying emotional prosody (Heilman, Blonder, Bowers, & Crucian, 2000; Ross, 1981; Tucker, Watson, & Heilman, 1977), automatic speech (Speedie, Wertman, Tair, & Heilman, 1993), and singing (Wildgruber, Ackerman, Klose, Kardatzki, & Grodd, 1996). In patients with aphasia after left hemisphere injury, comprehension and production of affective vocal prosody and emotional facial expressions may also be relatively spared (Barrett, Crucian, Raymer, & Heilman, 1999; Kanter, Day, Heilman, & Rothi, 1986). This double dissociation argues against left hemisphere dominance for comprehending, imitating, or producing emotional facial expression or prosody.

Barrett et al. (2005) note that right-handed subjects with limb apraxia and gestural production and imitation deficits are hypothesised to have lost function in brain regions supporting time-space-movement representations. Most have damage to posterior, rather than anterior, cortical areas, usually the inferior parietal lobe (Rothi, Raade, & Heilman, 1994). Further, Buxbaum, Kyle, and Menon (2005) argue that the system for pantomiming object-related actions is mediated (at least in part) by the left IPL and is plausibly built on the mirror neuron system, but that symbolic, non-object-related gestures are much less well localised, are bi-hemispheric, and are probably less closely tied to object-related mirror neuron systems. Systems for articulation of the tongue and soft/hard palates are also bi-hemispheric and probably not very closely linked to grasping. So to further MSH we need to develop an account of the different strengths of the level of evolutionary linkage of these varied systems to the pre-existing mirror neuron system. In this regard, recall (Figure 3) that the mirror system for manual actions in macaque involves the whole STS-PP-F5 system, and other areas as well, not just F5 alone. However, the differential effects of posterior and frontal lesions generally remains poorly understood—our present models must be expanded along the lines sketched above (which include a variety of features not made explicit in Figure 4) so that the resultant model can explain how the cooperative computation of many brain regions can provide some compensation in the human patient to yield varied patterns of behaviour in response to diverse lesions.

In particular, it will be important to understand lateralisation in terms of *predisposition* that favours differential learning in the two hemispheres, rather than conceiving of a genetic specification of different mature circuitry in the two hemispheres. The left and right hemispheres of the human brain are homologous to the left and right hemispheres of the monkey brain, and the left and right hemispheres of the monkey brain are homologous to each other—thus implying a homology in the human brain between structures with dissociable functions in the adult. To understand this more clearly, we need to place the observation in developmental perspective. Although most people have left-hemisphere language dominance, a child who has the left hemisphere removed early enough can acquire far greater language capacity with the right hemisphere than is possible for an adult who has a left hemispherectomy, although a child with a right hemispherectomy can do even better (Dennis & Kohn, 1975). Thus it is not the case that an innate syntax machine is wired into the left hemisphere and not the right, but rather (to speculate somewhat) that although both hemispheres can learn syntax, the left hemisphere in most people has capabilities that allow it to "win the race" to acquire early elements of syntax, and that the presence of these assemblies in one hemisphere biases the system to acquire similar structures in nearby areas of cortex. This returns us to our earlier discussion of self-organisation in the MNS model (Oztop & Arbib, 2002)—the way in which some aspects of brain organisation may reflect structures emergent from patterns of learning rather than specific genetic preprogramming of function.

A developmental perspective

Continuing with this theme, we ask: are the various dissociations noted above (e.g., that between pantomime and signing) evidence for genetic specification of separate circuitry or rather for the self-organisation through experience of shared circuitry? Two examples from connectionist modelling (Plaut, 1995) show that the issue is not straightforward. The first provides a case where apparently different schemas may prove to be properties of a single distributed network. The second shows that the opposite may also be possible—through learning, an essentially homogeneous network may organise itself into subnetworks with distinctive properties.

Deep dyslexic patients (Coltheart, Patterson, & John Marshall, 1980) may make semantic errors, such as reading the word *river* as "ocean", as well as visual errors, such as reading scandal as "sandals". This suggests two separate impairments, yet visual errors almost always co-occur with semantic errors. Hinton and Shallice (1991) developed a model in which this co-occurrence is a natural consequence of a single lesion to an attractor network trained to derive the meanings of written words. They trained a recurrent back-propagation network to map from the visual form (orthography) of 40 three- or four-letter words to a simplified representation of their semantics, described in terms of 68 predetermined semantic features (e.g., brown, made-of-wood, for-cooking). After training, lesions throughout the network resulted in both semantic errors (e.g., reading cat as "dog") and visual errors (e.g., reading cat as "cot"). The key point is that the layout of attractor basins must be sensitive to both visual and semantic similarity. Indeed, Plaut and Shallice (1993) were able to show that the co-occurrence of visual and semantic errors did not depend on particular characteristics of the network architecture, the training procedure, or the way responses are generated from semantic activity; and extended the approach to account for other characteristics of deep dyslexia.

By contrast, the basic idea of a self-organising feature map or Kohonen map (Kohonen, 1982) is that all the cells of a two-dimensional array receive the same inputs. Then, when an input pattern is received, the cell that responds most vigorously and (to a lesser extent) cells nearby in the array have their input synapses adjusted in a Hebbian fashion; i.e., a synapse changes by an amount proportional to the product of the input activity of the synapse and some decreasing function of the post-synaptic cell's distance from the "winning" cell. The fascinating property of such a network is that over time the array organises itself into a relatively small set of neighbourhoods or regions such that in each region nearby neurons respond best to very similar input patterns—the array becomes organised into a set of topographical maps of regions of the input space, with the size of the map of a region increasing with the frequency with which input patterns occur within the corresponding ensemble relative to the set of all patterns presented. The resultant maps thus depend on random variations of the initial synaptic weights as much as on the input statistics. In any case, a lesion of the resultant array may greatly impair one function (i.e., one region of similar input patterns) but not another, even though the two functions had no specific encoding in the original "wiring specification" of the network. In an evolutionary framework, then, the emergence of a new function for a brain region might require not so much the genetic specification for new circuitry appropriate to that function as the availability of novel input patterns from elsewhere in the brain to serve as the basis of the self-organisation of novel subsystems within that brain region. (Recall the discussion of "Evolutionary Parcellation of the Brain" on p. 1129)

Note that these examples provide evidence neither for nor against the Barrett et al. (2005) critique of MSH. Rather, they are intended to make clear that the types of dissociation of various functions presented by Barrett et al. (2005) cannot a priori be taken as evidence that the mechanisms underlying these functions lack the evolutionary cousinage posited by MSH. Indeed, the whole thrust of this article has been to show how confrontation of the MNS and FARS models of the macaque system for the control and recognition of manual actions with the rich database on human language and aphasia, and praxis and apraxia, sets specific goals for an integrative approach to the modelling of the brain mechanisms supporting human praxis and language. Comparative neurobiological modelling will allow us to better delineate what mechanisms are common to the macaque and human brains, and then devise more rigorous tests of their evolutionary relationship.

REFERENCES

Alstermark, B., Lundberg, A., Norrsell, U., & Sybirska, E. (1981). Integration in descending motor pathways controlling the forelimb in the cat: 9. Differential behavioural defects after spinal cord lesions interrupting defined pathways from higher centres to motoneurones. *Experimental Brain Research, 42*(3), 299–318.

Arbib, M. A. (1981). Perceptual structures and distributed motor control. In V. B. Brooks (Ed.), *Handbook of physiology, Section 2: The nervous system, Vol. II, Motor control, Part 1* (pp. 1449–1480). Bethesda, MD: American Physiological Society.

Arbib, M. A. (1989). *The metaphorical brain 2: Neural networks and beyond.* New York: Wiley-Interscience.

Arbib, M. A. (2002). The mirror system, imitation, and the evolution of language. In C. Nehaniv & K. Dautenhahn (Eds.), *Imitation in animals and artefacts* (pp. 229–280). Cambridge, MA: The MIT Press.

Arbib, M. A. (2005a). From monkey-like action recognition to human language: An evolutionary framework for neurolinguistics. *Behavioral and Brain Sciences, 28*, 105–167 [Supplemental commentaries and the author's "electronic response" are at *Behavioral and Brain Sciences*, http://www.bbsonline.org/Preprints/Arbib-05012002/Supplemental/Arbib.E-Response_Supplemental.pdf]

Arbib, M. A. (2005b). Interweaving protosign and protospeech: Further developments beyond the mirror. *Interaction Studies: Social Behaviour and Communication in Biological and Artificial Systems, 6*, 145–171.

Arbib, M. A., & Bota, M. (2006). Neural homologies and the grounding of neurolinguistics. In M. A. Arbib (Ed.), *Action to language via the mirror neuron system* (pp. 136–173). Cambridge, UK: Cambridge University Press.

Arbib, M. A., & Caplan, D. (1979). Neurolinguistics must be computational. *Behavioral and Brain Sciences, 2*, 449–483.

Arbib, M. A., Caplan, D., & Marshall, J. C. (Eds.). (1982). *Neural models of language processes.* New York: Academic Press.

Arbib, M. A., Conklin, E. J., & Hill, J. C. (1987). *From schema theory to language.* Oxford, UK: Oxford University Press.

Arbib, M. A., & Didday, R. L. (1975). Eye-movements and visual perception: A two-visual system model. *International Journal of Man-Machine Studies, 7*, 547–569.

Arbib, M. A., Érdi, P., & Szentágothai, J. (1998). *Neural organisation: Structure, function, and dynamics.* Cambridge, MA: The MIT Press.

Arbib, M. A., & Rizzolatti, G. (1997). Neural expectations: A possible evolutionary path from manual skill to language. *Communication and Cognition, 29*, 393–424.

Barrett, A. M., Crucian, G. P., Raymer, A. M., & Heilman, K. M. (1999). Spared comprehension of emotional prosody in a patient with global aphasia. *Neuropsychiatry, Neuropsychology, and Behavioral Neurology, 12*, 117–120.

Barrett, A. M., Foundas, A. L., & Heilman, K. M. (2005). Speech and gesture are mediated by independent systems. *Behavioral and Brain Sciences, 28*, 125–126.

Bischoff-Grethe, A., Crowley, M. G., & Arbib, M. A. (2003). Movement inhibition and next sensory state prediction in basal ganglia. In A. M. Graybiel, M. R. Delong, & S. T. Kitai (Eds.), *The basal ganglia VI* (pp. 267–277). New York: Kluwer Academic/Plenum Publishers.

Bonaiuto, J., Rosta, E., & Arbib, M. A. (in press). Extending the mirror neuron system model, I: Audible actions and invisible grasps. *Biological Cybernetics*.

Bonaiuto, J., Rosta, E., & Arbib, M. A. (2006b). *From Alstermark's cat to Byrne's gorillas: Hierarchical motor programs and insight learning.* Manuscript in preparation.

Broca, P. (1861). Nouvelle observation d'aphémie produite par une lésion de la moitié posteriérieure des deuxième et troisième circonvolutions frontales. *Bulletin de la Société Anatomique, 6,* 398–407.

Butler, A. B., & Hodos, W. (1996). *Comparative vertebrate neuroanatomy: Evolution and adaptation.* New York: John Wiley & Sons.

Buxbaum, L. J., Kyle, K., & Menon, R. (2005). On beyond mirror neurons: Internal representations subserving imitation and recognition of skilled object-related actions in humans. *Cognitive Brain Research, 25*(1), 226–239.

Buxbaum, L. J., Sirigu, A., Schwartz, M. F., & Klatzky, R. (2003). Cognitive representations of hand posture in ideomotor apraxia. *Neuropsychologia, 41,* 1091–1113.

Byrne, R. W. (2003). Imitation as behaviour parsing. *Philosophical Transactions of the Royal Society of London. Series B: Biological Sciences, 358,* 529–536.

Carey, D. P., Perrett, D. I., & Oram, M. W. (1997). Recognising, understanding, and producing action. In M. Jeannerod & J. Grafman (Eds.), *Handbook of neuropsychology: Action and cognition, Vol. 11* (pp. 111–130). Amsterdam: Elsevier.

Chersi, F., Fogassi, L., Rozzi, S., Rizzolatti, G., & Ferrari, P. F. (2005). Neuronal chains for actions in the parietal lobe: A computational model. *2005 abstract viewer/itinerary planner.* Washington, DC: Society for Neuroscience, Program No. 412.8.

Code, C. (1998). Models, theories and heuristics in apraxia of speech. *Clinical Linguistics & Phonetics, 12,* 47–65.

Cole, J., Gallagher, S., & McNeill, D. (2002). Gesture following deafferentation: A phenomenologically informed experimental study. *Phenomenology and the Cognitive Sciences, 1,* 49–67.

Coltheart, M., Patterson, K. E., & Marshall, J. C. (Eds.). (1980). *Deep dyslexia.* London: Routledge & Kegan Paul.

Corina, D. P., Poizner, H., Bellugi, U., Feinberg, T., Dowd, D., & O'Grady-Batch, L. (1992). Dissociation between linguistic and nonlinguistic gestural systems: A case for compositionality. *Brain & Language, 43*(3), 414–447.

Dennis, M., & Kohn, B. (1975). Comprehension of syntax in infantile hemiplegics after cerebral hemidecortication: Left-hemisphere superiority. *Brain & Language, 2,* 472–482.

DeRenzi, E., Pieczuro, A., & Vignolo, L. A. (1966). Oral apraxia and aphasia. *Cortex, 2,* 50–73.

Deutsch, S. E. (1984). Oral stereognosis. In C. Code & M. J. Ball (Eds.), *Experimental clinical phonetics.* London: Croom Helm.

Distler, C., Boussaoud, D., Desimone, R., & Ungerleider, L. G. (1993). Cortical connections of inferior temporal area TEO in macaque monkeys. *Journal of Comparative Neurology, 334,* 125–150.

Dominey, P. F., Arbib, M. A., & Joseph, J-P. (1995). A model of corticostriatal plasticity for learning associations and sequences. *Journal of Cognitive Neuroscience, 7,* 311–336.

Draper, B. A., Collins, R. T., Brolio, J., Hanson, A. R., & Riseman, E. M. (1989). The schema system. *International Journal of Computer Vision, 2,* 209–250.

Escola, L., Intskirveli, I., Umiltà, M. A., Rochat, M., Rizzolatti, G., & Gallese, V. (2004). Goal-relatedness in area F5 of the macaque monkey during tool use. *Society of Neuroscience Abstracts.* 191.8.

Fagg, A. H., & Arbib, M. A. (1998). Modelling parietal-premotor Interactions in primate control of grasping. *Neural Networks, 11,* 1277–1303.

Ferrari, P. F., Gallese, V., Rizzolatti, G., & Fogassi, L. (2003). Mirror neurons responding to the observation of ingestive and communicative mouth actions in the monkey ventral premotor cortex. *European Journal of Neuroscience, 17*(8), 1703–1714.

Fillmore, C. J., Kay, P., & O'Connor, M. K. (1988). Regularity and idiomaticity in grammatical constructions: The case of *let alone. Language, 64,* 501–538.

Fogassi, L., & Ferrari, P. F. (2004). Mirror neurons, gestures and language evolution. *Interaction Studies: Social Behavior and Communication in Biological and Artificial Systems, 5,* 345–363.

Fogassi, L., Ferrari, P. F., Gesierich, B., Rozzi, S., Chersi, F., & Rizzolatti, G. (2005). Parietal lobe: From action organisation to intention understanding. *Science, 308,* 662–667.

Frey, S. H., Funnell, M. G., Gerry, V. E., & Gazzaniga, M. S. (2005). A dissociation between the representation of tool-use skills and hand dominance: Insights from left- and right-handed callosotomy patients. *Journal of Cognitive Neuroscience, 17*(2), 262–272.

Gentilucci, M. (2003). Grasp observation influences speech production. *European Journal of Neuroscience, 17*(1), 179–184.

Gentilucci, M., Santunione, P., Roy, A. C., & Stefanini, S. (2004a). Execution and observation of bringing a fruit to the mouth affect syllable pronunciation. *European Journal of Neuroscience, 19,* 190–202.

Gentilucci, M., Stefanini, S., Roy, A. C., & Santunione, P. (2004b). Action observation and speech production: Study on children and adults. *Neuropsychologia*, *42*, 1554–1567.

Gerlach, C., Law, I., & Paulson, O. B. (2002). When action turns into words. Activation of motor-based knowledge during categorization of manipulable objects. *Journal of Cognitive Neuroscience*, *14*(8), 1230–1239.

Ghazanfar, A. A. (Ed.) (2003). *Primate audition: Ethology and neurobiology*. Boca Raton, FL: CRC Press.

Gibson, J. J. (1979). *The ecological approach to visual perception*. New York: Houghton Mifflin.

Glover, S., & Dixon, P. (2002). Semantics affect the planning but not control of grasping. *Experimental Brain Research*, *146*, 383–387.

Glover, S., Rosenbaum, D. A., Graham, J., & Dixon, P. (2004). Grasping the meaning of words. *Experimental Brain Research*, *154*(1), 103–108.

Goodale, M. A., Milner, A. D., Jakobson, L. S., & Carey, C. P. (1991). A neurological dissociation between perceiving objects and grasping them. *Nature*, *349*, 154–156.

Heilman, K. M., Blonder, L. X., Bowers, D., & Crucian, G. P. (2000). Neurological disorders and emotional dysfunction. In J. C. Borod (Ed.), *The neuropsychology of emotion. Series in affective science*. Oxford, UK: Oxford University Press.

Heilman, K. M., Coyle, J. M., Gonyea, E. F., & Geschwind, N. (1973). Apraxia and agraphia in a left-hander. *Brain*, *96*, 21–28.

Heilman, K. M., & Rothi, L. J. G. (2003). Apraxia. In K. M. Heilman & E. Valenstein (Eds.), *Clinical neuropsychology, 4th edition* (pp. 215–235). Oxford, UK: Oxford University Press.

Hickok, G., & Poeppel, D. (2004). Dorsal and ventral streams: A framework for understanding aspects of the functional anatomy of language. *Cognition*, *92*, 67–99.

Hinton, G. E., & Shallice, T. (1991). Lesioning an attractor network: Investigations of acquired dyslexia. *Psychological Review*, *98*, 74–95.

Houghton, G., & Hartley, T. (1995). Parallel Models of Serial Behavior: Lashley Revisited. *Psyche*, *2*, 25.

Itti, L., & Arbib, M. A. (2006). Attention and the minimal subscene. In M. A. Arbib (Ed.), *Action to language via the mirror neuron system* (pp. 289–346). Cambridge, UK: Cambridge University Press.

Jeannerod, M., Arbib, M. A., Rizzolatti, G., & Sakata, H. (1995). Grasping objects – the cortical mechanisms of visuomotor transformation. *Trends in Neuroscience*, *18*, 314–320.

Jeannerod, M., Decety, J., & Michel, F. (1994). Impairment of grasping following a bilateral posterior parietal lesion. *Neurophysiologia*, *32*, 369–380.

Johnson-Frey, S. H. (2003). What's so special about human tool use? *Neuron*, *39*, 201–204.

Johnson-Frey, S. H., Funnell, M. G., Gerry, V. E., & Gazzaniga, M. S. (2005). A dissociation between tool use skills and hand dominance: Insights from left and right-handed callosotomy patients. *Journal of Cognitive Neuroscience*, *17*, 262–272.

Kaas, J. H. (1993). Evolution of multiple areas and modules within neocortex. *Perspectives on Developmental Neurobiology*, *1*, 101–107.

Kanter, S. L., Day, A. L., Heilman, K. M., & Rothi, L. J. (1986). Pure word deafness: A possible explanation of transient deterioration following EC-IC bypass. *Neurosurgery*, *18*, 186–189.

Kemmerer, D. (2006). Action verbs, argument structure constructions, and the mirror neuron system. In M. A. Arbib (Ed.), *Action to language via the mirror neuron system* (pp. 347–373). Cambridge, UK: Cambridge University Press.

Kertesz, A., Ferro, J. M., & Shewan, C. M. (1984). Apraxia and aphasia: The functional-anatomical basis for their dissociation. *Neurology*, *34*, 40–47.

Kimura, D. (1993). *Neuromotor mechanisms in human communication* (Oxford Psychology Series No. 20). Oxford & New York: Oxford University Press/Clarendon Press.

Kohler, E., Keysers, C., Umiltà, M. A., Fogassi, L., Gallese, V., & Rizzolatti, G. (2002). Hearing sounds, understanding actions: Action representation in mirror neurons. *Science*, *297*, 846–868.

Kohonen, T. (1982). Self-organised formation of topologically correct feature maps. *Biological Cybernetics*, *43*, 59–69.

Krubitzer, L. (1998). Constructing the neocortex: Influences on the pattern of organisation in mammals. In M. S. Gazzaniga & J. S. Altman (Eds.), *Brain and mind: Evolutionary perspectives* (pp. 19–34). Strasbourg: HFSP.

Liepmann, H. (1920). Apraxia. *Ergebnisse der Gesamten Medizin*, *1*, 516–543.

MacNeilage, P. F., & Davis, B. L. (2005). The frame/content theory of evolution of speech: Comparison with a gestural origins theory. *Interaction Studies: Social Behavior and Communication in Biological and Artificial Systems*, *6*, 173–199.

Mahon, B. Z., & Caramazza, A. (2005). The orchestration of the sensory-motor systems: Clues from neuropsychology. *Cognitive Neuropsychology, 22,* 480–494.

Marquardt, T. P., & Sussman, H. (1984). The elusive lesion – apraxia of speech link in Broca's aphasia. In J. C. Rosenbek, M. R. McNeil, & A. E. Aronson (Eds.), *Apraxia of speech: Physiology, acoustics, linguistics, management.* San Diego, CA: College-Hill Press.

Marshall, J., Atkinson, J., Smulovitch, E., Thacker, A., & Woll, B. (2004). Aphasia in a user of British Sign Language: Dissociation between sign and gesture. *Cognitive Neuropsychology, 21,* 537–554.

Meador, K. J., Loring, D. W., Lee, K., Hughes, M., Lee, G., & Nichols, M. et al. (1999). Cerebral lateralisation: Relationship of language and ideomotor praxis. *Neurology, 53*(9), 2028–2031.

Miall, R. C. (2003). Connecting mirror neurons and forward models. *Neuroreport, 14,* 2135–2137.

Ochipa, C., Rothi, L. J., & Heilman, K. M. (1994). Conduction apraxia. *Journal of Neurology, Neurosurgery and Psychiatry, 57,* 1241–1244.

Oztop, E., & Arbib, M. A. (2002). Schema design and implementation of the grasp-related mirror neuron system. *Biological Cybernetics, 87,* 116–140.

Oztop, E., Kawato, M., & Arbib, M. A. (2006). Mirror neurons and imitation: A computationally guided review. *Neural Networks, 19,* 254–271.

Papagno, C., della Sala, S., & Basso, A. (1993). Ideomotor apraxia without aphasia and aphasia without apraxia: The anatomical support for a double dissociation. *Journal of Neurology, Neurosurgery and Psychiatry, 56,* 286–289.

Paulesu, E., Goldacre, B., Scifo, P., Cappa, S. F., Gilardi, M. C., & Castiglioni, I. et al. (1997). Functional heterogeneity of left inferior frontal cortex as revealed by MRI. *Neuroreport, 8,* 2011–2017.

Perrett, D. I., Mistlin, A. J., Harries, M. H., & Chitty, A. J. (1990). Understanding the visual appearance and consequence of hand actions. In M. A. Goodale (Ed.), *Vision and action: The control of grasping* (pp. 163–342). Norwood, NJ: Ablex.

Plaut, D. C. (1995). Lesioned attractor networks as models of neuropsychological deficits. In M. A. Arbib (Ed.), *The handbook of brain theory and neural networks* (pp. 540–543). Cambridge, MA: The MIT Press.

Plaut, D. C., & Shallice, T. (1993). Deep dyslexia: A case study of connectionist neuropsychology. *Cognitive Neuropsychology, 10,* 377–500.

Rhodes, B. J., Bullock, D., Verwey, W. B., Averbeck, B. B., & Page, M. P. A. (2004). Learning and production of movement sequences: Behavioral, neurophysiological, and modelling perspectives. *Human Movement Science, 23,* 699–746.

Rizzolatti, G., & Arbib, M. A. (1998). Language within our grasp. *Trends in Neurosciences, 21*(5), 188–194.

Rizzolatti, G., Fadiga, L., Gallese, V., & Fogassi, L. (1996). Premotor cortex and the recognition of motor actions. *Cognitive Brain Research, 3,* 131–141.

Rizzolatti, G., Fogassi, L., & Gallese, V. (2001). Neurophysiological mechanisms underlying the understanding and imitation of action. *Nature Reviews Neuroscience, 2,* 661–670.

Rizzolatti, G., & Luppino, G. (2003). Grasping movements: Visuomotor transformations. In M. A. Arbib (Ed.), *The handbook of brain theory and neural networks* (2nd ed., pp. 501–504). Cambridge, MA: The MIT Press.

Rizzolatti, G., Luppino, G., & Matelli, M. (1998). The organisation of the cortical motor system: New concepts. *Electroencephalography and Clinical Neurophysiology, 106,* 283–296.

Romanski, L. M., Tian, B., Fritz, J., Mishkin, M., Goldman-Rakic, P. S., & Rauschecker, J. P. (1999). Dual streams of auditory afferents target multiple domains in the primate prefrontal cortex. *Nature Neuroscience, 12,* 1131–1136.

Ross, E. D. (1981). The aprosodias. Functional-anatomic organisation of the affective components of language in the right hemisphere. *Archives of Neurology, 38*(9), 561–569.

Rothi, L. J. G., Raade, A. S., & Heilman, K. M. (1994). Localisation of lesions in limb and buccofacial apraxia. In A. Kertesz (Ed.), *Localisation and neuroimaging in neuropsychology.* New York: Academic Press.

Roy, A. C., & Arbib, M. A. (2005). The syntactic motor system. *Gesture, 5,* 7–37.

Sereno, M. E., Trinath, T., Augath, M., & Logothetis, N. K. (2002). Three-dimensional shape representation in monkey cortex. *Neuron, 33,* 635–652.

Speedie, L. J., Wertman, E., Tair, J., & Heilman, K. M. (1993). Disruption of automatic speech following a right basal ganglia lesion. *Neurology, 43,* 1768–1774.

Striedter, G. F. (2004). *Principles of brain evolution.* Sunderland, MA: Sinauer Associates.

Sutton, R. S., & Barto, A. G. (1998). *Reinforcement learning: An introduction.* Cambridge, MA: MIT Press.

Taira, M., Mine, S., Georgopoulos, A. P., Murata, A., & Sakata, H. (1990). Parietal cortex neurons of the monkey related to the visual guidance of hand movement. *Experimental Brain Research, 83*, 29–36.

Tonkonogy, J., & Goodglass, H. (1981). Language function, foot of the third frontal gyrus, and rolandic operculum. *Archives of Neurology, 38*, 486–490.

Tucker, D. M., Watson, R. T., & Heilman, K. M. (1977). Affective discrimination and evocation in patients with right parietal disease. *Neurology, 17*, 947–950.

Umiltà, M. A., Kohler, E., Gallese, V., Fogassi, L., Fadiga, L., & Keysers, C. et al. (2001). I know what you are doing. A neurophysiological study. *Neuron, 31*(1), 155–165.

Valenstein, E., & Heilman, K. M. (1979). Apraxic agraphia with neglect-induced paragraphia. *Archives of Neurology, 36*, 506–508.

Voelkl, B., & Huber, L. (2000). True imitation in marmosets. *Animal Behavior, 60*, 195–202.

Webster, M. J., Bachevalier, J., & Ungerleider, L. G. (1994). Connections of inferior temporal areas TEO and TE with parietal and frontal cortex in macaque monkeys. *Cerebral Cortex, 4*, 470–483.

Wildgruber, D., Ackermann, H., Klose, U., Kardatzki, B., & Grodd, W. (1996). Functional lateralisation of speech production at primary motor cortex: A fMRI study. *Neuroreport, 7*, 2791–2795.

Wohlschläger, A., Gattis, M., & Bekkering, H. (2003). Action generation and action perception in imitation: An instance of the ideomotor principle. *Philosophical Transactions of the Royal Society, London B, 358*, 501–515.

Zhong, Y. M., & Rockland, K. S. (2003). Inferior parietal lobule projections to anterior inferotemporal cortex (area TE) in macaque monkey. *Cerebral Cortex, 13*(5), 527–540.

Author Index

Ackermann, H., 1148
Aggujaro, S., 1051
Alexander, J. R. M., 876
Alexander, M. P., 960
Aliminosa, D., 852, 861, 1107, 1109
Allport, D. A., 820, 944, 946, 1117
Alstermark, B., 1136–1137
Andreewsky, A., 965
Andrews, S., 830
Annoni, J. M., 854
Arbib, M. A., 1123, 1125, 1126–1127, 1131, 1132, 1133, 1136, 1137, 1139, 1140, 1141, 1142, 1143, 1145, 1146, 1147, 1148, 1149
Archimedes 1110
Ardilà, A., 825, 844, 845, 960
Ardilà, O., 960
Arduino, L. S., 830
Arens, K., 1090
Aristotle 1092
Armstrong, D. F., 1055
Atkins, P., 845, 880
Augath, M., 1130
Averbeck, B. B., 1136

Baars, D. J., 1096
Bachevalier, J., 1130
Baddeley, A. D., 861, 1053, 1054, 1144
Badecker, W., 852, 1007, 1010, 1011
Baginsky A., 1082
Ball, M. J., 1036, 1037, 1038
Barbey, A. K., 1113
Barca, L., 826, 830, 847
Baron, R., 965
Barresi, B., 1022

Barrett, A., 1125n, 1127, 1145, 1146, 1147, 1149, 1150
Barry, C., 826, 840, 847, 848
Barsalou, L. W., 1113
Barto, A. G., 1137
Basili, G., 1053
Basso, A., 1145, 1146
Bastiaanse, R., 1046, 1051
Bastian, H. C., 1082, 1095, 1100
Bateman, D., 968
Bates, E., 826, 844
Bates, T. C., 876
Bay, E., 1094
Bayard, D., 961
Bayer, J., 1008, 1055
Beauvois, M. F., 873
Bekkering, H., 1138
Bellugi, U., 1140, 1147
Benke, T., 1110
Berndt, R. S., 926, 944, 1041, 1046, 1051, 1052, 1053
Best, W., 921n, 926, 945, 946
Bickerton, D., 1097
Binder, J. R., 846
Bird, H. 994, 995, 996, 1009, 1011
Bischoff-Grethe, A., 1135
Bishop, D. V. M., 1022
Black, M. 1048
Blazely, A., 889
Blonder, L. X., 1148
Blumstein, S. E., 1122
Blumstein, S., 960
Boberg, C., 961
Boder, E., 875
Bonaiuto, J., 1133, 1136
Bonin, P., 826
Boring, E. G., 1076
Bota, M., 1142, 1147
Boussaoud, D., 1130
Bowers, D., 1148

Bowey, J., 876
Bozeat, S., 971, 1020
Braber, N., 1018n
Brinkman, U., 2008
Broca, P., 820, 823, 846, 928, 944, 1019, 1079, 1082, 1099, 1146
Brolio, J., 1145
Broussolle, E., 1053
Brown, G. D. A., 933, 946
Brown-Sequard, C., 1098
Bruce, C., 921n, 940, 946
Brucke, E., 1095
Brugmann, K., 1087, 1092
Bryant, P., 874
Bub, D. N., 1118, 1122
Buckingham, H. W., 1085, 1088, 1089, 1090, 1091, 1092, 1094, 1096, 1097, 1098, 1099, 1100
Bukach, C. M., 1118
Bullock, D., 1136
Bumann, W., 1074, 1076
Burani, C., 826, 830, 847
Burns, R., 1064
Butler, A. B., 1127
Butterworth, B., 826, 875, 923, 945, 1105, 1110
Buxbaum, L., 1125n, 1143, 1148, 1149
Bybee, J. L., 994, 1011
Byng, S., 873, 1048
Byrne, R. W., 1138, 1139

Campbell, L., 1087
Campbell, R., 875
Capasso, R., 844, 1107
Caplan, D., 893, 894, 898, 918, 1053, 1055, 1125n, 1127
Caramazza, A., 844, 851, 852, 854, 865, 890, 922, 923–924, 933, 944, 945, 947, 963, 994, 1007,

Subject Index

Indexes compiled by Frank Pert

For Product Safety Concerns and Information please contact our EU
representative GPSR@taylorandfrancis.com Taylor & Francis Verlag GmbH,
Kaufingerstraße 24, 80331 München, Germany

Batch number: 08158492

Printed by Printforce, the Netherlands